JAVA PROGRAMMING

FROM PROBLEM ANALYSIS TO PROGRAM DESIGN

FIFTH EDITION

D.S. MALIK

COURSE TECHNOLOGY
CENGAGE Learning

Australia • Brazil • Japan • Korea • Mexico • Singapore • Spain • United Kingdom • United States

COURSE TECHNOLOGY
CENGAGE Learning™

Java Programming: From Problem Analysis to Program Design, Fifth Edition, International Edition
D.S. Malik

Executive Editor: Marie Lee

Acquisitions Editor: Brandi Shailer

Senior Product Manager: Alyssa Pratt

Editorial Assistant: Jacqueline Lacaire

Content Project Manager: Lisa Weidenfeld

Associate Marketing Manager:
Shanna Shelton

Art Director: Faith Brosnan

Proofreader: Andrea Schein

Indexer: Alexandra Nickerson

Print Buyer: Julio Esperas

Cover Designer: Roycroft Design/
www.roycroftdesign.com

Cover Photo: © photolibrary/Richard
Cummins

Compositor: Integra

Library of Congress Control Number: 2010940363

International Edition:
ISBN-13: 978-1-111-57764-3

ISBN-10: 1-111-57764-1

Cengage Learning International Offices

Asia
www.cengageasia.com
tel: (65) 6410 1200

Australia/New Zealand
www.cengage.com.au
tel: (61) 3 9685 4111

Brazil
www.cengage.com.br
tel: (55) 11 3665 9900

India
www.cengage.co.in
tel: (91) 11 4364 1111

Latin America
www.cengage.com.mx
tel: (52) 55 1500 6000

UK/Europe/Middle East/ Africa
www.cengage.co.uk
tel: (44) 0 1264 332 424

Represented in Canada by Nelson Education, Ltd.
www.nelson.com
tel: (416) 752 9100 /
(800) 668 0671

Cengage Learning is a leading provider of customized learning solutions with office locations around the globe, including Singapore, the United Kingdom, Australia, Mexico, Brazil, and Japan. Locate your local office at: **www.cengage.com/global**

For product information and free companion resources:
www.cengage.com/international

Visit your local office: **www.cengage.com/global**

Visit our corporate website: **www.cengage.com**

Printed in China
2 3 4 5 6 7 15 14 13 12

TO

My Daughter

Shelly Malik

BRIEF CONTENTS

TABLE OF CONTENTS

6 GRAPHICAL USER INTERFACE (GUI) AND OBJECT-ORIENTED DESIGN (OOD) 327

7 USER-DEFINED METHODS 383

PREFACE TO THE FIFTH EDITION

Welcome to *Java Programming: From Problem Analysis to Program Design, Fifth Edition.* Designed for a first Computer Science (CS1) Java course, this text will provide a breath of fresh air to you and your students. The CS1 course serves as the cornerstone of the Computer Science curriculum. My primary goal is to motivate and excite all programming students, regardless of their level. Motivation breeds excitement for learning. Motivation and excitement are critical factors that lead to the success of the programming student. This text is the culmination and development of my classroom notes throughout more than fifty semesters of teaching successful programming.

Warning: This text can be expected to create a serious reduction in the demand for programming help during your office hours. Other side effects include significantly diminished student dependency on others while learning to program.

The primary focus in writing this text is on student learning. Therefore, in addition to clear explanations, we address the key issues that otherwise impede student learning. For example, a common question that arises naturally during an early programming assignment is: "How many variables and what kinds are needed in this program?" We illustrate this important and crucial step by helping students learn why variables are needed and how data in a variable is manipulated. Next students learn that the analysis of the problem will spill the number and types of the variables. Once students grasp this key concept, control structures (selection and loops) become easier to learn. The second major impediment in learning programming is parameter passing. We pay special attention to this topic. First students learn how to use predefined methods and how actual and formal parameters relate. Next students learn about user-defined methods. They see visual diagrams that help them learn how methods are called and how formal parameters affect actual parameters. Once students have a clear understanding of these two key concepts, they readily assimilate advanced topics.

The topics are introduced at a pace that is conducive to learning. The writing style is friendly, engaging, and straightforward. It parallels the learning style of the contemporary CS1 student. Before introducing a key concept, the student learns why the concept is needed, and then sees examples illustrating the concept. Special attention is paid to topics that are essential in mastering the Java programming language and in acquiring a foundation for further study of computer science.

Other important topics include debugging techniques and techniques for avoiding programming bugs. When a beginner compiles his/her first program and sees that the number of errors exceeds the length of this first program, he/she becomes frustrated by the plethora of errors, only some of which can be interpreted. To ease this frustration and help students learn to produce correct programs, debugging and bug avoidance techniques are presented systematically throughout the text.

Changes in the Fifth Edition

The main changes are:

- In the fifth edition, new debugging sections have been added and some of the old ones have been rewritten. These sections are indicated with a debugging icon.

- The fifth edition contains more than 125 new exercises, 27 new programming exercises, and numerous new examples spread throughout the book.

- In Chapters 6 and 12 the GUI figures have been captured and replaced in Windows 7 Professional environment.

- Appendix D contains screen images illustrating how to compile and execute a Java program using the command-line statements as well as how to set the path in Windows 7 Professional environment.

These changes were implemented based on comments from the text reviewers of the fifth edition. The source code and the programming exercises are developed and tested using Java 6.0 and the version of Java 7.0 available at the time this book was being typeset.

Approach

Once conceived as a Web programming language, Java slowly but surely found its way into classrooms where it now serves as a first programming language in computer science curricula (CS1). Java is a combination of traditional style programming—programming with a non-graphical user interface—and modern style programming with a graphical user interface (GUI). This book introduces you to both styles of programming. After giving a brief description of each chapter, we discuss how to read this book.

Chapter 1 briefly reviews the history of computers and programming languages. The reader can quickly skim and become familiar with some of the hardware and software components of the computer. This chapter also gives an example of a Java program and describes how a Java program is processed. The two basic problem-solving techniques, structured programming and object-oriented design, are also presented.

After completing Chapter 2, students become familiar with the basics of Java and are ready to write programs that are complicated enough to do some computations. The debugging section in this chapter illustrates how to interpret and correct syntax errors.

The three terms that you will encounter throughout the book are—primitive type variables, reference variables, and objects. Chapter 3 makes clear distinctions between these terms and sets the tone for the rest of the book. An object is a fundamental entity in an object-oriented programming language. This chapter further explains how an object works. The `class` `String` is one of the most important classes in Java. This chapter introduces this class and explains how various methods of this class can be used to manipulate strings. Because input/ output is fundamental to any programming language, it is introduced early, and is covered in detail in Chapter 3. The debugging section in this chapter illustrates how to find and correct logical errors.

Chapters 4 and 5 introduce control structures used to alter the sequential flow of execution. The debugging sections in these chapters discuss and illustrate logical errors associated with selection and looping structures.

Java is equipped with powerful yet easy-to-use graphical user interface (GUI) components to create user-friendly graphical programs. Chapter 6 introduces various GUI components and gives examples of how to use these components in Java application programs. Because Java is an object-oriented programming language, the second part of Chapter 6 discusses and gives examples of how to solve various problems using object-oriented design methodology.

Chapter 7 discusses user-defined methods. Parameter passing is a fundamental concept in any programming language. Several examples, including visual diagrams, help readers understand this concept. It is recommended that readers with no prior programming background spend extra time on this concept. The debugging section in this chapter discuss how to debug a program using stubs and drivers.

Chapter 8 discusses user-defined classes. In Java, a class is an important and widely used element. It is used to create Java programs, group related operations, and it allows users to create their own data types. This chapter uses extensive visual diagrams to illustrate how objects of classes manipulate data.

Chapter 9 describes arrays. This chapter also introduces variable length formal parameter lists. In addition, this chapter introduces foreach loops and explains how this loop can be used to process the elements of an array. This chapter also discusses the sequential searching algorithm and the `class` `Vector`.

Inheritance is an important principle of object-oriented design. It encourages code reuse. Chapter 10 discusses inheritance and gives various examples to illustrate how classes are derived from existing classes. In addition, this chapter also discusses polymorphism, abstract classes, inner classes, and composition.

An occurrence of an undesirable situation that can be detected during program execution is called an exception. For example, division by zero is an exception. Java provides extensive support for handing exceptions. Chapter 11 shows how to handle exceptions in a program. Chapter 11 also discusses event handling, which was introduced in Chapter 6. Chapter 12 picks up the discussion of GUI components started in Chapter 6. This chapter introduces additional GUI components and discusses how to create applets.

Chapter 13 introduces recursion. Several examples illustrate how recursive methods execute.

Chapter 14 discusses a binary search algorithm as well as bubble sort, selection sort, insertion sort, and quick sort algorithms. Additional content covering the sorting algorithms bubble sort and quick sort is provided online at *www.cengagebrain.com*.

Appendix A lists the reserved words in Java. Appendix B shows the precedence and associativity of the Java operators. Appendix C lists the ASCII (American Standard Code for Information Interchange) portion of the Unicode character set as well as the EBCDIC (Extended Binary Code Decimal Interchange) character set.

Appendix D contains additional topics in Java. The topics covered are converting a base 10 number to binary (base 2) number and vice versa, converting a number from base 2 to base 8 (base 16) and vice versa, how to compile and execute a Java program using command line statements, how to create Java style documentation of the user-defined classes, how to create packages, how to use user-defined classes in a Java program, and **enum** type. Appendix E gives answers to the odd-numbered exercises in the text. Those odd-numbered exercises with very long solutions will not be in the text, but will be provided to students online at *www.cengagebrain.com*.

How To Use This Book

Java is a complex and very powerful language. In addition to traditional (non-GUI) programming, Java provides extensive support for creating programs that use a graphical user interface (GUI). Chapter 3 introduces graphical input and output dialog boxes. Chapter 6 introduces the most commonly used GUI components such as labels, buttons, and text fields. More extensive coverage of GUI components is provided in Chapter 12.

This book can be used in two ways. One way is an integrated approach in which readers learn how to write both non-GUI and GUI programs as they learn basic programming concepts and skills. The other approach focuses on illustrating fundamental programming concepts with non-GUI programming first, and later incorporating GUI components. The recommended chapter sequence for each of these approaches is as follows:

- **Integrated approach:** Study all chapters in sequence.
- **Non-GUI first, then GUI:** Study Chapters 1–5 in sequence. Then study Chapters 7–11 and Chapters 13 and 14. This approach initially skips Chapters 6 and 12, the primary GUI chapters. After studying Chapters 1–5, 7–11, 13, and 14, the reader can come back to study Chapters 6 and 12, the GUI chapters. Also note that Chapter 14 can be studied after Chapter 9.

If you choose the second approach, it should also be noted that the Programming Examples in Chapters 8 and 10 are developed first without any GUI components, and then the programs are extended to incorporate GUI components. Also, if Chapter 6 is skipped, the reader can skip the event handling part of Chapter 11. Chapter 13 (recursion) contains two Programming Examples: one creates a non-GUI application program, while the other creates a program that uses GUI. If you skip Chapters 6 and 12, you can skip the GUI part of the Programming Examples in Chapters 8, 10, 11, and 13. Once you have studied Chapter 6 and 12, you can study the GUI part of the Programming Examples of Chapters 8, 10, 11, and 13.

Figure 1 shows a chapter dependency diagram for this book. Solid arrows indicate that the chapter at the beginning of the arrow is required before studying the chapter at the end of the arrow. A dotted arrow indicates that the chapter at the beginning of the arrow is not essential to studying the chapter at the end of the dotted arrow.

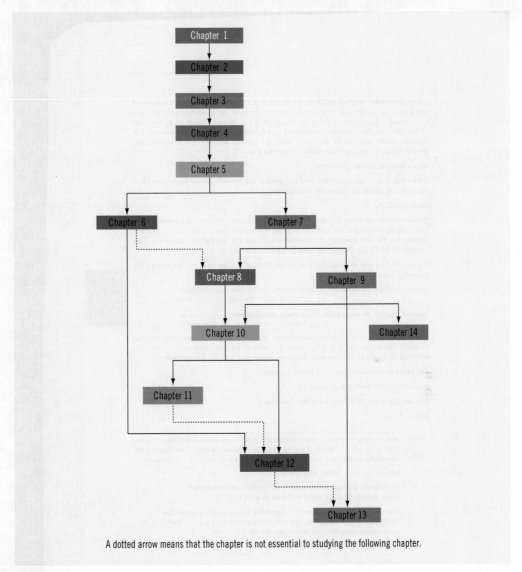

A dotted arrow means that the chapter is not essential to studying the following chapter.

FIGURE 1   Chapter dependency diagram

All source code and solutions have been written, compiled, and quality assurance tested with Java 6.0 and the version of Java 7.0 available at the time this book was being typeset.

FEATURES OF THE BOOK

called a **nonstatic** method. Similarly, the heading of a method may contain the reserved word `public`. In this case, it is called a `public` method. An important property of a `public` and `static` method is that (in a program) it can be used (called) using the name of the class, the dot operator, the method name, and the appropriate parameters. For example, all the methods of the `class Math` are `public` and `static`. Therefore, the general syntax to use a method of the `class Math` is:

```
Math.methodName(parameters)
```

(Note that, in fact, the parameters used in a method call are called actual parameters.) For example, the following expression determines $2.5^{3.5}$:

```
Math.pow(2.5, 3.5)
```

(In the previous statement, `2.5` and `3.5` are actual parameters.) Similarly, if a method of the `class Character` is `public` and `static`, you can use the name of the `class`, which is `Character`, the dot operator, the method name, and the appropriate parameters. The methods of the `class Character` listed in Table 7–2 are `public` and `static`.

To simplify the use of (`public`) `static` methods of a class, Java 5.0 introduces the following import statements:

```
import static packageName.ClassName.*;   //to use any (public)
                                    //static method of the class

import static packageName.ClassName.methodName;   //to use a
                                    //specific method of the class
```

These are called `static import` **statements**. After including such statements in your program, when you use a (`public`) `static` method (or any other `public static` member) of a `class`, you can omit the name of the class and the dot operator.

For example, after including the `import` statement:

```
import static java.lang.Math.*;
```

you can determine $2.5^{3.5}$ by using the expression:

```
pow(2.5, 3.5)
```

 NOTE After including the `static import` statement, in reality, you have a choice. When you use a (`public`) `static` method of a `class`, you can either use the name of the class and the dot operator or omit them. For example, after including the `static import` statement:

```
import static java.lang.Math.*;
```

in a program, you can determine $2.5^{3.5}$ by using either the expression `Math.pow(2.5, 3.5)` or the expression `pow(2.5, 3.5)`.

The `static import` statement is *not* available in versions of Java lower than 5.0. Therefore, if you are using, say, Java 4.0, then you must use a `static` method of the `class Math` using the name of the class and the dot operator.

7

Four-color interior design shows accurate code and related comments.

Debugging: Using Drivers and Stubs

In this and previous chapters you learned how to write methods to divide a problem into subproblems, solve each subproblem, and then combine the methods to form the complete program to get a solution of the problem. A program may contain a number of methods. In a complex program, usually, when a method is written, it is tested and debugged alone. You can write a separate program to test the method. The program that tests a method is called a **driver** program. For example, the program in Example 7-12, contains methods to convert the length from inches to centimeters and vice versa. Before writing the complete program, you could write separate driver programs to make sure that each method is working properly.

Sometimes the results calculated by one method are needed in another method. In that case, the method that depends on another method cannot be tested alone. For example, consider the following program that determines the time to fill a swimming pool:

```java
import java.util.*;

public class Pool
{
    static Scanner console = new Scanner(System.in);

    static final double GALLONS_IN_A_CUBIC_FEET = 7.48;

    public static void main(String[] args)
    {
        double length, width, depth;
        double fillRate;
        int fillTime;

        System.out.print("Enter the length, width, and the "
                        + "depth of the pool, (in feet): ");
        length = console.nextDouble();
        width = console.nextDouble();
        depth = console.nextDouble();
        System.out.println();

        System.out.print("Enter the rate of the water, "
                        + "(in gallons per minute): ");
        fillRate = console.nextInt();
        System.out.println();

        fillTime = poolFillTime(length, width, depth, fillRate);
        print(fillTime);
    }

    public static double poolCapacity(double len, double wid,
                                        double dep)
```

The debugging sections show how to find and correct syntax and semantic (logical) errors.

The preceding program works as follows: The statement in Line 5 declares **str** to be a reference variable of the **StringBuffer** type and assigns the string **"Hello"** to it (see Figure 7-13).

FIGURE 7-13 Variable after the statement in Line 5 executes

The statement in Line 6 outputs the first line of output. The statement in Line 7 calls the method **stringBufferParameter**. The actual parameter is **str** and the formal parameter is **pStr**. The value of **str** is copied into **pStr**. Because both of these parameters are reference variables, **str** and **pStr** point to the same string, which is **"Hello"** (see Figure 7-14).

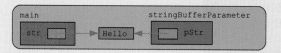

FIGURE 7-14 Variable before the statement in Line 7 executes

Then control is transferred to the method **stringBufferParameter**. The next statement executed is in Line 12, which produces the second line of the output. The statement in Line 13 produces the third line of the output. This statement also outputs the string to which **pStr** points, and the printed value is that string. The statement in Line 14 uses the method **append** to append the string **" There"** to the string pointed to by **pStr**. After this statement executes, **pStr** points to the string **"Hello There"**. However, this also changes the string that was assigned to the variable **str**. When the statement in Line 14 executes, **str** points to the same string as **pStr** (see Figure 7-15).

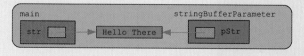

FIGURE 7-15 Variable after the statement in Line 14 executes

ACTUAL PARAMETER LIST

An actual parameter list has the following syntax:

```
expression or variable, expression or variable, ...
```

As with value-returning methods, in a method call the number of actual parameters, together with their data types, must match the formal parameters in the order given. Actual and formal parameters have a one-to-one correspondence. A method call causes the body of the called method to execute. Two examples of void methods with parameters follow.

EXAMPLE 7-5

Consider the following method heading:

```
public static void funexp(int a, double b, char c, String name)
```

The method **funexp** has four formal parameters: (1) **a**, a parameter of type int;, (2) **b**, a parameter of type double;, (3) **c**, a parameter of type char, and (4) **name**, a parameter of type String.

EXAMPLE 7-6

Consider the following method heading:

```
public static void expfun(int one, char two, String three, double four)
```

The method **expfun** has four formal parameters: (1) **one**, a parameter of type int;, (2) **two**, a parameter of type char;, (3) **three**, a parameter of type String, and (4) **four**, a parameter of type double.

Parameters provide a communication link between the calling method (such as **main**) and the called method. They enable methods to manipulate different data each time they are called.

EXAMPLE 7-7

Suppose that you want to print a pattern (a triangle of stars) similar to the following:

The first line has one star with some blanks before the star, the second line has two stars, some blanks before the stars, and a blank between the stars, and so on. Let's write the

Because this is a value-returning method of type int, it must return a value of type int. Suppose the value of **x** is 10. Then, the expression, **x > 5**, in Line 1, evaluates to true. So the return statement in Line 2 returns the value 20. Now suppose that **x** is 3. The expression, **x > 5**, in Line 1, now evaluates to false. The if statement therefore fails and the return statement in Line 2 *does not* execute. However, the body of the method has no more statements to be executed. It thus follows that if the value of **x** is less than or equal to 5, the method does not contain any valid return statements to return the value of **x**. In this case, in fact, the compiler generates an error message such as **missing return statement**.

The correct definition of the method **secret** is:

```
public static int secret(int x)
{
    if (x > 5)              //Line 1
        return 2 * x;       //Line 2

    return x;              //Line 3
}
```

Here, if the value of **x** is less than or equal to 5, the return statement in Line 3 executes, which returns the value of **x**. On the other hand, if the value of **x** is, say, 10, the return statement in Line 2 executes, which returns the value 20 and also terminates the method.

NOTE

(return statement: A precaution) If the compiler can determine that during execution certain statements in a program can never be reached, then it will generate syntax errors. For example, consider the following methods:

```
public static int funcReturnStatementError(int z)
{
    return z;

    System.out.println(z);
}
```

The first statement in the method **funcReturnStatementError** is the return statement. Therefore, if this method executes, then the output statement, **System.out.println(z);**, will never be executed. In this case, when the compiler compiles this method, it will generate two syntax errors, one specifying that the statement **System.out.println(z);** is unreachable, and the second specifying that there is a missing return statement after the output statement. Even if you include a return statement after the output statement, the compiler will still generate the error that the statement **System.out.println(z);** is unreachable. Therefore, you should be careful when writing the definition of a method. Additional methods illustrating such errors can be found at *www.cengagebrain.com*. The name of the program is **TestReturnStatement.java**.

Notes highlight important facts about the concepts introduced in the chapter.

If the call is `larger(5, 3)`, for example, the first method executes because the actual parameters match the formal parameters of the first method. If the call is `larger('A', '9')`, the second method executes, and so on.

Method overloading is used when you have the same action for different types of data. Of course, for method overloading to work, you must give the definition of each method.

PROGRAMMING EXAMPLE: Data Comparison

Two groups of students at a local university are enrolled in special courses during the summer semester. The courses are offered for the first time and are taught by different teachers. At the end of the semester, both groups are given the same tests for the same courses and their scores are recorded in separate files. The data in each file is in the following form:

```
courseID   score1, score2, ..., scoreN -999
courseID   score1, score2, ..., scoreM -999
.
.
.
```

This programming example illustrates:

1. How to read data from more than one file in the same program.
2. How to send the output to a file.
3. How to generate bar graphs.
4. With the help of methods and parameter passing, how to use the same program segment on different (but similar) sets of data.
5. How to use structured design to solve a problem and how to perform parameter passing.

This program is broken into two parts. First, you learn how to read data from more than one file. Second, you learn how to generate bar graphs.

Next we write a program that finds the average course score for each course for each group. The output is of the following form:

```
Course ID   Group No   Course Average
   CSC         1           83.71
               2           80.82

   ENG         1           82.00
               2           78.20
.
.
.
Avg for group 1: 82.04
Avg for group 2: 82.01
```

7

- An identifier **x** declared within a method (block) is accessible:
  - Only within the block from the point at which it is declared until the end of the block.
  - By those blocks that are nested within that block.
- Suppose **x** is an identifier declared within a class and outside every method's definition (block):
  - If **x** is declared without the reserved word `static` (such as a named constant or a method name), then it cannot be accessed within a `static` method.
  - If **x** is declared with the reserved word `static` (such as a named constant or a method name), then it can be accessed within a method (block), provided the method (block) does not have any other identifier named **x**.

38. Two methods are said to have different formal parameter lists if both methods have:
    - A different number of formal parameters, or
    - If the number of formal parameters is the same, then the data type of the formal parameters, in the order you list, must differ in at least one position.

39. The signature of a method consists of the method name and its formal parameter list. Two methods have different signatures if they have either different names or different formal parameter lists.

40. If a method is overloaded, then in a call to that method, the signature, that is, the formal parameter list of the method, determines which method to execute.

EXERCISES

1. Mark the following statements as true or false:
   a. To use a predefined method of a `class` contained in the package `java.lang` in a program, you only need to know what the name of the method is and how to use it.
   b. A value-returning method returns only one value via the return statement.
   c. Parameters allow you to use different values each time the method is called.

Exercises further reinforce learning and ensure that students have, in fact, mastered the material.

```
public static void traceMe(double x, double y)
{
    double z;

    if (x != 0)
        z = Math.sqrt(y) / x;
    else
    {
        System.out.print("Enter a nonzero number: ");
        x   = console.nextDouble();
        System.out.println();
        z = Math.floor(Math.pow(y, x));
    }

    System.out.printf("%.2f, %.2f, %.2f, %n", x, y, z);
}
```

a. What is the output if the input is 3 625?

b. What is the output if the input is 24 1024?

c. What is the output if the input is 0 196?

29. In Exercise 28, determine the scope of each identifier.

30. Write the definition of a void method that takes as input a decimal number and outputs 3 times the value of the decimal number. Format your output to two decimal places.

31. Write the definition of a void method that takes as input two decimal numbers. If the first number is nonzero, it outputs the second number divided by the first number; otherwise, it outputs a message indicating that the second number cannot be divided by the first number because the first number is 0.

32. Write the definition of a method that takes as input two parameters of type int, say sum and testScore. The method updates the value of sum by adding the value of testScore, and then returns the updated value of sum.

PROGRAMMING EXERCISES

Programming Exercises challenge students to write Java programs with a specified outcome.

1. Write a value-returning method, isVowel, that returns the value true if a given character is a vowel, and otherwise returns false. Also write a program to test your method.

2. Write a program that prompts the user to input a sequence of characters and outputs the number of vowels. (Use the method isVowel written in Programming Exercise 1.)

3. Write a program that uses the method sqrt of the class Math and outputs the square roots of the first 25 positive integers. (Your program must output each number and its square root.)

SUPPLEMENTAL RESOURCES

The following supplemental materials are available when this book is used in a classroom setting.

Most instructor teaching tools, outlined below, are available with this book on a single CD-ROM, and are also available for instructor access at *login.cengage.com*.

Electronic Instructor's Manual

The Instructor's Manual that accompanies this textbook includes:

- Additional instructional material to assist in class preparation, including suggestions for lecture topics.
- Solutions to all the end-of-chapter materials, including the Programming Exercises.

ExamView®

This textbook is accompanied by ExamView, a powerful testing software package that allows instructors to create and administer printed, computer (LAN-based), and Internet exams. ExamView includes hundreds of questions that correspond to the topics covered in this text, enabling students to generate detailed study guides that include page references for further review. These computer-based and Internet testing components allow students to take exams at their computers, and save the instructor time because each exam is graded automatically.

PowerPoint Presentations

Microsoft PowerPoint slides are available for each chapter. These slides are provided as a teaching aid for classroom presentations, either to make available to students on the network for chapter review, or to be printed for classroom distribution. Instructors can add their own slides for additional topics that they introduce to the class.

Distance Learning

Course Technology is proud to present online courses in WebCT and Blackboard to provide the most complete and dynamic learning experience possible. For more information on how to bring distance learning to your course, contact your local Course Technology sales representative.

Source Code

The source code is available for students at *www.cengagebrain.com*. At the *cengagebrain.com* home page, search for the ISBN of your title (from the back cover of your book) using the search box at the top of the page. This will take you to the product page where these resources can be found. The source code is also available on the Instructor Resources CD-ROM. The input files needed to run some of the programs are also included with the source code.

Additional Student Files

The Additional Student Files referenced throughout the text are available on the Instructor Resources CD. Students can download these files directly at *www.cengagebrain.com*. At the *cengagebrain.com* home page, search for the ISBN of your title using the search box at the top of the page. This will take you to the product page where these resources can be found. Click the *Access Now* link below the book cover to find all study tools and additional files available directly to students. Additional Student Files appear on the left navigation and provide access to additional Java programs, selected solutions, and more.

Solution Files

The solution files for all programming exercises are available for instructor download at *http://login.cengage.com* and are also available on the Instructor Resources CD-ROM. The input files needed to run some of the programming exercises are also included with the solution files.

ACKNOWLEDGMENTS

There are many people I must thank who, in one way or another, contributed to the success of this book. First, I would like to thank those who e-mailed numerous comments that helped to improve on the fourth edition. I am thankful to Professors S.C. Cheng and Randall Crist for constantly supporting this project.

I owe a great deal to the following reviewers, who patiently read each page of every chapter of the current version and made critical comments that helped to improve the book: Nadimpalli Mahadev, Fitchburg State College and Baoqiang Yan, Missouri Western State University. Additionally, I would like to thank Brian Candido, Springfield Technical Community College, for his review of the proposal package. The reviewers will recognize that their suggestions have not been overlooked and, in fact, made this a better book.

Next, I express thanks to Brandi Shailer, Acquisitions Editor, for recognizing the importance and uniqueness of this project. All this would not have been possible without the careful planning of Senior Product Manager Alyssa Pratt. I extend my sincere thanks to Alyssa, as well as to Content Project Manager, Lisa Weidenfeld. I also thank Sreejith Govindan of Integra Software Services for assisting us in keeping the project on schedule. I would like to thank Chris Scriver and Serge Palladino of the MQA department of Course Technology for patiently and carefully proofreading the text, testing the code, and discovering typos and errors.

I am thankful to my parents for their blessings.

Finally, I am thankful to the support of my wife Sadhana, and especially my daughter Shelly, to whom this book is dedicated. They cheered me up whenever I was overwhelmed during the writing of this book.

We welcome any comments concerning the text. Comments may be forwarded to the following e-mail address: `malik@creighton.edu`.

D.S. Malik

AN OVERVIEW OF COMPUTERS AND PROGRAMMING LANGUAGES

IN THIS CHAPTER, YOU WILL:

- Learn about different types of computers
- Explore the hardware and software components of a computer system
- Learn about the language of a computer
- Learn about the evolution of programming languages
- Examine high-level programming languages
- Discover what a compiler is and what it does
- Examine how a Java program is processed
- Learn about the Internet and World Wide Web
- Learn what an algorithm is and explore problem-solving techniques
- Become familiar with structured and object-oriented programming design methodologies

Introduction

Terms such as "the Internet," which was unfamiliar just a few years ago, are now common. Elementary school students regularly "surf" the Internet and use computers to design their classroom projects. Many people use the Internet to look up information and to communicate with others. These Internet activities are all made possible by the availability of different software, also known as computer programs. Software is developed by using programming languages. The Java programming language is especially well suited for developing software to accomplish specific tasks. Our main objective is to teach you how to write programs in the Java programming language. Before you begin programming, it is useful if you understand some of the basic terminology and different components of a computer. We begin with an overview of the history of computers.

An Overview of the History of Computers

The first device known to carry out calculations was the abacus. The abacus was invented in Asia but was used in ancient Babylon, China, and throughout Europe until the late middle ages. The abacus uses a system of sliding beads on a rack for addition and subtraction. In 1642, the French philosopher and mathematician Blaise Pascal invented the calculating device called the Pascaline. It had eight movable dials on wheels that could calculate sums up to eight figures long. Both the abacus and Pascaline could perform only addition and subtraction operations. Later in the seventeenth century, Gottfried von Leibniz invented a device that was able to add, subtract, multiply, and divide. In 1819, Joseph Jacquard, a French weaver, discovered that the weaving instructions for his looms could be stored on cards with holes punched in them. While the cards moved throughout the loom in sequence, needles passed through the holes and picked up threads of the correct color and texture. A weaver could rearrange the cards and change the pattern being woven. In essence, the cards programmed a loom to produce patterns in cloth. The weaving industry seems to have little in common with the computer industry. However, the idea of storing information by punching holes on a card turned out to be of great importance in the later development of computers.

In the early and mid-1800s, Charles Babbage, an English mathematician and physical scientist, designed two calculating machines—the difference engine and the analytical engine. The difference engine could automatically perform complex operations, such as squaring numbers. Babbage built a prototype of the difference engine, but did not build the actual device. The first complete difference engine was completed in London in 2002, 153 years after it was designed. It consists of 8,000 parts, weighs five tons, and measures 11 feet long. A replica of the difference engine was completed in 2008 and is on display at the Computer History Museum in Mountain View, California (*http://www.computerhistory.org/babbage/*). Most of Babbage's work is known through the writings of his colleague Ada Augusta, Countess of Lovelace. Augusta is considered to be the first computer programmer.

At the end of the 19th century, U.S. Census officials needed help in accurately tabulating the census data. Herman Hollerith invented a calculating machine that ran on electricity and used punched cards to store data. Hollerith's machine was immensely successful. Hollerith founded the Tabulating Machine Company, which later became the computer and technology corporation known as IBM.

The first computer-like machine was the Mark I. It was built, in 1944, jointly by IBM and Harvard University under the leadership of Howard Aiken. Punched cards were used to feed data into the machine. Mark I was 52 feet long, weighed 50 tons, and had 750,000 parts. In 1946, ENIAC (Electronic Numerical Integrator and Calculator) was built at the University of Pennsylvania. It contained 18,000 vacuum tubes and weighed some 30 tons.

The computers that we know today use the design rules given by John von Neumann in the late 1940s. His design included components such as arithmetic logic unit, control unit, memory, and input/output devices. These components are described in the next section. Von Neumann computer design makes it possible to store the programming instruction and the data in the same memory space. In 1951, the UNIVAC (Universal Automatic Computer) was built and sold to the U.S. Census Bureau.

In 1956, the invention of the transistors resulted in smaller, faster, more reliable, and more energy-efficient computers. This era also saw the emergence of the software development industry with the introduction of FORTRAN and COBOL, two early programming languages. In the next major technological advancement, transistors were replaced by tiny integrated circuits or "chips." Chips are smaller and cheaper than transistors and can contain thousands of circuits on a single chip. They give computers tremendous processing speed.

In 1970, the microprocessor, an entire CPU on a single chip, was invented. In 1977, Stephen Wozniak and Steven Jobs designed and built the first Apple computer in their garage. In 1981, IBM introduced its personal computer (PC). In the 1980s, clones of the IBM PC made the personal computer even more affordable. By the mid-1990s, people from many walks of life were able to afford them. Computers continue to become faster and less expensive as technology advances.

Modern-day computers are very powerful, reliable, and easy to use. They can accept spoken-word instructions and imitate human reasoning through artificial intelligence. Expert systems assist doctors in making diagnoses. Mobile computing applications are growing significantly. Using hand-held devices, delivery drivers can access global positioning satellites (GPS) to verify customer locations for pickups and deliveries. Cell phones can check your e-mail, make airline reservations, see how stocks are performing, and access your bank accounts.

Although there are several categories of computers, such as mainframe, midsize, and micro, all computers share some basic elements.

Elements of a Computer System

A computer is an electronic device capable of performing commands. The basic commands that a computer performs are input (get data), output (display results), storage, and performance of arithmetic and logical operations. There are two main components of a computer system—hardware and software. In the next few sections, we give a brief overview of these components. Let's look at hardware first.

Hardware

Major hardware components include the central processing unit (CPU); main memory (MM), also called random access memory (RAM); input/output devices; and secondary storage. Some examples of input devices are the keyboard, mouse, and secondary storage. Examples of output devices are the monitor, printer, and secondary storage.

CENTRAL PROCESSING UNIT AND MAIN MEMORY

The **central processing unit (CPU)** is the "brain" of the computer and the single most expensive piece of hardware in a computer. The more powerful the CPU, the faster the computer. Arithmetic and logical operations are carried out inside the CPU. Figure 1-1(a) shows some hardware components.

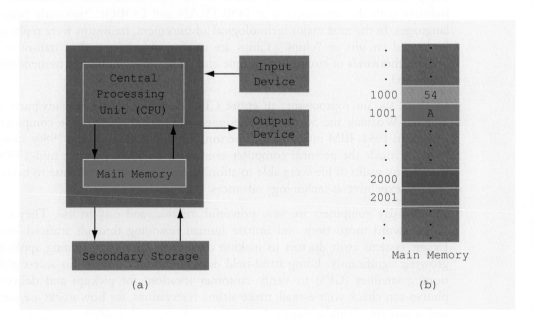

FIGURE 1-1 Hardware components of a computer and main memory

Main memory, or random access memory (RAM), is connected directly to the CPU. All programs must be loaded into main memory before they can be executed. Similarly, all data must be brought into main memory before a program can manipulate it. When the computer is turned off, everything in main memory is lost.

Main memory is an ordered sequence of cells, called **memory cells**. Each cell has a unique location in main memory, called the **address** of the cell. These addresses help you access the information stored in the cell. Figure 1-1(b) shows main memory with some data.

Today's computers come with main memory consisting of millions to billions of cells. Although Figure 1-1(b) shows data stored in cells, the content of a cell can be either a programming instruction or data. Moreover, this figure shows the data as numbers and letters. However, as explained later in this chapter, main memory stores everything as sequences of 0s and 1s. The memory addresses are also expressed as sequences of 0s and 1s.

SECONDARY STORAGE

Because programs and data must be stored in main memory before processing, and because everything in main memory is lost when the computer is turned off, information stored in main memory must be transferred to some other device for longer-term storage. A device that stores longer-term information (unless the device becomes unusable or you change the information by rewriting it) is called **secondary storage**. To be able to transfer information from main memory to secondary storage, these components must be connected directly to each other. Examples of secondary storage are hard disks, floppy disks, flash memory, ZIP disks, CD-ROMs, and tapes.

INPUT/OUTPUT DEVICES

For a computer to perform a useful task, it must be able to take in data and programs and display the results of the manipulation of the data. The devices that feed data and programs into computers are called **input devices**. The keyboard, mouse, and secondary storage are examples of input devices. The devices that the computer uses to display and store results are called **output devices**. A monitor, printer, and secondary storage are examples of output devices. Figure 1-2 shows some input and output devices.

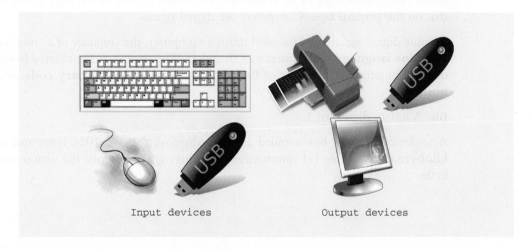

Input devices   Output devices

FIGURE 1-2 Some input and output devices

Software

Software consists of programs written to perform specific tasks. For example, you use word-processing programs to write letters, papers, and books. The two types of programs are system programs and application programs.

System programs control the computer. The system program that loads first when you turn on your PC is called the **operating system**. Without an operating system, the computer is useless. The operating system monitors the overall activity of the computer and provides services, such as memory management, input/output activities, and storage management. The operating system has a special program that organizes secondary storage so that you can access information conveniently. The operating system is the program that runs the application programs. **Application programs** perform specific tasks. Word processors, spreadsheets, and games are examples of application programs. Both operating systems and application programs are written in programming languages.

Language of a Computer

When you press A on your keyboard, the computer displays A on the screen, but what is actually stored inside the computer's main memory? What is the language of the computer? How does it store whatever you type on the keyboard?

Remember that a computer is an electronic device. Electrical signals move along channels inside the computer. There are two types of electrical signals: analog and digital. **Analog signals** are continuous waveforms used to represent things, such as sound. Audio tapes, for example, store data in analog signals. **Digital signals** represent information with a sequence of 0s and 1s. A 0 represents a low voltage, and a 1 represents a high voltage. Digital signals are more reliable carriers of information than analog signals and can be copied from one device to another with exact precision. You might have noticed that when you make a copy of an audio tape, the sound quality of the copy is not as good as that on the original tape. Computers use digital signals.

Because digital signals are processed inside a computer, the language of a computer, called **machine language**, is a sequence of 0s and 1s. The digit 0 or 1 is called a **binary digit**, or **bit**. Sometimes a sequence of 0s and 1s is referred to as a **binary code** or a **binary number**.

Bit: A binary digit 0 or 1.

A sequence of eight bits is called a **byte**. Moreover, $2^{10} = 1024$ bytes and is called a **kilobyte (KB)**. Table 1-1 summarizes the terms used to describe the various numbers of bytes.

TABLE 1-1 Binary Units

Unit	Symbol	Bits/Bytes
Byte		8 bits
Kilobyte	KB	2^{10} bytes = 1024 bytes
Megabyte	MB	1024 KB = 2^{10} KB = 2^{20} bytes = 1,048,576 bytes
Gigabyte	GB	1024 MB = 2^{10} MB = 2^{30} bytes = 1,073,741,824 bytes
Terabyte	TB	1024 GB = 2^{10} GB = 2^{40} bytes = 1,099,511,627,776 bytes
Petabyte	PB	1024 TB = 2^{10} TB = 2^{50} bytes = 1,125,899,906,842,624 bytes
Exabyte	EB	1024 PB = 2^{10} PB = 2^{60} bytes = 1,152,921,504,606,846,976 bytes
Zettabyte	ZB	1024 EB = 2^{10} EB = 2^{70} bytes = 1,180,591,620,717,411,303,424 bytes

Every letter, number, or special symbol (such as * or {) on your keyboard is encoded as a sequence of bits, each having a unique representation. The most commonly used encoding scheme on personal computers is the seven-bit **American Standard Code for Information Interchange (ASCII)**. The ASCII data set consists of 128 characters, numbered 0 through 127. (Note that $2^7 = 128$ and $2^8 = 256$.) That is, in the ASCII data set, the position of the first character is 0, the position of the second character is 1, and so on. In this scheme, A is encoded as 1000001. In fact, A is the 66th character in the ASCII character code, but its position is 65 because the position of the first character is 0. Furthermore, 1000001 is the binary representation of 65. The character 3 is encoded as 0110011. For a complete list of the printable ASCII character set, refer to Appendix C.

NOTE The number system that we use in our daily life is called the **decimal system** or **base 10**. Because everything inside a computer is represented as a sequence of 0s and 1s, that is, binary numbers, the number system that a computer uses is called binary or **base 2**. We indicated in the preceding paragraph that the number 1000001 is the binary representation of 65. Appendix D describes how to convert a number from base 10 to base 2 and vice versa. Appendix D also describes how to convert a number between base 2 and base 16 (hexadecimal) and between base 2 and base 8 (octal).

Inside the computer, every character is represented as a sequence of eight bits, that is, as a byte. Because ASCII is a seven-bit code, you must add 0 to the left of the ASCII encoding of a character. Hence, inside the computer, the character A is represented as 01000001, and the character 3 is represented as 00110011.

Other encoding schemes include Unicode, which is a more recent development. **Unicode** consists of 65,536 characters. To store a Unicode character, you need two bytes. Java uses the Unicode character set. Therefore, in Java, every character is represented as a sequence of 16 bits, that is, 2 bytes. In Unicode, the character A is represented as 0000000001000001.

The ASCII character set is a subset of Unicode; the first 128 characters of Unicode are the same as the characters in ASCII. If you are dealing with only the English language, the ASCII character set is sufficient to write Java programs. The advantage of the Unicode character set is that symbols from languages other than English can be handled easily.

Evolution of Programming Languages

The most basic computer language, machine language, provides program instructions in bits. Even though most computers perform the same kinds of operations, the designers of different CPUs sometimes choose different sets of binary codes to perform those operations. Therefore, the machine language of one computer is not necessarily the same as the machine language of another computer. The only consistency among computers is that in any computer, all data are stored and manipulated as a binary code.

Early computers were programmed in machine language. To see how instructions are written in machine language, suppose you want to use the equation:

```
wages = rate · hours
```

to calculate weekly wages. Assume that the memory locations of rate, hours, and wages are 010001, 010010, and 010011, respectively. Further suppose that the binary code 100100 stands for load, 100110 stands for multiplication, and 100010 stands for store. In machine language, you might need the following sequence of instructions to calculate the weekly wages:

```
100100 010001
100110 010010
100010 010011
```

To represent the weekly wages equation in machine language, the programmer had to remember the machine language codes for various operations. Also, to manipulate data, the programmer had to remember the locations of the data in main memory. Remembering specific codes made programming difficult and error prone.

Assembly languages were developed to make the programmer's job easier. In **assembly language**, an instruction is an easy-to-remember form called a **mnemonic**. Table 1-2 shows some examples of instructions in assembly language and their corresponding machine language code.

TABLE 1-2 Examples of Instructions in Assembly Language and Machine Language

Assembly Language	Machine Language
LOAD	100100
STOR	100010
MULT	100110
ADD	100101
SUB	100011

Using assembly language instructions, you can write the equation to calculate the weekly wages as follows:

```
LOAD    rate
MULT    hours
STOR    wages
```

As you can see, it is much easier to write instructions in assembly language. However, a computer cannot execute assembly language instructions directly. The instructions first have to be translated into machine language. A program called an **assembler** translates the assembly language instructions into machine language.

Assembler: A program that translates a program written in assembly language into an equivalent program in machine language.

Moving from machine language to assembly language made programming easier, but a programmer was still forced to think in terms of individual machine instructions. The next step toward making programming easier was to devise **high-level languages** that were closer to spoken languages, such as English and Spanish. Basic, FORTRAN, COBOL, Pascal, C, C++, and Java are all high-level languages. You will learn the high-level language Java in this book.

In Java, you write the weekly wages equation as follows:

```
wages = rate * hours;
```

The instruction written in Java is much easier to understand and is self-explanatory to a novice user who is familiar with basic arithmetic. As in the case of assembly language, however, the computer cannot directly execute instructions written in a high-level language. To run on a computer, these Java instructions first need to be translated into an intermediate language called **bytecode** and then interpreted into a particular machine language. A program called a **compiler** translates instructions written in Java into bytecode.

Compiler: A program that translates a program written in a high-level language into the equivalent machine language. (In the case of Java, this machine language is the bytecode.)

Recall that the computer understands only machine language. Moreover, different types of CPUs use different machine languages. To make Java programs **machine independent**, that is, able to run on many different types of computer platforms, the designers of Java introduced a hypothetical computer called the **Java Virtual Machine (JVM)**. In fact, bytecode is the machine language for the JVM.

NOTE In languages such as C and C++, the compiler translates the source code directly into the machine language of your computer's CPU. For such languages, a different compiler is needed for each type of CPU. Therefore, programs in these languages are not easily portable from one type of machine to another. The source code must be recompiled for each type of CPU. To make Java programs machine independent and easily portable, and to allow them to run on a Web browser, the designers of Java introduced the Java Virtual Machine (JVM) and bytecode as the (machine) language of this machine. It is easier to translate a bytecode into a particular type of CPU. This concept is covered further in the following section, Processing a Java Program.

Processing a Java Program

Java has two types of programs—applications and applets. The following is an example of a Java application program:

```java
public class MyFirstJavaProgram
{
    public static void main(String[] args)
    {
        System.out.println("My first Java program.");
    }
}
```

At this point you need not be too concerned with the details of this program. However, if you run (execute) this program, it will display the following line on the screen:

```
My first Java program.
```

Recall that a computer can understand only machine language. Therefore, in order to run this program successfully, the code must first be translated into the machine language. In this section we review the steps required to execute programs written in Java.

To process a program written in Java, you carry out the following steps, as illustrated in Figure 1-3.

1. You use a text editor, such as Notepad, to create (that is, type) a program in Java following the rules, or syntax, of the language. This program is called the **source program**. The program must be saved in a text file named `ClassName.java`, where `ClassName` is the name of the Java class contained in the file. For example, in the Java program

1

given above, the name of the (`public`) class containing the Java program is `MyFirstJavaProgram`. Therefore, this program must be saved in the text file named `MyFirstJavaProgram.java`. Otherwise an error will occur.

Source program: A program written in a high-level language.

2. You must verify that the program obeys the rules of the programming language—that is, the program must be syntactically correct—and translate the program into the equivalent bytecode. The compiler checks the source program for syntax errors and, if no error is found, translates the program into bytecode. The bytecode is saved in the file with the `.class` extension. For example, the bytecode for `MyFirstJavaProgram.java` is stored in the `MyFirstJavaProgram.class` file by the compiler.

3. To run a Java application program, the `.class` file must be loaded into computer memory. To run a Java applet, you must use either a Web browser or an applet viewer, a stripped-down Web browser for running applets. The programs that you write in Java are typically developed using an **integrated development environment (IDE)**. The IDE contains many programs that are useful in creating your program. For example, it contains the necessary code to display the results of the program and several mathematical functions to make the programmer's job somewhat easier. Because certain code is already available to you, you can use this code rather than writing your own. You can also develop your own libraries (called *packages* in Java). (Note that in Java, typically, a package is a set of related classes. So, typically, a Java program is a collection of classes. We will explain this further in Chapters 2 and 8. At this point, you need not be too concerned with these details.) In general, to successfully run a Java program, the bytecode for classes used in the program must be connected. The program that automatically does this in Java is known as the **loader**.

4. The next step is to execute the Java program. In addition to connecting the bytecode from various classes, the loader also loads your Java program's bytecode into main memory. As the classes are loaded into main memory, the *bytecode verifier* verifies that the bytecode for the classes is valid and does not violate Java's security restrictions. Finally, a program called an **interpreter** translates each bytecode instruction into your computer's machine language, and then executes it.

Interpreter: A program that reads and translates each bytecode instruction into your computer's machine language, and then executes it.

Note that the Java interpreter translates and executes one bytecode instruction at a time. It does not first translate the entire bytecode into your computer's machine language. As noted earlier, in languages such as C++, a different compiler is needed for each type of CPU, whereas a Java compiler translates a Java source program into bytecode, the machine language of JVM, which is independent of any particular type of CPU.

The Java interpreter translates each bytecode instruction into a particular type of CPU machine language and then executes the instruction. Thus, in the case of the Java language, a different type of interpreter is needed for a particular type of CPU. However, interpreters are programs that are simpler than compilers. Because the Java interpreter translates one bytecode instruction at a time, Java programs run more slowly.

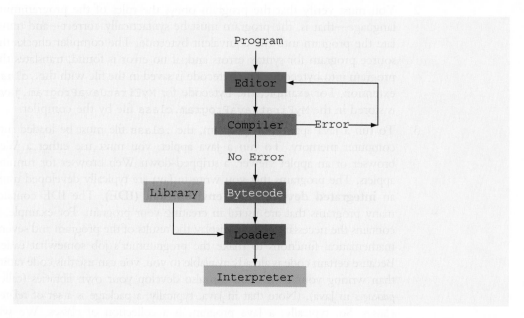

FIGURE 1-3 Processing a Java program

As a programmer, one of your primary concerns is with Step 1. That is, you must learn, understand, and master the rules of the programming language to create source programs. Programs are developed using an IDE. Well-known IDEs used to create programs in Java include JBuilder (from Borland), CodeWarrior (Metrowerks), and jGrasp (Auburn University). These IDEs contain an editor to create the program, a compiler to check the program for syntax errors, a program to load the object codes of the resources used from the IDE, and a program to execute the program. These IDEs are also quite user friendly. When you compile your program, the compiler not only identifies the syntax errors, but also typically suggests how to correct them.

> **NOTE**   Other software that can be used to develop Java programs include Eclipse, TextPad, JCreator, BlueJ, and DrJava.

In Chapter 2, after being introduced to some basic elements of Java, you will see how a Java program is created.

Internet, World Wide Web, Browser, and Java

We often hear the terms Internet, World Wide Web (or simply, Web) and Web browser (or simply, browser). What do these terms mean, and what is Java's connection with them?

The *Internet* is an interconnection of networks that allows computers around the world to communicate with each other. In 1969, the U.S. Department of Defense's Advanced Research Project Agency (ARPA) funded research projects to investigate and develop techniques and technologies to interlink networks. The objective was to develop communication protocols so that networked computers could communicate with each other. This was called the *internetting* project, and the funding resulted into ARPANET, which eventually became known as the "Internet."

Over the last four decades, the Internet has grown manyfold. In 1973, approximately 25 computers were connected via the Internet. This number grew to 700,000 computers by 1991, and to over 10,000,000 by 2000. Each day, more and more computers are getting connected via the Internet.

The terms Internet and World Wide Web are often used interchangeably. However, there is a difference between the two. The Internet allows computers to be connected and communicate with each other. On the other hand, the *World Wide Web* (WWW), or Web, uses software programs that enable computer users to access documents and files (including images, audio, and video) on almost any subject over the Internet with the click of a mouse. Undoubtedly, the Internet has become one of the world's leading communication mechanisms. Computers around the world communicate via the Internet; the World Wide Web makes that communication a fun activity.

The primary language for the Web is known as *Hypertext Markup Language* (HTML). It is a simple language for laying out and linking documents, as well as for viewing images and listening to sound. However, HTML is not capable of interacting with the user, except to collect information via simple forms. Therefore, Web pages are essentially static. As noted previously, Java has two types of programs—applications and applets. In terms of programming, both types are similar. Application programs are stand-alone programs that can run on your computer. Java applets are programs that run from a *Web browser* and make the Web responsive and interactive. Two well-known *browsers* are Mozilla Firefox and Internet Explorer. Java applets can run in either browser. Moreover, through the use of applets, the Web becomes responsive, interactive, and fun to use. (Note that to run applets, the browser you use must be Java enabled.)

Programming with the Problem Analysis–Coding–Execution Cycle

Programming is a process of problem solving. Different people use different techniques to solve problems. Some techniques are clearly outlined and easy to follow; they solve the problem and give insight into how the solution was reached. Such problem-solving techniques can be easily modified if the domain of the problem changes.

To be a skillful problem solver, and, therefore, to become a skillful programmer, you must use good problem-solving techniques. One common problem-solving technique includes analyzing a problem, outlining the problem requirements, and designing steps, called an **algorithm**, to solve the problem.

Algorithm: A step-by-step problem-solving process in which a solution is arrived at in a finite amount of time.

In the programming environment, the problem-solving process involves the following steps:

1. Analyze the problem and outline the problem and its solution requirements.
2. Design an algorithm to solve the problem.
3. Implement the algorithm in a programming language, such as Java.
4. Verify that the algorithm works.
5. Maintain the program by using and improving it, and modifying it if the problem domain changes.

Figure 1-4 summarizes this programming process.

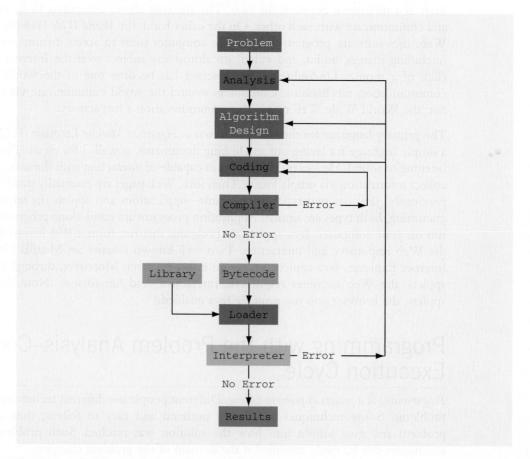

FIGURE 1-4 Problem analysis–coding–execution cycle

To develop a program to solve a problem, you start by analyzing the problem, then outlining the problem and the options for a solution. You then design the algorithm; write the program instructions in a high-level language, or code the program; and enter the program into a computer system.

Analyzing the problem is the first, and most important, step in the process. This step requires that you do the following:

- Thoroughly understand the problem.

- Understand the problem requirements. Requirements can include whether the program requires interaction with the user, whether it manipulates data, whether it produces output, and what the output looks like. If the program manipulates data, the programmer must know what the data are and how they are represented. To do this, you need to look at sample data.

- If the program produces output, you should know how the results should be generated and formatted.

- If the problem is complex, divide the problem into subproblems and repeat Steps 1 and 2 by analyzing each subproblem and understanding each subproblem's requirements. You also need to know how the subproblems relate to each other.

After you carefully analyze the problem, the next step is to design an algorithm to solve it. If you broke the problem into subproblems, you need to design an algorithm for each subproblem. Once you design an algorithm, you must check it for correctness. You can sometimes do this using sample data; other times, you might need to perform some mathematical analysis to test the algorithm's correctness. You also need to integrate the subproblem solutions.

Once you have designed the algorithm and verified its correctness, the next step is to convert the algorithm into a high-level language. You use a text editor to enter the program into a computer, making sure that the program follows the language's syntax. To verify the correctness of the syntax, you run the code through a compiler. If the compiler generates error messages, you must identify the errors in the code, resolve them, and then run the code through the compiler again. When all syntax errors are removed, the compiler generates the machine code (bytecode in Java).

The final step is to execute the program. The compiler guarantees only that the program follows the language's syntax; it does not guarantee that the program will run correctly. During execution, the program might terminate abnormally due to logical errors, such as division by zero. Even if the program terminates normally, it may still generate erroneous results. Under these circumstances, you may have to reexamine the code, the algorithm, or even your analysis of the problem.

Your overall programming experience will benefit if you spend enough time to thoroughly complete the problem analysis before attempting to write the programming instructions. Usually, you do this work on paper using a pen or pencil. Taking this careful approach to programming has a number of advantages. It is much easier to discover errors in a program that is well analyzed and well designed. Furthermore, a thoroughly analyzed and carefully designed program is much easier to follow and modify. Even the most experienced programmers spend a considerable amount of time analyzing a problem and designing an algorithm.

Throughout this book, you will learn not only the rules of writing programs in Java, but also problem-solving techniques. Each chapter discusses several programming problems, each of which is clearly marked as a Programming Example. The Programming Examples teach techniques to analyze and solve the problems and also help you understand the concepts discussed in the chapter. To gain the full benefit of this book, we recommend that you work through the Programming Examples at the end of each chapter.

EXAMPLE 1-1

In this example, we design an algorithm to find the perimeter and area of a rectangle.

To find the perimeter and area of a rectangle, you need to know the rectangle's length and width. The perimeter and area of the rectangle are then given by the following formulas:

```
perimeter = 2 · (length + width)
area = length · width
```

The algorithm to find the perimeter and area of the rectangle is:

1. Get the length of the rectangle.
2. Get the width of the rectangle.
3. Find the perimeter using the following equation:

   ```
   perimeter = 2 · (length + width)
   ```

4. Find the area using the following equation:

   ```
   area = length · width
   ```

EXAMPLE 1-2

In this example, we design an algorithm that calculates the monthly paycheck of a salesperson at a local department store.

Every salesperson has a base salary. The salesperson also receives a bonus at the end of each month, based on the following criteria: If the salesperson has been with the store for five years or less, the bonus is $10 for each year that he or she has worked there. If the salesperson has been with the store for more than five years, the bonus is $20 for each year that he or she has worked there. The salesperson can earn an additional bonus as follows: If the total sales made by the salesperson for the month are greater than or equal to $5,000 but less than $10,000, he or she receives a 3% commission on the sale. If the total sales made by the salesperson for the month are at least $10,000, he or she receives a 6% commission on the sale.

To calculate a salesperson's monthly paycheck, you need to know the base salary, the number of years that the salesperson has been with the company, and the total sales made by the salesperson for that month. Suppose baseSalary denotes the base salary, noOfServiceYears denotes the number of years that the salesperson has been with the store, bonus denotes the bonus, totalSales denotes the total sales made by the salesperson for the month, and additionalBonus denotes the additional bonus.

You can determine the bonus as follows:

```
if (noOfServiceYears is less than or equal to five)
    bonus = 10 · noOfServiceYears
otherwise
    bonus = 20 · noOfServiceYears
```

Next, you can determine the additional bonus of the salesperson as follows:

```
if (totalSales is less than 5000)
    additionalBonus = 0
otherwise
        if (totalSales is greater than or equal to 5000 and
                    totalSales is less than 10000)
            additionalBonus = totalSales · (0.03)
        otherwise
            additionalBonus = totalSales · (0.06)
```

Following the above discussion, you can now design the algorithm to calculate a salesperson's monthly paycheck:

1. Get baseSalary.

2. Get noOfServiceYears.

3. Calculate bonus using the following formula:

```
if (noOfServiceYears is less than or equal to five)
    bonus = 10 · noOfServiceYears
otherwise
    bonus = 20 · noOfServiceYears
```

4. Get totalSales.

5. Calculate additionalBonus using the following formula:

```
if (totalSales is less than 5000)
    additionalBonus = 0
otherwise
    if (totalSales is greater than or equal to 5000 and
        totalSales is less than 10000)
        additionalBonus = totalSales · (0.03)
otherwise
        additionalBonus = totalSales · (0.06)
```

6. Calculate payCheck using the following equation:

```
payCheck = baseSalary + bonus + additionalBonus
```

EXAMPLE 1-3

In this example, we design an algorithm to play a number-guessing game.

The objective is to randomly generate an integer greater than or equal to 0 and less than 100. Then, prompt the player (user) to guess the number. If the player guesses the number correctly, output an appropriate message. Otherwise, check whether the guessed number is less than the random number. If the guessed number is less than the random number generated, output the message, "Your guess is lower than the number. Guess again!"; otherwise, output the message, "Your guess is higher than the number. Guess again!". Then, prompt the player to enter another number. The player is prompted to guess the random number until the player enters the correct number.

The first step is to generate a random number, as described above. Java provides the means to do so, which is discussed in Chapter 5. Suppose num stands for the random number and guess stands for the number guessed by the player.

After the player enters the guess, you can compare the guess with the random number as follows:

```
if (guess is equal to num)
    Print "You guessed the correct number."
otherwise
    if guess is less than num
       Print "Your guess is lower than the number. Guess again!"
otherwise
       Print "Your guess is higher than the number. Guess again!"
```

You can now design an algorithm as follows:

1. Generate a random number and call it num.

2. *Repeat* the following steps until the player has guessed the correct number:

   a. Prompt the player to enter guess.

   b.
```
      if (guess is equal to num)
          Print "You guessed the correct number."
      otherwise
          if guess is less than num
             Print "Your guess is lower than the number. Guess again!"
      otherwise
             Print "Your guess is higher than the number. Guess again!"
```

In Chapter 5, we write a program that uses this algorithm to play the number-guessing game.

The type of coding used in Examples 1-1 to 1-3 is called **pseudocode**, which is an "outline" of a program that could be translated into actual code. Pseudocode is not written in a particular language, nor does it have syntax rules; it is mainly a technique to show the programming steps.

Programming Methodologies

Two popular approaches to programming design are the structured approach and the object-oriented approach, which are outlined below.

Structured Programming

Dividing a problem into smaller subproblems is called **structured design**. Each subproblem is then analyzed, and a solution for the subproblem is obtained. The solutions to all the subproblems are then combined to solve the overall problem. This process of implementing a structured design is called **structured programming**. The structured design approach is also known as **top-down design**, **bottom-up design**, **stepwise refinement**, and **modular programming**.

Object-Oriented Programming

Object-oriented design (OOD) is a widely used programming methodology. In OOD, the first step in the problem-solving process is to identify the components called **objects**, which form the basis of the solution, and to determine how these objects interact with one another. For example, suppose you want to write a program that automates the video rental process for a local video store. The two main objects in this problem are the video and the customer.

After identifying the objects, the next step is to specify for each object the relevant data and possible operations to be performed on that data. For example, for a video object, the *data* might include:

- movie name
- starring actors
- producer
- production company
- number of copies in stock

Some of the operations on a video object might include:

- checking the name of the movie
- reducing the number of copies in stock by one after a copy is rented
- incrementing the number of copies in stock by one after a customer returns a copy

This illustrates that each **object** consists of data and the operations on those data. An object combines data and operations on that data into a single unit. In OOD, the final program is a collection of interacting objects. A programming language that implements OOD is called an **object-oriented programming (OOP)** language. You will learn about the many advantages of OOD in later chapters.

Because an object consists of data and operations on the data, before you can design and use objects, you need to learn how to represent data in computer memory, how to manipulate data, and how to implement operations. In Chapter 2, you will learn the basic data types of Java and discover how to represent and manipulate data in computer memory. Chapter 3 discusses how to input data into a Java program and output the results generated by a Java program.

To create operations, you write algorithms and implement them in a programming language. Because a data element in a complex program usually has many operations, to separate operations from each other and use them effectively and in a convenient manner, you use **methods** to implement algorithms. You will learn the details of methods in Chapter 7. Certain algorithms require that a program make decisions, a process called selection. Other algorithms might require that certain statements be repeated until certain conditions are met, a process called repetition. Still other algorithms might require both selection and repetition. You will learn about selection and repetition mechanisms, called control structures, in Chapters 4 and 5.

Finally, to work with objects, you need to know how to combine data and operations on that data into a single unit. In Java, the mechanism that allows you to combine data and operations on the data into a single unit is called a **class**. In Chapter 8, you will learn how to create your own classes.

In Chapter 9, using a mechanism called an array, you will learn how to manipulate data when data items are of the same type, such as the items in a list of sales figures. As you can see, you need to learn quite a few things before working with the OOD methodology.

For some problems, the structured approach to program design is very effective. Other problems are better addressed by OOD. For example, if a problem requires manipulating sets of numbers with mathematical functions, you might use the structured design approach and outline the steps required to obtain the solution. The Java library supplies a wealth of functions that you can use to manipulate numbers effectively. On the other hand, if you want to write a program that would make a candy machine operational, the OOD approach is more effective. Java was designed especially to implement OOD. Furthermore, OOD works well and is used in conjunction with structured design. Chapter 6 explains how to use an existing class to create a Graphical User Interface (GUI) and then gives several examples explaining how to solve problems using OOD concepts.

Both the structured design and OOD approaches require that you master the basic components of a programming language to be an effective programmer. In the next few chapters, you will learn the basic components of Java required by either approach to programming.

QUICK REVIEW

1. A computer is an electronic device capable of performing arithmetic and logical operations.

2. A computer system has two kinds of components: hardware and software.

3. The central processing unit (CPU) and the main memory are examples of hardware components.

4. All programs must be brought into main memory before they can be executed.

5. When the power to the computer is switched off, everything in main memory is lost.

6. Secondary storage provides permanent storage for information. Hard disks, floppy disks, flash-memory, ZIP disks, CD-ROMs, and tapes are examples of secondary storage.

7. Input to the computer is done via an input device. Two common input devices are the keyboard and the mouse.

8. The computer sends output to an output device, such as the computer monitor.

9. Software refers to programs run by the computer.

10. The operating system monitors the overall activity of the computer and provides services.

11. Application programs perform a specific task.

12. The most basic language of a computer is a sequence of 0s and 1s called machine language. Every computer directly understands its own machine language.

13. A bit is a binary digit, 0 or 1.

14. A sequence of 0s and 1s is called a binary code or a binary number.

15. A byte is a sequence of eight bits.

16. One kilobyte (KB) is $2^{10} = 1024$ bytes; one megabyte (MB) is $2^{20} = 1,048,576$ bytes; one gigabyte (GB) is $2^{30} = 1,073,741,824$ bytes; one terabyte (TB) is $2^{40} = 1,099,511,627,776$ bytes; one petabyte (PB) is $2^{50} = 1,125,899,906,842,624$ bytes; one exabyte (EB) is $2^{60} = 1,152,921,504,606,846,976$ bytes; and one zettabyte (ZB) is $2^{70} = 1,180,591,620,717,411,303,424$ bytes.

17. Assembly language uses easy-to-remember instructions called mnemonics.

18. Assemblers are programs that translate a program written in assembly language into machine language.

19. To run a Java program on a computer, the program must first be translated into an intermediate language called bytecode and then interpreted into a particular machine language.

20. To make Java programs machine independent, the designers of the Java language introduced a hypothetical computer called the Java Virtual Machine (JVM).

21. Bytecode is the machine language for the JVM.

22. Compilers are programs that translate a program written in a high-level language into an equivalent machine language. In the case of Java, this machine language is the bytecode.

23. In Java, the necessary steps to process a program are edit, compile, load, and execute.

24. A Java loader transfers into main memory the bytecode of the classes needed to execute the program.

25. An interpreter is a program that reads, translates each bytecode instruction into the machine language of your computer, and then executes it.

26. The Internet is a network of networks through which computers around the world are connected.

27. The World Wide Web, or Web, uses software programs that allow computer users to view documents on almost any subject over the Internet with the click of a mouse.

28. Java application programs are stand-alone programs that can run on your computer. Java applets are programs that run from a Web browser, or simply a browser.

29. A problem-solving process for programming has five steps: analyze the problem, design an algorithm, implement the algorithm in a programming language, verify that the algorithm works, and maintain the program.

30. An algorithm is a step-by-step problem-solving process in which a solution is arrived at in a finite amount of time.

31. The two basic approaches to programming design are structured design and object-oriented design.

32. In structured design, a problem is divided into smaller subproblems. Each subproblem is solved, and the subproblem solutions are integrated.

33. In object-oriented design (OOD), the programmer identifies components called objects, which form the basis of the solution, and determines how these objects interact with one another. In OOD, a program is a collection of interacting objects.

34. An object consists of data and the operations on those data.

EXERCISES

1. Mark the following statements as true or false.

   a. The first device known to carry out calculations was the Pascline.

   b. Modern-day computers can accept spoken-word instructions, but cannot imitate human reasoning.

   c. In Unicode, every character is coded as a sequence of sixteen bits.

   d. The arithmetic operations are performed inside the CPU and, if an error is found, it outputs the logical errors.

   e. A sequence of 0s and 1s is called a decimal code.

   f. A Java compiler is a program that translates a Java program into bytecode.

   g. Bytecode is the machine language of the JVM.

   h. The CPU stands for command performing unit.

   i. RAM stands for readily available memory.

   j. A program written in a high-level programming language is called a source program.

   k. ZB stands for zero byte.

   l. The first step in the problem-solving process is to analyze the problem.

2. Name two input devices.

3. Name two output devices.

4. Why is secondary storage needed?

5. What is the function of an operating system?

6. What are the two types of programs?

7. What are the differences between machine languages and high-level languages?

8. What is a source program?

9. What kind of errors are reported by a compiler?

10. Why do you need to translate a program written in a high-level language into machine language?

11. Why would you prefer to write a program in a high-level language rather than a machine language?

12. What are the advantages of problem analysis and algorithm design over directly writing a program in a high-level language?

13. Design an algorithm to find the weighted average of four test scores. The four test scores and their respective weights are given in the following format:

    ```
    testScore1 weightTestScore1
    ...
    ```

For example, a sample data is as follows:

```
75 0.20
95 0.35
85 0.15
65 0.30
```

14. Given the radius, in inches, and price of a pizza, design an algorithm and write the pseudocode to find the price of the pizza per square inch.

15. To make a profit, the prices of the items sold in a furniture store are marked up by 80%. After marking up the prices each item is put on sale at a discount of 10%. Design an algorithm to find the selling price of an item sold at the furniture store. What information do you need to find the selling price?

16. Suppose a, b, and c denote the lengths of the sides of a triangle. Then, the area of the triangle can be calculated using the formula:

$$\sqrt{s(s-a)(s-b)(s-c)}$$

where $s = (1/2)(a + b + c)$. Design an algorithm that uses this formula to find the area of a triangle. What information do you need to find the area?

17. Suppose that the cost of sending an international fax is calculated as follows: Service charges $3.00, $0.20 per page for the first 10 pages, and $0.10 for each additional page. Design an algorithm that asks the user to enter the number of pages to be faxed. The algorithm then uses the number of pages to be faxed to calculate the amount due.

18. You are given a list of students' names and their test scores. Design an algorithm that does the following:

   a. Calculates the average test scores.

   b. Determines and prints the names of all the students whose test score is below the average test score.

   c. Determines the highest test score.

   d. Prints the names of all the students whose test score is the same as the highest test score.

   (You must divide this problem into subproblems as follows: The first subproblem determines the average test score. The second subproblem determines and prints the names of all the students whose test score is below the average test score. The third subproblem determines the highest test score. The fourth subproblem prints the names of all the students whose test score is the same as the highest test score. The main algorithm combines the solutions of the subproblems.)

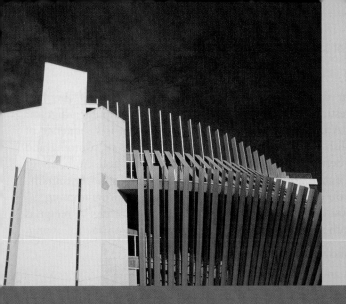

CHAPTER 2

BASIC ELEMENTS OF JAVA

IN THIS CHAPTER, YOU WILL:

- Become familiar with the basic components of a Java program, including methods, special symbols, and identifiers
- Explore primitive data types
- Discover how to use arithmetic operators
- Examine how a program evaluates arithmetic expressions
- Explore how mixed expressions are evaluated
- Learn about type casting
- Become familiar with the `String` type
- Learn what an assignment statement is and what it does
- Discover how to input data into memory by using input statements
- Become familiar with the use of increment and decrement operators
- Examine ways to output results using output statements
- Learn how to import packages and why they are necessary
- Discover how to create a Java application program
- Learn how to understand and correct syntax errors
- Explore how to properly structure a program, including using comments to document a program
- Learn how to avoid bugs using consistent and proper formatting, and code walk-through
- Learn how to do a code walk-through

In this chapter, you will learn the basics of Java. As you begin to learn the Java programming language, two questions naturally arise: First, what is a computer program? Second, what is programming? A **computer program**, or a program, is a sequence of statements intended to accomplish a task. **Programming** is a process of planning and creating a program. These two definitions tell the truth, but not the whole truth, about programming. It might take an entire book to give a satisfactory definition of programming. An analogy might help you gain a better grasp of the nature of programming, so we'll use a topic on which almost everyone has some knowledge—cooking. A recipe is also a program, and everyone with some cooking experience can agree on the following:

1. It is usually easier to follow a recipe than to create one.
2. There are good recipes and there are bad recipes.
3. Some recipes are easy to follow and some are difficult to follow.
4. Some recipes produce reliable results and some do not.
5. You must have some knowledge of how to use cooking tools to follow a recipe to completion.
6. To create good new recipes, you must have significant knowledge and understanding of cooking.

These same six points can also be applied to programming. Let us take the cooking analogy one step further. Suppose you want to teach someone how to become a chef. How would you go about it? Would you introduce the person to good food, hoping the person develops a taste for it? Would you have the person follow recipe after recipe in the hope that some of the techniques rub off? Or, would you first teach the use of the tools, the nature of ingredients and foods and spices, and then explain how these concepts fit together?

Just as there are many ways to teach cooking, there are also different ways to teach programming. However, some fundamentals apply to programming, just as they do to cooking or other activities, such as music.

Learning a programming language is like learning to become a chef or learning to play a musical instrument. All three skills require direct interaction with the tools. You cannot become a good chef just by reading recipes. Similarly, you cannot learn to play musical instruments by reading books about musical instruments. The same is true of programming. You must have a fundamental knowledge of the language, and you must test your programs on the computer to make sure that each program does what it is supposed to do.

A Java Program

In this and the next chapter, you will learn the basic elements and concepts of the Java programming language used to create a Java program. In addition to giving examples to illustrate various concepts, we also include Java programs to help clarify the concepts. This section gives an example of a Java program. At this point you need not be too concerned with the details of this program. You only need to understand the effect of an *output* statement, which is introduced in the program.

Consider the following Java (application) program:

```
//********************************************************
// This is a simple Java program. It displays three lines
// of text, including the sum of two numbers.
//********************************************************

public class ASimpleJavaProgram
{
    public static void main(String[] args)
    {
        System.out.println("My first Java program.");
        System.out.println("The sum of 2 and 3 = " + 5);
        System.out.println("7 + 8 = " + (7 + 8));
    }
}
```

Sample Run: (When you compile and execute this program, the following three lines are displayed on the screen.)

```
My first Java program.
The sum of 2 and 3 = 5
7 + 8 = 15
```

This output is displayed on the screen when the following three lines are executed:

```
System.out.println("My first Java program.");
System.out.println("The sum of 2 and 3 = " + 5);
System.out.println("7 + 8 = " + (7 + 8));
```

To explain how this happens, let's first consider the statement:

```
System.out.println("My first Java program.");
```

This is an example of a Java *output* statement. It causes the program to evaluate whatever is in the parentheses and display the result on the screen. Typically, anything in double quotation marks, called a *string*, evaluates to itself, that is, its value is the string itself. Therefore, the statement causes the system to display the following line on the screen:

```
My first Java program.
```

(In general, when a string is printed, it is printed without the double quotation marks.) Now let's consider the statement:

```
System.out.println("The sum of 2 and 3 = " + 5);
```

In this output statement, the parentheses contain the string "The sum of 2 and 3 = ", + (the plus sign), and the number 5. Here the symbol + is used to concatenate (join) the operands. In this case, the system automatically converts the number 5 into a string, joins that string with the first string, and displays the following line on the screen:

```
The sum of 2 and 3 = 5
```

Now let's consider the statement:

```
System.out.println("7 + 8 = " + (7 + 8));
```

In this output statement, the parentheses contain the string "7 + 8 = ", + (the plus sign), and the expression (7 + 8). In the expression (7 + 8), notice the parentheses around 7 + 8. This causes the system to add the numbers 7 and 8, resulting in 15. The number 15 is then converted to the string "15" and then joined with the string "7 + 8 = ". Therefore, the output of this statement is:

```
7 + 8 = 15
```

In this and the next chapter, until we explain how to construct a Java program properly, we will use output statements such as the preceding ones to explain concepts.

Before closing this section, let's look at some other features of the preceding Java program. The basic unit of a Java program is a `class`. Typically, every Java `class` consists of one or more methods. Roughly speaking, a method is a sequence of statements or instructions whose objective is to accomplish something. The first line of the program is:

```
public class ASimpleJavaProgram
```

`ASimpleJavaProgram` is the name of the Java `class`. The second line of the program consists of the left brace, which is matched with the second right brace (the very last brace). These braces together mark the beginning and end of (the body of) the `class` `ASimpleJavaProgram`. The third line consists of:

```
public static void main(String[] args)
```

This is the heading of the method named `main`. A Java `class` can have at most one method `main`. If a Java `class` contains an application program, such as the preceding program, it must contain the method `main`. When you execute (run) a Java (application) program, execution always begins with the method `main`.

The eighth line consists of a left brace (the second left brace of the program). This marks the beginning of (the body of) the method `main`. The first right brace (on the 12th line of the program) matches this left brace and marks the end of (the body of) the method `main`. The method `main` is indented to set it apart.

In the next section, you will learn about the purpose of the lines shown in green in the program.

Basics of a Java Program

As we stated in the previous chapter, the two types of Java programs are Java applets and Java application programs. Java applets are programs designed to run on a Web browser. Java application programs do not require a Web browser. To introduce the basic Java components, in the next few chapters we develop Java application programs. Java applets are considered later.

If you have never seen a program written in a programming language, the Java program, `ASimpleJavaProgram`, given in the previous section, may seem to be written in a foreign language. To make meaningful sentences in any foreign language, you must learn its alphabet, words, and grammar. The same is true of a programming language. To write meaningful programs, you must learn the programming language's special symbols, words, and syntax rules. The **syntax rules** tell you which statements (instructions) are legal, or accepted by the programming language, and which are not. You must also learn the **semantic rules**, which determine the meaning of the instructions. The programming language's rules, symbols, special words, and their meanings enable you to write programs to solve problems.

Programming language: A set of rules, symbols, and special words used to construct programs.

In the remainder of this section, you will learn about some of the special symbols used in a Java program. Additional symbols are introduced as other concepts are encountered in later chapters. Similarly, syntax and semantic rules are introduced and discussed throughout the book.

Comments

The program that you write should be clear not only to you, but also to the reader of your program. Part of good programming is the inclusion of comments in the program. Typically, comments can be used to identify the authors of the program, give the date when the program is written or modified, give a brief explanation of the program, and explain the meaning of key statements in a program. In the programming examples, for the programs that we write, we will not include the date when the program is written, consistent with the standard convention for writing such books.

Comments are for the reader, not for the compiler. So when a compiler compiles a program to check for the syntax errors, it completely ignores comments. Throughout this book, comments are shown in green.

`ASimpleJavaProgram`, given in the previous section, contains the following comments:

```
//*******************************************************
// This is a simple Java program. It displays three lines
// of text, including the sum of two numbers.
//*******************************************************
```

A Java program has two common types of comments—single-line comments and multiple-line comments.

Single-line comments begin with `//` and can be placed anywhere in the line. Everything encountered in that line after `//` is ignored by the compiler. For example, consider the following statement:

```
System.out.println("7 + 8 = " + (7 + 8));
```

You can put comments at the end of this line as follows:

```
System.out.println("7 + 8 = " + (7 + 8)); //prints: 7 + 8 = 15
```

This comment could be meaningful for a beginning programmer.

Multiple-line comments are enclosed between /* and */. The compiler ignores anything that appears between /* and */. For example, the following is an example of a multiple-line comment:

```
/*
    You can include comments that can
    occupy several lines.
*/
```

Special Symbols

The following are some of the special symbols:

```
+     -     *     /
.     ;     ?     ,
<=    !=    ==    >=
```

The first row includes mathematical symbols for addition, subtraction, multiplication, and division. The second row consists of punctuation marks taken from English grammar. Note that the comma is a special symbol. In Java, commas are used to separate items in a list. Semicolons are used to end a Java statement. The third row contains symbols used for comparisons. Note that a blank, which is not shown above, is also a special symbol. You create a blank symbol by pressing the spacebar (only once) on the keyboard. The third row consists of tokens made up of two characters, but which are regarded as single symbols. No character can come between the two characters in these symbols, not even a blank.

Reserved Words (Keywords)

A second category of tokens is reserved words. Some reserved words include the following:

```
int, float, double, char, void, public, static, throws, return
```

Reserved words are also called **keywords**. The letters in a reserved word are always lowercase. Like the special symbols, each reserved word is considered a single symbol. Furthermore, reserved words cannot be redefined within any program; that is, they cannot be used for anything other than their intended use. For a complete list of reserved words in Java, see Appendix A.

NOTE   Throughout this book, the reserved words are shown in blue.

2

Identifiers

A third category of tokens is identifiers. **Identifiers** are names of things, such as variables, constants, and methods, that appear in programs. Some identifiers are predefined; others are defined by the user. All identifiers must obey Java's rules for identifiers.

Identifier: A Java identifier consists of letters, digits, the underscore character (_), and the dollar sign ($) and must begin with a letter, underscore, or the dollar sign.

Identifiers can be made of only letters, digits, the underscore character (_), and the dollar sign ($); no other symbols are permitted to form an identifier.

 NOTE   Java is case sensitive—uppercase and lowercase letters are considered different. Thus, the identifier NUMBER is not the same as the identifier number or the identifier Number. Similarly, the identifiers X and x are different.

In Java, identifiers can be any length. Some predefined identifiers that you will encounter frequently are print, println, and printf, which are used when generating output, and nextInt, nextDouble, next, and nextLine, which are used to input data. Unlike reserved words, predefined identifiers can be redefined, but it would be unwise to do so.

EXAMPLE 2-1

The following are legal identifiers in Java:

```
first
conversion
payRate
counter1
$Amount
```

Table 2-1 shows some illegal identifiers and explains why they are illegal.

TABLE 2-1 Examples of Illegal Identifiers

Illegal Identifier	Description
employee Salary	There can be no space between employee and Salary.
Hello!	The exclamation mark cannot be used in an identifier.
one+two	The symbol + cannot be used in an identifier.
2nd	An identifier cannot begin with a digit.

Data Types

The objective of a Java program is to manipulate data. Different programs manipulate different data. A program designed to calculate an employee's paycheck will add, subtract, multiply, and divide numbers; some of the numbers might represent hours worked and pay rate. Similarly, a program designed to alphabetize a class list will manipulate names. You wouldn't expect a cherry pie recipe to help you bake cookies. Similarly, you wouldn't manipulate alphabetic characters with a program designed to perform arithmetic calculations. Furthermore, you wouldn't multiply or subtract names. Reflecting such underlying differences, Java categorizes data into different types, and only certain operations can be performed on a particular type of data. At first, it may seem confusing, but by being so type conscious, Java has built-in checks to guard against errors.

Data type: A set of values together with a set of operations on those values.

Primitive Data Types

The primitive data types are the fundamental data types in Java. There are three categories of primitive data types:

- **Integral**, which is a data type that deals with integers, or numbers without a decimal part (and characters)
- **Floating-point**, which is a data type that deals with decimal numbers
- **Boolean**, which is a data type that deals with logical values

Integral data types are further classified into five categories: `char`, `byte`, `short`, `int`, and `long`.

Why are there so many categories of integral data types? Every data type has a different set of values associated with it. For example, the `int` data type is used to represent integers between -2147483648 ($= -2^{32}$) and 2147483647 ($= 2^{32} - 1$). The data type `short` is used to represent integers between -32768 ($= -2^{15}$) and 32767 ($= 2^{15} - 1$).

Which data type you use depends on how big a number your program needs to deal with. In the early days of programming, computers and main memory were very expensive. Only a small amount of memory was available to execute programs and manipulate data. As a result, programmers had to optimize the use of memory. Because writing a program and making it work is already a complicated process, not having to worry about the size of the memory makes for one less thing to think about. To effectively use memory, a programmer can look at the type of data used in a program and figure out which data type to use. (Memory constraints may still be a concern for programs written for applications such as a wrist watch.)

Table 2-2 gives the range of possible values associated with the five integral data types and the size of memory allocated to manipulate these values.

TABLE 2-2 Values and Memory Allocation for Integral Data Types

Data Type	Values	Storage (in bytes)
char	0 to 65535 ($= 2^{16} - 1$)	2 (16 bits)
byte	-128 ($= -2^7$) to 127 ($= 2^7 - 1$)	1 (8 bits)
short	-32768 ($= -2^{15}$) to 32767 ($= 2^{15} - 1$)	2 (16 bits)
int	-2147483648 ($= -2^{31}$) to 2147483647 ($= 2^{31} - 1$)	4 (32 bits)
long	-9223372036854775808 ($= -2^{63}$) to 9223372036854775807 ($= 2^{63} - 1$)	8 (64 bits)

The most commonly used integral data type is `int`. Note that the following discussion of the `int` data type also applies to the integral types `byte`, `short`, and `long`.

`int` DATA TYPE

This section describes the `int` data type, but this discussion also applies to other integral data types. Integers in Java, as in mathematics, are numbers such as the following:

`-6728, -67, 0, 78, 36782, +763`

Note the following two rules from these examples:

- Positive integers do not require a + sign in front of them.
- No commas are used within an integer. Recall that in Java, commas are used for separating items in a list. Thus, `36,782` is interpreted as two integers: `36` and `782`.

`char` DATA TYPE

As indicated in Table 2-2, the `char` data type has 65536 values, 0 to 65535. However, the main purpose of this data type is to represent single characters—that is, letters, digits, and special symbols. Therefore, the `char` data type can represent any key on your keyboard. When using the `char` data type, you enclose each character represented within single quotation marks. Examples of values belonging to the `char` data type include the following:

`'A', 'a', '0', '*', '+', '$', '&', ' '`

Note that a blank space is a character and is written as `' '`, with a space between the single quotation marks.

The data type `char` *allows only one symbol* to be placed between the single quotation marks. Thus, the value `'abc'` is not of type `char`. Furthermore, even though `!=` and similar special symbols are considered to be one symbol, they are not regarded as possible values of the data type `char` when enclosed in single quotation marks. All the individual symbols located on the keyboard that are printable are considered possible values of the `char` data type.

As stated in Chapter 1, each character has a specific representation in computer memory, and there are several different coding schemes for characters. Java uses the Unicode character set, which contains 65536 values numbered 0 to 65535. The position of the first character is 0, the position of the second character is 1, and so on. Other commonly used character data sets are the American Standard Code for Information Interchange (ASCII) and Extended Binary-Coded Decimal Interchange Code (EBCDIC). The ASCII character set has 128 values. ASCII is a subset of Unicode. That is, the first 128 characters of Unicode are the same as the characters in ASCII. The EBCDIC character set has 256 values and was created by IBM.

Each of the 65536 values of the Unicode character set represents a different character. For example, the value 65 represents `'A'`, and the value 43 represents `'+'`. Thus, each character has a specific non-negative integer value in the Unicode character set, which is called a **collating sequence**, of the character. It follows that the collating sequence of `'A'` is 65. The collating sequence is used when you compare characters. For example, the value representing `'B'` is 66, so `'A'` is smaller than `'B'`. Similarly, `'+'` is smaller than `'A'` because 43 is smaller than 65.

The 14th character in the Unicode (and ASCII) character set is called the newline character and is represented as `'\n'`. (Note that the position of the newline character in the Unicode and ASCII character sets is 13 because the position of the first character is 0.) Even though the newline character is a combination of two characters, it is treated as one character. Similarly, the horizontal tab character is represented in Java as `'\t'`, and the null character is represented as `'\0'` (a backslash followed by zero). (Later in this chapter, we elaborate on these special characters.) Furthermore, the first 32 characters in the Unicode and ASCII character sets are nonprintable. (See Appendix C for a list of these characters.)

`boolean` DATA TYPE

The data type `boolean` has only two values: `true` and `false`. Also, `true` and `false` are called the logical (Boolean) values. The primary purpose of this data type is to manipulate logical (Boolean) expression. An expression that evaluates to `true` or `false` is called a **logical (Boolean) expression**. Logical (Boolean) expressions are formally defined and discussed in detail in Chapter 4. In Java, `boolean`, `true`, and `false` are reserved words. The memory allocated for the `boolean` data type is 1 bit.

FLOATING-POINT DATA TYPES

To deal with decimal numbers, Java provides the floating-point data type. To facilitate our discussion of this data type, we will review a concept from a high school or college algebra course.

You may be familiar with scientific notation. For example:

```
43872918 = 4.3872918 * 10^7
.0000265 = 2.65 * 10^-5
47.9832 = 4.7983 * 10^1
```

To represent real numbers, Java uses a form of scientific notation called **floating-point notation**. Table 2-3 shows how Java might print a set of real numbers. In the Java floating-point notation, the letter e stands for the exponent.

TABLE 2-3 Examples of Real Numbers Printed in Java Floating-Point Notation

Real Number	Java Floating-Point Notation
75.924	7.592400e+01
0.18	1.800000e-01
0.0000453	4.530000e-05
-1.482	-1.482000e+00
7800.0	7.800000e+03

Java provides two data types to represent decimal numbers: float and double. As in the case of integral data types, the data types float and double differ in the set of values.

float: The data type float is used in Java to represent any real number between −3.4E+38 and 3.4E+38. The memory allocated for the float data type is 4 bytes.

double: The data type double is used in Java to represent any real number between −1.7E+308 and 1.7E+308. The memory allocated for the double data type is 8 bytes.

Other than the set of values, there is one more difference between the data types float and double. The maximum number of significant digits—that is, the number of decimal places—in float values is 6 or 7. The maximum number of significant digits in values belonging to the double type is typically 15. The maximum number of significant digits is called the **precision**. Sometimes float values are called **single precision**, and values of type double are called **double precision**.

NOTE

In Java, by default, floating-point numbers are considered to be of type double. Therefore, if you use the data type float to represent floating-point numbers in a program, you might get a warning or an error message, such as "truncation from double to float" or "possible loss of data." To avoid such messages, you should use the double data type. For illustration purposes and to avoid such messages in programming examples, this book mostly uses the data type double to represent floating-point numbers. However, if you need to explicitly use a float value in a program, specify that the decimal value is a float value using the letter f at the end of the number. For example, 28.75f represents a float value while 28.75 represents a double value.

LITERALS (CONSTANTS)

Some authors call values such as 23 and -67 **integer literals** or **integer constants** or simply **integers**; values such as 12.34 and 25.60 are called **floating-point literals** or **floating-point constants** or simply **floating-point numbers**; and values such as 'a' and '5' are called **character literals**, **character constants**, or simply **characters**.

Arithmetic Operators and Operator Precedence

One of the most important features of a computer is its ability to calculate. You can use the standard arithmetic operators to manipulate integral and floating-point data types.

Java has five arithmetic operators:

Arithmetic Operators: + (addition), - (subtraction or negation), * (multiplication), / (division), % (**mod**, (**modulus** or **remainder**))

You can use these operators with both integral and floating-point data types. When you use / with the integral data type, it gives the quotient in integer form. That is, integral division truncates any fractional part; there is no rounding. Similarly, when you use % with the integral data type, it gives the remainder in integer form. (Examples 2-2 and 2-3 clarify how the operators / and % work with integral and floating-point data types.)

Since junior high school, you have probably worked with arithmetic expressions such as the following:

   (i)   -5
   (ii)   8 - 7
   (iii) 3 + 4
   (iv)   2 + 3 * 5
   (v)   5.6 + 6.2 * 3
   (vi)   x + 2 * 5 + 6 / y

In expression (vi), **x** and **y** are some unknown numbers. Formally, an **arithmetic expression** is constructed by using arithmetic operators and numbers. The numbers and alphabetical symbols in the expression are called **operands**. Moreover, the numbers and alphabetical symbols used to evaluate an operator are called the operands for that operator.

In expression (i), the operator - (subtraction) is used to specify that the number 5 is negative. Moreover, in the expression -5, - has only one operand, which is 5. Operators that have only one operand are called **unary operators**.

In expression (ii), the symbol - is used to subtract 7 from 8. In this expression, - has two operands, 8 and 7. Operators that have two operands are called **binary operators**.

Unary operator: An operator that has only one operand.

Binary operator: An operator that has two operands.

In the expression (iii), 3 and 4 are the operands for the operator +. Because the operator + has two operands, in this expression, + is a binary operator. Now consider the following expression:

+27

In this expression, the operator + is used to indicate that the number 27 is positive. Here, because + has only one operand, it acts as a unary operator.

From the preceding discussion, it follows that − and + can be unary or binary arithmetic operators. However, the arithmetic operators *, /, and % are binary and must have two operands.

The following examples show how arithmetic operators—especially / and %—work with integral data types. As you can see from these examples, the operator / represents the quotient in ordinary division when used with integral data types.

EXAMPLE 2-2

Arithmetic Expression	Result	Description
2 + 5	7	
13 + 89	102	
34 − 20	14	
45 − 90	−45	
2 * 7	14	
5 / 2	2	In the division 5 / 2, the quotient is 2 and the remainder is 1. Therefore, 5 / 2 with the integral operands evaluates to the quotient, which is 2.
14 / 7	2	
34 % 5	4	In the division 34 / 5, the quotient is 6 and the remainder is 4. Therefore, 34 % 5 evaluates to the remainder, which is 4.
4 % 6	4	In the division 4 / 6, the quotient is 0 and the remainder is 4. Therefore, 4 % 6 evaluates to the remainder, which is 4.

The following Java program evaluates the preceding expressions:

```java
// This program illustrates how integral expressions evaluate.

public class Example2_2
{
    public static void main(String[] args)
    {
        System.out.println("2 + 5 = " + (2 + 5));
        System.out.println("13 + 89 = " + (13 + 89));
        System.out.println("34 - 20 = " + (34 - 20));
        System.out.println("45 - 90 = " + (45 - 90));
```

```
        System.out.println("2 * 7 = " + (2 * 7));
        System.out.println("5 / 2 = " + (5 / 2));
        System.out.println("14 / 7 = " + (14 / 7));
        System.out.println("34 % 5 = " + (34 % 5));
        System.out.println("4 % 6 = " + (4 % 6));
    }
}
```

Sample Run:

```
2 + 5 = 7
13 + 89 = 102
34 - 20 = 14
45 - 90 = -45
2 * 7 = 14
5 / 2 = 2
14 / 7 = 2
34 % 5 = 4
4 % 6 = 4
```

NOTE You should be careful when evaluating the mod operator with negative integer operands. You might not get the answer you would expect. For example, −34 % 5 = −4, because in the division −34 / 5, the quotient is −6 and the remainder is −4. Similarly, 34 % −5 = 4, because in the division −34 / 5, the quotient is −6 and the remainder is 4. Also −34 % −5 = −4, because in the division −34 / −5, the quotient is 6 and the remainder is −4.

EXAMPLE 2-3

The following Java program evaluates various floating-point expressions. (The details are left as an exercise for you.)

```
// This program illustrates how floating-point expressions evaluate.

public class Example2_3
{
    public static void main(String[] args)
    {
        System.out.println("5.0 + 3.5 = " + (5.0 + 3.5));
        System.out.println("3.0 + 9.4 = " + (3.0 + 9.4));
        System.out.println("16.4 - 5.2 = " + (16.4 - 5.2));
        System.out.println("4.2 * 2.5 = " + (4.2 * 2.5));
        System.out.println("5.0 / 2.0 = " + (5.0 / 2.0));
        System.out.println("34.5 / 6.0 = " + (34.5 / 6.0));
        System.out.println("34.5 % 6.0 = " + (34.5 % 6.0));
        System.out.println("34.5 / 6.5 = " + (34.5 / 6.5));
        System.out.println("34.5 % 6.5 = " + (34.5 % 6.5));
    }
}
```

Sample Run:

```
5.0 + 3.5 = 8.5
3.0 + 9.4 = 12.4
16.4 - 5.2 = 11.2
4.2 * 2.5 = 10.5
5.0 / 2.0 = 2.5
34.5 / 6.0 = 5.75
34.5 % 6.0 = 4.5
34.5 / 6.5 = 5.3076923076923075
34.5 % 6.5 = 2.0
```

Order of Precedence

When more than one arithmetic operator is used in an expression, Java uses the operator precedence rules to determine the order in which the operations are performed to evaluate the expression. According to the order of precedence rules for arithmetic operators:

```
*,    /,    %
```

have a higher level of precedence than:

```
+,    -
```

Note that the operators *, /, and % have the same level of precedence. Similarly, the operators + and - have the same level of precedence.

When arithmetic operators have the same level of precedence, operations are performed from left to right. To avoid confusion, you can use parentheses to group arithmetic expressions.

EXAMPLE 2-4

Using the order of precedence rules,

```
3 * 7 - 6 + 2 * 5 / 4 + 6
```

means the following:

```
    (((3 * 7) - 6) + ((2 * 5) / 4 )) + 6
= ((21 - 6) + (10 / 4)) + 6      (Evaluate *)
= ((21 - 6) + 2) + 6             (Evaluate /. Note that this is an integer division.)
= (15 + 2) + 6                   (Evaluate -)
=   17 + 6                       (Evaluate first +)
=   23                           (Evaluate +)
```

Note that using parentheses in the preceding expression clarifies the order of precedence.

Because arithmetic operators are evaluated from left to right, unless parentheses are present, the **associativity** of arithmetic operators is said to be from left to right.

Character arithmetic: Since the `char` data type is also an integral data type, Java allows you to perform arithmetic operations on `char` data. You should use this ability carefully. There is a difference between the character `'8'` and the integer 8. The integer value of 8 is 8. The integer value of `'8'` is 56, which is the Unicode collating sequence of the character `'8'`.

When evaluating arithmetic expressions, 8 + 7 = 15, `'8'` + `'7'` = 56 + 55, yields 111, and `'8'` + 7 = 56 + 7, yields 63. Furthermore, `'8'` * `'7'` = 56 * 55 = 3080.

These examples illustrate that many things can go wrong when you perform character arithmetic. If you must use arithmetic operations on the `char` type data, do so with caution.

Expressions

To this point, we have discussed only arithmetic operators. In this section, we discuss arithmetic expressions in detail. (Arithmetic expressions were introduced in the last section.)

If all operands (that is, numbers) in an expression are integers, the expression is called an **integral expression**. If all operands in an expression are floating-point numbers, the expression is called a **floating-point** or **decimal expression**. An integral expression yields an integral result; a floating-point expression yields a floating-point result. Looking at some examples will help clarify these definitions.

EXAMPLE 2-5

Consider the following Java integral expressions:

```
2 + 3 * 5
3 + x - y / 7
x + 2 * (y - z) + 18
```

In these expressions, x, y, and z represent variables of the integral type; that is, they can hold integer values. (Variables are discussed later in this chapter.)

EXAMPLE 2-6

Consider the following Java floating-point expressions:

```
12.8 * 17.5 - 34.50
x * 10.5 + y - 16.2
```

Here, x and y represent variables of the floating-point type; that is, they can hold floating-point values. (Variables are discussed later in this chapter.)

Evaluating an integral or a floating-point expression is straightforward. As already noted, when operators have the same precedence, the expression is evaluated from left to right. To avoid confusion, you can always use parentheses to group operands and operators.

Mixed Expressions

An expression that has operands of different data types is called a **mixed expression**. A mixed expression contains both integers and floating-point numbers. The following expressions are examples of mixed expressions:

```
2 + 3.5
6 / 4 + 3.9
5.4 * 2 - 13.6 + 18 / 2
```

In the first expression, the operand + has one integer operand and one floating-point operand. In the second expression, both operands for the operator / are integers; the first operand of + is the result of 6 / 4, and the second operand of + is a floating-point number. The third example is a more complicated mix of integers and floating-point numbers. How does Java evaluate such mixed expressions?

Two rules apply when evaluating a mixed expression:

1. When evaluating an operator in a mixed expression:

   a. If the operator has the same types of operands (that is, both are integers or both are floating-point numbers), the operator is evaluated according to the type of the operand. Integer operands yield an integer result; floating-point numbers yield a floating-point number result.

   b. If the operator has both types of operands (that is, one is an integer and the other is a floating-point number), during calculation the integer is treated temporarily as a floating-point number with the decimal part of zero, and then the operator is evaluated. The result is a floating-point number.

2. The entire expression is evaluated according to the precedence rules. The multiplication, division, and modulus operators are evaluated before the addition and subtraction operators. Operators having the same level of precedence are evaluated from left to right. Grouping is allowed for clarity.

Following these rules, when you evaluate a mixed expression, you concentrate on one operator at a time, using the rules of precedence. If the operator to be evaluated has operands of the same data type, evaluate the operator using Rule 1(a). That is, an operator with integer operands yields an integer result, and an operator with floating-point operands yields a floating-point result. If the operator to be evaluated has one integer operand and one floating-point operand, before evaluating this operator, you treat the integer operand as a floating-point number with a decimal part of zero. Example 2-7 shows how to evaluate mixed expressions.

EXAMPLE 2-7

Mixed Expression	Evaluation	Rule Applied
3 / 2 + 5.0	= 1 + 5.0	3 / 2 = 1 (integer division; Rule 1(a))
	= 6.0	(1 + 5.0 = 1.0 + 5.0 (Rule 1(b)) = 6.0)
15.6 / 2 + 5	= 7.8 + 5	15.6 / 2 = 15.6 / 2.0 (Rule 1(b)) = 7.8
	= 12.8	7.8 + 5 = 7.8 + 5.0 (Rule1(b)) = 12.8
4 + 5 / 2.0	= 4 + 2.5	5 / 2.0 = 5.0 / 2.0 (Rule 1(b)) = 2.5
	= 6.5	4 + 2.5 = 4.0 + 2.5 (Rule 1(b)) = 6.5
4 * 3 + 7 / 5 - 25.5	= 12 + 7 / 5 - 25.5	4 * 3 = 12; (Rule 1(a))
	= 12 + 1 - 25.5	7 / 5 = 1 (integer division; Rule 1(a))
	= 13 - 25.5	12 + 1 = 13; (Rule 1(a))
	= -12.5	13 - 25.5 = 13.0 - 25.5 (Rule 1(b)) = -12.5

The following Java program evaluates the preceding expressions:

```
// This program illustrates how mixed expressions are evaluated.

public class Example2_7
{
    public static void main(String[] args)
    {
        System.out.println("3 / 2 + 5.0 = " + (3 / 2 + 5.0));
        System.out.println("15.6 / 2 + 5 = " + (15.6 / 2 + 5));
        System.out.println("4 + 5 / 2.0 = " + (4 + 5 / 2.0));
        System.out.println("4 * 3 + 7 / 5 - 25.5 = "
                          + (4 * 3 + 7 / 5 - 25.5));
    }
}
```

Sample Run:

```
3 / 2 + 5.0 = 6.0
15.6 / 2 + 5 = 12.8
4 + 5 / 2.0 = 6.5
4 * 3 + 7 / 5 - 25.5 = -12.5
```

These examples illustrate that an integer is not treated as a floating-point number unless the operator to be evaluated has one integer and one floating-point operand.

Type Conversion (Casting)

In the previous section, you learned that when evaluating an arithmetic expression if the operator has mixed operands, the integer value is treated as a floating-point value with the zero decimal part. When a value of one data type is automatically treated as another data type, an **implicit type coercion** has occurred. As the examples in the preceding section illustrate, if you are not careful about data types, implicit type coercion can generate unexpected results.

To avoid implicit type coercion, Java provides for explicit type conversion through the use of a cast operator. The **cast operator**, also called **type conversion** or **type casting**, takes the following form:

`(dataTypeName) expression`

First, the `expression` is evaluated. Its value is then treated as a value of the type specified by `dataTypeName`.

When using the cast operator to treat a floating-point (decimal) number as an integer, you simply drop the decimal part of the floating-point number. That is, the floating-point number is truncated. The following examples show how cast operators work. Be sure you understand why the last two expressions evaluate as they do.

EXAMPLE 2-8

Expression	Evaluates to
`(int)(7.9)`	7
`(int)(3.3)`	3
`(double)(25)`	25.0
`(double)(5 + 3)`	= `(double)(8)` = 8.0
`(double)(15) / 2`	= 15.0 / 2 (because `(double)(15)` = 15.0)
	= 15.0 / 2.0 = 7.5

```
(double)(15 / 2)                          = (double)(7) (because 15 / 2 = 7)
                                          = 7.0


(int)(7.8 + (double)(15) / 2)             = (int)(7.8 + 7.5)
                                          = (int)(15.3)
                                          = 15


(int)(7.8 + (double)(15 / 2))             = (int)(7.8 + 7.0)
                                          = (int)(14.8)
                                          = 14
```

The following Java program evaluates the preceding expressions:

```java
// This program illustrates how explicit type conversion works.

public class Example2_8
{
    public static void main(String[] args)
    {
        System.out.println("(int)(7.9) = " + (int)(7.9));
        System.out.println("(int)(3.3) = " + (int)(3.3));
        System.out.println("(double)(25) = " + (double)(25));
        System.out.println("(double)(5 + 3) = "
                           + (double)(5 + 3));
        System.out.println("(double)(15) / 2 = "
                           + ((double)(15) / 2));
        System.out.println("(double)(15 / 2) = "
                           + ((double)(15 / 2)));
        System.out.println("(int)(7.8 + (double)(15) / 2) = "
                           + ((int)(7.8 + (double)(15) / 2)));
        System.out.println("(int)(7.8 + (double)(15 / 2)) = "
                           + ((int)(7.8 + (double)(15 / 2))));
    }
}
```

Sample Run:

```
(int)(7.9) = 7
(int)(3.3) = 3
(double)(25) = 25.0
(double)(5 + 3) = 8.0
(double)(15) / 2 = 7.5
(double)(15 / 2) = 7.0
(int)(7.8 + (double)(15) / 2) = 15
(int)(7.8 + (double)(15 / 2)) = 14
```

2

You can also use cast operators to explicitly treat `char` data values as `int` data values, and `int` data values as `char` data values. To treat `char` data values as `int` data values, you use a collating sequence. For example, in the Unicode character set, `(int) ('A')` is 65 and `(int) ('8')` is 56. Similarly, `(char) (65)` is `'A'` and `(char) (56)` is `'8'`.

class String

In the preceding sections, we discussed primitive types to deal with data consisting of numbers and characters. What about data values such as a person's name? A person's name contains more than one character. Such values are called strings. More formally, a **string** is a sequence of zero or more characters. Strings in Java are enclosed in double quotation marks (not in single quotation marks, as are the `char` data types).

Most often, we process strings as a single unit. To process strings effectively, Java provides the `class String`. The `class String` contains various operations to manipulate a string. You will see this class used throughout the book. Chapter 3 discusses various operations provided by the `class String`. Moreover, technically speaking, the `class String` is not a primitive type.

A string that contains no characters is called a **null** or **empty** string. The following are examples of strings. Note that `""` is the empty string.

```
"William Jacob"
"Mickey"
""
```

A string, such as `"hello"`, is sometimes called a **character string** or **string literal** or **string constant**. However, if no confusion arises, we refer to characters between double quotation marks simply as strings.

Every character in a string has a specific position in the string. The position of the first character is 0, the position of the second character is 1, and so on. The **length** of a string is the number of characters in it.

EXAMPLE 2-9

String	"Sunny Day"								
Character in the string	`'S'`	`'u'`	`'n'`	`'n'`	`'y'`	`' '`	`'D'`	`'a'`	`'y'`
Position of the character in the string	0	1	2	3	4	5	6	7	8

The length of the string `"Sunny Day"` is 9.

When determining the length of a string, you must also count any spaces contained in the string. For example, the length of the string `"It is a beautiful day."` is 22.

Strings and the Operator +

One of the most common operations performed on strings is the concatenation operation, which allows a string to be appended at the end of another string. The operator + can be used to concatenate (or join) two strings as well as a string and a numeric value or a character.

Next we illustrate how the operator + works with strings. Consider the following expression:

```
"Sunny" + " Day"
```

This expression evaluates to

```
"Sunny Day"
```

Now consider the following expression:

```
"Amount Due = $" + 576.35
```

When the operator + evaluates, the numeric value 576.35 is converted to the string "576.35", which is then concatenated with the string:

```
"Amount Due = $"
```

Therefore, the expression "Amount Due = $" + 576.35 evaluates to

```
"Amount Due = $576.35"
```

Example 2-10 further explains how the operator + works with the String data type.

EXAMPLE 2-10

Consider the following expression:

```
"The sum = " + 12 + 26
```

This expression evaluates to

```
"The sum = 1226"
```

This is not what you might have expected. Rather than adding 12 and 26, the values 12 and 26 are concatenated. This is because the associativity of the operator + is from left to right, so the operator + is evaluated from left to right. The expression

```
"The sum = " + 12 + 26
```

is evaluated as follows:

```
"The sum = " + 12 + 26   = ("The sum = " + 12) + 26
                         = "The sum = 12" + 26
                         = "The sum = 12" + 26
                         = "The sum = 1226"
```

Now consider the following expression:

```
"The sum = " + (12 + 26)
```

This expression evaluates as follows:

```
    "The sum = " + (12 + 16)
=   "The sum = " + 38
=   "The sum = 38"
```

Next, consider the expression:

```
12 + 26 + " is the sum"
```

This expression evaluates as follows:

```
    12 + 26 + " is the sum"
=   (12 + 26) + " is the sum"
=   38 + " is the sum"
=   "38 is the sum"
```

Now consider the expression:

```
"The sum of " + 12 + " and " + 26 + " = " + (12 + 26)
```

Notice the parentheses around 12 + 26. This expression evaluates as follows:

```
    "The sum of " + 12 + " and " + 26 + " = " + (12 + 26)
=   "The sum of 12" + " and " + 26 + " = " + (12 + 26)
=   "The sum of 12 and " + 26 + " = " + (12 + 26)
=   "The sum of 12 and 26" + " = " + (12 + 26)
=   "The sum of 12 and 26 = " + (12 + 26)
=   "The sum of 12 and 26 = " + 38
=   "The sum of 12 and 26 = 38"
```

The following Java program shows the effect of the preceding statements:

```java
// This program illustrates how the String concatenation works.
public class Example2_10
{
    public static void main(String[] args)
    {
        System.out.println("The sum = " + 12 + 26);

        System.out.println("The sum = " + (12 + 26));

        System.out.println(12 + 26 + " is the sum");

        System.out.println("The sum of " + 12 + " and " + 26
                    + " = " + (12 + 26));
    }
}
```

Sample Run:

```
The sum = 1226
The sum = 38
38 is the sum
The sum of 12 and 26 = 38
```

> **NOTE** The **class** String contains many useful methods to manipulate strings. We will take a closer look at this class in Chapter 3 and illustrate how to manipulate strings. The complete description of this class can be found at the Web site *http://java.sun.com/javase/7/docs/api/*.

Input

As noted earlier, the main objective of Java programs is to perform calculations and manipulate data. Recall that the data must be loaded into main memory before it can be manipulated. In this section, you will learn how to put data into the computer's memory. Storing data in the computer's memory is a two-step process:

1. Instruct the computer to allocate memory.
2. Include statements in the program to put the data into the allocated memory.

Allocating Memory with Named Constants and Variables

When you instruct the computer to allocate memory, you tell it what names to use for each memory location and what type of data to store in those locations. Knowing the location of the data is essential because data stored in one memory location might be needed at several places in the program. As you learned earlier, knowing what data type you have is crucial for performing accurate calculations. It is also critical to know whether your data must remain constant throughout program execution or whether it could change.

Some data must not be changed. For example, the pay rate might be the same for all part-time employees. The value in a conversion formula that converts inches into centimeters is fixed, because 1 inch is always equal to 2.54 centimeters. When stored in memory, this type of data must be protected from accidental changes during program execution. In Java, you can use a **named constant** to instruct a program to mark those memory locations in which data is constant throughout program execution.

Named constant: A memory location whose content is not allowed to change during program execution.

To allocate memory, we use Java's declaration statements. The syntax to declare a named constant is:

```
static final dataType IDENTIFIER = value;
```

In Java, `static` and `final` are reserved words. The reserved word `final` specifies that the value stored in the identifier is fixed and cannot be changed.

NOTE In syntax, the shading indicates the part of the definition that is optional.

Because the reserved word `static` is shaded, it may or may not appear when a named constant is declared. The section, Creating a Java Application Program, later in this chapter, explains when this reserved word might be required. Also, notice that the identifier for a named constant is in uppercase letters. This is because Java programmers typically use uppercase letters for a named constant. (If the name of a named constant is a combination of more than one word, called a *run-together-word*, then the words are separated using an underscore; see the next example.)

EXAMPLE 2-11

Consider the following Java statements:

```
final double CENTIMETERS_PER_INCH = 2.54;
final int NO_OF_STUDENTS = 20;
final char BLANK = ' ';
final double PAY_RATE = 15.75;
```

The first statement tells the compiler to allocate enough memory to store a value of type `double`, call this memory space `CENTIMETERS_PER_INCH`, and store the value `2.54` in it. Throughout a program that uses this statement, whenever the conversion formula is needed, the memory space `CENTIMETERS_PER_INCH` can be accessed. The other statements have similar meanings.

NOTE As noted earlier, the default type of floating-point numbers is `double`. Therefore, if you declare a named constant of type `float`, then you must specify that the value is of type `float` as follows:

```
final float PAY_RATE = 15.75f;
```

otherwise, the compiler will generate an error message. Notice that in `15.75f`, the letter `f` at the end specifies that `15.75` is a `float` value. Recall that the memory size for `float` values is 4 bytes; for `double` values, 8 bytes. We will mostly use the type `double` to work with floating-point values.

Using a named constant to store fixed data, rather than using the data value itself, has one major advantage. If the fixed data changes, you do not need to edit the entire program and change the old value to the new value. Instead, you can make the change at just one place, recompile the program, and execute it using the new value throughout. In addition, by storing a value and referring to that memory location whenever the value is needed, you avoid typing the same value again and again and you prevent typos. If you misspell the name of the location, the computer might warn you through an error message, but it will not warn you if the value is mistyped.

Certain data must be modifiable during program execution. For example, after each test, a student's average test score may change; the number of tests also changes. Similarly, after each pay increase, an employee's salary changes. This type of data must be stored in memory cells whose contents can be modified during program execution. In Java, memory cells whose contents can be modified during program execution are called **variables**.

Variable: A memory location whose content may change during program execution.

The syntax for declaring one variable or multiple variables is:

```
dataType identifier1, identifier2, ..., identifierN;
```

EXAMPLE 2-12

Consider the following statements:

```
double amountDue;
int counter;
char ch;
int num1, num2;
```

The first statement tells the compiler to allocate enough memory to store a value of type `double` and call it `amountDue`. Statements 2 and 3 have similar conventions. The fourth statement tells the compiler to allocate two different memory spaces (each large enough to store a value of the type `int`), name the first memory space `num1`, and name the second memory space `num2`.

 NOTE | Java programmers typically use lowercase letters to declare variables. If a variable name is a combination of more than one word, then the first letter of each word, except the first word, is uppercase. (For example, see the variable `amountDue` in the preceding example.)

From now on, when we say "variable," we mean a variable memory location.

NOTE In Java (within a method), you must declare all identifiers before you can use them. If you refer to an identifier without declaring it, the compiler will generate an error message indicating that the identifier is not declared.

2

Putting Data into Variables

Now that you know how to declare variables, the next question is: How do you put data into those variables? The two common ways to place data into a variable are:

1. Use an assignment statement.
2. Use input (read) statements.

ASSIGNMENT STATEMENT

The assignment statement takes the following form:

```
variable = expression;
```

In an assignment statement, the value of the **expression** should match the data type of the **variable**. The expression on the right side is evaluated, and its value is assigned to the variable (and thus to a memory location) on the left side.

A variable is said to be **initialized** the first time a value is placed in the variable.

In Java, = (the equal sign) is called the **assignment operator**.

EXAMPLE 2-13

Suppose you have the following variable declarations:

```
int num1;
int num2;
double sale;
char first;
String str;
```

Now consider the following assignment statements:

```
num1 = 4;
num2 = 4 * 5 - 11;
sale = 0.02 * 1000;
first = 'D';
str = "It is a sunny day.";
```

For each of these statements, the computer first evaluates the expression on the right and then stores that value in a memory location named by the identifier on the left. The first statement stores the value 4 in num1, the second statement stores 9 in num2, the third statement stores 20.00 in sale, and the fourth statement stores the character 'D' in first. The fifth statement assigns the string "It is a sunny day." to the variable str.

The following Java program shows the effect of the preceding statements:

```java
// This program illustrates how data in the variables are
// manipulated.

public class Example2_13
{
    public static void main(String[] args)
    {
        int num1;
        int num2;

        double sale;

        char first;

        String str;

        num1 = 4;
        System.out.println("num1 = " + num1);

        num2 = 4 * 5 - 11;
        System.out.println("num2 = " + num2);

        sale = 0.02 * 1000;
        System.out.println("sale = " + sale);

        first = 'D';
        System.out.println("first = " + first);

        str = "It is a sunny day.";
        System.out.println("str = " + str);
    }
}
```

Sample Run:

```
num1 = 4
num2 = 9
sale = 20.0
first = D
str = It is a sunny day.
```

For the most part, the preceding program is straightforward. Let us take a look at the output statement:

```java
System.out.println("num1 = " + num1);
```

This output statement consists of the string "num1 = ", +, and the variable num1. Here, the value of num1 is concatenated with the string "num1 = ", resulting in the string "num1 = 4", which is then output. The meanings of other output statements are similar.

A Java statement such as:

```
num = num + 2;
```

means "evaluate whatever is in num, add 2 to it, and assign the new value to the memory location num." The expression on the right side must be evaluated first; that value is then assigned to the memory location specified by the variable on the left side. Thus, the sequence of Java statements:

```
num = 6;
num = num + 2;
```

and the statement:

```
num = 8;
```

both assign 8 to num. Note that the statement num = num + 2 is meaningless if num has not been initialized.

The statement num = 5; is read as "num becomes 5" or "num gets 5" or "num is assigned the value 5." Each time a new value is assigned to num, the old value is erased.

 NOTE Suppose that num is an `int` variable. Consider the statement: num = num + 2;. This statement adds 2 to the value of num, and the new value is assigned to the variable num. If the variable num is not properly initialized, then the Java compiler will generate a syntax error. So to use the value of a variable in an expression, the variable must be properly initialized. Variable initialization is further covered in the next section, "Declaring and Initializing Variables."

EXAMPLE 2-14

Suppose that num1, num2, and num3 are `int` variables and the following statements are executed in sequence.

1. num1 = 18;
2. num1 = num1 + 27;
3. num2 = num1;
4. num3 = num2 / 5;
5. num3 = num3 / 4;

Table 2-4 shows the values of the variables after the execution of each statement. (A ? indicates that the value is unknown. The orange color in a box shows that the value of that variable is changed.)

TABLE 2-4 Values of the Variables num1, num2, and num3

Values of the Variables	Variables			Statement/Explanation
Before Statement 1	num1 ?	num2 ?	num3 ?	
After Statement 1	num1 18	num2 ?	num3 ?	num1 = 18; Store 18 into num1.
After Statement 2	num1 45	num2 ?	num3 ?	num1 = num1 + 27; num1 + 27 = 18 + 27 = 45. This value is assigned to num1, which replaces the old value of num1.
After Statement 3	num1 45	num2 45	num3 ?	num2 = num1; Copy the value of num1 into num2.
After Statement 4	num1 45	num2 45	num3 9	num3 = num2 / 5; num2 / 5 = 45 / 5 = 9. This value is assigned to num3. So num3 = 9.
After Statement 5	num1 45	num2 45	num3 2	num3 = num3 / 4; num3 / 4 = 9 / 4 = 2. This value is assigned to num3, which replaces the old value of num3.

Thus, after the execution of the statement in Line 5, num1 = 45, num2 = 45, and num3 = 2.

NOTE   The Java language is strongly typed, which means that you cannot assign a value to a variable that is not compatible with its data type. For example, a string cannot be stored in an int variable. If you try to store an incompatible value in a variable, an error is generated when you compile the program or during program execution. Therefore, in an assignment statement, the expression on the right side must evaluate to a value compatible with the data type of the variable on the left side.

NOTE   Suppose that x, y, and z are `int` variables. The following is a legal statement in Java:

```
x = y = z;
```

In this statement, first the value of z is assigned to y, and then the new value of y is assigned to x. Because the assignment operator = is evaluated from right to left, the **associativity** of the **assignment operator** is said to be from right to left.

Earlier, you learned that if a variable is used in an expression, the expression yields a meaningful value only if the variable has been initialized previously. You also learned that after declaring a variable, you can use an assignment statement to initialize it. It is possible to initialize and declare variables simultaneously. Before we discuss how to use an input (read) statement, we address this important issue.

Declaring and Initializing Variables

When a variable is declared, Java might not automatically put a meaningful value into it. In other words, Java might not automatically initialize all the variables you declare. For example, the `int` and `double` variables might not be initialized to 0, as happens in some programming languages.

If you declare a variable and then use it in an expression without first initializing it, when you compile the program you are likely to get an error. To avoid these pitfalls, Java allows you to initialize variables while they are being declared. Consider the following Java statements, in which variables are first declared and then initialized:

```
int first;
int second;
char ch;
double x;
double y;
first = 13;
second = 10;
ch = ' ';
x = 12.6;
y = 123.456;
```

You can declare and initialize these variables at the same time using the following Java statements:

```
int first = 13;
int second = 10;
char ch = ' ';
double x = 12.6;
double y = 123.456;
```

The first Java statement declares the `int` variable `first` and stores 13 in it. The second Java statement declares the `int` variable `second` and stores 10 in it. The other statements have similar meanings. Declaring and initializing variables simultaneously is another way to place meaningful data into a variable.

NOTE Not all variables are initialized during declaration. The nature of the program or the programmer's choice dictates which variables should be initialized during declaration.

Input (Read) Statement

In an earlier section, you learned how to put data into variables using the assignment statement. In this section, you will learn how to put data into variables from the standard input device using Java's input (or read) statements.

NOTE In most cases, the standard input device is the keyboard.

When the computer gets the data from the keyboard, the user is said to be acting interactively.

READING DATA USING THE Scanner class

To put data into variables from the standard input device, Java provides the **class Scanner**. Using this class, we first create an input stream object and associate it with the standard input device. The following statement accomplishes this:

```
static Scanner console = new Scanner(System.in);
```

This statement creates the input stream object `console` and associates it with the standard input device. (Note that `Scanner` is a predefined Java class and the preceding statement creates `console` to be an object of this class.) The object `console` reads the next input as follows:

a. If the next input token can be interpreted as an integer, then the expression:

```
console.nextInt()
```

retrieves that integer; that is, the value of this expression is that integer.

b. If the next input token can be interpreted as a floating-point number, then the expression:

```
console.nextDouble()
```

retrieves that floating-point number; that is, the value of this expression is that floating-point number. (Note that an integer can be treated as a floating-point number with 0 decimal part.)

c. The expression:

```
console.next()
```

retrieves the next input token as a string; that is, the value of this expression is the next input string. (Note that if the next input token is a number, this expression interprets that number as a string.)

d. The expression:

```
console.nextLine()
```

retrieves the next input as a string until the end of the line; that is, the value of this expression is the next input line. (Note that this expression also reads the newline character, but the newline character is not stored as part of the string.)

While scanning for the next input, the expressions `console.nextInt()`, `console.nextDouble()`, and `console.next()` skip whitespace characters. Whitespace characters are blanks and certain nonprintable characters, such as newline and tab.

NOTE `System.in` is called a **standard input stream object** and is designed to input data from the standard input device. However, the object `System.in` extracts data in the form of bytes from the input stream. Therefore, using `System.in`, we first create a `Scanner` object, such as `console`, as shown previously, so that the data can be extracted in a desired form. (The meaning of the word `new` is explained in Chapter 3.)

NOTE The `class` Scanner is added to the Java library in Java version 5.0. Therefore, this class is *not* available in Java versions lower than 5.0.

EXAMPLE 2-15

Suppose that `miles` is a variable of type `double`. Further suppose that the input is 73.65. Consider the following statements:

```
miles = console.nextDouble();
```

This statement causes the computer to get the input, which is 73.65, from the standard input device, and stores it in the variable `miles`. That is, after the execution of this statement, the value of the variable `miles` is 73.65.

Example 2-16 further explains how to input numeric data into a program.

EXAMPLE 2-16

Suppose we have the following declaration:

```
static Scanner console = new Scanner(System.in);
```

Consider the following statements:

```
int feet;
int inches;
```

Suppose the input is:

23 7

Next, consider the following statements:

```
feet = console.nextInt();           //Line 1
inches = console.nextInt();         //Line 2
```

The statement in Line 1 stores the number 23 into the variable feet. The statement in Line 2 stores the number 7 into the variable inches. Notice that when these numbers are entered at the keyboard, they are separated with a blank. In fact, they can be separated with one or more blanks, lines, or even the tab character. (Note that we have numbered the statements as Line 1 and Line 2, so that we can conveniently refer to a particular statement and explain its meaning.)

The following Java program shows the effect of the preceding input statements:

```
// This program illustrates how input statements work.

import java.util.*;

public class Example2_16
{
    static Scanner console = new Scanner(System.in);

    public static void main(String[] args)
    {
        int feet;
        int inches;

        System.out.println("Enter two integers separated by spaces.");

        feet = console.nextInt();
        inches = console.nextInt();

        System.out.println("feet = " + feet);
        System.out.println("inches = " + inches);
    }
}
```

Sample Run: (In this sample run, the user input is shaded.)

```
Enter two integers separated by spaces.
23 7
feet = 23
inches = 7
```

In the preceding program, notice the first line:

```
import java.util.*;
```

This line is required to use the class Scanner.

> **NOTE** If the next input token cannot be expressed as an appropriate number, then the expressions `console.nextInt()` and `console.nextDouble()` will cause the program to terminate with an error message (unless some care is taken in the program), indicating an input mismatch. For example, if the next input cannot be expressed as an integer, then the expression `console.nextInt()` will cause the program to terminate, with the error message indicating an input mismatch. Examples of invalid integers are 24w5 and 12.50. Chapter 12 explains why the program terminates with the error message indicating an input mismatch and how to include the necessary code to handle this problem. Until then, we assume that the user enters valid numbers.

The Java program in Example 2-17 illustrates how to read strings and numeric data.

EXAMPLE 2-17

```java
// This program illustrates how to read strings and numeric data.

import java.util.*;

public class Example2_17
{
    static Scanner console = new Scanner(System.in);

    public static void main(String[] args)
    {
        String firstName;                                  //Line 1
        String lastName;                                   //Line 2

        int age;                                           //Line 3
        double weight;                                     //Line 4

        System.out.println("Enter first name, last name, "
                    + "age, and weight separated "
                    + "by spaces.");                        //Line 5

        firstName = console.next();                        //Line 6
        lastName = console.next();                         //Line 7
        age = console.nextInt();                           //Line 8
        weight = console.nextDouble();                     //Line 9

        System.out.println("Name: " + firstName
                    + " " + lastName);                     //Line 10

        System.out.println("Age: " + age);                 //Line 11
        System.out.println("Weight: " + weight);           //Line 12
    }
}
```

Sample Run: (In this sample run, the user input is shaded.)

```
Enter first name, last name, age, and weight separated by spaces.
Sheila Mann 23 120.5
Name: Sheila Mann
Age: 23
Weight: 120.5
```

The preceding program works as follows: The statements in Lines 1 to 4 declare the variables `firstName` and `lastName` of type `String`, `age` of type `int`, and `weight` of type `double`. The statement in Line 5 is an output statement and tells the user what to do. (Such output statements are called prompt lines.) As shown in the sample run, the input to the program is:

```
Sheila Mann 23 120.5
```

The statement in Line 6 reads and assigns the string `Sheila` to the variable `firstName`; the statement in Line 7 skips the space after `Sheila` and reads and assigns the string `Mann` to the variable `lastName`. Next, the statement in Line 8 skips the blank after `Mann` and reads and stores `23` into the variable `age`. Similarly, the statement in Line 9 skips the blank after `23` and reads and stores `120.5` into the variable `weight`.

The statements in Lines 10, 11, and 12 produce the third, fourth, and fifth lines of the sample run.

VARIABLE INITIALIZATION

Remember, there are two ways to initialize a variable: by using the assignment statement and by using a read statement. Consider the following declaration:

```
int feet;
int inches;
```

Consider the following two sets of code:

```
(a) feet = 35;
    inches = 6;
    System.out.println("Total inches = " + (12 * feet + inches));
```

```
(b) System.out.print("Enter feet: ");
    feet = console.nextInt();
    System.out.println();
    System.out.print("Enter inches: ");
    inches = console.nextInt();
    System.out.println();
    System.out.print("Total inches = " + (12 * feet + inches));
```

In (a), `feet` and `inches` are initialized using assignment statements, and in (b), these variables are initialized using input statements. However, each time the code in (a) executes, `feet` and `inches` are initialized to the same value, unless you edit the source code, change the value, recompile, and run. On the other hand, in (b), each time the program runs, you are prompted to enter values for `feet` and `inches`. Therefore, a read statement is much more versatile than an assignment statement.

Sometimes it is necessary to initialize a variable by using an assignment statement. This is especially true if the variable is only used for internal calculation and not for reading and storing data.

NOTE   Recall that Java might not automatically initialize all the variables when they are declared. Some variables can be initialized when they are declared, whereas others must be initialized using either an assignment statement or a read statement. (Variable initialization is covered in more detail in Chapter 8.)

NOTE   Suppose you want to store a character into a `char` variable using an input statement. During program execution, when you input the character, you do not include the single quotation marks. Suppose that `ch` is a `char` variable. Consider the following input statement:

```
ch = console.next().charAt(0);
```

If you want to store `K` in `ch` using this statement, during program execution you type `K` without the single quotation marks. Similarly, if you want to store a string in a `String` variable using an input statement, during program execution you enter only the string without the double quotation marks.

Reading a Single Character

Suppose the next input is a single printable character, say, `A`. Further suppose that `ch` is a `char` variable. To input `A` into `ch`, you can use the following statement:

```
ch = console.next().charAt(0);
```

where `console` is as declared previously.

When something goes wrong in a program and the results it generates are not what you expect, you should do a walk-through of the statements that assign values to your variables. Example 2-18 illustrates how to do this. The walk-through is an effective debugging technique.

EXAMPLE 2-18

This example further illustrates how assignment statements and input statements manipulate variables. Consider the following declarations:

```
static Scanner console = new Scanner(System.in);

int firstNum;
int secondNum;
char ch;
double z;
```

Also suppose that the following statements execute in the order given:

1. `firstNum = 4;`
2. `secondNum = 2 * firstNum + 6;`
3. `z = (firstNum + 1) / 2.0;`
4. `ch = 'A';`
5. `secondNum = console.nextInt();`
6. `z = console.nextDouble();`
7. `firstNum = (int)(z) + 8;`
8. `secondNum = secondNum + 1;`
9. `ch = console.next().charAt(0);`
10. `firstNum = firstNum + (int)(ch);`

In addition, suppose the input is:

`8 16.3 D`

Let's now determine the values of the declared variables after the last statement executes. To show explicitly how a particular statement changes the value of a variable, the values of the variables after each statement executes are shown. (In the following table, a question mark, ?, in a box indicates that the value in the box is unknown.)

Values of the Variables	Variables				Statement/Explanation
	firstNum	secondNum	ch	z	
Before Statement 1	?	?	?	?	
After Statement 1	4	?	?	?	`firstNum = 4;` Store 4 into `firstNum`.
After Statement 2	4	14	?	?	`secondNum = 2 * firstNum + 6;` `2 * firstNum + 6 =` `2 * 4 + 6 = 14.` Store 14 into `secondNum`.
After Statement 3	4	14	?	2.5	`z = (firstNum + 1) / 2.0;` `(firstNum + 1) / 2.0 =` `(4 + 1) / 2.0 = 5 /` `2.0 = 2.5.` Store 2.5 into `z`.
After Statement 4	4	14	A	2.5	`ch = 'A';` Store `'A'` into `ch`.

2

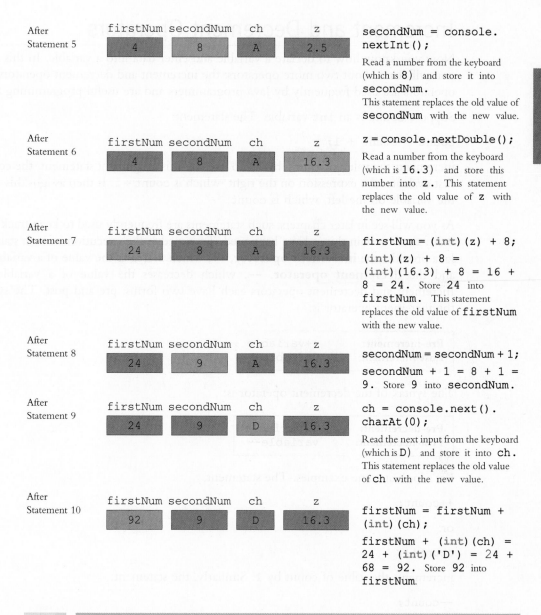

	firstNum	secondNum	ch	z
After Statement 5	4	8	A	2.5

secondNum = console.nextInt();

Read a number from the keyboard (which is 8) and store it into secondNum.
This statement replaces the old value of secondNum with the new value.

	firstNum	secondNum	ch	z
After Statement 6	4	8	A	16.3

z = console.nextDouble();

Read a number from the keyboard (which is 16.3) and store this number into z. This statement replaces the old value of z with the new value.

	firstNum	secondNum	ch	z
After Statement 7	24	8	A	16.3

firstNum = (int)(z) + 8;
(int)(z) + 8 =
(int)(16.3) + 8 = 16 +
8 = 24. Store 24 into
firstNum. This statement replaces the old value of firstNum with the new value.

	firstNum	secondNum	ch	z
After Statement 8	24	9	A	16.3

secondNum = secondNum + 1;
secondNum + 1 = 8 + 1 =
9. Store 9 into secondNum.

	firstNum	secondNum	ch	z
After Statement 9	24	9	D	16.3

ch = console.next().charAt(0);

Read the next input from the keyboard (which is D) and store it into ch. This statement replaces the old value of ch with the new value.

	firstNum	secondNum	ch	z
After Statement 10	92	9	D	16.3

firstNum = firstNum + (int)(ch);

firstNum + (int)(ch) =
24 + (int)('D') = 24 +
68 = 92. Store 92 into
firstNum.

NOTE To access a Java program that shows the effect of the 10 statements listed at the beginning of Example 2-18, download the Additional Student Files from *www.cengagebrain.com*. The program is named Example2_18.java.

NOTE If you assign the value of an expression that evaluates to a floating-point value—without using the cast operator—to a variable of type int, then a (syntax) error will occur.

Increment and Decrement Operators

Now you know how to declare a variable and enter data into a variable. In this section, you will learn about two more operators: the increment and decrement operators. These operators are used frequently by Java programmers and are useful programming tools.

Suppose `count` is an `int` variable. The statement:

```
count = count + 1;
```

increments the value of `count` by 1. To execute this assignment statement, the computer first evaluates the expression on the right, which is `count + 1`. It then assigns this value to the variable on the left, which is `count`.

As you will see in later chapters, such statements are frequently used to keep track of how many times certain things have happened. To expedite the execution of such statements, Java provides the **increment operator**, ++, which increases the value of a variable by 1, and the **decrement operator**, --, which decreases the value of a variable by 1. Increment and decrement operators each have two forms: pre and post. The syntax of the increment operator is:

Pre-increment:	`++variable`
Post-increment:	`variable++`

The syntax of the decrement operator is:

Pre-decrement:	`--variable`
Post-decrement:	`variable--`

Let's look at some examples. The statement:

```
++count;
```

or:

```
count++;
```

increments the value of count by 1. Similarly, the statement:

```
--count;
```

or:

```
count--;
```

decrements the value of count by 1.

Because increment and decrement operators are built into Java, the value of a variable is quickly incremented or decremented without having to use the form of an assignment statement.

As you can see from these examples, both the pre- and post-increment operators increment the value of the variable by 1. Similarly, the pre- and post-decrement operators decrement the value of the variable by 1. What is the difference between the pre and post forms of these operators? The difference becomes apparent when the variable using these operators is employed in an expression.

Suppose that x is a variable of type int. If ++x is used in an expression, first the value of x is incremented by 1, and then the new value of x is used to evaluate the expression. On the other hand, if x++ is used in an expression, first the current value of x is used in the expression, and then the value of x is incremented by 1. The following example clarifies the difference between the pre- and post-increment operators.

Suppose that x and y are int variables. Consider the following statements:

```
x = 5;
y = ++x;
```

The first statement assigns the value 5 to x. To evaluate the second statement, which uses the pre-increment operator, first the value of x is incremented to 6, and then this value, 6, is assigned to y. After the second statement executes, both x and y have the value 6.

Now consider the following statements:

```
x = 5;
y = x++;
```

As before, the first statement assigns 5 to x. In the second statement, the post-increment operator is applied to x. To execute the second statement, first the value of x, which is 5, is used to evaluate the expression, and then the value of x is incremented to 6. Finally, the value of the expression, which is 5, is stored in y. After the second statement executes, the value of x is 6 and the value of y is 5.

The following example further illustrates how the pre- and post-increment operators work.

EXAMPLE 2-19

Suppose a and b are int variables and:

```
a = 5;
b = 2 + (++a);
```

The first statement assigns 5 to a. To execute the second statement, first the expression 2 + (++a) is evaluated. As the pre-increment operator is applied to a, first the value of a is incremented to 6. Then, 2 is added to 6 to get 8, which is then assigned to b. Therefore, after the second statement executes, a is 6 and b is 8. On the other hand, after the execution of:

```
a = 5;
b = 2 + (a++);
```

the value of a is 6 while the value of b is 7.

NOTE This book most often uses the increment and decrement operators with a variable in a stand-alone statement. That is, the variable using the increment or decrement operator will not be part of any expression.

Output

In the preceding sections, you have seen how to put data into the computer's memory and how to manipulate that data. We also used certain output statements to show the results. This section explains, in some detail, how to further use output statements to generate the desired results.

NOTE The standard output device is usually the monitor.

In Java, output on the standard output device is accomplished by using the **standard output object** System.out. The object System.out has access to two methods, print and println, to output a string on the standard output device.

NOTE As of Java 5.0, you can also use the method printf to generate the output of a program. Chapter 3 discusses this method in detail.

The syntax to use the object System.out and the methods print and println is:

```
System.out.print(expression);
System.out.println(expression);
System.out.println();
```

These are **output statements**. The expression is evaluated, and its value is printed at the current insertion point on the output device. After outputting the value of expression, the method print leaves the insertion point after the last character of the value of expression, while the method println positions the insertion point at the beginning of the next line. Moreover, the statement:

```
System.out.println();
```

only positions the insertion point at the beginning of the next line. In this statement, notice the empty parentheses after println. They are still needed even though there is no expression between them.

> **NOTE** On the screen, the insertion point is where the cursor is.

In an output statement, if **expression** consists of only one string or a single constant value, then **expression** evaluates to itself. If **expression** consists of only one variable, then **expression** evaluates to the value of the variable. Also note, as explained in this chapter, how the operator + works with strings and numeric values. Example 2-20 illustrates how the output statements work and also gives examples of **expressions**.

When an output statement outputs **char** values, it outputs the character without the single quotation marks (unless the single quotation marks are part of the output statement). For example, suppose ch is a **char** variable and ch = 'A';. The statement:

```
System.out.println(ch);
```

or:

```
System.out.println('A');
```

outputs:

```
A
```

Similarly, when an output statement outputs the value of a string, it outputs the string without the double quotation marks (unless you include double quotation marks as part of the string, using an escape sequence).

EXAMPLE 2-20

Consider the following statements. The output is shown to the right of each statement.

	Statement	Output
1	`System.out.println(29 / 4);`	7
2	`System.out.println("Hello there.");`	Hello there.
3	`System.out.println(12);`	12
4	`System.out.println("4 + 7");`	4 + 7
5	`System.out.println(4 + 7);`	11
6	`System.out.println('A');`	A
7	`System.out.println("4 + 7 = " + (4 + 7));`	4 + 7 = 11
8	`System.out.println(2 + 3 * 5);`	17
9	`System.out.println("Hello \nthere.");`	Hello there.

Look at the output of statement 9. Recall that in Java, the newline character is '\n'; it causes the insertion point to move to the beginning of the next line before printing.

Therefore, when \n appears in a string in an output statement, it moves the insertion point to the beginning of the next line on the output device. This explains why Hello and there. are printed on separate lines.

> **NOTE** In Java, \ is called the **escape character** and \n is called the **newline escape sequence**.

Let's take a closer look at the newline character, '\n'. Consider the following Java statements:

```
System.out.print("Hello there. ");
System.out.print("My name is James.");
```

If these statements are executed in sequence, the output is:

```
Hello there. My name is James.
```

Consider the following Java statements:

```
System.out.print("Hello there.\n");
System.out.print("My name is James.");
```

The output of these Java statements is:

```
Hello there.
My name is James.
```

When \n is encountered in the string, the insertion point is positioned at the beginning of the next line. Note also that \n may appear anywhere in the string. For example, the output of the statement:

```
System.out.print("Hello \nthere. \nMy name is James.");
```

is:

```
Hello
there.
My name is James.
```

Also, note that the output of the statement:

```
System.out.print("\n");
```

is the same as the output of the statement:

```
System.out.println();
```

Thus, the output of the sequence of statements:

```
System.out.print("Hello there.\n");
System.out.print("My name is James.");
```

is equivalent to the output of the sequence of statements:

```
System.out.println("Hello there.");
System.out.print("My name is James.");
```

EXAMPLE 2-21

Consider the following Java statements:

```
System.out.print("Hello there.\nMy name is James.");
```

or:

```
System.out.print("Hello there.");
System.out.print("\nMy name is James.");
```

or:

```
System.out.println("Hello there.");
System.out.print("My name is James.");
```

In each case, the output of the statements is:

```
Hello there.
My name is James.
```

EXAMPLE 2-22

Suppose you want to output the following sentence in one line as part of a message:

```
It is sunny, warm, and not a windy day. We can go golfing.
```

Obviously, you will use the methods `print` and/or `println` to produce this output. However, in the programming code, this statement may not fit in one line as part of the output statement. Of course, you can use more than one output statement, as follows:

```
System.out.print("It is sunny, warm, and not a windy day. ");
System.out.println("We can go golfing.");
```

Two output statements are used to output the sentence in one line. You can also use the following statement to output this sentence:

```
System.out.println("It is sunny, warm, and not a windy day. " +
                "We can go golfing.");
```

In this statement, note that because there is no semicolon at the end of the first line, this output statement continues at the second line. Also, note that the first line is followed by the operator +, and there is a double quotation mark at the beginning of the second line. The string is broken into two strings, but both strings are part of the same output statement.

If a string appearing in an output statement is long and you want to output the string in one line, you can break the string by using either of these two approaches. However, the following statement using the **Enter** (or return) key would be incorrect:

```
System.out.println("It is sunny, warm, and not a windy day.
                We can go golfing.")
```

The Enter (or return) key on your keyboard cannot be part of the string—in programming code, a string *cannot* be broken into more than one line by using the Enter (return) key.

Recall that the newline character is \n, which moves the insertion point to the beginning of the next line. In Java, there are many other escape sequences that allow you to control the output. Table 2-5 lists some of the commonly used escape sequences.

TABLE 2-5 Commonly Used Escape Sequences

	Escape Sequence	Description
\n	Newline	Cursor moves to the beginning of the next line
\t	Tab	Cursor moves to the next tab stop
\b	Backspace	Cursor moves one space to the left
\r	Return	Cursor moves to the beginning of the current line (not the next line)
\\	Backslash	Backslash is printed
\'	Single quotation	Single quotation mark is printed
\"	Double quotation	Double quotation mark is printed

Example 2-23 shows the effect of some of these escape sequences.

EXAMPLE 2-23

The output of the statement:

```
System.out.println("The newline escape sequence is \\n");
```

is:

```
The newline escape sequence is \n
```

The output of the statement:

```
System.out.println("The tab character is represented as \'\\t\'");
```

is:

```
The tab character is represented as '\t'
```

Note that the single quote can also be printed without using the escape sequence. Therefore, the preceding statement is equivalent to the following output statement:

```
System.out.println("The tab character is represented as '\\t'");
```

The output of the statement:

```
System.out.println("The string \"Sunny\" contains five characters");
```

is:

```
The string "Sunny" contains five characters
```

 NOTE To access a Java program that shows the effect of the statements in Example 2-23, download Additional Student Files from *www.cengagebrain.com*. (The program is named `Example2_23.java`.)

Packages, Classes, Methods, and the `import` Statement

Only a small number of operations, such as arithmetic and assignment operations, are explicitly defined in Java. Many of the methods and identifiers needed to run a Java program are provided as a collection of libraries, called packages. A **package** is a collection of related classes. Moreover, every package has a name.

In Java, *class* is a broadly used term. The term **class** is used to create Java programs, either application or applet; it is used to group a set of related operations; and it is used to allow users to create their own data types. For example, there are various mathematical operations, such as determining the absolute value of a number, determining one number raised to the power of another number, and determining the logarithm of a number. Each of these operations is implemented using the Java mechanism of *methods*. Think of a **method** as a set of instructions designed to accomplish a specific task. For example, the name of the method implementing the operation of one number raised to the power of another number is `pow`. This and other mathematical methods are contained in the **class** Math. The name of the package containing the **class** Math is `java.lang`.

The package `java.util` contains the **class** Scanner. This class contains the methods `nextInt`, `nextDouble`, `next`, and `nextLine` for inputting data into a program. In the next section, you will learn how class(es) are used to create a Java application program.

 NOTE To see the complete definitions of the (predefined) Java classes, such as `String`, `Math`, and `Scanner`, as well as the class hierarchy, you can visit the Web site *http://java.sun.com/javase/7/docs/api/*.

To make use of the existing classes, methods, and identifiers, you must tell the program which package contains the appropriate information. The `import` statement helps you do this.

The general syntax to import the contents of a package in a Java program is:

```
import packageName.*;
```

In Java, `import` is a reserved word. For example, the following statement imports the necessary classes from the package `java.util`:

```
import java.util.*;
```

To import a specific class from a package, you can specify the name of the class in place of the `*`. The following statement imports the **class** `Scanner` from the package `java.util`:

```
import java.util.Scanner;
```

Import statements are placed at the top of the program.

NOTE   If you use the character `*` in the `import` statement, as in the statement:

```
import java.util.*;
```

then the compiler determines the relevant class(es) used in the program.

NOTE   The primitive data types are directly part of the Java language and do not require that any package be imported into the program. Also, the **class** `String` is contained in the package `java.lang`. You do not need to import classes from the package `java.lang`. The system automatically does it for you.

Creating a Java Application Program

In previous sections, you learned enough Java concepts to write meaningful programs. In this section, you will learn how to create a complete Java application program.

The basic unit of a Java program is called a class. A Java application program is, therefore, a collection of one or more classes. Roughly speaking, a class is a collection of methods and data members. As described in the previous section, a method is a set of instructions designed to accomplish a specific task. Some **predefined** or **standard** methods, such as `nextInt`, `print`, and `println`, are already written and are provided as part of the system. But to accomplish most tasks, programmers must learn to write their own methods.

One of the classes in a Java application program must have the method called `main`. Moreover, there can only be one method `main` in a Java class. If a Java application program has only one class, it *must* contain the method `main`. Until Chapter 6, other than using some predefined methods, you will mainly deal with Java application programs that have only one class.

Statements to declare memory spaces (named constants and variables), statements to create input stream objects, statements to manipulate data (such as assignments), and statements to input and output data will be placed within the class.

Statements to declare named constants and input stream objects are usually placed outside the method `main`, and statements to declare variables are usually placed within the method `main`. Statements to manipulate data and input and output statements are placed within the method `main`.

The syntax of a class to create a Java application program is:

```
public class ClassName
{
      classMembers
}
```

where `ClassName` is a user-defined Java identifier; `classMembers` consists of the data members and methods (such as the method `main`). In Java, `public` and `class` are reserved words. (Typically, the name of a class begins with an uppercase letter.)

A typical syntax of the method `main` is:

```
public static void main(String[] args)
{
      statement1
          .
          .
          .
      statementn
}
```

Recall that in a syntax example, the shading indicates the part of the definition that is optional.

A Java application program might be using the resources provided by the IDE, such as the necessary code to input data, which require your program to import certain packages. You can, therefore, divide a Java application program into two parts: import statements and the program itself. The import statements tell the compiler which packages are needed by the program. The program contains statements (placed in a class) that accomplish some meaningful results. Together, the import statements and the program statements constitute the Java **source code**. To be useful, this source code must be saved in a file, called a **source file**, that has the file extension `.java`. Moreover, the name of the class and the name of the file containing the Java program must be the same. For example, if the name of the class to create the Java program is `Welcome`, then the name of the source file must be `Welcome.java`.

Because the programming instructions are placed in the method `main`, let us elaborate on the method `main` a bit more.

The basic parts of the method `main` are the heading and the body. The first line of the method `main`:

```
public static void main(String[] args)
```

is called the **heading** of the method `main`.

The statements enclosed between braces (`{` and `}`) form the **body** of the method `main`. The body of the method `main` contains two types of statements:

- Declaration statements
- Executable statements

Declaration statements are used to declare things such as variables.
Executable statements perform calculations, manipulate data, create output, accept input, and so on.

In Java, variables or identifiers can be declared anywhere within a method, but they must be declared before they can be used.

EXAMPLE 2-24

The following statements are examples of variable declarations:

```
int    num1;
int    num2;
double salary;
String name;
```

EXAMPLE 2-25

Some executable statements that you have encountered so far are the assignment, input, and output statements.

Suppose that `num1` and `num2` are `int` variables. The following statements are examples of executable statements:

```
num1 = 4;                              //assignment statement
num2 = console.nextInt();              //input and
                                       //assignment statement

System.out.println(num1 + " " + num2); //output statement
```

2

In skeleton form, a Java application program looks like the following:

```
import statements if any

public class ClassName
{
    named constants and/or stream objects declarations

    public static void main(String[] args)
    {
        variable declaration

        statements
    }
}
```

 NOTE Notice that the heading of the method `main` contains the reserved word `static`. The statements to declare the named constants and the input stream objects are placed outside the definition of the method `main`. Therefore, to use these named constants and stream objects in the method `main`, Java requires that you declare the named constants and the input stream objects with the reserved word `static`. Example 2-26 illustrates this concept.

EXAMPLE 2-26

The following is a simple Java application program showing where in a Java program the import statements, the method `main`, and statements such as named constants, declarations, assignment statements, and input and output statements typically appear.

```
//*****************************************************************
// Author: D.S. Malik
//
// This program shows where the import statements, named constants,
// variable declarations, assignment statements, and input and
// output statements typically appear.
//*****************************************************************

import java.util.*;                                       //Line 1

public class FirstJavaProgram                             //Line 2
{                                                         //Line 3
    static final int NUMBER = 12;                         //Line 4

    static Scanner console = new Scanner(System.in);      //Line 5

    public static void main(String[] args)               //Line 6
    {                                                     //Line 7
        int firstNum;                                     //Line 8
        int secondNum;                                    //Line 9

        firstNum = 18;                                    //Line 10
        System.out.println("Line 11: firstNum = "
                          + firstNum);                    //Line 11
```

```
        System.out.print("Line 12: Enter an integer: ");    //Line 12
        secondNum = console.nextInt();                        //Line 13
        System.out.println();                                 //Line 14

        System.out.println("Line 15: secondNum = "
                       + secondNum);                           //Line 15

        firstNum = firstNum + NUMBER + 2 * secondNum;          //Line 16

        System.out.println("Line 17: The new value of " +
                       "firstNum = " + firstNum);              //Line 17
    }                                                          //Line 18
}                                                              //Line 19
```

Sample Run: (In this sample run, the user input is shaded.)

```
Line 11: firstNum = 18
Line 12: Enter an integer: 15

Line 15: secondNum = 15
Line 17: The new value of firstNum = 60
```

The preceding program works as follows: The statement in Line 1 imports the `class` Scanner. The statement in Line 2 names the `class` containing statements of the program as `FirstJavaProgram`. The left brace in Line 3 marks the beginning of the `class FirstJavaProgram`.

The statement in Line 4 declares the named constant `NUMBER` and sets its value to 12. The statement in Line 5 declares and initializes the object `console` to input data from the keyboard.

The statement in Line 6 contains the heading of the method `main`, and the left brace in Line 7 marks the beginning of the method `main`. The statements in Lines 8 and 9 declare the variables `firstNum` and `secondNum`.

The statement in Line 10 sets the value of `firstNum` to 18, and the statement in Line 11 outputs the value of `firstNum`.

Next, the statement in Line 12 prompts the user to enter an integer. The statement in Line 13 reads and stores the integer into the variable `secondNum`, which is 15 in the sample run. The statement in Line 14 positions the insertion point on the screen at the beginning of the next line. The statement in Line 15 outputs the value of `secondNum`.

The statement in Line 16 evaluates the expression:

```
firstNum + NUMBER + 2 * secondNum
```

and assigns the value of this expression to the variable `firstNum`, which is 60 in the sample run. The statement in Line 17 outputs the new value of `firstNum`. The right brace in Line 18 marks the end of the method `main`, and the right brace in Line 19 marks the end of the `class FirstJavaProgram`.

Debugging: Understanding and Fixing Syntax Errors

2

The previous sections of this chapter described the basic components of a Java program. When you type a program, typos and unintentional syntax errors are likely to occur. Therefore, when you compile a program, the compiler will identify the syntax errors. In this section, we will show how to identify and fix syntax errors.

Consider the following Java program:

```
1.   import java.util.*;
2.
3.   public class ProgramNum1
4.   {
5.       static Scanner console = new Scanner(System.in);
6.
7.       public static void main(String[] args)
8.       {
9.           int num
10.
11.          num = 18;
12.
13.          tempNum = 2 * num;
14.
15.          System.out.println("Num = " + num + ", tempNum = " - tempNum);
16.      }
```

(Note that the numbers 1 to 16 on the left side are not part of the program. We have numbered the statements for easy references.) This program contains syntax errors. When you compile this program, the compiler produces the following errors:

```
ProgramNum.java:9: ';' expected
      int num
            ^
ProgramNum.java:16: reached end of file while parsing
      }
       ^
2 errors
```

The expression `ProgramNum.java:9` indicates that there is error in Line 9. The remaining error indicates that `;` is expected. The next line indicates that there is a missing semicolon at the end of the statement `int num`. Therefore, we must insert `;` at the end of the statement in Line 9.

Next, consider the second error:

ProgramNum.java:16: reached end of file while parsing

This error occurs in Line 16 and it specifies that the end of the file is reached. This error is not very clear at this point. However, if you look at the source code, you will realize that there is a missing `}` , which should match `{` at Line 4. (Note that every `{` must have a matching `}` .)

Let us correct these errors. After correcting these errors we will rename this program as ProgramNum2.java. The program after correcting these errors is:

```
1.   import java.util.*;
2.
3.   public class ProgramNum2
4.   {
5.       static Scanner console = new Scanner(System.in);
6.
7.       public static void main(String[] args)
8.       {
9.           int num;
10.
11.          num = 18;
12.
13.          tempNum = 2 * num;
14.
15.          System.out.println("Num = " + num + ", tempNum = " - tempNum);
16.      }
17.  }
```

When you compile this program, it will generate the following errors:

```
ProgramNum2.java:13: cannot find symbol
symbol  : variable tempNum
location: class ProgramNum2
      tempNum = 2 * num;
         ^

ProgramNum2.java:15: cannot find symbol
symbol  : variable tempNum
location: class ProgramNum2
      System.out.println("Num = " + num + ", tempNum = " - tempNum);
                                                                  ^

2 errors
```

The first error is in Line 13 and it specifies that a symbol cannot be found. The next line indicates that the symbol is the variable tempNum. If we look at the program, we find that the variable tempNum is not declared, so we must declare it. The next error is in Line 15 and it also specifies that the variable tempNum cannot be found.

Let us declare the variable tempNum and also rename the program as ProgramNum3.java. The new program is now:

```
1.   import java.util.*;
2.
3.   public class ProgramNum3
4.   {
5.       static Scanner console = new Scanner(System.in);
6.
7.       public static void main(String[] args)
8.       {
9.           int num;
```

```
10.          int tempNum;
11.
12.          num = 18;
13.
14.          tempNum = 2 * num;
15.
16.          System.out.println("Num = " + num + ", tempNum = " - tempNum);
17.     }
18. }
```

When this program is compiled, it generates the following error:

```
ProgramNum3.java:16: operator - cannot be applied to java.lang.String,int
     System.out.println("Num = " + num + ", tempNum = " - tempNum);
                                                        ^
1 error
```

It specifies that the error is in Line 16 and it indicates that the operator – cannot be applied to strings. Recall that to join two strings, we use the operator +. So in Line 16, we must replace – with + at the place indicated by ^. After correcting this error and renaming this program, the program is:

```
1.  import java.util.*;
2.
3.  public class ProgramNum4
4.  {
5.      static Scanner console = new Scanner(System.in);
6.
7.      public static void main(String[] args)
8.      {
9.          int num;
10.         int tempNum;
11.
12.         num = 18;
13.
14.         tempNum = 2 * num;
15.
16.         System.out.println("Num = " + num + ", tempNum = " + tempNum);
17.     }
18. }
```

When we compile this program, the compiler will not generate any syntax errors and it will create the file ProgramNum4.class, which can be executed using the appropriate Java command.

When we execute this program it will generate the following output:

```
Num = 18, tempNum = 36
```

As you learn Java and practice writing and executing programs, you will learn how to spot and fix syntax errors. It is possible that the list of errors reported by the compiler is longer than the program itself. This is because a syntax error in one line can cause syntax errors in subsequent lines. In situations like this, correct the syntax errors in the order they are listed and compile your program, if necessary, after each correction. You will see how quickly the syntax errors list shrinks. The important thing is not to panic.

In the next section, we describe some simple rules that you can follow so that your program is properly structured.

Programming Style and Form

In previous sections, you learned how to create a Java application program. Here, we describe the proper structure of a program. Using the proper structure makes a Java program easier to understand and modify. It is frustrating trying to follow, and perhaps modify, a program that is syntactically correct but has no structure.

Every Java application program must satisfy certain language rules. It must also satisfy the syntax rules, which, like grammar rules, tell what is correct and what is incorrect, and what is legal and what is illegal in the language. Other rules give precise meaning to the language; that is, they support the language's semantics. The sections that follow are designed to help you learn more about how to put together the Java programming elements you have learned so far and how to create a functioning program. These sections cover syntax; the use of blanks; the use of semicolons, brackets, and commas; semantics; prompt lines; documentation, including comments and naming identifiers; and form and style.

Syntax

As noted earlier, the syntax rules of a language tell what is legal and what is illegal. Errors in syntax are detected during compilation. Consider the following Java statements:

```
int    x;         //Line 1
int    y          //Line 2
double z;         //Line 3

y = w + x;        //Line 4
```

When these statements are compiled, a compilation error will occur at Line 2 because there is no semicolon after the declaration of the variable y. A second compilation error will occur at Line 4 because the identifier w is used but has not been declared. (If w has been declared and x has not been properly initialized, then a syntax error will occur at Line 4.)

As discussed in Chapter 1, you enter a program into the computer by using an editor. When a program is typed, errors are almost unavoidable. Therefore, when the program is compiled, you most likely will see syntax errors. It is possible that a syntax error at a particular place might lead to syntax errors in several subsequent statements. It is common for the omission of a single character to cause four or five error messages. However, when the first syntax error is removed and the program is recompiled, subsequent syntax errors caused by the first syntax error may disappear. Therefore, you should correct syntax errors in the order in which the compiler lists them. As you become more experienced with Java, you will learn how to spot and fix syntax errors quickly. Note that compilers not only discover syntax errors, but also provide hints and sometimes tell the user where the syntax errors are and how to fix them.

USE OF BLANKS

In Java, you use one or more blanks to separate numbers when data is input. Blanks are also used to separate reserved words and identifiers from each other and from other symbols. Blanks must never appear within a reserved word or identifier.

USE OF SEMICOLONS, BRACES, AND COMMAS

In Java, a semicolon is used to terminate a statement. The semicolon is also called a **statement terminator**.

Note that braces, { and }, are not Java statements, even though they often appear on a line with no other code. You might regard braces as delimiters because they enclose the body of a method and set it off from other parts of the program. (Braces have other uses, which will be explained in Chapter 4.)

Recall that commas are used to separate items in a list. For example, you use commas when you declare more than one variable following a data type.

SEMANTICS

The set of rules that gives meaning to a language is called **semantics**. For example, the order-of-precedence rules for arithmetic operators are semantic rules.

If a program contains syntax errors, the compiler will warn you. What happens when a program contains semantic errors? It is quite possible to eradicate all syntax errors in a program and still not have it run. And if it runs, it may not do what you meant it to do. For example, the following two expressions are both syntactically correct expressions, but they have different meanings:

```
2 + 3 * 5
```

and:

```
(2 + 3) * 5
```

If you substitute one of these expressions for the other in a program, you will not get the same results—even though the numbers are the same, the semantics are different. You will learn about semantics throughout this book.

PROMPT LINES

Part of good documentation is the use of clearly written prompts so that users will know what to do when they interact with a program. It is frustrating for a user to sit in front of a running program and not have the foggiest notion of whether to enter something, and if so, what to enter. **Prompt lines** are executable statements that inform the user what to do. Consider the following Java statements, in which num is an `int` variable:

```
System.out.println("Please enter a number between 1 and 10 and "
                   + "then press Enter");
num = console.nextInt();
```

When these two statements execute in the order given, first the output statement causes the following line of text to appear on the screen:

```
Please enter a number between 1 and 10 and then press Enter
```

After seeing this line, an example of a prompt line, users know that they must enter a number and press the Enter key. If the program contained only the second statement, users would not know that they must enter a number, and the computer would wait indefinitely for the input. The preceding output statement is an example of a prompt line.

In a program, whenever users must provide input, you should include the necessary prompt lines. The prompt lines should include sufficient information about what input is acceptable. For example, the preceding prompt line not only tells the user to input a number, but also informs the user that the number should be between 1 and 10.

FORM AND STYLE

You might think that Java has too many rules. However, in practice, the rules give Java a great degree of freedom. For example, consider the following two ways of declaring variables:

```
int feet;
int inch;

double x;
double y;
```

and:

```
int feet; int inch;double x;double y;
```

The computer has no difficulty understanding either of these formats, but the first form is easier for a person to read and follow.

What about blank spaces? Where are they significant and where are they meaningless?

Consider the following two statements:

```
int a;
```

and:

```
int     a;
```

Both of these declarations mean the same thing. Here, the extra blanks between the identifiers in the second statement are meaningless. On the other hand, consider the following statement:

```
inta;
```

This statement contains a syntax error. The lack of a blank between the t in `int` and the identifier `a` changes the reserved word `int` and the identifier `a` into a new identifier, `inta`.

The clarity provided by the rules of syntax and semantics frees you to adopt formats that are pleasing to you and easier to understand.

The following example further elaborates on form and style.

EXAMPLE 2-27

Consider the following Java program:

```java
//An improperly formatted Java program.

import java.util.*;

public class Example2_27A
{
        static Scanner console = new Scanner(System.in);
public static void main(String[] args)
{
int num; double height;
String name;
System.out.print("Enter an integer: ");
num=console.nextInt(); System.out.println();
    System.out.println("num: "+num);
System.out.print("Enter first name: ");
name=console.next();
    System.out.println();System.out.print("Enter height: ");
height = console.nextDouble(); System.out.println();

System.out.println("Name: "+name);System.out.println("Height: "
+height);
}}
```

This program is syntactically correct; the Java compiler would have no difficulty reading and compiling this program. However, this program is very hard for a human to read. The program that you write should be properly indented and formatted. Next, we rewrite the preceding program and properly format it.

```java
//Properly formatted Java program.

import java.util.*;

public class Example2_27B
{
    static Scanner console = new Scanner(System.in);

    public static void main(String[] args)
    {
        int num;
        double height;
        String name;
```

```
System.out.print("Enter an integer: ");
num = console.nextInt();
System.out.println();

System.out.println("num: " + num);

System.out.print("Enter first name: ");
name = console.next();
System.out.println();

System.out.print("Enter height: ");
height = console.nextDouble();
System.out.println();

System.out.println("Name: " + name);
System.out.println("Height: " + height);
    }
}
```

As you can see, this program is easier to read. Your programs should be properly indented and formatted. To document the variables, programmers typically declare one variable per line. Also, always put a space before and after an operator.

DEBUGGING
Avoiding Bugs: Consistent, Proper Formatting and Code Walk-Through

Java is a free-format language in the sense that programming instructions need not be typed in specific columns. For example, you can declare one or more variables in a line and input and/or output statements can follow the declarations of variables as illustrated in the first program given in Example 2-27, which is an improperly formatted program. The compiler will have no trouble compiling this program. However, for us, this program is very hard to follow and if there are syntax or semantic (logical) errors, it will be very tedious and tiresome to debug this program. The second program in Example 2-27 is properly formatted and easier to read and follow. As you will discover, consistent and proper formatting will make it easier to develop, debug, and maintain programs. Throughout the book, you will see consistent and predictable use of blanks, tabs, and newline characters to separate the elements of a program. For example, we have indented statements four spaces to the right within a block (that is, between { and } .) Rather than four spaces, you can indent statements three spaces to the right; the important thing is to be consistent. We will list a few more indenting rules when we introduce selection and looping structures in a program.

Examples 2-14 and 2-18 illustrate how to walk-through a program. When you write programs unintentional typos and errors are unavoidable. The Java compiler will find the syntax rules and give some hints how to correct them. However, the compiler may not find logical (semantic) errors. Typically, programmers try to find and fix these problems themselves by walking carefully through their programs. They do so by looking at the output of the program and comparing it with what should be done at each step, which often reveals the problem. Sometimes after multiple readings a programmer may not be able to find the bug because the programmer may overlook the piece of the code that contains the bug; therefore they may seek outside help. In this case, if your program is properly formatted and you have used good names for identifiers, the person reading your program will have an easier time reading and debugging the program. Before you seek outside help, you should be prepared to explain what your program intended to do and answer questions raised by the person reading your program.

The examination of your program by yourself, by another person, or a group of persons is a walk-through. A walk-through is helpful for all phases of the software development process. In the next chapter, we will illustrate how to debug logical errors.

More on Assignment Statements (Optional)

Corresponding to the five arithmetic operators +, -, *, /, and %, Java provides five compound operators +=, -=, *=, /=, and %=, respectively. Consider the following simple assignment statement, where x and y are int variables:

```
x = x * y;
```

Using the compound operator *=, this statement can be written as:

```
x *= y;
```

In general, using the compound operator *=, you can rewrite the simple assignment statement:

```
variable = variable * (expression);
```

as:

```
variable *= expression;
```

Similar conventions apply to the other arithmetic compound operators. For example, using the compound operator +=, you can rewrite the simple assignment statement

```
variable = variable + (expression);
```

as:

```
variable += expression;
```

Thus, the compound assignment statement lets you write simple assignment statements in a concise fashion by combining an arithmetic operator with an assignment operator.

EXAMPLE 2-28

This example shows several compound assignment statements that are equivalent to simple assignment statements.

Simple Assignment Statement	**Compound Assignment Statement**
`i = i + 5;`	`i += 5;`
`counter = counter + 1;`	`counter += 1;`
`sum = sum + number;`	`sum += number;`
`amount = amount * (interest + 1);`	`amount *= interest + 1;`
`x = x / ( y + 5);`	`x /= y + 5;`

 NOTE Any compound assignment statement can be converted into a simple assignment statement. However, a simple assignment statement may not be (easily) converted into a compound assignment statement. Consider the following simple assignment statement:

`x = x * y + z - 5;`

To write this statement as a compound assignment statement, the variable x must be a common factor in the right side, which is not the case. Therefore, you cannot immediately convert this statement into a compound assignment statement. In fact, the equivalent compound assignment statement is:

`x *= y + (z - 5)/x;`

which is more complicated than the simple assignment statement. Furthermore, in the preceding compound statement, x cannot be zero. We recommend avoiding such compound expressions.

PROGRAMMING EXAMPLE: Convert Length

Write a program that takes as input given lengths expressed in feet and inches. The program should then convert and output the lengths in centimeters. Assume that the lengths given in feet and inches are integers.

Input: Length in feet and inches

Output: Equivalent length in centimeters

PROBLEM
ANALYSIS
AND
ALGORITHM
DESIGN

The lengths are given in feet and inches, and you need to find the equivalent length in centimeters. One inch is equal to 2.54 centimeters. The first thing the program needs to do is convert the length given in feet and inches to all inches. To convert the length from feet and inches to inches, you multiply the number of feet by 12 (1 foot is equal to 12 inches), and add your answer to the given inches. Then you can use the conversion formula, 1 inch = 2.54 centimeters, to find the equivalent length in centimeters.

Suppose the input is 5 feet and 7 inches. You find the total inches as follows:

```
totalInches = (12 * feet) + inches
            = 12 * 5 + 7
            = 67
```

You can then apply the conversion formula, 1 inch = 2.54 centimeters, to find the length in centimeters.

```
centimeters = totalInches * 2.54
            = 67 * 2.54
            = 170.18
```

Based on this analysis, you can design an algorithm as follows:

1. Get the length in feet and inches.
2. Convert the length into total inches.
3. Convert total inches into centimeters.
4. Output centimeters.

VARIABLES

The input for the program is two numbers: one for feet and one for inches. Thus, you need two variables: one to store feet and the other to store inches. Because the program will first convert the given length into inches, you need a third variable to store the total inches. You need a fourth variable to store the equivalent length in centimeters. In summary, you need the following variables:

```
int feet;           //variable to store feet
int inches;         //variable to store inches
int totalInches;    //variable to store total inches

double centimeters; //variable to store length in centimeters
```

NAMED
CONSTANTS

Recall that to calculate the equivalent length in centimeters, you need to multiply the total inches by 2.54. Instead of using the value 2.54 directly in the program, you will declare this value as a named constant. Similarly, to find the total inches, you need to multiply the feet by 12 and add the inches. Instead of using 12 directly in the program, you will also declare this value as a named constant. Using named constants makes it easier to modify the program later. Because the named constants will be placed before the method main, you must use the modifier static to declare these named constants (see the earlier section, Creating a Java Application Program).

```
static final double CENTIMETERS_PER_INCH = 2.54;
static final int INCHES_PER_FOOT = 12;
```

MAIN
ALGORITHM

In the preceding sections, we analyzed the problem and determined the formulas to perform the calculations. We also determined the necessary variables and named constants. We can now expand the algorithm given in the section Problem Analysis and Algorithm Design to solve the problem given at the beginning of this programming example (converting feet and inches to centimeters).

1. Prompt the user for the input. (Without a prompt line, the user will stare at a blank screen and not know what to do.)
2. Get feet.
3. Prompt the user to enter a value for inches.
4. Get inches.
5. Echo the input by outputting what the program read as input. (Without this step, after the program has executed, you will not know what the input was.)
6. Find the length in inches.
7. Output the length in inches.
8. Convert the length to centimeters.
9. Output the length in centimeters.

PUTTING IT
TOGETHER

Now that the problem has been analyzed and the algorithm has been designed, the next step is to translate the algorithm into Java code. Because this is the first complete Java program you are writing, let's review the necessary steps in sequence.

The program will begin with comments that document its purpose and functionality. Because there is both input to this program (the length in feet and inches) and output (the equivalent length in centimeters), you will use the system resources for input/output. In other words, the program will use input statements to get the data into the program and output statements to print the results. Because the data will be entered from the keyboard, the program must import the class Scanner from the package java.util. Thus, the first statement of the program, following the comments described previously, will be the import statement to import the class Scanner from the package java.util.

This program requires two types of memory locations for data manipulation: named constants and variables. Recall that named constants are usually placed before the method main so that they can be used throughout the program.

This program has only one class, which contains the method main. The method main will contain all of the programming instructions in its body. In addition, the program needs variables to manipulate the data; these variables will be declared in the body of the method main. (The reasons for declaring variables in the body of the method main are explained in Chapter 7.) The body of the method main will also contain the Java statements that implement the algorithm. Therefore, for this program, the definition of the method main has the following form:

```
public static void main(String[] args)
{
    declare variables
    statements
}
```

To write the complete conversion program, follow these steps:

1. Begin the program with comments for documentation.
2. Use import statements to import the classes required by the program.
3. Declare the named constants, if any.
4. Write the definition of the method main.

COMPLETE PROGRAM LISTING

```java
//*********************************************************
// Author: D. S. Malik
//
// Program Convert: This program converts measurements
// in feet and inches into centimeters using the formula
// that 1 inch is equal to 2.54 centimeters.
//*********************************************************

import java.util.*;

public class Conversion
{
    static Scanner console = new Scanner(System.in);

    static final double CENTIMETERS_PER_INCH = 2.54;
    static final int INCHES_PER_FOOT = 12;
    public static void main(String[] args)
    {
            //declare variables
        int feet;
        int inches;
        int totalInches;

        double centimeters;

        System.out.print("Enter feet: ");                //Step 1
        feet = console.nextInt();                        //Step 2
```

```
        System.out.println();
        System.out.print("Enter inches: ");              //Step 3
        inches = console.nextInt();                      //Step 4
        System.out.println();
        System.out.println("The numbers you entered are "
                        + feet + " for feet and "
                        + inches + " for inches.");       //Step 5

        totalInches = INCHES_PER_FOOT * feet + inches;    //Step 6

        System.out.println();
        System.out.println("The total number of inches = "
                        + totalInches);                   //Step 7

        centimeters = totalInches * CENTIMETERS_PER_INCH; //Step 8

        System.out.println("The number of centimeters = "
                        + centimeters);                   //Step 9
    }
}
```

Sample Run: (In this sample run, the user input is shaded.)

Enter feet: 15

Enter inches: 7

The numbers you entered are 15 for feet and 7 for inches.

The total number of inches = 187
The number of centimeters = 474.98

The programming code of this program must be saved in the file Conversion. java because we named the class containing the method main Conversion.

NOTE   The preceding program uses comments such as //Step 1, //Step 2, and so on. The only purpose of these comments is to show which step of the algorithm (shown before the program listing) corresponds to which statement in the program. We typically use this convention in all the programming examples in this book.

PROGRAMMING EXAMPLE: Make Change

Write a program that takes as input any change expressed in cents. It should then compute the number of half-dollars, quarters, dimes, nickels, and pennies to be returned, using as many half-dollars as possible, then quarters, dimes, nickels, and pennies, in that order. For example, 483 cents would be returned as 9 half-dollars, 1 quarter, 1 nickel, and 3 pennies.

Input: Change in cents

Output: Equivalent change in half-dollars, quarters, dimes, nickels, and pennies

PROBLEM
ANALYSIS
AND
ALGORITHM
DESIGN

Suppose the given change is 646 cents. To find the number of half-dollars, you divide 646 by 50, the value of a half-dollar, and find the quotient, which is 12, and the remainder, which is 46. The quotient, 12, is the number of half-dollars, and the remainder, 46, is the remaining change.

Next, divide the remaining change by 25, to find the number of quarters. The remaining change is 46, so division by 25 gives the quotient 1, which is the number of quarters, and a remainder of 21, which is the remaining change. This process continues for dimes and nickels. To calculate the remainder (pennies) in integer division, you use the mod operator, %.

Applying this discussion to 646 cents yields the following calculations:

1. Change = 646
2. Number of half-dollars = 646 / 50 = 12
3. Remaining change = 646 % 50 = 46
4. Number of quarters = 46 / 25 = 1
5. Remaining change = 46 % 25 = 21
6. Number of dimes = 21 / 10 = 2
7. Remaining change = 21 % 10 = 1
8. Number of nickels = 1 / 5 = 0
9. Number of pennies = remaining change = 1 % 5 = 1

This discussion translates into the following algorithm:

1. Get the change in cents.
2. Find the number of half-dollars.
3. Calculate the remaining change.
4. Find the number of quarters.
5. Calculate the remaining change.
6. Find the number of dimes.

7. Calculate the remaining change.

8. Find the number of nickels.

9. Calculate the remaining change.

10. The remaining change is the number of pennies.

VARIABLES

From the previous discussion and algorithm, it appears that the program needs variables to hold the number of half-dollars, quarters, and so on. However, the numbers of half-dollars, quarters, and so on are not used in later calculations, so the program can simply output these values without saving them in variables. The only thing that keeps changing is the change, so the program needs only one variable:

```
int change;
```

NAMED
CONSTANTS

The program performs calculations using the values of a half-dollar, 50; a quarter, 25; a dime, 10; and a nickel, 5. Because these data are special and the program uses these values more than once, it makes sense to declare them as named constants. (Using named constants also simplifies later modification of the program.)

```
static final int HALFDOLLAR = 50;
static final int QUARTER  = 25;
static final int DIME = 10;
static final int NICKEL = 5;
```

MAIN
ALGORITHM

In the preceding sections, we analyzed the problem and determined the formulas to do the calculations. We also determined the necessary variables and named constants. We can now expand the algorithm given in the section Problem Analysis and Algorithm Design to solve the problem given at the beginning of this programming example (expressing change in cents).

1. Prompt the user for the input.

2. Get the input.

3. Echo the input by displaying the entered change on the screen.

4. Compute and print the number of half-dollars.

5. Calculate the remaining change.

6. Compute and print the number of quarters.

7. Calculate the remaining change.

8. Compute and print the number of dimes.

9. Calculate the remaining change.

10. Compute and print the number of nickels.

11. Calculate the remaining change.

12. Print the remaining change.

2

COMPLETE PROGRAM LISTING

```java
//************************************************************
//  Author: D. S. Malik
//
// Program Make Change: Given any amount of change expressed
// in cents, this program computes the number of half-dollars,
// quarters, dimes, nickels, and pennies to be returned,
// returning as many half-dollars as possible, then quarters,
// dimes, nickels, and pennies, in that order.
//************************************************************

import java.util.*;

public class MakeChange
{
    static Scanner console = new Scanner(System.in);

    static final int HALFDOLLAR = 50;
    static final int QUARTER = 25;
    static final int DIME = 10;
    static final int NICKEL = 5;

    public static void main(String[] args)
    {
        //declare variables
        int change;

        //Statements: Step 1 - Step 12
        System.out.print("Enter the change in cents: ");    //Step 1
        change = console.nextInt();                          //Step 2
        System.out.println();

        System.out.println("The change you entered is "
                    + change);                               //Step 3

        System.out.println("The number of half dollars "
                    + "to be returned is "
                    + change / HALFDOLLAR);                  //Step 4

        change = change % HALFDOLLAR;                        //Step 5

        System.out.println("The number of quarters to be "
                    + "returned is "
                    + change / QUARTER);                     //Step 6

        change = change % QUARTER;                           //Step 7

        System.out.println("The number of dimes to be "
                    + "returned is "
                    + change / DIME);                        //Step 8
```

```
        change = change % DIME;                              //Step 9

        System.out.println("The number of nickels to be "
                         + "returned is "
                         + change / NICKEL);                 //Step 10

        change = change % NICKEL;                            //Step 11

        System.out.println("The number of pennies to be "
                         + "returned is " + change);         //Step 12
    }
}
```

Sample Run: (In this sample run, the user input is shaded.)

```
Enter the change in cents: 583

The change you entered is 583
The number of half dollars to be returned is 11
The number of quarters to be returned is 1
The number of dimes to be returned is 0
The number of nickels to be returned is 1
The number of pennies to be returned is 3
```

QUICK REVIEW

1. A Java program is a collection of classes.
2. Every Java application program has a method called `main`.
3. A single-line comment starts with the pair of symbols // anywhere in the line. Multiple-line comments are enclosed between /* and */.
4. The compiler ignores comments.
5. In Java, identifiers are names of things.
6. A Java identifier consists of letters, digits, the underscore character (_), and the dollar sign ($) and must begin with a letter, underscore, or the dollar sign.
7. Reserved words cannot be used as identifiers in a program.
8. All reserved words in Java consist of lowercase letters (see Appendix A).
9. Java is case sensitive.
10. A data type is a set of values with a set of operations.
11. The three categories of primitive data types are integral, floating-point, and Boolean.
12. Integral data types are used to deal with integers.
13. There are five categories of integral data types—`char`, `byte`, `short`, `int`, and `long`.

2

14. The `int` data type is used to represent integers between -2147483648 $(= -2^{31})$ and $2147483647 = (2^{31} - 1)$. The memory allocated for the `int` data type is 4 bytes.

15. The data type `short` is used to represent integers between -32768 $(= -2^{15})$ and 32767 $(2^{15} - 1)$. The memory allocated for the `short` data type is 2 bytes.

16. Java uses the Unicode character set, which is a set of 65536 characters. The ASCII character set, which has 128 values, is a subset of Unicode. The first 128 characters of Unicode, 0–127, are the same as those of ASCII.

17. The collating sequence of a character is its preset number in the Unicode character data set.

18. The data types `float` and `double` are used to deal with floating-point numbers.

19. The data type `float` can be used in Java to represent any real number between $-3.4E+38$ and $3.4E+38$. The memory allocated for the `float` data type is 4 bytes.

20. The data type `double` can be used in Java to represent any real number between $-1.7E+308$ and $1.7E+308$. The memory allocated for the `double` data type is 8 bytes.

21. The maximum number of significant digits—that is, the number of decimal places—in `float` values is 6 or 7. The maximum number of significant digits in values belonging to the `double` type is 15. The maximum number of significant digits is called the precision.

22. Values of type `float` are called single precision, and values of type `double` are called double precision.

23. The arithmetic operators in Java are addition (+), subtraction (-), multiplication (*), division (/), and mod (%).

24. The mod operator, %, gives the remainder upon division.

25. All operands in an integral expression, or integer expression, are integers, and all operands in a floating-point expression are decimal numbers.

26. A mixed expression is an expression that consists of both integers and decimal numbers.

27. When evaluating an operator in an expression, an integer is treated as a floating-point number, with a decimal part of zero, only if the operator has mixed operands.

28. You can use the cast operator to explicitly treat values of one data type as another.

29. The `class` `String` is used to manipulate strings.

30. A string is a sequence of zero or more characters.

31. Strings in Java are enclosed in double quotation marks.

32. A string containing no characters is called a null or empty string.

33. The operator + can be used to concatenate two strings.

34. During program execution, the contents of a named constant cannot be changed.

35. A named constant is declared by using the reserved word `final`.

36. A named constant is initialized when it is declared.

37. All variables must be declared before they can be used.

38. Java may not automatically initialize all the variables you declare.

39. Every variable has a name, a value, a data type, and a size.

40. When a new value is assigned to a variable, the old value is overwritten.

41. Only an assignment statement or an input (read) statement can change the value of a variable.

42. Input from the standard input device is accomplished by using a `Scanner` object initialized to the standard input device.

43. If `console` is a `Scanner` object initialized to the standard input device, then the expression `console.nextInt()` retrieves the next integer from the standard input device. Similarly, the expression `console.nextDouble()` retrieves the next floating number, and the expression `console.next()` retrieves the next string from the standard input device.

44. When data is input in a program, the data items, such as numbers, are usually separated by blanks, lines, or tabs.

45. The increment operator, `++`, increases the value of its operand by 1.

46. The decrement operator, `--`, decreases the value of its operand by 1.

47. Output of the program to the standard output device is accomplished by using the standard output object `System.out` and the methods `print` and `println`.

48. The character `\` is called the escape character.

49. The sequence `\n` is called the newline escape sequence.

50. A package is a collection of related classes. A class consists of methods, and a method is designed to accomplish a specific task.

51. The `import` statement is used to import the components of a package into a program. For example, the statement:

    ```
    import java.util.*;
    ```

    imports the (components of the) `package java.util` into the program.

52. In Java, `import` is a reserved word.

53. Because the primitive data types are directly part of the Java language, they do not require any import statement to use them.

54. The `class String` is contained in the package `java.lang`. You do not need to import classes from the package `java.lang`. The system automatically does it for you.

55. In Java, a semicolon is used to terminate a statement. The semicolon in Java is called the statement terminator.

56. A file containing a Java program always ends with the extension `.java`.

57. Prompt lines are executable statements that tell the user what to do.

58. Corresponding to five arithmetic operators +, -, *, /, and %, Java provides five compound operators +=, -=, *=, /=, and %=, respectively.

EXERCISES

1. Mark the following statements as true or false.

    a. An identifier can be any sequence of digits and letters.

    b. In Java, there is no difference between a reserved word and a predefined identifier.

    c. A Java identifier can start with a digit.

    d. The operands of the modulus operator must be integers.

    e. If the value of a is 4 and the value of b is 3, then after the statement a = b; the value of b is still 3.

    f. In an output statement, the newline character may be a part of the string.

    g. The following is a legal Java program:

    ```
    public class JavaProgram
    {
        public static void main(String[] args)
        {
        }
    }
    ```

    h. In a mixed expression, all operands are converted to floating-point numbers.

    i. Suppose x = 5. After the statement y = x++; executes, y is 5 and x is 6.

    j. Suppose a = 5. After the statement ++a; executes, the value of a is still 5 because the value of the expression is not saved in another variable.

2. Which of the following are valid Java identifiers?

    a. `myFirstProgram`   b. `MIX-UP`   c. `JavaProgram2`
    d. `quiz7`   e. `ProgrammingLecture2`   f. `1footEquals12Inches`
    g. `Mike'sFirstAttempt`   h. `Update Grade`   i. `4th`
    j. `New_Student`

3. Which of the following is a reserved word in Java?

    a. `int`   b. `INT`   c. `Char`   d. `CHAR`

4. What is the difference between a keyword and a user-defined identifier?

5. Are the identifiers `firstName` and `FirstName` the same?

6. Evaluate the following expressions:

   a. 25 / 3

   b. 20 - 12 / 4 * 2;

   c. 32 % 7

   d. 3 - 5 % 7

   e. 18.0 / 4

   f. 28 - 5 / 2.0

   g. 17 + 5 % 2 - 3

   h. 15.0 + 3.0 * 2.0 / 5.0

7. If x = 5, y = 6, z = 4, and w = 3.5, evaluate each of the following expressions, if possible. If it is not possible, state the reason.

   a. (x + z) % y

   b. (x + y) % w

   c. (y + w) % x

   d. (x + y) * w

   e. (x % y) % z

   f. (y % z) % x

   g. (x * z) % y

   h. ((x * y) * w) * z

8. Given:

   ```
   int num1, num2, newNum;
   double x, y;
   ```

   Which of the following assignments are valid? If an assignment is not valid, state the reason. When not given, assume that each variable is declared.

   a. num1 = 35;

   b. newNum = num1 - num2;

   c. num1 = 5; num2 = 2 + num1; num1 = num2 / 3;

   d. num1 * num2 = newNum;

   e. x = 12 * num1 - 15.3;

   f. num1 * 2 = newNum + num2;

   g. x / y = x * y;

   h. num2 = num1 % 2.0;

   i. newNum = (int) (x) % 5;

j. `x = x + y - 5;`

k. `newNum = num1 + (int) (4.6 / 2);`

9. Do a walk-through to find the value assigned to `e`. Assume that all variables are properly declared.

```
a = 3;
b = 4;
c = (a % b) * 6;
d = c / b;
e = (a + b + c + d)/ 4;
```

10. Which of the following variable declarations are correct? If a variable declaration is not correct, give the reason(s) and provide the correct variable declaration.

```
n = 12;                  //Line 1
char letter = ;          //Line 2
int one = 5, two;        //Line 3
double x, y, z;          //Line 4
```

11. Which of the following are valid Java assignment statements? Assume that `i`, `x`, and `percent` are `double` variables.

a. `i = i + 5;`

b. `x + 2 = x;`

c. `x = 2.5 * x;`

d. `percent = 10%`

12. Write Java statements that accomplish the following.

a. Declare `int` variables `x` and `y`.

b. Initialize an `int` variable `x` to 10 and a `char` variable `ch` to `'B'`.

c. Update the value of an `int` variable `x` by adding 5 to it.

d. Declare and initialize a `double` variable `payRate` to 12.50.

e. Copy the value of an `int` variable `firstNum` into an `int` variable `tempNum`.

f. Swap the contents of the `int` variables `x` and `y`. (Declare additional variables, if necessary.)

g. Suppose `x` and `y` are `double` variables. Output the contents of `x`, `y`, and the expression $x + 12 / y - 18$.

h. Declare a `char` variable `grade` and set the value of `grade` to `'A'`.

i. Declare `int` variables to store four integers.

j. Copy the value of a `double` variable `z` to the nearest integer into an `int` variable `x`.

13. Write each of the following as a Java expression.

a. 32 times a plus b

b. The character that represents 8

c. The string that represents the name `Julie Nelson`.

d. (b^2 – 4ac) / 2a

e. (a + b)/c(ef)-gh

f. (-b + (b^2 – 4ac)) / 2a

14. Suppose `x`, `y`, `z`, and `w` are `int` variables. What value is assigned to each variable after the last statement executes?

```
x = 5;
z = 3;
y = x - z;
z = 2 * y + 3;
w = x - 2 * y + z;
z = w - x;
w++;
```

15. Suppose `x`, `y`, and `z` are `int` variables and `w` and `t` are `double` variables. What is the value of each variable after the last statement executes?

```
x = 17;
y = 15;
x = x + y / 4;
z = x % 3 + 4;
w = 17 / 3 + 6.5;
t = x / 4.0 + 15 % 4 - 3.5;
```

16. Suppose `x` and `y` are `int` variables and `x = 25` and `y = 35`. What is the output of each of the following statements?

a. `System.out.println(x + ' ' + y);`

b. `System.out.println(x + " " + y);`

17. Suppose `x`, `y`, and `z` are `int` variables and `x = 2`, `y = 5`, and `z = 6`. What is the output of each of the following statements?

a. `System.out.println("x = " + x + ", y = " + y + ", z = " + z);`

b. `System.out.println("x + y = " + (x + y));`

c. `System.out.println("Sum of " + x + " and " + z + " is " + (x + z));`

d. `System.out.println("z / x = " + (z / x));`

e. `System.out.println(" 2 times " + x + " = " + (2 * x));`

18. What is the output of the following statements? Suppose `a` and `b` are `int` variables, `c` is a `double` variable, and `a = 13`, `b = 5`, and `c = 17.5`.

a. `System.out.println(a + b - c);`

b. `System.out.println(15 / 2 + c);`

c. `System.out.println(a / (double)(b) + 2 * c);`

d. `System.out.println(14 % 3 + 6.3 + b / a);`

e. `System.out.println((int)(c) % 5 + a - b);`

f. `System.out.println(13.5 / 2 + 4.0 * 3.5 + 18);`

19. Write Java statements that accomplish the following:

   a. Outputs the newline character.

   b. Outputs the tab character.

   c. Outputs a double quotation mark.

20. Which of the following are correct Java statements?

   a. `System.out.println("Hello There!");`

   b. ```
      System.out.println("Hello");
                         (" There!");
      ```

   c. ```
      System.out.println("Hello" +
                         " There!");
      ```

   d. `System.out.println('Hello There!');`

21. Give meaningful identifiers for the following variables:

   a. A variable to store the first name of a student.

   b. A variable to store the discounted price of an item.

   c. A variable to store the number of juice bottles.

   d. A variable to store the number of miles traveled.

   e. A variable to store the highest test score.

22. Write Java statements to do the following:

   a. Declare `int` variable num1 and num2.

   b. Prompt the user to input two numbers.

   c. Input the first number in num1 and the second number in num2.

   d. Output num1, num2, and 2 times num1 minus num2. Your output must identify each number and the expression.

23. The following program has syntax errors. Correct them. On each successive line, assume that any preceding error has been corrected. After you have corrected the syntax errors, type and compile the program to check if all errors have been found.

```
public class Exercise23
{
    static final int  SECRET_NUM = 11,213;
    static final PAY_RATE = 18.35
    public void main(String[] arg)
    {
        int one, two;
        double first, second;

        one = 18;
        two = 11;

        first = 25;
        second = first * three;
```

```
        second = 2 * SECRET_NUM;
        SECRET_NUM = SECRET_NUM + 3;
        System.out.println(first + " " + second + " " + SECRET_NUM);

        paycheck = hoursWorked * PAY_RATE

        System.out.println("Wages = "  paycheck);
    }
}
```

24. The following program has syntax errors. Correct them. On each successive line, assume that any preceding error has been corrected.

```
import java.util.*;

public class Exercise24
{
    static Scanner console = new Scanner(System.in);

    public static void main(String[] args)
    {
        int temp;
        String first;

        System.out.print("Enter first name: );
        first = next();
        System.out.println();

        System.out.print("Enter last name: );
        Last = console.next();
        System.out.println();

        System.out.print("Enter today's temperature: ");
        temperature = nextInt();
        System.out.println();

        System.out.println(first + " " - last
                            + " today's temperature is: ";
                            + temperature);
    }
}
```

25. The following program has syntax errors. Correct them. On each successive line, assume that any preceding error has been corrected. After you have corrected the syntax errors, type and compile the program to check if all errors have been found.

```
public class Exercise25
{
    static final char = STAR = '*'
    static final int  PRIME = 71;
```

```
public static void main(String[] arg)
{
    count = 1;
    sum = count + PRIME;
    x := 25.67;
    newNum = count * ONE + 2;
    sum + count = sum;
    x = x + sum * COUNT;
    System.out.println(" count = " + count + ", sum = "
                        + sum + ", PRIME = " + Prime);
}
}
```

26. What action must be taken, before a variable can be used in a program?

27. Explain why the **class** String need not be explicitly imported in a program using an **import** statement.

28. Write equivalent compound statements for the following, if possible.

    a. x = 2 * x;

    b. x = x + y - 2;

    c. sum = sum + num;

    d. z = z * x + 2 * z;

    e. y = y / (x + 5);

29. Write the following compound statements as equivalent simple statements.

    a. x += 5 - z;

    b. y *= 2 * x + 5 - z;

    c. w += 2 * z + 4;

    d. x -= z + y - t;

    e. sum += num;

    f. x /= y - 2;

30. Suppose a, b, and c are **int** variables and a = 5 and b = 6. What value is assigned to each variable after each statement executes? If a variable is undefined at a particular statement, report UND (undefined).

    $$\begin{array}{ccc} & a & b & c \end{array}$$

    ```
    a = (b++) + 3;
    c = 2 * a + (++b);
    b = 2 * (++c) - (a++);
    ```

31. Suppose a, b, and sum are **int** variables and c is a **double** variable. What value is assigned to each variable after each statement executes? Suppose a = 3, b = 5, and c = 14.1.

```
                                          a      b      c     sum
sum = a + b + (int) c;
c /= a;
b += (int) c - a;
a *= 2 * b + (int) c;
```

32. What is printed by the following program? Suppose the input is:

    20 15

```java
import java.util.*;
public class Mystery
{
    static Scanner console = new Scanner(System.in);

    static final int NUM = 10;
    static final double X = 20.5;

    public static void main(String[] arg)
    {
        int a, b;
        double z;
        char grade;

        a = 25;

        System.out.println("a = " + a);

        System.out.print("Enter the first integers: ");
        a = console.nextInt();
        System.out.println();

        System.out.print("Enter the second integers: ");
        b = console.nextInt();
        System.out.println();

        System.out.println("The numbers you entered are "
                            + a + " and " + b);

        z = X + 2 * a - b;

        System.out.println("z = " + z);

        grade = 'A';
        System.out.println("Your grade is " + grade);

        a = 2 * NUM + (int) z;
        System.out.println("The value of a = " + a);
    }
}
```

33. What is printed by the following program? Suppose the input is:

```
Miller
34
340
```

```java
import java.util.*;

public class Exercise33
{
    static Scanner console = new Scanner(System.in);

    static final int PRIME_NUM = 11;

    public static void main(String[] arg)
    {
        final int SECRET = 17;

        String name;
        int id;
        int num;
        int mysteryNum;

        System.out.print("Enter last name: ");
        name = console.next();
        System.out.println();

        System.out.print("Enter a two digit number: ");
        num = console.nextInt();
        System.out.println();

        id = 100 * num + SECRET;

        System.out.print("Enter a positive integer less than 1000: ");
        num = console.nextInt();
        System.out.println();

        mysteryNum = num * PRIME_NUM - 3 * SECRET;

        System.out.println("Name: " + name);
        System.out.println("Id: " + id);
        System.out.println("Mystery number: " + mysteryNum);
    }
}
```

34. Rewrite the following program so that it is formatted properly.

```java
import java.util.*;
public class Exercise34
{ static Scanner console = new Scanner(System.in);
static final double X = 13.45; static final int Y=34;
static final char BLANK= ' ';
public static void main(String[] arg)
```

```
{String firstName,lastName;int num;
double salary;
System.out.print("Enter first name: "); firstName=
console.next();System.out.println();
System.out.print("Enter last name: ");
lastName=console.next();System.out.println();
    System.out.print("Enter a positive integer less than 70:";
num = console.nextInt();System.out.println();salary=num*X;
 System.out.println("Name: " + firstName + BLANK + lastName);
System.out.println("Wages: $"+salary); System.out.println("X = " + X);
 System.out.println("X+Y = " + (X+Y));
}}
```

35. What type of input does the following program require, and in what order must the input be provided?

```
import java.util.*;

public class Strange
{
    static Scanner console = new Scanner(System.in);

    public static void main(String[] arg)
    {
        int x;
        int y;

        String name;

        x = console.nextInt();
        name = console.nextLine();
        y = console.nextInt();
    }
}
```

PROGRAMMING EXERCISES

1. Write a program that produces the following output:

```
**********************************
*     Programming Assignment 1    *
*       Computer Programming I     *
*         Author: Duffy Ducky       *
*     Due Date: Thursday, Jan. 24  *
**********************************
```

2. Consider the following program segment:

```
//import classes

public class Exercise2
{
    public static void main(String[] args)
```

2

```
    {
        //variable declaration

        //executable statements
    }
}
```

a. Write Java statements that declare the following variables: num1, num2, and num3, and average of type int.

b. Write Java statements that store 125 into num1, 28 into num2, and -25 into num3.

c. Write a Java statement that stores the average of num1, num2, and num3 into average.

d. Write Java statements that output the values of num1, num2, num3, and average.

e. Compile and run your program.

3. Repeat Exercise 2 by declaring num1, num2, and num3, and average of type double. Store 75.35 into num1, -35.56 into num2, and 15.76 into num3.

4. Consider the following program segment:

```
//import classes

public class Exercise4
{
    public static void main(String[] args)
    {
        //variable declaration

        //executable statements
    }
}
```

a. Write a Java statement that imports the class Scanner.

b. Write a Java statement that declares console to be a Scanner object for inputting data from the standard input device.

c. Write Java statements that declare and initialize the following named constants: SECRET of type int initialized to 11; RATE of type double initialized to 12.50.

d. Write Java statements that declare the following variables: num1, num2, and newNum of type int; name of type String; hoursWorked and wages of type double.

e. Write Java statements that prompt the user to input two integers and store the first number into num1 and the second number into num2.

f. Write a Java statement(s) that outputs the value of num1 and num2, indicating which is num1 and which is num2. For example, if num1 is 8 and num2 is 5, then the output is:

```
The value of num1 = 8 and the value of num2 = 5.
```

g. Write a Java statement that multiplies that value of num1 by 2, adds the value of num2 to it, and then stores the result in newNum. Then write a Java statement that outputs the value of newNum.

h. Write a Java statement that updates the value of newNum by adding the value of the named constant SECRET. Then, write a Java statement that outputs the value of newNum with an appropriate message.

i. Write Java statements that prompt the user to enter a person's last name and then store the last name into the variable name.

j. Write Java statements that prompt the user to enter a decimal number between 0 and 70 and then store the number entered into hoursWorked.

k. Write a Java statement that multiplies that value of the named constant RATE with the value of hoursWorked and stores the result into the variable wages.

l. Write Java statements that produce the following output:

```
Name:            //output the value of the variable name
Pay Rate: $      //output the value of the named constant RATE
Hours Worked:    //output the value of the variable hoursWorked
Salary: $        //output the value of the variable wages
```

For example, if the value of name is "Rainbow" and hoursWorked is 45.50, then the output is:

```
Name: Rainbow
Pay Rate: $12.50
Hours Worked: 45.50
Salary: $568.75
```

m. Write a Java program that tests each of the Java statements in parts (a)—(l). Place the statements at the appropriate place in the preceding Java program segment. Test run your program (twice) on the following input data:

i. num1 = 13, num2 = 28; name = "Jacobson"; hoursWorked = 48.30.

ii. num1 = 32, num2 = 15; name = "Cynthia"; hoursWorked = 58.45.

5. Consider the following Java program in which the statements are in the incorrect order. Rearrange the statements so that it prompts the user to input the length and width of a rectangle and output the area and perimeter of the rectangle.

2

```
public class Ch2_PrExercise5
{
    static Scanner console = new Scanner(System.in);

    import java.util.*;
    {
        public static void main(String[] args)
        int width;

        System.out.print("Enter the length: ");
        width = console.nextInt();
        System.out.println();
        int length;

        System.out.print("Enter the width: ");
        length = console.nextInt();

        System.out.println();

        area = length * width;

        System.out.println("Area = " + area);
        System.out.println("Perimeter = " + perimeter);
        perimeter = 2 * (length + width);

        int area;
        int perimeter;

    }
}
```

6. Write a program that prompts the user to input a decimal number and outputs the number rounded to the nearest integer.

7. Write a program that prompts the user to enter five test scores and then prints the average test score.

8. Write a program that prompts the user to input five decimal numbers. The program should then add the five decimal numbers, convert the sum to the nearest integer, and print the result.

9. Write a program that does the following:

    a. Prompts the user to input five decimal numbers

    b. Prints the five decimal numbers

    c. Converts each decimal number to the nearest integer

    d. Adds the five integers

    e. Prints the sum and average of the five integers

10. Write a program that prompts the capacity, in gallons, of an automobile fuel tank and the miles per gallons the automobile can be driven. The program outputs the number of miles the automobile can be driven without refueling.

11. Write a Java program that prompts the user to input the elapsed time for an event in seconds. The program then outputs the elapsed time in hours, minutes, and seconds. (For example, if the elapsed time is 9630 seconds, then the output is 2:40:30.)

12. Write a Java program that prompts the user to input the elapsed time for an event in hours, minutes, and seconds. The program then outputs the elapsed time in seconds.

13. To make a profit, a local store marks up the prices of its items by a certain percentage. Write a Java program that reads the original price of the item sold, the percentage of the marked-up price, and the sales tax rate. The program then outputs the original price of the item, the marked-up percentage of the item, the store's selling price of the item, the sales tax rate, the sales tax, and the final price of the item. (The final price of the item is the selling price plus the sales tax.)

14. A milk carton can hold 3.78 liters of milk. Each morning, a dairy farm ships cartons of milk to a local grocery store. The cost of producing one liter of milk is $0.38, and the profit of each carton of milk is $0.27. Write a program that does the following:

    a. Prompts the user to enter the total amount of milk produced in the morning

    b. Outputs the number of milk cartons needed to hold milk (Round your answer to the nearest integer.)

    c. Outputs the cost of producing milk

    d. Outputs the profit for producing milk

15. Redo Programming Exercise 14 so that the user can also input the cost of producing one liter of milk and the profit on each carton of milk.

16. You found an exciting summer job for five weeks. It pays $15.50 per hour. Suppose that the total tax you pay on your summer job income is 14%. After paying the taxes, you spend 10% of your net income to buy new clothes and other accessories for the next school year and 1% to buy school supplies. After buying clothes and school supplies, you use 25% of the remaining money to buy savings bonds. For each dollar you spend to buy savings bonds, your parents spend $0.50 to buy additional savings bonds for you. Write a program that prompts the user to enter the pay rate for an hour and the number of hours you worked each week. The program then outputs the following:

    a. Your income before and after taxes from your summer job

    b. The money you spend on clothes and other accessories

    c. The money you spend on school supplies

    d. The money you spend to buy savings bonds

    e. The money your parents spend to buy additional savings bonds for you

17. A permutation of three objects, *a*, *b*, and *c*, is any arrangement of these objects in a row. For example, some of the permutations of these objects are *abc*, *bca*, and *cab*. The number of permutations of three objects is 6. Suppose that these three objects are strings. Write a program that prompts the user to enter three strings. The program then outputs the six permutations of those strings.

18. Write a program that computes the cost of painting and installing carpet in a room. Assume that the room has one door, two windows, and one book-shelf. Your program must do the following:

   a. Prompts the user to enter, in feet, the length, width, and height of a room. Read the dimensions of the room.

   b. Prompts the user to enter the widths and heights, in feet, of the door, each window, and the bookshelf. Read these quantities.

   c. Prompts the user to enter the cost, per square foot, of painting the walls. Read these quantities.

   d. Prompts the user to enter of cost, per square foot, of installing carpet. Read these quantities.

   e. Outputs the cost of painting the walls and installing the carpet.

19. Write a program that prompts the user to input the amount of rice, in pounds, in a bag. The program outputs the number of bags needed to store one metric ton of rice.

20. Cindy uses the services of a brokerage firm to buy and sell stocks. The firm charges 1.5% service charges on the total amount for each transaction, buy or sell. When Cindy sells stocks, she would like to know if she gained or lost on a particular investment. Write a program that allows Cindy to input the number of shares sold, the purchase price of each share, and the selling price of each share. The program outputs the amount invested, the total service charges, amount gained or lost, and the amount received after selling the stock.

CHAPTER 3

INTRODUCTION TO OBJECTS AND INPUT/OUTPUT

IN THIS CHAPTER, YOU WILL:

- Learn about objects and reference variables
- Explore how to use predefined methods in a program
- Become familiar with the `class String`
- Explore how to format output using the method `printf`
- Learn how to use input and output dialog boxes in a program
- Become familiar with the `String` method `format`
- Become familiar with file input and output
- Learn debugging by understanding error messages

Chapter 2 introduced you to the basic elements of Java programs, including special symbols and identifiers, primitive data types, arithmetic operators, and the order of precedence of arithmetic operators. You were briefly introduced to the **class** `String` for processing strings, the **class** `Scanner` for inputting data into a program, and general rules on programming style. In this chapter, you will learn more about input and output and how to use predefined methods in your programs. You will also learn, in some detail, how to use the **class** `String` to process strings.

Objects and Reference Variables

Three terms that you will encounter repeatedly throughout this book are variables, reference variables, and objects. We define these terms now so you will be familiar with them.

In Chapter 2, you learned about the primitive data types, such as `int`, `double`, and `char`. You also worked with strings. We used `String` variables to manipulate or process strings.

Consider the following statement:

```
int x;            //Line 1
```

This statement declares `x` to be an `int` variable. Now consider the statement:

```
String str;       //Line 2
```

This statement declares `str` to be a variable of type `String`.

The statement in Line 1 allocates memory space to store an `int` value and calls this memory space `x`. The variable `x` can store an `int` value in its memory space. For example, the following statement stores 45 in `x`, as shown in Figure 3-1:

```
x = 45;           //Line 3
```

FIGURE 3-1 Variable x and its data

Next, let us see what happens with the statement in Line 2. This statement allocates memory space for the variable `str`. However, unlike the variable `x`, the variable `str` *cannot* directly store data in its memory space. The variable `str` stores the memory location, that is, the address of the memory space where the actual data is stored. For example, the effect of the statement:

```
str = "Java Programming";      //Line 4
```

is shown in Figure 3-2.

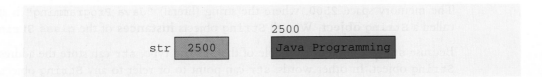

FIGURE 3-2 Variable `str` and the data it points to

For the `String` variable `str`, the statement in Line 4 causes the system to allocate memory space starting at, say, location 2500, stores the string (literal) `"Java Programming"` in this memory space, and then stores the address 2500 in the memory space of `str`.

The next obvious question is: How does this happen? In reality, *for the most part*, the effect of the statement in Line 4 is the same as the effect of the following statement:

```
str = new String("Java Programming");   //Line 5
```

In Java, `new` is an operator. It causes the system to allocate memory space of a specific type, store specific data in that memory space, and return the address of the memory space. Therefore, the statement in Line 4 causes the system to allocate memory space large enough to store the string (literal) `"Java Programming"`, stores this string in that memory space, and returns the address of the allocated memory space. The assignment operator stores the address of that memory space into the variable `str`.

NOTE As noted, for the most part the effects of the statements in Lines 4 and 5 are the same. In both the cases, the `String` variable `str` will point to a memory location that contains the string `"Java Programming"`. Note that in the statement in Line 5, the operator `new` is used explicitly, while the statement in Line 4 does not explicitly use the operator `new`. In reality, when the statement in Line 4 executes, it first looks if the program has already created the string `"Java Programming"`. If this is the case, then the `String` variable `str` will point to that memory location. However, when the statement in Line 5 executes, the system will allocate a memory space, store the string `"Java Programming"` into that memory space, and then store the address of that memory space into `str`. This is a key difference and plays an important role when strings and `String` variables are compared, which we will explain in Chapter 4.

`String` is not a primitive data type. In Java terminology, the data type `String` is defined by the **class** `String`. In this and subsequent chapters, you will encounter some other classes provided by the Java system. In Chapter 8, you will learn how to create your own classes.

In Java, variables such as `str` are called **reference variables**. More formally, reference variables are variables that store the address of a memory space. In Java, any variable declared using a **class** (such as the variable `str`) is a reference variable. Because `str` is a reference variable declared using the **class** `String`, we say that `str` is a reference variable of the `String` type.

The memory space 2500, where the string (literal) `"Java Programming"` is stored, is called a **String object**. We call `String` objects **instances** of the `class` `String`.

Because `str` is a reference variable of the `String` type, `str` can store the address of any `String` object. In other words, `str` can point to or refer to any `String` object. Moreover, it follows that we are dealing with two different things—the reference variable `str` and the `String` object that `str` points to. We call the `String` object that `str` points to, which is at memory space 2500 in Figure 3-2, the object `str`.

To emphasize that the `String` object at memory space 2500 is the object `str`, we can redraw Figure 3-2 as Figure 3-3.

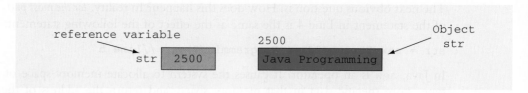

FIGURE 3-3 Variable `str` and object `str`

Using the operator `new` to create a `class` object is called **instantiating** an object of that `class`.

Let us summarize the Java terminology used in the preceding paragraphs, especially the use of the terms *variable* and *object*. While working with classes, we declare a reference variable of a `class` type and then, typically, we use the operator `new` to instantiate an object of that `class` type and store the address of the object into the reference variable. For example, suppose that `refVar` is a reference variable of a `class` type. When we use the term *variable* `refVar`, we mean the value of `refVar`, that is, the address stored in `refVar`. When we use the term *object* `refVar`, we mean the object whose address is stored in `refVar`. The object that `refVar` points to can be accessed via the variable `refVar`.

The next question is: How can you change the value of the object from `"Java Programming"`, as shown in Figure 3-3, to `"Hello there!"`? To do so, you must look at the `class` `String` and see if it provides a method that allows you to change the value of the (*existing*) object from `"Java Programming"` to `"Hello there!"`. (The next section briefly describes what a method is.) Unfortunately, the `class` `String` does not provide any such method. (The `class` `String` is discussed in some detail later in this chapter.) In other words, the value of the `String` object at memory space 2500 cannot be altered. It thus follows that `String` objects are *immutable*; that is, once they are created, they cannot be changed.

You could execute another statement, similar to the statement in Line 4, with the value `"Hello there!"`. Suppose that the following statement is executed:

```
str = "Hello there!";
```

This statement would again cause the system to allocate memory space to store the string `"Hello there!"`, if no such string already exists, and the address of that memory space would be stored in `str`. However, the address of the allocated memory space will be different from that in the first statement. To be specific, suppose that the address of the allocated memory space is 3850. Figure 3-4 illustrates the result.

FIGURE 3-4 Variable `str`, its value, and the object `str`

This is an important property of reference variables of the `String` type and `String` objects, and must be recognized and understood. Furthermore, it is especially important to understand this property when we start comparing strings.

To simplify Figure 3-4, we usually use the format shown in Figure 3-5.

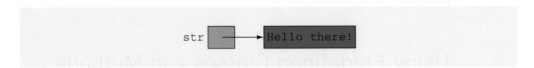

FIGURE 3-5 Variable `str` and the object `str`

In Figure 3-5, the arrow originating in the box `str` means that `str` contains an address. The arrow pointing to the memory space containing the value `"Hello there!"` means that the variable `str` contains the address of the object containing the value `"Hello there!"`. We will use this arrow notation to help explain various examples.

You might ask: What happened to memory space 2500 and the string `"Java Programming"` stored in it? If no other `String` variable refers to it, then sometime during program execution, the Java system reclaims this memory space for later use. This is called **garbage collection**.

NOTE | If you do not want to depend on the system to choose when to perform garbage collection, then you can include the statement:

```
System.gc();
```

in your program to instruct the computer to run the garbage collector (immediately). In general, it is not necessary to do so.

We can now summarize the discussion of the preceding sections. You can declare two types of variables in Java: primitive type variables and reference variables, as shown in Figure 3-6.

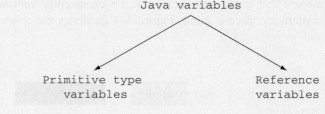

FIGURE 3-6 Java variables

Primitive type variables store data *directly* into their own memory spaces. Reference variables store the address of the object containing the data. An object is an instance of a `class` and the operator `new` is used to instantiate an object. In some languages, such as C++, reference variables are called *pointers*.

Before discussing the `class` `String`, we first discuss how to use predefined methods in a program.

Using Predefined Classes and Methods in a Program

Recall that a **method** is a collection of instructions. When a method executes, it accomplishes something. The method `main`, which you used in Chapter 2, executes automatically when you run a Java program. Other methods execute only when they are activated—that is, called. Java comes with a wealth of classes called **predefined classes**. In addition, every predefined `class` contains many predefined methods, which accomplish useful results. In this section, you do not learn how to write your own methods, but you do learn how to use some of the predefined classes and methods that accompany Java.

Recall from Chapter 2 that predefined classes are organized as a collection of packages, called **class libraries**. A particular `package` can contain several classes and each `class` can contain several methods. Therefore, to use a predefined `class` and/or a method, you need to know the name of the `package`, the name of the `class`, and the name of the method. To use a method, you also need to know a few other things, which are described shortly.

There are two types of methods in a `class`: `static` and non-`static`. A `static` method can be used, that is, called, using the name of the `class` containing the method. (Chapter 8 describes these methods in detail. At this point, you need to know only how to use predefined methods, which may be `static` or non-`static`.)

The Java system contains the `class` `Math`, which in turn contains powerful and useful mathematical functions. The `class` `Math` is contained in the `package` `java.lang`. Every method of the `class` `Math` is a `static` method. Therefore, you can use every method of the `class` `Math` using the name of the `class`, which is `Math`.

The **class** Math contains a very useful method, pow, called the method power, which is used to calculate x^y in a program, that is, Math.pow(x, y) = x^y. For example, Math.pow(2,3) = 2^3 = 8 and Math.pow(4, 0.5) = $4^{0.5}$ = $\sqrt{4}$ = 2. The numbers x and y used in the method pow are called the (*actual*) **parameters** of the method pow. For example, in Math.pow(2, 3), the parameters are 2 and 3.

An expression such as Math.pow(2, 3) is called a method call, and causes the code attached to the method pow to execute and, in this case, computes 2^3. The method pow computes a value of type **double**. Therefore, we say that the return type of the method pow is **double** or the method pow is of type **double**.

In general, to use a predefined method in a program:

1. You need to know the name of the **class** containing the method.
2. You need to know the name of the **package** containing the **class** and import this **class** from the **package** in the program.
3. You need to know the name of the method as well as the number of parameters the method takes, the type of each parameter, and the order of the parameters. You must also be aware of the return type of the method or, loosely speaking, what the method produces.

For example, to use the method nextInt, you import the **class** Scanner from the **package** java.util.

 NOTE As noted in Chapter 2, the Java system automatically imports methods and **classes** from the **package** java.lang. Therefore, you do not need to import any contents of the **package** java.lang explicitly. Because the **class** Math is contained in the **package** java.lang, to use the method pow, you need to know that the name of the method is pow, that the method pow has two parameters, both of which are numbers, and that the method calculates the first parameter to the power of the second parameter.

The program in the following example illustrates how to use predefined methods in a program. More specifically, we use some math methods. Later in this chapter, after introducing the **class** String, we will show how to use String methods in a program.

EXAMPLE 3-1

```
public class PredefinedMethods
{
    public static void main(String[] args)
    {
        double u, v;

        System.out.println("Line 1: 2 to the power "
                    + "of 6 = " + Math.pow(2, 6));    //Line 1
```

```
    u = 12.5;                                            //Line 2
    v = 3.0;                                             //Line 3
    System.out.println("Line 4: " + u + " to "
                  + "the power of " +  v
                  + " = " + Math.pow(u, v));             //Line 4

    System.out.println("Line 5: Square root of "
                  + "42.25 = "
                  + Math.sqrt(42.25));                   //Line 5

    u = Math.pow(8.5, 2.0);                              //Line 6
    System.out.println("Line 7: u = " + u);             //Line 7
  }
}
```

Sample Run:

```
Line 1: 2 to the power of 6 = 64.0
Line 4: 12.5 to the power of 3.0 = 1953.125
Line 5: Square root of 42.25 = 6.5
Line 7: u = 72.25
```

The preceding program works as follows. The statement in Line 1 uses the function pow to determine and output 2^6. The statement in Line 2 sets u to 12.5, and the statement in Line 3 sets v to 3.0. The statement in Line 4 determines and outputs u^v. The statement in Line 5 uses the method sqrt, of the **class** Math, to determine and output the square root of 42.25. The statement in Line 6 determines and assigns 8.5^2 to u. The statement in Line 7 outputs the value of u.

Dot Between Class (Object) Name and Class Member: A Precaution

In Chapter 2, you learned how to use the method nextInt of the **class** Scanner to input the next token, which can be expressed as an integer. In the preceding section, you learned how to use the method pow of the **class** Math.

Consider the following statement:

```
x = console.nextInt();
```

where x is a variable of type **int**. Notice the dot between console and nextInt; the name of the object console and the name of the method nextInt are separated by the dot.

In Java, the dot (.) is an operator called the **member access operator**.

Omitting the dot between console and nextInt results in a syntax error. In the statement:

```
x = consolenextInt();
```

`consolenextInt` becomes a new identifier. If you used `consolenextInt` in a program, the compiler (could) generate an undeclared identifier syntax error. Similarly, omitting the parentheses, as in `console.nextInt`, also results in a syntax error.

Usually, several methods and/or variables are associated with a particular `class`, each doing a specific job. In the dot notation, the dot separates the `class` variable name, that is, the object name from the member, or method, name. *It is also worth noting that* `methods` *are distinguished from (reference) variables by the presence of parentheses, and methods that have no parameters must have empty parentheses* (like in `nextInt()`). For example, `console` is the name of a (reference) variable, and `nextInt` is the name of a method.

3

class String

This section explains how to use `String` methods to manipulate strings. First, we review some terminology that we typically use while working with strings and the `class` `String`.

Consider the following statements:

```
String name;              //Line 1
name = "Lisa Johnson";    //Line 2
```

The statement in Line 1 declares `name` to be a `String` variable. The statement in Line 2 creates the string `"Lisa Johnson"` and assigns it to `name`.

In the statement in Line 2, we usually say that the `String` object, or the string `"Lisa Johnson"`, is assigned to the `String` variable or the variable `name`. In reality, as explained before, a `String` *object* with the value `"Lisa Johnson"` is instantiated (if it has not already been created) and the address of the object is stored in `name`. Whenever we use the term "the string `name`", we are referring to the object containing the string `"Lisa Johnson"`. Similarly, when we use the terms (reference) variable `name` or `String` variable `name`, we simply mean `name`, whose value is an address.

The remainder of this section describes various features of the `class` `String`. In Chapter 2, you learned that two strings can be joined using the operator +. The `class` `String` provides various methods that allow us to process strings in various ways. For example, we can find the length of a string, extract part of a string, find the position of a particular string in another string, convert a number into a string, and convert a numeric string into a number.

Each method associated with the `class` `String` implements a specific operation and has a specific name. For example, the method for determining the length of a string is named `length`, and the method for extracting a string from within another string is named `substring`.

As explained in the earlier section, Using Predefined Classes and Methods in a Program, in general, to use a method you must know the name of the `class` containing the method and the name of the **package** containing the **class**; you must import the **class**; and you must know the method name, its parameters, and what the method does. However, because the Java system automatically makes the **class** String available, you do not need to import this **class**. Therefore, in order to use a String method, you need to know its name, parameters, and what the method does.

Recall that a string (literal) is a sequence of 0 or more characters, and string literals are enclosed in double quotation marks. The **index** (position) of the first character is 0, the index of the second character is 1, and so on. The length of a string is the number of characters in it, not the largest index.

 NOTE   If length denotes the length of a string and length is not zero (that is, string is not null), then length − 1 gives the index of the last character in the string.

The general expression to use a String method on a String variable is:

StringVariable.StringMethodName(parameters)

In this statement, the variable name and the method name are separated with the dot (.). For example, if name is a String variable, and name = "Lisa Johnson", then the value of the expression

name.length()

is 12.

Table 3-1 lists commonly used methods of the **class** String. Suppose that sentence is a String. Suppose that sentence = "Programming with Java";. Then each character in sentence and its position is as follows:

sentence = "Programming with Java";																				
P	r	o	g	r	a	m	m	i	n	g	' '	w	i	t	h	' '	J	a	v	a
0	1	2	3	4	5	6	7	8	9	10	11	12	13	14	15	16	17	18	19	20

TABLE 3-1   Some Commonly Used String Methods

```
char charAt(int index)
   //Returns the character at the position specified by index
   //Example: sentence.charAt(3) returns 'g'
```

```
int indexOf(char ch)
   //Returns the index of the first occurrence of the character
   //specified by ch; If the character specified by ch does not
   //appear in the string, it returns -1
   //Example: sentence.indexOf('J') returns 17
   //          sentence.indexOf('a') returns 5
```

TABLE 3-1 Some Commonly Used `String` Methods (continued)

```
int indexOf(char ch, int pos)
   //Returns the index of the first occurrence of the character
   //specified by ch; The parameter pos specifies where to
   //begin the search; If the character specified by ch does not
   //appear in the string, it returns -1
   //Example: sentence.indexOf('a', 10) returns 18
```

```
int indexOf(String str)
   //Returns the index of the first occurrence of the string
   //specified by str; If the string specified by str does not
   //appear in the string, it returns -1
   //Example: sentence.indexOf("with") returns 12
   //         sentence.indexOf("ing") returns 8
```

```
int indexOf(String str, int pos)
   //Returns the index of the first occurrence of the String
   //specified by str; The parameter pos specifies where to begin
   //the search; If the string specified by str does not appear
   //in the string, it returns -1
   //Example: sentence.indexOf("a", 10) returns 18
   //         sentence.indexOf("Pr", 10) returns -1
```

```
String concat(String str)
   //Returns the string that is this string concatenated with str
   //Example: The expression
   //         sentence.concat(" is fun.")
   //         returns the string "Programming with Java is fun."
```

```
int compareTo(String str)
   //Compares two strings character by character
   //Returns a negative value if this string is less than str
   //Returns 0 if this string is same as str
   //Returns a positive value if this string is greater than str
```

```
boolean equals(String str)
   //Returns true if this string is same as str
```

```
int length()
   //Returns the length of the string
   //Example: sentence.length() returns 21, the number of characters in
   //         "Programming with Java"
```

```
String replace(char charToBeReplaced, char charReplacedWith)
   //Returns the string in which every occurrence of
   //charToBeReplaced is replaced with charReplacedWith
   //Example: sentence.replace('a', '*') returns the string
   //         "Progr*mming with J*v*"
   //         Each occurrence of a is replaced with *
```

TABLE 3-1 Some Commonly Used `String` Methods (continued)

```
String substring(int beginIndex)
  //Returns the string which is a substring of this string
  //beginning at beginIndex until the end of the string.
  //Example: sentence.substring(12) returns the string
  //          "with Java"
```

```
String substring(int beginIndex, int endIndex)
  //Returns the string which is a substring of this string
  //beginning at beginIndex until endIndex - 1
```

```
String toLowerCase()
  //Returns the string that is the same as this string, except
  //that all uppercase letters of this string are replaced with
  //their equivalent lowercase letters
  //Example: sentence.toLowerCase() returns "programming with java"
```

```
String toUpperCase()
  //Returns the string that is the same as this string, except
  //that all lowercase letters of this string are replaced with
  //their equivalent uppercase letters
  //Example: sentence.toUpperCase() returns "PROGRAMMING WITH JAVA"
```

```
boolean startsWith(String str)
  //Returns true if the string begins with the string specified by str;
  //otherwise, this methods returns false.
```

```
boolean endsWith(String str)
  //Returns true if the string ends with the string specified by str
  //otherwise, this methods returns false.
```

```
boolean regionMatches(int ind, String str, int strIndex, int len)
  //Returns true if the substring of str starting at strIndex and length
  //specified by len is same as the substring of this String
  //object starting at ind and having the same length
```

```
boolean regionMatches(boolean ignoreCase, int ind,
                      String str, int strIndex, int len)
  //Returns true if the substring of str starting at strIndex and length
  //specified by len is same as the substring of this String
  //object starting at ind and having the same length. If ignoreCase
  //is true, then during character comparison, case is ignored.
```

NOTE | Table 3-1 lists only some of the methods for string manipulation. Moreover, the table gives only the name of the method, the number of parameters, and the type of the method. The reader can find a list of `String` methods at the Web site *http://java.sun.com/javase/7/docs/api/*. The methods `equals` and `compareTo` are explained in Chapter 4 and the methods, `startsWith`, `endsWith`, and `regionMatches` are explained in Example 3-3.

EXAMPLE 3-2

Consider the following statements:

```
String sentence;
String str1;
String str2;
int index;

sentence = "Now is the time for the birthday party.";
```

The following statements further show how `String` methods work.

Statement	Effect / Explanation
`sentence.charAt(16)`	Returns: `'f'` In `sentence`, the character at position 16 is `'f'`.
`sentence.length()`	Returns: 38 The number of characters in sentence is 38.
`sentence.indexOf('t')`	Returns: 7 This is the index of the first `'t'` in `sentence`.
`sentence.indexOf("for")`	Returns: 16 In `sentence`, the starting index of the string `"for"`.
`sentence.substring(0, 6)`	Returns: `"Now is"` In `sentence`, the substring starting at index 0 until the index 5 (= 6 − 1) is `"Now is"`.
`sentence.substring(7, 12)`	Returns: `"the t"` In `sentence`, the substring starting at index 7 until the index 11 (= 12 − 1) is `"the t"`.
`sentence.substring(7, 22)`	Returns: `"the time for th"` In `sentence`, the substring starting at index 7 until the index 21 (= 22 − 1) is `"the time for th"`.
`sentence.substring(4, 10)`	Returns: `"is the"` In `sentence`, the substring starting at index 4 until the index 9 (= 10 − 1) is `"is the"`.
`str1 = sentence.substring(0, 8);`	`str1 = "Now is t"` In `sentence`, the substring starting at index 0 until the index 7 (= 8 − 1) is `"Now is t"`. So the value assigned to `str1` is `"Now is t"`.

Statement	Effect / Explanation
`str2 = sentence.substring(2, 12);`	`str2 = "w is the t"` In `sentence`, the substring starting at index 2 until the index 11 (= 12 − 1) is `"w is the t"`. So the value assigned to `str2` is `"w is the t"`.

`index =`
`    sentence.indexOf("birthday");`
`str1 = sentence.substring(index,`
`                index + 14);`
	`index = 24`
	`str1 = "birthday party"`
	The starting index of `"birthday"` in `sentence` is 24. So the value of index is 24. Now index is 24, so index + 14 is 38. The substring starting at the position 24 until the position 37 (= 38 − 1) is `"birthday party"`.

`sentence.replace('t', 'T')`	Returns: `"Now is The Time for The birThday parTy"`
`sentence.toUpperCase()`	Returns: `"NOW IS THE TIME FOR THE BIRTHDAY PARTY"`

The following program tests the preceding statements:

```java
// This program illustrate how various String methods work.

public class VariousStringMethods
{
    public static void main(String[] args)
    {
        String sentence;
        String str1;
        String str2;
        String str3;
        int index;

        sentence = "Now is the time for the birthday party";

        System.out.println("sentence = \"" + sentence + "\"");
        System.out.println("The length of sentence = "
                        + sentence.length());

        System.out.println("The character at index 16 in "
                        + "sentence = " + sentence.charAt(16));

        System.out.println("The index of first t in sentence = "
                        + sentence.indexOf('t'));

        System.out.println("The index of for in sentence = "
                        + sentence.indexOf("for"));
```

```
System.out.println("sentence.substring(0, 6) = \""
                    + sentence.substring(0, 6) + "\"");

System.out.println("sentence.substring(7, 12) = \""
                    + sentence.substring(7, 12) + "\"");

System.out.println("sentence.substring(7, 22) = \""
                    + sentence.substring(7, 22) + "\"");

System.out.println("sentence.substring(4, 10) = \""
                    + sentence.substring(4, 10) + "\"");

str1 = sentence.substring(0, 8);

System.out.println("str1 = \"" + str1 + "\"");

str2 = sentence.substring(2, 12);
System.out.println("str2 = \"" + str2 + "\"");

System.out.println("sentence in uppercase = \""
                    + sentence.toUpperCase() + "\"");

index = sentence.indexOf("birthday");

str1 = sentence.substring(index, index + 14);

System.out.println("str1 = \"" + str1 + "\"");

System.out.println("sentence.replace('t', 'T') = \""
                    + sentence.replace('t', 'T') + "\"");
    }
}
```

Sample Run:

```
sentence = "Now is the time for the birthday party"
The length of sentence = 38
The character at index 16 in sentence = f
The index of first t in sentence = 7
The index of for in sentence = 16
sentence.substring(0, 6) = "Now is"
sentence.substring(7, 12) = "the t"
sentence.substring(7, 22) = "the time for th"
sentence.substring(4, 10) = "is the"
str1 = "Now is t"
str2 = "w is the t"
sentence in uppercase = "NOW IS THE TIME FOR THE BIRTHDAY PARTY"
str1 = "birthday party"
sentence.replace('t', 'T') = "Now is The Time for The birThday parTy"
```

EXAMPLE 3-3

Consider the following statements:

```
String sentence;
String str1;
String str2;
String str3;
String str4;

sentence = "It is sunny and warm.";
str1 = "warm.";
str2 = "Programming with Java";
str3 = "sunny";
str4 = "Learning Java Programming is exciting";
```

The following statements show how String methods startsWith, endsWith, and regionMatches work.

Expression	Effect
sentence.startsWith("It")	Returns true
sentence.startsWith(str1)	Returns false
sentence.endsWith("hot")	Returns false
sentence.endsWith(str1)	Returns true
sentence.regionMatches(6, str3, 0, 5)	Returns true
sentence.regionMatches(true, 6, "Sunny", 0, 5)	Returns true
str4.regionMatches(9, str2, 17, 4)	Returns true

For the most part, the statements are straightforward. Let's look at the last three statements, which use the method regionMatches:

```
sentence.regionMatches(6, str3, 0, 5)
```

In this statement, we want to determine whether str3 appears as a substring in the string sentence starting at position 6. Notice that the last three arguments, str3, 0, and 5, specify that in str3 the starting index is 0 and the length of the substring is 5. The substring in sentence starting at position 6 and of length 5 matches str3. So this expression returns true.

The expression:

```
sentence.regionMatches(true, 6, "Sunny", 0, 5)
```

is similar to the previous expression, except that when the substrings are compared, the case is ignored, that is, uppercase and lowercase letters are considered the same. Next, let's look at the expression:

```
str4.regionMatches(9, str2, 17, 4)
```

In this expression, we want to determine whether the substring in `str2` starting at position `17` and of length `4` is the same as the substring in `str4` starting at position `9` and of length `4`. This expression returns `true` because these substrings are the same.

The program `Ch3_SomeStringMethods.java`, which shows the effect of the preceding statements, can be found in the Additional Student Files folder at *www.cengagebrain.com*.

To summarize the preceding discussion of the `class` `String`:

1. `String` variables are reference variables.
2. A string object is an instance of the `class` `String`.
3. The `class` `String` contains various methods to process strings.
4. A `String` variable invokes a `String` method using the dot operator, the method name, and the set of arguments (if any) required by the method.

Input/Output

A program performs three basic operations: it gets data into the program, it manipulates the data, and it outputs the results. In Chapter 2, you learned how to manipulate numeric data using arithmetic operations. Because writing programs for input/output (I/O) is quite complex, Java offers extensive support for I/O operations by providing a substantial number of I/O classes, such as the `class` `Scanner`. In the remainder of this chapter, you will:

- Learn how to format output using the method `printf`.
- Learn other ways to input data and output results in Java.
- Learn how to format the output of decimal numbers to a specific number of decimal places.
- Learn how to instruct the program to read data from, or write output to, a file. If there is a large amount of data, inputting data from the keyboard every time you execute your program is not practical. Similarly, if the output is large or you want to save the output for later use, you must save a program's output to a file.

Formatting Output with `printf`

In Chapter 2, you learned how to show the output of a program on the standard output device using the standard output object `System.out` and the methods `print` and `println`. More specifically, to output the results, you used statements such as `System.out.print(expression)` and/or `System.out.println(expression)`, where `expression` is evaluated and its value is output. However, the methods `print` and `println` cannot *directly* format certain outputs in a specific manner. For example, the default output of floating-point numbers is typically up to 6 decimal places for `float` values and up to 15 decimal places for `double` values. Moreover, sometimes we would like to align the output in certain columns. To format the output in a specific manner, you can use the method `printf`.

A syntax to use the method `printf` to produce the output on the standard output device is:

```
System.out.printf(formatString);
```

or:

```
System.out.printf(formatString, argumentList);
```

where `formatString` is a string specifying the format of the output and `argumentList` is a list of arguments. The `argumentList` is a list of arguments that consists of constant values, variables, or expressions. If `argumentList` has more than one argument, then the arguments are separated with commas.

For example, the statement:

```
System.out.printf("Hello there!");                          //Line 1
```

consists of only the format string, and the statement:

```
System.out.printf("There are %.2f inches in %d centimeters.%n",
                  centimeters / 2.54, centimeters);         //Line 2
```

consists of both the format string and `argumentList`, where `centimeters` is a variable of type `int`. Notice that the argument list consists of the expression `centimeters / 2.54` and the variable `centimeters`. Also notice that the format string consists of the two expressions, `%.2f` and `%d`; these are called **format specifiers**. By default, format specifiers and the arguments in `argumentList` have a one-to-one correspondence. Here, the first format specifier `%.2f` is matched with the first argument, which is the expression `centimeters / 2.54`. It says to output the value of the expression `centimeters / 2.54` to two decimal places. The second format specifier `%d` is matched with the second argument, which is `centimeters`. It says to output the value of `centimeters` as a (decimal) integer. (The format specifier `%n` positions the insertion point at the beginning of the next line.)

The output of the statement in Line 1 is:

```
Hello there!
```

Suppose that the value of `centimeters` is 150. Now (to 14 decimal places):

```
centimeters / 2.54 = 150 / 2.54 = 59.05511811023622
```

Therefore, the output of the statement in Line 2 is:

```
There are 59.06 inches in 150 centimeters.
```

Notice that the value of the expression `centimeters / 2.54` is rounded and printed to two decimal places.

It follows that when outputting the format string, the format specifiers are replaced with the formatted values of the corresponding arguments.

A format specifier for general, character, and numeric types has the following syntax:

```
%[argument_index$][flags][width][.precision]conversion
```

The expressions in square brackets are optional. That is, they may or may not appear in a format specifier.

The option *argument_index* is a (decimal) integer indicating the position of the argument in the argument list. The first argument is referenced by "1$", the second by "2$", and so on.

The option *flags* is a set of characters that modifies the output format. The set of valid flags depends on the conversion.

The option *width* is a (decimal) integer indicating the minimum number of characters to be written to the output.

The option *precision* is a (decimal) integer usually used to restrict the number of characters. The specific behavior depends on the conversion.

The required *conversion* is a character indicating how the argument should be formatted. The set of valid conversions for a given argument depends on the argument's data type. Table 3-2 summarizes some of the supported conversions.

TABLE 3-2 Some of Java's Supported Conversions

's'	general	The result is a string
'c'	character	The result is a Unicode character
'd'	integral	The result is formatted as a (decimal) integer
'e'	floating point	The result is formatted as a decimal number in computerized scientific notation
'f'	floating point	The result is formatted as a decimal number
'%'	percent	The result is '%'
'n'	line separator	The result is the platform-specific line separator

The method `printf` is available in Java 5.0 and higher versions.

The following example shows how the conversions f and e work to output floating-point numbers in fixed decimal and scientific formats.

EXAMPLE 3-4

```
//Example: Fixed and scientific format

public class ScientificVsFixed
{
    public static void main(String[] args)
    {
        double hours = 35.45;
        double rate = 15.00;
        double tolerance = 0.01000;

        System.out.println("Fixed decimal notation:");
        System.out.printf("hours = %.2f, rate = %.2f, pay = %.2f,"
                        + " tolerance = %.2f%n%n",
                          hours, rate, hours * rate, tolerance);

        System.out.println("Scientific notation:");
        System.out.printf("hours = %e, rate = %e, pay = %e,%n"
                        + "tolerance = %e%n",
                          hours, rate, hours * rate, tolerance);
    }
}
```

Sample Run:

```
Fixed decimal notation:
hours = 35.45, rate = 15.00, pay = 531.75, tolerance = 0.01

Scientific notation:
hours = 3.545000e+01, rate = 1.500000e+01, pay = 5.317500e+02,
tolerance = 1.000000e-02
```

The sample run shows how the value of hours, rate, pay, and tolerance are printed in fixed decimal format and in scientific notation. First the values are printed in fixed decimal format using the conversion f and then the values are printed in scientific notation using the conversion e.

EXAMPLE 3-5

```
//Program to illustrate how to format the outputting of        //Line 1
//decimal numbers.

public class FormattingDecimalNumNew                           //Line 1
{                                                              //Line 2
    static final double PI = 3.14159265;                       //Line 3

    public static void main(String[] args)                     //Line 4
    {                                                          //Line 5
        double radius = 12.67;                                 //Line 6
        double height = 12.00;                                 //Line 7
```

```
        System.out.println("Two decimal places: ");            //Line 8

        System.out.printf("Line 9: radius = %.2f, "
                  + "height = %.2f, volume = %.2f, "
                  + "PI = %.2f%n%n", radius, height,
                  PI * radius * radius * height, PI);           //Line 9

        System.out.println("Three decimal places: ");           //Line 10
        System.out.printf("Line 11: radius = %.3f, "
                  + "height = %.3f, volume = %.3f,%n"
                  + "            PI = %.3f%n%n", radius,
                  height,PI * radius * radius * height, PI);     //Line 11

        System.out.println("Four decimal places: ");            //Line 12
        System.out.printf("Line 13: radius = %.4f, "
                  + "height = %.4f, volume = %.4f,%n "
                  + "            PI = %.4f%n%n", radius,
                  height,PI * radius * radius * height, PI);     //Line 13

        System.out.printf("Line 14: radius = %.3f, "
                  + "height = %.2f, PI = %.5f%n",
                  radius, height, PI);                           //Line 14
    }                                                           //Line 15
}                                                               //Line 16
```

Sample Run:

```
Two decimal places:
Line 9: radius = 12.67, height = 12.00, volume = 6051.80, PI = 3.14

Three decimal places:
Line 11: radius = 12.670, height = 12.000, volume = 6051.797,
         PI = 3.142

Four decimal places:
Line 13: radius = 12.6700, height = 12.0000, volume = 6051.7969,
         PI = 3.1416

Line 14: radius = 12.670, height = 12.00, PI = 3.14159
```

In this program, the statement in Line 9 outputs the values of radius, height, the volume, and PI to two decimal places. The statement in Line 11 outputs the values of radius, height, the volume, and PI to three decimal places. The statement in Line 13 outputs the values of radius, height, the volume, and PI to four decimal places. The statement in Line 14 outputs the value of radius to three decimal places, the value of height to two decimal places, and the value of PI to five decimal places.

Notice how the values of radius are printed at Lines 11, 13, and 14. The value of radius printed in Line 11 contains a trailing 0. This is because the stored value of radius has only two decimal places, a 0 is printed at the third decimal place. In a similar manner, the value of height is printed in Lines 11, 13, and 14.

Also, notice how the statements in Lines 9, 11, and 13, calculate and output the volume to two, three, and four decimal places.

Note that the value of PI printed in Lines 9, 11, 13, and 14 is rounded.

In a format specifier, by using the option *width* you can also specify the number of columns to be used to output the value of an expression. For example, suppose num is an **int** variable and **rate** is a **double** variable. Furthermore, suppose that:

```
num = 96;
rate = 15.50;
```

Consider the following statements:

```
System.out.println("123456789012345");        //Line 1
System.out.printf("%5d %n", num);              //Line 2
System.out.printf("%5.2f %n", rate);           //Line 3
System.out.printf("%5d%6.2f %n", num, rate);   //Line 4
System.out.printf("%5d %6.2f %n", num, rate);  //Line 5
```

The output of the statement in Line 1 shows the column positions. The statement in Line 2 outputs the value of num in five columns. Because the value of num is 96, we need only two columns to output the value of num. The (*default*) output is right justified, so the first three columns are left blank.

The statement in Line 3 outputs the value of **rate** in five columns with two decimal places. Note that the decimal point also requires a column. That is, the width specifiers for floating-point values also include a column for the decimal point.

The statements in Lines 4 and 5 output the values of num in five columns, followed by the value of **rate** in six columns with two decimal places. The output of these statements is:

```
123456789012345
   96
15.50
   96 15.50
   96  15.50
```

Let us take a close look at the output of the statements in Lines 4 and 5. First, consider the statement in Line 4, that is:

```
System.out.printf("%5d%6.2f %n", num, rate);
```

In this statement, the format string is `"%5d%6.2f %n"`. Notice that there is no space between the format specifiers `%5d` and `%6.2f`. Therefore, after outputting the value of num in the first five columns, the value of **rate** is output starting at column 6 (see the fourth line of output). Because only five columns are needed to output the value of **rate** and the output is right justified, column 6 is left blank.

Now consider the statement in Line 5. Here, the format string is `"%5d %6.2f %n"`. Notice that there is a space between the format specifiers `%5d` and `%6.2f`. Therefore, after outputting the value of num in the first five columns, the sixth column is left blank. The value of **rate** is output starting at column 7 (see the fifth line of output). Because only five columns are needed to output the value of `rate` and the output is right justified, column 7 is (also) left blank.

> **NOTE**
>
> In a format specifier, if the number of columns in the option *width* is less than the number of columns required to output the value of the expression, the output is expanded to the required number of columns. That is, the output is not truncated. For example, the output of the statement:
>
> ```
> System.out.printf("%2d", 8756);
> ```
>
> is:
>
> ```
> 8756
> ```
>
> even though only two columns are specified to output 8756, which requires four columns.

Example 3-6 further illustrates the use of the method `printf`.

EXAMPLE 3-6

The following program illustrates how to format output using the `printf` method and the format specifier:

```java
public class FormattingOutputWithprintf
{
    public static void main(String[] args)
    {
        int num = 763;                              //Line 1

        double x = 658.75;                          //Line 2

        String str = "Java Program.";               //Line 3

        System.out.println("1234567890123456789"
                    + "01234567890");               //Line 4
        System.out.printf("%5d%7.2f%15s%n",
                    num, x, str);                   //Line 5
        System.out.printf("%15s%6d%9.2f%n",
                    str, num, x);                   //Line 6
        System.out.printf("%8.2f%7d%15s%n",
                    x, num, str);                   //Line 7

        System.out.printf("num = %5d%n", num);      //Line 8
        System.out.printf("x = %10.2f%n", x);       //Line 9
        System.out.printf("str = %15s%n", str);     //Line 10
        System.out.printf("%10s%7d%n",
                    "Program No.", 4);              //Line 11
    }
}
```

Sample Run:

```
12345678901234567890123 4567890
   763 658.75  Java Program.
   Java Program.   763    658.75
   658.75     763  Java Program.
num =    763
x =      658.75
str =    Java Program.
Program No.       4
```

For the most part, the preceding output is self-explanatory. Let us consider some of these statements. Notice that for each output statement, the output is right justified.

The statement in Line 4 outputs the first line of the sample run, which shows the column positions. The statements in Lines 5 through 11 produce the remaining lines of output. Let us consider the statement in Line 5, that is:

```
System.out.printf("%5d%7.2f%15s%n", num, x, str);
```

In this statement, the format string is `"%5d%7.2f%15s%n"` and the argument list is `num`, `x`, `str`. The value of `num` is output in five columns, the value of `x` is output in seven columns with two decimal places, and the value of `str` is output in 15 columns. Because only three columns are needed to output the value of `num`, the first two columns are left blank. There is no space between the format specifiers `%5d` and `%7.2f`; therefore, the output of `x` begins at column 6. Because only six columns are needed to output the value of `x` and the format specifier `%7.2f` specifies seven columns, column 6 is left blank. Once again, there is no space between the format specifiers `%7.2f` and `%15s`. The output of the object's value that `str` points to begins at column 13. The reference variable `str` refers to the `String` object with the value `"Java Program."`. Because the format specifier `%15s` specifies 15 columns and only 13 columns are needed to output the string `"Java Program."`, the first two columns, columns 13 and 14, are left blank. The format specifier `%n` positions the insertion point at the beginning of the next line. The statements in Lines 6 and 7 work similarly.

Let us consider the statement in Line 8, that is:

```
System.out.printf("num = %5d%n", num);
```

Note that in this statement, the format string, `"num = %5d%n"`, consists of a string and the format specifier. This statement first outputs the string `"num = "`, which requires six columns. Then, starting at column 7, the value of `num` is output in five columns. Because only three columns are needed to output the value of `num`, columns 7 and 8 are left blank.

If the number of columns specified in a format specifier is more than the number of columns needed to output the result, then the (default) output is right justified. However, strings such as names, typically, are left justified. To force the output to be left justified, you can use the format specifier flag. If the flag is set to `'-'`, then the output of the result is left justified.

For example, consider the following statements:

```
System.out.println("123456789012345678901234567890");   //Line 1
System.out.printf("%-15s ***%n", "Java Program.");      //Line 2
```

The output of these statements is:

```
123456789012345678901234567890
Java Program.   ***
```

Notice that the string `"Java Program."` is printed in 15 columns and the output is left justified. Because in Line 2, in the format specifier, there is a space between s and ***, the sixteenth column is left blank. Then, *** is printed.

The following example further clarifies this.

EXAMPLE 3-7

```
public class Example3_7
{
    public static void main(String[] args)
    {
        int num = 763;                                //Line 1
        double x = 658.75;                            //Line 2
        String str = "Java Program.";                 //Line 3

        System.out.println("1234567890123456789"
                        + "01234567890");             //Line 4
        System.out.printf("%-5d%-7.2f%-15s ***%n",
                        num, x, str);                 //Line 5
        System.out.printf("%-15s%-6d%-9.2f ***%n",
                        str, num, x);                 //Line 6
        System.out.printf("%-8.2f%-7d%-15s ***%n",
                        x, num, str);                 //Line 7

        System.out.printf("num = %-5d ***%n", num);   //Line 8
        System.out.printf("x = %-10.2f ***%n", x);    //Line 9
        System.out.printf("str = %-15s ***%n", str);  //Line 10
        System.out.printf("%-10s%-7d ***%n",
                        "Program No.", 4);            //Line 11
    }
}
```

Sample Run:

```
123456789012345678901234567890
763   658.75 Java Program.   ***
Java Program.   763   658.75   ***
658.75   763    Java Program.   ***
num = 763   ***
x = 658.75     ***
str = Java Program.   ***
Program No.4       ***
```

The output of this program is similar to the output of the program in Example 3-5. Here, the output is left justified. Notice that in the Sample Run, Lines 2 through 8 contain ***. This is to show how the value of the last argument is printed. The details are left as an exercise for you.

Soon, we will explain how to use input/output dialog boxes to input data into a program and then display the output of the program. However, input to a program using input dialog boxes is in string format. Even numeric data is input as strings. Therefore, you first need to learn how to convert numeric strings, called **parsing numeric strings**, into numeric form.

PARSING NUMERIC STRINGS

A string consisting of only an integer or a floating-point number, optionally preceded by a minus sign, is called a **numeric string**. For example, the following are numeric strings:

```
"6723"
"-823"
"345.78"
"-782.873"
```

To process these strings as numbers for addition or multiplication, we first must convert them into numeric form. Java provides special methods to convert numeric strings into their equivalent numeric form.

1. To convert a string consisting of an integer to a value of the type `int`, we use the following expression:

    ```
    Integer.parseInt(strExpression)
    ```

    For example:

    ```
    Integer.parseInt("6723") = 6723
    Integer.parseInt("-823") = -823
    ```

2. To convert a string consisting of a floating-point number to a value of the type `float`, we use the following expression:

    ```
    Float.parseFloat(strExpression)
    ```

    For example:

    ```
    Float.parseFloat("34.56") = 34.56
    Float.parseFloat("-542.97") = -542.97
    ```

3. To convert a string consisting of a floating-point number to a value of the type `double`, we use the following expression:

    ```
    Double.parseDouble(strExpression)
    ```

    For example:

    ```
    Double.parseDouble("345.78") = 345.78
    Double.parseDouble("-782.873") = -782.873
    ```

Note that Integer, Float, and Double are classes that contain methods to convert a numeric string into a number. These classes are called **wrapper** classes. Moreover, parseInt is a method of the class Integer, which converts a numeric integer string into a value of the type int. Similarly, parseFloat is a method of the class Float and is used to convert a numeric decimal string into an equivalent value of the type float, and the method parseDouble is a method of the class Double, which is used to convert a numeric decimal string into an equivalent value of the type double. At this point, do not be overly concerned with the details of these classes and methods; just continue to use them as shown previously whenever you need them. (Chapter 6 discusses these wrapper classes in more detail.)

EXAMPLE 3-8

1.
```
Integer.parseInt("34")              = 34
Integer.parseInt("-456")            = -456
Double.parseDouble("754.89")        = 754.89
```

2.
```
Integer.parseInt("34") + Integer.parseInt("75")       = 34 + 75 = 109
Integer.parseInt("87") + Integer.parseInt("-67")      = 87 - 67 = 20
```

3.
```
    Double.parseDouble("754.89") - Double.parseDouble("87.34")
=   754.89 - 87.34
=   667.55
```

Using Dialog Boxes for Input/Output

Recall that you have already used the class Scanner to input data into a program from the keyboard, and you used the object System.out to output the results to the screen.

Another way to gather input and output results is to use a graphical user interface (GUI). Java provides the class JOptionPane, which allows the programmer to use GUI components for I/O. This section describes how to use these facilities to make I/O more efficient and the program more attractive.

The class JOptionPane is contained in the package javax.swing. The two methods of this class that we use are: showInputDialog and showMessageDialog. The method showInputDialog allows the user to input a string from the keyboard; the method showMessageDialog allows the programmer to display the results.

The syntax to use the method showInputDialog is:

```
str = JOptionPane.showInputDialog(stringExpression);
```

where `str` is a `String` variable and `stringExpression` is an expression evaluating to a string. When this statement executes, a dialog box containing `stringExpression` appears on the screen prompting the user to enter the data. (The `stringExpression` usually informs the user what to enter.) The data entered is returned as a string and assigned to the variable `str`.

Consider the following statement (suppose that `name` is a `String` variable):

```
name = JOptionPane.showInputDialog("Enter your name and press OK");
```

When this statement executes, the dialog box shown in Figure 3-7 appears on the screen. (The arrow and the words `Text Field` are not part of the dialog box.)

FIGURE 3-7 Input dialog box prompting the user to input name

The user enters the name in the white area, called a **text field**, as shown in Figure 3-8.

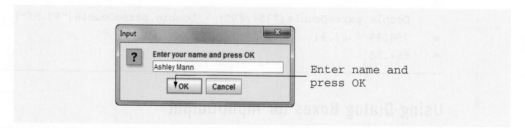

FIGURE 3-8 Input dialog box with user input

After you enter a name and click the OK button (or press the Enter key), the dialog box disappears and the entered name is assigned to the variable `name`. In this case, the string `"Ashley Mann"` is assigned to `name`.

Now that you know how to use an input dialog box, let's turn to the method `showMessageDialog` for output.

The syntax to use the method `showMessageDialog` is:

```
JOptionPane.showMessageDialog(parentComponent,
                        messageStringExpression,
                        boxTitleString, messageType);
```

The method `showMessageDialog` has four parameters, which are described in Table 3-3.

TABLE 3-3 Parameters for the Method `showMessageDialog`

Parameter	Description
parentComponent	This is an object that represents the parent of the dialog box. For now, we will specify the `parentComponent` to be `null`, in which case the program uses a default component that causes the dialog box to appear in the middle of the screen. Note that `null` is a reserved word in Java.
messageStringExpression	The `messageStringExpression` is evaluated and its value appears in the dialog box.
boxTitleString	The `boxTitleString` represents the title of the dialog box.
messageType	An `int` value representing the type of icon that will appear in the dialog box. Alternatively, you can use certain `JOptionPane` options described below.

Table 3-4 describes the options of the **class** `JOptionPane` that can be used with the parameter `messageType`. The option name is shown in bold. Examples 3-9 through 3-11 illustrate these options.

TABLE 3-4 `JOptionPane` Options for the Parameter `messageType`

messageType	Description
JOptionPane.**ERROR_MESSAGE**	The error icon, , is displayed in the dialog box.
JOptionPane.**INFORMATION_MESSAGE**	The information icon, , is displayed in the dialog box.
JOptionPane.**PLAIN_MESSAGE**	No icon appears in the dialog box.
JOptionPane.**QUESTION_MESSAGE**	The question icon, , is displayed in the dialog box.
JOptionPane.**WARNING_MESSAGE**	The warning icon, , is displayed in the dialog box.

3

EXAMPLE 3-9

The output of the statement:

```
JOptionPane.showMessageDialog(null, "Hello World!", "Greetings",
                        JOptionPane.INFORMATION_MESSAGE);
```

is shown in Figure 3-9.

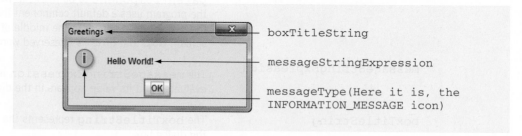

FIGURE 3-9 Message dialog box showing its various components

Notice the `INFORMATION_MESSAGE` icon to the left of `Hello World!` and the word `Greetings` in the title bar. After you click the OK button, the dialog box disappears.

EXAMPLE 3-10

Figure 3-10 shows the output of the following statement:

```
JOptionPane.showMessageDialog(null, "Amount Due = $" + 500.45,
                        "Invoice", JOptionPane.PLAIN_MESSAGE);
```

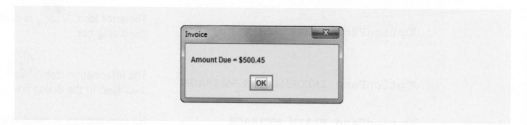

FIGURE 3-10 Message box with no icon

In the message dialog box in Figure 3-10, no icon appears to the left of the `messageStringExpression`. This is because the `messageType` is `JOptionPane.PLAIN_MESSAGE`.

EXAMPLE 3-11

Consider the following statements:

```
String str;
int num1 = 45;
int num2 = 56;
int sum;

str = "The two numbers are: " + num1 + " and " + num2 + "\n";
sum = num1 + num2;

str = str + "The sum of the numbers is: " + sum  + "\n";
str = str + "That is all for now!";
```

Figure 3-11 shows the output of the statement:

```
JOptionPane.showMessageDialog(null, str, "Summing Numbers",
                         JOptionPane.ERROR_MESSAGE);
```

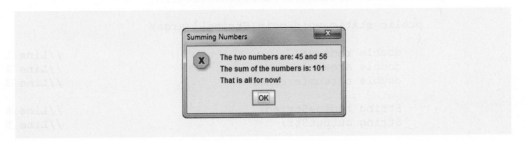

FIGURE 3-11 Message dialog box showing the output of the string `str`

The **class** JOptionPane is contained in the **package** javax.swing. Therefore, to use this **class** in a program, the program must import it from the **package** javax.swing. The following statements illustrate how to import the **class** JOptionPane (you can use either format):

```
import javax.swing.JOptionPane;
```

or:

```
import javax.swing.*;
```

```
System.exit
```

In order to use the input/output dialog boxes and properly terminate program execution, the program must include the following statement:

```
System.exit(0);
```

Note that this statement is needed only for programs that have GUI components such as input/output dialog boxes.

Example 3-12 shows a program that calculates the area and circumference of a circle and uses input/output dialog boxes.

EXAMPLE 3-12

The following program prompts the user to enter the radius of a circle. The program then outputs the circle's radius, area, and circumference. The class Math defines the named constant PI (π), which is PI = 3.141592653589793. We will use this value to find the area and circumference. (Note that to use this value, we use the expression Math.PI.)

```
//Program to determine the area and circumference of a circle

import javax.swing.JOptionPane;

public class AreaAndCircumferenceProgram
{
    public static void main(String[] args)
    {
        double radius;                                  //Line 1
        double area;                                    //Line 2
        double circumference;                           //Line 3

        String radiusString;                            //Line 4
        String outputStr;                               //Line 5

        radiusString =
          JOptionPane.showInputDialog
                    ("Enter the radius: ");             //Line 6

        radius = Double.parseDouble(radiusString);      //Line 7

        area = Math.PI * radius * radius;               //Line 8
        circumference = 2 * Math.PI * radius;           //Line 9

        outputStr = "Radius: " + radius + "\n" +
                    "Area: " + area + " square units\n" +
                    "Circumference: " + circumference +
                    " units";                           //Line 10

        JOptionPane.showMessageDialog(null, outputStr,
                            "Circle",
                    JOptionPane.INFORMATION_MESSAGE);    //Line 11

        System.exit(0);                                 //Line 12
    }
}
```

Sample Run: (Figure 3-12 shows a sample run of this program. The input screen is shown first, then the output screen.)

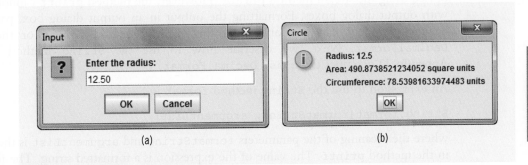

FIGURE 3-12 Sample run of program to calculate a circle's area and perimeter

The preceding program works as follows. The statements in Lines 1 through 5 declare the appropriate variables to manipulate the data. The statement in Line 6 displays the input dialog box with the message `Enter the radius:` (in Figure 3-12(a), the entered value is 12.50).

The string containing the input data is assigned to the `String` variable `radiusString`. The statement in Line 7 converts the string containing the radius into a value of the type `double` and stores it in the variable `radius`.

The statements in Lines 8 and 9 calculate the area and circumference of the circle and store them in the variables `area` and `circumference`, respectively. The statement in Line 10 constructs the string containing the radius, area, and circumference of the circle. The string is assigned to the variable `outputStr`. The statement in Line 11 uses the message dialog box to display the circle's radius, area, and circumference, as shown in Figure 3-12(b).

The statement in Line 12 terminates the program after the user clicks the OK button in the dialog box.

The program in Example 3-12 does not output the area and circumference to two decimal places. The next section explains how to format the output in an output dialog box.

NOTE If the amount of input data is small and the output is small, dialog boxes are an effective and attractive way to build an application.

Formatting the Output Using the `String` Method `format`

Earlier in this chapter, you learned how to format the output on the standard output device using the stream method `printf`. However, the method `printf` cannot be used with output dialog boxes. Formatting the output in an output dialog box, particularly decimal numbers, can be done using the `String` method `format` or the `class` `DecimalFormat`. Next, we describe how to use the `String` method `format`. Appendix D describes the `class` `DecimalFormat`.

An expression to use the `String` method `format` is:

```
String.format(formatString, argumentList)
```

where the meaning of the parameters `formatString` and `argumentList` is the same as in the method `printf`. The value of the expression is a formatted string. The following example shows how the method `format` works.

EXAMPLE 3-13

Suppose we have the following declarations and initializations:

```
double x = 15.674;
double y = 235.73;
double z = 9525.9864;

int num = 83;

String str;
```

Expression	Value
`String.format("%.2f", x)`	`"15.67"`
`String.format("%.3f", y)`	`"235.730"`
`String.format("%.2f", z)`	`"9525.99"`
`String.format("%7s", "Hello")`	`"  Hello"`
`String.format("%5d%7.2f", num, x)`	`"   83   15.67"`
`String.format("The value of num = %5d", num)`	`"The value of num =    83"`
`str = String.format("%.2f", z)`	`str = "9525.99"`

Because the value of the `String` method `format` is a string, the method `format` can also be used as an argument to the methods `print`, `println`, or `printf`. Example 3-14 illustrates this concept.

EXAMPLE 3-14

```
public class StringMethodformat
{
    public static void main (String[] args)
```

```
    {
        double x = 15.674;
        double y = 235.73;
        double z = 9525.9864;
        int num = 83;
        String str;

        System.out.println("123456789012345678901234567890");
        System.out.println(String.format("%.2f", x));
        System.out.println(String.format("%.3f", y));
        System.out.println(String.format("%.2f", z));

        System.out.println(String.format("%7s", "Hello"));
        System.out.println(String.format("%5d%7.2f", num, x));
        System.out.println(String.format("The value of "
                                 + "num = %5d", num));

        str = String.format("%.2f", z);

        System.out.println(str);
    }
}
```

Sample Run:

```
123456789012345678901234567890
15.67
235.730
9525.99
  Hello
   83  15.67
The value of num =    83
9525.99
```

The preceding sample run is self-explanatory. The details are left as an exercise for you.

The following example illustrates how the `String` method `format` can be used to format the output in an output dialog box.

EXAMPLE 3-15

```
import javax.swing.JOptionPane;

public class Example3_15
{
    public static void main(String[] args)
    {
        double x = 15.674;
        double y = 235.73;
        double z = 9525.9864;
        String str;
```

```
        str = String.format("The value of x with two decimal "
                        + "places = %.2f%n", x)
            + String.format("The value of y with two decimal "
                        + "places = %.2f%n", y)
            + String.format("The value of z with two decimal "
                        + "places = %.2f%n", z);

        JOptionPane.showMessageDialog(null, str,
                "Formatting with the String Method format",
                JOptionPane.INFORMATION_MESSAGE);

        System.exit(0);
    }
}
```

Sample Run: (Figure 3-13 shows the output of this program.)

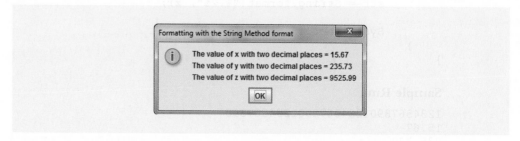

FIGURE 3-13 Output dialog box showing the values of x, y, and z with two decimal places

Note that in the preceding program, first we constructed `str` using the `String` method `format` and then used `str` in the output dialog box. However, you could have used the `String` method `format` directly in the output dialog box. That is, you can replace the statements:

```
str = String.format("The value of x with two decimal "
                + "places = %.2f%n", x)
    + String.format("The value of y with two decimal "
                + "places = %.2f%n", y)
    + String.format("The value of z with two decimal "
                + "places = %.2f%n", z);

JOptionPane.showMessageDialog(null, str,
        "Formatting with the String Method format",
        JOptionPane.INFORMATION_MESSAGE);
```

with the following statement:

```
JOptionPane.showMessageDialog(null,
        String.format("The value of x with two decimal "
                + "places = %.2f%n", x)
```

```
              + String.format("The value of y with two decimal "
                      + "places = %.2f%n", y)
              + String.format("The value of z with two decimal "
                      + "places = %.2f%n", z),
        "Formatting with the String Method format",
        JOptionPane.INFORMATION_MESSAGE);
```

3

File Input/Output

The previous sections discussed in some detail how to get input from the keyboard (standard input device) and send output to the screen (standard output device). However, getting input from the keyboard and sending output to the screen has limitations. If the amount of input data is large, it is inefficient to type it at the keyboard each time you run a program. In addition to the inconvenience of typing large amounts of data, typing can generate errors, and unintentional typos cause erroneous results. Sending output to the screen works well if the amount of data is small (no larger than the size of the screen), but suppose you want to distribute the output in a printed format? The solution to these problems is to use an alternate form of input and output: files. By using a file as a source of input data, you can prepare the data before running a program, and the program can access the data each time it runs. Saving output to a file allows the output to be saved and distributed to others, and the output produced by one program can be used as input to other programs.

This section discusses how to obtain data from other input devices, such as a disk (that is, secondary storage), and how to save the output to a disk. Java allows a program to get data from, and save output to, secondary storage. A program can use the file I/O and read data from or write data to a file. Formally, a **file** is defined as follows:

File: An area in secondary storage used to hold information.

In Chapter 2, you learned how to use a `Scanner` object to input data from the standard input device. Recall that the following statement creates the `Scanner` object `console` and initializes it to the standard input device:

`Scanner console = new Scanner(System.in);`

You can also initialize a `Scanner` object to input sources other than the standard input device by passing an appropriate argument in place of the object `System.in`. To do this, we use the **class** `FileReader` as follows. (The **class** `FileReader` is contained in the **package** `java.io`.) Suppose that the input data is stored in a file, say, `prog.dat`. The following statement creates the `Scanner` object `inFile` and initializes it to the file `prog.dat`:

```
Scanner inFile = new Scanner(new FileReader("prog.dat"));   //Line 1
```

Next, you use the object `inFile` to input the data from the file `prog.dat`, just the way you used the object `console` to input the data from the standard input device using the methods `next`, `nextInt`, `nextDouble`, and so on.

NOTE | The statement in Line 1 assumes that the file `prog.dat` is in the same directory (subdirectory) as your program. However, if this is in a different directory (subdirectory), then you must specify the path where the file is located, along with the name of the file. For example, suppose that the file `prog.dat` is on a flash memory in drive H. Then, the statement in Line 1 should be modified as follows:

```
Scanner inFile = new Scanner(new FileReader("h:\\prog.dat"));
```

Note that there are two \ after `h:`. Recall from Chapter 2 that in Java \ is the escape character. Therefore, to produce a \ within a string you need \\. (Moreover, to be absolutely sure about specifying the source where the input file is stored, such as the flash drive `h:\\`, check your system's documentation.)

NOTE | Suppose that a program reads data from a file. Because different computers have drives labeled differently, for simplicity, throughout the book we assume that the file containing the data and the program reading data from the file are in the same directory (subdirectory).

To send the output to a file, you use the **class** `PrintWriter`. This class is contained in the **package** `java.io`.

To summarize, Java file I/O is a four-step process:

1. Import the necessary classes from the **packages** `java.util` and `java.io` into the program.
2. Create and associate the appropriate objects with the input/output sources.
3. Use the appropriate methods associated with the variables created in Step 2 to input/output the data.
4. Close the files.

We now explain these four steps and then provide a skeleton program that shows how the steps might appear in a program.

Step 1 requires that the necessary classes be imported from the **packages** `java.util` and `java.io`. The following statements accomplish this task:

```
import java.util.*;
import java.io.*;
```

Step 2 requires that you create and associate appropriate `class` variables with the input/output sources. We already discussed how to declare and associate `Scanner` objects for inputting the data from a file. The next section describes how to create the appropriate objects to send the output to a file.

Step 3 requires us to read the data from the input file using the variables created in Step 2. Example 3-16 describes how to read the data from a file.

In Step 4, you close the input and output files. To do so, you use the method `close`, as described later in this section.

EXAMPLE 3-16

Suppose an input file, say `employeeData.txt`, consists of the following data:

```
Emily Johnson 45 13.50
```

The file consists of an employee's name, the number of hours the employee worked, and the pay rate. The following statements declare the appropriate variables to read and store the data into the variables:

```
    //Create and associate the Scanner object to the input source
Scanner inFile = new Scanner(new FileReader("employeeData.txt"));

String firstName;    //variable to store first name
String lastName;     //variable to store last name

double hoursWorked;  //variable to store hours worked
double payRate;      //variable to store pay rate
double wages;        //variable to store wages

firstName = inFile.next();  //get the first name
lastName = inFile.next();   //get the last name

hoursWorked = inFile.nextDouble(); //get hours worked
payRate = inFile.nextDouble();     //get pay rate

wages = hoursWorked * payRate;
```

The following statement closes the input file to which `inFile` is associated:

```
inFile.close();  //close the input file
```

Storing (Writing) Output to a File

To store the output of a program in a file, you use the **class** PrintWriter. You declare a PrintWriter variable and associate this variable with the destination, that is, the file where the output will be stored. Suppose the output is to be stored in the file prog.out. Consider the following statement:

```
PrintWriter outFile = new PrintWriter("prog.out");
```

This statement creates the PrintWriter object outFile and associates it with the file prog.out. (This statement assumes that the file prog.out is to be created in the directory [subdirectory] where the main program is.)

 NOTE If you want the output file to be stored, say, on a flash memory in drive H, then the previous statement takes the following form:

```
PrintWriter outFile = new PrintWriter("h:\\prog.out");
```

You can now use the methods print, println, and printf with outFile in the same way they have been used with the object System.out.

For example, the statement:

```
outFile.println("The paycheck is: $" + pay);
```

stores the output—The paycheck is: $565.78—in the file prog.out. This statement assumes that the value of the variable pay is 565.78.

Once the output is completed, Step 4 requires closing the file. You close the input and output files by using the method close. For example, assuming that inFile and outFile are as declared before, the statements to close these files are:

```
inFile.close();
outFile.close();
```

Closing the output file ensures that the buffer holding the output will be emptied, that is, the entire output generated by the program will be sent to the output file.

Step 3 requires that you create appropriate objects for file I/O. In the case of an input file, the file must exist before the program executes. If the input file does not exist, then the statement to associate the object with the input file fails and it **throws** a FileNotFoundException. At this time, we will not require the program to handle this exception, so the method main will also throw this exception. Therefore, the heading of the method main must contain an appropriate command to throw a FileNotFoundException.

An output file does not have to exist before it is opened; if the output file does not exist, the computer prepares an empty file for output. *If the designated output file already exists, by default, the old contents are erased (lost) when the file is opened.* Note that if the program is not able to create or access the output file, it throws a FileNotFoundException.

NOTE (throws **clause**) During program execution, various things can happen—for example, division by zero or inputting a letter for a number. If such things happen, the system would not tolerate it. In such cases, we say that an exception has occurred. If an exception occurs in a method, then the method should either handle the exception or *throw* it for the calling environment to handle. If an input file does not exist, the program throws a **FileNotFoundException**. Similarly, if an output file cannot be created or accessed, the program throws a **FileNotFoundException**. For the next few chapters, we will not be concerned with the handling of the exceptions; we will simply throw the exceptions. Because we do not need the method **main** to handle the **FileNotFoundException**, we will include a command in the heading of the method **main** to throw the **FileNotFoundException**. Chapter 11 describes exception handling.

In skeleton form, a program that uses file I/O is usually of the following form:

```java
import java.io.*;
import java.util.*;

//Add additional import statements as needed

public class ClassName
{
    //Declare appropriate variables
    public static void main(String[] args)
                            throws FileNotFoundException
    {
        //Create and associate the stream objects
        Scanner inFile =
            new Scanner(new FileReader("prog.dat"));

        PrintWriter outFile = new PrintWriter("prog.out");

        //Code for data manipulation

        //Close file
        inFile.close();
        outFile.close();
    }
}
```

The remainder of this chapter gives two programming examples—one illustrates dialog boxes for input/output; the other illustrates file input/output.

PROGRAMMING EXAMPLE: Movie Ticket Sale and Donation to Charity

A movie in a local theater is in great demand. The theater owner has decided to donate to a local charity a portion of the gross amount generated from the movie. This example designs and implements a program that prompts the user to input the movie name, adult ticket price, child ticket price, number of adult tickets sold, number of child tickets sold, and percentage of the gross amount to be donated to the charity. The output of the program is shown in Figure 3-14.

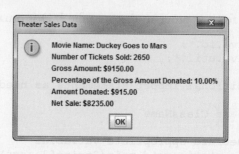

FIGURE 3-14 Output of theater sales program

Note that the decimal numbers are output with two decimal places.

Input: The input to the program consists of the movie name, adult ticket price, child ticket price, number of adult tickets sold, number of child tickets sold, and percentage of the gross amount to be donated to the charity.

Output: The output is as shown in Figure 3-14.

PROBLEM
ANALYSIS
AND
ALGORITHM
DESIGN

To calculate the amount donated to the local charity and the net sale, you first need to determine the gross amount. To calculate the gross amount, you multiply the number of adult tickets sold by the price of an adult ticket, multiply the number of child tickets sold by the price of a child ticket, and then add these two numbers:

```
grossAmount = adultTicketPrice * noOfAdultTicketsSold
            + childTicketPrice * noOfChildTicketsSold;
```

Next, you determine the percentage of the amount donated to the charity, and then calculate the net sale amount by subtracting the amount donated from the gross amount. The formulas to calculate the amount donated and the net sale amount are given below. This analysis leads to the following algorithm:

1. Get the movie name.
2. Get the price of an adult ticket.
3. Get the price of a child ticket.
4. Get the number of adult tickets sold.
5. Get the number of child tickets sold.
6. Get the percentage of the gross amount donated to the charity.
7. Calculate the gross amount using the following formula:

```
grossAmount = adultTicketPrice * noOfAdultTicketsSold
            + childTicketPrice * noOfChildTicketsSold;
```

8. Calculate the amount donated to the charity using the following formula:

```
amountDonated = grossAmount * percentDonation / 100;
```

9. Calculate the net sale amount using the following formula:

```
netSaleAmount = grossAmount - amountDonated;
```

VARIABLES   From the preceding discussion, it follows that you need variables to store the movie name, adult ticket price, child ticket price, number of adult tickets sold, number of child tickets sold, percentage of the gross amount donated to the charity, gross amount, amount donated, and net sale amount. You also need a variable to get the string containing the sales data and a string to format the output. Therefore, the following variables are needed:

```
String movieName;
String inputStr;
String outputStr;

double adultTicketPrice;
double childTicketPrice;
int noOfAdultTicketsSold;
int noOfChildTicketsSold;

double percentDonation;
double grossAmount;
double amountDonated;
double netSaleAmount;
```

FORMATTING THE OUTPUT   To show the desired output, you first create the string consisting of the strings and the values required. The following string accomplishes this:

```
outputStr = "Movie Name: " + movieName + "\n"
          + "Number of Tickets Sold: "
          + (noOfAdultTicketsSold +
```

```
                          noOfChildTicketsSold) + "\n"
          + "Gross Amount: $"
          + String.format("%.2f", grossAmount) + "\n"
          + "Percentage of Gross Amount Donated: "
          + String.format("%.2f%%", percentDonation) + "\n"
          + "Amount Donated: $"
          + String.format("%.2f", amountDonated) + "\n"
          + "Net Sale: $"
          + String.format("%.2f", netSaleAmount);
```

Notice that we have used the method format of the **class** String to output decimal numbers to two decimal places.

MAIN ALGORITHM   In the preceding sections, we analyzed the problem and determined the formulas to do the calculations. We also determined the necessary variables and the output string. We can now expand the algorithm given in the section Problem Analysis and Algorithm Design to solve the problem given at the beginning of this programming example.

1. Declare the variables.
2. Display the input dialog box to enter a movie name and retrieve the movie name.
3. Display the input dialog box to enter the price of an adult ticket.
4. Retrieve the price of an adult ticket.
5. Display the input dialog box to enter the price of a child ticket.
6. Retrieve the price of a child ticket.
7. Display the input dialog box to enter the number of adult tickets sold.
8. Retrieve the number of adult tickets sold.
9. Display the input dialog box to enter the number of child tickets sold.
10. Retrieve the number of child tickets sold.
11. Display the input dialog box to enter the percentage of the gross amount donated.
12. Retrieve the percentage of the gross amount donated.
13. Calculate the gross amount.
14. Calculate the amount donated.
15. Calculate the net sale amount.
16. Format the output string.
17. Display the message dialog box to show the output.
18. Terminate the program.

COMPLETE PROGRAM LISTING

```
//****************************************************************
// Author D.S. Malik
//
// Program: Movie ticket sale and donation to charity.
// This program prompts the user to input the movie name, adult
// ticket price, child ticket price, number of adult tickets
// sold, number of child tickets sold, and the percentage of the
// gross amount to be donated to the charity.
// The program outputs the movie name, the number of tickets
// sold, the gross amount, the percentage of the gross amount
// donated to the charity, the amount donated to the charity,
// and the net amount.
//****************************************************************

import javax.swing.JOptionPane;

public class MovieTicketSale
{
    public static void main(String[] args)
    {
            //Step 1
        String movieName;
        String inputStr;
        String outputStr;

        double adultTicketPrice;
        double childTicketPrice;

        int noOfAdultTicketsSold;
        int noOfChildTicketsSold;

        double percentDonation;
        double grossAmount;
        double amountDonated;
        double netSaleAmount;

        movieName = JOptionPane.showInputDialog
                    ("Enter the movie name");            //Step 2

        inputStr = JOptionPane.showInputDialog
                    ("Enter the price of an adult ticket"); //Step 3
        adultTicketPrice = Double.parseDouble(inputStr);   //Step 4

        inputStr = JOptionPane.showInputDialog
                    ("Enter the price of a child ticket"); //Step 5
        childTicketPrice = Double.parseDouble(inputStr);   //Step 6
```

```
            inputStr = JOptionPane.showInputDialog
                    ("Enter the number of adult tickets sold");   //Step 7
        noOfAdultTicketsSold = Integer.parseInt(inputStr);        //Step 8

            inputStr = JOptionPane.showInputDialog
                    ("Enter the number of child tickets sold");   //Step 9
        noOfChildTicketsSold = Integer.parseInt(inputStr);        //Step 10

            inputStr = JOptionPane.showInputDialog
                    ("Enter the percentage of the donation");     //Step 11
        percentDonation = Double.parseDouble(inputStr);           //Step 12

        grossAmount = adultTicketPrice * noOfAdultTicketsSold +
                    childTicketPrice * noOfChildTicketsSold;      //Step 13

        amountDonated = grossAmount * percentDonation / 100;      //Step 14
        netSaleAmount = grossAmount - amountDonated;              //Step 15

        outputStr = "Movie Name: " + movieName + "\n"
                    + "Number of Tickets Sold: "
                    + (noOfAdultTicketsSold +
                      noOfChildTicketsSold) + "\n"
                    + "Gross Amount: $"
                    + String.format("%.2f", grossAmount) + "\n"
                    + "Percentage of the Gross Amount Donated: "
                    + String.format("%.2f%%", percentDonation) + "\n"
                    + "Amount Donated: $"
                    + String.format("%.2f", amountDonated) + "\n"
                    + "Net Sale: $"
                    + String.format("%.2f", netSaleAmount);       //Step 16
        JOptionPane.showMessageDialog(null, outputStr,
                        "Theater Sales Data",
                        JOptionPane.INFORMATION_MESSAGE);         //Step 17
        System.exit(0);                                          //Step 18
    }
}
```

Sample Run: (In this sample run, the user input is in the input dialog boxes.)

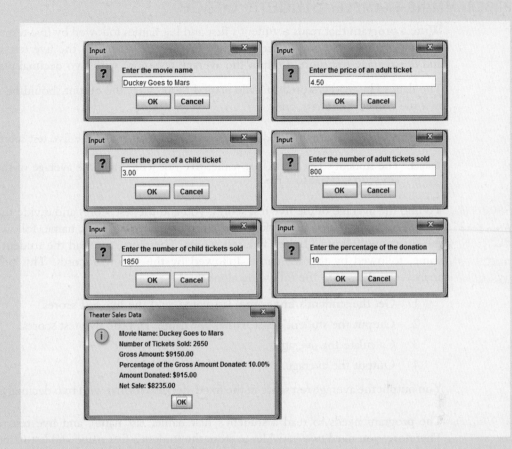

FIGURE 3-15 Sample run of movie sales program

In this output (see Figure 3-15), the first six dialog boxes (from left to right) get the necessary data to generate the last message dialog box.

PROGRAMMING EXAMPLE: Student Grade

Write a program that reads a student's first and last names followed by five test scores. The program should output the student's first name, last name, the five test scores, and the average test score. Output the average test score with two decimal places.

The data to be read is stored in a file named `test.txt`; the output should be stored in a file named `testavg.out`.

Input: A file containing the student's first name, last name, and the five test scores

Output: The student's first name, last name, five test scores, and the average of the five test scores, saved to a file

PROBLEM
ANALYSIS
AND
ALGORITHM
DESIGN

To find the average of the five test scores, you add the test scores and divide the sum by 5. The input data is in the following form: the student's first name, followed by the last name, followed by the five test scores. Therefore, we read the student's first name, followed by the last name, followed by the five test scores. This problem analysis translates into the following algorithm:

1. Get the student's first name, last name, and the five test scores.
2. Output the student's first name, last name, and the five test scores.
3. Calculate the average.
4. Output the average.

You output the average test score in the fixed-decimal format with two decimal places.

VARIABLES

The program needs to read a student's first name, last name, and five test scores. Therefore, you need two variables to store the student's first name and last name, and five variables to store the five test scores. To find the average, you must add the five test scores and then divide the sum by 5. Thus, you also need a variable to store the average test score. Furthermore, because the input data is in a file and the output is to be stored in a file, you must declare and initialize the appropriate variables. The program needs at least the following variables:

```
double test1, test2, test3, test4, test5; //variables to store
                                          //five test scores
double average;      //variable to store average test score

String firstName;    //variable to store the first name
String lastName;     //variable to store the last name

Scanner inFile = new Scanner(new FileReader("test.txt"));

PrintWriter outFile = new PrintWriter("testavg.out");
```

MAIN
ALGORITHM

In the preceding sections, we analyzed the problem and determined the formulas to perform the calculations. We also determined the necessary variables. Now we can expand the algorithm given in the Problem Analysis and Algorithm Design section to solve the Student Grade problem given at the beginning of this programming example.

1. Declare the variables.
2. Create a `Scanner` object and associate it with the input source.
3. Create a `PrintWriter` object and associate it with the output source.
4. Get the student's first name and last name.
5. Output the student's first name and last name.
6. Read the five test scores.
7. Output the five test scores.
8. Find the average test score.
9. Output the average test score.
10. Close the files.

This program reads the data from a file and outputs the data to a file, so it must import the necessary classes from the packages `java.io` and `java.util`.

COMPLETE PROGRAM LISTING

```
//****************************************************************
// Author D.S. Malik
//
// Program to calculate the average test score.
// Given a student's name and five test scores, this program
// calculates the average test score. The student's name, the
// five test scores, and the average test score is stored in the
// file testavg.out. The data is input from the file test.txt.
//****************************************************************
import java.io.*;
import java.util.*;

public class StudentGrade
{
    public static void main(String[] args) throws
                                        FileNotFoundException
    {
        //declare and initialize the variables          //Step 1
        double test1, test2, test3, test4, test5;
        double average;
```

```
        String firstName;
        String lastName;

        Scanner inFile =
            new Scanner(new FileReader("test.txt"));          //Step 2

        PrintWriter outFile = new
                        PrintWriter("testavg.out");           //Step 3

        firstName = inFile.next();                            //Step 4
        lastName = inFile.next();                             //Step 4

        outFile.println("Student Name: "
                    + firstName + " " + lastName);            //Step 5

            //Step 6 - retrieve the five test scores
        test1 = inFile.nextDouble();
        test2 = inFile.nextDouble();
        test3 = inFile.nextDouble();
        test4 = inFile.nextDouble();
        test5 = inFile.nextDouble();

        outFile.printf("Test scores: %5.2f %5.2f %5.2f "
                    + "%5.2f %5.2f %n", test1, test2,
                    test3, test4, test5);                     //Step 7

        average = (test1 + test2 + test3 + test4
                    + test5) / 5.0;                           //Step 8
        outFile.printf("Average test score: %5.2f %n",
                    average);                                 //Step 9

        inFile.close();                                       //Step 10
        outFile.close();                                      //Step 10
    }
}
```

Sample Run:

Input File (contents of the file `test.txt`):

Andrew Miller 87.50 89 65.75 37 98.50

Output File (contents of the file `testavg.out`):

```
Student Name: Andrew Miller
Test scores: 87.50 89.00 65.75 37.00 98.50
Average test score: 75.55
```

The preceding program uses five variables: `test1`, `test2`, `test3`, `test4`, and `test5` to read the five test scores and then find the average test score. The Additional Student Files folder at *www.cengagebrain.com* contains a modified version of this program that uses only one variable, `testscore`, to read the test scores and another variable, `sum`, to find the sum of the test scores. The program is named `StudentGradeVersion2.java`.

Debugging: Understanding Logic Errors and Debugging with **print** or **println** Statements

In the debugging section of Chapter 2, we illustrated how to understand and correct syntax errors. As we have seen, syntax errors are reported by the compiler, and the compiler not only reports syntax errors, it also gives some explanation about the errors. On the other hand, logic errors are typically not caught by the compiler except the trivial ones such as using a variable without properly initializing it. In this section, we illustrate how to spot and correct logic errors using print statements. Suppose that we want to write a program that takes as input the temperature in Fahrenheit and output the equivalent temperature in Celsius. The formula to convert the temperature is: *Celsius* = 5 / 9 ⋆ (*Fahrenheit* − 32). So consider the following program.

```
import java.util.*;                                    //Line 1

public class LogicError1                               //Line 2
{                                                      //Line 3
    static Scanner console = new Scanner(System.in);   //Line 4

    public static void main(String[] args)             //Line 5
    {                                                  //Line 4
        int fahrenheit;                                //Line 6
        int celsius;                                   //Line 7

        System.out.print("Enter temperature in "
                    + "Fahrenheit: ");                 //Line 8
        fahrenheit = console.nextInt();                //Line 9
        System.out.println();                          //Line 10

        celsius = 5 / 9 * (fahrenheit - 32);           //Line 11

        System.out.println(fahrenheit + " degree F = "
                    + celsius + " degree C.");         //Line 12
    }                                                  //Line 13
}                                                      //Line 14
```

Sample Run 1: The user input is shaded.

```
Enter temperature in Fahrenheit: 32

32 degree F = 0 degree C.
```

Sample Run 2: The user input is shaded.

```
Enter temperature in Fahrenheit: 110

110 degree F = 0 degree C.
```

The result shown in the first calculation looks correct. However, the result in the second calculation is clearly not correct even though the same formula is used, because 110 degree F = 43 degree C. Thus, the value of `celsius` calculated in Line 10 is incorrect. Now the value of `celsius` is given by the expression 5 / 9 * (fahrenheit - 32). So we should look at this expression closely. To see the effect of this expression, we can separately print the values of the two expression 5 / 9 and `fahrenheit` - 32. This can be accomplished by temporarily inserting an output statement as shown in the following program:

```
import java.util.*;                                        //Line 1

public class LogicError2                                   //Line 2
{                                                          //Line 3
    static Scanner console = new Scanner(System.in);       //Line 4

    public static void main(String[] args)                 //Line 5
    {                                                      //Line 4
        int fahrenheit;                                    //Line 6
        int celsius;                                       //Line 7

        System.out.print("Enter temperature in "
                        + "Fahrenheit: ");                 //Line 8
        fahrenheit = console.nextInt();                    //Line 9
        System.out.println();                              //Line 10

        System.out.println("5 / 9 = " + 5 / 9
                          + ";  fahrenheit - 32 = "
                          + (fahrenheit - 32));            //Line 10a

        celsius = 5 / 9 * (fahrenheit - 32);               //Line 11

        System.out.println(fahrenheit + " degree F = "
                          + celsius + " degree C.");       //Line 12
    }                                                      //Line 13
}                                                          //Line 14
```

Sample Run: In this sample run, the user input is shaded.

```
Enter temperature in Fahrenheit: 110

5 / 9 = 0;  fahrenheit - 32 = 78
110 degree F = 0 degree C.
```

Let us look at the sample run. We see that the value of 5 / 9 = 0 and the value of `fahrenheit` - 32 = 78. Because `fahrenheit` = 110, the value of the expression `fahrenheit` - 32 is correct. Now let us look at the expression 5 / 9. The value of this expression is 0. Because both the operands, 5 and 9, of the operator / are integers, using integer division, the value of the expression is 0. That is, the value of the expression 5 / 9 = 0 is also calculated correctly. So by the precedence of the operators, the value of the expression 5 / 9 * (`fahrenheit` - 32) will always be 0 regardless of the value of `fahrenheit`. So the problem is in the integer division. There are two solutions to this problem. In the first solution, we can replace the expression 5 / 9 with 5.0 / 9. In this case, the value of the expression 5.0 / 9 * (`fahrenheit` - 32) will be a decimal number. Because `fahrenheit` and `celsius` are `int` variables, we can use the cast operators to convert this value to an integer, that is, we use the following expression:

```
celsius = (int) (5.0 / 9 * (fahrenheit - 32) + 0.5);
```

(Note that in the preceding expression we added 0.5 to round the number to the nearest integer.)

The revised program is:

```
import java.util.*;                                     //Line 1

public class LogicErrorCorrection                       //Line 2
{                                                       //Line 3
    static Scanner console = new Scanner(System.in);    //Line 4

    public static void main(String[] args)              //Line 5
    {                                                   //Line 4
        int fahrenheit;                                 //Line 6
        int celsius;                                    //Line 7

        System.out.print("Enter temperature in "
                        + "Fahrenheit: ");              //Line 8
        fahrenheit = console.nextInt();                 //Line 9
        System.out.println();                           //Line 10

        celsius = (int) (5.0 / 9 * (fahrenheit - 32)
                        + 0.5);                         //Line 11

        System.out.println(fahrenheit + " degree F = "
                        + celsius + " degree C.");      //Line 12
    }                                                   //Line 13
}                                                       //Line 14
```

Sample Run: In this sample run, the user input is shaded.

Enter temperature in Fahrenheit: `110`

110 degree F = 43 degree C.

As we can see, using temporary `println` statements, we were able to find the problem. After correcting the problem, the temporary `println` statements are removed.

The temperature conversion program contained logic errors not syntax errors. Using `println` statements to print the values of expressions and/or variables to see the results of calculation is an effective way to find and correct logic errors.

QUICK REVIEW

1. A reference variable is a variable that stores the address of a memory space.
2. In Java, all variables declared using a `class` are reference variables.
3. A reference variable does not directly store data in its memory space. It stores the address of the memory space where the actual data is stored.
4. Class objects are instances of that `class`.
5. Using the operator `new` to create a `class` object is called instantiating an object of that `class`.

6. To use a predefined method in a program, you need to know the name of the `class` containing the method (unless the class, such as the `class` `String`, is automatically imported) and the name of the `package` containing the `class`, and then you need to import the `class` into the program. In addition, you need to know the name of the method, the number of parameters the method takes, and the type of each parameter. You must also be aware of the method's return type or, loosely speaking, what the method produces.

7. In Java, the dot (.) is called the member access operator. The dot separates the `class` name from the member, or method, name. Dot notation is also used when a reference variable of a `class` type accesses a member of that `class`.

8. The `class` `String` is used to process strings.

9. The assignment operator is defined for the `class` `String`.

10. The method `substring` of the `class` `String` returns a substring from another string.

11. The `class` `String` contains many other useful methods, such as: `charAt`, `indexOf`, `concat`, `length`, `replace`, `toLowerCase`, and `toUpperCase`.

12. You can use the method `printf` to format the output in a specific manner.

13. A format specifier for general, character, and numeric types has the following syntax:

    `%[argument_index$][flags][width][.precision]conversion`

    The expressions in square brackets are optional. The required `conversion` is a character indicating how the argument should be formatted.

14. The method `printf` is available in Java 5.0 and its higher versions.

15. In a format specifier, using the option `width` you can also specify the number of columns to be used to output the value of an expression. The (*default*) output is right justified.

16. In a format specifier, if the number of columns in the option `width` is less than the number of columns required to output the value of the expression, the output is expanded to the required number of columns. That is, the output is not truncated.

17. To force the output to be *left* justified, you use the format specifier flag. If the flag is set to `'-'`, then the output of the result is left justified.

18. A numeric string consists of an integer or a decimal number with an optional minus sign.

19. To convert a numeric integer string into an integer, you use the expression:

    `Integer.parseInt(strExpression)`

    where `strExpression` is an expression containing a numeric integer string.

20. To convert a numeric decimal string into a `double` value, you use the expression:

```
Double.parseDouble(strExpression)
```

where `strExpression` is an expression containing a numeric string.

21. The method `showInputDialog` of the `class` `JOptionPane` is used to create an input dialog box.

22. The method `showMessageDialog` of the `class` `JOptionPane` is used to create an output message dialog box.

23. The `class` `JOptionPane` is contained in the `package` `javax.swing`.

24. If a program uses input and output dialog boxes, it must also use the statement:

```
System.exit(0);
```

25. To format a floating-point number to a specific number of decimal places, you can use the `String` method `format`.

26. To input data from a file, you use the `class`es `Scanner` and `FileReader`; to send output to a file, you use the `class` `PrintWriter`.

27. File I/O is a four-step process: (i) import the necessary classes from the `package`s `java.util` and `java.io` into the program; (ii) create and associate the appropriate objects with the input/output sources; (iii) use the appropriate methods associated with the objects created in Step ii to input/output the data; and (iv) close the file(s).

EXERCISES

1. Mark the following statements as true or false.

   a. A variable declared using a `class` is called an object.

   b. In the statement `x = console.nextInt() ;`, `x` must be a variable.

   c. You generate the newline character by pressing Enter (return) on the keyboard.

   d. The methods `printf` and `format` are used to format a decimal number to a specific number of decimal places.

2. How does a variable of a primitive type differ from a reference variable?

3. What is an object?

4. What does the operator `new` do?

5. Suppose that `str` is a `String` variable. Write a Java statement that uses the operator `new` to instantiate the object `str` and assign the string `"Java Programming"` to `str`.

6. What is garbage collection? Write the statement that instructs the Java system to (immediately) perform garbage collection.

7. Which package contains `class` `String`? If a program uses this class, explain why it is not necessary to explicitly import this class using the import statement.

8. Consider the following statements:

```
String str = "Going to the amusement park";
char ch;
int len;
int position;
```

   a. What value is stored in ch by the following statement?

   ```
   ch = str.charAt(0);
   ```

   b. What value is stored in ch by the following statement?

   ```
   ch = str.charAt(10);
   ```

   c. What value is stored in len by the following statement?

   ```
   len = str.length();
   ```

   d. What value is stored in position by the following statement?

   ```
   position = str.indexOf('t');
   ```

   e. What value is stored in position by the following statement?

   ```
   position = str.indexOf("park");
   ```

9. Assume the declaration in Exercise 8. What is the output of the following statements?

   a. `System.out.println(str.substring(0, 5));`

   b. `System.out.println(str.substring(13, 22));`

   c. `System.out.println(str.toUpperCase());`

   d. `System.out.println(str.toLowerCase());`

   e. `System.out.println(str.replace('t', '*'));`

10. Suppose that you have the following statements:

```
String str;
str = "Java programming: from problem analysis to program design";
```

   What is the value of the following expressions?

   a. `str.indexOf("analysis")`

   b. `str.substring(5, 16)`

   c. `str.startsWith("Java")`

   d. `str.startsWith("J")`

   e. `str.endsWith(".")`

11. Suppose that you have the following statements:

```
String str;
String str1 = "programming";
str = "Java programming: from problem analysis to program design";
```

   What is the value of the following expressions?

a. `str.regionMatches(6, str1, 0, str1.length())`

b. `str.regionMatches(true, 31, "Analysis", 0, 8)`

12. Which class contains the function `pow`? Write the statement to use the method `pow` to compute and output $6.5^{3.5}$.

13. Suppose that `name` is a variable of type `String`. Write the input statement to read and store the input `Brenda Clinton` in `name`. (Assume that the input is from the standard input device and it is the only input in a line; and `console` is a `Scanner` object initialized to the standard input device.)

14. a. What method is used to create an input dialog box?

b. What method is used to create an output dialog box?

c. What is the name of the `class` that contains the methods to create input and output dialog boxes?

d. What is the name of the `package` that contains the `class` described in part c?

15. What does the following statement do? (Assume that `scoreStr` is a `String` variable.)

`scoreStr = JOptionPane.showInputDialog("Enter the score:");`

16. Write a Java statement that creates the output dialog box in Figure 3-16.

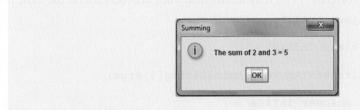

FIGURE 3-16   Figure for Exercise 16, Chapter 3

17. Write a Java statement that creates the output dialog box in Figure 3-17.

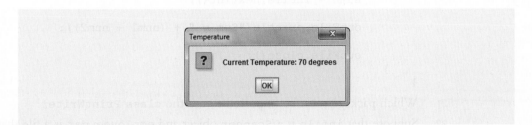

FIGURE 3-17   Figure for Exercise 17, Chapter 3

18. Consider the statements:

```
double x = 75.3987;
double y = 982.89764;
```

What is the output of the following statements?

a. `System.out.printf("%.2f %n", x);`

b. `System.out.printf("%.2f %n", y);`

c. `System.out.printf("%.3f %n", x);`

d. `System.out.printf("%.3f %n", y);`

19. Consider the statements:

```
int x, y;
char ch;
```

and the input:

```
46 A 49
```

Write the Java statements that would store 46 into x, 'A' into ch, and 49 into y.

20. The following program is supposed to read two numbers from a file named Ex20Input.txt, and write the sum of the numbers to a file named Ex20Output.dat. However, it fails to do so. Rewrite the program so that it performs correctly. (You may assume that both numbers are on the same line.)

```java
import java.util.*;

public class Ch3Ex20
{
    public static void main(String[] args)
    {
        Scanner inFile =
            new Scanner(new FileReader("Ex20Input.txt"));

        int num1, num2;

        num1 = inFile.nextInt();
        num2 = inFile.nextInt();

        outFile.println("Sum = " + (num1 + num2));

        outFile.close();
    }
}
```

21. Which package must be imported to use the **class** PrintWriter?

22. Suppose that infile is a Scanner object and employee.dat is a file that contains employees' information. Write the Java statement that opens this file using the variable infile.

23. Suppose that `infile` is a `Scanner` object associated with the file that contains the following data: 27306 savings 7503.35. Write the Java statements that read and store the first input in the `int` variable `acctNumber`, the second input in the `String` variable `accountType`, and the third input in the `double` variable `balance`.

24. Suppose that you have the following statements:

```
PrintWriter outfile;
double distance = 375;
double speed = 58;
double travelTime;
```

Write Java statements to do the following:

a. Open the file `travel.dat` using the variable `outfile`.

b. Write the values of the variables `distance` and `speed`, to two decimal places, in the file `travel.dat`.

c. Calculate and write the `travelTime`, to two decimal places, in the file `travel.dat`.

25. A program reads data from a file called `inputFile.dat` and, after doing some calculations, writes the results to a file called `outFile.dat`. Answer the following questions:

a. After the program executes, what are the contents of the file `inputFile.dat`?

b. After the program executes, what are the contents of the file `outFile.dat` if this file was empty before the program executed?

c. After the program executes, what are the contents of the file `outFile.dat` if this file contained 100 numbers before the program executed?

d. What would happen if the file `outFile.dat` did not exist before the program executed?

PROGRAMMING EXERCISES

1. Consider the following incomplete Java program:

```
public class Ch3_PrExercise1
{
    public static void main(String[] args)
    {
        .
        .
        .
    }
}
```

a.   Write Java statements that import the classes Scanner, FileReader, and PrintWriter from the packages java.util and java.io.

b.   Write statements that declare inFile to be a reference variable of type Scanner and outFile to be a reference variable of type PrintWriter.

c.   The program will read data from the file inData.txt and write output to the file outData.dat. Write statements to open both these files, associate inFile with inData.txt, and associate outFile with outData.dat.

d.   Suppose that the file inData.txt contains the following data:

```
10.20 5.35
15.6
Randy Gill 31
18500 3.5
A
```

The numbers in the first line represent the length and width, respectively, of a rectangle. The number in the second line represents the radius of a circle. The third line contains the first name, last name, and the age of a person. The first number in the fourth line is the savings account balance at the beginning of the month and the second number is the interest rate per year. (Assume that $\pi = 3.1416$.) The fifth line contains an uppercase letter between A and Y (inclusive). Write statements so that after the program executes, the contents of the file outData.txt are as shown below. If necessary, declare additional variables. Your statements should be general enough so that if the content of the input file changes and the program is run again (without editing and recompiling), it outputs the appropriate results.

```
Rectangle:
Length = 10.20, width = 5.35, area = 54.57, parameter = 31.10

Circle:
Radius = 15.60, area = 764.54, circumference = 98.02

Name: Randy Gill, age: 31
Beginning balance = $18500.00, interest rate = 3.50
Balance at the end of the month = $18553.96

The character that comes after A in the ASCII set is B
```

e.   Write the statement that closes the output file.

f.   Write a Java application program that tests the Java statements that you wrote in parts a–e.

2.   Consider the following program in which the statements are in the incorrect order. Rearrange the statements so that the program prompts the user to input the height and the radius of the base of a cylinder, and outputs the volume and surface area of the cylinder. Also modify the relevant output statements to format the output to two decimal places.

```
public class Ch3_PrExercise2
{
    public static void main(String[] args)
    {
        System.out.print("Enter the height of the cylinder: ");
        radius = console.nextDouble();
        System.out.println();

        static Scanner console = new Scanner(System.in);

        System.out.println("Volume of the cylinder = "
                            + PI * Math.pow(radius, 2.0) * height);

        System.out.print("Enter the radius of the base of the "
                         + " cylinder: ");
        height = console.nextDouble();
        System.out.println();

        double height;
        double radius;

        System.out.println("Surface area: "
                            + (2 * PI * Math.pow(radius, 2.0))
                            + (2 * PI * radius * height));
        static final double PI = 3.14159;
    }
}
import java.util.*;
```

3. Write a program that prompts the user to enter the weight of a person in kilograms and outputs the equivalent weight in pounds. Output both the weights rounded to two decimal places. (Note that 1 kilogram = 2.2 pounds.) Format your output with two decimal places.

4. During each summer John and Jessica grow vegetables in their back yard and buy seeds and fertilizer from a local nursery. The nursery carries different types of vegetable fertilizers in various bag sizes. When buying a particular fertilizer, they want to know the price of the fertilizer per pound and the cost of fertilizing per square foot. The following program prompts the user to enter the size of the fertilizer bag, in pounds, the cost of the bag, and the area, in square feet, that can be covered by the bag. The program should output the desired result. However, the program contains logic errors. Find and correct the logic errors so that the program works properly.

```
//Logic errors.

import java.util.*;

public class Ch3_PrExercise4
```

```
{
    static Scanner console = new Scanner(System.in);

    public static void main(String[] args)
    {
        double cost;
        double area;

        double bagSize;

        System.out.print("Enter the amount of fertilizer, "
                         + "in pounds, in one bag: ");
        bagSize = console.nextDouble();
        System.out.println();

        System.out.print("Enter the cost of the " + bagSize
                         + " pound fertilizer bag: ");
        cost = console.nextDouble();
        System.out.println();

        System.out.print("Enter the area, in square feet, that "
                         + "can be fertilized by one bag: ");
        area = console.nextDouble();
        System.out.println();

        System.out.printf("The cost of the fertilizer per pound is: "
                         + "$%.2f%n", bagSize / cost);
        System.out.printf("The cost of fertilizing per square "
                         + "foot is: $%.4f%n", area / cost);
    }
}
```

5. The manager of a football stadium wants you to write a program that calculates the total ticket sales after each game. There are four types of tickets—box, sideline, premium, and general admission. After each game, data is stored in a file in the following form:

    ticketPrice   numberOfTicketsSold
    .
    .
    .

Sample data are shown below:

    250 5750
    100 28000
    50 35750
    25 18750

The first line indicates that the box ticket price is $250 and that 5750 tickets were sold at that price. Output the number of tickets sold and the total sale amount. Format your output with two decimal places.

6. Write a program that calculates and prints the monthly paycheck for an employee. The net pay is calculated after taking the following deductions:

Federal Income Tax:	15%
State Tax:	3.5%
Social Security Tax:	5.75%
Medicare/Medicaid Tax:	2.75%
Pension Plan:	5%
Health Insurance:	$75.00

Your program should prompt the user to input the gross amount and the employee name. The output will be stored in a file. Format your output to have two decimal places. A sample output follows:

```
Bill Robinson
Gross Amount:              $ 3575.00
Federal Tax:               $  536.25
State Tax:                 $  125.13
Social Security Tax:       $  205.56
Medicare/Medicaid Tax: $     98.31
Pension Plan:              $  178.75
Health Insurance:          $   75.00
Net Pay:                   $ 2356.00
```

7. Three employees in a company are up for a special pay increase. You are given a file, say Ch3_Ex7Data.txt, with the following data:

```
Miller Andrew 65789.87 5
Green Sheila 75892.56 6
Sethi Amit 74900.50 6.1
```

Each input line consists of an employee's last name, first name, current salary, and percent pay increase. For example, in the first input line, the last name of the employee is Miller, the first name is Andrew, the current salary is 65789.87, and the pay increase is 5%. Write a program that reads data from the specified file and stores the output in the file Ch3_Ex7Output.dat. For each employee, the data must be output in the following form: firstName lastName updatedSalary. Format the output of decimal numbers to two decimal places.

8. Write a program that accepts as input the mass (in grams) and density (in grams per cubic centimeters), and outputs the volume of the object using the formula: *density = mass / volume*. Format your output to two decimal places.

CHAPTER 4

CONTROL STRUCTURES I: SELECTION

Chapter 2 defined a program as a sequence of statements whose objective is to accomplish some task. The programs you have examined so far have been simple and straightforward. In executing programs, the computer starts at the first (executable) statement and executes the statements in order until it comes to the end. In this chapter and in Chapter 5, you will learn how to tell a computer that it does not have to follow a simple sequential order of statements; it can also make decisions and/or repeat certain statements over and over until certain conditions are met.

Control Structures

A computer can process a program in one of three ways:

- In **sequence**
- By making a selection or a choice, which is also called a **branch**
- By repetition, executing a statement over and over using a structure called a **loop**

These three types of program flow are shown in Figure 4-1. The programming examples in Chapters 2 and 3 show simple sequential programs. With such a program, the computer starts at the beginning and follows the statements in order. No decisions are made and there is no repetition.

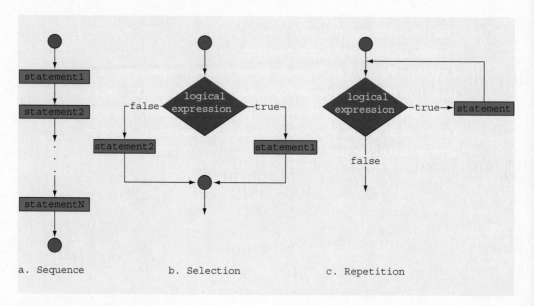

a. Sequence   b. Selection   c. Repetition

FIGURE 4-1   Flow of execution

Control structures provide alternatives to sequential program execution and are used to alter the flow of execution. The two most common control structures are selection and repetition. In **selection**, the program executes particular statements depending on one or more conditions. In **repetition**, the program repeats particular statements a certain number of times depending on one or more conditions. This chapter introduces selection (branching); Chapter 5 introduces repetition (looping).

Branch: Altering the flow of program execution by making a selection or choice.

Loop: Altering the flow of program execution by the repetition of statement(s).

Before you can learn about selection and repetition, you must understand the nature of conditional expressions and how to use them. Consider the following three statements (notice that these are not Java statements):

1. `if (score is greater than or equal to 90)`
   `    grade is A`

2. `if (hours worked are less than or equal to 40)`
   `        wages = rate * hours`
   `otherwise`
   `        wages = (rate * 40) + 1.5 * (rate * (hours - 40))`

3. `if (temperature is greater than 50 degrees and it is not`
   `        raining)`
   `        recommended activity is golfing`

These statements include conditional expressions. For example, in 1, the conditional expression is: `score is greater than or equal to 90`.

You can see that a statement such as `grade is A` is to be executed only if a certain condition is met.

A condition is met if it evaluates to `true`. For example, in statement 1:

`score is greater than or equal to 90`

is `true` if the value of `score` is greater than or equal to 90; it is `false` otherwise. For example, if the value of `score` is 95, the statement evaluates to `true`. Similarly, if the value of `score` is 86, the statement evaluates to `false`. So if the value of `score` is greater than or equal to 90, then the statement, `grade is A`, executes.

It is useful for the computer to be able to recognize expressions, such as `score is greater than or equal to 90`, to be `true` for appropriate values. Furthermore, in certain situations, the truth of a statement could depend on more than one condition. For example, in statement 3, both `temperature is greater than 50 degrees` and `it is not raining` must be `true` for the recommended activity to be `golfing`.

As you can see from these examples, to make decisions, the computer must be able to react to conditions that exist when the program executes. The next few sections discuss how to represent and evaluate conditional statements in Java.

4

Relational Operators

To make decisions, you must be able to express conditions and make comparisons. For example, the interest rate paid and service charges imposed on a checking account might depend on the balance at the end of the month. If the balance is less than some minimum balance, not only is the interest rate lower, but there is also usually a service charge. Therefore, to determine the interest rate, you must be able to state the minimum balance (a condition) and compare the account balance with the minimum balance. The premium on an insurance policy is also determined by determining conditions and making comparisons. For example, to determine an insurance premium, you must be able to check the smoking behavior of the policyholder. Nonsmokers (the condition) receive lower premiums than smokers. Both of these examples involve comparing items. Items can be compared in various ways. For example, you can compare items for equality or inequality. You can also determine whether one item is greater than another item, and so on.

An expression that has a value of either `true` or `false` is called a **logical (boolean) expression**. The values `true` and `false` are called **logical (boolean) values**. In Java, a condition is represented by a logical (boolean) expression; conditions are either `true` or `false`.

Logical (boolean) expression: An expression that has a value of either `true` or `false`.

Suppose i and j are integers. Consider the expression:

```
i > j
```

This is a logical expression. It will have the value `true` if the value of i is greater than the value of j; otherwise, it will have the value `false`. The symbol > is called a **relational operator** because the value of i > j is `true` only when the relationship "greater than" holds for i relative to j.

Relational operator: An operator that allows you to make comparisons in a program.

Java includes six relational operators that enable you to make comparisons. Table 4-1 lists the relational operators.

TABLE 4-1 Relational Operators in Java

Operator	Description
==	equal to
!=	not equal to
<	less than
<=	less than or equal to
>	greater than
>=	greater than or equal to

NOTE In Java, the symbol ==, which consists of two equal signs, is called the **equality operator**. Recall that the symbol = is called the assignment operator. The equality operator, ==, determines whether two expressions are equal, whereas the assignment operator, =, assigns the value of an expression to a variable.

Each of the relational operators is a binary operator; that is, it requires two operands. Because the result of a comparison is `true` or `false`, expressions using these operators evaluate to `true` or `false`.

Relational Operators and Primitive Data Types

You can use the relational operators with integral and floating-point primitive data types. For example, the following expressions use both integers and floating-point numbers:

Expression	Meaning	Value
8 < 15	8 is less than 15	true
6 != 6	6 is not equal to 6	false
2.5 > 5.8	2.5 is greater than 5.8	false
5.9 <= 7.5	5.9 is less than or equal to 7.5	true

For `char` values, whether an expression using relational operators evaluates to `true` or `false` depends on the collating sequence of the Unicode character set. Table 4-2 gives the collating sequence (Unicode value as a decimal integer) of some of the characters in the character set.

TABLE 4-2 Some Characters of the Unicode Character Set and their Unicode Value as a Decimal Integer

Unicode Value	Character	Unicode Value	Character	Unicode Value	Character	Unicode Value	Character
32	' '	61	=	81	Q	105	i
33	!	62	>	82	R	106	j
34	"	65	A	83	S	107	k
42	*	66	B	84	T	108	l
43	+	67	C	85	U	109	m
45	–	68	D	86	V	110	n
47	/	69	E	87	W	111	o
48	0	70	F	88	X	112	p

TABLE 4-2 Some Characters of the Unicode Character Set and their Unicode Value as a Decimal Integer (continued)

Unicode Value	Character	Unicode Value	Character	Unicode Value	Character	Unicode Value	Character
49	9	71	G	89	Y	113	q
50	2	72	H	90	Z	114	r
51	3	73	I	97	a	115	s
52	4	74	J	98	b	116	t
53	5	75	K	99	c	117	u
54	6	76	L	100	d	118	v
55	7	77	M	101	e	119	w
56	8	78	N	102	f	120	x
57	9	79	O	103	g	121	y
60	<	80	P	104	h	122	z

The first 128 characters of the Unicode character set are described in Appendix C. Table 4-3 shows how expressions using the Unicode character set are evaluated.

TABLE 4-3 Evaluating Expressions Using Relational Operators and the Unicode (ASCII) Collating Sequence

Expression	Value of the Expression	Explanation
`' ' < 'a'`	true	The Unicode value of `' '` is 32, and the Unicode value of `'a'` is 97. Because 32 < 97 is `true`, it follows that `' ' < 'a'` is `true`.
`'R' > 'T'`	false	The Unicode value of `'R'` is 82, and the Unicode value of `'T'` is 84. Because 82 > 84 is `false`, it follows that `'R' > 'T'` is `false`.
`'+' < '*'`	false	The Unicode value of `'+'` is 43, and the Unicode value of `'*'` is 42. Because 43 < 42 is `false`, it follows that `'+' < '*'` is `false`.
`'6' <= '>'`	true	The Unicode value of `'6'` is 54, and the Unicode value of `'>'` is 62. Because 54 <= 62 is `true`, it follows that `'6' <= '>'` is `true`.

NOTE Consider the following expression:

`8 < '5'`

You might think that 8 is being compared with 5. This is not the case. Here, the integer 8 is being compared with the character 5. That is, 8 is being compared with the Unicode collating sequence of `'5'`, which is 53. The Java system uses implicit type conversion, changes `'5'` to 53, and compares 8 with 53. Therefore, the expression `8 < '5'` always evaluates to `true`. However, the expression 8 < 5 always evaluates to `false`. Note that `char` and `int` are of integral type and using explicit or implicit type conversion, values of `char` type can be converted to `int` type and vice versa.

4

Expressions such as 4 < 6 and `'R' > 'T'` are examples of logical (boolean) expressions. When Java evaluates a logical expression, it returns the `boolean` value `true` if the logical expression evaluates to `true`; it returns the `boolean` value `false` otherwise.

Logical (Boolean) Operators and Logical Expressions

This section describes how to form and evaluate logical expressions that are combinations of other logical expressions. **Logical (Boolean) operators** enable you to combine logical expressions. Java has three logical (boolean) operators, as shown in Table 4-4.

TABLE 4-4 Logical (Boolean) Operators in Java

Operator	Description
!	not
&&	and
||	or

Logical operators take only logical values as operands and yield only logical values as results. The operator ! is unary, so it has only one operand. The operators && and || are binary.

Table 4-5 shows that when you use the ! operator, `!true` is `false` and `!false` is `true`. Putting ! in front of a logical expression reverses the value of that logical expression. Table 4-5 is called the **truth table** of the operator !. Example 4-1 gives examples of the ! operator.

TABLE 4-5 ! (not) Operator

Expression	!(Expression)
true	false
false	true

EXAMPLE 4-1

Expression	Value	Explanation
!('A' > 'B')	true	Because 'A' > 'B' is false, !('A' > 'B') is true.
!(6 <= 7)	false	Because 6 <= 7 is true, !(6 <= 7) is false.

Table 4-6 defines the operator && (and). From this table, it follows that Expression1 && Expression2 is true if and only if both Expression1 and Expression2 are true; otherwise, Expression1 && Expression2 evaluates to false. Table 4-6 is called the **truth table** of the operator &&. Example 4-2 gives examples of the && operator.

TABLE 4-6 && (and) Operator

Expression1	Expression2	Expression1 && Expression2
true	true	true
true	false	false
false	true	false
false	false	false

EXAMPLE 4-2

Expression	Value	Explanation
(14 >= 5) && ('A' < 'B')	true	Because (14 >= 5) is true, ('A' < 'B') is true, and true && true is true, the expression evaluates to true.
(24 >= 35) && ('A' < 'B')	false	Because (24 >= 35) is false, ('A' < 'B') is true, and false && true is false, the expression evaluates to false.

Table 4–7 defines the operator `||` (or). From this table, it follows that `Expression1 || Expression2` is `true` if and only if at least one of the expressions, `Expression1` or `Expression2`, is `true`; otherwise, `Expression1 || Expression2` evaluates to `false`. Table 4–7 is called the **truth table** of the operator `||`. Example 4-3 gives examples of the `||` operator.

TABLE 4-7   `||` (or) Operator

Expression1	Expression2	Expression1 `||` Expression2
true	true	true
true	false	true
false	true	true
false	false	false

EXAMPLE 4-3

Expression	Value	Explanation
`(14 >= 5) || ('A' > 'B')`	true	Because `(14 >= 5)` is `true`, `('A' > 'B')` is `false`, and `true || false` is `true`, the expression evaluates to `true`.
`(24 >= 35) || ('A' > 'B')`	false	Because `(24 >= 35)` is `false`, `('A' > 'B')` is `false`, and `false || false` is `false`, the expression evaluates to `false`.
`('A' <= 'a') || (7 != 7)`	true	Because `('A' <= 'a')` is `true`, `(7 != 7)` is `false`, and `true || false` is `true`, the expression evaluates to `true`.

Order of Precedence

To work with complex logical expressions, there must be some priority scheme for determining which operators to evaluate first. Because an expression might contain arithmetic, relational, and logical operators, as in the expression `5 + 3 <= 9 && 2 > 3`, an order of precedence for the Java operators must be established. Table 4-8 shows the order of precedence of some Java operators, including the arithmetic, relational, and logical operators. (See Appendix B for the precedence of all Java operators.)

TABLE 4-8 Precedence of Operators

Operators	Precedence
!, +, − (unary operators)	first (highest)
*, /, %	second
+, −	third
<, <=, >=, >	fourth
==, !=	fifth
&&	sixth
||	seventh
= (assignment operator)	last (lowest)

Using the precedence rules given in Table 4-8, in an expression, relational and logical operators are evaluated from left to right, and consequently the **associativity** of these operators is said to be from left to right.

You can insert parentheses into an expression to clarify its meaning or to affect the precedence.

EXAMPLE 4-4

Evaluate the following expression:

```
(17 < 4 * 3 + 5) || (8 * 2 == 4 * 4) && !(3 + 3 == 6)
```

Now:

```
      (17 < 4 * 3 + 5) || (8 * 2 == 4 * 4) && !(3 + 3 == 6)
 =    (17 < 12 + 5) || (16 == 16) && !(6 == 6)
 =    (17 < 17) || true && !(true)
 =    false || true && false
 =    false || false (because true && false is false)
 =    false
```

Therefore, the value of the original logical expression is `false`.

You can also use parentheses to override the precedence of operators. For example, in the expression:

```
(7 >= 8 || 'A' < 'B') && 5 * 4 == 20
```

the operator || evaluates before the operator &&; whereas, in the expression:

7 >= 8 || 'A' < 'B' && 5 * 4 == 20

the operator && evaluates before the operator ||.

Example 4-5 illustrates how logical expressions consisting of variables are evaluated.

EXAMPLE 4-5

Suppose you have the following declarations:

```
boolean found = true;
double hours = 45.30;
double overTime = 15.00;
int count = 20;
char ch = 'B';
```

Consider the following expressions:

Expression	Value / Explanation
!found	false Because found is true, !found is false.
hours > 40.00	true Because hours is 45.30 and 45.30 > 40.00 is true, the expression hours > 40.00 evaluates to true.
!found && (hours >= 0)	false !found is false; hours >= 0 is 45.30 >= 0 is true. Therefore, !found && (hours >= 0) is false && true, which evaluates to false.
!(found && (hours >= 0))	false Now, found && (hours >= 0) is true && true, which evaluates to true. Therefore, !(found && (hours >= 0)) is !true, which evaluates to false.
hours + overTime <= 75.00	true Because hours + overTime is 45.30 + 15.00 = 60.30 and 60.30 <= 75.00 is true, it follows that hours + overTime <= 75.00 evaluates to true.
(count >= 0) && (count <= 100)	true Now count is 20. Because 20 >= 0 is true, count >= 0 is true. Also, 20 <= 100 is true, so count <= 100 is true. Therefore, (count >= 0) && (count <= 100) is true && true, which evaluates to true.
('A' <= ch && ch <= 'Z')	true Here, ch is 'B'. Because 'A' <= 'B' is true, 'A' <= ch evaluates to true. Also, because 'B' <= 'Z' is true, ch <= 'Z' evaluates to true. Therefore, ('A' <= ch && ch <= 'Z') is true && true, which evaluates to true.

4

The following program evaluates and outputs the values of these logical expressions.

```
//Logical operators

public class LogicalOperators
{
    public static void main(String[] args)
    {
        boolean found = true;
        double hours = 45.30;
        double overTime = 15.00;
        int count = 20;
        char ch = 'B';

        System.out.printf("found = %b, hours = %.2f, overTime = "
                        + "%.2f, count = %2d, ch = %c%n%n",
                        found, hours, overTime, count, ch);

        System.out.println("!found evaluates to " + !found);
        System.out.println("hours > 40.00 evaluates to "
                        + (hours > 40.00));
        System.out.println("!found && (hours >= 0) evaluates to "
                        + (!found && (hours >= 0)));
        System.out.println("!(found && (hours >= 0)) evaluates to "
                        + (!(found && (hours >= 0))));
        System.out.println("hours + overTime <= 75.00 evaluates to "
                        + (hours + overTime <= 75.00));
        System.out.println("(count >= 0) && (count <= 100) "
                        + "evaluates to "
                        + ((count >= 0) && (count <= 100)));
        System.out.println("('A' <= ch && ch <= 'Z') evaluates to "
                        + ('A' <= ch && ch <= 'Z'));
    }
}
```

Sample Run:

```
found = true, hours = 45.30, overTime = 15.00, count = 20, ch = B

!found evaluates to false
hours > 40.00 evaluates to true
!found && (hours >= 0) evaluates to false
!(found && (hours >= 0)) evaluates to false
hours + overTime <= 75.00 evaluates to true
(count >= 0) && (count <= 100) evaluates to true
('A' <= ch && ch <= 'Z') evaluates to true
```

NOTE

Be careful when forming logical expressions. Some beginners make the following common mistake: Suppose that num is an `int` variable. Further suppose that you want to write a logical expression that evaluates to `true` if the value of num is between 0 and 10, including 0 and 10, and that evaluates to `false` otherwise. The following expression appears to represent a comparison of 0, num, and 10 that will yield the desired result:

```
0 <= num <= 10
```

This statement is *not* legal in Java and you will get a syntax error. This is because the associativity of the operator <= is from left to right. Therefore, the preceding expression is equivalent to:

```
(0 <= num) <= 10
```

The value of the expression (0 <= num) is either `true` or `false`. Because you cannot compare the `boolean` values `true` and `false` with other data types, the expression would result in a syntax error. A correct way to write this expression in Java is:

```
0 <= num && num <= 10
```

4

When creating a complex logical expression, take care to use the proper logical operators.

`boolean` Data Type and Logical (Boolean) Expressions

Recall that Java contains the built-in data type `boolean`, which has the logical (boolean) values `true` and `false`. Therefore, you can manipulate logical (boolean) expressions using the `boolean` data type. Also, recall that in Java, `boolean`, `true`, and `false` are reserved words.

Suppose that you have the following statements:

```
boolean legalAge;
int age;
```

The statement:

```
legalAge = true;
```

sets the value of the variable `legalAge` to `true`. The statement:

```
legalAge = (age >= 21);
```

assigns the value `true` to `legalAge` if the value of `age` is greater than or equal to 21. This statement assigns the value `false` to `legalAge` if the value of `age` is less than 21. For example, if the value of `age` is 25, the value assigned to `legalAge` is `true`. Similarly, if the value of `age` is 16, the value assigned to `legalAge` is `false`.

Selection: `if` and `if...else`

Although there are only two logical values, `true` and `false`, they are extremely useful because they permit programs to incorporate decision making that alters the processing flow. The remainder of this chapter discusses ways to incorporate decisions into a program. Java has three selection or branch control structures: `if` and `if...else` statements, and the `switch` structure. This section discusses how `if` and `if...else` statements can be used to create one-way selection, two-way selection, and multiple selections. The `switch` structure is discussed later in this chapter.

One-Way Selection

A bank wants to send a notice to a customer if her or his checking account balance falls below the required minimum balance. That is, if the balance is below the required minimum, the bank should send a notice to the customer; otherwise, it should do nothing. Similarly, if the policyholder of an insurance policy is a nonsmoker, the company wants to apply a 10% discount to the policy premium. Both of these examples involve one-way selection. In Java, one-way selections are incorporated using the `if` statement. The syntax of one-way selection is:

```
if (logical expression)
    statement
```

Note the elements of this syntax. It begins with the reserved word `if`, followed by a `logical expression` contained within parentheses, followed by a `statement`. The `logical expression` is also called a **condition**; it decides whether to execute the `statement` that follows it. If `logical expression` is `true`, the `statement` executes. If it is `false`, the `statement` does not execute and the computer goes on to the next statement in the program. The `statement` following the `logical expression` is sometimes called the **action statement**. (Note the indentation of the action `statement`. We have indented it four spaces to the right of the `if` statement in the previous line.)

Figure 4-2 shows the flow of execution of the `if` statement (one-way selection).

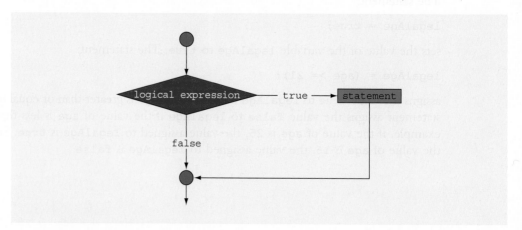

FIGURE 4-2 One-way selection

Next, we give various examples to show how an `if` statement works. We also show some common syntax and/or semantic errors that beginning programmers often make.

EXAMPLE 4-6

```
if (score >= 90)
    grade = 'A';
```

In this code, if the logical expression, `score >= 90`, evaluates to `true`, the assignment statement, `grade = 'A';`, executes. If `score >= 90` evaluates to `false`, the assignment statement, `grade = 'A';`, is skipped. For example, if the value of `score` is 95, the value assigned to the variable `grade` is A.

EXAMPLE 4-7

The following Java program finds the absolute value of an integer.

```
//Program to determine the absolute value of an integer.

import javax.swing.JOptionPane;

public class AbsoluteValue
{
    public static void main(String[] args)
    {
        int number;
        int temp;

        String numString;

        numString =
            JOptionPane.showInputDialog("Enter an integer:"); //Line 1

        number = Integer.parseInt(numString);                 //Line 2
        temp = number;                                        //Line 3

        if (number < 0)                                       //Line 4
            number = -number;                                 //Line 5

        JOptionPane.showMessageDialog(null,
                    "The absolute value of " + temp
                + " is " + number,
                    "Absolute Value",
                    JOptionPane.INFORMATION_MESSAGE);         //Line 6
        System.exit(0);
    }
}
```

Sample Run: Figure 4–3 shows a sample run of this program.

FIGURE 4-3 Sample run of Example 4-7

The statement in Line 1 displays the input dialog box and prompts the user to enter an integer. The entered number is stored as a string in numString. The statement in Line 2 uses the method parseInt of the class Integer, converts the value of numString into the number, and stores the number in the variable number. The statement in Line 3 copies the value of number into temp. The statement in Line 4 checks whether number is negative. If number is negative, the statement in Line 5 changes number to a positive number. The statement in Line 6 displays the message dialog box and shows the original number, stored in temp, and the absolute value of the number stored in number.

EXAMPLE 4-8

Consider the following statement:

```
if score >= 90
    grade = 'A';
```

This statement illustrates an incorrect version of an if statement. The parentheses around the logical expression are missing, which is a syntax error.

Putting a semicolon after the parentheses following the logical expression in an if statement (that is, before the statement) is a semantic error. If the semicolon immediately follows the closing parenthesis, the if statement will operate on the empty statement.

EXAMPLE 4-9

Consider the following Java statements:

```
if (score >= 90);          //Line 1
    grade = 'A';           //Line 2
```

This statement represents a one-way selection. Because there is a semicolon at the end of the logical expression in Line 1, the `if` statement terminates at Line 1, the action of the `if` statement is null, and the statement in Line 2 is not part of the `if` statement. The statement in Line 2 executes regardless of how the `if` statement evaluates. Note that the semicolon in Line 1 is a logical error and this can be hard to debug. So be careful when forming one-way selection.

Two-Way Selection

In the previous section, you learned how to implement one-way selections in a program. There are many situations in which you must choose between two alternatives. For example, if a part-time employee works overtime, the paycheck is calculated using the overtime payment formula; otherwise, the paycheck is calculated using the regular formula. This is an example of two-way selection. To choose between two alternatives—that is, to implement two-way selections—Java provides the `if...else` statement. Two-way selection uses the following syntax:

```
if (logical expression)
    statement1
else
    statement2
```

Take a moment to examine this syntax. It begins with the reserved word `if`, followed by a `logical expression` contained within parentheses, followed by a statement, followed by the reserved word `else`, followed by a second statement. Statements 1 and 2 can be any valid Java statements. In a two-way selection, if the value of the `logical expression` is `true`, then `statement1` executes. If the value of the `logical expression` is `false`, then `statement2` executes. Figure 4-4 shows the flow of execution of the `if...else` statement (two-way selection).

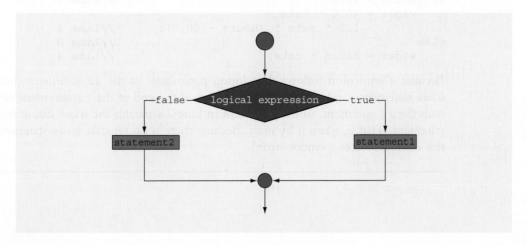

FIGURE 4-4 Two-way selection

EXAMPLE 4-10

Consider the following statements:

```
if (hours > 40.0)                                    //Line 1
    wages = 40.0 * rate +
            1.5 * rate * (hours - 40.0);             //Line 2
else                                                 //Line 3
    wages = hours * rate;                            //Line 4
```

If the value of the variable hours is greater than 40.0, then the wages include overtime payment. Suppose that hours is 50. The logical expression in the if statement in Line 1 evaluates to true, so the statement in Line 2 executes. On the other hand, if hours is 30, or any number less than or equal to 40, the logical expression in the if statement in Line 1 evaluates to false. In this case, the program skips the statement in Line 2 and executes the statement in Line 4—that is, the statement following the reserved word else executes.

In a two-way selection statement, putting a semicolon after the right parenthesis and before statement1 creates a syntax error. If the if statement ends with a semicolon, statement1 is no longer part of the if statement, and the else part of the if...else statement stands by itself. There is no stand-alone else statement in Java; that is, the else statement cannot be separated from the if statement. This also creates a syntax error.

EXAMPLE 4-11

The following statements show an example of a syntax error:

```
if (hours > 40.0);                       //Line 1
    wages = 40.0 * rate +
            1.5 * rate * (hours - 40.0); //Line 2
else                                     //Line 3
    wages = hours * rate;                //Line 4
```

Because a semicolon follows the closing parenthesis of the if statement (Line 1), the else statement stands alone. The semicolon at the end of the if statement (see Line 1) ends the if statement, so the statement in Line 2 separates the else clause from the if statement. That is, else is by itself. Because there is no separate else statement in Java, this code generates a syntax error.

EXAMPLE 4-12

The following program determines an employee's weekly wages. If the `hours` worked exceed `40`, then `wages` include overtime payment.

```java
//Weekly Wages

import java.util.*;

public class WeeklyWages
{
    static Scanner console = new Scanner(System.in);

    public static void main(String[] args)
    {
        double wages, rate, hours;                          //Line 1

        System.out.print("Line 2: Enter the working "
                        + "hours: ");                       //Line 2
        hours = console.nextDouble();                       //Line 3
        System.out.println();                               //Line 4

        System.out.print("Line 5: Enter the pay "
                        + "rate: ");                        //Line 5
        rate = console.nextDouble();                        //Line 6
        System.out.println();                               //Line 7

        if (hours > 40.0)                                   //Line 8
            wages = 40.0 * rate +
                    1.5 * rate * (hours - 40.0);            //Line 9
        else                                                //Line 10
            wages = hours * rate;                           //Line 11

        System.out.printf("Line 12: The wages are $%.2f %n",
                        wages);                             //Line 12
        System.out.println();                               //Line 13
    }
}
```

Sample Run: (In this sample run, the user input is shaded.)

Line 2: Enter working hours: `60`

Line 5: Enter pay rate: `10`

Line 12: The wages are $700

The statement in Line 1 declares the appropriate variables. The statement in Line 2 prompts the user to input the number of hours worked. The statement in Line 3 inputs and stores the working hours in the variable `hours`. The statement in Line 5 prompts the user to input the pay rate. The statement in Line 6 inputs and stores the pay rate into the variable `rate`. The statement in Line 8 checks whether the value of the variable `hours` is greater than `40.0`. If `hours` is greater than `40.0`, then the wages are calculated by the statement in Line 9, which includes overtime payment; otherwise, the wages are calculated by the statement in Line 11. The statement in Line 12 outputs the wages.

Let's now consider more examples of `if` statements and examine some of the common errors made by beginning programmers.

EXAMPLE 4-13

Consider the following statements:

```
if (score >= 90)                                        //Line 1
    grade = 'A';                                        //Line 2
    System.out.println("The grade is " + grade);        //Line 3
```

Here, you might think that because the statements in Lines 2 and 3 are aligned, both statements are the action statements of the `if` statement. However, this is not the case. The `if` statement acts on only one statement, which is `grade = 'A';`. The output statement executes regardless of whether `(score >= 90)` is `true` or `false`.

Example 4-14 illustrates another common mistake.

EXAMPLE 4-14

Consider the following statements:

```
if (score >= 60)
    System.out.println("Passing");
    System.out.println("Failing");
```

If the logical expression, `score >= 60`, evaluates to `false`, the output would be `Failing`. That is, this set of statements performs the same action as an `else` statement. It will execute the second output statement rather than the first. For example, if the value of `score` is 50, these statements will output the following line:

```
Failing
```

However, if the logical expression, `score >= 60`, evaluates to `true`, the program will write both statements, giving an unsatisfactory result. For example, if the value of `score` is 70, these statements will output the following lines:

```
Passing
Failing
```

The correct code to print `Passing` or `Failing`, depending on the value of `score`, is:

```java
if (score >= 60)
    System.out.println("Passing");
else
    System.out.println("Failing");
```

Compound (Block of) Statements

The `if` and `if...else` structures select only one statement at a time. Suppose, however, that you want to execute more than one statement if the `logical expression` in an `if` or `if...else` statement evaluates to `true`. To permit more complex statements, Java provides a structure called a **compound statement** or a **block** of statements. A compound statement takes the following form:

```
{
    statement1
    statement2
        .
        .
        .
    statementn
}
```

That is, a compound statement or block consists of a sequence of statements enclosed in braces. In an `if` or `if...else` structure, a compound statement functions as if it were a single statement. Thus, instead of having a simple two-way selection similar to the following code:

```java
if (age > 18)
    System.out.println("Eligible to vote.");
else
    System.out.println("Not eligible to vote.");
```

you could include compound statements, similar to the following code:

```java
if (age > 18)
{
    System.out.println("Eligible to vote.");
    System.out.println("No longer a minor.");
}
else
{
    System.out.println("Not eligible to vote.");
    System.out.println("Still a minor.");
}
```

The compound statement is useful and will be used in most of the ensuing structured statements in this chapter.

Multiple Selections: Nested `if`

In the previous sections, you learned how to implement one-way and two-way selections in a program. However, some problems require the implementation of more than two alternatives. For example, suppose that if the checking account balance is greater than or equal to $50000, the interest rate is 5%; if the balance is greater than or equal to $25000 and less than $50000, the interest rate is 4%; if the balance is greater than or equal to $1000 and less than $25000, the interest rate is 3%; otherwise, the interest rate is 0%. This particular problem has four alternatives—that is, multiple selection paths. You can include multiple selection paths in a program by using an `if...else` structure—if the action statement itself is an `if` or `if...else` statement. When one control statement is located within another, it is said to be **nested**.

<hr/>

EXAMPLE 4-15

Suppose that `balance` and `interestRate` are variables of type `double`. The following statements determine the `interestRate` depending on the value of `balance`:

```
if (balance >= 50000.00)                        //Line 1
    interestRate = 0.05;                        //Line 2
else                                            //Line 3
    if (balance >= 25000.00)                    //Line 4
        interestRate = 0.04;                    //Line 5
    else                                        //Line 6
        if (balance >= 1000.00)                 //Line 7
            interestRate = 0.03;                //Line 8
        else                                    //Line 9
            interestRate = 0.00;                //Line 10
```

Suppose that the value of `balance` is 60000.00. Then, the expression `balance >= 50000.00` in Line 1 evaluates to `true` and the statement in Line 2 executes. Now suppose the value of `balance` is 40000.00. Then, the expression `balance >= 50000.00` in Line 1 evaluates to `false`. So the `else` part at Line 3 executes. The statement part of this `else` is an `if...else` statement. Therefore, the expression `balance >= 25000.00` is evaluated, which evaluates to `true` and the statement in Line 5 executes. Note that the expression in Line 4 is evaluated only when the expression in Line 1 evaluates to `false`. The expression in Line 1 evaluates to `false` if `balance < 50000.00` and then the expression in Line 4 is evaluated. It follows that the expression in Line 4 determines if the value of `balance` is greater than or equal to 25000 and less than 50000. In other words, the expression in Line 4 is equivalent to the expression `(balance >= 25000.00 && balance < 50000.00)`. The expression in Line 7 works the same way.

The statements in Example 4-15 illustrate how to incorporate multiple selections using a nested `if...else` structure.

A nested `if...else` structure presents an important question: How do you know which `else` is paired with which `if`? Recall that in Java there is no stand-alone `else` statement. Every `else` must be paired with an `if`. The rule to pair an `else` with an `if` is as follows:

Pairing an `else` with an `if`: In a nested `if` statement, Java associates an `else` with the most recent incomplete `if`—that is, the most recent `if` that has not been paired with an `else`.

Using this rule, in Example 4-15, the `else` in Line 3 is paired with the `if` in Line 1. The `else` in Line 6 is paired with the `if` in Line 4, and the `else` in Line 9 is paired with the `if` in Line 7.

To avoid excessive indentation, the code in Example 4-15 can be rewritten as follows:

```
if (balance >= 50000.00)                    //Line 1
    interestRate = 0.05;                    //Line 2
else if (balance >= 25000.00)               //Line 3
    interestRate = 0.04;                    //Line 4
else if (balance >= 1000.00)                //Line 5
    interestRate = 0.03;                    //Line 6
else                                        //Line 7
    interestRate = 0.00;                    //Line 8
```

EXAMPLE 4-16

Assume that `score` is a variable of type `int`. Based on the value of `score`, the following code determines the grade:

```
if (score >= 90)
    System.out.println("The grade is A");
else if (score >= 80)
    System.out.println("The grade is B");
else if (score >= 70)
    System.out.println("The grade is C");
else if (score >= 60)
    System.out.println("The grade is D");
else
    System.out.println("The grade is F");
```

The following examples will further help you see the various ways in which you can use nested `if` structures to implement multiple selection.

EXAMPLE 4-17

Assume that all variables are properly declared, and consider the following statements:

```
if (temperature >= 50)                                      //Line 1
    if (temperature >= 80)                                  //Line 2
        System.out.println("Good day for swimming.");  //Line 3
    else                                                    //Line 4
        System.out.println("Good day for golfing.");   //Line 5
else                                                        //Line 6
    System.out.println("Good day to play tennis.");    //Line 7
```

In this Java code, the `else` in Line 4 is paired with the `if` in Line 2, and the `else` in Line 6 is paired with the `if` in Line 1. Note that the `else` in Line 4 cannot be paired with the `if` in Line 1. If you pair the `else` in Line 4 with the `if` in Line 1, the `if` in Line 2 becomes the action statement part of the `if` in Line 1, leaving the `else` in Line 6 dangling. Also, the statements in Lines 2 though 5 form the statement part of the `if` in Line 1.

EXAMPLE 4-18

Assume that all variables are properly declared, and consider the following statements:

```
if (temperature >= 60)                                      //Line 1
    if (temperature >= 80)                                  //Line 2
        System.out.println("Good day for swimming.");  //Line 3
    else                                                    //Line 4
        System.out.println("Good day for golfing.");   //Line 5
```

In this code, the `else` in Line 4 is paired with the `if` in Line 2. Note that for the `else` in Line 4, the most recent incomplete `if` is the `if` in Line 2. In this code, the `if` in Line 1 has no `else` and is a one-way selection.

Comparing `if...else` Statements with a Series of `if` Statements

Consider the following Java program segments, both of which accomplish the same task:

(a)
```
if (month == 1)                           //Line 1
    System.out.println("January");    //Line 2
else if (month == 2)                      //Line 3
    System.out.println("February");   //Line 4
else if (month == 3)                      //Line 5
    System.out.println("March");      //Line 6
```

```
else if (month == 4)                           //Line 7
    System.out.println ("April");              //Line 8
else if (month == 5)                           //Line 9
    System.out.println ("May");                //Line 10
else if (month == 6)                           //Line 11
    System.out.println ("June");               //Line 12
```

```
(b)
if (month == 1)
    System.out.println ("January");
if (month == 2)
    System.out.println ("February");
if (month == 3)
    System.out.println ("March");
if (month == 4)
    System.out.println ("April");
if (month == 5)
    System.out.println ("May");
if (month == 6)
    System.out.println ("June");
```

Program segment (a) is written as a sequence of `if...else` statements; program segment (b) is written as a series of `if` statements. Both program segments accomplish the same thing. If month is 3, then both program segments output March. If month is 1, then in program segment (a), the expression in the `if` statement in Line 1 evaluates to `true`. The statement (in Line 2) associated with this `if` then executes. The rest of the structure, which is the `else` of this `if` statement, is skipped, and the remaining `if` statements are not evaluated. In program segment (b), the computer has to evaluate the logical expression in each `if` statement because there is no `else` statement. As a consequence, program segment (b) executes more slowly than does program segment (a).

Short-Circuit Evaluation

Logical expressions in Java are evaluated using an efficient algorithm. This algorithm is illustrated with the help of the following statements:

```
(x > y) || (x == 5)
(a == b) && (x >= 7)
```

In the first statement, the two operands of the operator `||` are the expressions `(x > y)` and `(x == 5)`. This expression evaluates to `true` if either the operand `(x > y)` is `true` or the operand `(x == 5)` is `true`. With **short-circuit evaluation**, the computer evaluates the logical expression from left to right. As soon as the value of the entire logical expression can be determined, the evaluation stops. For example, in the first statement, if the operand `(x > y)` evaluates to `true`, then the entire expression evaluates to `true` because `true || true` is `true` and `true || false` is `true`. Therefore, the value of the operand `(x == 5)` has no bearing on the final outcome.

Similarly, in the second statement, the two operands of the operator `&&` are `(a == b)` and `(x >= 7)`. Now, if the operand `(a == b)` evaluates to `false`, then the entire expression evaluates to `false` because `false && true` is `false` and `false && false` is `false`.

Short-circuit evaluation (of a logical expression): A process in which the computer evaluates a logical expression from left to right and stops as soon as the value of the expression is determined.

EXAMPLE 4-19

Consider the following expressions:

```
(age >= 21) || (x == 5)        //Line 1
(grade == 'A') && (x >= 7)     //Line 2
```

For the expression in Line 1, suppose that the value of `age` is 25. Because `(25 >= 21)` is `true` and the logical operator used in the expression is `||`, the expression evaluates to `true`. Because of short-circuit evaluation, the computer does not evaluate the expression `(x == 5)`. Similarly, for the expression in Line 2, suppose that the value of `grade` is `'B'`. Because `('A' == 'B')` is `false` and the logical operator used in the expression is `&&`, the expression evaluates to `false`. The computer does not evaluate `(x >= 7)`.

 NOTE   In Java, `&` and `|` are also operators. You can use the operator `&` in place of the operator `&&` in a logical expression. Similarly, you can use the operator `|` in place of the operator `||` in a logical expression. However, there is no short-circuit evaluation of the logical expressions if `&` is used in place of `&&` or `|` is used in place of `||`. For example, suppose that a and b are `int` variables, and a = 10 and b = 18. After the evaluation of the expression `(a > 10) && (b++ < 5)`, the value of b is still 18. This is because the expression a > 10 evaluates to `false`, and `false && false` is `false` as well as `false && true` is `false`, so using short-circuit evaluation the expression `(a > 10) && (b++ < 5)` evaluates to `false` and the expression `(b++ < 5)` does not get evaluated.

Comparing Floating-Point Numbers for Equality: A Precaution

Comparison of floating-point numbers for equality may not behave as you would expect. For example, consider the following program.

```java
public class FloatingPointNumbers
{
    public static void main(String[] args)
    {
        double x = 1.0;
        double y = 3.0 / 7.0 + 2.0 / 7.0 + 2.0 / 7.0;
```

```
        System.out.println("3.0 / 7.0 + 2.0 / 7.0 + 2.0 / 7.0 = "
                        + (3.0 / 7.0 + 2.0 / 7.0 + 2.0 / 7.0));

        System.out.println("x = " + x);
        System.out.println("y = " + y);

        if (x == y)
            System.out.println("x and y are the same.");
        else
            System.out.println("x and y are not the same.");

        if (Math.abs(x - y) < 0.000001)
            System.out.println("x and y are the same within the "
                + "tolerance 0.000001.");
        else
            System.out.println(" x and y are not the same within "
                            + "the tolerance 0.000001.");
    }
}
```

Sample Run:

```
3.0 / 7.0 + 2.0 / 7.0 + 2.0 / 7.0 = 0.9999999999999999
x = 1.0
y = 0.999999999999999
x and y are not the same.
x and y are the same within the tolerance 0.000001.
```

In this program, x is initialized to 1.0 and y is initialized to 3.0 / 7.0 + 2.0 / 7.0 + 2.0 / 7.0. Now because of rounding, as shown by the output, this expression evaluates to 0.99999999999999989. Therefore, the expression (x == y) evaluates to **false**. However, if you evaluate the expression 3.0 / 7.0 + 2.0 / 7.0 + 2.0 / 7.0 by hand using a paper and a pencil, you will get 3.0 / 7.0 + 2.0 / 7.0 + 2.0 / 7.0 = (3.0 + 2.0 + 2.0) / 7.0 = 7.0 / 7.0 = 1.0. That is, the value of y should be set to 1.0.

The preceding program and its output show that you should be careful when comparing floating-point numbers for equality. One way to check whether two floating-point numbers are equal is to check whether the absolute value of their difference is less than a certain tolerance. For example, suppose the tolerance is 0.000001. Then x and y are equal if the absolute value of (x - y) is less than 0.000001. To find the absolute value, you can use the function Math.abs of the class Math, as shown in the program. Therefore, the expression Math.abs(x - y) < 0.000001 determines whether the absolute value of (x - y) is less than 0.000001.

Conditional Operator (? :) (Optional)

Certain `if...else` statements can be written more concisely by using Java's conditional operator. The **conditional operator**, written as `? :`, is a **ternary operator**, which means that it takes three arguments. The syntax for using the conditional operator is:

```
expression1 ? expression2 : expression3
```

This type of statement is called a **conditional expression**. The conditional expression is evaluated as follows: If `expression1` evaluates to `true`, the result of the conditional expression is `expression2`; otherwise, the result of the conditional expression is `expression3`. Note that `expression1` is a logical expression.

Consider the following statements:

```
if (a >= b)
    max = a;
else
    max = b;
```

You can use the conditional operator to simplify the writing of this `if...else` statement as follows:

```
max = (a >= b) ? a : b;
```

DEBUGGING

Avoiding Bugs by Avoiding Partially Understood Concepts and Techniques

The debugging sections in Chapters 2 and 3 illustrated how to understand and fix syntax and logic errors. In this section, we will illustrate how to avoid bugs by avoiding partially understood concepts and techniques.

The programs that you have written until now should have illustrated that a small error such as omission of a semicolon at the end of a variable declaration or using a variable without properly declaring it can prevent a program from successfully compiling. Similarly, using a variable without properly initializing it can prevent a program from running correctly. Recall that the condition associated with an `if` statement must be enclosed in parentheses. Therefore, the following expression will result in a syntax error:

```
if score >= 90
```

Example 4-11 illustrates that an unintended semicolon following the condition of the following `if` statement:

```
if (hours > 40.0);
```

can prevent successful compilation or correct execution.

The approach you take to solve a problem must use concepts and techniques correctly; otherwise, your solution will be either incorrect or deficient. If you do not understand a concept or technique completely, don't use it until your understanding is complete. The problem of using partially understood concepts and techniques can be illustrated by the following program.

Suppose that we want to write a program that analyzes a student's GPA. If the GPA is greater than or equal to 3.9, the student makes the dean's honor list. If the GPA is less than 2.00, the student is sent a warning letter indicating that the GPA is below the graduation requirement. So consider the following program:

```java
//GPA program with bugs.

import java.util.*;                                         //Line 1

public class GPABugProg                                     //Line 2
{                                                           //Line 3
    static Scanner console = new Scanner(System.in);        //Line 4

    public static void main(String[] args)                  //Line 5
    {                                                       //Line 6
        double gpa;                                         //Line 7

        System.out.print("Enter the GPA: ");               //Line 8
        gpa = console.nextDouble();                         //Line 9
        System.out.println();                              //Line 10

        if (gpa >= 2.0)                                     //Line 11
            if (gpa >= 3.9)                                 //Line 12
                System.out.println("Dean\'s Honor List."); //Line 13
        else                                               //Line 14
            System.out.println("The GPA is below the "
                 + " graduation requirement. \nSee your   "
                 + "academic advisor.");                   //Line 15
    }                                                       //Line 16
}                                                           //Line 17
```

Sample Runs: (In these sample runs, the user input is shaded.)

Sample Run 1:

Enter the GPA: 3.91

Dean's Honor List.

Sample Run 2:

Enter the GPA: 3.8

The GPA is below the graduation requirement.
See your academic advisor.

Sample Run 3:

Enter the GPA: 1.95

4

Let's look at these sample runs. Clearly, the output in Sample Run 1 is correct. In Sample Run 2, the input is 3.8 and the output indicates that this GPA is below the graduation requirement. However, a student with a GPA of 3.8 would graduate with some type of honor, so the output in Sample Run 2 is incorrect. In Sample Run 3, the input is 1.95 and the output does not show any warning message. Therefore, the output in Sample Run 3 is also incorrect. It means that the if...else statement in Lines 11 to 15 is incorrect. Let us look at these statements:

```
if (gpa >= 2.0)                                        //Line 11
    if (gpa >= 3.9)                                    //Line 12
        System.out.println("Dean\'s Honor List.");     //Line 13
else                                                   //Line 14
    System.out.println("The GPA is below the "
        + " graduation requirement. \nSee your  "
        + "academic advisor.");                        //Line 15
```

Following the rule of pairing an else with an if, the else in Line 14 is paired with the if in Line 12. In other words, using the correct indentation, the code is:

```
if (gpa >= 2.0)                                        //Line 11
    if (gpa >= 3.9)                                    //Line 12
        System.out.println("Dean\'s Honor List.");     //Line 13
    else                                               //Line 14
        System.out.println("The GPA is below the "
            + " graduation requirement. \nSee your  "
            + "academic advisor.");                    //Line 15
```

Now we can see that the if statement in Line 11 is a one-way selection. Therefore, if the input number is less than 2.0, no action will take place, that is, no warning message will be printed. Now suppose the input is 3.8. Then the expression in Line 11 evaluates to true, so the expression in Line 12 is evaluated, which evaluate to false. This means the output statement in Line 13 executes, resulting in an unsatisfactory result.

In fact, the program should print the warning message only if the GPA is less than 2.0, and the message:

Dean's Honor List.

if the GPA is greater than or equal to 3.9.

To achieve that result, the else in Line 14 needs to be paired with the if in Line 11. To pair the else in Line 14 with the if in Line 11, you need to use a compound statement as follows:

```
if (gpa >= 2.0)                                             //Line 11
{                                                           //Line 12
    if (gpa >= 3.9)                                         //Line 13
        System.out.println("Dean\'s Honor List."); //Line 14
}                                                           //Line 15
else                                                        //Line 16
    System.out.println("The GPA is below the "
        + " graduation requirement. \nSee your  "
        + "academic advisor.");                             //Line 17
```

The correct program is as follows:

```
//GPA program without bugs.

import java.util.*;                                             //Line 1

public class GPABugProgCorrect                                  //Line 2
{                                                               //Line 3
    static Scanner console = new Scanner(System.in);            //Line 4

    public static void main(String[] args)                      //Line 5
    {                                                           //Line 6
        double gpa;                                             //Line 7

        System.out.print("Enter the GPA: ");                   //Line 8
        gpa = console.nextDouble();                            //Line 9
        System.out.println();                                  //Line 10

        if (gpa >= 2.0)                                         //Line 11
        {                                                       //Line 12
            if (gpa >= 3.9)                                    //Line 13
                System.out.println("Dean\'s Honor List.");    //Line 14
        }                                                       //Line 15
        else                                                    //Line 16
            System.out.println("The GPA is below the "
                + " graduation requirement. \nSee your   "
                + "academic advisor.");                        //Line 17
    }                                                           //Line 18

}                                                               //Line 19
```

Sample Runs: (In these sample runs, the user is shaded.)

Sample Run 1:

Enter the GPA: 3.91

Dean's Honor List.

Sample Run 2:

Enter the GPA: 3.8

Sample Run 3:

Enter the GPA: 1.95

The GPA is below the graduation requirement.
See your   academic advisor.

In cases such as this one, the general rule is that you cannot look inside a block (that is, inside the braces) to pair an `else` with an `if`. The `else` in Line 16 cannot be paired with the `if` in Line 13 because the `if` statement in Line 13 is enclosed within braces, and the `else` in Line 16 cannot look inside those braces. Therefore, the `else` in Line 16 is paired with the `if` in Line 11.

In this book, the Java programming concepts and techniques are presented in a logical order. When these concepts and techniques are learned one at a time in a logical order, they are simple enough to be understood completely. Understanding a concept or technique completely before using it will save you an enormous amount of debugging time.

Program Style and Form (Revisited): Indentation

In the section "Program Style and Form" of Chapter 2, we specified some guidelines to write programs. Now that we have started discussing control structures, in this section, we give some general guidelines to properly indent your program.

As you write programs, typos and errors are unavoidable. If your program is properly indented, you can spot and fix errors quickly as shown by several examples in this chapter. Typically, the IDE that you use will automatically indent your program. If for some reason your IDE does not indent your program, you can indent your program yourself.

Proper indentation can show the natural grouping of statements. You should insert a blank line between statements that are naturally separate. In this book, the statements inside braces, the statements of selection structures, an `if` statement within an `if` statement are all indented four spaces to the right. Throughout the book, we use four spaces of indentation for statements; we especially use indentation to show the level of a control structure within another control structure. You can also use four spaces for indentation.

There are two commonly used styles for placing braces. In this book, we place braces on a line by themselves. Also, matching left and right braces are in the same column, that is, they are the same number of spaces away from the left side of the program. This style of placing braces easily shows the grouping of the statements as well as matching left and right braces. You can also follow this style to place and indent braces.

In the second style of placing braces, the left brace need not be on a line by itself. Typically, for control structures, the left brace is placed after the last right parenthesis of the (logical) expression and the right brace is on a line by itself. This style might save some space. However, sometimes this style might not immediately show the grouping or the block of the statements.

No matter what style of indentation you use, you should be consistent within your programs and the indentation should show the structure of the program.

`switch` Structures

Recall that there are three selection, or branch, structures in Java. The two-selection structure, which is implemented with `if` and `if...else` statements, usually requires the evaluation of a (logical) expression. The third selection structure, which does not require the evaluation of a logical expression, is called a `switch` structure. Java's `switch` structure gives the computer the power to choose from many alternatives.

The general syntax of a `switch` statement is:

```
switch (expression)
{
case value1:
    statements1
    break;

case value2:
    statements2
    break;

        .
        .
        .
case valuen:
    statementsn
    break;

default:
    statements
}
```

In Java, `switch`, `case`, `break`, and `default` are reserved words. In a `switch` structure, the `expression` is evaluated first. The value of the `expression` is then used to perform the actions specified in the statements that follow the reserved word `case`. (Recall that, in a syntax template, the shading indicates an optional part of the definition.)

Although it need not be, the `expression` is usually an identifier. Whether it is an identifier or an expression, *the value of the identifier or the expression can only be of type* `int`, `byte`, `short`, or `char`. The `expression` is sometimes called the selector. Its value determines which statements are selected for execution. A particular `case` value must appear only once. One or more statements may follow a `case` label, so you do not need to use braces to turn multiple statements into a single compound statement. The `break` statement may or may not appear after each `statements1`, `statements2`, ..., `statementsn`. A `switch` structure may or may not have the `default` label. Figure 4-5 shows the flow of execution of a `switch` statement.

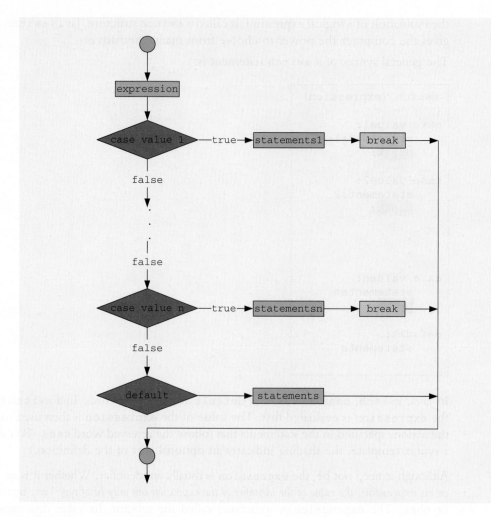

FIGURE 4-5 `switch` statement

A `switch` statement executes according to the following rules:

1. When the value of the `expression` is matched against a `case` value (also called a label), the statements execute until either a `break` statement is found or the end of the `switch` structure is reached.

2. If the value of the `expression` does not match any of the `case` values, the statements following the `default` label execute. If the `switch` structure has no `default` label, and if the value of the `expression` does not match any of the `case` values, the entire `switch` statement is skipped.

3. A `break` statement causes an immediate exit from the `switch` structure.

EXAMPLE 4-20

Consider the following statements (assume that `grade` is a `char` variable):

```
switch (grade)
{
case 'A':
   System.out.println("The grade is A.");
   break;

case 'B':
   System.out.println("The grade is B.");
   break;

case 'C':
   System.out.println("The grade is C.");
   break;

case 'D':
   System.out.println("The grade is D.");
   break;

case 'F':
   System.out.println("The grade is F.");
   break;

default:
   System.out.println("The grade is invalid.");
}
```

In this example, the expression in the `switch` statement is a variable identifier. The variable `grade` is of type `char`, which is an integral type. The valid values of `grade` are `'A'`, `'B'`, `'C'`, `'D'`, and `'F'`. Each `case` label specifies a different action to take, depending on the value of `grade`. If the value of `grade` is `'A'`, the output is:

```
The grade is A.
```

EXAMPLE 4-21

The following program illustrates the effect of the `break` statement. It asks the user to input a number between 0 and 10.

```java
//Effect of break statements in a switch structure

import java.util.*;

public class BreakStatementsInSwitch
{
    static Scanner console = new Scanner(System.in);

    public static void main(String[] args)
    {
        int num;

        System.out.print("Enter an integer between "
                         + "0 and 10: ");                    //Line 1
        num = console.nextInt();                             //Line 2
        System.out.println();                                //Line 3

        System.out.println("The number you entered "
                           + "is " + num);                   //Line 4

        switch (num)                                         //Line 5
        {
        case 0:                                              //Line 6
        case 1:                                              //Line 7
            System.out.print("Hello ");                      //Line 8
        case 2:                                              //Line 9
            System.out.print("there. ");                     //Line 10
        case 3:                                              //Line 11
            System.out.print("I am ");                       //Line 12
        case 4:                                              //Line 13
            System.out.println("Mickey.");                   //Line 14
            break;                                           //Line 15

        case 5:                                              //Line 16
            System.out.print("How ");                        //Line 17
        case 6:                                              //Line 18
        case 7:                                              //Line 19
        case 8:                                              //Line 20
            System.out.println("are you?");                  //Line 21
            break;                                           //Line 22

        case 9:                                              //Line 23
            break;                                           //Line 24

        case 10:                                             //Line 25
            System.out.println("Have a nice day.");          //Line 26
            break;                                           //Line 27
        default:                                             //Line 28
            System.out.println("Sorry the number is "
                               + "out of range.");           //Line 29
        }
```

```
        System.out.println("Out of switch "
                         + "structure.");              //Line 30
    }
}
```

Sample Runs

These outputs were obtained by executing the preceding program several times. In each of these outputs, the user input is shaded.

Sample Run 1:

```
Enter an integer between 0 and 10: 0

The number you entered is 0
Hello there. I am Mickey.
Out of switch structure.
```

Sample Run 2:

```
Enter an integer between 0 and 10: 3

The number you entered is 3
I am Mickey.
Out of switch structure.
```

Sample Run 3:

```
Enter an integer between 0 and 10: 4

The number you entered is 4
Mickey.
Out of switch structure.
```

Sample Run 4:

```
Enter an integer between 0 and 10: 7

The number you entered is 7
are you?
Out of switch structure.
```

Sample Run 5:

```
Enter an integer between 0 and 10: 9

The number you entered is 9
Out of switch structure.
```

A walk-through of this program, using certain values of the switch expression num, can help you understand how the break statement functions. If the value of num is 0, the value of the switch expression matches the case value 0. All statements following case 0: execute until a break statement appears.

The first **break** statement appears at Line 15, just before the **case** value of 5. Even though the value of the **switch** expression does not match any of the **case** values (1, 2, 3, or 4), the statements following these values execute.

When the value of the **switch** expression matches a **case** value, *all* statements execute until a **break** is encountered, and the program skips all **case** labels in between. Similarly, if the value of num is 3, it matches the **case** value of 3 and the statements following this label execute until the **break** statement is encountered at Line 15. If the value of num is 9, it matches the **case** value of 9. In this situation, the action is empty, because only the **break** statement, at Line 24, follows the **case** value of 9.

EXAMPLE 4-22

Although a **switch** structure's **case** values (labels) are limited, the **switch** statement **expression** can be as complex as necessary. Consider the following **switch** statement:

```
switch (score / 10)
{
case 0:
case 1:
case 2:
case 3:
case 4:
case 5:
    grade = 'F';
    break;

case 6:
    grade = 'D';
    break;

case 7:
    grade = 'C';
    break;

case 8:
    grade = 'B';
    break;

case 9:
case 10:
    grade = 'A';
    break;

default:
    System.out.println("Invalid test score.");
}
```

Assume that `score` is an `int` variable with values between 0 and 100. If `score` is 75, then `score / 10 = 75 / 10 = 7` and the grade assigned is `'C'`. If the value of `score` is between 0 and 59, then the grade is `'F'`. If `score` is between 0 and 59, `score / 10` is 0, 1, 2, 3, 4, or 5; each of these values corresponds to the grade `'F'`.

Therefore, in this `switch` structure, the action statements of `case 0`, `case 1`, `case 2`, `case 3`, `case 4`, and `case 5` are all the same. Rather than write the statement `grade = 'F';` followed by the `break` statement for each of the `case` values of 0, 1, 2, 3, 4, and 5, you can simplify the programming code by first specifying all of the case values (as shown in the preceding code) and then specifying the desired action statement. The `case` values of 9 and 10 follow similar conventions.

4

CHOOSING BETWEEN AN `if...else` AND A `switch` STRUCTURE

As you can see from the preceding examples, the `switch` statement is an elegant way to implement multiple selections. You will see a `switch` statement used in the programming examples in this chapter. There are no fixed rules that can be applied to decide whether to use an `if...else` structure or a `switch` structure to implement multiple selections, but you should remember the following consideration: If multiple selections involve a range of values, you should use either an `if...else` structure or a `switch` structure wherein you convert each range to a finite set of values.

For instance, in Example 4-22, the value of `grade` depends on the value of `score`. If `score` is between 0 and 59, `grade` is `'F'`. Because `score` is an `int` variable, 60 values correspond to the grade of `'F'`. If you list all 60 values as `case` values, the `switch` statement could be very long. However, dividing by 10 reduces these 60 values to only 6 values: 0, 1, 2, 3, 4, and 5.

If the range of values is infinite and you cannot reduce them to a set containing a finite number of values, you must use the `if...else` structure. For example, suppose that `score` is a `double` variable. The number of `double` values between 0 and 60 is (practically) infinite. However, you can use the expression `(int)(score) / 10` and reduce the infinite number of values to just six values.

EBUGGING

Avoiding Bugs by Avoiding Partially Understood Concepts and Techniques (Revisited)

Earlier in this chapter, we discussed how a partial understanding of a concept or technique can lead to errors in a program. In this section, we give another example to illustrate the problem of using partially understood concepts and techniques. In Example 4-22, we illustrated how to assign a grade based on a test score between 0 and 100. Next consider the following program that assigns a grade based on a test score.

```
//Grade program with bugs.
import java.util.*;                                      //Line 1

public class BugInSwitch                                 //Line 2
{                                                        //Line 3
    static Scanner console = new Scanner(System.in);     //Line 4

    public static void main(String[] args)               //Line 5
    {                                                    //Line 6
        int testScore;                                   //Line 7

        System.out.print("Enter the test score: ");      //Line 8
        testScore = console.nextInt();                   //Line 9
        System.out.println();                            //Line 10

        switch (testScore / 10)                          //Line 11
        {                                                //Line 12
        case 0:                                          //Line 13
        case 1:                                          //Line 14
        case 2:                                          //Line 15
        case 3:                                          //Line 16
        case 4:                                          //Line 17
        case 5:                                          //Line 18
            System.out.println("The grade is F.");       //Line 19
        case 6:                                          //Line 20
            System.out.println("The grade is D.");       //Line 21
        case 7:                                          //Line 22
            System.out.println("The grade is C.");       //LIne 23
        case 8:                                          //Line 24
            System.out.println("The grade is B.");       //Line 25
        case 9:                                          //Line 26
        case 10:                                         //Line 27
            System.out.println("The grade is A.");       //Line 28
        default:                                         //Line 29
            System.out.println("Invalid test score.");   //Line 30
        }                                                //Line 31
    }                                                    //Line 32
}                                                        //Line 33
```

Sample Runs: (In these sample runs, the user input is shaded.)

Sample Run 1:

Enter the test score: 110

Invalid test score.

Sample Run 2:

Enter the test score: -70

Invalid test score.

Sample Run 3:

```
Enter the test score: 75

The grade is C.
The grade is B.
The grade is A.
Invalid test score.
```

From these sample runs, it follows that if the value of `testScore` is less than 0 or greater than 100, the program produces correct results, but if the value of `testScore` is between 0 and 100, say 75, the program produces incorrect results. Can you see why?

As in Sample Run 3, suppose that the value of `testScore` is 75. Then `testScore % 10 = 7`, and this value matched the `case` label 7. So as we indented, it should print `The grade is C`. However, the output is:

```
The grade is C.
The grade is B.
The grade is A.
Invalid test score.
```

But why? Clearly, at most, only one `println` statement is associated with each `case` label. The problem is a result of having only a partial understanding of how the `switch` structure works. As we can see, the `switch` statement does not include any `break` statement. Therefore, after executing the statement(s) associated with the matching case label, execution continues with the statement(s) associated with the next case label, resulting in the printing of four unintended lines.

To output results correctly, the `switch` structure must include a `break` statement after each `println` statement, except the last `println` statement. We leave it as an exercise for you to modify this program so that it outputs correct results.

Once again, we can see that a partially understood concept can lead to serious errors in a program. Therefore, taking the time to understand each concept and technique completely will save you hours of debugging time.

PROGRAMMING EXAMPLE: Cable Company Billing

This programming example demonstrates a program that calculates a customer's bill for a local cable company. There are two types of customers: residential and business. There are two rates for calculating a cable bill: one for residential customers and one for business customers.

For residential customers, the following rates apply:

- Bill-processing fee: $4.50
- Basic service fee: $20.50

- Premium channels: $7.50 per channel
  For business customers, the following rates apply:
- Bill-processing fee: $15.00
- Basic service fee: $75.00 for the first 10 connections; $5.00 for each additional connection
- Premium channels: $50.00 per channel for any number of connections

The program should ask the user for an account number (an integer) and a customer code. Assume that R or r stands for a residential customer, and B or b stands for a business customer.

Input: Input to the program is the customer's account number, customer code, number of premium channels to which the customer subscribes, and, in the case of business customers, the number of basic service connections.

Output: Customer's account number and the billing amount.

PROBLEM ANALYSIS AND ALGORITHM DESIGN

The purpose of this program is to calculate and print the billing amount. To calculate the billing amount, you need to know the customer for whom the billing amount is calculated (whether the customer is residential or business) and the number of premium channels to which the customer subscribes. In the case of a business customer, you also need to know the number of basic service connections. Other data needed to calculate the bill, such as bill-processing fees and the cost of a premium channel, are known quantities. The program should print the billing amount to two decimal places, which is standard for monetary amounts. This problem analysis translates into the following algorithm:

1. Prompt the user for the account number and customer type.
2. Determine the number of premium channels and basic service connections, compute the bill, and print the bill based on the customer type:

   a. If the customer type is R or r:

      i. Prompt the user for the number of premium channels.
      ii. Compute the bill.
      iii. Print the bill.

   b. If the customer type is B or b:

      i. Prompt the user for the number of basic service connections and number of premium channels.
      ii. Compute the bill.
      iii. Print the bill.

VARIABLES

Because the program will ask the user to input the customer account number, customer code, number of premium channels, and number of basic service connections, you need variables to store all of this information. Also, because the program will calculate the billing amount, you need a variable to store the billing amount. Thus, the program needs at least the following variables to compute and print the bill:

```
int accountNumber;        //variable to store customer's
                          //account number
char customerType;        //variable to store customer code
int noOfPremChannels;     //variable to store number
                          //of premium channels to which
                          //the customer subscribes
int noOfBasicServConn;    //variable to store number of
                          //basic service connections
                          //to which the customer subscribes
double amountDue;         //variable to store the billing amount
```

NAMED
CONSTANTS

As you can see, the bill-processing fees, the cost of a basic service connection, and the cost of a premium channel are fixed; these values are needed to compute the bill. Although these values are constants in the program, they do change periodically. To simplify the process of modifying the program later, instead of using these values directly in the program, you should declare them as named constants. Based on the problem analysis, you need to declare the following named constants:

```
        //Named constants - residential customers
static final double R_BILL_PROC_FEE = 4.50;
static final double R_BASIC_SERV_COST = 20.50;
static final double R_COST_PREM_CHANNEL = 7.50;

        //Named constants - business customers
static final double B_BILL_PROC_FEE = 15.00;
static final double B_BASIC_SERV_COST = 75.00;
static final double B_BASIC_CONN_COST = 5.00;
static final double B_COST_PREM_CHANNEL = 50.00;
```

FORMULAS

The program uses a number of formulas to compute the billing amount. To compute the residential bill, you need to know only the number of premium channels to which the user subscribes. The following statement calculates the billing amount for a residential customer:

```
amountDue = R_BILL_PROC_FEE + R_BASIC_SERV_COST +
            noOfPremChannels * R_COST_PREM_CHANNEL;
```

To compute the business bill, you need to know the number of basic service connections and the number of premium channels to which the user subscribes. If the number of basic service connections is less than or equal to 10, the cost of the basic service connections is fixed. If the number of basic service connections exceeds

10, you must add the cost for each connection over 10. The following statement calculates the business billing amount:

```
if (noOfBasicServConn <= 10)
    amountDue =  B_BILL_PROC_FEE + B_BASIC_SERV_COST +
                 noOfPremChannels * B_COST_PREM_CHANNEL;
else
    amountDue =  B_BILL_PROC_FEE + B_BASIC_SERV_COST +
                 (noOfBasicServConn - 10) *
                 B_BASIC_CONN_COST +
                 noOfPremChannels * B_COST_PREM_CHANNEL;
```

MAIN ALGORITHM

Based on the preceding discussion, you can now write the main algorithm.

1. Prompt the user to enter the account number.
2. Get the customer account number.
3. Prompt the user to enter the customer code.
4. Get the customer code.
5. If the customer code is r or R:
    a. Prompt the user to enter the number of premium channels.
    b. Get the number of premium channels.
    c. Calculate the billing amount.
    d. Print the account number.
    e. Print the billing amount.
6. If the customer code is b or B:
    a. Prompt the user to enter the number of basic service connections.
    b. Get the number of basic service connections.
    c. Prompt the user to enter the number of premium channels.
    d. Get the number of premium channels.
    e. Calculate the billing amount.
    f. Print the account number.
    g. Print the billing amount.
7. If the customer code is something other than r, R, b, or B, output an error message.

For Steps 5 and 6, the program uses a `switch` statement to calculate the bill for the desired customer. (You can also use an `if...else` statement to implement Steps 5 and 6.)

COMPLETE PROGRAM LISTING

```java
//***********************************************************
// Author: D.S. Malik
//
// Program: Cable Company Billing
// This program calculates and prints a customer's bill for
// a local cable company. The program processes two types of
// customers: residential and business.
//***********************************************************

import java.util.*;

public class CableCompanyBilling
{
    static Scanner console = new Scanner(System.in);

        //Named constants - residential customers
    static final double R_BILL_PROC_FEE = 4.50;
    static final double R_BASIC_SERV_COST = 20.50;
    static final double R_COST_PREM_CHANNEL = 7.50;

      //Named constants - business customers
    static final double B_BILL_PROC_FEE = 15.00;
    static final double B_BASIC_SERV_COST = 75.00;
    static final double B_BASIC_CONN_COST = 5.00;
    static final double B_COST_PREM_CHANNEL = 50.00;

    public static void main(String[] args)
    {
          //Variable declaration
        int accountNumber;
        char customerType;
        int noOfPremChannels;
        int noOfBasicServConn;
        double amountDue;

        System.out.println("This program computes "
                         + "a cable bill.");

        System.out.print("Enter the account "
                       + "number: ");                    //Step 1
        accountNumber = console.nextInt();               //Step 2
        System.out.println();

        System.out.print("Enter the customer type: "
                       + "R or r (Residential), "
                       + "B or b(Business): ");           //Step 3
```

4

```
       customerType = console.next().charAt(0);        //Step 4
       System.out.println();

       switch (customerType)
       {
       case 'r':                                        //Step 5
       case 'R':
           System.out.print("Enter the number of "
                          + "premium channels: ");      //Step 5a
           noOfPremChannels = console.nextInt();        //Step 5b
           System.out.println();

           amountDue = R_BILL_PROC_FEE +                //Step 5c
                       R_BASIC_SERV_COST +
                       noOfPremChannels *
                       R_COST_PREM_CHANNEL;

           System.out.println("Account number = "
                          + accountNumber);             //Step 5d
           System.out.printf("Amount due = $%.2f %n",
                          amountDue);                   //Step 5e
           break;

       case 'b':                                        //Step 6
       case 'B':
           System.out.print("Enter the number of "
                          + "basic service "
                          + "connections: ");           //Step 6a
           noOfBasicServConn = console.nextInt();       //Step 6b
           System.out.println();

           System.out.print("Enter the number of "
                          + "premium channels: ");      //Step 6c
           noOfPremChannels = console.nextInt();        //Step 6d
           System.out.println();

           if (noOfBasicServConn <= 10)                 //Step 6e
               amountDue = B_BILL_PROC_FEE +
                           B_BASIC_SERV_COST +
                           noOfPremChannels *
                           B_COST_PREM_CHANNEL;
           else
               amountDue = B_BILL_PROC_FEE +
                           B_BASIC_SERV_COST +
                           (noOfBasicServConn - 10) *
                           B_BASIC_CONN_COST +
                           noOfPremChannels *
                           B_COST_PREM_CHANNEL;

           System.out.println("Account number = "
                          + accountNumber);             //Step 6f
```

```
            System.out.printf("Amount due = $%.2f %n",
                             amountDue);              //Step 6g
         break;
    default:                                         //Step 7
         System.out.println("Invalid customer type.");
    }//end switch
    }
}
```

Sample Run: (In this sample run, the user input is shaded.)

```
This program computes a cable bill.
Enter the account number: 12345

Enter the customer type: R or r (Residential), B or b (Business): b

Enter the number of basic service connections: 16

Enter the number of premium channels: 8

Account number = 12345
Amount due = $520.00
```

Comparing Strings

In Java, strings are compared character by character, starting with the first character and using the Unicode collating sequence. The character-by-character comparison continues until one of the following three conditions is met: a mismatch is found, the last characters have been compared and are equal, or one string is exhausted.

For example, the string `"Air"` is less than the string `"Big"` because the first character `'A'` of `"Air"` is less than the first character `'B'` of `"Big"`. The string `"Air"` is less than the string `"An"` because the first characters of `"Air"` and `"An"` are the same, but the second character `'i'` of `"Air"` is less than the second character `'n'` of `"An"`. The string `"Hello"` is less than the string `"hello"` because the first character `'H'` of `"Hello"` is less than the first character `'h'` of `"hello"`.

If two strings of different lengths are compared and the character-by-character comparison is equal through the last character of the shorter string, the shorter string is evaluated as less than the larger string. For example, the string `"Bill"` is less than the string `"Billy"` and the string `"Sun"` is less than the string `"Sunny"`.

The **class** `String` provides the method `compareTo` to compare objects of the **class** `String`. The syntax to use the method `compareTo` is:

```
str1.compareTo(str2)
```

where `str1` and `str2` are `String` variables. Moreover, `str2` can also be a `String` constant (literal). This expression returns an integer value as follows:

$$
\text{str1.compareTo(str2)} = \begin{cases} \text{an integer value less than 0 if string } \texttt{str1} \\ \quad \text{is less than string } \texttt{str2} \\ \text{0 if string } \texttt{str1} \text{ is equal to string } \texttt{str2} \\ \text{an integer value greater than 0 if string } \texttt{str1} \\ \quad \text{is greater than string } \texttt{str2} \end{cases}
$$

Consider the following statements:

```
String str1 = "Hello";
String str2 = "Hi";
String str3 = "Air";
String str4 = "Bill";
String str5 = "Bigger";
```

Using these variable declarations, Table 4-9 shows how the method `compareTo` works.

TABLE 4-9 Comparing Strings with the Method `compareTo`

Expression	Value	Explanation
`str1.compareTo(str2)`	< 0	`str1` = `"Hello"` and `str2` = `"Hi"`. The first character of `str1` and `str2` are the same, but the second character `'e'` of `str1` is less than the second character `'i'` of `str2`. Therefore, `str1.compareTo(str2)` < 0.
`str1.compareTo("Hen")`	< 0	`str1` = `"Hello"`. The first two characters of `str1` and `"Hen"` are the same, but the third character `'l'` of `str1` is less than the third character `'n'` of `"Hen"`. Therefore, `str1.compareTo("Hen")` < 0.
`str4.compareTo(str3)`	> 0	`str4` = `"Bill"` and `str3` = `"Air"`. The first character `'B'` of `str4` is greater than the first character `'A'` of `str3`. Therefore, `str4.compareTo(str3)` > 0.
`str1.compareTo("hello")`	< 0	`str1` = `"Hello"`. The first character `'H'` of `str1` is less than the first character `'h'` of `"hello"` because the Unicode value of `'H'` is 72, and the Unicode value of `'h'` is 104. Therefore, `str1.compareTo("hello")` < 0.

TABLE 4-9 Comparing Strings with the Method `compareTo` (continued)

Expression	Value	Explanation
`str2.compareTo("Hi")`	= 0	`str2` = `"Hi"`. The strings `str2` and `"Hi"` are of the same length and their corresponding characters are the same. Therefore, `str2.compareTo("Hi")` = 0.
`str4.compareTo("Billy")`	< 0	`str4` = `"Bill"` has four characters and `"Billy"` has five characters. Therefore, `str4` is the shorter string. All four characters of `str4` are the same as the corresponding first four characters of `"Billy"`, and `"Billy"` is the larger string. Therefore, `str4.compareTo("Billy")` < 0.
`str5.compareTo("Big")`	> 0	`str5` = `"Bigger"` has six characters and `"Big"` has three characters. Therefore, `str5` is the larger string. The first three characters of `str5` are the same as the corresponding first three characters of `"Big"`. Therefore, `str5.compareTo("Big")` > 0.
`str1.compareTo("Hello ")`	< 0	`str1` = `"Hello"` has five characters and `"Hello "` has six characters. Therefore, `str1` is the shorter string. All five characters of `str1` are the same as the corresponding first five characters of `"Hello "`, and `"Hello "` is the larger string. Therefore, `str1.compareTo("Hello ")` < 0.

The program in Example 4-23 evaluates the expressions in Table 4-9.

EXAMPLE 4-23

```
//The String method compareTo

public class StringComparison
{
    public static void main(String[] args)
```

```
        {
            String str1 = "Hello";                              //Line 1
            String str2 = "Hi";                                 //Line 2
            String str3 = "Air";                                //Line 3
            String str4 = "Bill";                               //Line 4
            String str5 = "Bigger";                             //Line 5

            System.out.println("Line 6: " +
                    "str1.compareTo(str2) evaluates to "
                    + str1.compareTo(str2));                    //Line 6

            System.out.println("Line 7: " +
                    "str1.compareTo(\"Hen\") evaluates to "
                    + str1.compareTo("Hen"));                   //Line 7

            System.out.println("Line 8: " +
                    "str4.compareTo(str3) evaluates to "
                    + str4.compareTo(str3));                    //Line 8

            System.out.println("Line 9: " +
                    "str1.compareTo(\"hello\") evaluates to "
                    + str1.compareTo("hello"));                 //Line 9

            System.out.println("Line 10: " +
                    "str2.compareTo(\"Hi\") evaluates to "
                    + str2.compareTo("Hi"));                    //Line 10

            System.out.println("Line 11: " +
                    "str4.compareTo(\"Billy\") evaluates to "
                    + str4.compareTo("Billy"));                 //Line 11

            System.out.println("Line 12: " +
                    "str5.compareTo(\"Big\") evaluates to "
                    + str5.compareTo("Big"));                   //Line 12

            System.out.println("Line 13: " +
                    "str1.compareTo(\"Hello \") evaluates to "
                    + str1.compareTo("Hello "));                //Line 13
        }
    }
```

Sample Run:

```
Line 6: str1.compareTo(str2) evaluates to -4
Line 7: str1.compareTo("Hen") evaluates to -2
Line 8: str4.compareTo(str3) evaluates to 1
Line 9: str1.compareTo("hello") evaluates to -32
Line 10: str2.compareTo("Hi") evaluates to 0
Line 11: str4.compareTo("Billy") evaluates to -1
Line 12: str5.compareTo("Big") evaluates to 3
Line 13: str1.compareTo("Hello ") evaluates to -1
```

Notice that the values, such as -4, -2, 1, and so on, printed in Lines 6 through 13 are the differences of the collating sequences of the first unmatched characters of the strings.

The only thing we need to know is whether the value is positive, negative, or zero. The output is self-explanatory.

The following example shows how to use strings in Boolean expressions as part of an `if` statement.

EXAMPLE 4-24

The following program assigns standard exemption depending on the filing status of a person.

```java
import java.util.*;

public class Example4_24
{
    static Scanner console = new Scanner(System.in);

    public static void main(String[] args)
    {
        String status1;
        String status2 = "";
        double standardExemption = 0.0;

        System.out.print("Enter the tax filing status: ");
        status1 = console.next();
        System.out.println();

        if (status1.compareTo("married") == 0)
        {
            System.out.print("Enter filing joint/separately: ");
            status2 = console.next();
            System.out.println();

            if (status2.compareTo("joint") == 0)
                standardExemption = 12000.00;
            else if (status2.compareTo("separately") == 0)
                standardExemption = 6000.00;
            else
                System.out.println("Invalid status.");
        }
        else if (status1.compareTo("single") == 0)
            standardExemption = 9000.00;
        else if (status1.compareTo("headHouseHold") == 0)
            standardExemption = 10000.00;
        else
            System.out.println("Invalid status.");

        System.out.println("Filing status: " + status1 + " " + status2);
        System.out.printf("Standard exemption: $%.2f %n",
                    standardExemption);
    }
}
```

4

Sample Run: (In this sample run, the user input is shaded.)

Enter the tax filing status: `married`

Enter filing joint/separately: `joint`

Filing status: married joint
Standard exemption: $12000.00

The preceding output is self-explanatory. The details are left as an exercise.

In addition to the method `compareTo`, you can also use the method `equals` of the `class` String to determine whether two String objects contain the same value. However, the method `equals` returns the value **true** or **false**. For example, the expression:

`str1.equals("Hello")`

evaluates to **true**, while the expression:

`str1.equals(str2)`

evaluates to **false**, where `str1` and `str2` are as defined in Example 4-26.

> **NOTE** You can apply the relational operators `==` and `!=` to variables of the String type, such as the variables `str1` and `str2`. However, when these operators are applied to these variables they compare the values of the variables, not the values of the String objects they point to. For example, suppose, as in Figure 4-6:
>
> ```
> str1 = "Hello";
> str2 = "Hi";
> ```

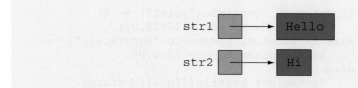

FIGURE 4-6 Variables `str1`, `str2`, and the objects to which they point

The expression (`str1 == str2`) determines whether the values of `str1` and `str2` are the same, that is, if `str1` and `str2` point to the same String object. Similarly, the expression (`str1 != str2`) determines whether the values of `str1` and `str2` are *not* the same, that is, if `str1` and `str2` do not point to the same String object.

Strings, the Assignment Operator, and the Operator new

Suppose that `str` is a `String` variable and we want to assign the string `"Sunny"` to `str`. As explained in Chapter 3, this can be accomplished by using the statement:

```
str = "Sunny";                //Line 1
```

or the statement:

```
str = new String("Sunny");    //Line 2
```

After the execution of the statement in Line 1 or Line 2, `str` will point to the `String` object with the value `"Sunny"`. Recall from Chapter 3 that the statement in Line 2 explicitly uses the operator `new`. Also recall that there is a slight difference in the way these statements execute. When the statement in Line 1 executes, the computer checks whether there already is a `String` object with the value `"Sunny"`; if so, then the address of that object is stored in `str`. On the other hand, when the statement in Line 2 executes, the computer will create a new `String` object with the value `"Sunny"` regardless of whether such a `String` object already exits. Let us further explain this concept.

Consider the following statements:

```
String str1 = "Hello";
String str2 = "Hello";
```

When the first statement executes, a `String` object with the value `"Hello"` is created and its address is assigned to `str1`. When the second statement executes, because there already exists a `String` object with the value `"Hello"`, the address of this `String` object is stored in `str2` (see Figure 4-7).

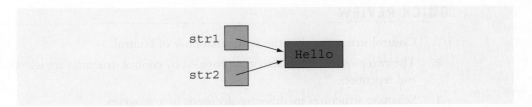

FIGURE 4-7 Variables `str1`, `str2`, and the objects to which they point

Therefore, if you evaluate the expression (`str1 == str2`) after these statements, this expression evaluates to `true`. Moreover, here the expression `str1.equals(str2)` also evaluates to `true`.

If you later assigned a different string, say, `"Cloudy"`, to `str2`, then if no `String` object exists with the value `"Cloudy"`, a `String` object with this value is created and its address is stored in `str2`. However, `str1` would still point to the string `"Hello"`. In other words, changing the value of the string `str2` does not change the value of the string `str1`.

Next, consider the following statements:

```
String str3 = new String("Hello");
String str4 = new String("Hello");
```

When the first statement executes, a `String` object with the value `"Hello"` is created and its address is assigned to `str3`. When the second statement executes, another `String` object with the value `"Hello"` is created and its address is assigned to `str4` (see Figure 4-8).

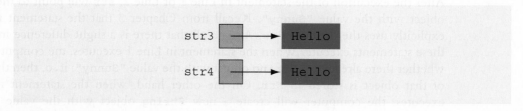

FIGURE 4-8 Variables `str3`, `str4`, and the objects to which they point

It follows that the expression `(str3 == str4)` evaluates to `false`. However, the expression `str3.equals(str4)` evaluates to `true`.

 NOTE The program `StringObjectsAndTheOprNew.java`, which shows the effect of the preceding statements, can be found in the Additional Student Files folder at *www.cengagebrain.com*.

QUICK REVIEW

1. Control structures alter the sequential flow of control.

2. The two most common activities provided by control structures are selection and repetition.

3. Selection structures incorporate decisions in a program.

4. The Java relational operators are `==` (equality), `!=` (not equal to), `<` (less than), `<=` (less than or equal to), `>` (greater than), and `>=` (greater than or equal to).

5. Including a space within the relational operators `==`, `<=`, `>=`, and `!=` creates a syntax error. (For example, `= =` will create a syntax error.)

6. Characters are compared using the collating sequence of the Unicode character set.

7. Logical (boolean) expressions evaluate to `true` or `false`.

8. In Java, `boolean` variables are used to store the value of a logical expression.

9. In Java, the logical operators are ! (not), && (and), and || (or).

10. In Java, there are three selection structures.

11. One-way selection takes the following form:

    ```
    if (logical expression)
        statement
    ```

    If logical expression is true, then the statement executes; otherwise, the computer executes the statement following the if statement.

12. Two-way selection takes the following form:

    ```
    if (logical expression)
        statement1
    else
        statement2
    ```

    If logical expression is true, then statement1 executes; otherwise, statement2 executes.

13. The expression in an if or if...else structure is a logical expression.

14. Including a semicolon before the statement in a one-way selection creates a semantic error. In this case, the action of the if statement is empty.

15. Including a semicolon before statement1 in a two-way selection creates a syntax error.

16. There is no stand-alone else statement in Java. Every else has a related if.

17. An else is paired with the most recent if that has not been paired with any other else.

18. A sequence of statements enclosed between braces, { and }, is called a compound statement or block of statements. A compound statement is treated as a single statement.

19. A switch structure is used to handle multiple selections.

20. The expression in a switch statement must evaluate to an integral value.

21. A switch statement executes according to the following rules:

    a. When the value of the expression is matched against a case value, the statements execute until either a break statement is found or the end of the switch structure is reached.

    b. If the value of the expression does not match any of the case values, the statements following the default label execute. If the switch structure has no default label, and if the value of the expression does not match any of the case values, the entire switch statement is skipped.

    c. A break statement causes an immediate exit from the switch structure.

22. To compare strings, you use the method compareTo of the class String.

4

23. To use the method `compareTo`, you use the expression:

`str1.compareTo(str2)`

where `str1` and `str2` are `String` variables. Moreover, `str2` can also be a `String` constant (literal). The expression `str1.compareTo(str2)` evaluates as follows:

$$str1.compareTo(str2) = \begin{cases} \text{an integer value less than 0 if string } str1 \\ \quad \text{is less than string } str2 \\ 0 \text{ if string } str1 \text{ is equal to string } str2 \\ \text{an integer value greater than 0 if string } str1 \\ \quad \text{is greater than string } str2 \end{cases}$$

EXERCISES

1. Mark the following statements as true or false.

   a. The result of a logical expression cannot be assigned to an `int` variable.

   b. In a one-way selection, if a semicolon is placed after the expression in an `if` statement, the expression in the `if` statement is always `true`.

   c. Every `if` statement must have a corresponding `else`.

   d. The expression:

      `(ch >= 'A' && ch <= 'Z')`

      evaluates to `false` if either `ch < 'A'` or `ch >= 'Z'`.

   e. Suppose the input is 5. (Assume that all variables are properly declared.) The output of the code:

      ```
      num = console.nextInt();
      if (num > 5)
          System.out.println(num);
          num = 0;
      else
          System.out.println("Num is zero");
      ```

      is:

      `Num is zero.`

   f. The expression in a `switch` statement should evaluate to a value of any primitive data type.

   g. The expression `!(x > 0)` is true only if `x` is a negative number.

   h. In Java, both `!` and `!=` are logical operators.

   i. The order in which statements execute in a program is called the flow of control.

2. Select the best answer.

    a. ```
        if (6 < 2 * 5)
            System.out.print("Hello");
            System.out.print(" There");
        ```

    outputs the following:

    i. Hello There      ii. Hello      iii. Hello      iv. There

                                                                  There

    b.  ```
        if ('a' > 'b' || 66 > (int)('A'))
            System.out.println("#*#");
        ```

    outputs the following:

    i. #*#   ii. #   iii. *   iv. none of these

                                        *

                                        #

    c. ```
        if (7 <= 7)
            System.out.println(6 - 9 * 2 / 6);
        ```

    outputs the following:

    i. -1      ii. 3      iii. 3.0      iv. none of these

    d.  ```
        if (7 < 8)
        {
            System.out.println("2 4 6 8");
            System.out.println("1 3 5 7");
        }
        ```

    outputs the following:

    i. 2 4 6 8   ii. 1 3 5 7   iii. none of these
       1 3 5 7

    e. ```
        if (5 < 3)
            System.out.println("*");
        else if (7 == 8)
            System.out.println("&");
        else
            System.out.println("$");
        ```

    outputs the following:

    i. *      ii. &      iii. $      iv. none of these
        ```

3. Suppose that x, y, and z are `int` variables and x = 10, y = 15, and z = 20. Determine whether the following expressions evaluates to `true` or `false`.

   a. `!(x > 10)`

   b. `x <= 5 || y < 15`

   c. `(x != 5) && (y != z)`

   d. `x >= z || (x + y >= z)`

   e. `(x <= y – 2) && (y >= z) || (z – 2 != 20)`

4. Suppose that x, y, z, and w are `int` variables and x = 3, y = 4, z = 7, and w = 1. What is the output of the following statements?

   a. `System.out.println("x == y: " + (x == y));`

   b. `System.out.println("x != z: " + (x != z));`

   c. `System.out.println("y == z – 3: " + (y == z – 3));`

   d. `System.out.println("!(z > w): " + !(z > w));`

   e. `System.out.println("x + y < z: " + (x + y < z));`

5. What is the output of the following Java code?

```java
int x = 100;
int y = 200;

if (x > 100 && y <= 200)
    System.out.println(x + " " + y + " " + (x + y));
else
    System.out.println(x + " " + y + " " + (2 * x - y));
```

6. Write Java statements that output `Democrat` if the party affiliation code is `'D'`, `Republican` if the party affiliation code is `'R'`, and `independent` otherwise.

7. Correct the following code so that it prints the correct message.

```java
if (score >= 60)
    System.out.println("You pass.");
else;
    System.out.println("You fail.");
```

8. Suppose that you have the following declaration:

```java
int j = 0;
```

   The output of the statement:

```java
if ((8 > 4) || (j++ == 7))
    System.out.println("j = " + j);
```

   is:

```java
j = 0
```

while the output of the statement:

```
if ((8 > 4) | (j++ == 7))
    System.out.println("j = " + j);
```

is:

```
j = 1
```

Explain why.

9. What is the output of the following program?

```
public class Exercise9
{
    public static void main(String[] args)
    {
        int myNum = 10;
        int yourNum = 30;

        if (yourNum % myNum == 3)
        {
            yourNum = 3;
            myNum = 1;
        }
        else if (yourNum % myNum == 2)
        {
            yourNum = 2;
            myNum = 2;
        }
        else
        {
            yourNum = 1;
            myNum = 3;
        }

        System.out.println(myNum + " " + yourNum);
    }
}
```

10. What is the output of the program in Exercise 9, if myNum = 5 and yourNum = 12?

11. What is the output of the program in Exercise 9, if myNum = 30 and yourNum = 33?

12. Suppose that sale and bonus are double variables. Write an if...else statement that assigns a value to bonus as follows: If sale is greater than $20,000, the value assigned to bonus is 0.10; if sale is greater than $10,000 and less than or equal to $20,000, the value assigned to bonus is 0.05; otherwise, the value assigned to bonus is 0.

13. Suppose that overSpeed and fine are double variables. Assign the value to fine as follows: If 0 < overSpeed <= 5, the value assigned to fine is $20.00; if 5 < overSpeed <= 10, the value assigned to fine is $75.00; if 10 < overSpeed <= 15, the value assigned to fine is $150.00; if overSpeed > 15, the value assigned to fine is $150.00 plus $20.00 per mile over 15.

14. Suppose that `score` is an `int` variable. Consider the following `if` statements:

```
if (score >= 90);
    System.out.println("Discount = 10%");
```

a. What is the output if the value of `score` is 95? Justify your answer.

b. What is the output if the value of `score` is 85? Justify your answer.

15. Suppose that `score` is an `int` variable. Consider the following `if` statements:

i.
```
if (score == 70)
    System.out.println("Grade is C.");
```

ii.
```
if (score = 70)
    System.out.println("Grade is C.");
```

Answer the following questions:

a. What is the output in (i) and (ii) if the value of `score` is 70? What is the value of `score` after the `if` statement executes?

b. What is the output in (i) and (ii) if the value of `score` is 80? What is the value of `score` after the `if` statement executes?

16. Rewrite the following expressions using the conditional operator. (Assume that all variables are declared properly.)

a.
```
if (x >= y)
    z = x - y;
else
    z = y - x;
```

b.
```
if (hours >= 40.0)
    wages = 40 * 7.50 + 1.5 * 7.5 * (hours - 40);
else
    wages = hours * 7.50;
```

c.
```
if (score >= 60)
    str = "Pass";
else
    str = "Fail";
```

17. Rewrite the following expressions using an `if...else` statement. (Assume that all variables are declared properly.)

a. `(x < 5) ? y = 10 : y = 20;`

b. `(fuel >= 10) ? drive = 150 : drive = 30;`

c. `(booksBought >= 3) ? discount = 0.15 : discount = 0.0;`

18. Suppose that you have the following conditional expression. (Assume that all the variables are properly declared.)

```
(0 < backyard && backyard <= 5000) ? fertilizingCharges = 40.00
                : fertilizingCharges = 40.00 + (backyard - 5000) * 0.01;
```

   a. What is the value of `fertilizingCharges` if the value of `backyard` is 3000?

   b. What is the value of `fertilizingCharges` if the value of `backyard` is 5000?

   c. What is the value of `fertilizingCharges` if the value of `backyard` is 6500?

19. State whether the following are valid `switch` statements. If not, explain why. Assume that n and `digit` are `int` variables.

   a.
```
switch (n <= 2)
{
case 0:
    System.out.println("Draw.");
    break;

case 1:
    System.out.println("Win.");
    break;

case 2:
    System.out.println("Lose.");
    break;
}
```

   b.
```
switch (digit / 4)
{
case 0:
case 1:
    System.out.println("low.");
    break;

case 1:
case 2:
    System.out.println("middle.");
    break;

case 3:
    System.out.println("high.");
}
```

   c.
```
switch (n % 6)
{
case 1:
case 2:
```

```
        case 3:
        case 4:
        case 5:
            System.out.println(n);
            break;

        case 0:
            System.out.println();
            break;
        }
```

d.
```
    switch (n % 10)
    {
    case 0:
    case 2:
    case 4:
    case 6:
    case 8:
        System.out.println("Even");
        break;

    case 1:
    case 3:
    case 5:
    case 7:
        System.out.println("Odd");
        break;
    }
```

20. Suppose the input is 5. What is the value of `alpha` after the following Java code executes? (Assume that `alpha` is an `int` variable and `console` is a Scanner object initialized to the keyboard.)

```
alpha = console.nextInt();

switch (alpha)
{
case 1:
case 2:
    alpha = alpha + 2;
    break;

case 4:
    alpha++;

case 5:
    alpha = 2 * alpha;

case 6:
    alpha = alpha + 5;
    break;
default:
    alpha--;
}
```

21. Suppose the input is 3. What is the value of beta after the following Java code executes? (Assume that all variables are declared properly.)

```java
beta = console.nextInt();

switch (beta)
{
case 3:
    beta = beta + 3;
case 1:
    beta++;
    break;

case 5:
    beta = beta + 5;
case 4:
    beta = beta + 4;
}
```

22. Suppose the input is 6. What is the value of a after the following Java code executes? (Assume that all variables are declared properly.)

```java
a = console.nextInt();

if (a > 0)
    switch (a)
    {
    case 1:
        a = a + 3;

    case 3:
        a++;
        break;

    case 6:
        a = a + 6;
    case 8:
        a = a * 8;
        break;

    default:
        a--;
    }
else
    a = a + 2;
```

23. In the following code, correct any errors that would prevent the program from compiling or running:

```java
public class Errors
{
    public static void main(String[] args)
    {
        int a, b;
        boolean found;
```

4

```
System.out.print("Enter the first integer: ");
a = console.nextInt();;
System.out.println();

System.out.print("Enter the second integer: ");
b = console.nextInt();;

if a > a * b && 10 < b
    found = 2 * a > b;
else
{
    found = 2 * a < b;
    if found
       a = 3;
       c = 15;
    if b
    {
        b = 0;
        a = 1;
    }
}
}
}
```

24. The following program contains errors. Correct them so that the program will run and output w = 21.

```
public class Mystery
{
    static final int ONE = 5;

    public static void main(String[] args)
    {
        int  x, y, w, z;
        z = 9;

        if z > 10
            x = 12;  y = 5,   w = x + y + one;
        else
            x = 12;  y = 4,   w = x + y + one;

        System.out.println("w = " + w);
    }
}
```

25. Suppose that str1, str2, and str3 are String variables, and str1 = "English", str2 = "Computer Science", and str3 = "Programming". Evaluate the following expressions:

a. str1.compareTo(str2) >= 0

b. str1.compareTo("english") != 0

c. str3.compareTo(str2) < 0

d. str2.compareTo("Chemistry") >= 0

26. Write the missing statements in the following program so that it prompts the user to input two numbers. If one of the numbers is 0, the program should output a message indicating that both numbers must be nonzero. If the first number is greater than the second number, it outputs the first number divided by the second number; if the first number is less than the second number, it outputs the second number divided by the first number; otherwise, it outputs the product of the numbers. Format your output to two decimal places.

```java
import java.util.*;

public class Exercise26
{
    static Scanner console = new Scanner(System.in);

    public static void main(String[] args)
    {
        double firstNum, secondNum;

        System.out.print("Enter two nonzero numbers: ");
        firstNum = console.nextDouble();
        secondNum = console.nextDouble();
        System.out.println();

        //Missing statements
    }
}
```

PROGRAMMING EXERCISES

1. Write a program that prompts the user to input a number. The program should then output the number and a message saying whether the number is positive, negative, or zero.

2. Write a program that prompts the user to input three numbers. The program should then output the numbers in nondescending order.

3. Write a program that prompts the user to input an integer between 0 and 35. If the number is less than or equal to 9, the program should output the number; otherwise, it should output A for 10, B for 11, C for 12, ..., and Z for 35. (*Hint:* Use the cast operator, (char)( ), for numbers >= 10.)

4. The statements in the following program are in incorrect order. Rearrange the statements so that it prompts the user to input the shape type (rectangle, circle, or cylinder), and the appropriate dimension of the shape. The program then outputs the following information about the shape: For a rectangle, it outputs the area and perimeter; for a circle, it outputs the area and circumference; and for a cylinder, it outputs the volume and surface area. After rearranging the statements, your program should be properly indented.

```
public class Ch4_PrExercise4
{
    public static void main(String[] args)
    {
        System.out.print("Enter the shape type: (rectangle, "
                        +" circle, cylinder) ");
        shape = console.next();
        System.out.println();

        String shape

        if (shape.compareTo("rectangle") == 0)
        {
            System.out.print("Enter the height of the cylinder: ");
            height = console.nextDouble();
            System.out.println();

            System.out.print("Enter the width of the rectangle: ");
            width = console.nextDouble();;
            System.out.println();

            System.out.printf("Area of the circle = %.2f%n",
                        (PI * Math.pow(radius, 2.0)));

            System.out.printf("Perimeter of the rectangle = %.2f%n",
                        (2 * (length + width)));
        }
        double length;
        double width;
        else if (shape.compareTo("circle") == 0)
        {
            System.out.print("Enter the length of the rectangle: ");
            length = console.nextDouble();;
            System.out.println();

            System.out.printf("Volume of the cylinder = %.2f%n",
                        (PI * Math.pow(radius, 2.0)* height));
            System.out.printf("Circumference of the circle: %.2f%n",
                        (2 * PI * radius));
        }
        else if (shape.compareTo("cylinder") == 0)
        {
            double height;
            double radius;

            System.out.print("Enter the radius of the circle: ");
            radius = console.nextDouble();;
            System.out.println();

            System.out.print("Enter the radius of the base of "
                        + "the cylinder: ");
            radius = console.nextDouble();
```

```
            System.out.println();

            System.out.printf("Area of the rectangle = %.2f%n",
                              (length * width));

            System.out.printf("Surface area of the cylinder: %.2f%n",
                              (2 * PI * radius * height
                             + 2 * PI * Math.pow(radius, 2.0)));
        }
      else
            System.out.println("The program does not handle "
                             + shape);
    }

    static Scanner console = new Scanner(System.in);
    static final double PI = 3.1416;
}
import java.util.*;
```

5. Write a program to implement the algorithm you designed in Exercise 17 of Chapter 1.

6. In a right triangle, the square of the length of one side is equal to the sum of the squares of the lengths of the other two sides. Write a program that prompts the user to enter the lengths of three sides of a triangle and then outputs a message indicating whether the triangle is a right triangle.

7. A box of cookies can hold 24 cookies and a container can hold 75 boxes of cookies. Write a program that prompts the user to enter the total number of cookies. The program then outputs the number of boxes and the number of containers to ship the cookies. Note that each box must contain the specified number of cookies and each container must contain the specified number of boxes. If the last box of cookies contains less than the number of specified cookies, you can discard it, and output the number of leftover cookies. Similarly, if the last container contains less than the number of specified boxes, you can discard it, and output the number of leftover boxes.

8. The roots of the quadratic equation $ax^2 + bx + c = 0$, $a \neq 0$ are given by the following formula:

$$\frac{-b \pm \sqrt{b^2 - 4ac}}{2a}$$

In this formula, the term $b^2 - 4ac$ is called the **discriminant**. If $b^2 - 4ac = 0$, then the equation has a single (repeated) root. If $b^2 - 4ac > 0$, the equation has two real roots. If $b^2 - 4ac < 0$, the equation has two complex roots. Write a program that prompts the user to input the value of a (the coefficient of x^2), b (the coefficient of x), and c (the constant term), and outputs the type of roots of the equation. Furthermore, if $b^2 - 4ac \geq 0$, the program should output the roots of the quadratic equation. (*Hint:* Use the method `pow` or `sqrt` from the `class` Math to calculate the square root. Chapter 3 explains how to use these methods.)

9. Write a program that mimics a calculator. The program should take as input two integers and an arithmetic operation (+, −, *, or /) to be performed. It should then output the numbers, the operator, and the result. (For division, if the denominator is zero, output an appropriate message.) Some sample outputs follow:

```
3 + 4 = 7
13 * 5 = 65
```

10. Redo Exercise 9 to handle floating-point numbers. (Format your output to two decimal places.)

11. Redo Programming Exercise 16 of Chapter 2, taking into account that your parents buy additional savings bonds for you as follows:

   a. If you do not spend any money to buy savings bonds, then because you had a summer job, your parents buy savings bonds for you in an amount equal to 1% of the money you save after paying taxes and buying clothes, school supplies, and other accessories.

   b. If you spend up to 25% of your net income to buy savings bonds, your parents spend $0.25 for each dollar you spend to buy savings bonds, plus money equal to 1% of the money you save after paying taxes and buying clothes, school supplies, and other accessories.

   c. If you spend more than 25% of your net income to buy savings bonds, your parents spend $0.40 for each dollar you spend to buy savings bonds, plus money equal to 2% of the money you save after paying taxes and buying clothes, school supplies, and other accessories.

12. A bank in your town updates its customers' accounts at the end of each month. The bank offers two types of accounts: savings and checking. Every customer must maintain a minimum balance. If a customer's balance falls below the minimum balance, there is a service charge of $10.00 for savings accounts and $25.00 for checking accounts. If the balance at the end of the month is at least the minimum balance, the account receives interest as follows:

   a. Savings accounts receive 4% interest.

   b. Checking accounts with balances of up to $5000 more than the minimum balance receive 3% interest; otherwise, the interest is 5%.

Write a program that reads a customer's account number (`int` type), account type (`char` type; s or S for savings, c or C for checking), minimum balance that the account should maintain, and current balance. The program should then output the account number, account type, current balance, and new balance or an appropriate error message. Test your program by running it five times, using the following data:

```
46728  S  1000  2700
87324  C  1500  7689
79873  S  1000  800
89832  C  2000  3000
98322  C  1000  750
```

13. Write a program that implements the algorithm given in Example 1-2 (Chapter 1), which determines the monthly wages of a salesperson.

14. The number of lines that can be printed on a piece of paper depends on the paper size, the point size of each character in a line, whether lines are double-spaced or single-spaced, the top and bottom margin, and the left and right margins of the paper. Assume that all characters are of the same point size, and all lines are either single-spaced or double-spaced. Note that 1 inch = 72 points. Moreover, assume that the lines are printed along the width of the paper. For example, if the length of the paper is 11 inches and the width is 8.5 inches, then the maximum length of a line is 8.5 inches. Write a program that calculates the number of characters in a line and the number of lines that can be printed on a paper based on the following input from the user:

a. The length and width, in inches, of the paper.

b. The top, bottom, left, and right margins.

c. The point size of a line.

d. If the lines are double-spaced, then double the point size of each character.

15. Write a program that calculates and prints the bill for a cellular telephone company. The company offers two types of service: regular and premium. Rates vary based on the type of service and are computed as follows:

Regular service: $10.00 plus first 50 minutes are free. Charges for over 50 minutes are $0.20 per minute.

Premium service: $25.00 plus:

a. For calls made from 6:00 a.m. to 6:00 p.m., the first 75 minutes are free; charges for over 75 minutes are $0.10 per minute.

b. For calls made from 6:00 p.m. to 6:00 a.m., the first 100 minutes are free; charges for over 100 minutes are $0.05 per minute.

Your program should prompt the user to enter an account number, a service code (type char), and the number of minutes the service was used. A service code of r or R means regular service; a service code of p or P means premium service. Treat any other character as an error. Your program should output the account number, type of service, number of minutes the telephone service was used, and the amount due from the user. For the premium service, the customer may be using the service during the day and the night. Therefore, to calculate the bill, you must ask the user to input the number of minutes the service was used during the day and the number of minutes the service was used during the night.

16. You have several pictures of different sizes that you would like to frame. A local picture framing store offers two types of frames—regular and fancy. The frames are available in white and can be ordered in any color the customer desires. Suppose that each frame is 1 inch wide. The cost of coloring the frame is $0.10 per inch. The cost of a regular frame is $0.15 per inch and the cost of a fancy frame is $0.25 per inch. The cost of putting a cardboard paper behind the picture is $0.02 per square inch and the cost of putting glass on top of the picture is $0.07 per square inch. The customer can also choose to put crowns on the corners, which costs $0.35 per crown. Write a program that prompts the user to input the following information and then output the cost of framing the picture:

    a. The length and width, in inches, of the picture.

    b. The type of the frame.

    c. Customer's choice of color to color the frame.

    d. If the user wants to add the crowns, then the number of crowns.

17. Samantha and Vikas are looking to buy a house in a new development. After looking at various models the three models they like are colonial, split-entry, and single-story. The builder gave them the base price and the finished area in square feet of the three models. They want to know the price per square foot of the three models and the model with the least price per square foot. Write a program that accepts as input the base price and the finished area in square feet of the three models. The program outputs the price per square foot of the three models and the model with the least price per square foot.

18. One way to determine how healthy a person is by measuring the body fat of the person. The formulas to determine the body fat for female and male are as follows:

    Body fat formula for women:

    $$A1 = (\text{Body weight} \times 0.732) + 8.987$$
    $$A2 = \text{Wrist measurement (at fullest point)} / 3.140$$
    $$A3 = \text{Waist measurement (at navel)} \times 0.157$$
    $$A4 = \text{Hip measurement (at fullest point)} \times 0.249$$
    $$A5 = \text{Forearm measurement (at fullest point)} \times 0.434$$
    $$B = A1 + A2 - A3 - A4 + A5$$

Body fat = body weight − B

Body fat percentage = body fat × 100 / body weight

Body fat formula for men:

A1 = (Body weight × 1.082) + 94.42

A2 = Waist measurement × 4.15

B = A1 − A2

Body fat = body weight − B

Body fat percentage = body fat × 100 / body weight

Write a program to calculate the body fat of a person.

19. Rewrite the program in Example 4-24, using the `String` method `equals`.

4

CHAPTER 5

CONTROL STRUCTURES II: REPETITION

IN THIS CHAPTER, YOU WILL:

- · Learn about repetition (looping) control structures
- · Explore how to construct and use counter-controlled, sentinel-controlled, flag-controlled, and EOF-controlled repetition structures
- · Examine **break** and **continue** statements
- · Learn how to avoid bugs by avoiding patches
- · Discover how to form and use nested control structures

In Chapter 4, you learned how decisions are incorporated in programs. In this chapter, you will learn how repetitions are incorporated in programs.

Why Is Repetition Needed?

Suppose you want to add five integers to find their average. From what you have learned so far, you know that you could proceed as follows (assume that all the variables are properly declared):

```
num1 = console.nextInt();   //get the first number
num2 = console.nextInt();   //get the second number
num3 = console.nextInt();   //get the third number
num4 = console.nextInt();   //get the fourth number
num5 = console.nextInt();   //get the fifth number

sum = num1 + num2 + num3 + num4 + num5;   //add the numbers
average = sum / 5;                         //find the average
```

But suppose you want to add and average 1000 or more numbers. You would have to declare that many variables, and list them again in the input statements, and perhaps again in the output statements. This would take an exorbitant amount of typing as well as time. Also, if you wanted to run this program again with a different number of values, you would have to rewrite the program.

Suppose you want to add the following numbers:

5 3 7 9 4

Assume that the input is these five numbers. Consider the following statements, in which sum and num are variables of type int:

```
sum = 0;                    //Line 1
num = console.nextInt();    //Line 2
sum = sum + num;            //Line 3
```

The statement in Line 1 initializes sum to 0. Let's execute the statements in Lines 2 and 3. The statement in Line 2 stores 5 in num; the statement in Line 3 updates the value of sum by adding num to it. After Line 3 executes, the value of sum is 5.

Let's repeat the statements in Lines 2 and 3. After the statement in Line 2 executes (after the programming code reads the next number):

num = 3

After the statement in Line 3 executes:

sum = sum + num = 5 + 3 = 8

At this point, sum contains the sum of the first two numbers. Let's repeat the statements in Lines 2 and 3 a third time. After the statement in Line 2 executes (after the programming code reads the next number):

```
num = 7
```

After the statement in Line 3 executes:

```
sum = sum + num = 8 + 7 = 15
```

Now, sum contains the sum of the first three numbers. If you repeat the statements in Lines 2 and 3 two more times, sum will contain the sum of all five numbers.

If you want to add 10 integers, you can repeat the statements in Lines 2 and 3 ten times. And if you want to add 100 numbers, you can repeat the statements 100 times. In either case, you do not have to declare any additional variables as you did in the code shown previously. By repeating the statements in Lines 2 and 3 you can add any set of integers, whereas the earlier code requires that you drastically change the code.

There are many situations in which it is necessary to repeat a set of statements. For example, for each student in a class, the formula to determine the course grade is the same. Java has three repetition, or looping, structures that let you repeat statements over and over until certain conditions are met: while, for, and do...while. The following sections discuss these three looping (repetition) structures.

while Looping (Repetition) Structure

In the previous section, you saw that sometimes it is necessary to repeat a set of statements several times. One way to do this is to type the set of statements in the program over and over. For example, if you want to repeat a set of statements 100 times, you type the set of statements 100 times in the program. However, this way of repeating a set of statements is impractical, if not impossible. Fortunately, there is a simpler approach. As noted earlier, Java has three repetition, or looping, structures that allow you to repeat a set of statements until certain conditions are met. This section discusses the first looping structure, a while loop.

The general form of the while statement is:

```
while (logical expression)
    statement
```

In Java, while is a reserved word. The logical expression is called a **loop condition** or simply a **condition**. The statement is called the body of the loop. Moreover, the statement can be either a simple or compound statement. Also, note that the parentheses around the logical expression are part of the syntax. Figure 5-1 shows the flow of execution of a while loop.

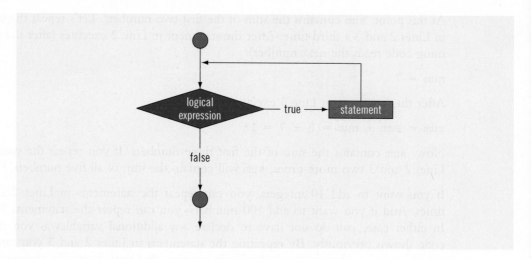

FIGURE 5-1 `while` loop

The `logical expression` provides an entry condition. If it initially evaluates to `true`, the `statement` executes. The loop condition—the `logical expression`—is then reevaluated. If it again evaluates to `true`, the `statement` executes again. The `statement` (body of the loop) continues to execute until the `logical expression` is no longer `true`. A loop that continues to execute endlessly is called an **infinite loop**. To avoid an infinite loop, make sure that the loop's body contains one or more statements that ensure that the loop condition—the `logical expression` in the `while` statement—will eventually be `false`.

EXAMPLE 5-1

Consider the following Java program segment:

```
int i = 0;                              //Line 1

while (i <= 20)                         //Line 2
{
    System.out.print(i + " ");          //Line 3
    i = i + 5;                          //Line 4
}

System.out.println();                   //Line 5
```

Sample Run:

```
0 5 10 15 20
```

In Line 1, the variable `i` is set to 0. The logical expression in the `while` statement (in Line 2), `i <= 20`, is then evaluated. Because the expression `i <= 20` evaluates to `true`, the body of the `while` loop executes next. The body of the `while` loop consists of the statements in

Lines 3 and 4. The statement in Line 3 outputs the value of i, which is 0; the statement in Line 4 changes the value of i to 5. After executing the statements in Lines 3 and 4, the logical expression in the while loop (Line 2) is evaluated again. Because i is 5, the expression i <= 20 evaluates to true and the body of the while loop executes again. This process of evaluating the logical expression and executing the body of the while loop continues until the expression i <= 20 (Line 2) no longer evaluates to true.

The variable i (Line 2) in the expression is called the **loop control variable**. Note the following from the preceding example:

1. Eventually, within the loop, i becomes 25, but is not printed because the entry condition is false.

2. If you omit the statement:

   ```
   i = i + 5;
   ```

   from the body of the loop, you will have an infinite loop, continually printing rows of zeros.

3. You must initialize the loop control variable i before you execute the loop. If the statement:

   ```
   i = 0;
   ```

   (in Line 1) is omitted, either the compiler will generate an error or the loop might not execute at all. (Recall that not all variables in Java are automatically initialized.)

4. In the previous program segment, if the two statements in the body of the loop are interchanged, the result may be altered. For example, consider the following statements:

   ```
   int i = 0;

   while (i <= 20)
   {
       i = i + 5;
       System.out.print(i + " ");
   }

   System.out.println();
   ```

   Here, the output is:

   ```
   5 10 15 20 25
   ```

   Typically, this would be a semantic error because you rarely want a condition to be true for i <= 20, and yet produce results for i > 20.

Designing `while` Loops

As shown in Example 5-1, the body of a `while` loop executes only when the `expression` in the `while` statement evaluates to `true`. Typically, the `expression` checks whether a variable(s), called the loop control variable (LCV), satisfies certain conditions. For example, in Example 5-1, the `expression` in the `while` statement checks whether i <= 20. (Recall that in Java, when variables are declared, they are not automatically initialized.) The LCV must be properly initialized before the `while` loop, and its value should eventually make the `logical expression` evaluate to `false`. We do this by updating the LCV in the body of the `while` loop. Therefore, `while` loops are typically written in the following form:

```
//initialize the loop control variable(s)

while (logical expression)     //expression tests the LCV
{
        .
        .
        .
    //update the loop control variable(s)
        .
        .
        .

}
```

For instance, in Example 5-1, the statement in Line 1 initializes the LCV i to 0. The expression i <= 20 in Line 2 checks whether i is less than or equal to 20, and the statement in Line 4 updates the value of i.

EXAMPLE 5-2

Consider the following Java program segment:

```
int i = 20;                            //Line 1

while (i < 20)                         //Line 2
{
    System.out.print(i + " ");         //Line 3
    i = i + 5;                         //Line 4
}

System.out.println();                  //Line 5
```

It is easy to overlook the difference between this example and Example 5-1. Here, in Line 1, i is set to 20. Because i is 20, the expression i < 20 in the `while` statement (Line 2) evaluates to `false`. Initially, the loop entry condition, i < 20, is `false`, so the body of the `while` loop never executes. Hence, no values are output and the value of i remains 20.

The next few sections describe the various forms of while loops.

Counter-Controlled while Loops

Suppose you know exactly how many times certain statements need to be executed. For example, suppose you know exactly how many pieces of data (or entries) need to be read. In such cases, the while loop assumes the form of a **counter-controlled** while **loop**. (If you know the number of iterations in advance, a for loop should be used.) Suppose that a set of statements needs to be executed N times. You can set up a counter (initialized to 0 before the while statement) to track how many items have been read. Before executing the body of the while statement, the counter is compared with N. If counter < N, the body of the while statement executes. The body of the loop continues to execute until the value of counter >= N. Thus, inside the body of the while statement, the value of counter increments after it reads a new item. In this case, the while loop might look like the following:

```
counter = 0;          //initialize the loop control variable

while (counter < N) //test the loop control variable
{
      .
      .
      .
      counter++;      //update the loop control variable
      .
      .
      .
}
```

If N represents the number of data items in a file, then the value of N can be determined several ways: The program can prompt you to specify the number of items in the file; an input statement can read the value; or you can specify the first item in the file as the number of items in the file, so that you need not remember the number of input values (items). This is useful if someone other than the programmer enters the data. Consider Example 5-3.

EXAMPLE 5-3

Suppose the input is:

8 9 2 3 90 38 56 8 23 89 7 2

Suppose you want to add these numbers and find their average. Consider the following program.

```
//Counter-controlled while loop

import java.util.*;

public class CounterControlledWhileLoop
{
    static Scanner console = new Scanner(System.in);
```

```java
public static void main(String[] args)
{
    int limit;          //store the number of items
                        //in the list
    int number;         //variable to store the number
    int sum;            //variable to store the sum
    int counter;        //loop control variable

    System.out.print("Line 1: Enter the number of "
                    + "integers in the list: ");        //Line 1

    limit = console.nextInt();                          //Line 2
    System.out.println();                               //Line 3

    sum = 0;                                            //Line 4
    counter = 0;                                        //Line 5
    System.out.println("Line 6: Enter " + limit
                    + " integers.");                    //Line 6

    while (counter < limit)                             //Line 7
    {
        number = console.nextInt();                     //Line 8
        sum = sum + number;                             //Line 9
        counter++;                                      //Line 10
    }

    System.out.printf("Line 11: The sum of the %d " +
                    "numbers = %d%n", limit, sum);      //Line 11

    if (counter != 0)                                   //Line 12
        System.out.printf("Line 13: The average = %d%n",
                        (sum / counter));               //Line 13
    else                                                //Line 14
        System.out.println("Line 15: No input.");       //Line 15
}
}
```

Sample Run: (In this sample run, the user input is shaded).

```
Line 1: Enter the number of integers in the list: 12

Line 6: Enter 12 integers.
8 9 2 3 90 38 56 8 23 89 7 2
Line 11: The sum of the 12 numbers = 335
Line 13: The average = 27
```

The preceding program works as follows: The statement in Line 1 prompts the user to input the data for processing. The statement in Line 2 reads the next input and stores it in the variable limit. The value of limit indicates the number of items to be read. The statements in Lines 4 and 5 initialize the variables sum and counter to 0. The while statement in Line 7 checks the value of counter to determine how many items have been read. If counter is less than limit, the while loop proceeds for the next iteration.

The statement in Line 8 stores the next number in the variable number. The statement in Line 9 updates the value of sum by adding the value of number to the previous value. The statement in Line 10 increments the value of counter by 1. The statement in Line 11 outputs the sum of the numbers. The statements in Lines 12 through 15 output either the average or the text: Line 15: No input.

Note that in this program, in Line 4, sum is initialized to 0. In Line 9, after storing the next number in number in Line 8, the program adds the next number to the sum of all the numbers scanned before the current number. The first number read is added to zero (because sum is initialized to 0), giving the correct sum of the first number. To find the average, divide sum by counter. If counter is 0, then dividing by 0 terminates the program and you get an error message. Therefore, before dividing sum by counter, you must check whether or not counter is 0.

Notice that in this program, the statement in Line 5 initializes the LCV counter to 0. The expression counter < limit in Line 7 evaluates whether counter is less than limit. The statement in Line 8 updates the value of counter. Note that in this program, the while loop can also be written without using the variable number as follows:

```
while (counter < limit)
{
    sum = sum + console.nextInt();
    counter++;
}
```

Sentinel-Controlled while Loops

You might not know exactly how many times a set of statements needs to be executed, but you do know that the statements need to be executed until a special value is met. This special value is called a **sentinel**. For example, while processing data, you might not know how many pieces of data (or entries) need to be read, but you do know that the last entry is a special value. In such cases, you read the first item before entering the while statement. If this item does not equal the sentinel, the body of the while statement executes. The while loop continues to execute as long as the program has not read the sentinel. Such a while loop is called a **sentinel-controlled while loop**. In this case, a while loop might look like the following:

```
input the first data item into variable //initialize the
                                         //loop control variable
while (variable != sentinel)     //test the loop control variable
{
    .
    .
    .
    input a data item into variable  //update the loop
                                     //control variable
}
```

EXAMPLE 5-4

Suppose you want to read some positive integers and average them, but you do not have a preset number of data items in mind. Suppose you choose the number -999 to mark the end of the data. You can proceed as follows:

```java
//Sentinel-controlled while loop

import java.util.*;

public class SentinelControlledWhileLoop
{
    static Scanner console = new Scanner(System.in);

    static final int SENTINEL = -999;

    public static void main(String[] args)
    {
        int number;         //variable to store the number
        int sum = 0;        //variable to store the sum
        int count = 0;      //variable to store the total
                            //numbers read

        System.out.println("Line 1: Enter positive integers "
                        + "ending with " + SENTINEL);    //Line 1

        number = console.nextInt();                      //Line 2

        while (number != SENTINEL)                       //Line 3
        {
            sum = sum + number;                          //Line 4
            count++;                                     //Line 5
            number = console.nextInt();                  //Line 6
        }

        System.out.printf("Line 7: The sum of %d " +
                        "numbers = %d%n", count, sum);    //Line 7

        if (count != 0)                                   //Line 8
            System.out.printf("Line 9: The average = %d%n",
                            (sum / count));               //Line 9
        else                                              //Line 10
            System.out.println("Line 11: No input.");     //Line 11
    }
}
```

Sample Run: (In this sample run, the user input is shaded.)

```
Line 1: Enter positive integers ending with -999
34 23 9 45 78 0 77 8 3 5 -999
Line 7: The sum of 10 numbers = 282
Line 9: The average = 28
```

This program works as follows: The statement in Line 1 prompts the user to enter numbers and to terminate by entering -999. The statement in Line 2 reads the first number and stores it in the variable number. The while statement in Line 3 checks whether number is not equal to SENTINEL. If number is not equal to SENTINEL, the body of the while loop executes. The statement in Line 4 updates the value of sum by adding number to it. The statement in Line 5 increments the value of count by 1. The statement in Line 6 stores the next number in the variable number. The statements in Lines 4 through 6 repeat until the program reads -999. The statement in Line 7 outputs the sum of the numbers, and the statements in Lines 8 through 11 output the average of the numbers.

Notice that the statement in Line 2 initializes the LCV number. The expression number != SENTINEL in Line 3 checks whether the value of number is not equal to SENTINEL. The statement in Line 6 updates the LCV number. Also, note that the program continues to read data as long as the user has not entered -999.

5

Next, consider another example of a sentinel-controlled while loop. In this example, the user is prompted to enter the value to be processed. If the user wants to stop the program, he or she can enter the value chosen for the sentinel.

EXAMPLE 5-5 TELEPHONE DIGITS

The following program reads the letter codes 'A' through 'Z' and prints the corresponding telephone digit. This program uses a sentinel-controlled while loop. To stop the program, the user is prompted for the sentinel, which is '#'. This is also an example of a nested control structure, where if... else, switch, and the while loop are nested.

```java
//*******************************************************
// Program: Telephone Digits
// This is an example of a sentinel-controlled while loop.
// This program converts uppercase letters to their
// corresponding telephone digits.
//*******************************************************

import javax.swing.JOptionPane;

public class TelephoneDigitProgram
{
    public static void main (String[] args)
    {
        char letter;                             //Line 1

        String inputMessage;                     //Line 2
        String inputString;                      //Line 3
        String outputMessage;                    //Line 4
```

```
        inputMessage = "Program to convert uppercase "
                     + "letters to their corresponding "
                     + "telephone digits.\n"
                     + "To stop the program enter #.\n"
                     + "Enter a letter:";              //Line 5
        inputString =
            JOptionPane.showInputDialog(inputMessage); //Line 6

        letter = inputString.charAt(0);                //Line 7

        while (letter != '#' )                         //Line 8
        {
            outputMessage = "The letter you entered is: "
                          + letter + "\n"
                          + "The corresponding telephone "
                          + "digit is: ";               //Line 9

            if (letter >= 'A' && letter <= 'Z')        //Line 10
            {
                switch (letter)                         //Line 11
                {
                case 'A':
                case 'B':
                case 'C':
                    outputMessage = outputMessage
                                  + "2";                //Line 12
                    break;                              //Line 13

                case 'D':
                case 'E':
                case 'F':
                    outputMessage = outputMessage
                                  + "3";                //Line 14
                    break;                              //Line 15

                case 'G':
                case 'H':
                case 'I':
                    outputMessage = outputMessage
                                  + "4";                //Line 16
                    break;                              //Line 17

                case 'J':
                case 'K':
                case 'L':
                    outputMessage = outputMessage
                                  + "5";                //Line 18
                    break;                              //Line 19
```

```
            case 'M':
            case 'N':
            case 'O':
                outputMessage = outputMessage
                              + "6";                    //Line 20
                break;                                  //Line 21

            case 'P':
            case 'Q':
            case 'R':
            case 'S':
                outputMessage = outputMessage
                              + "7";                    //Line 22
                break;                                  //Line 23

            case 'T':
            case 'U':
            case 'V':
                outputMessage = outputMessage
                              + "8";                    //Line 24
                break;                                  //Line 25

            case 'W':
            case 'X':
            case 'Y':
            case 'Z':
                outputMessage = outputMessage
                              + "9";                    //Line 26
            }
        }
        else                                            //Line 27
            outputMessage = outputMessage
                          + "Invalid input";            //Line 28

        JOptionPane.showMessageDialog(null, outputMessage,
                      "Telephone Digit",
                      JOptionPane.PLAIN_MESSAGE); //Line 29

        inputMessage = "Enter another uppercase letter "
                     + "to find its corresponding "
                     + "telephone digit.\n"
                     + "To stop the program enter #.\n"
                     + "Enter a letter:";               //Line 30

        inputString =
          JOptionPane.showInputDialog(inputMessage); //Line 31
        letter = inputString.charAt(0);                 //Line 32
    }//end while

    System.exit(0);                                     //Line 33
    }
}
```

Sample Run: (Figure 5-2 shows the sample run.)

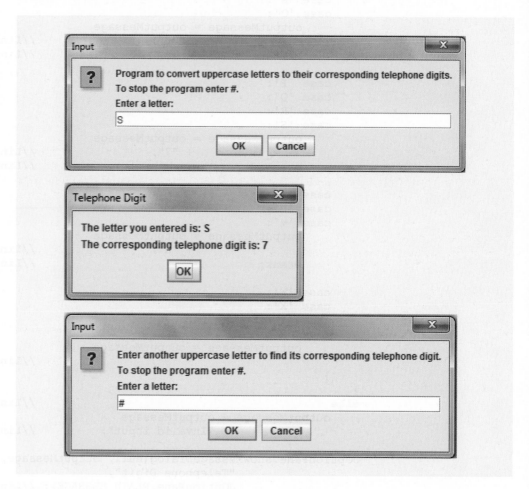

FIGURE 5-2 Sample run of `TelephoneDigitProgram`

The program in Example 5-5 works as follows: The statements in Lines 1 through 4 declare the appropriate variables. The statement in Line 5 creates the appropriate string to be included in the input dialog box. The statement in Line 6 displays the input dialog box informing the user what to do. This statement also retrieves the string entered by the user and assigns the string to the object `inputString`. (Notice that even though the user enters a single letter, it is still treated as a string.) The statement in Line 7 retrieves the letter from `inputString` and stores it in `letter`. The expression in the `while` statement in Line 8 checks that the letter is not #. If the letter entered by the user is not #, the body of the `while` loop executes. The statement in Line 9 creates the appropriate string to be displayed in the output dialog box.

The `if` statement in Line 10 checks whether the letter entered by the user is uppercase. If the letter entered by the user is uppercase, the **logical expression** in the `if` statement (in Line 10) evaluates to `true` and the `switch` statement executes, which determines the appropriate telephone digit and appends the telephone digit to `outputMessage` (see the statements in Lines 11 through 26). If the letter entered by the user is not uppercase, the `else` statement (in Line 27) executes and the statement in Line 28 appends the string `"Invalid input"` to `outputMessage`. The statement in Line 29 displays the output dialog box showing the result of the input.

Once the current letter is processed, the statement in Line 30 creates the message string, and the statement in Line 31 displays the input dialog box informing the user what to do next. The statement in Line 32 copies the letter entered by the user into `letter`. (Note that the statement in Line 30 is similar to the statement in Line 5, and that the statements in Lines 31 and 32 are the same as the statements in Lines 6 and 7.) After the statement in Line 32 (at the end of the `while` loop) executes, the control goes back to the top of the `while` loop and the same process begins again. When the user enters #, the program terminates.

> **NOTE**
> In the program in Example 5-5, you can write the statements between Lines 10 and 28 using just a `switch` structure, that is, without the `if` in Line 10 and the `else` in Line 27. (See Programming Exercise 3 at the end of this chapter.)

Flag-Controlled `while` Loops

A **flag-controlled** `while` **loop** uses a `boolean` variable to control the loop. Suppose `found` is a `boolean` variable. The flag-controlled `while` loop takes the following form:

```
found = false;       //initialize the loop control variable

while (!found)        //test the loop control variable
{
    .
    .
    .

    if (logical expression)
        found = true; //update the loop control variable
    .
    .
    .
}
```

The variable, such as `found`, which is used to control the execution of the `while` loop, is called a **flag variable**.

Example 5-6 further illustrates the use of a flag-controlled `while` loop.

EXAMPLE 5-6 GUESSING THE NUMBER GAME

The following program randomly generates an integer greater than or equal to 0 and less than 100. The program then prompts the user to guess the number. If the user guesses the number correctly, the program outputs an appropriate message. Otherwise, the program checks whether the guessed number is less than the random number. If the guessed number is less than the random the number generated by the program, the program outputs the message, "Your guess is lower than the number"; otherwise, the program outputs the message, "Your guess is higher than the number". The program then prompts the user to enter another number. The user is prompted to guess the random number until the user enters the correct number.

The program uses the method `random` of the `class` Math to generate a random number. To be specific, the expression:

`Math.random()`

returns a value of type `double` greater than or equal to 0.0 and less than 1.0. To convert it to an integer greater than or equal to 0 and less than 100, the program uses the following expression:

`(int) (Math.random() * 100);`

Furthermore, the program uses the `boolean` variable done to control the loop. The `boolean` variable done is initialized to `false`. It is set to `true` when the user guesses the correct number.

```java
//Flag-controlled while loop.
//Guessing the number game.

import java.util.*;

public class FlagControlledLoop
{
    static Scanner console = new Scanner(System.in);

    public static void main(String[] args)
    {
            //declare the variables
        int num;        //variable to store the random number
        int guess;      //variable to store the number
                        //guessed by the user

        boolean done;   //boolean variable to control the loop

        num = (int) (Math.random() * 100);          //Line 1

        done = false;                               //Line 2

        while (!done)                               //Line 3
        {                                           //Line 4
```

```java
        System.out.print ("Enter an integer greater"
                 + " than or equal to 0 and "
                 + "less than 100: ");              //Line 5
        guess = console.nextInt();                  //Line 6
        System.out.println();                       //Line 7

        if (guess == num)                           //Line 8
        {                                           //Line 9
            System.out.println("You guessed the "
                     + "correct number.");          //Line 10
            done = true;                            //Line 11
        }                                           //Line 12
        else if (guess < num)                       //Line 13
            System.out.println("Your guess is "
                     + "lower than "
                     + "the number.\n"
                     + "Guess again!");             //Line 14
        else                                        //Line 15
            System.out.println("Your guess is "
                     + "higher than "
                     + "the number.\n"
                     + "Guess again!");             //Line 16
    } //end while                                   //Line 17
    }                                               //Line 18
}
```

Sample Runs: (In the following sample run, the user input is shaded.)

```
Enter an integer greater than or equal to 0 and less than 100: 25

Your guess is higher than the number.
Guess again!
Enter an integer greater than or equal to 0 and less than 100: 5

Your guess is lower than the number.
Guess again!
Enter an integer greater than or equal to 0 and less than 100: 10

Your guess is higher than the number.
Guess again!
Enter an integer greater than or equal to 0 and less than 100: 8

Your guess is higher than the number.
Guess again!
Enter an integer greater than or equal to 0 and less than 100: 6

Your guess is lower than the number.
Guess again!
Enter an integer greater than or equal to 0 and less than 100: 7

You guessed the correct number.
```

The preceding program works as follows: The statement in Line 1 creates an integer greater than or equal to 0 and less than 100 and stores this number in the variable num.

The statement in Line 2 sets the `boolean` variable `done` to `false`. The `while` loop starts at Line 3 and ends at Line 17. The expression in the `while` loop at Line 3 evaluates the expression `!done`. If `done` is `false`, then `!done` is `true` and the body of the `while` loop executes; if `done` is `true`, then `!done` is `false`, so the `while` loop terminates.

The statement in Line 5 prompts the user to enter an integer greater than or equal to 0 and less than 100. The statement in Line 6 stores the number entered by the user in the variable `guess`. The expression in the `if` statement in Line 8 determines whether the value of `guess` is the same as `num`, that is, if the user guessed the number correctly. If the value of `guess` is the same as `num`, then the statements in Lines 10 and 11 execute. The statement in Line 10 outputs the message:

```
You guessed the correct number.
```

The statement in Line 11 sets the variable `done` to `true`. The control then goes back to Line 3. Because `done` is `true`, `!done` is `false` and the `while` loop terminates.

If the expression in Line 8 evaluates to `false`, then the `else` statement in Line 13 executes. The statement part of this `else` is an `if...else` statement, starting at Line 13 and ending at Line 16. The `if` statement in Line 13 determines whether the value of `guess` is less than `num`. In this case, the statement in Line 14 outputs the message:

```
Your guess is lower than the number.
Guess again!
```

If the expression in the `if` statement in Line 13 evaluates to `false`, then the statement in Line 16 executes, which outputs the message:

```
Your guess is higher than the number.
Guess again!
```

The program then prompts the user to enter an integer greater than or equal to 0 and less than 100.

EOF-Controlled `while` Loops

If the data file is frequently altered (for example, if data is frequently added or deleted), it's best not to read the data with a sentinel value. Someone might accidentally erase the sentinel value or add data past the sentinel, especially if the programmer and data entry person are different people. Also, the programmer sometimes does not know what the sentinel is. In such situations, you can use an **EOF (End Of File)-controlled `while` loop**.

In Java, the form of the EOF-controlled `while` loop depends on the type of stream object used to input data into a program. Because we have been using the `Scanner` object to input data into a program, next we describe the EOF-controlled `while` loop that uses a `Scanner` object to input data.

Recall that the following statement creates the Scanner object console and initializes it to the standard input device:

```
static Scanner console = new Scanner(System.in);    //Line 1
```

This statement is equivalent to the following statements:

```
static Scanner console;              //Line 2
console = new Scanner(System.in);    //Line 3
```

The statement in Line 2 declares console to be the Scanner variable; the statement in Line 3 initializes console to the standard input device. On the other hand, the statement in Line 1 both declares and initializes the Scanner variable console.

The method hasNext, of the class Scanner, returns true if there is an input in the input stream, otherwise it returns false. In other words, the expression console.hasNext() evaluates to true if there is an input in the input stream; otherwise, it returns false. Therefore, the expression console.hasNext() acts as the loop condition.

It now follows that a general form of the EOF-controlled while loop that uses the Scanner object console to input data is of the following form (we assume that console has been created and initialized using either the statement in Line 1 or the statements in Lines 2 and 3):

```
while (console.hasNext())
{
    //Get the next input (token) and store it in an
    //appropriate variable
    //Process the data
}
```

NOTE In the Windows console environment, the end-of-file marker is entered using Ctrl+z. (Hold the Ctrl key and press z.) In the UNIX environment, the end-of-file marker is entered using Ctrl+d. (Hold the Ctrl key and press d.)

Suppose that inFile is a Scanner object initialized to the input file. In this case, the EOF-controlled while loop takes the following form:

```
while (inFile.hasNext())
{
    //Get the next input (token) and store it in an
    //appropriate variable
    //Process the data
}
```

EXAMPLE 5-7

The following code uses an EOF-controlled `while` loop to find the sum of a set of numbers:

```
static Scanner console = new Scanner(System.in);

int sum = 0;
int num;

while (console.hasNext())
{
    num = console.nextInt(); //Get the next number
    sum = sum + num;         //Add the number to sum
}

System.out.printf("Sum = %d%n", sum);
```

EXAMPLE 5-8

Suppose we are given a file consisting of students' names and their test scores, a number between 0 and 100 (inclusive). Each line in the file consists of a student name followed by the test score. We want a program that outputs each student's name followed by the test score and the grade. The program also needs to output the average test score for the class. Consider the following program.

```
// This program reads data from a file consisting of students'
// names and their test scores. The program outputs each
// student's name followed by the test score and the grade. The
// program also outputs the average test score for all students.

import java.io.*;                                         //Line 1
import java.util.*;                                       //Line 2

public class ClassAverage                                 //Line 3
{                                                         //Line 4
    public static void main(String[] args)
                    throws FileNotFoundException           //Line 5
    {                                                     //Line 6
        String firstName;                                 //Line 7
        String lastName;                                  //Line 8
        double testScore;                                 //Line 9
        char grade = ' ';                                 //Line 10
        double classAverage;                              //Line 11

        double sum = 0;                                   //Line 12
        int count = 0;                                    //Line 13
```

```
Scanner inFile =
      new Scanner(new FileReader("stData.txt"));    //Line 14

PrintWriter outFile =
      new PrintWriter("stData.out");                //Line 15

while (inFile.hasNext())                            //Line 16
{                                                  //Line 17
    firstName = inFile.next();//read the first name Line 18
    lastName = inFile.next(); //read the last name  Line 19
    testScore =
        inFile.nextDouble(); //read the test score  Line 20

    sum = sum + testScore; //update sum             Line 21
    count++;               //increment count        Line 22

        //determine the grade
    switch ((int) testScore / 10)                  //Line 23
    {                                              //Line 24
    case 0:                                        //Line 25
    case 1:                                        //Line 26
    case 2:                                        //Line 27
    case 3:                                        //Line 28
    case 4:                                        //Line 29
    case 5:                                        //Line 30
        grade = 'F';                               //Line 31
        break;                                     //Line 32

    case 6:                                        //Line 33
        grade = 'D';                               //Line 34
        break;                                     //Line 35

    case 7:                                        //Line 36
        grade = 'C';                               //Line 37
        break;                                     //Line 38

    case 8:                                        //Line 39
        grade = 'B';                               //Line 40
        break;                                     //Line 41

    case 9:                                        //Line 42
    case 10:                                       //Line 43
        grade = 'A';                               //Line 44
        break;                                     //Line 45

    default:                                       //Line 46
        System.out.println("Invalid score.");      //Line 47
    }//end switch                                  //Line 48

    outFile.printf("%-12s %-12s %4.2f %c %n",
                firstName, lastName,
                testScore, grade);                 //Line 49
}//end while                                       //Line 50
```

5

```
        outFile.println();                          //Line 51

        if (count != 0)                             //Line 52
            outFile.printf("Class Average: %.2f %n",
                                sum / count);       //Line 53
        else                                        //Line 54
            outFile.println("No data.");            //Line 55

        outFile.close();                            //Line 56
    }                                               //Line 57
}                                                   //Line 58
```

Sample Run:

Input File:

```
Steve Gill 89
Rita Johnson 91.5
Randy Brown 85.5
Seema Arora 76.5
Samir Mann 73
Samantha McCoy 88.5
```

Output File:

```
Steve       Gill        89.00 B
Rita        Johnson     91.50 A
Randy       Brown       85.50 B
Seema       Arora       76.50 C
Samir       Mann        73.00 C
Samantha    McCoy       88.50 B
```

```
Class Average: 84.00
```

The preceding program works as follows. The statements in Lines 7 to 11 declare variables required by the program. The statements in Lines 12 and 13 initialize the variables sum and count. The statement in Line 14 declares inFile to be a reference variable of type Scanner and associates it with the input file. The statement in Line 15 declares outFile to be a reference variable of type PrintWriter and associates it with the output file.

The while loop from Lines 16 to 50 reads each student's first name, last name, and test score, and outputs the name followed by the test score and grade. Specifically, the statement in Line 18 reads the first name, the statement in Line 19 reads the last name, and the statement in Line 20 reads the test score. The statement in Line 21 updates the value of sum. (After reading all the data, the value of sum stores the sum of all the test scores.) The statement in Line 22 updates the value of count. (The variable count stores the number of students in the class.) The switch statement from Lines 23 to 48 determines the grade from testScore and stores it in the variable grade. The statement in Line 49 outputs a student's first name, last name, test score, and grade.

The if...else statement in Lines 52 to 55 outputs the class average, and the statement in Line 56 closes the file associated with outFile, which is stData.out.

The Programming Example Checking Account Balance, available with the Additional Student Files at *www.cengagebrain.com*, further illustrates how to use an EOF-controlled while loop in a program.

More on Expressions in while Statements

In the examples in the previous sections, the expression in the while statement is quite simple. In other words, the while loop is controlled by a single variable. However, there are situations where the logical expression in the while statement may be more complex.

For example, the program in Example 5-6 uses a flag-controlled while loop to implement the Guessing the Number game. However, the program gives as many tries as the user needs to guess the number. Suppose you want to give the user, at most, five tries to guess the number. If the user does not guess the number correctly within five tries, then the program outputs the random number generated by the program, as well as a message that they lost the game. In this case, you can write the while loop as follows. (Assume that numOfGuesses is an int variable initialized to 0.)

```
while ((numOfGuesses < 5) && (!done))
{
    System.out.print ("Enter an integer greater "
                    + "than or equal to 0 and "
                    + "less than 100: ");
    guess = console.nextInt();
    System.out.println();

    numOfGuesses++;

    if (guess == num)
    {
        System.out.println("Winner!. You guessed the "
                        + "correct number.");
        done = true;
    }
    else if (guess < num)
        System.out.println("Your guess is "
                        + "lower than "
                        + "the number.\n"
                        + "Guess again!");
    else
        System.out.println("Your guess is "
                        + "higher than "
                        + "the number.\n"
                        + "Guess again!");
}//end while
```

You also need the following code, to be included after the `while` loop, in case the user cannot guess the correct number in five tries:

```
if (!done)
    System.out.println("You lose! The correct "
                        + "number is " + num);
```

We leave it as an exercise for you to write a complete Java program to implement the Guessing the Number game in which the user has, at most, five tries to guess the number. (See Programming Exercise 16 at the end of this chapter.)

As you can see from the preceding `while` loop, the logical expression in a `while` statement can be complex. The main objective of a `while` loop is to repeat certain statement(s) until certain conditions are met.

Next, consider the following `while` loop:

```
int count = 0;

while (count++ < 5)
    System.out.println("Iteration: " + count);
System.out.println("The value of count after the while loop: " + count);
```

Note that the loop control variable count is initialized before the `while` loop and its value is updated in the `while` loop test condition (logical expression). The expression count++ < 5 uses the post-increment operator. So first the value of count is used to evaluate the expression and then the value of count is incremented. The output of the previous `while` loop is:

```
Iteration: 1
Iteration: 2
Iteration: 3
Iteration: 4
Iteration: 5
The value of count after the while loop: 6
```

Now consider the following `while` loop:

```
int count = 0;

while (++count < 5)
    System.out.println("Iteration: " + count);
System.out.println("The value of count after the while loop: " + count);
```

In this `while` loop, the expression ++count < 5 uses the pre-increment operator. So first the value of count is incremented and then its value is used to evaluate the expression. The output of the previous `while` loop is:

```
Iteration: 1
Iteration: 2
Iteration: 3
Iteration: 4
The value of count after the while loop: 5
```

PROGRAMMING EXAMPLE: Fibonacci Number

So far, you have seen several examples of loops. Recall that in Java, `while` loops are used when a certain statement(s) must be executed repeatedly until certain conditions are met. The following program uses a `while` loop to find a **Fibonacci number**.

Consider the following sequence of numbers:

1, 1, 2, 3, 5, 8, 13, 21, 34, ...

Given the first two numbers of the sequence (say, a_1 and a_2), the nth number a_n, $n >= 3$, of this sequence is given by:

$$a_n = a_{n-1} + a_{n-2}$$

Thus:

$$a_3 = a_2 + a_1 = 1 + 1 = 2,$$

$$a_4 = a_3 + a_2 = 2 + 1 = 3,$$

and so on.

Such a sequence is called a **Fibonacci sequence**. In the preceding sequence, $a_2 = 1$ and $a_1 = 1$. However, given any first two numbers, using this process, you can determine the nth number, a_n, $n >= 3$, of the sequence. The number determined this way is called the nth **Fibonacci number**. Suppose $a_2 = 6$ and $a_1 = 3$.

Then:

$$a_3 = a_2 + a_1 = 6 + 3 = 9; a_4 = a_3 + a_2 = 9 + 6 = 15.$$

Next, we write a program that determines the nth Fibonacci number given the first two numbers.

Input: The first two numbers of the Fibonacci sequence and the position of the desired Fibonacci number in the Fibonacci sequence

Output: The nth Fibonacci number

PROBLEM
ANALYSIS
AND
ALGORITHM
DESIGN

To find, say, the 10th Fibonacci number of a sequence, you must first find a_9 and a_8, which requires you to find a_7 and a_6 and so on. Therefore, to find a_{10}, you must first find $a_3, a_4, a_5, \ldots, a_9$. This discussion translates into the following algorithm:

1. Get the first two Fibonacci numbers.

2. Get the position of the desired number in the Fibonacci sequence. That is, get the position, n, of the number in the Fibonacci sequence.

3. Calculate the next Fibonacci number by adding the previous two elements of the Fibonacci sequence.

4. Repeat Step 3 until the nth Fibonacci number is found.

5. Output the nth Fibonacci number.

Note that the program assumes that the first number of the Fibonacci sequence is less than or equal to the second number of the Fibonacci sequence, and both numbers are non-negative. Moreover, the program also assumes that the user enters a valid value for the position of the desired number in the Fibonacci sequence; that is, it is a positive integer. (See Programming Exercise 12 at the end of this chapter.)

VARIABLES

Because you must know the last two numbers to find the current Fibonacci number, you need the following variables: two variables—say, previous1 and previous2—to hold the previous two numbers of the Fibonacci sequence, and one variable—say, current—to hold the current Fibonacci number. The number of times that Step 2 of the algorithm repeats depends on the position of the Fibonacci number you are calculating. For example, if you want to calculate the 10th Fibonacci number, you must execute Step 3 eight times. (Remember, the user gives the first two numbers of the Fibonacci sequence.) Therefore, you need a variable to store the number of times that Step 3 should execute. You also need a variable—the loop control variable—to track the number of times that Step 3 has executed. Therefore, you need five variables for the data manipulation:

```
int previous1;     //Variable to store the first
                   //Fibonacci number
int previous2;     //Variable to store the second
                   //Fibonacci number
int current;       //Variable to store the current
                   //Fibonacci number
int counter;       //Loop control variable
int nthFibonacci;  //Variable to store the desired
                   //Fibonacci number
```

To calculate the third Fibonacci number, add the value of previous1 and previous2 and store the result in current. To calculate the fourth Fibonacci number, add the value of the second Fibonacci number (that is, previous2) and the value of the third Fibonacci number (that is, current). Thus, when the fourth Fibonacci number is calculated, you no longer need the first Fibonacci number. Instead of declaring additional variables, which could be several, after calculating a Fibonacci number to determine the next Fibonacci number, current becomes previous2 and previous2 becomes previous1. Therefore, you can again use the variable current to store the next Fibonacci number. This process is repeated until the desired Fibonacci number is calculated. Initially, previous1 and previous2 are the first two numbers of the sequence, supplied by the user. From the preceding discussion, it follows that you need five variables.

<table>
<tr>
<td>MAIN
ALGORITHM</td>
<td>

1. Display the input dialog box to prompt the user for the first Fibonacci number—that is, `previous1`. Store the string representing `previous1` into `inputString`.

2. Retrieve the string from `inputString`, and store the first Fibonacci number into `previous1`.

3. Display the input dialog box to prompt the user for the second Fibonacci number—that is, `previous2`. Store the string representing `previous2` into `inputString`.

4. Retrieve the string from `inputString`, and store the second Fibonacci number into `previous2`.

5. Create the `outputString` and append `previous1` and `previous2`.

6. Display the input dialog box to prompt the user for the desired Fibonacci number, that is, `nthFibonacci`. Store the string representing `nthFibonacci` into `inputString`.

7. Retrieve the string from `inputString`, and store the desired *n*th Fibonacci number into `nthFibonacci`.

8. a. `if (nthFibonacci == 1)`

   the desired Fibonacci number is the first Fibonacci number. Copy the value of `previous1` into `current`.

   b. `else if (nthFibonacci == 2)`

   the desired Fibonacci number is the second Fibonacci number. Copy the value of `previous2` into `current`.

   c. `else` calculate the desired Fibonacci number as follows:

   Since you already know the first two Fibonacci numbers of the sequence, start by determining the third Fibonacci number.

      i. Initialize `counter` to 3, to keep track of the calculated Fibonacci numbers.

      ii. Calculate the next Fibonacci number, as follows:

   `current = previous2 + previous1;`

      iii. Assign the value of `previous2` to `previous1`.

      iv. Assign the value of `current` to `previous2`.

      v. Increment `counter`.

   Repeat Steps 8c(ii) through 8c(v) until the Fibonacci number you want is calculated.

   The following `while` loop executes Steps 8c(ii) through 8c(v) and determines the *n*th Fibonacci number:

</td>
</tr>
</table>

5

```
                    while (counter <= nthFibonacci)
                    {
                        current = previous2 + previous1;
                        previous1 = previous2;
                        previous2 = current;
                        counter++;
                    }
```

9. Append the *n*th Fibonacci number to outputString. Notice that the *n*th Fibonacci number is stored in current.

10. Display the output dialog box showing the first two and the *n*th Fibonacci numbers.

COMPLETE PROGRAM LISTING

```
//***************************************************************
// Author: D.S. Malik
//
// Program: nth Fibonacci number
// Given the first two numbers of a Fibonacci sequence, this
// determines and outputs the desired number of the Fibonacci
// sequence.
//***************************************************************
import javax.swing.JOptionPane;

public class FibonacciNumber
{
    public static void main (String[] args)
    {
            //Declare variables

        String inputString;
        String outputString;

        int    previous1;
        int    previous2;
        int    current = 0;
        int    counter;
        int    nthFibonacci;

        inputString =
            JOptionPane.showInputDialog("Enter the first "
                            + "Fibonacci number: ");   //Step 1
        previous1 = Integer.parseInt(inputString);       //Step 2

        inputString =
            JOptionPane.showInputDialog("Enter the second "
                            + "Fibonacci number: ");  //Step 3
        previous2 = Integer.parseInt(inputString);       //Step 4
```

```java
outputString = "The first two numbers of the "
             + "Fibonacci sequence are: "
             + previous1 + " and " + previous2;   //Step 5

inputString =
    JOptionPane.showInputDialog("Enter the position "
             + "of the desired number in "
             + "the Fibonacci sequence: ");   //Step 6
nthFibonacci = Integer.parseInt(inputString);   //Step 7

if (nthFibonacci == 1)                          //Step 8.a
    current = previous1;
else if (nthFibonacci == 2)                     //Step 8.b
    current = previous2;
else                                            //Step 8.c
{
    counter = 3;                                //Step 8.c.1

        //Steps 8.c.2 - 8.c.5
    while (counter <= nthFibonacci)
    {
        current = previous2 + previous1;        //Step 8.c.2
        previous1 = previous2;                  //Step 8.c.3
        previous2 = current;                    //Step 8.c.4
        counter++;                              //Step 8.c.5
    }
}

outputString = outputString + "\nThe "
             + nthFibonacci
             + "th Fibonacci number of "
             + "the sequence is: "
             + current;                         //Step 9

JOptionPane.showMessageDialog(null, outputString,
                    "Fibonacci Number",
             JOptionPane.INFORMATION_MESSAGE);   //Step 10
System.exit(0);
    }
}
```

5

Sample Run: (Figure 5-3 shows the sample run.)

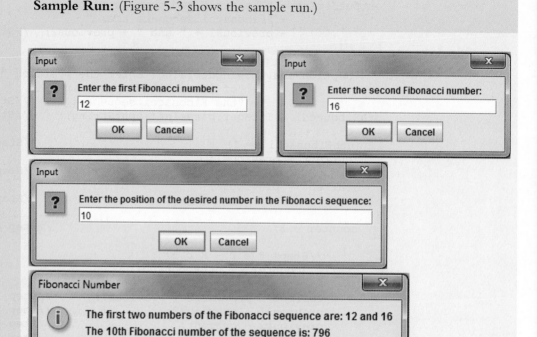

FIGURE 5-3 Sample run `FibonacciNumber`

`for` Looping (Repetition) Structure

The `while` loop discussed in the previous section is general enough to implement all forms of repetitions. As noted earlier, Java provides three looping structures. The previous section discussed `while` loops in detail. This section explains how to use Java's `for` loop.

The general form of the `for` statement is:

```
for (initial expression; logical expression; update expression)
    statement
```

In Java, `for` is a reserved word. The `logical expression` is called the **loop condition**. The `initial expression`, `logical expression`, and `update expression` (called `for` loop **control expressions**) are enclosed within parentheses and control the body (`statement`) of the `for` statement. Note that the `for` loop control expressions are separated by semicolons, and that the body of a `for` loop can have either a simple or compound statement. Figure 5-4 shows the flow of execution of a `for` loop.

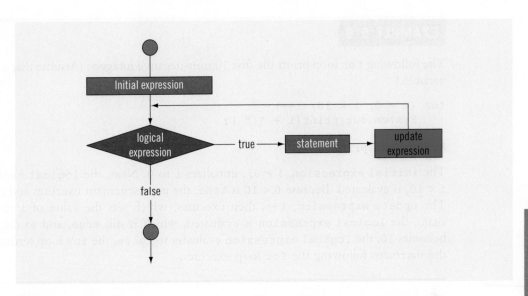

FIGURE 5-4 for loop

The **for** loop executes as follows:

1. The `initial expression` executes.
2. The `logical expression` is evaluated. If the `loop condition` evaluates to `true`:

    a. Execute the body of the `for` loop.

    b. Execute the `update statement` (the third expression in the parentheses).

3. Repeat Step 2 until the `loop condition` evaluates to `false`.

The `initial statement` usually initializes a variable (called the `for` loop control, or indexed, variable).

NOTE   As the name implies, the `initial expression` in the `for` loop is the first statement to execute; it executes only once.

Primarily, `for` loops are used to implement counter-controlled loops. For this reason, the `for` loop is typically called a **counted** or **indexed** `for` loop. Next, we give various examples to illustrate how a `for` loop works.

EXAMPLE 5-9

The following `for` loop prints the first 10 non-negative integers: (Assume that `i` is an `int` variable.)

```
for (i = 0; i < 10; i++)
    System.out.print(i + " " );

System.out.println();
```

The initial expression, `i = 0;`, initializes `i` to 0. Next, the logical expression, `i < 10`, is evaluated. Because `0 < 10` is `true`, the print statement executes and outputs 0. The update expression, `i++`, then executes, which sets the value of `i` to 1. Once again, the logical expression is evaluated, which is still `true`, and so on. When `i` becomes 10, the logical expression evaluates to `false`, the `for` loop terminates, and the statement following the `for` loop executes.

The following examples further illustrate how a `for` loop executes.

EXAMPLE 5-10

1. The following `for` loop outputs the word `Hello` and a star (on separate lines) five times:

   ```
   for (i = 1; i <= 5; i++)
   {
       System.out.println("Hello");
       System.out.println("*");
   }
   ```

2. Now consider the following `for` loop:

   ```
   for (i = 1; i <= 5; i++)
       System.out.println("Hello");
       System.out.println("*");
   ```

This loop outputs the word `Hello` five times and the star only once. In this case, the `for` loop controls only the first output statement because the two output statements are not made into a compound statement using braces. Therefore, the first output statement executes five times because the `for` loop executes five times. After the `for` loop executes, the second output statement executes only once.

EXAMPLE 5-11

The following `for` loop executes five empty statements:

```
for (i = 0; i < 5; i++);          //Line 1
    System.out.println("*");      //Line 2
```

The semicolon at the end of the `for` statement (before the output statement in Line 2) terminates the `for` loop. The action of this `for` loop is empty. The statement in Line 2 outputs a star.

The preceding examples show that care is required to get a `for` loop to perform the desired action.

Some additional comments on `for` loops follow:

- If the `logical expression` is initially `false`, the loop body does not execute.

- The update expression, when executed, should change the value of the loop control variable, which eventually sets the value of the loop condition to `false`. The `for` loop executes indefinitely if the loop condition is always `true`.

- If you put a semicolon at the end of a `for` statement (just before the body of the loop), the action of the `for` loop is empty.

- In a `for` statement, if the `logical expression` is omitted, it is assumed to be `true`.

- In a `for` statement, you can omit all three statements—initial expression, `logical expression`, and `update expression`. The following is a legal `for` loop:

  ```
  for (;;)
      System.out.println("Hello");
  ```

  This is an infinite `for` loop, continuously printing the world `Hello`.

More examples of `for` loops follow.

EXAMPLE 5-12

1. You can count backward using a `for` loop if the `for` loop control expressions are set correctly. For example, consider the following `for` loop:

   ```
   for (i = 10; i >= 1; i--)
       System.out.print(i + " ");

   System.out.println();
   ```

The output is:

```
10 9 8 7 6 5 4 3 2 1
```

In this `for` loop, the variable `i` is initialized to 10. After each iteration of the loop, `i` is decremented by 1. The loop continues to execute as long as `i >= 1`.

2. You can increment (or decrement) the loop control variable by any fixed number (or modify it in any way you please). In the following `for` loop, the variable is initialized to 0; at the end of the `for` loop, `i` is incremented by 2. This `for` loop outputs 10 even integers 0 through 18:

```java
for (i = 0; i < 20; i = i + 2)
    System.out.print(i + " ");

System.out.println();
```

EXAMPLE 5-13

Consider the following examples, where `i` is an `int` variable.

1.
```java
for (i = 10; i <= 9; i++)
    System.out.print(i + " ");

System.out.println();
```

In this `for` loop, the initial expression sets `i` to 10. Because initially the logical expression (`i <= 9`) is `false`, the body of the `for` loop does not execute.

2.
```java
for (i = 9; i >= 10; i--)
    System.out.print(i + " ");

System.out.println();
```

In this `for` loop, the initial expression sets `i` to 9. Because initially the logical expression (`i >= 10`) is `false`, the body of the `for` loop does not execute.

3.
```java
for (i = 10; i <= 10; i++)        //Line 1
    System.out.print(i + " ");    //Line 2

System.out.println();             //Line 3
```

In this `for` loop, the output statement in Line 2 executes once.

4.
```java
for (i = 1; i <= 10; i++);
    System.out.print(i + " ");

System.out.println();
```

This **for** loop has no effect on the output statement. The semicolon at the end of the **for** statement terminates the **for** loop; the action of the **for** loop is thus empty. Both output statements are outside the scope of the **for** loop, so the **for** loop has no effect on them. Note that this code will output 11.

5.  ```
    for (i = 1; ; i++)
        System.out.print(i + " ");

    System.out.println();
    ```

In this **for** loop, because the `logical expression` is omitted from the **for** statement, the loop condition is always **true**. This is an infinite loop.

5

EXAMPLE 5-14

In this example, a **for** loop reads five integers and finds their sum and average. Consider the following programming code, in which i, newNum, sum, and average are **int** variables:

```
sum = 0;

for (i = 0; i < 5; i++)
{
    newNum = console.nextInt();
    sum = sum + newNum;
}

average = sum / 5;
System.out.println("The sum is " + sum);
System.out.println("The average is " + average);
```

In the preceding **for** loop, after getting a newNum, this value is added to the previously calculated (partial) sum of all the numbers read before the current number. The variable sum is initialized to 0 before the **for** loop. Thus, after the program gets the first number and adds it to the value of sum, the variable sum holds the correct sum of the first number.
```

NOTE   The syntax of the `for` loop, which is

```
for (initial expression; logical expression; update expression)
    statement
```

is functionally equivalent to the following `while` statement:

```
initial expression
while (logical expression)
{
        statement
        update expression
}
```

For example, the following `for` and `while` loops are equivalent:

```
for (int i = 0; i < 10; i++)        int i = 0;
    system.out.print(i + " ");      while (i < 10)
system.out.println();               {
                                            system.out.print(i + " ");
                                            i++;
                                    }
                                    system.out.println();
```

If the number of iterations of a loop is known or can be determined in advance, then typically, programmers use a `for` loop.

EXAMPLE 5-15 (FIBONACCI NUMBER PROGRAM: REVISITED)

The programming example Fibonacci Number given in the previous section uses a `while` loop to determine the desired Fibonacci number. You can replace the `while` loop with an equivalent `for` loop as follows:

```
for (counter = 3; counter <= nthFibonacci; counter++)
{
    current = previous2 + previous1;
    previous1 = previous2;
    previous2 = current;
    counter++;
}//end for
```

The complete program listing of the program that uses a `for` loop to determine the desired Fibonacci number is given with the Additional Student Files at *www.cengagebrain.com*. The program is named Ch5_FibonacciNumberUsingAForLoop.java.

Recall that putting one control structure statement inside another is called **nesting**. The following programming example demonstrates a simple instance of nesting, and also nicely demonstrates counting.

PROGRAMMING EXAMPLE: Classify Numbers

This program reads a given set of integers and then prints the number of odd integers, the number of even integers, and the number of zeros.

The program reads 20 integers, but you can easily modify it to read any set of numbers. In fact, you can modify the program so that it first prompts the user to specify how many integers are to be read.

Input: 20 integers—positive, negative, or zeros

Output: The number of zeros, even numbers, and odd numbers

PROBLEM
ANALYSIS
AND
ALGORITHM
DESIGN

After reading a number, you need to check whether it is even or odd. Suppose the value is stored in the variable number. Divide number by 2 and check the remainder. If the remainder is zero, number is even. Increment the even count and then check whether number is zero. If it is, increment the zero count. If the remainder is not zero, increment the odd count.

The program uses a `switch` statement to decide whether number is odd or even. Suppose that number is odd. Dividing by 2 gives the remainder 1 if number is positive, and the remainder -1 if negative. If number is even, dividing by 2 gives the remainder 0 whether number is positive or negative. You can use the mod operator, %, to find the remainder. For example:

```
6 % 2 = 0, -4 % 2 = 0, -7 % 2 = -1, 15 % 2 = 1
```

Repeat the preceding process of analyzing a number for each number in the list.

This discussion translates into the following algorithm:

1. For each number in the list:
   a. Get the number.
   b. Analyze the number.
   c. Increment the appropriate count.
2. Print the results.

VARIABLES

Because you want to count the number of zeros, even numbers, and odd numbers, you need three variables of the type int—say, zeros, evens, and odds—to track the counts. You also need a variable—say, number—to read and store the number to be analyzed, and another variable—say, counter—to count the numbers analyzed. Your program thus needs the following variables:

```
int counter;    //loop control variable
int number;     //variable to store the number read
int zeros;      //variable to store the zero count
int evens;      //variable to store the even count
int odds;       //variable to store the odd count
```

Clearly, you must initialize the variables zeros, evens, and odds to zero. You can initialize these variables when you declare them.

MAIN
ALGORITHM

1. Initialize the variables.

2. Prompt the user to enter 20 numbers.

3. For each number in the list:

   a. Get the next number.

   b. Output the number (echo input).

   c. If the number is even:

      {

      i. Increment the even count.

      ii. If the number is zero, increment the zero count.

      }

   otherwise,

      Increment the odd count.

4. Print the results.

Before writing the Java program, let's describe Steps 1 through 4 in more detail. It will be much easier for you to then write the instructions in Java.

1. Initialize the variables. You can initialize the variables zeros, evens, and odds when you declare them.

2. Use an output statement to prompt the user to enter 20 numbers.

3. For Step 3, you can use a `for` loop to process and analyze the 20 numbers. In pseudocode, this step is written as follows:

```
for (counter = 1; counter <= 20; counter++)
{
    a.  get the number;
    b.  output the number;
    c.  switch (number % 2)      //check the remainder
        {
        case 0:
            increment the even count;
            if (number == 0)
                increment the zero count;
            break;
```

```
                    case 1:
                    case -1:
                          increment the odd count;
                    }//end switch
              }//end for
```

4. Print the result. Output the values of the variables zeros, evens, and odds.

COMPLETE PROGRAM LISTING

```java
//*********************************************************
// Author: D.S. Malik
//
// Program: Classify Numbers
// This program counts the number of odd and even numbers.
// The program also counts the number of zeros.
//*********************************************************

import java.util.*;

public class ClassifyNumbers
{
    static Scanner console = new Scanner(System.in);

    static final int N = 20;

    public static void main (String[] args)
    {
            //Declare the variables
        int counter;  //loop control variable
        int number;    //variable to store the new number

        int zeros = 0;                              //Step 1
        int odds = 0;                               //Step 1
        int evens = 0;                              //Step 1

        System.out.println("Please enter " + N
                    + " integers, positive, "
                    + "negative, or zeros.");  //Step 2

        for (counter = 1; counter <= N; counter++)  //Step 3
        {
            number = console.nextInt();             //Step 3a
            System.out.print(number + " ");         //Step 3b

                //Step 3c
            switch (number % 2)
```

```
            {
            case 0:
                evens++;
                if (number == 0)
                    zeros++;
                break;

            case 1:
            case -1:
                odds++;
            }//end switch

      }//end for loop

      System.out.println();

            //Step 4
      System.out.println("There are " + evens + " evens, "
                    + "which also includes "
                    + zeros + " zeros");
      System.out.println("Total number of odds is: " + odds);
    }
}
```

Sample Run: (In this sample run, the user input is shaded.)

```
Please enter 20 integers, positive, negative, or zeros.
0 0 -2 -3 -5 6 7 8 0 3 0 -23 -8 0 2 9 0 12 67 54
0 0 -2 -3 -5 6 7 8 0 3 0 -23 -8 0 2 9 0 12 67 54
There are 13 evens, which also includes 6 zeros
Total number of odds is: 7
```

We recommend that you do a walk-through of this program using the above sample input.

Note that the `switch` statement in Step 3c can also be written as an `if...else` statement as follows:

```
if (number % 2 == 0)
{
    evens++;
    if (number == 0)
        zeros++;
}
else
    odds++;
```

do...while Looping (Repetition) Structure

This section describes the third type of looping or repetition structure—a do...while loop. The general form of a do...while statement is:

```
do
    statement
while (logical expression);
```

In Java, `do` is a reserved word. As with the other repetition structures, the `do...while` statement can be either a simple or compound statement. If it is a compound statement, enclose it between braces. The `logical expression` is called the **loop condition**. Figure 5-5 shows the flow of execution of a `do...while` loop.

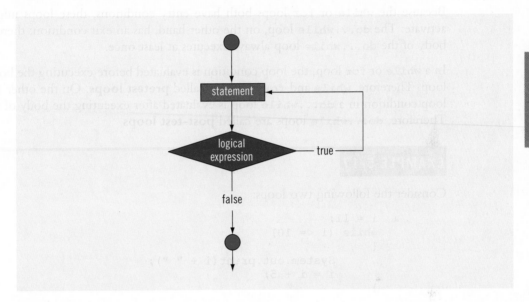

FIGURE 5-5 `do...while` loop

The `statement` executes first, and then the `logical expression` is evaluated. If the `logical expression` evaluates to `true`, the `statement` executes again. As long as the `logical expression` in a `do...while` statement is `true`, the `statement` executes. To avoid an infinite loop, you must, as before, make sure that the body of the loop contains a statement that ultimately makes the `logical expression` evaluate to `false` and assures that it exits properly.

EXAMPLE 5-16

```
i = 0;
do
{
    System.out.print(i + " ");
    i = i + 5;
}
while (i <= 20);
```

The output of this code is:

```
0 5 10 15 20
```

After the value 20 is output, the statement:

```
i = i + 5;
```

changes the value of i to 25, so i <= 20 becomes `false`, which halts the loop.

Because the `while` or `for` loops both have entry conditions, these loops might never activate. The `do...while` loop, on the other hand, has an exit condition; therefore, the body of the `do...while` loop always executes at least once.

In a `while` or `for` loop, the loop condition is evaluated before executing the body of the loop. Therefore, `while` and `for` loops are called **pretest loops**. On the other hand, the loop condition in a `do...while` loop is evaluated after executing the body of the loop. Therefore, `do...while` loops are called **post-test loops**.

EXAMPLE 5-17

Consider the following two loops:

```
a.  i = 11;
    while (i <= 10)
    {
            System.out.print(i + " ");
            i = i + 5;
    }

    System.out.println();

b.  i = 11;
    do
    {
        System.out.print(i + " ");
        i = i + 5;
    }
    while (i <= 10);

    System.out.println();
```

In (a), the `while` loop produces nothing. In (b), the `do...while` loop outputs the number 11 and also changes the value of i to 16.

A `do...while` loop can be used for input validation. Suppose that a program prompts a user to enter a test score, which must be greater than or equal to 0 and less than or equal to 50. If the user enters a score less than 0 or greater than 50, the user should be prompted to re-enter the score. The following `do...while` loop can be used to accomplish this objective:

```
int score;

do
{
    System.out.print("Enter a score between 0 and 50: ");
    score = console.nextInt();
    System.out.println();
}
while (score < 0 || score > 50);
```

EXAMPLE 5-18 DIVISIBILITY TEST BY 3 AND 9

Suppose that m and n are integers and m is nonzero. Then m is called a **divisor** of n if $n = mt$ for some integer t; that is, when m divides n, the remainder is 0.

Let $n = a_k a_{k-1} a_{k-2} \ldots a_1 a_0$ be an integer. Let $s = a_k + a_{k-1} + a_{k-2} + \ldots + a_1 + a_0$ be the sum of the digits of n. It is known that n is divisible by 3 and 9 if s is divisible by 3 and 9. In other words, an integer is divisible by 3 and 9 if and only if the sum of its digits is divisible by 3 and 9.

For example, suppose $n = 27193257$. Then, $s = 2 + 7 + 1 + 9 + 3 + 2 + 5 + 7 = 36$. Because 36 is divisible by both 3 and 9, it follows that 27193257 is divisible by both 3 and 9.

Next, we write a program that determines whether a positive integer is divisible by 3 and 9 by first finding the sum of its digits and then checking whether the sum is divisible by 3 and 9.

To find the sum of the digits of a positive integer, we need to extract each digit of the number. Consider the number 951372. Note that 951372 % 10 = 2, which is the last digit of 951372. Also note that 951372 / 10 = 95137, that is, when the number is divided by 10, it removes the last digit. Next, we repeat this process on the number 95137. Of course, we need to add the extracted digits.

Suppose that sum and num are `int` variables and the positive integer is stored in num. We thus have the following algorithm to find the sum of the digits:

```
sum = 0;

do
{
    sum = sum + num % 10;   //extract the last digit
                            //and add it to sum
    num = num / 10;         //remove the last digit
}
while (num > 0);
```

Using this algorithm, we can write the following program that uses a do...while loop to implement the preceding divisibility test algorithm.

5

```java
//Program: Divisibility test by 3 and 9

import java.util.*;

public class DivisibilityTest
{
    static Scanner console = new Scanner(System.in);

    public static void main (String[] args)
    {
        int num;
        int temp;
        int sum;

        System.out.print("Enter a positive integer: ");
        num = console.nextInt();
        System.out.println();

        temp = num;

        sum = 0;

        do
        {
            sum = sum + num % 10; //extract the last digit
                                  //and add it to sum
            num = num / 10;       //remove the last digit
        }
        while (num > 0);

        System.out.println("The sum of the digits = " + sum);

        if (sum % 3 == 0)
            System.out.println(temp + " is divisible by 3");
        else
            System.out.println(temp + " is not divisible by 3");

        if (sum % 9 == 0)
            System.out.println(temp + " is divisible by 9");
        else
            System.out.println(temp + " is not divisible by 9");
    }
}
```

Sample Runs: (In these sample runs, the user input is shaded.)

Sample Run 1:
Enter a positive integer: 27193257

The sum of the digits = 36
27193257 is divisible by 3
27193257 is divisible by 9

Sample Run 2:
```
Enter a positive integer: 609321

The sum of the digits = 21
609321 is divisible by 3
609321 is not divisible by 9
```

Sample Run 3:
```
Enter a positive integer: 161905102

The sum of the digits = 25
161905102 is not divisible by 3
161905102 is not divisible by 9
```

5

Choosing the Right Looping Structure

All three loops have a place in Java. If you know or the program can determine in advance the number of repetitions needed, the `for` loop is the correct choice. If you do not know, and the program cannot determine in advance, the number of repetitions needed, and it could be zero, the `while` loop is the right choice. If you do not know, and the program cannot determine in advance, the number of repetitions needed, and it is at least one, the `do...while` loop is the right choice.

break and continue Statements

The `break` and `continue` statements alter the flow of control in a program. As you have seen, the `break` statement, when executed in a `switch` structure, provides an immediate exit from the `switch` structure. Similarly, you can use the `break` statement in `while`, `for`, and `do...while` loops to immediately exit from these structures. The `break` statement is typically used for two purposes:

- To exit early from a loop

- To skip the remainder of the `switch` structure

After the `break` statement executes, the program continues to execute starting at the first statement after the structure.

Suppose that you have the following declaration:

```
static Scanner console = new Scanner(System.in);

int sum;
int num;

boolean isNegative;
```

The use of a `break` statement in a loop can eliminate the use of certain `boolean` variables. The following Java code segment helps illustrate this idea:

```
sum = 0;
isNegative = false;

while (console.hasNext() && !isNegative)
{
    num = console.nextInt();

    if (num < 0)  //if the number is negative, terminate the
                  //loop after this iteration
    {
        System.out.println("Negative number found in the data.");

        isNegative = true;
    }
    else
        sum = sum + num;
}
```

This `while` loop is supposed to find the sum of a set of positive numbers. If the data set contains a negative number, the loop terminates with an appropriate error message. This `while` loop uses the flag variable `isNegative` to accomplish the desired result. The variable `isNegative` is initialized to `false` before the `while` loop. Before adding num to sum, the code checks whether num is negative. If num is negative, an error message appears on the screen and `isNegative` is set to `true`. In the next iteration, when the expression in the `while` statement is evaluated, it evaluates to `false` because `!isNegative` is `false`. (Note that because `isNegative` is `true`, `!isNegative` is `false`.)

The following `while` loop is written without using the variable `isNegative`:

```
sum = 0;

while (console.hasNext())
{
    num = console.nextInt();

    if (num < 0)    //if the number is negative, terminate the loop
    {
        System.out.println("Negative number found in the data.");

        break;
    }

    sum = sum + num;
}
```

In this form of the `while` loop, when a negative number is found, the expression in the `if` statement evaluates to `true`; after printing an appropriate message, the `break` statement terminates the loop. (After executing the `break` statement in a loop, the remaining statements in the loop are skipped.)

The `continue` statement is used in `while`, `for`, and `do...while` structures. When the `continue` statement is executed in a loop, it skips the remaining statements in the loop and proceeds with the next iteration of the loop. In a `while` or `do...while` structure, the `logical expression` is evaluated immediately after the `continue` statement. In a `for` structure, the `update statement` is executed after the `continue` statement, and then the `logical expression` executes.

If the previous program segment encounters a negative number, the `while` loop terminates. If you want to ignore the negative number and read the next number rather than terminate the loop, replace the `break` statement with the `continue` statement, as shown in the following example:

```
sum = 0;

while (console.hasNext())
{
    num = console.nextInt();

    if (num < 0) //if the number is negative, go to the
                 //next iteration
    {
        System.out.println("Negative number found in the data.");

        continue;
    }

    sum = sum + num;
}
```

> **NOTE** The `break` and `continue` statements are an effective way to avoid extra variables to control a loop and produce an elegant code. However, these statements must be used very sparingly within a loop. An excessive use of these statements in a loop will produce a spaghetti-code (loops with many exit conditions) and could be very hard to understand and manage.

> **NOTE** As stated earlier, all three loops have their place in Java and one loop can often replace another. The execution of a `continue` statement, however, is where a `while` structure differs from a `for` structure. In a `while` loop, when the `continue` statement is executed, if the `update statement` appears after the `continue` statement, the `update statement` is not executed. In a `for` loop, the `update statement` always executes.

Avoiding Bugs by Avoiding Patches

Debugging sections in the previous chapters illustrated how to debug syntax and logical errors, and how to avoid partially understood concepts. In this section, we illustrate how to avoid a software patch to fix a code. A software patch is a piece of code written on top of an existing piece of code intended to fix a bug in the original code.

Suppose that the following data is in the file `Ch5_LoopWithBugsData.txt`:

```
87 78 83 94
23 89 92 70
92 78 34 56
```

The objective is to find the sum of the numbers in each line. For each line, output the numbers together with their sum. Let us consider the following program:

```java
import java.io.*;
import java.util.*;

public class LoopWithBugsData1
{
    public static void main(String[] args)
                        throws FileNotFoundException
    {
        int i;
        int j;
        int sum;
        int num;

        Scanner infile =
            new Scanner(new FileReader("Ch5_LoopWithBugsData.txt"));

        for (i = 1; i <= 4; i++)
        {
            sum = 0;

            for (j = 1; j <= 4; j++)
            {
                num = infile.nextInt();
                System.out.print(num + " ");
                sum = sum + num;
            }

            System.out.println("sum = " + sum);
        }
    }
}
```

Sample Run:

```
87 78 83 94 sum = 342
23 89 92 70 sum = 274
92 78 34 56 sum = 260
Exception in thread "main" java.util.NoSuchElementException
        at java.util.Scanner.throwFor(Scanner.java:838)
        at java.util.Scanner.next(Scanner.java:1461)
        at java.util.Scanner.nextInt(Scanner.java:2091)
        at java.util.Scanner.nextInt(Scanner.java:2050)
        at LoopWithBugsData1.main(LoopWithBugsData1.java:23)
```

The Sample Run shows that there is a bug in the program because after correctly producing the three lines of output, the program crashes with error messages. (This is an example of a run (execution) time error. That is, the program compiled correctly, but crashed during execution.) The last line of output shows that the error is in line 23 of the code, which is the input statement: num = infile.nextInt();. The program is trying to read data from the input file, but there is no more input in the file. At this point the value of the outer loop variable i is 4. Clearly, there is a bug in the program and we must fix the code. Some programmers, especially some beginners, address the symptom of the problem by adding a software patch. A beginning programmer might fix the code by adding a software patch as shown in the following modified program:

```java
import java.io.*;
import java.util.*;

public class LoopWithBugsData2
{
    public static void main(String[] args)
                        throws FileNotFoundException
    {
        int i;
        int j;
        int sum;
        int num;

        Scanner infile =
            new Scanner(new FileReader("Ch5_LoopWithBugsData.txt"));

        for (i = 1; i <= 4; i++)
        {
            sum = 0;

            if (i != 4)
            {
                for (j = 1; j <= 4; j++)
                {
                    num = infile.nextInt();
                    System.out.print(num + " ");
                    sum = sum + num;
                }

                System.out.println("sum = " + sum);
            }
        }
    }
}
```

Sample Run:

```
87 78 83 94 sum = 342
23 89 92 70 sum = 274
92 78 34 56 sum = 260
```

Clearly, the program is working correctly now.

As we can see, the programmer merely observed the symptom and addressed the problem by adding a software patch. However, if you look at the code, not only will the program execute extra statements, it is also an example of a partially understood concept. It appears that the programmer does not have a good grasp of why the earlier program produced four lines rather than three. Adding a patch eliminated the symptom, but it is a poor programming practice. The programmer must resolve why the program produced four lines. Looking at the program closely, we can see that the four lines are produced because the outer loop executes four times. The values assigned to loop control variable i are 1, 2, 3, and 4. This is an example of the classic "off by one" problem. (In the "off by one" problem, either the loop executes one too many or one too few times.) We can eliminate this problem by correctly setting the values of the loop control variable. For example, we can rewrite the loops as follows:

```
for (i = 1; i <= 3; i++)
{
    sum = 0;

    for (j = 1; j <= 4; j++)
    {
        num = infile.nextInt();
        System.out.print(num + " ");
        sum = sum + num;
    }

    System.out.println("sum = " + sum);
}
```

This code fixes the original problem without using a software patch. It also represents good programming practice. The complete modified program is available with the Additional Student Files at *www.cengagebrain.com*. The program is named `Ch5_LoopWithBugsCorrectedProgram.cpp`.

DEBUGGING

Debugging Loops

As we have seen in the earlier debugging sections, no matter how carefully a program is designed and coded, errors are likely to occur. If there are syntax errors, the compiler will identify them. However, if there are logical errors, we must carefully look at the code or even maybe at the design to try to find the errors. To increase the reliability of the program, errors must be discovered and fixed before the program is released to the users.

Once an algorithm is written, the next step is to verify that it works properly. If the algorithm is a simple sequential flow or contains a branch, it can be hand traced or you can use the debugger, if any, provided by the IDE. Typically, loops are harder to debug. The correctness of a loop can be verified by using loop invariants. A loop invariant is a set of statements that remains true each time the loop body is executed. Let p be a loop invariant and q be the (logical) expression in a loop statement. Then p && q remains true before each iteration of the loop and p && $not(q)$ is true after the loop terminates. The full discussion of loop invariants is beyond the scope of the book. However, you can learn about loop invariants in the book: *Discrete Mathematics: Theory and Applications*, D.S. Malik and M.K. Sen, Cengage Learning, Asia, 2010. Here we give a few tips that you can use to debug a loop.

As discussed in the previous section, the most common error associated with loops is off by one. If a loop turns out to be an infinite loop, the error is most likely in the logical expression that controls the execution of the loop. Check the logical expression carefully and see if you have reversed an inequality, an assignment statement symbol appears in place of the equality operator, or && appears in place of ||. If the loop changes the values of variables, you can print the values of the variables before and/or after each iteration or you can use your IDE's debugger, if any, and watch the values of variables during each iteration.

The debugging sections in this book are designed to help you understand the debugging process. However, as you will realize, debugging can be a tiresome process. If your program is very bad, do not debug, throw it away and start over.

Nested Control Structures

5

In this section, we give examples that illustrate how to use nested loops to achieve useful results and process data.

EXAMPLE 5-19

Suppose you want to create the following pattern:

```
*
**
***
****
*****
```

Clearly, you want to print five lines of stars. In the first line you want to print one star, in the second line two stars, and so on. Because five lines will be printed, start with the following for statement:

```
for (i = 1; i <= 5; i++)
```

The value of i in the first iteration is 1, in the second iteration it is 2, and so on. You can use the value of i as the limiting condition in another for loop nested within this loop to control the number of stars in a line. A little more thought produces the following code:

```
for (i = 1; i <= 5; i++)                //Line 1
{                                        //Line 2
    for (j = 1; j <= i; j++)             //Line 3
        System.out.print("*");          //Line 4

    System.out.println();               //Line 5
}                                        //Line 6
```

A walk-through of this code shows that the for loop, in Line 1, starts with i = 1. When i is 1, the inner for loop, in Line 3, outputs one star and the insertion point moves to the next line. Then i becomes 2, the inner for loop outputs two stars, and the output statement in Line 5 moves the insertion point to the next line, and so on. This process continues until i becomes 6 and the loop stops.

What pattern does this code produce if you replace the for statement, in Line 1, with the following?

```
for (i = 5; i >= 1; i--)
```

EXAMPLE 5-20

Suppose you want to create the following multiplication table:

```
1  2  3  4  5  6  7  8  9 10
2  4  6  8 10 12 14 16 18 20
3  6  9 12 15 18 21 24 27 30
4  8 12 16 20 24 28 32 36 40
5 10 15 20 25 30 35 40 45 50
```

The multiplication table has five lines. Therefore, as in Example 5-19, we use a for statement to output these lines as follows:

```
for (i = 1; i <= 5; i++)
    //output a line of numbers
```

In the first line, we want to print the multiplication table of one, in the second line we want to print the multiplication table of 2, and so on. Notice that the first line starts with 1 and when this line is printed, i is 1. Similarly, the second line starts with 2 and when this line is printed, the value of i is 2, and so on. If i is 1, i * 1 is 1; if i is 2, i * 2 is 2; and so on. Therefore, to print a line of numbers we can use the value of i as the starting number and 10 as the limiting value. That is, consider the following for loop:

```
for (j = 1; j <= 10; j++)
    System.out.printf("%3d", i * j);
```

Let us take a look at this for loop. Suppose i is 1. Then we are printing the first line of the multiplication table. Also, j goes from 1 to 10 and so this for loop outputs the numbers 1 through 10, which is the first line of the multiplication table. Similarly, if i is 2, we are printing the second line of the multiplication table. Also, j goes from 1 to 10, and so this for loop outputs the second line of the multiplication table, and so on.

A little more thought produces the following nested loops to output the desired grid:

```
for (i = 1; i <= 5; i++)                    //Line 1
{                                           //Line 2
    for (j = 1; j <= 10; j++)               //Line 3
        System.out.printf("%3d", i * j);    //Line 4

    System.out.println();                   //Line 5
}                                           //Line 6
```

EXAMPLE 5-21

Consider the following data residing in a file:

```
65 78 65 89 25 98 -999
87 34 89 99 26 78 64 34 -999
23 99 98 97 26 78 100 63 87 23 -999
62 35 78 99 12 93 19 -999
```

The number -999 at the end of each line acts as a sentinel and, therefore, it is not part of the data. Our objective is to find the sum of the numbers in each line and output the sum. Moreover, assume that this data is to be read from a file, say, Exp_5_21.txt. We assume that the input file has been opened using the input file stream variable inFile.

This particular data set has four lines of input. So we can use a for loop or a counter-controlled while loop to process each line of data. Let us use a for loop to process these four lines. The for loop takes the following form:

```
for (counter = 0; counter < 4; counter++;)    //Line 1
{                                              //Line 2
    //process the line
    //output the sum
}
```

Let us now concentrate on processing a line. Each line has a varying number of data items. For example, the first line has 6 numbers, the second line has 8 numbers, and so on. Because each line ends with -999, we can use a sentinel-controlled while loop to find the sum of the numbers in each line. Remember how a sentinel-controlled loop works. Consider the following while loop:

```
sum = 0;                            //Line 3
num = inFile.nextInt();             //Line 4

while (num != -999)                 //Line 5
{                                   //Line 6
    sum = sum + num;                //Line 7
    num = inFile.nextInt();         //Line 8
}                                   //Line 9
```

The statement in Line 3 initializes sum to 0, and the statement in Line 4 reads and stores the first number of the line into num. The logical expression, num != -999, in Line 5, checks whether the number is -999. If num is not -999, the statements in Lines 7 and 8 execute. The statement in Line 7 updates the value of sum; the statement in Line 8 reads and stores the next number into num. The loop continues to execute as long as num is not -999.

It now follows that the nested loop to process the data is as follows (assuming that all variables are properly declared):

```
for (counter = 0; counter < 4; counter++;)    //Line 1
{                                              //Line 2
    sum = 0;                                   //Line 3
    num = inFile.nextInt();                    //Line 4
```

5

```
    while (num != -999)                         //Line 5
    {                                           //Line 6
        sum = sum + num;                        //Line 7
        num = inFile.nextInt();                 //Line 8
    }                                           //Line 9

    System.out.println("Line " + (counter + 1)
                   + ": Sum = " + sum);         //Line 10
}                                               //Line 11
```

EXAMPLE 5-22

Consider the following data:

```
101
Lance Smith
65 78 65 89 25 98 -999
102
Cynthia Marker
87 34 89 99 26 78 64 34 -999
103
Sheila Mann
23 99 98 97 26 78 100 63 87 23 -999
104
David Arora
62 35 78 99 12 93 19 -999
...
```

The number -999 at the end of a line acts as a sentinel and therefore is not part of the data.

Assume that this data describes certain candidates seeking the student council's presidential seat. For each candidate the data is in the following form:

```
ID
Name
Votes
```

The objective is to find the total number of votes received by each candidate.

We assume that the data is input from the file, Exp_5_22.txt, of unknown size. We also assume that the input file has been opened using the Scanner variable inFile.

Because the input file is of an unspecified length, we use an EOF-controlled while loop. For each candidate, the first data item is the ID of the type, say, int, on a line by itself; the second data item is the name, which may consist of more than one word; and the third line contains the votes received from the various departments.

To read the `ID` we use the method `nextInt`; to read the name we use the method `nextLine`. Notice that after reading the `ID`, the reading marker is after the `ID` and the character after the `ID` is the newline character. Therefore, after reading the `ID`, the reading marker is after the `ID` and at the newline character (of the line containing the `ID`).

The method `nextLine` reads until the end of the line. Therefore, if we read the name immediately after reading the `ID`, then the method `nextLine` will position the reading marker after the newline character following the `ID`, and nothing will be stored in the variable `name`. Because the reading marker is just before the name, if we use the method `nextInt` to read the voting data, the program will terminate with an error message. Therefore, it follows that to read the name, we must discard the newline character after the `ID`, which we can do using the method `nextLine`. (Assume that `discard` is a variable of type `String`.) Therefore, the statements to read the `ID` and name are as follows:

```
ID = inFile.nextInt();          //read the ID
discard = inFile.nextLine();    //discard the newline character
                                //after the ID
name = inFile.nextLine();       //read the name
```

The general loop to process the data is:

```
while (inFile.hasNext())                        //Line 1
{                                               //Line 2
    ID = inFile.nextInt();                      //Line 3
    discard = inFile.nextLine();                //Line 4
    name = inFile.nextLine();                   //Line 5
    //process the numbers in each line
}
```

The code to read and sum up the voting data uses a `while` loop as follows:

```
sum = 0;                            //Line 6
num = inFile.nextInt();             //Line 7; read the first number

while (num != -999)                 //Line 8
{                                   //Line 9
    sum = sum + num;                //Line 10; update sum
    num = inFile.nextInt();         //Line 11; read the next number
}                                   //Line 12
```

We can now write the following nested loop to process the data:

```
while (inFile.hasNext())                        //Line 1
{                                               //Line 2
    ID = inFile.nextInt();                      //Line 3
    discard = inFile.nextLine();                //Line 4
    name = inFile.nextLine();                   //Line 5

    sum = 0;                                    //Line 6

    num = inFile.nextInt();                     //Line 7; read the first number
```

5

```
    while (num != -999)            //Line 8
    {                              //Line 9
        sum = sum + num;           //Line 10; update sum
        num = inFile.nextInt();    //Line 11; read the next number
    }                              //Line 12

    System.out.println("Name: " + name
                 + ", Votes: " + sum);   //Line 13
}                                        //Line 14
```

QUICK REVIEW

1. Java has three looping (repetition) structures: `while`, `for`, and `do...while`.

2. The syntax of the `while` statement is:

   ```
   while (logical expression)
       statement
   ```

3. In Java, `while` is a reserved word.

4. In a `while` statement, the parentheses around the `logical expression`, the loop condition, are required; they mark the beginning and end of the expression.

5. The `statement` is called the body of the loop.

6. The body of the `while` loop typically contains statement(s) that eventually set the expression to `false` to terminate the loop.

7. A counter-controlled `while` loop uses a counter to control the loop.

8. In a counter-controlled `while` loop, you must initialize the counter before the loop, and the body of the loop must contain a statement that changes the value of the counter variable.

9. A sentinel is a special value that marks the end of the input data. The sentinel must be similar, yet different, from all the data items.

10. A sentinel-controlled `while` loop uses a sentinel to control the `while` loop. The `while` loop continues to execute until the sentinel is read.

11. An EOF-controlled `while` loop continues to execute until the program detects the end-of-file marker.

12. The method `hasNext` returns the value `true` if there is an input (token) in the input stream, otherwise it returns `false`.

13. In the Windows console environment, the end-of-file marker is entered using `Ctrl+z`. (Hold the `Ctrl` key and press `z`.) In the UNIX environment, the end-of-file marker is entered using `Ctrl+d`. (Hold the `Ctrl` key and press `d`.)

14. In Java, `for` is a reserved word.

15. A `for` loop simplifies the writing of a counter-controlled `while` loop.

16. The syntax of the `for` loop is:

    ```
    for (initialize expression; logical expression; update expression)
        statement
    ```

    The `statement` is called the body of the `for` loop.

17. If you put a semicolon at the end of the `for` loop (before the body of the `for` loop), the action of the `for` loop is empty.

18. The syntax of the `do...while` statement is:

    ```
    do
        statement
    while (logical expression);
    ```

19. The `statement` is called the body of the `do...while` loop.

20. The body of the `while` and `for` loops might not execute at all, but the body of a `do...while` loop always executes at least once.

21. In a `while` or `for` loop, the loop condition is evaluated before executing the body of the loop. Therefore, `while` and `for` loops are called pretest loops.

22. In a `do...while` loop, the loop condition is evaluated after executing the body of the loop. Therefore, `do...while` loops are called post-test loops.

23. Executing a `break` statement in the body of a loop immediately terminates the loop.

24. Executing a `continue` statement in the body of a loop skips the loop's remaining statements and proceeds with the next iteration.

25. When a `continue` statement executes in a `while` or `do...while` loop, the update statement in the body of the loop might not execute.

26. After a `continue` statement executes in a `for` loop, the update statement is the next statement executed.

5

EXERCISES

1. Mark the following statements as true or false:

   a. In a counter-controlled `while` loop, it is not necessary to initialize the loop control variable.

   b. It is possible that the body of a `while` loop might not execute at all.

   c. In an infinite `while` loop, the loop condition is initially false, but after the first iteration, it is always true.

   d. The `while` loop:

   ```
   j = 0;

   while (j <= 10)
       j++;
   ```

   terminates when j > 10.

   e. A sentinel-controlled `while` loop is an event-controlled `while` loop whose termination depends on a special value.

   f. A loop is a control structure that causes certain statements to execute over and over.

   g. To read data from a file of an unspecified length, an EOF-controlled loop is a good choice.

   h. When a `while` loop terminates, the control first goes back to the statement just before the `while` statement, and then the control goes to the statement immediately following the `while` loop.

2. What is the output of the following Java code?

   ```java
   count = 1;
   y = 100;

   while (count < 100)
   {
       y = y - 1;
       count++;
   }

   System.out.println("y = " + y + " and count = " + count);
   ```

3. What is the output of the following Java code?

   ```java
   num = 5;

   while (num > 5)
       num = num + 2;

   System.out.println(num);
   ```

4. What is the output of the following Java code?

```
num = 1;

while (num < 10)
{
    System.out.print(num + " ");
    num = num + 2;
}

System.out.println();
```

5. When does the following `while` loop terminate?

```
ch = 'D';

while ('A' <= ch && ch <= 'Z')
    ch = (char)((int)(ch) + 1));
```

6. Suppose that the input is:

```
38 35 71 14 -1
```

What is the output of the following code? Assume all variables are properly declared.

```
sum = console.nextInt();
num = console.nextInt();

for (j = 1; j <= 3; j++)
{
    num = console.nextInt();
    sum = sum + num;
}

System.out.println("Sum = " + sum);
```

7. Suppose that the input is:

```
38 35 71 14 -1
```

What is the output of the following code? Assume all variables are properly declared.

```
sum = console.nextInt();
num = console.nextInt();

while (num != -1)
{
    sum = sum + num;
    num = console.nextInt();
}

System.out.println("Sum = " + sum);
```

5

8. Suppose that the input is:

```
38 35 71 14 -1
```

What is the output of the following code? Assume all variables are properly declared.

```
num = console.nextInt();
sum = num;

while (num != -1)
{
    num = console.nextInt();
    sum = sum + num;
}

System.out.println("Sum = " + sum);
```

9. Suppose that the input is:

```
38 35 71 14 -1
```

What is the output of the following code? Assume all variables are properly declared.

```
sum = 0;
num = console.nextInt();

while (num != -1)
{
    sum = sum + num;
    num = console.nextInt();
}

System.out.println("Sum = " + sum);
```

10. Correct the following code so that it finds the sum of 10 numbers:

```
sum = 0;

while (count < 10)
    num = console.nextInt();
    sum = sum + num;
    count++;
```

11. What is the output of the following program?

```
public class WhatIsTheOutput
{
    public static void main(String[] args)
    {
        int x, y, z;

        x = 4;
        y = 5;
        z = y + 6;
```

```
        while (((z - x) % 4) != 0)
        {
            System.out.print(z + " ");
            z = z + 7;
        }
        System.out.println();
    }
}
```

12. Suppose that the input is:

    58 23 46 75 98 150 12 176 145 -999

    What is the output of the following program?

```
import java.util.*;

public class FindTheOutput
{
    static Scanner console = new Scanner(System.in);

    public static void main(String[] args)
    {
        int num;

        num = console.nextInt();

        while (num != -999)
        {
            System.out.print(num % 25 + "   ");
            num = console.nextInt();
        }

        System.out.println();
    }
}
```

13. The following program is designed to input two numbers and output their sum. It asks the user if he/she would like to run the program. If the answer is Y or y, it prompts the user to enter two numbers. After adding the numbers and displaying the results, it again asks the user if he/she would like to add more numbers. However, the program fails to do so. Correct the program so that it works properly.

```
import java.util.*;

public class Exercise13
{
    static Scanner console = new Scanner(System.in);

    public static void main(String[] args)
    {
        char response;
        double num1;
        double num2;
```

5

```
System.out.println("This program adds two numbers.");
System.out.print("Would you like to run the program: (Y/y) ");
response = console.next().charAt(0);
System.out.println();

while (response == 'Y' && response == 'y')
{
    System.out.print("Enter two numbers: ");
    num1 = console.nextInt();
    num2 = console.nextInt();
    System.out.println();

    System.out.printf("%.2f + %.2f  = %.2f %n",
                         num1, num2, (num1 - num2));

    System.out.print("Would you like to add again: (Y/y) ");
    response = console.next().charAt(0);
    System.out.println();
}
    }
}
```

14. What is the output of the following program segment?

```
int count = 0;

while (count++ < 10)
    System.out.println("This loop can repeat statements.");
```

15. What is the output of the following program segment?

```
int count = 5;

while (--count > 0)
    System.out.print(count + " ");
System.out.println();
```

16. What is the output of the following program segment?

```
int count = 5;

while (count-- > 0)
    System.out.print(count + " ");
System.out.println();
```

17. What is the output of the following program segment?

```
int count = 1;
while (count++ <= 5)
    System.out.print(((count * (count - 2)) + " ");

System.out.println();
```

18. What type of loop, such as counter control and sentinel control, will you use in each of the following situations?

    a. Sum the following series: 1 + (2 / 1) + (3 / 2) + (4 / 3) + (5 / 4) + ... + (10 / 9)

    b. Sum the following numbers, except the last number: 17, 32, 62, 48, 58, −1

    c. A file contains employees' salaries. Update employees' salaries.

19. Consider the following `for` loop:

```
int j, s;

s = 0;
for (j = 1; j <= 10; j++)
    s = s + j * (j - 1);
```

    In this `for` loop, identify the loop control variable, the initialization statement, loop condition, the update statement, and the statement that updates the value of s.

20. Given that the following code is correctly inserted into a program, state its entire output as to content and form:

```
num = 0;

for (i = 1; i <= 4; i++)
{
    num = num + 10 * (i - 1);
    System.out.print(num + " ");
}

System.out.println();
```

21. Given that the following code is correctly inserted into a program, describe the content and form of its entire output:

```
j = 2;

for (i = 0; i <= 5; i++)
{
    System.out.print(j + " ");
    j = 2 * j + 3;
}

System.out.println();
```

22. Assume that the following code is correctly inserted into a program:

```
s = 0;

for (i = 0; i < 5; i++)
{
    s = 2 * s + i;
    System.out.print(s + " ");
}
```

```
System.out.println();
```

a. What is the final value of s?

    i.   11 ii.   4 iii.   26 iv.   none of these

b. If a semicolon is inserted after the right parenthesis in the `for` loop control expressions, what is the final value of s?

    i.   0 ii.   1 iii.   2 iv.   5 v.   none of these

c. If the 5 is replaced with a 0 in the `for` loop control expression, what is the final value of s?

    i.   0 ii.   1 iii.   2 iv.   none of these

23. State what output, if any, results in each of the following statements:

a.
```
for (i = 1; i <= 1; i++)
    System.out.print("*");

System.out.println();
```

b.
```
for (i = 2; i >= 1; i++)
     System.out.print("*");

System.out.println();
```

c.
```
for (i = 1; i <= 1; i--)
     System.out.print("*");

System.out.println();
```

d.
```
for (i = 12; i >= 9; i--)
      System.out.print("*");
System.out.println();
```

e.
```
for (i = 0; i <= 5; i++)
      System.out.print("*");

System.out.println();
```

f.
```
for (i = 1; i <= 5; i++)
{

    System.out.print("*");
     i = i + 1;
}
System.out.println();
```

24. Write a `for` statement to add all multiples of 3 between 1 and 100.

25. What is the output of the following code? Is there a relationship between the variables x and y? If yes, state the relationship? What is the output?

```
int x = 19683;
int i;
int y = 0;

for (i = x; i >= 1; i = i / 3)
    y++;
System.out.println("x = " + x + ", y = " + y);
```

26. Suppose that the input is:

    5 3 8

    What is the output of the following code? Assume all variables are properly declared.

    ```
    a = console.nextInt();
    b = console.nextInt();
    c = console.nextInt();

    for (j = 1; j < a; j++)
    {
        d = b + c;
        b = c;
        c = d;

        System.out.print(c + "   ");
    }

    System.out.println();
    ```

27. What is the output of the following Java program segment? Assume all variables are properly declared.

    ```
    for (j = 0; j < 8; j++)
    {
        System.out.print(j * 25 + " - ");

        if (j != 7)
            System.out.println((j + 1) * 25 - 1);
        else
            System.out.println((j + 1) * 25);
    }
    ```

28. Suppose that the input is:

    38 35 71 14 -1

    What is the output of the following code? Assume all variables are properly declared.

    ```
    sum = console.nextInt();
    num = console.nextInt();

    for (j = 1; j <= 3; j++)
    ```

```
{
    num = console.nextInt();
    sum = sum + num;
}

System.out.println("Sum = " + sum);
```

29. Which of the following apply to the `while` loop only? To the `do...while` loop only? To both?

    a. It is considered a conditional loop.

    b. The body of the loop executes at least once.

    c. The logical expression controlling the loop is evaluated before the loop is entered.

    d. The body of the loop might not execute at all.

30. The following program has more than five mistakes that prevent it from compiling and/or running. Correct all such mistakes.

```
public class Exercise30
{
    final int N = 2,137;

    public static main(String[] args)
    {
        int a, b, c, d:

        a := 3;
        b = 5;
        c = c + d;
        N = a + n;

        for (i = 3; i <= N; i++)
        {
            System.out.print(" " + i);
            i = i + 1;
        }

        System.out.println();
    }
}
```

31. What is the difference between a pretest loop and a posttest loop?

32. How many times will each of the following loops execute? What is the output in each case?

    a.
```
    x = 5;   y = 50;
    do
        x = x + 10;
    while (x < y);

    System.out.println(x + " " + y);
```

b. ```
    x = 5;   y = 80;
    do
        x = x * 2;
    while (x < y);

    System.out.println(x + " " + y);
    ```

c.  ```
    x = 5;   y = 20;

    do
        x = x + 2;
    while (x >= y);

    System.out.println(x + " " + y);
    ```

d. ```
    x = 5;   y = 35;

    while (x < y)
        x = x + 10;

    System.out.println(x + " " + y);
    ```

e.  ```
    x = 5;   y = 30;

    while (x <= y)
        x = x * 2;

    System.out.println(x + " " + y);
    ```

f. ```
    x = 5;   y = 30;

    while (x > y)
        x = x + 2;

    System.out.println(x + " " + y);
    ```

33. Write an input statement validation loop that prompts the user to enter a number less than 20 or greater than 75.

34. Rewrite the following as a `for` loop:

```
int i = 0, value = 0;

while (i <= 20)
{
    if (i % 2 == 0 && i <= 10)
        value = value + i * i;
    else if (i % 2 == 0 && i > 10)
        value = value + i;
    else
        value = value - i;
    i = i + 1;
}

System.out.println("value = " + value);
```

What is the output of this loop?

<div style="text-align:right">5</div>
```

35. Write the `while` loop of Exercise 34 as a do...while loop.

36. The do...while loop in the following program is intended to read some numbers until it reaches a sentinel (in this case, -1). It is supposed to add all of the numbers except for the sentinel. If the data looks like:

```
12 5 30 48 -1
```

the program fails to work as intended. Make any necessary corrections.

```java
import java.util.*;

public class Strange
{
    static Scanner console = new Scanner(System.in);

    public static void main(String[] args)
    {
        int total = 0;
        int number;

        do
        {
            number = console.nextInt();
            total = total + number;
        }
        while (number != -1);

        System.out.println("The sum of the numbers entered is "
                            + total);
    }
}
```

37. Using the same data as in Exercise 36, the following loop also fails. Correct it.

```java
number = console.nextInt();
while (number != -1)
    total =  total + number;
    number = console.nextInt();
    System.out.println();
    System.out.println(total);
```

38. Using the same data as in Exercise 36, the following loop also fails. Correct it.

```java
number = console.nextInt();
while (number != -1)
{
    number = console.nextInt();
    total = total + number;
}
System.out.println();
System.out.println(total);
```

39. Given the following program segment:

```
for (number = 1; number <= 10; number++)
    System.out.print(number + " ");
System.out.println();
```

write a `while` loop and a `do...while` loop that have the same output.

40. Given the following program segment:

```
j = 2;

for (i = 1; i <= 5; i++)
{
    System.out.print(j + " ");
    j = j + 5;
}

System.out.println();
```

write a `while` loop and a `do...while` loop that have the same output.

41. What is the output of the following program?

```
public class Mystery
{
    public static void main(String[] args)
    {
        int  x, y, z;

        x = 4;
        y = 5;
        z = y + 6;

        do
        {
            System.out.print(z + " ");
            z = z + 7;
        }
        while(((z - x) % 4) != 0);

        System.out.println();
    }
}
```

42. To further learn how nested `for` loops work, do a walk-through of the following program segments and, in each case, determine the exact output.

    a. ```
        int i, j;

        for (i = 1; i <= 5; i++)
        {
            for (j = 1; j <= 5; j++)
                System.out.printf("%3d", i);
            System.out.println();
        }
        ```

5
        ```

b.
```
int i, j;

for (i = 1; i <= 5; i++)
{
    for (j = 1; j <= i; j++)
        System.out.printf("%3d", j);
    System.out.println();
}
```

c.
```
int i, j;

for (i = 1; i <= 5; i++)
{
    for (j = (i + 1); j <= 5; j++)
        System.out.printf("%5d", j);
    System.out.println();
}
```

d.
```
final int m = 10;
final int n = 10;
int i, j;

for (i = 1; i <= m; i++)
{
    for (j = 1; j <= n; j++)
        System.out.printf("%4d", (m * (i - 1) + j));
    System.out.println();
}
```

e.
```
int i, j;

for (i = 1; i <= 9; i++)
{
    for (j = 1; j <= (9 - i); j++)
        System.out.print(" ");
    for (j = 1; j <= i; j++)
        System.out.print(j);
    for (j = (i - 1); j >= 1; j--)
        System.out.print(j);

    System.out.println();
}
```

43. What is the output of the following program segment?

```
int count = 1;
do
    System.out.print((count * (count - 2)) + " ");
while (count++ <= 5);

System.out.println();
```

44. What is the output of the following code?

```
int num = 12;

while (num >= 0)
{
    if (num % 5 == 0)
        break;

    System.out.print(num + " ");
    num = num - 2;
}

System.out.println();
```

45. What is the output of the following code?

```
int num = 12;

while (num >= 0)
{
    if (num % 5 == 0)
    {
        num++;
        continue;
    }

    System.out.print(num + " ");
    num = num - 2;
}
System.out.println();
```

46. What does a `break` statement do in a loop?

PROGRAMMING EXERCISES

1. Write a program that prompts the user to input an integer and then outputs both the individual digits of the number and the sum of the digits. For example, the program should: output the individual digits of 3456 as 3 4 5 6 and the sum as 18, output the individual digits of 8030 as 8 0 3 0 and the sum as 11, output the individual digits of 2345526 as 2 3 4 5 5 2 6 and the sum as 27, output the individual digits of 4000 as 4 0 0 0 and the sum as 4, and output the individual digits of –2345 as 2 3 4 5 and the sum as 14.

2. The value of π can be approximated by using the following series:

$$\pi = 4\left(1 - \frac{1}{3} + \frac{1}{5} - \frac{1}{7} + \cdots + (-1)^{n-1}\frac{1}{2n-1} + (-1)^{n}\frac{1}{2n+1}.\right)$$

The following program uses this series to find the approximate value of π. However, the statements are in the wrong order and there is also a bug in this program. Rearrange the statements and also find and remove the bug so that this program can be used to approximate π.

```java
import java.util.*;

public class Ch5_PrExercise2
{
    static Scanner console = new Scanner(System.in);

    public static void main(String[] args)
    {
        double pi = 0;
        long i;
        long n;

        n = console.nextInt();
        System.out.print("Enter the value of n: ");
        System.out.println();

        if (i % 2 == 0)
            pi = pi + (1 / (2 * i + 1));
        else
            pi = pi - (1 / (2 * i + 1));

        for (i = 0; i < n; i++)
        {
            pi = 0;
            pi = 4 * pi;
        }

        System.out.println("pi = " + pi);
    }
}
```

3. Rewrite the program of Example 5-5, Telephone Digits. Replace the statements from Lines 10 to 28 so that the program uses only a `switch` structure to find the digit that corresponds to an uppercase letter.

4. The program Telephone Digits outputs only telephone digits that correspond to uppercase letters. Rewrite the program so that it processes both uppercase and lowercase letters and outputs the corresponding telephone digit. If the input is other than an uppercase or lowercase letter, the program must output an appropriate error message.

5. To make telephone numbers easier to remember, some companies use letters to show their telephone number. For example, the telephone number 438-5626 can be shown as GET-LOAN. In some cases, to make a telephone number meaningful, companies might use more than seven letters. For example, 225-5466 can be displayed as CALL-HOME, which uses eight letters. Write a program that prompts the user to enter a telephone number expressed in

letters and outputs the corresponding telephone number in digits. If the user enters more than eight letters, then process only the first seven letters. Also, output the — (hyphen) after the third digit. Allow the user to use uppercase and lowercase letters, as well as spaces between words. Moreover, your program should process as many telephone numbers as the user wants. (*Hint:* You can read the entered telephone number as a string and then use the charAt method of the **class** String to extract each character. For example, if str refers to a string, then the expression str.charAt(i) returns the character at the ith position. Recall that in a string, the position of the first character is 0.)

6. Write a program that reads a set of integers, and then finds and prints the sum of the even and odd integers.

7. Write a program that prompts the user to input a positive integer. It should then output a message indicating whether the number is a prime number. (*Note:* 2 is the only even number that is prime. An odd integer is prime if it is not divisible by any odd integer less than or equal to the square root of the number.)

8. Let $n = a_k a_{k-1} a_{k-2} \ldots a_1 a_0$ be an integer. Let $t = a_0 - a_1 + a_2 - \ldots + (-1)^k a_k$. It is known that n is divisible by 11 if and only if t is divisible by 11. For example, suppose that $n = 8784204$. Then, $t = 4 - 0 + 2 - 4 + 8 - 7 + 8 = 11$. Because 11 is divisible by 11, it follows that 8784204 is divisible by 11. If $n = 54063297$, then $t = 7 - 9 + 2 - 3 + 6 - 0 + 4 - 5 = 2$. Because 2 is not divisible by 11, 54063297 is not divisible by 11.

Write a program that prompts the user to enter a positive integer and then uses this criteria to determine whether the number is divisible by 11.

9. Write a program that uses **while** loops to perform the following steps:

   a. Prompt the user to input two integers: firstNum and secondNum. (firstNum must be less than secondNum.)

   b. Output all the odd numbers between firstNum and secondNum inclusive.

   c. Output the sum of all the even numbers between firstNum and secondNum inclusive.

   d. Output all the numbers and their squares between 1 and 10.

   e. Output the sum of the squares of all the odd numbers between firstNum and secondNum inclusive.

   f. Output all the uppercase letters.

10. Redo Exercise 9 using **for** loops.

11. Redo Exercise 9 using do...while loops.

12. The program in the Fibonacci Number programming example does not check whether the first number entered by the user is less than or equal to the second number and both the numbers are non-negative. Also, the program does not check whether the user entered a valid value for the position of the desired number in the Fibonacci sequence. Rewrite the program so that it checks for these conditions.

13. The population of a town A is less than the population of town B. However, the population of town A is growing faster than the population of town B. Write a program that prompts the user to enter the population and growth rate of each town. The program outputs after how many years the population of town A will be greater than or equal to the population of town B and the populations of both the towns at that time. (A sample input is: Population of town $A = 5,000$, growth rate of town $A = 4\%$, population of town $B = 8,000$, and growth rate of town $B = 2\%$.)

14. Suppose that the first number of a sequence is x, where x is an integer. Define $a_0 = x$; $a_{n+1} = a_n / 2$ if a_n is even; $a_{n+1} = 3 \times a_n + 1$ if a_n is odd. Then there exists an integer k such that $a_k = 1$. Write a program that prompts the user to input the value of x. The program outputs the integer k such that $a_k = 1$ and the numbers $a_0, a_1, a_2, \ldots, a_k$. (For example, if $x = 75$, then $k = 14$, and the numbers $a_0, a_1, a_2, \ldots, a_{14}$, respectively, are 75, 226, 113, 340, 170, 85, 256, 128, 64, 32, 16, 8, 4, 2, 1.) Test your program for the following values of x: 75, 111, 678, 732, 873, 2048, and 65535.

15. Enhance your program of Exercise 14, by outputting the position of the largest number and the largest number of the sequence $a_0, a_1, a_2, \ldots, a_k$. (For example, the largest number of the sequence 75, 226, 113, 340, 170, 85, 256, 128, 64, 32, 16, 8, 4, 2, 1 is 340, and its position is 4.) Test your program for the following values of x: 75, 111, 678, 732, 873, 2048, and 65535.

16. The program in Example 5-6 implements the Guessing the Number game. However, in that program, the user is given as many tries as needed to guess the correct number. Rewrite that program so that the user has, at most, five tries to guess the correct number. Your program should print an appropriate message, such as "You win!" or "You lose!"

17. Example 5-6 implements the Guessing the Number game program. If the guessed number is not correct, the program outputs a message indicating whether the guess is low or high. Modify the program as follows: Suppose that the variables num and guess are as declared in Example 5-6 and diff is an int variable. Let diff = the absolute value of (num - guess). If diff is 0, then guess is correct and the program outputs a message indicating that the user guessed the correct number. Suppose diff is not 0. Then, the program outputs the message as follows:

a. If diff is greater than or equal to 50, the program outputs the message indicating that the guess is very high (if guess is greater than num) or very low (if guess is less than num).

b. If diff is greater than or equal to 30 and less than 50, the program outputs the message indicating that the guess is high (if guess is greater than num) or low (if guess is less than num).

c. If diff is greater than or equal to 15 and less than 30, the program outputs the message indicating that the guess is moderately high (if guess is greater than num) or moderately low (if guess is less than num).

d. If diff is greater than 0 and less than 15, the program outputs the message indicating that the guess is somewhat high (if guess is greater than num) or somewhat low (if guess is less than num).

As in Programming Exercise 16, give the user, at most, five tries to guess the number. (To find the absolute value of num – guess, use the expression Math.abs(num - guess).)

18. A high school has 1000 students and 1000 lockers, one locker for each student. On the first day of school, the principal plays the following game: She asks the first student to open all the lockers. She then asks the second student to close all the even-numbered lockers. The third student is asked to check every third locker. If it is open, the student closes it; if it is closed, the student opens it. The fourth student is asked to check every fourth locker. If it is open, the student closes it; if it is closed, the student opens it. The remaining students continue this game. In general, the nth student checks every nth locker. If the locker is open, the student closes it; if it is closed, the student opens it. After all the students have taken their turns, some of the lockers are open and some are closed. Write a program that prompts the user to enter the number of lockers in a school. After the game is over, the program outputs the number of lockers and the locker numbers of the lockers that are open. Test run your program for the following inputs: 1000, 5000, and 10,000. Do you see any pattern developing for the locker numbers that are open in the output?

(Hint: Consider locker number 100. This locker is visited by student numbers 1, 2, 4, 5, 10, 20, 25, 50, and 100. These are the positive divisors of 100. Similarly, locker number 30 is visited by student numbers 1, 2, 3, 5, 6, 10, 15, and 30. Note that if the number of positive divisors of a locker number is odd, then at the end of the game the locker is open. If the number of positive divisors of a locker number is even, then at the end of the game the locker is closed.)

19. When you borrow money to buy a house, a car, or for some other purpose, you repay the loan by making periodic payments over a certain time. Of course the lending company will charge interest on the loan. Every periodic

payment consists of the interest on the loan and the payment toward the principal amount. To be specific, suppose that you borrow $1000 at the interest rate of 7.2% per year and the payments are monthly. Suppose that your monthly payment is $25. The interest is 7.2% per year and the payments are monthly, so the interest rate per month is $7.2/12 = 0.6\%$. The first month's interest on $1000 is $1000 * 0.006 = 6$. Because the payment is $25 and interest for the first month is $6, the payment toward the principal amount is $25 - 6 = 19$. This means that after making the first payment, the loan amount is $1000 - 19 = 981$. For the second payment, the interest is calculated on $981. So the interest for the second month is $981 * 0.006 = 5.886$, that is, approximately $5.89. This implies that the payment toward the principal is $25 - 5.89 = 19.11$, and the remaining balance after the second payment is $981 - 19.11 = 961.89$. This process is repeated until the loan is paid. Write a program that accepts as input the loan amount, the interest rate per year, and the monthly payment. (Enter the interest rate as a percentage. For example, if the interest rate is 7.2% per year, then enter 7.2.) The program then outputs the number of months it would take to repay the loan. (*Note:* If the monthly payment is less then the first month's interest, then after each payment, the loan amount will increase. In this case, the program must warn the borrower that the monthly payment is too low and with this monthly payment the loan amount could not be repaid.)

20. Enhance your program of Exercise 19, by first telling the user the minimum monthly payment and then prompting the user to enter the monthly payment. The last payment might be more than the remaining loan amount and interest on it. In this case, output the loan amount before the last payment and the actual amount of the last payment. Also, output the total interest paid.

21. Write a program that reads in a line consisting of a student's name, Social Security number, user id, and password (separated by one space). The program outputs the string in which all the digits of the Social Security number and all the characters in the password are replaced by **x**. (The Social Security number is in the form 000-00-0000. The student name does not contain any digits, and the user id and the password do not contain any spaces.) Use the appropriate string methods described in Table 3-1.

22. Write a complete program to generate the pattern given in Example 5-19.

23. Write a complete program to generate the multiplication table given in Example 5-20.

24. Write a complete program to process the data given in Example 5-21.

25. Write a complete program to process the data given in Example 5-22.

26. You have been given the contract for making little conical cups that are used for bottled water. These cups are to be made from a circular waxed paper die

of 4 inches in radius, by removing a sector of length x (see Figure 5-6). By closing the remaining part of the circle, a conical cup is made. Your objective is to remove the sector so that the cup is of maximum volume.

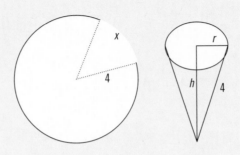

FIGURE 5-6   Conical paper cup

Write a program that prompts the user to enter the radius of the circular waxed paper. The program should then output the length of the removed sector so that the resulting cup is of maximum volume. Calculate your answer to two decimal places.

27.   A real estate office handles 50 apartment units. When the rent is $600 per month, all the units are occupied. However, for each $40 increase in rent, one unit becomes vacant. Each occupied unit requires an average of $27 per month for maintenance. How many units should be rented to maximize the profit?

Write a program that prompts the user to enter:

a.   The number of apartment units

b.   The rent to occupy all the units

c.   The increase in rent that results in a vacant unit

d.   Amount to maintain a rented unit

The program then outputs the number of units to be rented to maximize the profit.

GRAPHICAL USER INTERFACE (GUI) AND OBJECT-ORIENTED DESIGN (OOD)

IN THIS CHAPTER, YOU WILL:

- Learn about basic GUI components
- Explore how the GUI components **JFrame**, **JLabel**, **JTextField**, and **JButton** work
- Become familiar with the concept of event-driven programming
- Discover events and event handlers
- Explore object-oriented design
- Learn how to identify objects, classes, and members of a class
- Learn about wrapper classes
- Become familiar with the autoboxing and auto-unboxing of primitive data types

Java is equipped with many powerful, yet easy-to-use graphical user interface (GUI) components, such as the input and output dialog boxes you learned about in Chapter 3. You can use these to make your programs attractive and user-friendly. The first half of this chapter introduces you to some basic Java GUI components. Chapter 12 covers GUI in some detail.

In Chapter 1, you were introduced to the object-oriented design (OOD) problem-solving methodology. The second half of this chapter outlines a general approach to solving problems using OOD, and provides several examples to clarify this problem-solving methodology.

Graphical User Interface (GUI) Components

In Chapter 3, you learned how to use input and output dialog boxes to input data into a program and show the output of a program. Before introducing the various GUI components, we will use input and output dialog boxes to write a program to determine the area and perimeter of a rectangle. We will then discuss how to use additional GUI components to create a different graphical user interface to determine the area and perimeter of a rectangle.

The program in Example 6-1 prompts the user to input the length and width of a rectangle and then displays its area and perimeter. We will use the method `showInputDialog` to create an input dialog box and the method `showMessageDialog` to create an output dialog box. Recall that these methods are contained in the `class JOptionPane` and this class is contained in the package `javax.swing`.

EXAMPLE 6-1

```java
// This Java Program determines the area and
// perimeter of a rectangle.

import javax.swing.JOptionPane;

public class Rectangle
{
    public static void main(String[] args)
    {
        double width, length, area, perimeter;           //Line 1

        String lengthStr, widthStr, outputStr;           //Line 2

        lengthStr =
            JOptionPane.showInputDialog("Enter the length: "); //Line 3
        length = Double.parseDouble(lengthStr);          //Line 4
```

```
        widthStr =
             JOptionPane.showInputDialog("Enter the width: ");  //Line 5
        width = Double.parseDouble(widthStr);                   //Line 6

        area = length * width;                                  //Line 7
        perimeter = 2 * (length + width);                       //Line 8

        outputStr = "Length: " + length + "\n" +
                    "Width: " + width + "\n" +
                    "Area: " + area + " square units\n" +
                    "Perimeter: " + perimeter + " units\n";      //Line 9

        JOptionPane.showMessageDialog(null, outputStr,
                          "Rectangle",
                          JOptionPane.INFORMATION_MESSAGE);       //Line 10

        System.exit(0);                                          //Line 11
    }
}
```

Sample Run: (Figure 6-1 shows the sample run.)

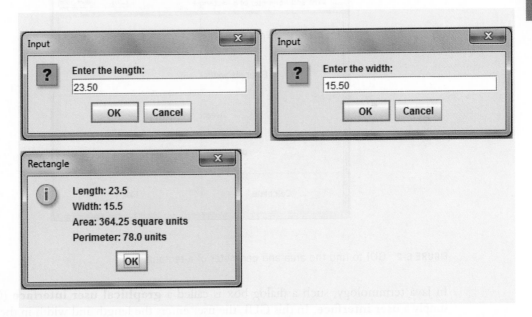

FIGURE 6-1 Sample run for `Rectangle`

The program in Example 6-1 works as follows: The statements in Lines 1 and 2 declare various variables to manipulate the data. The statement in Line 3 displays the first dialog box of the sample run and prompts the user to enter the length of the rectangle. The entered length is assigned as a string to `lengthStr`. The statement in Line 4 retrieves the length and stores it in the variable `length`.

The statement in Line 5 displays the second dialog box of the sample run and prompts the user to enter the width of the rectangle. The entered width is assigned as a string to widthStr. The statement in Line 6 retrieves the width and stores it in the variable width.

The statement in Line 7 determines the area, and the statement in Line 8 determines the perimeter of the rectangle. The statement in Line 9 creates the string containing the desired output and assigns it to outputStr. The statement in Line 10 uses the output dialog box to display the desired output, which is shown in the third dialog box of the sample run. Finally, the statement in Line 11 terminates the program.

The program in Example 6-1 uses input and output dialog boxes to accomplish its job. When you run this program, you see only one dialog box at a time.

However, suppose that you want the program to display all the input and output in one dialog box, as shown in Figure 6-2.

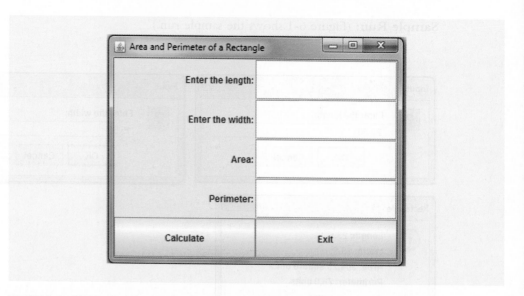

FIGURE 6-2 GUI to find the area and perimeter of a rectangle

In Java terminology, such a dialog box is called a **graphical user interface** (GUI), or simply a **user interface**. In this GUI, the user enters the length and width in the top two white boxes. When the user clicks the Calculate button, the program displays the area and the perimeter in their respective locations. When the user clicks the Exit button, the program terminates.

In this interface, the user can:

- See the entire input and output simultaneously
- Input values for length and width, in any order of preference
- Input values that can be corrected after entering them and before clicking the `Calculate` button
- Enter another set of input values and click the `Calculate` button to obtain the area and perimeter of another rectangle

The interface shown in Figure 6-2 contains various Java GUI components that are labeled in Figure 6-3.

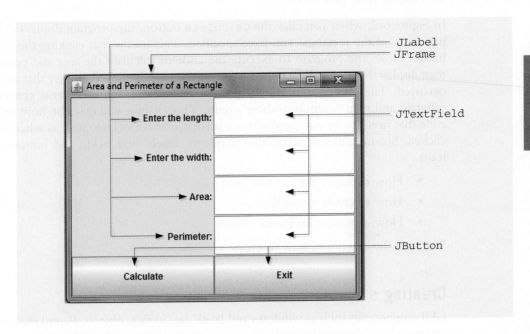

FIGURE 6-3 Java GUI components

As you can see in Figure 6-3, the white areas used to get the input and show the results are called `JTextFields`. The labels for these text fields, such as `Enter the length:`, are called `JLabels`; the buttons `Calculate` and `Exit` are each called a `JButton`. All these components are placed in a window, called `JFrame`.

Creating this type of user interface is not difficult. Java has done all the work; you merely need to learn how to use the tools provided by Java to create such an interface. For example, to create an interface like the one shown in Figures 6-2 and 6-3 that contains labels, text fields, buttons, and windows, you need to learn how to write the statements that create these components. The next sections describe how to create the following GUI components:

- Windows
- Labels
- Text fields
- Buttons

GUI components, such as labels, are placed in an area called the **content pane** of the window. You can think of a content pane as the inner area of the window, below the title bar and inside the border. You will also learn how to place these GUI components in the content pane of a window.

In Figure 6-2, when you click the `Calculate` button, the program displays the area and perimeter of the rectangle you have specified. This means that clicking the `Calculate` button causes the program to execute the code to calculate the area and perimeter and then display the results. When the `Calculate` button is clicked, we say that an **event** has occurred. The Java system is very prompt in listening for the events generated by a program and then reacting to those events. This chapter will describe how to write the code that needs to be executed when a particular event occurs, such as when a button is clicked. So, in addition to creating windows, labels, text fields, and buttons, you will learn:

- How to access the content pane
- How to create event listeners
- How to process or handle events

We begin by describing how to create a window.

Creating a Window

GUI components such as windows and labels are, in fact, objects. Recall that an object is an instance of a particular class. Therefore, these components (objects) are instances of a particular class type. `JFrame` is a `class` and the GUI component `window` can be created by using a `JFrame` object. Various attributes are associated with a window. For example:

- Every window has a title.
- Every window has width and height.

JFrame

The `class JFrame` provides various methods to control the attributes of a window. For example, it has methods to set the window title and methods to specify the height and width of the window. Table 6-1 describes some of the methods provided by the `class` `JFrame`.

TABLE 6-1 Some Methods Provided by the `class` JFrame

Method / Description / Example

public **JFrame**()
//This is used when an object of type JFrame is
//instantiated and the window is created without any title.
//Example: JFrame myWindow = new JFrame();
//   myWindow is a window with no title

public **JFrame**(String s)
//This is used when an object of type JFrame is
//instantiated and the title specified by the string s.
//Example: JFrame myWindow = new JFrame("Rectangle");
//   myWindow is a window with the title Rectangle

public void **setSize**(int w, int h)
//Method to set the size of the window.
//Example: The statement
//   myWindow.setSize(400, 300);
//   sets the width of the window to 400 pixels and
//   the height to 300 pixels.

public void **setTitle**(String s)
//Method to set the title of the window.
//Example: myWindow.setTitle("Rectangle");
//   sets the title of the window to Rectangle.

public void **setVisible**(boolean b)
//Method to display the window in the program. If the value of b is
//true, the window will be displayed on the screen.
//Example: myWindow.setVisible(true);
//   After this statement executes, the window will be shown
//   during program execution.

public void **setDefaultCloseOperation**(int operation)
//Method to determine the action to be taken when the user clicks
//on the window closing button, ×, to close the window.
//Choices for the parameter operation are the named constants —
//EXIT_ON_CLOSE, HIDE_ON_CLOSE, DISPOSE_ON_CLOSE, and
//DO_NOTHING_ON_CLOSE. The named constant EXIT_ON_CLOSE is defined
//in the class JFrame. The last three named constants are defined in
//javax.swing.WindowConstants.
//Example: The statement
//   setDefaultCloseOperation(EXIT_ON_CLOSE);
//sets the default close option of the window closing to close the
//window and terminate the program when the user clicks the
//window closing button, ×.

6

TABLE 6-1 Some Methods Provided by the **class** JFrame (continued)

Method / Description / Example
`public void addWindowListener(WindowEvent e)`   `//Method to register a window listener object to a JFrame.`

 NOTE The **class** JFrame also contains methods to set the color of a window. Chapter 12 describes these methods.

There are two ways to make an application program create a window. The first way is to declare an object of type JFrame, instantiate the object, and then use various methods to manipulate the window. In this case, the object created can use the various applicable methods of the class.

The second way is to create the class containing the application program by *extending* the definition of the **class** JFrame; that is, the class containing the application program is built "on top of" the **class** JFrame. In Java, this way of creating a class uses the mechanism of **inheritance**. Inheritance means that a new class can be derived from or based on an already existing class. The new class "inherits" features such as methods from the existing class, which saves a lot of time for programmers. For example, we could define a new **class** RectangleProgram that would extend the definition of JFrame. The class RectangleProgram would be able to use the variables and methods from JFrame, and also add some functionality of its own (such as the ability to calculate the area and perimeter of a rectangle).

When you use inheritance, the class containing your application program will have more than one method. In addition to the method main, you will have at least one other method that will be used to create a window object containing the required GUI components (such as labels and text fields). This additional method is a special type of method called a **constructor**. A constructor is a method of a class that is automatically executed when an object of the class is created. Typically, a constructor is used to initialize an object. The name of the constructor is always the same as the name of the class. For example, the constructor for the **class** RectangleProgram would be named RectangleProgram.

 NOTE Chapter 10 discusses the principles of inheritance in detail. Constructors are covered in detail in Chapter 8.

Because inheritance is an important concept in programming languages such as Java, we will use the second way of creating a window. We will extend the definition of the **class** JFrame by using the modifier **extends**. For example, the definition of the **class**

RectangleProgram, containing the application program to calculate the area and perimeter of a rectangle, is as follows:

```
public class RectangleProgram extends JFrame
{
    public RectangleProgram()       //constructor
    {
        //Necessary code
    }

    public static void main(String[] args)
    {
        //Code for the method main
    }
}
```

In Java, **extends** is a reserved word. The remainder of this section describes the necessary code to create a window.

An important property of inheritance is that the class (called a **subclass**) that extends the definition of an existing class (called a **superclass**) inherits all the properties of the superclass. For example, all `public` methods of the superclass can be *directly* accessed in the subclass. In our example, the `class RectangleProgram` is a subclass of the `class JFrame`, so it can access the `public` methods of the `class JFrame`. Therefore, to set the title of the window to `Area and Perimeter of a Rectangle`, you use the method `setTitle` of the `class JFrame` as follows:

```
setTitle("Area and Perimeter of a Rectangle");         //Line 1
```

Similarly, the statement:

```
setSize(400, 300);                                     //Line 2
```

sets the window's width to 400 pixels and its height to 300 pixels. (A **pixel** is the smallest unit of space on your screen. The term pixel stands for *picture element*.) Note that since the pixel size depends on the current monitor setting, it is impossible to predict the exact width and height of a window in centimeters or inches.

Next, to display the window, you must invoke the method `setVisible`. The following statement accomplishes this:

```
setVisible(true);                                      //Line 3
```

To terminate the application program when the user closes the window, use the following statement (as described in Table 6-1):

```
setDefaultCloseOperation(EXIT_ON_CLOSE);               //Line 4
```

The statements in Lines 1, 2, 3, and 4 will be placed in the constructor (that is, in the method whose heading is `public RectangleProgram()`). Thus, you can write the constructor as follows:

```
public RectangleProgram()
{
    setTitle("Area and Perimeter of a Rectangle");
    setSize(400, 300);
    setDefaultCloseOperation(EXIT_ON_CLOSE);
    setVisible(true);
}
```

You could create a window by using an object of type JFrame. However, for our program, if we do so, then the window created will not have a title or the required size unless we specify the necessary statements similar to the ones in the preceding code. Because RectangleProgram is also a class, we can create objects of type RectangleProgram. Because the class RectangleProgram extends the definition of the class JFrame, it inherits the properties of the class JFrame. If we create an object of type RectangleProgram, not only do we create a window, but the created window will also have a title and a specific size, and the window will be displayed when the program executes.

Consider the following statement:

```
RectangleProgram rectObject = new RectangleProgram();   //Line 5
```

This statement creates the object rectObject of type RectangleProgram.

The statement in Line 5 causes the window shown in Figure 6-4 to appear on the screen.

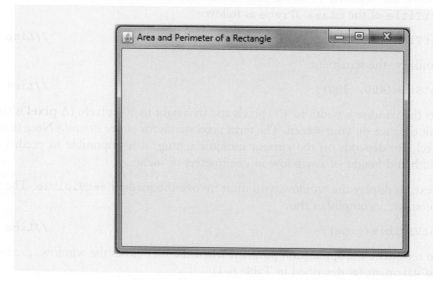

FIGURE 6-4 Window with the title Area and Perimeter of a Rectangle

You can close the window in Figure 6-4 by clicking the "close" button, the button containing the ×, in the upper-right corner. The window in Figure 6-4 is empty because we have not yet created labels, text fields, and so on.

The program to create the window shown in Figure 6-4 uses the class JFrame; this class is contained in the package javax.swing. Therefore, the program must include either of the following two statements:

```
import javax.swing.*;
```

or:

```
import javax.swing.JFrame;
```

After making the minor changes in the statements described in this section, the program to create the window shown in Figure 6-4 is as follows:

```java
//Java program to create a window.

import javax.swing.*;

public class RectangleProgramOne extends JFrame
{
    private static final int WIDTH = 400;
    private static final int HEIGHT = 300;

    public RectangleProgramOne()
    {
        setTitle("Area and Perimeter of a Rectangle");
        setSize(WIDTH, HEIGHT);

        setDefaultCloseOperation(EXIT_ON_CLOSE);
        setVisible(true);
    }

    public static void main(String[] args)
    {
        RectangleProgramOne rectProg = new RectangleProgramOne();
    }
}
```

Notice that the named constants WIDTH and HEIGHT are declared with the modifier private. This is because we want these named constants to be used only within the class RectangleProgram. In general, if a named constant, variable, or method is to be used only within the specified class, then it is declared with the modifier private. Also, note that private is a reserved word in Java. (Chapter 8 discusses the modifier private in detail.)

(Note that in the preceding program we have changed the name of the class to RectangleProgramOne. This is because we have not yet added all the GUI components to the program. After adding labels, we will call it class RectangleProgramTwo, and so on. After adding all the necessary GUI components, we will call it class RectangleProgram. These programs can be found with the Additional Student Files at *www.cengagebrain.com*.)

6

Let's review the important points introduced in this section:

- The preceding program has exactly one class: `RectangleProgramOne`.
- The `class` `RectangleProgramOne` contains the constructor `RectangleProgramOne` and the `main` method.
- You created the new `class` `RectangleProgramOne` by extending the existing class, `JFrame`. Therefore, `JFrame` is the superclass of `RectangleProgramOne`, and `RectangleProgramOne` is a subclass of `JFrame`.
- Whenever there is a superclass–subclass relationship, the subclass inherits all the data members and methods of the superclass. The methods `setTitle`, `setSize`, `setVisible`, and `setDefaultCloseOperation` are methods of the `class` `JFrame`, and these methods can be inherited by its subclasses.

The next few sections describe how to create GUI labels, text fields, and buttons, which can all be placed in the content pane of a window. Before you can place GUI components in the content pane, you must learn how to access the content pane.

Getting Access to the Content Pane

If you can visualize `JFrame` as a window, think of the content pane as the inner area of the window (below the title bar and inside the border). The `class` `JFrame` has the method `getContentPane` that you can use to access the content pane of the window. However, the `class` `JFrame` does not have the necessary tools to manage the components of the content pane. The components of the content pane are managed by declaring a reference variable of the `Container` type and then using the method `getContentPane`, as shown next.

Consider the following statements:

```
Container pane;                     //Line 1
pane = getContentPane();            //Line 2
```

The statement in Line 1 declares `pane` to be a reference variable of the `Container` type. The statement in Line 2 gets the content pane of the window as a container, that is, the reference variable `pane` now points to the content pane. You can now access the content pane to add GUI components to it by using the reference variable `pane`.

The statements in Lines 1 and 2 can be combined into one statement:

```
Container pane = getContentPane();     //Line 3
```

If you look back at Figure 6-2, you will see that the labels, text fields, and buttons are arranged in five rows and two columns. To control the placement of GUI components in the content pane, you set the layout of the content pane. The layout used in Figure 6-2 is called the grid layout. The `class` `Container` provides the method `setLayout`, as described in Table 6-2, to set the layout of the content pane. To add components such as labels and text fields to the content pane, you use the method `add` of the `class` `Container`, which is also described in Table 6-2.

TABLE 6-2 Some Methods of the **class** Container

Method / Description
public void **add**(Object obj)   //Method to add an object to the pane.
public void **setLayout**(Object obj)   //Method to set the layout of the pane.

The **class** Container is contained in the package java.awt. To use this **class** in your program, you need to include one of the following statements:

import java.awt.*;

or:

import java.awt.Container;

As noted earlier, the method setLayout is used to set the layout of the content pane, pane. To set the layout of the container to a grid, you use the **class** GridLayout. Consider the following statement:

pane.setLayout(**new** GridLayout(5, 2));

This statement creates an object belonging to the **class** GridLayout and assigns that object as the layout of the content pane, pane, by invoking the setLayout method. Moreover, this statement sets the layout of the content pane, pane, to five rows and two columns. This allows you to add 10 components arranged in five rows and two columns.

Note that the GridLayout manager arranges GUI components in a matrix formation with the number of rows and columns defined by the constructor and that the components are placed left to right, starting with the first row. For example, in the statement pane.setLayout(**new** GridLayout(5, 2));, the expression **new** GridLayout(5, 2), invokes the constructor of the **class** GridLayout and sets the number of rows to 5 and the number of columns to 2. Also, in this chapter, we only discuss the GridLayout manager; additional layout managers are discussed in Chapter 12. Layout managers allow you to manage GUI components in a content pane.

If you do not specify a layout, Java uses a default layout. If you specify a layout, you must set the layout before adding any components. Once the layout is set, you can use the method add to add the components to the pane; this process is described in the next section.

JLabel

Now you will learn how to create labels and add them to the pane. We assume the following statements:

Container pane = getContentPane();
pane.setLayout(**new** GridLayout(4, 1));

6

Labels are objects of a particular `class` type. The Java `class` that you use to create labels is JLabel. Therefore, to create labels, you instantiate objects of type `JLabel`. The `class` JLabel is contained in the package `javax.swing`.

Just like a window, various attributes are associated with a label. For example, every label has a title, width, and height. The `class` JLabel contains various methods to control the display of labels. Table 6–3 describes some of the methods provided by the `class` JLabel.

TABLE 6-3   Some Methods Provided by the `class` JLabel

Method / Description/ Example

public **JLabel**(String str)
  //Constructor to create a label with left-aligned text specified
  //by str.
  //Example: JLabel lengthL;
  //   lengthL = new JLabel("Enter the length:")
  //   Creates the label lengthL with the title Enter the length:

public **JLabel**(String str, int align)
  //Constructor to create a label with the text specified by str.
  //   The value of align can be any one of the following:
  //   SwingConstants.LEFT, SwingConstants.RIGHT,
  //   SwingConstants.CENTER
  //Example:
  // JLabel lengthL;
  // lengthL = new JLabel("Enter the length:",
  //   SwingConstants.RIGHT);
  // The label lengthL is right aligned.

public **JLabel**(String t, Icon icon, int align)
  //Constructs a JLabel with both text and an icon.
  //The icon is to the left of the text.

public **JLabel**(Icon icon)   //Constructs a JLabel with an icon.

NOTE   In Table 6-3, SwingConstants.LEFT, SwingConstants.RIGHT, and SwingConstants.CENTER are constants defined in the `class` SwingConstants. They specify whether to set the string describing the label as left-justified, right-justified, or centered.

Consider the statements:

```
JLabel lengthL;
lengthL = new JLabel("Enter the length:", SwingConstants.RIGHT);
```

After these statements execute, the label in Figure 6-5 is created.

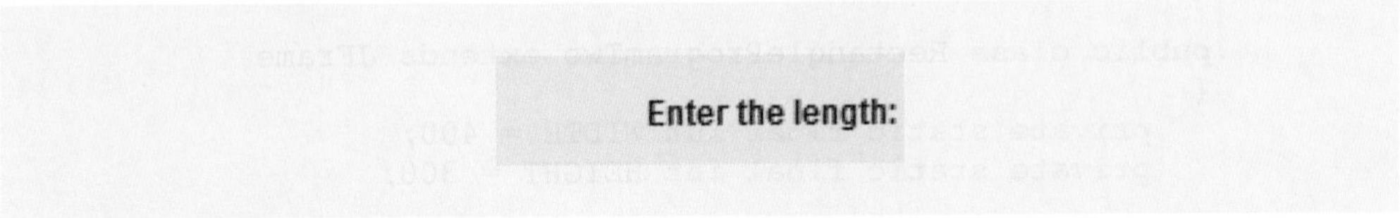

Enter the length:

FIGURE 6-5 JLabel with the text Enter the length:

Now consider the following statements:

```
private JLabel lengthL, widthL, areaL, perimeterL;           //Line 1

lengthL =
    new JLabel("Enter the length: ", SwingConstants.RIGHT); //Line 2

widthL =
    new JLabel("Enter the width: ", SwingConstants.RIGHT);  //Line 3

areaL = new JLabel("Area: ", SwingConstants.RIGHT);          //Line 4

perimeterL =
    new JLabel("Perimeter: ", SwingConstants.RIGHT);         //Line 5
```

The statement in Line 1 declares four reference variables, lengthL, widthL, areaL, and perimeterL, of the JLabel type. The statement in Line 2 instantiates the object lengthL, assigns it the title Enter the length:, and sets the title alignment to right-justified. The statements in Lines 3 through 5 instantiate the objects widthL, areaL, and perimeterL with appropriate titles and text alignment.

Next, we add these labels to the pane declared at the beginning of this section. The following statements accomplish this. (Recall from the preceding section that we use the method add to add components to a pane.)

```
pane.add(lengthL);
pane.add(widthL);
pane.add(areaL);
pane.add(perimeterL);
```

Because we have specified a grid layout for the pane with four rows and one column, the label lengthL is added to the first row, the label widthL is added to the second row, and so on.

Now that you know how to add the components to the pane, you can put together the program to create these labels. RectangleProgramTwo builds on the

RectangleProgramOne of the preceding section and, like RectangleProgramOne, is a subclass of JFrame.

```java
//Java program to create a window and place four labels

import javax.swing.*;
import java.awt.*;

public class RectangleProgramTwo extends JFrame
{
    private static final int WIDTH = 400;
    private static final int HEIGHT = 300;

    private JLabel lengthL, widthL, areaL, perimeterL;

    public RectangleProgramTwo()
    {
        setTitle("Area and Perimeter of a Rectangle");

        lengthL =
            new JLabel("Enter the length: ", SwingConstants.RIGHT);
        widthL =
            new JLabel("Enter the width: ", SwingConstants.RIGHT);
        areaL = new JLabel("Area: ", SwingConstants.RIGHT);
        perimeterL =
            new JLabel("Perimeter: ", SwingConstants.RIGHT);

        Container pane = getContentPane();
        pane.setLayout(new GridLayout(4, 1));

        pane.add(lengthL);
        pane.add(widthL);
        pane.add(areaL);
        pane.add(perimeterL);

        setSize(WIDTH, HEIGHT);
        setVisible(true);
        setDefaultCloseOperation(EXIT_ON_CLOSE);
    }

    public static void main(String[] args)
    {
        RectangleProgramTwo rectObject = new RectangleProgramTwo();
    }
}
```

Sample Run: (Figure 6-6 shows a sample run.)

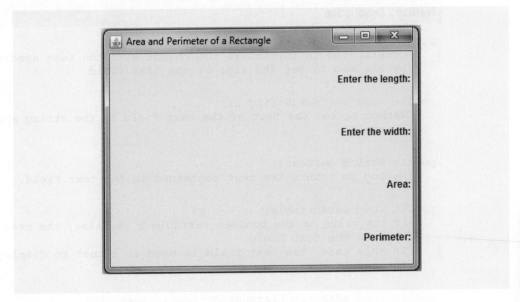

FIGURE 6-6 Sample run for `RectangleProgramTwo`

Now you are ready to create and place the text fields and buttons. The techniques for creating and placing components, such as `JTextField` and `JButton`, in a container are similar to the ones used for `JLabel`, and are described in the next two sections.

JTextField

As you may recall, text fields are objects belonging to the **class** `JTextField`. Therefore, you can create a text field by declaring a reference variable of type `JTextField` followed by an instantiation of the object.

Table 6-4 describes some of the methods of the **class** `JTextField`.

TABLE 6-4 Some Methods of the **class** `JTextField`

Method / Description
`public` **`JTextField`**`(int columns)` `//Constructor to set the size of the text field.`

`public` **`JTextField`**`(String str)`
`//Constructor to initialize the object with the text specified`
`//by str.`

TABLE 6-4 Some Methods of the **class** JTextField (continued)

Method / Description

public **JTextField**(String str, int columns)
//Constructor to initialize the object with the text specified
//by str and to set the size of the text field.

public void setText(String str)
//Method to set the text of the text field to the string specified
//by str.

public **String** getText() //Method to return the text contained in the text field.

public void **setEditable**(boolean b)
//If the value of the boolean variable b is false, the user cannot
//type in the text field.
//In this case, the text field is used as a tool to display
//the result.

public void **addActionListener**(ActionListener obj) //Method to register a listener object to a JTextField.

Consider the following statements:

```
private JTextField lengthTF, widthTF, areaTF,
                   perimeterTF;                        //Line 1

lengthTF = new JTextField(10);                         //Line 2
widthTF = new JTextField(10);                          //Line 3
areaTF = new JTextField(10);                           //Line 4
perimeterTF = new JTextField(10);                      //Line 5
```

The statement in Line 1 declares four reference variables, lengthTF, widthTF, areaTF, and perimeterTF, of type JTextField. The statement in Line 2 instantiates the object lengthTF and sets the width of this text field to 10 characters. That is, this text field can display no more than 10 characters. The meaning of the other statements is similar.

Placing these objects involves using the add method of the **class** Container as described in the previous section. The following statements add these components to the container:

```
pane.add(lengthTF);
pane.add(widthTF);
pane.add(areaTF);
pane.add(perimeterTF);
```

The container pane now would contain eight objects—four labels and four text fields. We want to place the object lengthTF adjacent to the label lengthL in the same row, and use similar placements for the other objects. So we need to expand the grid layout to four rows and two columns. The following statements create the required grid layout and the necessary objects:

```
pane.setLayout(new GridLayout(4, 2));
pane.add(lengthL);
pane.add(lengthTF);
pane.add(widthL);
pane.add(widthTF);
pane.add(areaL);
pane.add(areaTF);
pane.add(perimeterL);
pane.add(perimeterTF);
```

The following program, RectangleProgramThree, summarizes our discussion so far:

```
//Java program to create a window
//and place four labels and four text fields

import javax.swing.*;
import java.awt.*;

public class RectangleProgramThree extends JFrame
{
    private static final int WIDTH = 400;
    private static final int HEIGHT = 300;

    private JLabel lengthL, widthL, areaL, perimeterL;
    private JTextField lengthTF, widthTF, areaTF,
                       perimeterTF;

    public RectangleProgramThree()
    {
        setTitle("Area and Perimeter of a Rectangle");

        lengthL =
            new JLabel("Enter the length: ", SwingConstants.RIGHT);
        widthL =
            new JLabel("Enter the width: ", SwingConstants.RIGHT);
        areaL =
            new JLabel("Area: ", SwingConstants.RIGHT);
        perimeterL =
            new JLabel("Perimeter: ", SwingConstants.RIGHT);
```

6

```
        lengthTF = new JTextField(10);
        widthTF = new JTextField(10);
        areaTF = new JTextField(10);
        perimeterTF = new JTextField(10);

        Container pane = getContentPane();
        pane.setLayout(new GridLayout(4, 2));

        pane.add(lengthL);
        pane.add(lengthTF);
        pane.add(widthL);
        pane.add(widthTF);
        pane.add(areaL);
        pane.add(areaTF);
        pane.add(perimeterL);
        pane.add(perimeterTF);

        setSize(WIDTH, HEIGHT);
        setVisible(true);
        setDefaultCloseOperation(EXIT_ON_CLOSE);
    }

    public static void main(String[] args)
    {
        RectangleProgramThree rectObject =
                        new RectangleProgramThree();
    }
}
```

Sample Run: (Figure 6-7 shows the sample run.)

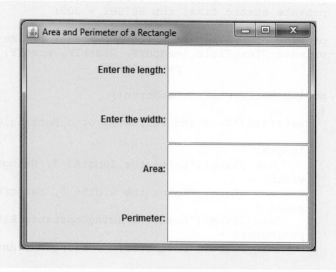

FIGURE 6-7 Sample run for `RectangleProgramThree`

To complete the design of the user interface, we will discuss how to create buttons.

JButton

To create a button, Java provides the `class` JButton. Thus, to create objects belonging to the `class` JButton, we use a technique similar to the one we used to create instances of JLabel and JTextField. Table 6-5 shows some methods of the `class` JButton.

TABLE 6-5 Commonly Used Methods of the `class` JButton

Method / Description

public **JButton**(Icon ic)
//Constructor to initialize the button object with the icon
//specified by ic.

public **JButton**(String str)
//Constructor to initialize the button object to the text specified
//by str.

public **JButton**(String str, Icon ic)
//Constructor to initialize the button object to the text specified
//by str and the icon specified by ic.

public void **setText**(String str) //Method to set the text of the button to the string specified by str.
public String **getText**() //Method to return the text contained in the button.
public void **addActionListener**(ActionListener obj) //Method to register a listener object to the button object.

The following three lines will create two buttons, Calculate and Exit, shown earlier in Figure 6-2:

```
JButton calculateB, exitB;                //Line 1

calculateB = new JButton("Calculate");   //Line 2
exitB = new JButton("Exit");             //Line 3
```

The statement in Line 1 declares calculateB and exitB to be reference variables of type JButton. The statement in Line 2 instantiates the button object calculateB and sets the text for the button to the string Calculate. Similarly, the statement in Line 3 instantiates the button object exitB and sets the text for exitB to the string Exit.

The buttons `calculateB` and `exitB` can be placed into the container `pane` by using the method `add`. The following statements add these buttons to the `pane`:

```
pane.add(calculateB);
pane.add(exitB);
```

Now you have two more objects in the container, so you need to modify the `GridLayout` to accommodate five rows and two columns, and then add all the components. The following statements create the required grid layout and add the labels, text fields, and buttons to the container `pane`:

```
pane.setLayout(new GridLayout(5,2));//specify the layout

pane.add(lengthL);          //add the label lengthL
pane.add(lengthTF);         //add the text field lengthTF
pane.add(widthL);           //add the label widthL
pane.add(widthTF);          //add the text field widthTF
pane.add(areaL);            //add the label areaL
pane.add(areaTF);           //add the text field areaTF
pane.add(perimeterL);       //add the label perimeterL
pane.add(perimeterTF);      //add the text field perimeterTF
pane.add(calculateB);       //add the button calculateB
pane.add(exitB);            //add the button exitB
```

Notice that the preceding `add` statements place the components from left to right and from top to bottom.

HANDLING AN EVENT

You have now learned how to create a window, how to create a container, and how to create labels, text fields, and buttons.

Now that you can create a button, such as `calculateB`, you need to specify how such a button should behave when you click it. For example, when you click the button `calculateB`, you want the program to calculate the area and perimeter of the rectangle and display these values in their respective text fields. Similarly, when you click the button `exitB`, the program should terminate.

Clicking a `JButton` creates an event, known as an **action event**, which sends a message to another object, known as an **action listener**. When the listener receives the message, it performs some action. Sending a message or an event to a listener object simply means that some method in the listener object is invoked with the event as the argument. This invocation happens automatically; you will not see the code corresponding to the method invocation. However, you must specify two things:

- For each JButton, you must specify the corresponding listener object. In Java, this is known as **registering** the listener.
- You must define the methods that will be invoked when the event is sent to the listener. Normally, you will write these methods and you will never write the code for invocation.

Java provides various classes to handle different kinds of events. The action event is handled by the class ActionListener, which contains only the method actionPerformed. In the method actionPerformed, you include the code that you want the system to execute when an action event is generated.

The class ActionListener that handles the action event is a special type of class, called an interface. In Java, interface is a reserved word. Roughly speaking, an interface is a class that contains only the method headings, and each method heading is terminated with a semicolon. For example, the definition of the interface ActionListener containing the method actionPerformed is:

```
public interface ActionListener
{
    public void actionPerformed(ActionEvent e);
}
```

Because the method actionPerformed does not contain a body, Java does not allow you to instantiate an object of type ActionListener. So how do you register an action listener with the object calculateB?

One way is as follows (there are other ways not discussed here): Because you cannot instantiate an object of type ActionListener, first you need to create a class on top of ActionListener so that the required object can be instantiated. The class created must provide the necessary code for the method actionPerformed. You will create the class CalculateButtonHandler to handle the event generated by clicking the button calculateB.

The class CalculateButtonHandler is created on top of the interface ActionListener. The definition of the class CalculateButtonHandler is:

```
private class CalculateButtonHandler implements
                                    ActionListener   //Line 1
{
    public void actionPerformed(ActionEvent e)       //Line 2
    {
        //The code for calculating the area and the perimeter
        //and displaying these quantities goes here
    }
}
```

Notice the following:

- The `class CalculateButtonHandler` starts with the modifier `private`. This is because you want this class to be used only within your `RectangleProgram`.

- This class uses another modifier, `implements`. This is how you build classes on top of classes that are interfaces. Notice that you have not yet provided the code for the method `actionPerformed`. You will do that shortly.

In Java, `implements` is a reserved word.

Next, we illustrate how to create a listener object of type `CalculateButtonHandler`. Consider the following statements:

```
CalculateButtonHandler cbHandler;

cbHandler = new CalculateButtonHandler();   //instantiate the object
```

As described, these statements create the listener object. Having created a listener, you next must associate (or in Java terminology, register) this handler with the corresponding JButton. The following line of code registers `cbHandler` as the listener object of `calculateB`:

```
calculateB.addActionListener(cbHandler);
```

The complete definition of the `class CalculateButtonHandler`, including the code for the method `actionPerformed`, is:

```
private class CalculateButtonHandler implements
                                    ActionListener        //Line 1
{
    public void actionPerformed(ActionEvent e)            //Line 2
    {
        double width, length, area, perimeter;           //Line 3

        length
            = Double.parseDouble(lengthTF.getText());     //Line 4
        width
            = Double.parseDouble(widthTF.getText());      //Line 5
        area = length * width;                            //Line 6
        perimeter = 2 * (length + width);                 //Line 7

        areaTF.setText("" + area);                        //Line 8
        perimeterTF.setText("" + perimeter);              //Line 9
    }
}
```

In the preceding program segment, Line 1 declares the `class CalculateButtonHandler` and makes it an action listener by including the phrase `implements ActionListener`. Note that all of this code is just a new class definition.

This class has one method; Line 2 is the first statement of that method. Let us look at the statement in Line 4:

```
length = Double.parseDouble(lengthTF.getText());
```

The length of the rectangle is stored in the text field `lengthTF`. We use the method `getText` to retrieve the string from this text field, specifying the length. Now the value of the expression `lengthTF.getText()` is the length, but it is in a string form. So we need to use the method `parseDouble` to convert the length string into an equivalent decimal number. The length is then stored in the variable `length`. The statement in Line 5 works similarly for the width.

The statements in Lines 6 and 7 compute the area and the perimeter, respectively. The statement in Line 8 uses the method `setText` of the `class` `JTextField` to display the area. Because `setText` requires that the argument be a string, you need to convert the value of the variable `area` into a string. The easiest way to do this is to concatenate the value of `area` to an empty string. Similar conventions apply for the statement in Line 9.

It follows that the method `actionPerformed` displays the area and perimeter in the corresponding `JTextFields`.

Before creating an action listener for the `JButton` `exitB`, let us summarize what we've done so far to create and register an action event listener:

1. Created a class that implements the `interface` ActionListener. For example, for the JButton `calculateB` we created the `class` CalculateButtonHandler.

2. Provided the definition of the method `actionPerformed` within the class that you created in Step 1. The method `actionPerformed` contains the code that the program executes when a specific event is generated. For example, when you click the JButton `calculateB`, the program should calculate and display the area and perimeter of the rectangle.

3. Created and instantiated an object of the class type created in Step 1. For example, for the JButton `calculateB` we created the object `cbHandler`.

4. Registered the event handler created in Step 3 with the object that generates an action event using the method `addActionListener`. For example, for JButton `calculateB` the following statement registers the object `cbHandler` to listen and register the action event:

```
calculateB.addActionListener(cbHandler);
```

6

We can now repeat these four steps to create and register the action listener with the JButton exitB.

```
private class ExitButtonHandler implements ActionListener
{
    public void actionPerformed(ActionEvent e)
    {
        System.exit(0);
    }
}
```

The following statements create the action listener object for the button exitB:

```
ExitButtonHandler ebHandler;

ebHandler = new ExitButtonHandler();
exitB.addActionListener(ebHandler);
```

The interface ActionListener is contained in the package java.awt.event. Therefore, to use this interface to handle events, your program must include the statement:

```
import java.awt.event.*;
```

or:

```
import java.awt.event.ActionListener;
```

The complete program to calculate the perimeter and area of a rectangle is:

```
//Given the length and width of a rectangle, this Java
//program determines its area and perimeter.

import javax.swing.*;
import java.awt.*;
import java.awt.event.*;

public class RectangleProgram extends JFrame
{
    private JLabel lengthL, widthL, areaL, perimeterL;

    private JTextField lengthTF, widthTF, areaTF, perimeterTF;

    private JButton calculateB, exitB;

    private CalculateButtonHandler cbHandler;
    private ExitButtonHandler ebHandler;

    private static final int WIDTH = 400;
    private static final int HEIGHT = 300;

    public RectangleProgram()
    {
            //Create the four labels
        lengthL = new JLabel("Enter the length: ",
                                SwingConstants.RIGHT);
```

```java
        widthL = new JLabel("Enter the width: ",
                                    SwingConstants.RIGHT);
        areaL = new JLabel("Area: ", SwingConstants.RIGHT);
        perimeterL = new JLabel("Perimeter: ",
                                    SwingConstants.RIGHT);

            //Create the four text fields
        lengthTF = new JTextField(10);
        widthTF = new JTextField(10);
        areaTF = new JTextField(10);
        perimeterTF = new JTextField(10);

            //Create Calculate Button
        calculateB = new JButton("Calculate");
        cbHandler = new CalculateButtonHandler();
        calculateB.addActionListener(cbHandler);

            //Create Exit Button
        exitB = new JButton("Exit");
        ebHandler = new ExitButtonHandler();
        exitB.addActionListener(ebHandler);

            //Set the title of the window
        setTitle("Area and Perimeter of a Rectangle");

            //Get the container
        Container pane = getContentPane();

            //Set the layout
        pane.setLayout(new GridLayout(5, 2));

            //Place the components in the pane
        pane.add(lengthL);
        pane.add(lengthTF);
        pane.add(widthL);
        pane.add(widthTF);
        pane.add(areaL);
        pane.add(areaTF);
        pane.add(perimeterL);
        pane.add(perimeterTF);
        pane.add(calculateB);
        pane.add(exitB);

            //Set the size of the window and display it
        setSize(WIDTH, HEIGHT);
        setVisible(true);
        setDefaultCloseOperation(EXIT_ON_CLOSE);
    }
```

6

```java
    private class CalculateButtonHandler implements ActionListener
    {
       public void actionPerformed(ActionEvent e)
       {
          double width, length, area, perimeter;

          length = Double.parseDouble(lengthTF.getText());
          width = Double.parseDouble(widthTF.getText());
          area = length * width;
          perimeter = 2 * (length + width);

          areaTF.setText("" + area);
          perimeterTF.setText("" + perimeter);
       }
    }

    private class ExitButtonHandler implements ActionListener
    {
       public void actionPerformed(ActionEvent e)
       {
           System.exit(0);
       }
    }

    public static void main(String[] args)
    {
       RectangleProgram rectObject = new RectangleProgram();
    }
}
```

Sample Run: (Figure 6-8 shows the sample run.)

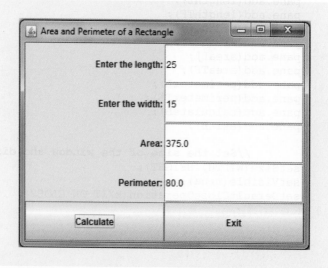

FIGURE 6-8 Sample run for the final `RectangleProgram`

PROGRAMMING EXAMPLE: Temperature Conversion

Write a program that creates the GUI shown in Figure 6-9, to convert the temperature from Fahrenheit to Celsius and from Celsius to Fahrenheit.

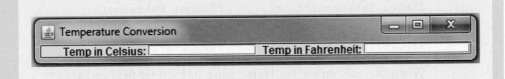

FIGURE 6-9 GUI for the temperature conversion program

When the user enters the temperature in the text field adjacent to the label `Temp in Celsius:` and presses the `Enter` key, the program displays the equivalent temperature in the text field adjacent to the label `Temp in Fahrenheit:` Similarly, when the user enters the temperature in Fahrenheit and presses the `Enter` key, the program displays the equivalent temperature in Celsius.

Input: Temperature in Fahrenheit or Celsius

Output: Temperature in Celsius if the input is Fahrenheit; the temperature in Fahrenheit if the input is Celsius

PROBLEM ANALYSIS, GUI DESIGN, AND ALGORITHM DESIGN

Suppose that the variable `celsius` represents the temperature in Celsius and the variable `fahrenheit` represents the temperature in Fahrenheit. If the user enters the temperature in Fahrenheit, the formula for calculating the equivalent temperature in Celsius is:

```
celsius = (5.0 / 9.0) * (fahrenheit - 32)
```

For example, if `fahrenheit` is 98.6, then:

```
celsius = 5.0 / 9.0 * (98.6 - 32) = 37.00
```

Similarly, if the user enters the temperature in Celsius, then the formula for calculating the equivalent temperature in Fahrenheit is:

```
fahrenheit = 9.0 / 5.0 * celsius + 32
```

For example, if `celsius` is 20, then:

```
fahrenheit = 9.0 / 5.0 * 20 + 32 = 68.0
```

The GUI in Figure 6-9 contains a window, a container, two labels, and two text fields. The labels and text fields are placed in the container of the window. As we did in the rectangle program earlier in this chapter, we can create the window by making the application extend the `class` JFrame. To get access to the container, we will use a reference variable of the `Container` type. To create labels, we use objects of type JLabel; to create text fields, we use objects of type `JTextField`. Suppose that we have the following declarations:

```
JLabel celsiusLabel;        //label Celsius
JLabel fahrenheitLabel;     //label Fahrenheit

JTextField celsiusTF;       //text field Celsius
JTextField fahrenheitTF;    //text field Fahrenheit
```

When the user enters the temperature in the text field `celsiusTF` and presses the Enter key, we want the program to show the equivalent temperature in the text field `fahrenheitTF` and vice versa.

Recall that when you click a JButton, it generates an action event. Moreover, the action event is handled by the method `actionPerformed` of the `interface` ActionListener. Similarly, when you press the Enter key in a text field, it generates an action event. Therefore, we can register an action event listener with the text fields `celsiusTF` and `fahrenheitTF` to take the appropriate action.

Based on this analysis and the GUI shown in Figure 6-9, you can design an event-driven algorithm as follows:

1. Have a listener in each text field.
2. Register an event handler with each text field.
3. Let each event handler registered with a text field do the following:
   a. Get the data from the text field once the user presses Enter.
   b. Apply the corresponding formula to perform the conversion.
   c. Set the value of the other text field.

This process of adding an event listener and then registering the event listener to a text field is similar to the process we used to register an event listener to a JButton earlier in the chapter. (This process will be described later in this programming example.)

VARIABLES, OBJECTS, AND NAMED CONSTANTS

The input to the program is either the temperature in Celsius or the temperature in Fahrenheit. If the input is a value for Celsius, then the program calculates the equivalent temperature in Fahrenheit. Similarly, if the input is a value for Fahrenheit, then the program calculates the equivalent temperature in Celsius. Therefore, the program needs the following variables:

```
double celsius;      //variable to hold Celsius
double fahrenheit;   //variable to hold Fahrenheit
```

Notice that these variables are needed in each event handler.

The formulas to convert the temperature from Fahrenheit to Celsius and vice versa use the special values 32, 9.0/5.0, and 5.0/9.0, which we will declare as named constants as follows:

```
private static final double FTOC = 5.0 / 9.0;
private static final double CTOF = 9.0 / 5.0;
private static final int OFFSET = 32;
```

As in the GUI, you need two labels—one to label the text field corresponding to the Celsius value and another to label the text field corresponding to the Fahrenheit value. Therefore, the following statements are needed:

```
private JLabel celsiusLabel;        //label Celsius
private JLabel fahrenheitLabel;     //label Fahrenheit

celsiusLabel = new JLabel("Temp in Celsius: ",
                SwingConstants.RIGHT);//object instantiation

fahrenheitLabel = new JLabel("Temp in Fahrenheit: ",
                SwingConstants.RIGHT);//object instantiation
```

You also need two `JTextField` objects. The necessary Java code is:

```
private JTextField celsiusTF;       //text field Celsius
private JTextField fahrenheitTF;    //text field Fahrenheit

celsiusTF = new JTextField(7);      //object instantiation
fahrenheitTF = new JTextField(7);   //object instantiation
```

Now you need a window to display the labels and the text fields. Because a window is an object of type `JFrame`, the class containing the application program that we create will extend the definition of the `class JFrame`. We will set the width of the window to 500 pixels and the height to 50 pixels. We'll call the class containing the application program `TempConversion`. The application will look like this:

```
//Java program to convert the temperature from Celsius to
//Fahrenheit and vice versa.

import javax.swing.*;

public class TempConversion extends JFrame
{
    private static final int WIDTH = 500;
    private static final int HEIGHT = 50;

    private static final double FTOC = 5.0 / 9.0;
    private static final double CTOF = 9.0 / 5.0;
    private static final int OFFSET = 32;
```

```
public TempConversion()
{
    setTitle("Temperature Conversion");
    setSize(WIDTH, HEIGHT);
    setDefaultCloseOperation(EXIT_ON_CLOSE);
    setVisible(true);
}

public static void main(String[] args)
{
    TempConversion tempConv = new TempConversion();
}
}
```

Now you need to access the container content pane to place the GUI components and set the required layout of the pane. Therefore, as before, you need the following statements:

```
Container c = getContentPane();    //get the container

c.setLayout(new GridLayout(1, 4)); //create a new layout

c.add(celsiusLabel);               //add the label celsiusLabel
                                   //to the container
c.add(celsiusTF);                  //add the text field celsiusTF
                                   //to the container
c.add(fahrenheitLabel);            //add the label fahrenheitLabel
                                   //to the container
c.add(fahrenheitTF);               //add the text field fahrenheitTF
                                   //to the container
```

You want your program to respond to the events generated by `JTextFields`. Just as when you click a `JButton` an action event is generated, when you press Enter in a `JTextField`, it generates an action event. Therefore, to register event listeners with `JTextFields`, we use the four steps outlined in the section Handling an Event earlier in this chapter: (1) create a class that implements the interface `ActionListener`; (2) provide the definition of the method `actionPerformed` within the class that you created in Step 1; (3) create and instantiate an object of the class created in Step 1; and (4) register the event handler created in Step 3 with the object that generates an action event using the method `addActionListener`.

Next, we create and register an action listener with the `JTextField celsiusTF`.

First we create the class `CelsHandler`, implementing the interface `ActionListener`. Then, we provide the definition of the method `actionPerformed` of the class `CelsHandler`. When the user enters the temperature in the `JTextField celsiusTF` and presses Enter, the program needs to calculate and display the equivalent temperature in the `JTextField` fahrenheitTF. The necessary code is placed within the body of the method actionPerformed.

We now describe the steps of the method actionPerformed. The temperature in Celsius is contained in the JTextField celsiusTF. We use the method getText of the class JTextField to retrieve the temperature in celsiusTF. However, the value returned by the method getText is in string form, so we use the method parseDouble of the class Double to convert the numeric string into a decimal value. It follows that we need a variable of type double, say, celsius, to store the temperature in Celsius. We accomplish this with the following statement:

```
celsius = Double.parseDouble(celsiusTF.getText());
```

We also need a variable of type double, say, fahrenheit, to store the equivalent temperature in Fahrenheit. Because we want to display the temperature to two decimal places, we use the method format of the class String.

We can now write the definition of the class CelsHandler as follows:

```
private class CelsHandler implements ActionListener
{
    public void actionPerformed(ActionEvent e)
    {
        double celsius, fahrenheit;

        celsius =
            Double.parseDouble(celsiusTF.getText());

        fahrenheit = celsius * CTOF + OFFSET;

        fahrenheitTF.setText(String.format("%.2f",
                                    fahrenheit));
    }
}
```

We can now create an object of type CelsHandler as follows:

```
private CelsHandler celsiusHandler;
celsiusHandler = new CelsHandler();
```

Having created a listener, you must associate this handler with the corresponding JTextField celsiusTF. The following code does this:

```
celsiusTF.addActionListener(celsiusHandler);
```

6

Similarly, we can create and register an action listener with the text field `fahrenheitTF`. The necessary code is:

```java
private class FahrHandler implements ActionListener
{
    public void actionPerformed(ActionEvent e)
    {
        double celsius, fahrenheit;

        fahrenheit =
            Double.parseDouble(fahrenheitTF.getText());

        celsius = (fahrenheit - OFFSET) * FTOC;

        celsiusTF.setText(String.format("%.2f",
                                        celsius));
    }
}

private FahrHandler fahrenheitHandler;

fahrenheitHandler = new FahrHandler(); //instantiate the object

fahrenheitTF.addActionListener(fahrenheitHandler);
                                //add the action listener
```

Now that we have created the necessary GUI components and the programming code, we can put everything together to create the complete program.

PUTTING IT
TOGETHER

You can start with the window creation program and then add all the components, handlers, and classes developed. You also need the necessary `import` statements. In this case, they are:

```java
import java.awt.*;          //for the class Container
import java.awt.event.*;    //for events
import javax.swing.*;       //for JLabel and JTextField
```

Thus, you have the following Java program:

```java
//*****************************************************************
//Author: D.S. Malik
//
//Java program to convert the temperature between Celsius and
//Fahrenheit.
//*****************************************************************

import java.awt.*;
import java.awt.event.*;
import javax.swing.*;
```

```java
public class TempConversion extends JFrame
{
    private JLabel celsiusLabel;
    private JLabel fahrenheitLabel;

    private JTextField celsiusTF;
    private JTextField fahrenheitTF;

    private CelsHandler celsiusHandler;
    private FahrHandler fahrenheitHandler;

    private static final int WIDTH = 500;
    private static final int HEIGHT = 50;
    private static final double FTOC = 5.0 / 9.0;
    private static final double CTOF = 9.0 / 5.0;
    private static final int OFFSET = 32;

    public TempConversion()
    {
        setTitle("Temperature Conversion");
        Container c = getContentPane();
        c.setLayout(new GridLayout(1, 4));

        celsiusLabel = new JLabel("Temp in Celsius: ",
                                SwingConstants.RIGHT);
        fahrenheitLabel = new JLabel("Temp in Fahrenheit: ",
                                SwingConstants.RIGHT);

        celsiusTF = new JTextField(7);
        fahrenheitTF = new JTextField(7);

        c.add(celsiusLabel);
        c.add(celsiusTF);
        c.add(fahrenheitLabel);
        c.add(fahrenheitTF);

        celsiusHandler = new CelsHandler();
        fahrenheitHandler = new FahrHandler();

        celsiusTF.addActionListener(celsiusHandler);
        fahrenheitTF.addActionListener(fahrenheitHandler);

        setSize(WIDTH, HEIGHT);
        setDefaultCloseOperation(EXIT_ON_CLOSE);
        setVisible(true);
    }
```

6

```java
private class CelsHandler implements ActionListener
{
    public void actionPerformed(ActionEvent e)
    {
        double celsius, fahrenheit;

        celsius =
            Double.parseDouble(celsiusTF.getText());

        fahrenheit = celsius * CTOF + OFFSET;

        fahrenheitTF.setText(String.format("%.2f",
                                    fahrenheit));
    }
}

private class FahrHandler implements ActionListener
{
    public void actionPerformed(ActionEvent e)
    {
        double celsius, fahrenheit;

        fahrenheit =
            Double.parseDouble(fahrenheitTF.getText());

        celsius = (fahrenheit - OFFSET) * FTOC;

        celsiusTF.setText(String.format("%.2f",
                                    celsius));
    }
}

public static void main(String[] args)
{
    TempConversion tempConv = new TempConversion();
}
}
```

Sample Run: (Figure 6-10 shows the display after the user typed 98.60 in the text field Temp in Fahrenheit and pressed Enter.)

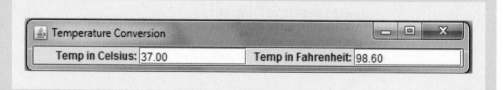

FIGURE 6-10 Sample run for TempConversion

Object-Oriented Design

Chapter 3 discussed the **class** **String** in detail. Using the **class** **String**, you can create various **String** objects. Moreover, using the methods of the **class** **String**, you can manipulate the string stored in a **String** object. Recall that **String** objects are instances of the **class** **String**. Similarly, a Java program that uses GUI components also uses various objects. For example, in the first part of this chapter, you used the **JFrame**, **JLabel**, **JTextField**, and **JButton** objects. Labels are instances of the **class** **JLabel**, buttons are instances of the **class** **JButton**, and so on. In general, an object is an instance of a particular class.

In this section, we delve a little deeper into the general concept of objects and how they are used in object-oriented design (OOD). OOD is a major field of study in its own right. Most colleges and universities offer courses on this topic. This section by no means presents an in-depth treatise on OOD. Rather, we review its general concepts and give a simplified methodology for using the OOD approach to problem solving.

Since Chapter 2, you have used **String** objects. Moreover, in the first part of this chapter, you used objects belonging to various classes, such as **JFrame**, **JLabel**, **JTextField**, **JButton**, and **String**. In fact, in your daily life you use objects such as a DVD player, CD player, and so on without realizing how they might be conceptualized as objects or classes. For example, regarding a DVD player, note the following facts:

- To use a DVD player, you do not need to know how the DVD player is made. You do not need to know the internal parts of a DVD player or how they work. These are hidden from you.

- To use a DVD player, you do need to know the functions of various buttons and how to use them.

- Once you know how to use a DVD player, you can use it either as a stand-alone device or you can combine it with other devices to create an entertainment system.

- You cannot modify the functions of a DVD player. The Play button will always function as a Play button.

Any Java objects, such as **String** objects, that you have encountered also have the properties mentioned above. You can use the objects and their methods, but you don't need to know how they work.

The aim of OOD is to build software from components called classes so that if someone wants to use a class, all they need to know is the various methods provided by that class.

Recall that in OOD, an object combines data and operations on that data in a single unit, a feature called **encapsulation**. In OOD, we first identify the object, then identify the relevant data, and then identify the operations needed to manipulate the object.

For example, the relevant data for a **String** object is the actual string and the length of the string, that is, the number of characters in the string. Every **String** object must have memory space to store the relevant data, that is, the string and its length. Next, we must identify the type of operations performed on a string. Some of the operations on a string might be to replace a particular character of a string, extract part of a string, change a string from uppercase to lowercase, and so on. The `class` `String` provides the necessary operations to be performed on a string.

As another example of how an object contains both data and operations on that data, consider objects of type `JButton`. Because every button has a label, which is a string, every button must have memory space to store its label. Some of the operations on a button that you have encountered are to set the label of the button and to add a listener object to a button. Other operations that can be performed on a button are to set its size and location. These operations are the methods of a class. Thus, the `class` `JButton` provides the methods to set a button's size and location.

A Simplified OOD Methodology

Now that you have an overview of objects and the essential components of OOD, you may be eager to learn how to solve a particular problem using OOD methodology. The best way to learn is by practice. A simplified OOD methodology can be expressed as follows:

1. Write down a detailed description of the problem.
2. Identify all the (relevant) nouns and verbs.
3. From the list of nouns, select the objects. Identify the data components of each object.
4. From the list of verbs, select the operations.

In item 3, after identifying the objects or classes, usually you will realize that several objects function in the same way. That is, they have the same data components and same operations. In other words, they will lead to the construction of the same class.

Remember that objects are nothing but instances of a particular class. Therefore, to create objects you have to learn how to create classes. In other words, to create objects you first need to create classes; to know what type of classes to create, you need to know what an object stores and what operations are needed to manipulate an object's data. You can see that objects and classes are closely related. Because an object consists of data and operations on the data in a single unit, in Java we use the mechanism of classes to combine data and its operations in a single unit. In OOD methodology, we therefore identify classes, data members of classes, and operations. In Java, data members are also known as **fields**.

The remainder of this section gives various examples to illustrate how objects, data components of objects, and operations on data are identified. In these examples, nouns (objects) are in bold type, and verbs (operations) are in italics.

EXAMPLE 6-2

Consider the problem presented in Example 6-1. In simple terms, the problem can be stated as follows:

"Write a **program** to *input* the **length** and **width** of a **rectangle** and *calculate* and *print* the **perimeter** and **area** of the **rectangle**."

Step 1: Identify all the (relevant) nouns.

- Length
- Width
- Perimeter
- Area
- Rectangle

Step 2: Identify the class(es).

Considering all five nouns, it is clear that:

- Length is the length of a rectangle.
- Width is the width of a rectangle.
- Perimeter is the perimeter of a rectangle.
- Area is the area of a rectangle.

Notice that four of the five nouns are related to the fifth one, namely, `rectangle`. Therefore, choose `Rectangle` as a class. From the `class` Rectangle, you can instantiate rectangles of various dimensions. The `class` Rectangle can be graphically represented as in Figure 6-11.

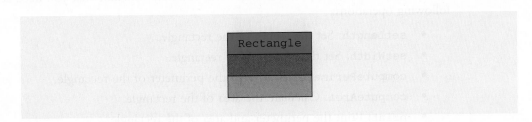

FIGURE 6-11 `class` Rectangle

Step 3: Identify the data members for each of the classes.

In this step, you evaluate the remaining nouns and determine the information that is essential to fully describing each class. Therefore, consider each noun—length, width, perimeter, and area—and ask: "Is each of these nouns essential for describing the rectangle?"

- Perimeter is not needed, because it can be computed from length and width. Perimeter is not a data member.
- Area is not needed, because it can be computed from length and width. Area is not a data member.
- Length is required. Length is a data member.
- Width is required. Width is a data member.

Having made these choices, the **class** Rectangle can be represented with data members, as shown in Figure 6-12.

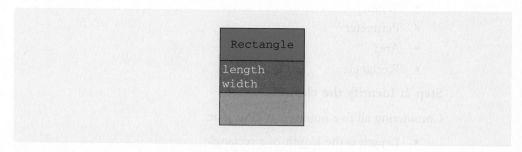

FIGURE 6-12 **class** Rectangle with data members

Step 4: Identify the operations for each of the classes.

Many operations for a class or an object can be determined by looking at the list of verbs. Let us consider the verbs *input*, *calculate*, and *print*. The possible operations on a rectangle object are *input* the length and width, *calculate* the perimeter and area, and *print* the perimeter and area. In this step, we focus on the functionalities of the class(es) involved. By carefully reading the problem statement, you may conclude that you need at least the following operations:

- setLength: Set the length of the rectangle.
- setWidth: Set the width of the rectangle.
- computePerimeter: Calculate the perimeter of the rectangle.
- computeArea: Calculate the area of the rectangle.
- print: Print the perimeter and area of the rectangle.

It is customary to include operations to retrieve the values of the data members of an object. Therefore, you also need the following operations:

- getLength: Retrieve the length of the rectangle.
- getWidth: Retrieve the width of the rectangle.

Figure 6-13 shows the **class** Rectangle with data members and operations.

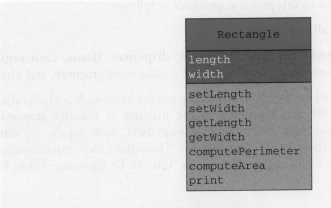

FIGURE 6-13 `class Rectangle` with data members and operations

With these steps completed, you can design an algorithm for each operation of an object (class) and implement each algorithm in Java.

 NOTE The diagram in Figure 6-13 is a form of a diagram known as the *class unified modeling language (UML) diagram*. After introducing a few more terms used in a class UML diagram, we formally introduce the class UML diagram in Chapter 8, when we discuss classes in general.

EXAMPLE 6-3

Consider the following problem:

A **place** to buy **candy** is from a **candy machine**. A new candy machine is purchased for the **cafeteria**, but it is not working properly. The candy machine has four **dispensers** to hold and release **items** sold by the candy machine as well as a **cash register**. The machine sells four products—**candies**, **chips**, **gum**, and **cookies**—each stored in a separate dispenser. You have been asked to write a program for this candy machine so that it can be put into operation.

The program should do the following:

- *Show* the **customer** the different **products** sold by the **candy machine**.
- Let the **customer** *make* the selection.
- *Show* the **customer** the **cost of the item** selected.
- *Accept* the **money** from the **customer**.
- *Return* the **change**.
- *Release* the **item**, that is, *make* the sale.

The OOD solution to this problem proceeds as follows:

Step 1: Identify all the nouns.

Place, **candy**, **candy machine**, **cafeteria**, **dispenser**, **items**, **cash register**, **chips**, **gum**, **cookies**, **customer**, **products**, **cost** (of the item), **money**, and **change**.

In this description of the problem, products stand for items such as candy, chips, gum, and cookies. In fact, the actual product in the machine is not that important. What is important is to note that there are four dispensers, each capable of dispensing one product. Further, there is one cash register. Thus, the candy machine consists of four dispensers and one cash register. Graphically, this can be represented as in Figure 6-14.

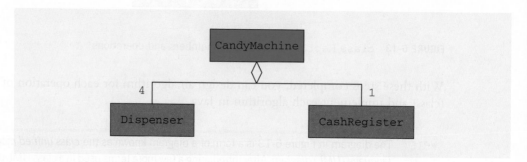

FIGURE 6-14 Candy Machine and its components

In Figure 6-14, the number 4 on top of the box `Dispenser` indicates that there are four dispensers in the candy machine. Similarly, the number 1 on top of the box `CashRegister` indicates that the candy machine has one cash register.

Step 2: Identify the class(es).

You can see that the program you are about to write is supposed to deal with dispensers and cash registers. That is, the main objects are four dispensers and a cash register. Because all the dispensers are of the same type, you need to create a class, say, `Dispenser`, to create the dispensers. Similarly, you need to create a class, say, `CashRegister`, to create a cash register. We will create the **class** `CandyMachine` containing the four dispensers, a cash register, and the application program.

Step 3: Identify the data members for each of the class(es).

Dispenser To make the sale, at least one item must be in the dispenser and the customer must know the cost of the product. Therefore, the data members of a dispenser are:

- Product cost
- Number of items in the dispenser

Cash Register The cash register accepts money and returns change. Therefore, the cash register has only one data member, which we call `cashOnHand`.

Candy Machine The `class` CandyMachine has four dispensers and a cash register. You can name the four dispensers by the items they store. Therefore, the candy machine has five data members—four dispensers and a cash register.

Step 4: Identify the operations for each of the objects (classes).

The relevant verbs are *show* (selection), *make* (selection), *show* (cost), *accept* (money), *return* (change), and *make* (sale).

The verbs *show* (selection) and *make* (selection) relate to the candy machine. The verbs *show* (cost) and *make* (sale) relate to the dispenser. Similarly, the verbs *accept* (money) and *return* (change) relate to the cash register.

Dispenser The verb *show* (cost) applies to either printing or retrieving the value of the data member `cost`. The verb *make* (sale) applies to reducing the number of items in the dispenser by 1. Of course, the dispenser has to be nonempty. You must also provide an operation to set the cost and the number of items in the dispenser. Thus, the operations for a dispenser object are:

- `getCount`: Retrieve the number of items in the dispenser.
- `getProductCost`: Retrieve the cost of the item.
- `makeSale`: Reduce the number of items in the dispenser by 1.
- `setProductCost`: Set the cost of the product.
- `setNumberOfItems`: Set the number of items in the dispenser.

Cash Register The verb *accept* (money) applies to updating the money in the cash register by adding the money deposited by the customer. Similarly, the verb *return* (change) applies to reducing the money in the cash register by returning the overpaid amount (by the customer) to the customer. You also need to (initially) set the money in the cash register and retrieve the money from the cash register. Thus, the possible operations on a cash register are:

- `acceptAmount`: Update the amount in the cash register.
- `returnChange`: Return the change.
- `getCashOnHand`: Retrieve the amount in the cash register.
- `setCashOnHand`: Set the amount in the cash register.

Candy Machine The verbs *show* (selection) and *make* (selection) apply to the candy machine. Thus, the two possible operations are:

- `showSelection`: Show the number of products sold by the candy machine.
- `makeSelection`: Allow the customer to select the product.

The result of the OOD for this problem is shown in Figure 6-15.

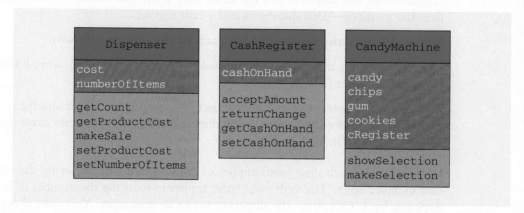

FIGURE 6-15 Classes `Dispenser`, `CashRegister`, `CandyMachine`, and their members

Implementing Classes and Operations

From the preceding examples, it is clear that once the relevant classes, data members of each class, and relevant operations for each class are identified, the next step is to implement these things in Java. Because objects are nothing but instances of classes, we need to learn how to implement classes in Java. Implementing data members, that is, fields, of classes is simple because you need variables to store the data.

What about operations? In Java, we write algorithms to implement operations. Because there is usually more than one operation on an object, each algorithm is implemented with the help of Java's methods. In Chapter 3, we briefly introduced methods and described some predefined methods. However, Java does not provide all the methods that you will ever need. Therefore, to learn how to design and implement classes, you first must learn how to construct and implement your own methods. Because methods are an essential part of Java (or any programming language), Chapter 7 is devoted to teaching you how to create methods.

Primitive Data Types and the Wrapper Classes

Chapter 3 discussed how to use the method `parseInt` of the `class Integer` to convert an integer string into an integer. Moreover, you learned that the `class Integer` is called a **wrapper** class, or simply a wrapper. It is used to wrap `int` values into `Integer` objects so that `int` values can be regarded as objects. Similarly, the `class Long` is used to wrap `long` values into `Long` objects, the `class Double` is used to wrap `double` values into `Double` objects, and the `class` `Float` is used to wrap `float` values into `Float` objects. In fact, Java provides a wrapper class corresponding to each primitive data type. For example, the wrapper class corresponding to the type `int` is `Integer`.

Next, we briefly discuss the `class` `Integer`. Table 6-6 describes some members of the `class` `Integer`.

TABLE 6-6 Some Members of the `class` `Integer`

Named Constants
`public static final int MAX_VALUE = 2147483647;`
`public static final int MIN_VALUE = -2147483648;`

Constructors

`public Integer(int num)`
`//Creates an object initialized to the value specified`
`//by num.`

`public Integer(String str)`
`//Creates an object initialized to the value specified`
`//by the num contained in str.`

Methods

`int compareTo(Integer anotherInteger)`
`//Compares two Integer objects numerically.`
`//Returns the value 0 if the value of this Integer object is`
`//equal to the value of anotherInteger object, a value less`
`//than 0 if the value of this Integer is less than the value of`
`//anotherInteger object, and a value greater than 0 if the value`
`//of this Integer object is greater than the value of`
`//anotherInteger object.`

`public int intValue()` `//Returns the value of the object as an int value.`
`public double doubleValue()` `//Returns the value of the object as a double value.`

`public boolean equals(Object obj)`
`//Returns true if the value of this object is equal`
`//to the value of the object specified by obj;`
`//otherwise returns false.`

6

TABLE 6-6 Some Members of the `class` Integer (continued)

```
public static int parseInt(String str)
  //Returns the value of the number contained in str.
```

```
public String toString()
  //Returns the int value, of the object, as a string.
```

```
public static String toString(int num)
  //Returns the value of num as a string.
```

```
public static Integer valueOf(String str)
  //Returns an Integer object initialized to the value
  //specified by str.
```

 NOTE The wrapper classes are contained in the package java.lang. As noted in Chapter 2, if a class is contained in the package java.lang, to use that class in a program, it is not necessary to explicitly import that class using the import statement. The system automatically imports classes contained in the package java.lang. Therefore, to use the `class` Integer in a program, it is not necessary to explicitly import this class using the import statement.

Consider the following statements:

```
Integer num;           //Line 1
num = new Integer(86)  //Line 2
```

The statement in Line 1 declares num to be a reference variable of type `Integer`. The statement in Line 2 creates an `Integer` object, stores the value 86 in it, and then stores the address of this object into num. (See Figure 6-16. Suppose that the address of the `Integer` object is 1350.)

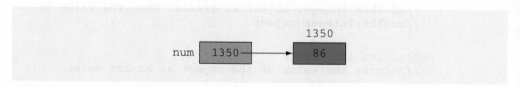

FIGURE 6-16 The reference variable num and the object it points to

As you can see, the `int` value 86 is wrapped into an `Integer` object. Just like the `class` `String`, the `class` Integer does not provide any method to change the value of an existing `Integer` object. That is, `Integer` objects are **immutable**. (In fact, wrapper class objects are immutable.)

As of Java 5.0, Java has simplified the wrapping and unwrapping of primitive type values, called the **autoboxing** and **auto-unboxing** of primitive types. For example, consider the following statements:

```
int x;                          //Line 3
Integer num;                    //Line 4
```

The statement in Line 3 declares the `int` variable `x`; the statement in Line 4 declares `num` to be a reference variable of type `Integer`.

Consider the statement:

```
num = 25;                       //Line 5
```

For the most part, this statement is equivalent to the statement:

```
num = new Integer(25);          //Line 6
```

That is, after the execution of either of these statements, num refers to or points to an `Integer` object with value 25. The expression in Line 5 is referred to as *autoboxing* of `int` type.

 NOTE   In reality, for the statement in Line 5, if an `Integer` object with value 25 already exists, then num would point to that object. On the other hand, if the statement in Line 6 executes, then an `Integer` object with value 25 will be created, even if such an object exists, and num would point to that object. In either case, num would point to an `Integer` object with value 25.

Now consider the statement:

```
x = num;                        //Line 7
```

This statement is equivalent to the statement:

```
x = num.intValue();             //Line 8
```

After the execution of either the statement in Line 7 or Line 8, the value of **x** is 25. The statement in Line 7 is referred to as *auto-unboxing* of `int` type.

 NOTE   Autoboxing and -unboxing of primitive types are features of Java 5.0 and are *not* available in Java versions lower than 5.0.

Next, consider the following statement:

```
x = 2 * num;                    //Line 9
```

This statement first unboxes the value of the object num, which is 25, multiplies this value by 2, and then stores the value, which is 50, into **x**. This illustrates that unboxing also occurs in an expression.

To compare the values of two `Integer` objects, you can use the method `compareTo`, described in Table 6-6. If you want to compare the values of two `Integer` objects only for equality, then you can use the method `equals`.

| NOTE | Suppose you have the following statements: |

```
Integer num1 = 24;
Integer num2 = 35;
```

Now consider the following statements:

```
if (num1.equals(num2))
    System.out.println("The values of the "
                    + "objects num1 and num2 "
                    + "are the same.");
else
    System.out.println("The values of the "
                    + "objects num1 and num2 "
                    + "are not the same.");
```

The expression in the `if` statement determines if the value of the object num1, which is 24, is the same as the value of the object num2, which is 35. Next, consider the following statements:

```
if (num1 == num2)
    System.out.println("Both num1 and num2 "
                    + "point to the same "
                    + "object.");
else
    System.out.println("num1 and num2 "
                    + "do not point to the "
                    + "same object.");
```

It follows that when the operator `==` is used with reference variables of the `Integer` type, it compares whether the objects point to the same object. Therefore, if you want to compare the values of two `Integer` objects, then you should use the method `equals` of the `class` `Integer`. On the other hand, if you want to determine whether two reference variables of `Integer` type points to the same `Integer` object, then you should use the operator `==`.

The preceding discussion of comparing Integer objects also applies to other wrapper classes' objects.

Autoboxing and -unboxing of primitive types is a new feature of Java and is available in Java 5.0 and higher versions. It automatically boxes and unboxes primitive type values into appropriate objects. For example, as explained above, `int` values can be automatically boxed and unboxed into `Integer` objects. Example 6-4 further illustrates autoboxing and auto-unboxing of `Integer` objects.

EXAMPLE 6-4

```
//Programm illustrating autoboxing and -unboxing
//of Integer objects.

public class IntegerClassExample
{
    public static void main(String[] args)
    {
        int   x, y;                                        //Line 1

        Integer num1, num2;                                //Line 2

        num1 = 8;        //Autobox 8                       //Line 3
        num2 = 16;       //Autobox 16                      //Line 4

        System.out.println("Line 5: num1 = " + num1
                        + ", num2 = " + num2);             //Line 5

        x = num1 + 4;                                      //Line 6

        System.out.println("Line 7: x = " + x);            //Line 7

        y = num1 + num2;                                   //Line 8

        System.out.println("Line 9: y = " + y);            //Line 9

        System.out.println("Line 10: The value of "
                        + "2 * num1 + num2 = "
                        + (2 * num1 + num2));              //Line 10

        System.out.println("Line 11: The value of "
                        + "x * num2 - num1 = "
                        + (x * num2 - num1));              //Line 11

        System.out.println("Line 12: The value of "
                        + "num1 <= num2 is "
                        + (num1 <= num2));                 //Line 12

        System.out.println("Line 13: The value of "
                        + "2 * num1 <= x is "
                        + (2 * num1 <= x));                //Line 13

        System.out.println("Line 14: The value of "
                        + "2 * num1 >= num2 is "
                        + (2 * num1 >= num2));             //Line 14
    }
}
```

Sample Run:

```
Line 5: num1 = 8, num2 = 16
Line 7: x = 12
```

```
Line 9: y = 24
Line 10: The value of 2 * num1 + num2 = 32
Line 11: The value of x * num2 - num1 = 184
Line 12: The value of num1 <= num2 is true
Line 13: The value of 2 * num1 <= x is false
Line 14: The value of 2 * num1 >= num2 is true
```

For the most part, the preceding sample run is self-explanatory. Let us look at some of the statements. The statement in Line 3 autoboxes the value 8 into an `Integer` object and stores the address of that object into the reference variable `num1`. The meaning of the statement in Line 4 is similar.

The statement in Line 6 unboxes the value of the object to which `num1` points, adds 4 to that value, and stores the result in `x`. Similarly, the statement in Line 8 unboxes the values of objects pointed to by `num1` and `num2`, adds the values, and stores the result in `y`.

The statement in Line 12 unboxes the values of the objects pointed by `num1` and `num2`, and then compares the values using the relational operator `<=`. (Note that we are not using the operator `==`, so autoboxing occurs here.)

The `class` `Double` also has methods similar to the methods shown in Table 6-6. A program that illustrates the autoboxing and -unboxing of `double` values into `Double` objects can be found with the Additional Student Files at *www.cengagebrain.com*. The program is named `DoubleClassExample.java`. However, to compare the values, for equality, of the wrapper classes objects, you should use the method `equals`. See the following example.

EXAMPLE 6-5

```java
//Program illustrating how the operator == and the
//method equals works with Double objects.

public class DoubleClassMethodEquals
{
    public static void main(String[] args)
    {
        Double num1, num2;                          //Line 1

        num1 = 2567.58;                             //Line 2
        num2 = 2567.58;                             //Line 3

        System.out.println("Line 4: num1 = " + num1
                       + ", num2 = " + num2);       //Line 4

        System.out.println("Line 5: The value of "
                       + "num1.equals(num2) is "
                       + num1.equals(num2));         //Line 5
```

```
    System.out.println("Line 6: The value of "
            + "num1 == num2 is "
            + (num1 == num2));              //Line 6
  }
}
```

Sample Run:

```
Line 4: num1 = 2567.58, num2 = 2567.58
Line 5: The value of num1.equals(num2) is true
Line 6: The value of num1 == num2 is false
```

In the preceding program, the statements in Lines 2 and 3 create two objects, each with the value 2567.58 and make num1 and num2, respectively, point to these objects. The expression num1.equals(num2), in Line 5, compares the values stored in the objects to which num1 and num2 point. Because both objects contain the same value, this expression evaluates to true; see the output of the statement in Line 5. On the other hand, the expression num1 == num2, in Line 6, determines whether num1 and num2 point to the same object.

6

NOTE   Note that the program in Example 6-5 also illustrates that when you create a Double object using the assignment operator without explicitly using the operator new, the system always creates a different Double object even if one with a given value already exists. For example, see the statements in Lines 2 and 3, and the output of the statement in Line 6.

QUICK REVIEW

1. GUI stands for graphical user interface.
2. Every GUI program requires a window.
3. Various components are added to the content pane of the window and not to the window itself.
4. You must create a layout before you can add a component to the content pane.
5. Pixel stands for picture element. Windows are measured in pixels of height and width.
6. JFrame is a class and the GUI component window can be created as an instance of JFrame.
7. JLabel is used to label other GUI components and to display information to the user.
8. A JTextField can be used for both input and output.
9. A JButton generates an event.
10. An event handler is a Java method that determines the action to be performed as the event happens.
11. When you click a button, an action event is created and sent to another object known as an action listener.

12. An action listener must have a method called `actionPerformed`.

13. A `class` is a collection of data members and methods associated with those data members.

14. OOD starts with a problem statement and tries to identify the classes required by identifying the nouns appearing in the problem statement.

15. Methods of a class are identified with the help of verbs appearing in the problem statement.

16. To wrap values of primitive data types into objects corresponding to each primitive type, Java provides a `class`, called a wrapper class. For example, to wrap an `int` value into an object, the corresponding wrapper `class` is `Integer`. Similarly, to wrap a `double` value into an object, the corresponding wrapper `class` is `Double`.

17. Java 5.0 simplifies the wrapping and unwrapping of primitive type values, called the autoboxing and auto-unboxing of primitive data types.

18. `Integer` objects are immutable. (In fact, wrapper classes' objects are immutable.)

19. To compare the values of two `Integer` objects, you can use the method `compareTo`. If you want to compare the values of two `Integer` objects only for equality, then you can use the method `equals`.

EXERCISES

1. Mark the following statements as true or false.

   a. Every window has a width and height.

   b. In Java, `JFrame` is a class.

   c. To display the window, you need not invoke a method such as `setVisible`.

   d. In Java, the reserved word `extends` allows you to create a new class from an existing one.

   e. The window you see displayed on your screen is a class.

   f. Labels are used to display the output of a program.

   g. Every GUI component you need has to be created and added to a container.

   h. In Java, `implements` is a keyword.

   i. Clicking a button is an example of an action event.

   j. In a problem statement, every verb is a possible class.

   k. In a problem statement, every noun is a possible method.

   l. To use an object, you must know how it is implemented.

2. Name some commonly used GUI components and their uses.

3. Name a GUI component that can be used for both input and output.

4. Name two input GUI components.

5. Why do you need labels in a GUI program?

6. Why would you prefer a GUI program over a non-GUI version?

7. What are the advantages of problem analysis, GUI design, and algorithm design over directly writing a program?

8. Modify the temperature conversion program to convert centimeters to inches, and vice versa.

9. Modify the program to compute the area and perimeter of a rectangle so that your new program will compute the sum and product of two numbers.

10. Fill in the blanks in each of the following:

a. A(n) _____ places GUI components in a container.

b. Clicking a button is a(n)_____.

c. The method _____ is invoked when a button is pressed and a(n) _____ is registered to handle the event.

d. _____operator is needed to instantiate an object.

e. A class has two types of members: _____ and _____.

f. To create a window, you extend the _____class.

g. Every GUI program is a(n)_____ program.

h. The method _____ gets the string in the JTextField and the method _____ changes the string displayed in a JTextField.

i. If Student is a class and you create a new **class** GradStudent by extending Student, then Student is a(n) _____ and GradStudent is a(n) _____.

j. Event and event listener classes are contained in the package _____.

k. The unit of measure of length in a window is _____.

11. Write necessary statements to create the following GUI components:

a. A JLabel with the text string "Enter the number of courses"

b. A JButton with the text string "Run"

c. A JTextField that can display 15 characters

d. A window with the title "Welcome Home!"

e. A window with a width of 200 pixels and a height of 400 pixels

f. A JTextField that displays the string "Apple tree"

12. Correct the syntax errors in the following program and add any additional statements necessary to make the program work:

```
import javax.jswing.*;

public class ROne extends JFrame
{
    static private final int WIDTH = 400;
    static private final int HEIGHT = 300;

    public RectangleProgramOne()
    {
        setTitle("Welcome");
        setSize(WIDTH,HEIGHT);
        SetVisible(true);
        setDefaultCloseOperation(EXIT_ON_CLOSE);
    }

    public static void main(String args[])
    {
        ROne r1 = r1();
    }
}
```

13. Correct the syntax errors in the following program:

```
public class RTwo extends JFrame
{
    public RTwoProgram()
    {
        private JLabel length, width, area;

        setTitle("Good day Area");

        length = JLabel("Enter the length);
        width = JLabel("Enter the width);
        area = JLabel("Area: ");
        containerPane  = ContentPane();
        pane.setLayout(GridLayout(4,1));
        setSize(WIDTH,HEIGHT);
        setVisible();
        setDefaultCloseOperation(EXIT_ON_CLOSE);
    }

    public static void main(String args[])
    {
        RTwoProgram R2 = new RTwoProgram();
    }
}
```

14. Consider a common DVD player. What are the methods of a DVD player?

15. What are the methods of an ATM?

16. Do an OOD analysis of the following problem: Write a program to input the dimensions of a cylinder, and calculate and print the surface area and volume.

17. Lead County Credit Union (LCCU) has recently upgraded its software systems to an OOD design. List at least five classes that you think should be included in this design. For each class, identify some of the data members and methods.

18. Your local public library wants to design new software to keep track of patrons, books, and lending activity. List at least three classes you think should be in the design. For each class, identify some data members and methods.

19. The Custom Consulting Company (CCC) places temporary computer professionals in companies that request such employees. CCC's business can be explained as follows:

CCC keeps a list of professionals willing to work or currently working on a temporary assignment. A professional may have up to three qualifications, including programmer, senior programmer, analyst, tester, designer, and so on. A company always requests a professional with a single specific qualification. CCC keeps a list of all its clients (that is, a list of other companies) and their current needs. If CCC can find a match, a professional with the required qualification is assigned to a specific opening at one of CCC's clients.

Identify at least five classes and, for each class, list possible data members and methods.

PROGRAMMING EXERCISES

1. Design a GUI program to find the weighted average of four test scores. The four test scores and their respective weights are given in the following format:

```
testscore1 weight1
...
```

For example, the sample data is as follows:

```
75 0.20
95 0.35
85 0.15
65 0.30
```

The user is supposed to enter the data and press a Calculate button. The program must display the weighted average.

2. Write a GUI program that converts seconds to years, weeks, days, hours, and minutes. For this problem, assume 1 year is 365 days.

3. Design and implement a GUI program to compare two strings and display the larger one.

4. Write a GUI program to convert a character to a corresponding integer, and vice versa.

5. Write a GUI program to convert all letters in a string to uppercase letters. For example, `Alb34ert` will be converted to `ALB34ERT`.

6. Write a GUI program to convert all lowercase letters in a string to uppercase letters, and vice versa. For example, `Alb34eRt` will be converted to `aLB34ErT`.

7. Write a GUI program to compute the amount of a certificate of deposit on maturity. The sample data follows:

   ```
   Amount deposited: 80000.00
   Years: 15
   Interest rate: 7.75
   ```

   Hint: To solve this problem, compute $80000.00 \ (1 + 7.75 \ / \ 100)^{15}$.

8. Write a GUI program that will accept three (integer) input values, say, x, y, and z, and then verify whether or not x * x + y * y = z * z.

9. Design and implement a GUI program to convert a positive number given in one base to another base. For this problem, assume that both bases are less than or equal to 10. Consider the sample data:

   `number = 2010, base = 3, and new base = 4.`

   In this case, first convert 2010 in base 3 into the equivalent number in base 10 as follows:

   $2 * 3^3 + 0 * 3^2 + 1 * 3 + 0 = 54 + 0 + 3 + 0 = 57$

   To convert 57 to base 4, you need to find the remainders obtained by dividing by 4, as shown in the following:

   ```
   57 % 4 = 1, quotient = 14
   14 % 4 = 2, quotient = 3
   3 % 4 = 3, quotient = 0.
   ```

   Therefore, 57 in base 4 is 321.

CHAPTER 7

USER-DEFINED METHODS

IN THIS CHAPTER, YOU WILL:

- Understand how methods are used in Java programming
- Explore predefined methods and how to use them in a program
- Learn about user-defined methods
- Examine value-returning methods
- Understand actual and formal parameters
- Explore how to construct and use a value-returning, user-defined method in a program
- Learn how to construct and use user-defined void methods in a program
- Explore variables as parameters
- Learn about the scope of an identifier
- Become acquainted with method overloading
- Learn how to avoid bugs by using stubs and drivers
- Learn how to avoid bugs by doing one-piece-at-a-time coding

In Chapter 2, you learned that a Java application program is a collection of classes, and that a class is a collection of methods and data members. One such method is `main`. The programs in Chapters 2 through 5 use only the method `main`; all the programming instructions are packed into one method. This technique, however, is appropriate only for short programs. For large programs, it is not practical (although it is possible) to put the entire programming instructions into one method, as you will soon discover. You must learn to break the problem into manageable pieces. This chapter first discusses previously defined methods and then user-defined methods.

Let's imagine an automobile factory. When an automobile is manufactured, it is not made from basic raw materials; it is put together from previously manufactured parts. Some parts are made by the company itself, others are manufactured by different companies at different locations.

Methods in Java are like automobile parts; they are building blocks. Methods are used to divide complicated programs into manageable pieces. There are both **predefined methods**, methods that are already written and provided by Java, and **user-defined methods**, methods that you create.

Using methods has several advantages:

- While working on one method, you can focus on just that part of the program and construct it, debug it, and perfect it.
- Different people can work on different methods simultaneously.
- If a method is needed in more than one place in a program, or in different programs, you can write it once and use it many times.
- Using methods greatly enhances the program's readability because it reduces the complexity of the method `main`.

Methods are often called *modules*. They are like miniature programs; you can put them together to form a larger program. When user-defined methods are discussed, you will see that this is the case. This ability is less apparent with predefined methods because their programming code is not available to us. However, because predefined methods are already written, you will learn these first so that you can use them when needed. To include a predefined method in your program(s), you only need to know how to use it.

Predefined Methods

Before formally discussing Java's predefined methods, let's review a concept from college algebra. In algebra, a function can be considered a rule or correspondence between values—called the function's arguments—and the unique value of the function associated with the arguments. Thus, if $f(x) = 2x + 5$, then $f(1) = 7$, $f(2) = 9$, and $f(3) = 11$, where 1, 2, and 3 are arguments of f, and 7, 9, and 11 are the corresponding values of the function f.

In Java, the concept of a method, whether predefined or user-defined, is similar to that of a function in algebra. For example, every method has a name and, depending on the values specified by the user, it does some computation. This section discusses various predefined methods.

Some of the predefined mathematical methods are `pow(x, y)` and `sqrt(x)`.

The *power* method, `pow(x, y)`, calculates x^y; that is, the value of `pow(x, y)` is x^y.

For example, `pow(2, 3)` is `8.0` and `pow(2.5, 3)` is `15.625`. Because the value of `pow(x, y)` is of type `double`, we say that the method `pow` is of type `double` or that the method `pow` returns a value of type `double`. Also, `x` and `y` are called the **parameters** (or **arguments**) of the method `pow`. The method `pow` has two parameters.

The *square root* method, `sqrt(x)`, calculates the nonnegative square root of `x` for `x >= 0.0`. For example, `sqrt(2.25)` is `1.5`. The method `sqrt` is of type `double` and has only one parameter.

In Java, predefined methods are organized as a collection of classes, called **class libraries**. For example, the `class Math` contains mathematical methods. Table 7-1 lists some of Java's predefined mathematical methods. The table gives the name of the method (in bold type), number of parameters, the data type of the parameters, and the method type. The **method type** is the data type of the value returned by the method. The table also shows how a method works. The `class Math` is contained in the package `java.lang`.

TABLE 7-1 Some Predefined Mathematical Methods and Named Constants

class Math (Package: java.lang)	
Named Constants	
double E;	E = 2.7182818284590455
double PI;	PI = 3.141592653589793
Methods	
Expression	**Description**
abs(x)	Returns the absolute value of x. If x is of type int, it returns a value of type int; if x is of type long, it returns a value of type long; if x is of type float, it returns a value of type float; if x is of type double, it returns a value of type double. **Example:** abs(-67) returns the value 67 abs(35) returns the value 35 abs(-75.38) returns the value 75.38

7

TABLE 7-1 Some Predefined Mathematical Methods and Named Constants (continued)

class Math (**Package:** java.lang)	
ceil(x)	x is of type double. Returns a value of type double, which is the smallest integer value that is not less than x. **Example:** ceil(56.34) returns the value 57.0
exp(x)	x is of type double. Returns e^x, where e is approximately 2.7182818284590455. **Example:** exp(3) returns the value 20.085536923187668
floor(x)	x is of type double. Returns a value of type double, which is the largest integer value less than x. **Example:** floor(65.78) returns the value 65.0
log(x)	x is of type double. Returns a value of type double, which is the natural logarithm (base e) of x. **Example:** log(2) returns the value 0.6931471805599453
log10(x)	x is of type double. Returns a value of type double, which is the common logarithm (base 10) of x. **Example:** log10(2) returns the value 0.3010299956639812
max(x, y)	Returns the larger of x and y. If x and y are of type int, it returns a value of type int; if x and y are of type long, it returns a value of type long; if x and y are of type float, it returns a value of type float; if x and y are of type double, it returns a value of type double. **Example:** max(15, 25) returns the value 25 max(23.67, 14.28) returns the value 23.67 max(45, 23.78) returns the value 45.00
min(x, y)	Returns the smaller of x and y. If x and y are of type int, it returns a value of type int; if x and y are of type long, it returns a value of type long; if x and y are of type float, it returns a value of type float; if x and y are of type double, it returns a value of type double. **Example:** min(15, 25) returns the value 15 min(23.67, 14.28) returns the value 14.28 min(12, 34.78) returns the value 12.00
pow(x, y)	x and y are of type double. Returns a value of type double, which is x^y. **Example:** pow(2.0, 3.0) returns the value 8.0 pow(4, 0.5) returns the value 2.0
round(x)	Returns a value that is the integer closest to x. **Example:** round(24.56) returns the value 25 round(18.35) returns the value 18

TABLE 7-1 Some Predefined Mathematical Methods and Named Constants (continued)

class Math (**Package:** java.lang)	
sqrt(x)	x is of type double. Returns a value of type double, which is the square root of x. **Example:** sqrt(4.0) returns the value 2.0 sqrt(2.25) returns the value 1.5
cos(x)	x is of type double. Returns the cosine of x measured in radians. **Example:** cos(0) returns the value 1.0 cos(PI / 3) returns the value 0.5000000000000001
sin(x)	x is of type double. Returns the sine of x measured in radians. **Example:** sin(0) returns the value 0.0 sin(PI / 2) returns the value 1.0
tan(x)	x is of type double. Returns the tangent of x measured in radians. **Example:** tan(0) returns the value 0.0

7

NOTE The method log10 is not available in Java versions lower than 5.0.

Java also provides methods, contained in the **class** Character, to manipulate characters. Table 7-2 describes some of the methods of the **class** Character contained in the package java.lang. As in Table 7-1, Table 7-2 shows the name of the method in bold and gives examples of how the methods work.

TABLE 7-2 Some Predefined Methods for Character Manipulation

class Character (**Package:** java.lang)	
Expression	**Description**
isDigit(ch)	ch is of type char. Returns true, if ch is a digit; false otherwise. **Example:** isDigit('8') returns the value true isDigit('*') returns the value false
isLetter(ch)	ch is of type char. Returns true, if ch is a letter; false otherwise. **Example:** isLetter('a') returns the value true isLetter('*') returns the value false

TABLE 7-2 Some Predefined Methods for Character Manipulation (continued)

class Character (**Package:** java.lang)	
Expression	**Description**
isLowerCase(ch)	ch is of type char. Returns true, if ch is a lowercase letter; false otherwise. **Example:** isLowerCase('a') returns the value true isLowerCase('A') returns the value false
isUpperCase(ch)	ch is of type char. Returns true, if ch is an uppercase letter; false otherwise. **Example:** isUpperCase('B') returns the value true isUpperCase('k') returns the value false
toLowerCase(ch)	ch is of type char. Returns the character that is the lowercase equivalent of ch. If ch does not have the corresponding lowercase letter, it returns ch. **Example:** toLowerCase('D') returns the value d toLowerCase('*') returns the value *
toUpperCase(ch)	ch is of type char. Returns the character that is the uppercase equivalent of ch. If ch does not have the corresponding uppercase letter, it returns ch. **Example:** toUpperCase('j') returns the value J toUpperCase('8') returns the value 8

Using Predefined Methods in a Program

In general, to use the predefined methods of a class in a program, you must import the class from the package containing the class. For example, to use the method nextInt of the class Scanner contained in the package java.util, we imported this class from the package java.util. However, as stated in Chapter 2, if a class is contained in the package java.lang and you want to use a (public) method of this class, Java does not require you to include an explicit import statement to import that class. For example, to use any (public) method of the class String contained in the package java.lang in a program, we do not need an import statement. By default, Java automatically imports classes from the package java.lang.

A method of a class may contain the reserved word static (in its heading). For example, the method main contains the reserved word static in its heading. If (the heading of) a method contains the reserved word static, it is called a static method; otherwise, it is called a **nonstatic** method. Similarly, the heading of a method may contain the reserved word `public`. In this case, it is called a `public` method. An important property of a `public` and `static` method is that (in a program) it can be used (called) using the name of the class, the dot operator, the method name, and the appropriate parameters. For example, all the methods of the `class Math` are `public` and `static`. Therefore, the general syntax to use a method of the `class Math` is:

```
Math.methodName(parameters)
```

(Note that, in fact, the parameters used in a method call are called actual parameters.) For example, the following expression determines $2.5^{3.5}$:

```
Math.pow(2.5, 3.5)
```

(In the previous statement, `2.5` and `3.5` are actual parameters.) Similarly, if a method of the `class Character` is `public` and `static`, you can use the name of the `class`, which is `Character`, the dot operator, the method name, and the appropriate parameters. The methods of the `class Character` listed in Table 7-2 are `public` and `static`.

To simplify the use of (`public`) `static` methods of a class, Java 5.0 introduces the following import statements:

```
import static pakageName.ClassName.*; //to use any (public)
                                      //static method of the class

import static packageName.ClassName.methodName; //to use a
                                                //specific method of the class
```

These are called `static import` **statements**. After including such statements in your program, when you use a (`public`) `static` method (or any other `public static` member) of a `class`, you can omit the name of the class and the dot operator.

For example, after including the `import` statement:

```
import static java.lang.Math.*;
```

you can determine $2.5^{3.5}$ by using the expression:

```
pow(2.5, 3.5)
```

NOTE After including the `static import` statement, in reality, you have a choice. When you use a (`public`) `static` method of a `class`, you can either use the name of the class and the dot operator or omit them. For example, after including the `static import` statement:

```
import static java.lang.Math.*;
```

in a program, you can determine $2.5^{3.5}$ by using either the expression `Math.pow(2.5, 3.5)` or the expression `pow(2.5, 3.5)`.

The `static import` statement is *not* available in versions of Java lower than 5.0. Therefore, if you are using, say, Java 4.0, then you must use a `static` method of the `class Math` using the name of the class and the dot operator.

NOTE Suppose that there are two **class**es Test1 and Test2. Both classes contain the **static** method printAll, and you want to use these classes in a program. To correctly use the method printAll, you should call this method using the name of the class and the dot operators.

The (**public**) **static** methods of the **class** Character have similar conventions.

Example 7-1 illustrates how to use predefined methods.

EXAMPLE 7-1

This example shows you how to use some of the predefined methods:

```java
//How to use the predefined methods

import static java.lang.Math.*;
import static java.lang.Character.*;

public class PredefinedMethods
{
    public static void main(String[] args)
    {
        int     x;
        double u;
        double v;

        System.out.println("Line 1: Uppercase a is "
                        + toUpperCase('a'));            //Line 1

        u = 4.2;                                        //Line 2
        v = 3.0;                                        //Line 3

        System.out.printf("Line 4: %.1f to the power "
                + "of %.1f = %.2f%n",
                    u, v, pow(u, v));                   //Line 4

        System.out.printf("Line 5: 5 to the power of "
                    + "4 = %.2f%n", pow(5, 4));         //Line 5

        u = u + Math.pow(3, 3);                         //Line 6
        System.out.printf("Line 7: u = %.2f%n", u);     //Line 7

        x = -15;                                        //Line 8
        System.out.printf("Line 9: The absolute value "
                    + "of %d = %d%n", x, abs(x));       //Line 9
    }
}
```

Sample Run:

```
Line 1: Uppercase a is A
Line 4: 4.2 to the power of 3.0 = 74.09
Line 5: 5 to the power of 4 = 625.00
Line 7: u = 31.20
Line 9: The absolute value of -15 = 15
```

This program works as follows: The statement in Line 1 outputs the uppercase letter that corresponds to `'a'`, which is `'A'`. In the statement in Line 4, the method `pow` (of the `class` `Math`) is used to output u^v. In Java terminology, it is said that the method `pow` is called with the (actual) parameters u and v. In this case, the values of u and v are passed to the method `pow`. The statement in Line 5 uses the method `pow` to output 5^4. The statement in Line 6 uses the method `pow` to determine 3^3, adds this value to the value of u, and then stores the new value into u. Notice that in this statement, the method `pow` is called using the name of the `class`, which is `Math`, and the dot operator. The statement in Line 7 outputs the value of u. The statement in Line 8 stores -15 into x, and the statement in Line 9 outputs the absolute value of x.

 NOTE Additional programming examples that show how to use some of the other methods of the `class`es `Math` and `Character` can be found with the Additional Student Files at *www.cengagebrain.com*.

User-Defined Methods

Because Java does not provide every method that you will ever need, and designers cannot possibly know a user's specific needs, you must learn to write your own methods.

User-defined methods in Java are classified into two categories:

- **Value-returning methods**—methods that have a return data type. These methods return a value of a specific data type using the `return` statement, which we will explain shortly.
- **Void methods**—methods that do not have a return data type. These methods *do not* use a `return` statement to return a value.

The next section discusses value-returning methods. Many concepts regarding value-returning methods also apply to void methods. Void methods are discussed later in this chapter.

Value-Returning Methods

The previous section introduced some predefined Java methods, such as `pow`, `sqrt`, `isLowerCase`, and `toUpperCase`. These are examples of value-returning methods, that is, methods that calculate and return a value. To use these methods in your programs, you must know the following properties:

1. The name of the method
2. The number of **parameters**, if any
3. The data type of each parameter
4. The data type of the value computed (that is, the value returned) by the method, called the type of the method

Typically, the value returned by a value-returning method is unique. So it is natural for you to use the value in one of three ways:

- Save the value for further calculation.
- Use the value in some calculation.
- Print the value.

This suggests that a value-returning method is used in either an assignment statement or an output statement. That is, a value-returning method is used in an expression.

In addition to the four properties just described, one more thing is associated with methods (both value-returning and void):

5. The code required to accomplish the task

Before we look at the syntax of a user-defined value-returning method, let's review the points associated with such methods. The first four properties become part of what is called the **heading** of the method; the fifth property (the code) is called the **body** of the method. Together, these five properties form what is called the **definition** of the method.

 NOTE For predefined methods, you only need to be concerned with the first four properties. Software companies typically do not give out the actual source code, which is the body of the method.

For example, for the method abs (*absolute*), the heading might look like:

```java
public static int abs(int number)
```

Similarly, the method abs might have the following definition:

```java
public static int abs(int number)
{
    if (number < 0)
        number = -number;

    return number;
}
```

The variable declared in the heading, within the parentheses, of the method abs is called the **formal parameter** of the method abs. Thus, the formal parameter of abs is number.

The program in Example 7-1 contains several statements that use the method pow. In Java terminology, we say that the method pow is *called* several times. Later in this chapter, we discuss what happens when a method is called.

Suppose that the heading of the method pow is:

```
public static double pow(double base, double exponent)
```

In this heading, you can see that the formal parameters of pow are base and exponent. Consider the following statements:

```
double u = 2.5;
double v = 3.0;
double x, y, w;

x = pow(u, v);          //Line 1
y = pow(2.0, 3.2);      //Line 2
w = pow(u, 7);          //Line 3
```

In Line 1, the method pow is called with the parameters u and v. In this case, the values of u and v are passed to the method pow. In fact, the value of u is copied into base and the value of v is copied into exponent. The variables u and v that appear in the call to the method pow in Line 1 are called **actual parameters** of that call. In Line 2, the method pow is called with the parameters 2.0 and 3.2. In this call, the value 2.0 is copied into base and 3.2 is copied into exponent. In this call to the method pow, the actual parameters are 2.0 and 3.2, respectively. Similarly, in Line 3, the actual parameters of the method pow are u and 7. The value of u is copied into base, and 7.0 is copied into exponent.

We now present the following two definitions:

Formal parameter: A variable declared in the method heading.

Actual parameter: A variable or expression listed in a call to a method.

SYNTAX: VALUE-RETURNING METHOD

The syntax of a value-returning method is:

```
modifier(s) returnType methodName(formal parameter list)
{
    statements
}
```

In this syntax:

- **modifier(s)** indicates the visibility of the method, that is, where in a program the method can be used (called). Some of the modifiers are public, private, protected, static, abstract, and final. If you include more than one modifier, they must be separated with spaces. You can select one modifier among public, protected, and private. The modifier public specifies that the method can be called outside the class; the modifier private specifies that the method cannot be used outside the class. Similarly, you can choose one of the modifiers static or `abstract`. More information about these modifiers is provided in Chapter 8. Meanwhile, we will use the modifiers `public` and/or `static`, as used in the method `main`.

- **`returnType`** is the type of value that the method returns. This type is also called the type of the value-returning method.
- **`methodName`** is a Java identifier, giving a name to the method.
- Statements enclosed between braces form the body of the method.

In Java, `public`, `protected`, `private`, `static`, and `abstract` are reserved words.

 NOTE Abstract methods are covered in Chapter 10. Chapter 8 describes, in detail, the meaning of the modifiers `public`, `private`, and `static`.

SYNTAX: FORMAL PARAMETER LIST

The syntax of a formal parameter list is:

```
dataType identifier, dataType identifier,....
```

METHOD CALL

The syntax to call a value-returning method is:

```
methodName(actual parameter list)
```

SYNTAX: ACTUAL PARAMETER LIST

The syntax of an actual parameter list is:

```
expression or variable, expression or variable, ...
```

Thus, to call a value-returning method, you use its name, with the actual parameters (if any) in parentheses.

A method's formal parameter list can be empty, but the parentheses are still needed. If the formal parameter list is empty, the method heading of the value-returning method takes the following form:

```
modifier(s) returnType methodName()
```

If the formal parameter list is empty, in a method call, the actual parameter list is also empty. In the case of an empty formal parameter list, in a method call, the empty parentheses are still needed. Thus, a call to a value-returning method with an empty formal parameter list is:

```
methodName()
```

In a method call, the number of actual parameters, together with their data types, must match the formal parameters in the order given. That is, actual and formal parameters have a one-to-one correspondence.

As stated previously, a value-returning method is called in an expression. The expression can be part of an assignment statement, or an output statement, or a parameter in a method call. A method call in a program causes the body of the called method to execute.

NOTE   Recall that the heading of the method `main` contains the modifier `static`. The main objective of this chapter is to learn how to write your own methods and use them in a Java application program. Therefore, the methods that you will learn to write in this chapter will be called (used) within the method `main` and/or in other methods of the `class` containing the application program. Because a `static` method cannot call another nonstatic method of the `class`, the heading of the methods that you will learn to write in this chapter will contain the modifier `static`. Chapter 8 discusses the `static` methods (members) of a `class` in detail.

Next, we describe how a value-returning method returns its value.

`return` **Statement**

A value-returning method uses a `return`(s) statement to return its value; that is, it passes a value back when the method completes its task.

SYNTAX: `return` STATEMENT

The `return` statement has the following syntax:

```
return expr;
```

where `expr` is a variable, constant value, or expression. The `expr` is evaluated and its value is returned. The data type of the value that `expr` computes should be compatible with the return type of the method.

In Java, `return` is a reserved word.

When a `return` statement executes in a method, the method immediately terminates and the control goes back to the caller.

To put the ideas of this section to work, we'll write a method that determines the larger of two numbers. Because the method compares two numbers, it follows that this method has two parameters and that both parameters are numbers. Assume that the data type of these numbers is a floating-point number—say, `double`. Because the larger number is of type `double`, the method's data type is also `double`. Let's name this method `larger`. The only thing you need to complete this method is the body of the method. Thus, following the syntax of a method, you can write this method as follows:

```
public static double larger(double x, double y)
{
    double max;

    if (x >= y)
        max = x;
    else
        max = y;

    return max;
}
```

Note that the method `larger` uses an additional variable `max` (called a **local declaration**, where `max` is a variable local to the method `larger`). Figure 7-1 describes the various parts of the method `larger`.

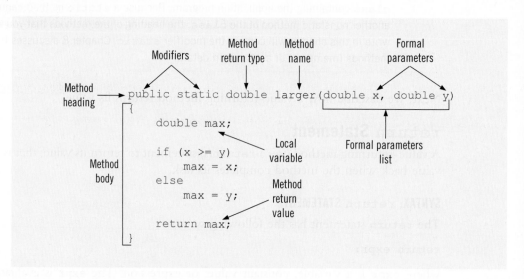

FIGURE 7-1 Various parts of the method `larger`

Suppose that num, num1, and num2 are `int` variables. Also suppose that num1 = 45.75 and num2 = 35.50. Figure 7-2 shows various calls to the method `larger`.

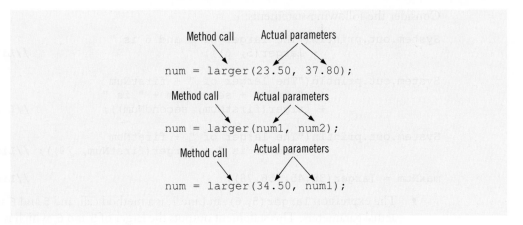

FIGURE 7-2 Method calls

Note that you can write the method `larger` as follows:

```java
public static double larger(double x, double y)
{
    if (x >= y)
        return x;
    else
        return y;
}
```

Because the execution of a `return` statement in a method terminates the method, the preceding definition of the method `larger` can also be written (without the word `else`) as:

```java
public static double larger(double x, double y)
{
    if (x >= y)
        return x;

    return y;
}
```

 NOTE The `return` statement can appear anywhere in the method. Recall that once a `return` statement executes, all subsequent statements are skipped. Thus, it's a good idea to return the value as soon as it is computed.

Example 7-2 further shows how to use the method `larger`.

EXAMPLE 7-2

Now that the method `larger` is written, the following Java code further illustrates how to use it:

```java
double firstNum = 13;
double secondNum = 36;
double maxNum;
```

7

Consider the following statements:

```
System.out.println("The larger of 5 and 6 is "
                + larger(5, 6));                              //Line 1

System.out.println("The larger of " + firstNum
            +  " and " + secondNum + " is "
            + larger(firstNum, secondNum));                  //Line 2

System.out.println("The larger of " + firstNum
            + " and 29 is " + larger(firstNum, 29));  //Line 3

maxNum = larger(38.45, 56.78);                               //Line 4
```

- The expression `larger(5, 6)`, in Line 1, is a method call, and 5 and 6 are actual parameters. This statement outputs the larger of 5 and 6, which is 6.

- The expression `larger(firstNum, secondNum)`, in Line 2, is a method call. Here, `firstNum` and `secondNum` are actual parameters. This statement outputs the larger of `firstNum` and `secondNum`, which is 36.

- The expression `larger(firstNum, 29)`, in Line 3, is also a method call. Here, `firstNum` and 29 are actual parameters.

- The expression `larger(38.45, 56.78)`, in Line 4, is a method call. In this call, the actual parameters are 38.45 and 56.78. In this statement, the value returned by the method `larger` is assigned to the variable `maxNum`.

NOTE | In a method call, you specify only the actual parameter, not its data type. For example, in Example 7-2, the statements in Lines 1, 2, 3, and 4 show how to call the method `larger` with the actual parameters. However, the following statements contain incorrect calls to the method `larger` and would result in syntax errors. (Assume that all variables are properly declared.)

```
x = larger(int one, 29);                    //illegal
y = larger(int one, int 29);                //illegal
System.out.println(larger(int one, int two));    //illegal
```

Final Program

You now know enough to write the entire program, compile it, and run it. The following program uses the method `larger` and `main` to determine the larger of two numbers:

```
//Program: Larger of two numbers

import java.util.*;

public class LargerNumber
{
    static Scanner console = new Scanner(System.in);

    public static void main(String[] args)
```

```
    {
        double num1;                                        //Line 1
        double num2;                                        //Line 2

        System.out.println("Line 3: The larger of "
                        + "5.6 and 10.8 is "
                        + larger(5.6, 10.8));               //Line 3

        System.out.print("Line 4: Enter two "
                    + "numbers: ");                         //Line 4
        num1 = console.nextDouble();                        //Line 5
        num2 = console.nextDouble();                        //Line 6
        System.out.println();                               //Line 7

        System.out.println("Line 8: The larger of "
                    + num1 + " and " + num2 + " is "
                    + larger(num1, num2));                  //Line 8
    }

    public static double larger(double x, double y)
    {
        double max;

        if (x >= y)
            max = x;
        else
            max = y;

        return max;
    }
}
```

Sample Run: (In this sample run, the user input is shaded.)

```
Line 3: The larger of 5.6 and 10.8 is 10.8
Line 4: Enter two numbers: 34 43

Line 8: The larger of 34.0 and 43.0 is 43.0
```

NOTE You can put methods within a class in any order.

NOTE A value-returning method must return a value. Consider the following method, secret, which takes as a parameter an int value. If the value of the parameter, x, is greater than 5, it should return twice the value of x; otherwise, it should return the value of x.

```
public static int secret(int x)
{
    if (x > 5)                  //Line 1
        return 2 * x;           //Line 2
}
```

7

Because this is a value-returning method of type `int`, it must return a value of type `int`. Suppose the value of `x` is 10. Then, the expression, `x > 5`, in Line 1, evaluates to `true`. So the `return` statement in Line 2 returns the value 20. Now suppose that `x` is 3. The expression, `x > 5`, in Line 1, now evaluates to `false`. The `if` statement therefore fails and the `return` statement in Line 2 *does not* execute. However, the body of the method has no more statements to be executed. It thus follows that if the value of `x` is less than or equal to 5, the method does not contain any valid `return` statements to return the value of `x`. In this case, in fact, the compiler generates an error message such as `missing return statement`.

The correct definition of the method `secret` is:

```
public static int secret(int x)
{
    if (x > 5)                  //Line 1
        return 2 * x;           //Line 2

    return x;                   //Line 3
}
```

Here, if the value of `x` is less than or equal to 5, the `return` statement in Line 3 executes, which returns the value of `x`. On the other hand, if the value of `x` is, say, 10, the `return` statement in Line 2 executes, which returns the value 20 and also terminates the method.

NOTE

(`return` statement: A precaution) If the compiler can determine that during execution certain statements in a program can never be reached, then it will generate syntax errors. For example, consider the following methods:

```
public static int funcReturnStatementError(int z)
{
    return z;

    System.out.println(z);
}
```

The first statement in the method `funcReturnStatementError` is the `return` statement. Therefore, if this method executes, then the output statement, `System.out.println(z);`, will never be executed. In this case, when the compiler compiles this method, it will generate two syntax errors, one specifying that the statement `System.out.println(z);` is unreachable, and the second specifying that there is a missing `return` statement after the output statement. Even if you include a `return` statement after the output statement, the compiler will still generate the error that the statement `System.out.println(z);` is unreachable. Therefore, you should be careful when writing the definition of a method. Additional methods illustrating such errors can be found with the Additional Student Files at *www.cengagebrain.com*. The name of the program is `TestReturnStatement.java`.

The following is an example of a method that returns a boolean value.

EXAMPLE 7-3 ROLLING A PAIR OF DICE

In this example, we write a method that rolls a pair of dice until the sum of the numbers rolled is a specific number. We also want to know the number of times the dice are rolled to get the desired sum.

The smallest number on each die is 1 and the largest number is 6. So the smallest sum of the numbers rolled is 2 and the largest sum of the numbers rolled is 12. Suppose that we have the following declarations:

```
int die1;
int die2;
int sum;
int rollCount = 0;
```

We use the random number generator, discussed in Chapter 5, to randomly generate a number between 1 and 6. Then the following statement randomly generates a number between 1 and 6 and stores that number into `die1`, which becomes the number rolled by `die1`.

```
die1 = (int) (Math.random() * 6) + 1;
```

Similarly, the following statement randomly generates a number between 1 and 6 and stores that number into `die2`, which becomes the number rolled by `die2`.

```
die2 = (int) (Math.random() * 6) + 1;
```

The sum of the numbers rolled by two dice is:

```
sum = die1 + die2;
```

Next, we determine whether `sum` contains the desired sum of the numbers rolled by the dice. If `sum` does not contain the desired sum, then we roll the dice again. This can be accomplished by the following `do...while` loop. (Assume that the `int` variable `num` contains the desired sum to be rolled.)

```
do
{
    die1 = (int) (Math.random() * 6) + 1;
    die2 = (int) (Math.random() * 6) + 1;
    sum = die1 + die2;
    rollCount++;
}
while (sum != num);
```

We can now write the method `rollDice` that takes as a parameter the desired sum of the numbers to be rolled and returns the number of times the dice are rolled to roll the desired sum.

```
public static int rollDice(int num)
{
    int die1;
    int die2;
    int sum;
    int rollCount = 0;
```

```
    do
    {
        die1 = (int) (Math.random() * 6) + 1;
        die2 = (int) (Math.random() * 6) + 1;
        sum = die1 + die2;
        rollCount++;
    }
    while (sum != num);

    return rollCount;
}
```

The following program shows how to use the method `rollDice` in a program:

```
//Program: Roll dice

public class RollDice
{
    public static void main(String[] args)
    {
        System.out.println("The number of times the dice are "
                         + "rolled to get the sum 10 = " + rollDice(10));
        System.out.println("The number of times the dice are "
                         + "rolled to get the sum 6 = " + rollDice(6));
    }

    public static int rollDice(int num)
    {
        int die1;
        int die2;
        int sum;
        int rollCount = 0;

        do
        {
            die1 = (int) (Math.random() * 6) + 1;
            die2 = (int) (Math.random() * 6) + 1;
            sum = die1 + die2;
            rollCount++;
        }
        while (sum != num);

        return rollCount;
    }
}
```

Sample Run:

```
The number of times the dice are rolled to get the sum 10 = 91
The number of times the dice are rolled to get the sum 6 = 7
```

We leave it as an exercise for you to modify this program so that it allows the user to enter the desired sum of the numbers to be rolled. (See Programming Exercise 7 at the end of this chapter.)

The following is an example of a method that returns a boolean value.

EXAMPLE 7-4

In this example, we write a method that determines whether a string is a palindrome. A string is a **palindrome** if it reads the same forward and backward. For example, the strings `"madam"` and `"789656987"` are both palindromes.

The method `isPalindrome` takes a string as a parameter and returns `true` if the string is a palindrome, `false` otherwise. Suppose that the `String` variable `str` refers to the string. To be specific, suppose that `str` refers to the string `"845548"`. The length of this string is 6. Recall that the position of the first character of a string is 0, the position of the second character is 1, and so on.

To determine whether the string `str` `"madam"` is a palindrome, first we compare the character at position 0 with the character at position 4. If these two characters are the same, then we compare the character at position 1 with the character at position 3; if these two characters are the same, then we compare the characters at position 2 and 2. If we find mismatched characters, the string `str` is not a palindrome, and the method returns `false`. It follows that we need two variables, `i` and `j`; `i` is initialized to 0 and `j` is initialized to the position of the last character of the string. We then compare the characters at positions `i` and `j`. If the characters at positions `i` and `j` are the same, we then increment `i` and decrement `j`, and continue this process. If the characters at positions `i` and `j` are not the same, then the method returns `false`. Note that we only need to compare the characters in the first half of the string with the characters in the second half of the string in the order described above. This discussion translates into the following algorithm:

1. Find the length of the string. Because `str` is a `String` variable, we can use the method `length` of the `class` `String` to find the length of the string. Suppose `len = str.length();`.

2. Set `j = len - 1`. (Recall that in a string, the position of the first character is 0, the position of the second character is 1, and so on. Therefore, the position of the last character in the string `str` is `len - 1`.)

3. Use a `for` loop to compare the characters in the first half of the string with those in the second half. Now `len` specifies the length of the string, so `len - 1` specifies the position of the last character in the string. Therefore, `(len - 1) / 2` gives the position of the character immediately in front of the midposition in the string. Initially, `j` is set to `len - 1` and we will use a variable, `i` (`for` loop control variable), initialized to 0. After each iteration, `i` is incremented by 1 and `j` is decremented by 1. Therefore, when `i` is `(len - 1) / 2`, the value of `i` gives the position of the character immediately in front of the midposition in the string. When `i` is at the last character of the first half of the string, `j` is at the first character of the second half of the string. The required `for` loop is:

```
for (i = 0; i <= (len - 1)/2; i++)
{
  a. if (str.charAt(i) is not equal to str.charAt(j))
       return false;
  b. j--;
}
```

4. Return true.

The following method implements this algorithm:

```
public static boolean isPalindrome(String str)
{
    int len = str.length();                          //Step 1
    int i, j;

    j = len - 1;                                     //Step 2

    for (i = 0; i <= (len - 1)/2; i++)               //Step 3
    {
        if (str.charAt(i) !=  str.charAt(j))         //Step 3.a
            return false;
        j--;                                         //Step 3.b
    }

    return true;                                     //Step 4
}
```

We leave it as an exercise for you to write a program to test the method isPalindrome. (See Programming Exercise 8 at the end of this chapter.)

Flow of Execution

As you know, a Java application program is a collection of classes, and a class is a collection of methods and data members. In a Java program, methods can appear in any order. However, when a (class containing the main) program executes, the first statement in the method main (of that class) always executes first, regardless of where in the program the method main is placed. Other methods execute only when they are called.

A method call statement transfers control to the first statement in the body of the method. In general, after the last statement of the called method executes, control is passed back to the point immediately following the method call. A value-returning method returns a value. *Therefore, for value-returning methods, after executing the method control goes back to the caller, and the value that the method returns replaces the method call statement.* The execution then continues at the point immediately following the method call.

PROGRAMMING EXAMPLE: Largest Number

In this programming example, the method `larger` is used to determine the largest number from a set of numbers, in this case, the largest number from a set of 10 numbers. You can easily modify this program to accommodate any set of numbers.

Input: A set of 10 numbers

Output: The largest of 10 numbers

PROBLEM
ANALYSIS
AND
ALGORITHM
DESIGN

Suppose that the input data is:

15 20 7 8 28 21 43 12 35 3

Read the first number of the data set. Because this is the only number read to this point, you can assume that it is the largest number and call it `max`. Next, read the second number and call it `num`. Now compare `max` and `num`, and store the larger number into `max`. Now `max` contains the larger of the first two numbers. Next, read the third number. Compare it with `max` and store the larger number into `max`. At this point, `max` contains the largest of the first three numbers. Read the next number, compare it with `max`, and store the larger into `max`. Repeat this process for each remaining number in the data set. Eventually, `max` will contain the largest number in the data set. This discussion translates into the following algorithm:

1. Get the first number. Because this is the only number that you have read so far, it is the largest number so far. Save it in a variable called `max`.

2. For each remaining number in the list:

   a. Get the next number. Store it in a variable called `num`.

   b. Compare `num` and `max`. If `max` < `num`, then `num` is the new largest number; update the value of `max` by copying `num` into `max`. If `max` >= `num`, discard `num`; that is, do nothing.

3. Because `max` now contains the largest number, print it.

To find the larger of two numbers, the program uses the method `larger`.

COMPLETE PROGRAM LISTING

```
//*********************************************************
// Author D.S. Malik
//
// Program: Largest number
// This program determines the largest number of a set of
// 10 numbers.
//*********************************************************
```

```java
import java.util.*;

public class LargestNumber
{
    static Scanner console = new Scanner(System.in);

    public static void main(String[] args)
    {
        double num;   //variable to hold the current number
        double max;   //variable to hold the larger number
        int count;    //loop control variable

        System.out.println("Enter 10 numbers:");

        num = console.nextDouble();                     //Step 1
        max = num;                                      //Step 1

        for (count = 1; count < 10; count++)            //Step 2
        {
            num = console.nextDouble();                 //Step 2a
            max = larger(max, num);                     //Step 2b
        }

        System.out.println("The largest number is "
                            + max);                     //Step 3
    }

    public static double larger(double x, double y)
    {
        double max;

        if (x >= y)
            max = x;
        else
            max = y;

        return max;
    }
}
```

Sample Run: (In this sample run, the user input is shaded.)

```
Enter 10 numbers:
10.5 56.34 73.3 42 22 67 88.55 26 62 11
The largest number is 88.55
```

Void Methods

Void methods (methods that do not have a `return` data type) and value-returning methods have similar structures. Both have a heading part and a statement part. You can place user-defined void methods either before or after the method `main`. However, program execution always begins with the first statement in the method `main`. Because a void method does not return a value of a specific data type using the `return` statement, the return type of these methods can be considered `void`. In a void method, you can use the `return` statement without any value; it is typically used to exit the method early. (Recall that if the compiler can determine that during execution certain statements in a program can never be reached, then it will generate syntax errors. So be careful when using a return statement in a void method.) Like value-returning methods, void methods may or may not have formal parameters.

Because void methods do not return a value of a data type, they are not used (that is, called) in an expression. A call to a void method is a stand-alone statement. Thus, to call a void method, you use the method name together with the actual parameters (if any) in a stand-alone statement. When a void method exits, control goes back to the calling environment at the statement immediately following the point where it was called. Before giving examples of void methods, next we give the syntax of void methods.

7

METHOD DEFINITION

The definition of a void method with parameters has the following syntax:

```
modifier(s) void methodName(formal parameter list)
{
    statements
}
```

The formal parameter list may be empty, in which case, in the method heading, the empty parentheses are still needed.

FORMAL PARAMETER LIST

A formal parameter list has the following syntax:

```
dataType variable, dataType variable, ...
```

METHOD CALL

A method call has the following syntax:

```
methodName(actual parameter list);
```

If the formal parameter list is empty, then in the method call statement, empty parentheses are still needed, that is, in this case the method call is: `methodName();`.

ACTUAL PARAMETER LIST

An actual parameter list has the following syntax:

```
expression or variable, expression or variable, ...
```

As with value-returning methods, in a method call the number of actual parameters, together with their data types, must match the formal parameters in the order given. Actual and formal parameters have a one-to-one correspondence. A method call causes the body of the called method to execute. Two examples of void methods with parameters follow.

EXAMPLE 7-5

Consider the following method heading:

```
public static void funexp(int a, double b, char c, String name)
```

The method `funexp` has four formal parameters: (1) a, a parameter of type `int;`, (2) b, a parameter of type `double;`, (3) c, a parameter of type `char`, and (4) `name`, a parameter of type `String`.

EXAMPLE 7-6

Consider the following method heading:

```
public static void expfun(int one, char two, String three, double four)
```

The method `expfun` has four formal parameters: (1) `one`, a parameter of type `int;`, (2) `two`, a parameter of type `char;`, (3) `three`, a parameter of type `String`, and (4) `four`, a parameter of type `double`.

Parameters provide a communication link between the calling method (such as `main`) and the called method. They enable methods to manipulate different data each time they are called.

EXAMPLE 7-7

Suppose that you want to print a pattern (a triangle of stars) similar to the following:

The first line has one star with some blanks before the star, the second line has two stars, some blanks before the stars, and a blank between the stars, and so on. Let's write the method `printStars`, which has two parameters: a parameter to specify the number of blanks before the stars in a line and another parameter to specify the number of stars in a line. The definition of the method `printStars` is:

```
public static void printStars(int blanks, int starsInLine)
{
    int count = 1;

       //print the number of blanks before the stars in a line
    for (count <= blanks; count++)
       System.out.print(" ");

       //print the number of stars with a blank between stars
    for (count = 1; count <= starsInLine; count++)
       System.out.print(" *");

    System.out.println();
} //end printStars
```

The first parameter, `blanks`, determines how many blanks to print preceding the star(s); the second parameter, `starsInLine`, determines how many stars to print in a line. If the value of the parameter `blanks` is 30, for instance, then the first `for` loop in the method `printStars` executes 30 times and prints 30 blanks. Also, because you want to print spaces between the stars, every iteration of the second `for` loop in the method `printStars` prints the string `" *"` (Line 30)—a blank followed by a star.

Next consider the following statements:

```
int numberOfLines = 15;
int numberOfBlanks = 30;
int counter = 1;

for (counter = 1; counter <= numberOfLines; counter++)
{
    printStars(numberOfBlanks, counter);
    numberOfBlanks--;
}
```

The `for` loop calls the method `printStars`. Every iteration of this `for` loop specifies the number of blanks followed by the number of stars to print in a line, using the variables `numberOfBlanks` and `counter`. Every invocation of the method `printStars` receives one fewer blank and one more star than the previous call. For example, the first iteration of the `for` loop in the method `main` specifies 30 blanks and 1 star (which are passed as the parameters, `numberOfBlanks` and `counter`, to the method `printStars`). The `for` loop then decrements the number of blanks by 1 by executing the statement, `numberOfBlanks--;`. At the end of the `for` loop, the number of stars is incremented by 1 for the next iteration. This is done by executing the update statement, `counter++`, in the `for` statement, which increments the value of the variable `counter` by 1. In other words, the second call of the method `printStars` receives 29 blanks and 2 stars as parameters. Thus, the previous statements will print a triangle of stars consisting of 15 lines.

The complete program is as follows:

```java
// Program: Print a triangle of stars
// Given the number of lines, this program prints a triangle of
// stars.

import java.util.*;

public class TriangleOfStars
{
    static Scanner console = new Scanner(System.in);

    public static void main(String[] args)
    {
        int numberOfLines;
        int numberOfBlanks;
        int counter = 1;

        System.out.print("Enter the number of star lines "
                         + "(1 to 20) to be printed: ");
        numberOfLines = console.nextInt();
        System.out.println();

        while (numberOfLines < 0 || numberOfLines > 20)
        {
            System.out.println("The number of star lines should "
                               + "be between 1 and 20");
            System.out.print("Enter the number of star lines "
                             + "(1 to 20) to be printed: ");
            numberOfLines = console.nextInt();
            System.out.println ();
        }

        numberOfBlanks = 30;

        for (counter = 1; counter <= numberOfLines; counter++)
        {
            printStars(numberOfBlanks, counter);
            numberOfBlanks--;
        }
    } // end main

    public static void printStars(int blanks, int starsInLine)
    {
        int count = 1;

        for (count = 1; count <= blanks; count++)
            System.out.print(" ");

        for (count = 1; count <= starsInLine; count++)
            System.out.print(" *");

        System.out.println();
    } //end printStars
}
```

Sample Run: (In this sample run, the user input is shaded.)

Enter the number of star lines (1 to 20) to be printed: 10

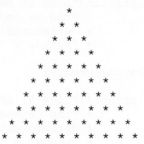

In the method `main`, the user is first asked to specify how many lines of stars to print. (In this program, the user is restricted to 20 lines because a triangular grid of up to 20 lines fits nicely on the screen.) Because the program is restricted to only 20 lines, the `while` loop in the method `main` ensures that the program prints the triangular grid of stars only if the number of lines is between 1 and 20.

Primitive Data Type Variables as Parameters

In Chapter 3, you learned that Java has two categories of variables—primitive type variables and reference variables. Before considering examples of void methods with parameters, let's make the following observation about variables of primitive types and reference variables. When a method is called, the value of the actual parameter is copied into the corresponding formal parameter. If a formal parameter is a variable of a primitive data type, then after copying the value of the actual parameter, there is no connection between the formal parameter and the actual parameter. That is, the formal parameter has its own copy of the data. Therefore, during program execution, the formal parameter manipulates the data stored in its own memory space. The program in Example 7-8 further illustrates how a formal parameter of a primitive data type works.

EXAMPLE 7-8

```
//Example 7-8
//Program illustrating how a formal parameter of a
//primitive data type works.

public class PrimitiveTypeParameters            //Line 1
{                                               //Line 2
    public static void main(String[] args)      //Line 3
```

```
{                                                       //Line 4
    int number = 6;                                     //Line 5

    System.out.println("Line 6: Before calling"
                    + "the method "
                    + "primFormalParam, "
                    + "number = " + number);            //Line 6

    primFormalParam(number);                            //Line 7

    System.out.println("Line 8: After calling "
                    + "the method "
                    + "primFormalParam, "
                    + "number = " + number);            //Line 8
} //end main                                            //Line 9

public static void primFormalParam(int num)             //Line 10
{                                                       //Line 11
    System.out.println("Line 12: In the method "
                    + "primFormalParam, "
                    + "before changing, num = "
                    + num);                             //Line 12

    num = 15;                                           //Line 13

    System.out.println("Line 14: In the method "
                    + "primFormalParam, "
                    + "after changing, num = "
                    + num);                             //Line 14
} //end primFormalParam                                 //Line 15
}                                                       //Line 16
```

Sample Run:

```
Line 6: Before calling the method primFormalParam, number = 6
Line 12: In the method primFormalParam, before changing, num = 6
Line 14: In the method primFormalParam, after changing, num = 15
Line 8: After calling the method primFormalParam, number = 6
```

The preceding program works as follows. The execution begins at the method main. The statement in Line 5 declares and initializes the int variable number (see Figure 7-3).

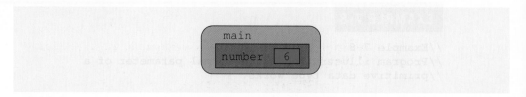

FIGURE 7-3 The method main and its variable number

The statement in Line 6 outputs the value of number before calling the method primFormalParam. The statement in Line 7 calls the method primFormalParam. The value of the variable `number` is passed to the formal parameter `num`. Control now transfers to the method `primFormalParam` (see Figure 7-4).

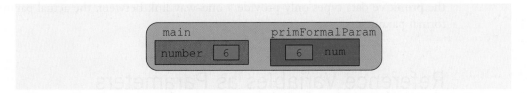

FIGURE 7-4 The variables `number` and `num` before execution of the statement in Line 13

The statement in Line 12 outputs the value of `num` before changing its value. The statement in Line 13 changes the value of `num` to 15 (see Figure 7-5).

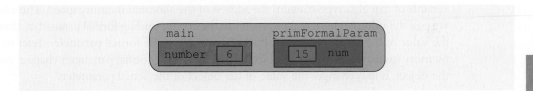

FIGURE 7-5 The variables `number` and `num` after execution of the statement in Line 13

The statement in Line 14 outputs the value of `num`. After this statement executes, the method `primFormalParam` exits and control goes back to the method `main` at Line 8 (see Figure 7-6).

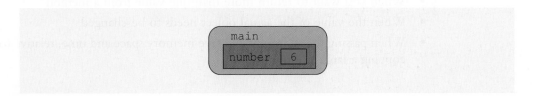

FIGURE 7-6 The variables `number` and `num` after execution of the statement in Line 13

The statement in Line 8 outputs the value of `number` after calling the method `primFormalParam`. As you can see from the output, the value of `number`, as shown by the output of the statements in Lines 6 and 8, remains the same even though the value of its corresponding formal parameter `num` was changed within the method `primFormalParam`.

After copying data, a formal parameter of the primitive data type has no connection with the actual parameter, so a formal parameter of the primitive data type cannot pass any result back to the calling method. When the method executes, any changes made to the formal parameters do not, in any way, affect the actual parameters. The actual parameter has no knowledge of what is happening to the formal parameter. Thus, formal parameters of the primitive data types cannot pass information outside the method; formal parameters of the primitive data types only provide a one-way link between the actual parameters and formal parameters.

Reference Variables as Parameters

The program in Example 7-8 illustrates how a formal parameter of a primitive data type works. Now suppose that a formal parameter is a reference variable. Here, also, the value of the actual parameter is copied into the corresponding formal parameter, but there is a slight difference. Recall that a reference variable does not store data directly in its own memory space. We use the operator `new` to allocate memory for an object belonging to a specific class, and a reference variable of that class type contains the address of the allocated memory space. Therefore, when we pass the value of the actual parameter to the corresponding formal parameter, after copying the value of the actual parameter, both the actual and the formal parameters refer to the same memory space, that is, the same object. Therefore, if the formal parameter changes the value of the object, it also changes the value of the object of the actual parameter.

Because a reference variable contains the address (that is, memory location) of the actual data, both the formal and the value parameters refer to the same object. Therefore, reference variables can pass one or more values from a method and can change the value of the actual parameter.

Reference variables as parameters are useful in three situations:

- When you want to return more than one value from a method
- When the value of the actual object needs to be changed
- When passing the address would save memory space and time, relative to copying a large amount of data

Parameters and Memory Allocation

When a method is called, memory for its formal parameters and variables declared in the body of the method, called **local variables**, is allocated in the method data area. The value of the actual parameter is copied into the memory cell of its corresponding formal parameter. If the parameter is an object (of a class type), both the actual parameter and the formal parameter refer to the same memory space.

Reference Variables of the `String` Type as Parameters: A Precaution

Recall that reference variables do not directly contain the data. Reference variables contain the address of the memory space where the data is stored. We use the operator `new` to allocate memory space of a specific type. However, in the case of reference variables of type `String`, we can also use the assignment operator to allocate memory space to store a string and assign the string to a `String` variable. Consider the following statements:

```
String str;                    //Line 1
```

The statement:

```
str = "Hello";                 //Line 2
```

creates a `String` object with the value `"Hello"`, if one does not exist, and stores the reference of that object in `str` (see Figure 7-7).

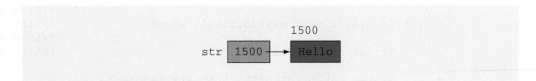

FIGURE 7-7   Variable `str` and the `string` object

We assume that the address of the memory space where the string `"Hello"` is stored is 1500. Now suppose that you execute either the statement:

```
str = "Hello There";
```

or the statement:

```
str = str + " There";
```

The effect of either of these statements is illustrated by Figure 7-8.

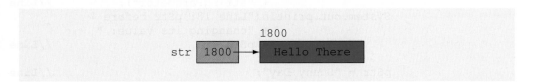

FIGURE 7-8   `str` after the statement `str = "Hello There";` or `str = str + " There";` executes

Note that the string `"Hello There"` is stored at a different location. It is now clear that any time you assign a different string to a `String` variable, the `String` variable points to a different object. In other words, when a string is created and assigned to a `String` variable, the *string cannot be changed*. Note that the **class** `String` does not contain any method that allows you to change an existing string.

If you pass a `String` variable, that is, a reference variable of the `String` type, as a parameter to a method, and within the method you use the assignment operator to change the string, you might think that you have changed the string assigned to the actual parameter. But this does not happen. The string of the actual parameter remains unchanged; a new string is assigned to the formal parameter. The following example further illustrates this concept.

EXAMPLE 7-9 String OBJECTS AS PARAMETERS

Consider the following program:

```java
// This program illustrates how String objects as parameters work.

public class StringObjectsAsParameters                   //Line 1
{                                                         //Line 2
    public static void main(String[] args)               //Line 3
    {                                                     //Line 4
        String str = "Hello";                             //Line 5

        System.out.println("Line 6: str before "
                         + "calling the method "
                         + "stringParameter: "+ str);     //Line 6

        stringParameter(str);                             //Line 7

        System.out.println("Line 8: str after "
                         + "calling the method "
                         + "stringParameter: " + str);    //Line 8
    } //end main                                          //Line 9

    public static void stringParameter(String pStr)       //Line 10
    {                                                     //Line 11
        System.out.println("Line 12: In the method "
                         + "stringParameter");            //Line 12
        System.out.println("Line 13: pStr before "
                         + "changing its value: "
                         + pStr);                         //Line 13

        pStr = "Sunny Day";                               //Line 14

        System.out.println("Line 15: pStr after "
                         + "changing its value: "
                         + pStr);                         //Line 15
    } //end stringParameter                               //Line 16
}                                                         //Line 17
```

Sample Run:

```
Line 6: str before calling the method stringParameter: Hello
Line 12: In the method stringParameter
Line 13: pStr before changing its value: Hello
Line 15: pStr after changing its value: Sunny Day
Line 8: str after calling the method stringParameter: Hello
```

The preceding program works as follows: The statement in Line 5 declares `str` to be a `String` variable and assigns the string `"Hello"` to it (see Figure 7-9).

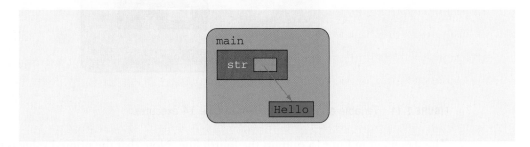

FIGURE 7-9 Variable after the statement in Line 5 executes

The statement in Line 6 outputs the first line of output. The statement in Line 7 calls the method `stringParameter`. The actual parameter is `str` and the formal parameter is `pStr`, so the value of `str` is copied into `pStr`. Because both these parameters are reference variables, `str` and `pStr` point to the same string, which is `"Hello"` (see Figure 7-10).

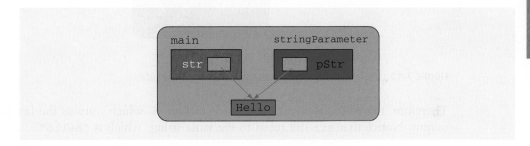

FIGURE 7-10 Variable before the statement in Line 7 executes

The control is transferred to the method `stringParameter`. The next statement executed is in Line 12, which outputs the second line of the output. The statement in Line 13 outputs the third line of the output. Notice that this statement also outputs the string referenced by `pStr` and the printed value is the string `"Hello"`. The next statement executed is in Line 14. This statement uses the assignment operator and assigns the string `"Sunny Day"` to `pStr`. After the execution of the statement in Line 14, `str` no longer refers to the same string as does `pStr` (see Figure 7-11).

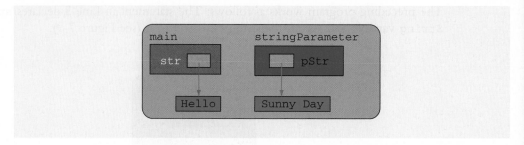

FIGURE 7-11   Variable after the statement in Line 14 executes

The statement in Line 15 outputs the fourth line. Note that the printed value is the string **"Sunny Day"**. After the execution of this statement, control goes back to the method **main** at Line 8 (see Figure 7-12).

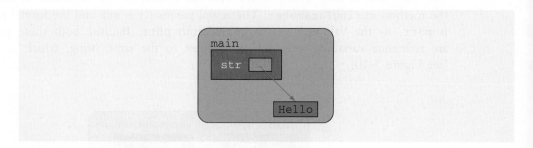

FIGURE 7-12   Variable after the statement in Line 15 executes

Therefore, the next statement executed is in Line 8, which outputs the last line of the output. Notice that **str** still refers to the same string, which is **"Hello"**.

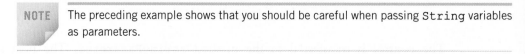

NOTE   The preceding example shows that you should be careful when passing **String** variables as parameters.

The **class StringBuffer**

If you want to pass strings as parameters to a method and want to change the actual parameters, you can use the **class StringBuffer**. The **class StringBuffer** is similar to the **class String**. However, strings assigned to **StringBuffer** variables can be altered.

The **class StringBuffer** contains the method **append**, which allows you to append a string to an existing string, and the method **delete**, which allows you to delete all the characters of the string. It also contains other methods to manipulate a string.

The assignment operator *cannot* be used with `StringBuffer` variables. You must use the operator `new` to (*initially*) allocate memory space for a string.

The following example illustrates how objects of type `StringBuffer` are passed as parameters.

EXAMPLE 7-10

```
// This program illustrates how StringBuffer objects as
// parameters work.

public class StringBufferObjectsAsParameters      //Line 1
{                                                 //Line 2
    public static void main(String[] args)        //Line 3
    {                                             //Line 4
        StringBuffer str = new StringBuffer("Hello");   //Line 5

        System.out.println("Line 6: str before "
                    + "calling the method "
                    + "stringBufferParameter: "
                    + str);                       //Line 6

        stringBufferParameter(str);               //Line 7

        System.out.println("Line 8: str after "
                    + "calling the method "
                    + "stringBufferParameter: "
                    + str);                       //Line 8
    } //end main                                  //Line 9

    public static void stringBufferParameter
                            (StringBuffer pStr)    //Line 10
    {                                             //Line 11
        System.out.println("Line 12: In the method "
                    + "stringBufferParameter ");   //Line 12
        System.out.println("Line 13: pStr before "
                    + "changing its value: "
                    + pStr);                      //Line 13

        pStr.append(" There");                    //Line 14

        System.out.println("Line 15: pStr after "
                    + "changing its value: "
                    + pStr);                      //Line 15
    } //end stringBufferParameter                 //Line 16
}                                                 //Line 17
```

Sample Run:

```
Line 6: str before calling the method stringBufferParameter: Hello
Line 12: In the method stringBufferParameter
Line 13: pStr before changing its value: Hello
Line 15: pStr after changing its value: Hello There
Line 8: str after calling the method stringBufferParameter: Hello There
```

The preceding program works as follows: The statement in Line 5 declares str to be a reference variable of the StringBuffer type and assigns the string "Hello" to it (see Figure 7-13).

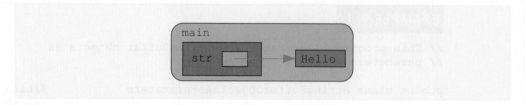

FIGURE 7-13 Variable after the statement in Line 5 executes

The statement in Line 6 outputs the first line of output. The statement in Line 7 calls the method stringBufferParameter. The actual parameter is str and the formal parameter is pStr. The value of str is copied into pStr. Because both of these parameters are reference variables, str and pStr point to the same string, which is "Hello" (see Figure 7-14).

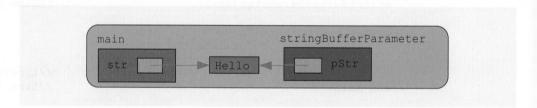

FIGURE 7-14 Variable before the statement in Line 7 executes

Then control is transferred to the method stringBufferParameter. The next statement executed is in Line 12, which produces the second line of the output. The statement in Line 13 produces the third line of the output. This statement also outputs the string to which pStr points, and the printed value is that string. The statement in Line 14 uses the method append to append the string " There" to the string pointed to by pStr. After this statement executes, pStr points to the string "Hello There". However, this also changes the string that was assigned to the variable str. When the statement in Line 14 executes, str points to the same string as pStr (see Figure 7-15).

FIGURE 7-15 Variable after the statement in Line 14 executes

The statement in Line 15 produces the fourth line of output. Notice that the printed value is the string **"Hello There"**, which is the string pointed to by **pStr**. After this statement executes, control goes back to the method **main** at Line 8 (see Figure 7-16).

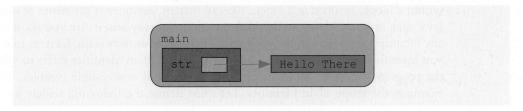

FIGURE 7-16   Variable after the statement in Line 7 executes

The next statement executed is in Line 8, which produces the last line of the output. Note that **str** points to the string **"Hello There"**.

Primitive Type Wrapper Classes as Parameters

As illustrated by the program in Example 7-8, if a formal parameter is of the primitive data type and the corresponding actual parameter is a variable, then the formal parameter cannot change the value of the actual parameter. In other words, changing the value of a formal parameter of the primitive data type has no effect on the actual parameter. So, how do we pass the values of primitive data types outside the method? As stated earlier, only reference variables can pass values outside the method (except, of course, for the return value). Corresponding to each primitive data type, Java provides a class so that the values of primitive data types can be wrapped in objects. For example, you can use the **class Integer** to wrap **int** values in objects, the **class Double** to wrap **double** values in objects, and so on. These wrapper classes were introduced in Chapter 6, "Graphical User Interface (GUI) and Object-Oriented Design (OOD)." Even though you can use the **class Integer** to wrap **int** values in objects, the **class Integer** does not provide a method to change the value of an existing **Integer** object. The same is true of other wrapper classes. That is, when passed as parameters, objects of wrapper classes have the same limitations as objects of the **class String**. If we want to pass a **String** object as a parameter and also change that object, we can use the **class StringBuffer**. However, Java does not provide any class that wraps primitive type values in objects and when passed as parameters change their values. If a method returns only one value of a primitive type, then you can write a value-returning method. However, if you encounter a situation that requires you to write a method that needs to pass more than one value of a primitive type, then you should design your own classes. Appendix D provides the definitions of such classes and shows how to use them in a program.

The file, **Chapter7_PrimitiveTypesAsObjects.java**, illustrating how to use user-defined classes to pass primitive type values as objects and change their values, can be found with the Additional Student Files at *www.cengagebrain.com*.

Scope of an Identifier Within a Class

The previous sections presented several examples of programs with user-defined methods. In these examples, and in Java in general, identifiers are declared in a method heading, within a block, or outside a block. (Recall that an identifier is the name of something in Java, such as a variable or method.) A question naturally arises: Are you allowed to access any identifier anywhere in the program? The general answer is no. Certain rules exist that you must follow to access an identifier. The **scope** of an identifier refers to what parts of the program can "see" an identifier, that is, where it is accessible (visible). This section examines the scope of an identifier. Let's first define the following widely used term:

Local identifier: An identifier declared within a method or block that is visible only within that method or block.

Before giving the scope rules of an identifier, let us note the following:

- Java does not allow the nesting of methods. That is, you cannot include the definition of one method in the body of another method.

- Within a method or a block, an identifier must be declared before it can be used. Note that a block is a collection of statements enclosed within braces. A method's definition can contain several blocks. The body of a loop or an `if` statement also forms a block.

- Within a class, outside every method definition (and every block), an identifier can be declared anywhere.

- Within a method, an identifier used to name a variable in the outer block of the method cannot be used to name any other variable in an inner block of the method. For example, in the following method definition, the second declaration of the variable **x** is illegal:

```
public static void illegalIdentifierDeclaration()
{
    int x;

    //block
    {
        double x;    //illegal declaration, x is already declared
        ...
    }
}
```

Next, we describe the scope rules of an identifier declared within a class and accessed within a method (block) of the class. (In Chapter 8, we describe the rules for an *object* to access the identifiers of its class.)

- An identifier, say, **x**, declared within a method (block) is accessible:
  - Only within the block from the point at which it is declared until the end of the block.
  - By those blocks that are nested within that block.

- Suppose x is an identifier declared within a class and outside every method's definition (block):

  - If x is declared *without* the reserved word static (such as a named constant or a method name), then it *cannot* be accessed within a static method.

  - If x is declared *with* the reserved word static (such as a named constant or a method name), then it *can* be accessed within a method (block), provided the method (block) does not have any other identifier named x.

Before considering an example that illustrates these scope rules, first note the scope of the identifier declared in the for statement. Java allows the programmer to declare a variable in the initialization statement of the for statement. For example, the following for statement:

```
for (int count = 1; count < 10; count++)
    System.out.println(count);
```

declares the variable count and initializes it to 1. The scope of the variable count is only limited to the body of the for loop.

Example 7-11 illustrates the scope rules.

7

EXAMPLE 7-11

```
public class ScopeRules
{
    static final double rate = 10.50;
    static int z;
    static double t;

    public static void main(String[] args)
    {
        int num;
        double x, z;
        char ch;

        //...
    }

    public static void one(int x, char y)
    {
        //...
    }

    public static int w;

    public static void two(int one, int z)
    {
        char ch;
        int a;
```

```
//block three
{
    int x = 12;

    //...
}//end block three
//...
}
}
```

Table 7-3 summarizes the scope (visibility) of the identifiers in Example 7-11.

TABLE 7-3 Scope (Visibility) of the Identifiers

Identifier	Visibility in one	Visibility in two	Visibility in block three	Visibility in main
rate (before main)	Y	Y	Y	Y
z (before main)	Y	N	N	N
t (before main)	Y	Y	Y	Y
main	Y	Y	Y	Y
local variables of main	N	N	N	Y
one (method name)	Y	Y	Y	Y
x (one's formal parameter)	Y	N	N	N
y (one's formal parameter)	Y	N	N	N
w (before method two)	Y	Y	Y	Y
two (method name)	Y	Y	Y	Y
one (two's formal parameter)	N	Y	Y	N
z (two's formal parameter)	N	Y	Y	N
local variables of two	N	Y	Y	N
x (Block three's local variable)	N	N	Y	N

The Additional Student Files folder at *www.cengagebrain.com* contains the programs ScopeRuleA.java and ScopeRuleB.java, and further demonstrates the scope of variables.

Before we look at some programming examples, we will explore the concept of method overloading.

EXAMPLE 7-12 (MENU DRIVEN PROGRAM)

The following is an example of a menu driven program. When the program executes, it gives the user a list of choices to choose from. It converts length from feet and inches to meters and centimeters and vice versa. The program contains three methods: showChoices, inchesToCentimeters, and centimetersToInches. The method showChoices informs the user how to use the program. The user has the choice to run the program as long as the user wishes.

```java
//Menu driven program.

import java.util.*;

public class Conversion
{
    static Scanner console = new Scanner(System.in);

    static final double CONVERSION = 2.54;

    public static void main(String[] args)
    {
        int inches;
        int centimeters;
        int choice;

        do
        {
            showChoices();
            choice = console.nextIn();
            System.out.println();

            switch (choice)
            {
            case 1:
                System.out.print("Enter inches: ");
                inches = console.nextInt();
                System.out.println();
                System.out.printf("%d inch(es) = %d centimeter(s)%n",
                            inches, inchesToCentimeters(inches));
                break;

            case 2:
                System.out.print("Enter centimeters: ");
                centimeters = console.nextInt();
                System.out.println();
                System.out.printf("%d centimeter(s) = %d inch(es)%n",
                            centimeters, centToInches(centimeters));
                break;

            case 99:
                break;
```

7

```
                default:
                    System.out.println("Invalid input.");
            }
        }
        while (choice != 99);
    }

    public static void showChoices()
    {
        System.out.println("Enter-");
        System.out.println("1: To convert from inches to "
                         + "centimeters.");
        System.out.println("2: To convert from centimeters to "
                         + "inches.");
        System.out.println("99: To quit the program.");
    }

    public static int inchesToCentimeters(int in)
    {
        return (int) (in * CONVERSION);
    }

    public static int centToInches(int ct)
    {
        return (int) (ct / CONVERSION);
    }
}
```

Sample Run: (In this sample run, the user input is shaded.)

```
Enter--
1: To convert from inches to centimeters.
2: To convert from centimeters to inches.
99: To quit the program.
2

Enter centimeters: 34

    34 centimeter(s) =    13 inch(es)
Enter--
1: To convert from inches to centimeters.
2: To convert from centimeters to inches.
99: To quit the program.
1

Enter inches: 45

45 inch(es) = 114 centimeter(s)
Enter--
1: To convert from inches to centimeters.
2: To convert from centimeters to inches.
99: To quit the program.
99
```

The `do...while` loop in the method `main` continues to execute as long as the user has not entered 99, which allows the user to run the program as long as the user wishes. The preceding sample run is self-explanatory.

Method Overloading: An Introduction

In Java, several methods can have the same name within a `class`. This is called **method overloading** or **overloading a method name**. Before we state the rules to overload a method, let us define the following:

Two methods are said to have **different formal parameter lists** if both methods have:

- A different number of formal parameters, or
- If the number of formal parameters is the same, then the data type of the formal parameters, in the order you list, must differ in at least one position.

For example, consider the following method headings:

```
public void methodOne(int x)
public void methodTwo(int x, double y)
public void methodThree(double y, int x)
public int methodFour(char ch, int x, double y)
public int methodFive(char ch, int x, String name)
```

These methods all have different formal parameter lists.

Now consider the following headings:

```
public void methodSix(int x, double y, char ch)
public void methodSeven(int one, double u, char firstCh)
```

The methods `methodSix` and `methodSeven` both have three formal parameters, and the data type of the corresponding parameters is the same. Therefore, these methods have the same formal parameter list.

To overload a method name, within a `class`, any two definitions of the method must have different formal parameter lists.

Method overloading: Creating several methods, within a `class`, with the same name.

The **signature** of a method consists of the method name and its formal parameter list. Two methods have different signatures if they have either different names or different formal parameter lists. (Note that the signature of a method does not include the return type of the method.)

7

If a method's name is overloaded, then all the methods (with the same name) have different signatures if they have different formal parameter lists. Thus, the following method headings correctly overload the method `methodXYZ`:

```
public void methodXYZ()
public void methodXYZ(int x, double y)
public void methodXYZ(double one, int y)
public void methodXYZ(int x, double y, char ch)
```

Consider the following method headings to overload the method `methodABC`:

```
public void methodABC(int x, double y)
public int methodABC(int x, double y)
```

Both method headings have the same name and same formal parameter list. Therefore, these method headings to overload the method `methodABC` are incorrect. In this case, the compiler will generate a syntax error. (Note that the return types of these method headings are different.)

If a method's name is overloaded, then in a call to that method, the formal parameter list of the method determines which method to execute.

NOTE Some authors define the signature of a method as the formal parameter list; other authors consider the entire heading of the method as its signature. In this book, the signature of a method consists of the method's name and its formal parameter list. If the method names are different, then, of course, the compiler would have no problem identifying which method is called and correctly translating the code. However, if a method name is overloaded, then, as noted, the method's formal parameter list determines which method's body executes.

Suppose you need to write a method that determines the larger of two items. Both items can be integers, floating-point numbers, characters, or strings. You could write several methods as follows (we give only the method heading):

```
int largerInt(int x, int y)
char largerChar(char first, char second)
double largerDouble(double u, double v)
String largerString(String first, String second)
```

The method `largerInt` determines the larger of two integers, the method `largerChar` determines the larger of two characters, and so on. All of these methods perform similar operations. Instead of giving different names to these methods, you can use the same name—say, `larger`—for each method; that is, you can overload the method `larger` as follows:

```
int larger(int x, int y)
char larger(char first, char second)
double larger(double u, double v)
String larger(String first, String second)
```

If the call is `larger(5, 3)`, for example, the first method executes because the actual parameters match the formal parameters of the first method. If the call is `larger('A', '9')`, the second method executes, and so on.

Method overloading is used when you have the same action for different types of data. Of course, for method overloading to work, you must give the definition of each method.

PROGRAMMING EXAMPLE: Data Comparison

Two groups of students at a local university are enrolled in special courses during the summer semester. The courses are offered for the first time and are taught by different teachers. At the end of the semester, both groups are given the same tests for the same courses and their scores are recorded in separate files. The data in each file is in the following form:

```
courseID   score1, score2, ..., scoreN -999
courseID   score1, score2, ..., scoreM -999
.
.
.
```

This programming example illustrates:

1. How to read data from more than one file in the same program.
2. How to send the output to a file.
3. How to generate bar graphs.
4. With the help of methods and parameter passing, how to use the same program segment on different (but similar) sets of data.
5. How to use structured design to solve a problem and how to perform parameter passing.

This program is broken into two parts. First, you learn how to read data from more than one file. Second, you learn how to generate bar graphs.

Next we write a program that finds the average course score for each course for each group. The output is of the following form:

```
Course ID   Group No    Course Average
   CSC          1           83.71
                2           80.82

   ENG          1           82.00
                2           78.20
    .
    .
    .
Avg for group 1: 82.04
Avg for group 2: 82.01
```

7

Input: Because the data for the two groups is recorded in separate files, the input data appears in two separate files

Output: As shown above

PROBLEM ANALYSIS AND ALGORITHM DESIGN

Reading the input data from both files is straightforward. Suppose the data is stored in the file `group1.txt` for group 1 and in the file `group2.txt` for group 2. After processing the data for one group, we can process the data for the second group for the same course, and continue until we run out of data. Processing the data for each course is similar and uses the following process:

    a.   Sum the scores for the course.

    b.   Count the number of students in the course.

    c.   Divide the total score by the number of students to find the course average.

    d.   Output the results.

We are only comparing the averages of the corresponding courses in each group. The data in each file is ordered according to the course ID. To ensure that only the averages of the corresponding courses are compared, we compare the course IDs for each group. If the corresponding course IDs are not the same, we output an error message and terminate the program.

This discussion suggests that we should write a method, `calculateAverage`, to find the course average. We should also write another method, `printResult`, to output the data in the form given. By passing the appropriate parameters, we can use the same methods, `calculateAverage` and `printResult`, to process each course's data for both groups. (In the second part of the program, we modify the method `printResult`.)

The preceding discussion translates into the following algorithm:

    1.   Initialize the variables.

    2.   Get the course IDs for group 1 and group 2.

    3.   If the course IDs are different, print an error message and exit the program.

    4.   Calculate the course average for group 1 and group 2.

    5.   Print the results in the form given earlier.

    6.   Repeat Steps 2 through 5 for each course.

    7.   Print the final results.

Variables (Method main)

The preceding discussion suggests that the program needs the following variables for data manipulation in the method `main`:

```
String courseId1;                    //course ID for group 1
String courseId2;                    //course ID for group 2
```

```
int numberOfCourses;

double avg1; //average for a course in group 1
double avg2; //average for a course in group 2

double avgGroup1;
double avgGroup2;

Scanner group1 =
        new Scanner(new FileReader("group1.txt"));
Scanner group2 =
        new Scanner(new FileReader("group2.txt"));

PrintWriter outfile = new PrintWriter("student.out");
```

Next, we discuss the methods `calculateAverage` and `printResult`. Then, we will put the method `main` together.

Method calculateAverage

This method calculates the average for a course. Because the input is stored in a file and the input file is opened in the method `main`, we must pass the variable associated with the input file to this method. Furthermore, after calculating the course average, this method must pass the course average to the method `main`. Therefore, this method has one parameter.

To find the course average, we must first find the sum of all the scores for the course and the number of students who took the course; we then divide the sum by the number of students. Thus, we need a variable to find the sum of the scores, a variable to find the number of students, a variable to find the course average, and a variable to read and store a score. Of course, we must initialize the variables to zero to find the sum and the number of students.

Local Variables (Method calculateAverage)

In the previous discussion of data manipulation, we identified four variables for the method `calculateAverage`:

```
double totalScore;      //to store the sum of scores
int numberOfStudents;   //to store the number of students
int score;              //to read and store a course score
double courseAvg;       //to store the course average
```

The preceding discussion translates into the following algorithm for the method `calculateAverage`:

    a. Declare the variables.

    b. Initialize `totalScore` to `0.0`.

    c. Initialize `numberOfStudents` to `0`.

    d. Get the (next) course score.

e. while (score != -999)

    i. Update `totalScore` by adding the course score read in Step d.

    ii. Increment `numberOfStudents` by 1.

    iii. Get the next course score.

f. `courseAvg = totalScore / numberOfStudents;`

g. `return courseAvg;`

We are now ready to write the definition of the method `calculateAverage`.

```
public static double calculateAverage(Scanner inp)
{
    double totalScore = 0.0;
    int numberOfStudents = 0;
    int score = 0;
    double courseAvg;

    score = inp.nextInt();

    while (score != -999)
    {
        totalScore = totalScore + score;
        numberOfStudents++;
        score = inp.nextInt();
    }//end while

    courseAvg = totalScore / numberOfStudents;

    return courseAvg;
}//end calculate Average
```

Method printResult The method `printResult` prints the group's course ID, group number, and course average. The output is stored in a file. We must pass four parameters to this method: the variable associated with the output file, the group number, the course ID, and the course average for the group. Also, from the output, it is clear that we print the course ID only before group 1. In pseudocode, the algorithm is:

```
if (group number == 1)
    print course ID
else
    print a blank

print group number and course average
```

The definition of the method `printResult` follows:

```
public static void printResult(PrintWriter outp, String courseId,
                               int groupNo, double avg)
```

```
{
    if (groupNo == 1)
        outp.print("   " + courseId + "    ");
    else
        outp.print("            ");

    outp.printf("%9d %15.2f%n", groupNo, avg);
}
```

Now that we have designed and defined the methods `calculateAverage` and `printResults`, we can describe the algorithm for the method `main`. Before outlining the algorithm, however, note the following: It is quite possible that in both input files the data is ordered according to the course IDs, but one file might have fewer courses than the other. We discover this error only after we have processed both files and discover that one file has unprocessed data. Make sure to check for this error before printing the final answer—that is, the average for group 1 and group 2.

Main
Algorithm:
Method
main

1. Declare the variables (local declaration).
2. Create and initialize the variables to open the input and output files.
3. Initialize the course average for group 1 to `0.0`.
4. Initialize the course average for group 2 to `0.0`.
5. Initialize the number of courses to 0.
6. Print the heading.
7. For each course in group 1 and group 2:

    a. Get `courseId1` for group 1.
    b. Get `courseId2` for group 2.
    c. `if (courseId1 != courseId2)`
        ```
        {
            System.out.println("Data error: Course IDs do not match");
            return;
        }
        ```
    d. `else`
        ```
        {
        ```
        i.   Calculate the course average for group 1 (call the method `calculateAverage` and pass the appropriate parameters).
        ii. Calculate the course average for group 2 (call the method `calculateAverage` and pass the appropriate parameters).

      iii. Print the results for group 1 (call the method `printResult` and pass the appropriate parameters).

      iv. Print the results for group 2 (call the method `printResult` and pass the appropriate parameters).

      v. Update the average for group 1.

      vi. Update the average for group 2.

      vii. Increment the number of courses.

    }

8. a. `if` not_end_of_file on group 1 and end_of_file on group 2

      print "Ran out of data for group 2 before group 1"

    b. `else if end_of_file` on group 1 and `not_end_of_file` on group 2

      print "Ran out of data for group 1 before group 2"

    c. `else`

      print the average of group 1 and group 2.

9. Close the files.

COMPLETE PROGRAM LISTING

```
//**********************************************************
// Author: D.S. Malik
//
// Program: Comparison of Class Averages
// This program computes and compares the class averages of
// two groups of students.
//**********************************************************

import java.io.*;
import java.util.*;

public class DataComparison
{
    public static void main (String[] args)
                            throws FileNotFoundException
    {
            //Step 1
        String courseId1;      //course ID for group 1
        String courseId2;      //course ID for group 2

        int numberOfCourses;

        double avg1; //average for a course in group 1
        double avg2; //average for a course in group 2
        double avgGroup1;   //average group 1
        double avgGroup2;   //average group 2
```

```
            //Step 2 Open the input and output files
Scanner group1 =
            new Scanner(new FileReader("group1.txt"));
Scanner group2 =
            new Scanner(new FileReader("group2.txt"));

PrintWriter outfile = new PrintWriter("student.out");


avgGroup1 = 0.0;                                  //Step 3
avgGroup2 = 0.0;                                  //Step 4

numberOfCourses = 0;                             //Step 5

            //print heading: Step 6
outfile.println("Course ID    Group No"
            + "    Course Average");

while (group1.hasNext() && group2.hasNext()) //Step 7
{
    courseId1 = group1.next();                   //Step 7a
    courseId2 = group2.next();                   //Step 7b

    if (!courseId1.equals(courseId2))            //Step 7c
    {
        System.out.println("Data error: Course IDs "
                    + "do not match.");
        System.out.println("Program terminates.");
        outfile.println("Data error: Course IDs "
                    + "do not match.");
        outfile.println("Program terminates.");
        outfile.close();
        return;
    }
    else                                         //Step 7d
    {
        avg1 = calculateAverage(group1);         //Step 7d.i
        avg2 = calculateAverage(group2);         //Step 7d.ii
        printResult(outfile, courseId1,
                    1, avg1);                    //Step 7d.iii
        printResult(outfile, courseId2,
                    2, avg2);                    //Step 7d.iv
        avgGroup1 = avgGroup1 + avg1;            //Step 7d.v
        avgGroup2 = avgGroup2 + avg2;            //Step 7d.vi
        outfile.println();
        numberOfCourses++;                       //Step 7d.vii
    }
}//end while

if (group1.hasNext() && !group2.hasNext())        //Step 8a
    System.out.println("Ran out of data for group 2 "
                    + "before group 1.");
```

```java
            else if (!group1.hasNext() && group2.hasNext()) //Step 8b

                System.out.println("Ran out of data for "
                                + "group 1 before group 2.");
            else                                        //Step 8c
            {
                outfile.printf("Avg for group 1: %.2f %n",
                          (avgGroup1 / numberOfCourses));
                outfile.printf("Avg for group 2: %.2f %n",
                          (avgGroup2 / numberOfCourses));
            }

            group1.close();                             //Step 9
            group2.close();                             //Step 9
            outfile.close();                            //Step 9
    }

    public static double calculateAverage(Scanner inp)
    {
        double totalScore = 0.0;
        int numberOfStudents = 0;
        int score = 0;
        double courseAvg;

        score = inp.nextInt();

        while (score != -999)
        {
            totalScore = totalScore + score;
            numberOfStudents++;
            score = inp.nextInt();
        }//end while

        courseAvg = totalScore / numberOfStudents;

        return courseAvg;
    }//end calculate Average

    public static void printResult(PrintWriter outp,
                                   String courseId,
                                   int groupNo, double avg)
    {
        if (groupNo == 1)
            outp.print("   " + courseId + "    ");
        else
            outp.print("            ");

        outp.printf("%9d %15.2f%n", groupNo, avg);
    }
}
```

Sample Run:

```
Course ID    Group No     Course Average
   CSC           1            83.71
                 2            80.82

   ENG           1            82.00
                 2            78.20

   HIS           1            77.69
                 2            84.15

   MTH           1            83.57
                 2            84.29

   PHY           1            83.22
                 2            82.60
```

```
Avg for group 1: 82.04
Avg for group 2: 82.01
```

7

Input Data Group 1:

```
CSC 80 100 70 80 72 90 89 100 83 70 90 73 85 90 -999
ENG 80 90 80 94 90 74 78 63 83 80 90 -999
HIS 90 70 80 70 90 50 89 83 90 68 90 60 80  -999
MTH 74 80 75 89 90 73 90 82 74 90 84 100 90 79 -999
PHY 100 83 93 80 63 78 88 89 75 -999
```

Input Data Group 2:

```
CSC 90 75 90 75 80 89 100 60 80 70 80 -999
ENG 80 80 70 68 70 78 80 90 90 76 -999
HIS 100 80 80 70 90 76 88 90 90 75 90 85 80 -999
MTH 80 85 85 92 90 90 74 90 83 65 72 90 84 100 -999
PHY 90 93 73 85 68 75 67 100 87 88 -999
```

BAR GRAPHS In the business world, company executives often like to see results in a visual form, such as bar graphs. Many software packages can analyze data in several forms and then display the results in such visual forms as bar graphs or pie charts. The second part of this program displays the earlier results in the form of bar graphs, as shown below:

```
Course           Course Average
   ID    0   10   20   30   40   50   60   70   80   90   100
         |....|....|....|....|....|....|....|....|....|....|
   CSC   *****************************************
         #####################################

   ENG   *******************************************
         #####################################
```

```
Group 1 -- ****
Group 1 -- ####
```

```
Avg for group 1: 82.04
Avg for group 2: 82.01
```

Each symbol (* or #) in the bar graph represents 2 points. If a course average is less than 2, no symbol is printed.

Because the output is in the form of a bar graph, we need to modify the method printResult.

Method printResult The method printResult prints the course ID and the bar graph representing the average for a course. The output is stored in a file. So we must pass four parameters to this method: the variable associated with the output file, the group number (to print * or #), the course ID, and the course average for the department.

To print the bar graph, we can use a loop to print a symbol for each two points. If the average is 78.45, for example, we must print 39 symbols to represent this average. To find the number of symbols to print, we can use integer division as follows:

```
numberOfSymbols = (int)(average) / 2;
```

For example, (int)(78.45) / 2 = 78 / 2 = 39.

Following this outline, the definition of the method printResult is:

```java
public static void printResult(PrintWriter outp,
                               String courseId,
                               int groupNo, double avg)
{
    int noOfSymbols;
    int count;

    if (groupNo == 1)
        outp.print(" " + courseId + "      ");
    else
        outp.print("            ");

    noOfSymbols = (int)(avg)/2;

    if (groupNo == 1)
        for (count = 1; count <= noOfSymbols; count++)
            outp.print("*");
    else
        for (count = 1; count <= noOfSymbols; count++)
            outp.print("#");

    outp.println();
}//end printResults
```

We also include a method, `printHeading`, to print the first two lines of the output. The definition of this method is:

```
public static void printHeading(PrintWriter outp)
{
    outp.println("Course           Course Average");
    outp.println("  ID    0   10   20   30   40   50   60   70"
              + "   80   90   100");
    outp.println("          |....|....|....|....|....|....|....|"
              + "....|....|....|");
}//end printHeading
```

If you replace the method `printResult` in the preceding program, include the method `printHeading`, include the statements to output—Group 1 -- **** and Group 2 -- #### —and rerun the program, then the output for the previous data is as follows:

Sample Output:

```
Course        Course Average
   ID    0   10   20   30   40   50   60   70   80   90   100
          |....|....|....|....|....|....|....|....|....|....|....|
   CSC    ****************************************
          ####################################

   ENG    *****************************************
          #####################################

   HIS    ****************************************
          ######################################

   MTH    ******************************************
          ######################################

   PHY    *******************************************
          #####################################
```

```
Group 1 -- ****
Group 2 -- ####

Avg for group 1: 82.04
Avg for group 2: 82.01
```

Compare both outputs. Which one do you think is better?

Debugging: Using Drivers and Stubs

In this and previous chapters you learned how to write methods to divide a problem into subproblems, solve each subproblem, and then combine the methods to form the complete program to get a solution of the problem. A program may contain a number of methods. In a complex program, usually, when a method is written, it is tested and debugged alone. You can write a separate program to test the method. The program that tests a method is called a **driver** program. For example, the program in Example 7-12, contains methods to convert the length from inches to centimeters and vice versa. Before writing the complete program, you could write separate driver programs to make sure that each method is working properly.

Sometimes the results calculated by one method are needed in another method. In that case, the method that depends on another method cannot be tested alone. For example, consider the following program that determines the time to fill a swimming pool:

```java
import java.util.*;

public class Pool
{
    static Scanner console = new Scanner(System.in);

    static final double GALLONS_IN_A_CUBIC_FEET = 7.48;

    public static void main(String[] args)
    {
        double length, width, depth;
        double fillRate;
        int fillTime;

        System.out.print("Enter the length, width, and the "
                        + "depth of the pool, (in feet): ");
        length = console.nextDouble();
        width = console.nextDouble();
        depth = console.nextDouble();
        System.out.println();

        System.out.print("Enter the rate of the water, "
                        + "(in gallons per minute): ");
        fillRate = console.nextInt();
        System.out.println();

        fillTime = poolFillTime(length, width, depth, fillRate);
        print(fillTime);
    }

    public static double poolCapacity(double len, double wid,
                                      double dep)
```

```
    {
        double volume;
        double poolWaterCapacity;

        volume = len * wid * dep;
        poolWaterCapacity = volume * GALLONS_IN_A_CUBIC_FEET;

        return poolWaterCapacity;
    }

    public static int poolFillTime(double len, double wid,
                                   double dep, double fRate)
    {
        double poolWaterCapacity;

        poolWaterCapacity = poolCapacity(len, wid, dep);
        return (int) (poolWaterCapacity / fRate + 0.5);
    }

    public static void print(int fTime)
    {
        System.out.println("The time to fill the pool is "
                  + "approximately: " + fTime / 60
                  + " hour(s) and " + fTime % 60
                  + " minute(s).");
    }
}
```

Sample Run: (In this sample run, the user input is shaded.)

Enter the length, width, and the depth of the pool, (in feet): `30 15 10`

Enter the rate of the water, (in gallons per minute): `100`

The time to fill the pool is approximately: 5 hour(s) and 37 minute(s).

As you can see the program contains the method `poolCapacity` to find the amount of water needed to fill the pool, the method `poolFillTime` to find the time to fill the pool, and some other methods. Now to calculate the time to fill the pool, you must know the amount of the water needed and the rate at which the water is released into the pool. Because the results of the method `poolCapacity` are needed in the method `poolFillTime`, the method `poolFillTime` cannot be tested alone. Does this mean that we must write the method in a specific order? Not necessarily, especially, when different people are working on different parts of the program. In situations such as these, we use method stubs. A method **stub** is a method that is not fully coded. For a void method, a method stub might consist of only a method header and a set of empty braces, { }, and for a value-returning method it might contain only a return statement with a plausible return value. For example, the method stub for the method `poolCapacity` can be:

```
public static double poolCapacity(double len, double wid, double dep)
{
    return 1000.00;
}
```

This allows the method `poolCapacity` to be called while the program is being coded. Ultimately, the stub for the method `poolCapacity` is replaced with a method that properly calculates the amount of water needed to fill the pool based on the values of the parameters. In the meantime, the method stub allows work to continue on other parts of the program that call the method `poolCapacity`.

DEBUGGING

Avoiding Bugs: One-Piece-at-a-Time Coding

It is evident from the programming examples given in this and the previous chapters, that before a programming code is written, the problem must be thoroughly understood and analyzed. If the problem is large and complex, it must be broken into subproblems, and if a subproblem is still complex, it must further be divided into subproblems. The subdivision of a problem should continue to the point where the solution is clear and obvious. After thoroughly understanding and analyzing a (sub) problem, an algorithm is designed, which can be coded into a programming language such as Java. Once a subproblem is solved, we can continue with the solution of another subproblem and if all the subproblems of a problem are solved, we can continue with the next level. Eventually, the overall solution of the problem must be assembled and tested to ensure that the programming code accomplishes the required task.

In general, a Java program is a collection of classes and a class is a collection of data members and methods. (Sometimes a class may also contain an inner class.) Each class and each method must work properly. To accomplish this, as explained in the previous section, once a method is written, it can be tested using stubs and drivers. (Note that for complex methods and algorithms sometimes a mathematical proof may be required to verify the correctness of the algorithm. The discussion of this is beyond the scope of this book.) Since a method can be tested in isolation, it is not necessary to code all the methods in order. However, once all the methods are written, the overall program must be tested.

The technique to solve a problem by subdividing into smaller problems is known as divide-and-conquer and top-down design approach. These techniques are suitable and work for many kinds of problems, including most of the problems given in this book and the problems you will encounter as a beginning programmer.

To simplify the overall solution of a problem that consists of many subproblems, we write and test the code one piece at a time. Typically, once a subproblem is solved and the code is tested, it is saved as the first version or a version of the program. We continue to add and save the program one piece at a time. Keep in mind that a working program with fewer features is better than a nonworking one with many features.

QUICK REVIEW

1. Methods enable you to divide a program into manageable tasks.
2. The Java system provides standard (predefined) methods.

3. In general, to use a predefined method, you must:

   a. Know the name of the class containing the method, and the name of the package containing the class that contains the method.

   b. Import the class into the program.

   c. Know the name and type of the method, and the number and types of the parameters (arguments).

4. To use a method of a class contained in the package `java.lang` in a program, you do not need to explicitly import these classes into your program.

5. To simplify the use of `static` methods (members) of a class, Java 5.0 and higher versions provide the `static import` statement.

6. The two types of user-defined methods are value-returning methods and void methods.

7. Variables defined in a method heading are called formal parameters.

8. Expressions, variables, or constant values used in a method call are called actual parameters.

9. In a method call, the number of actual parameters and their types must match the formal parameters in the order given.

10. To call a method, use its name together with the actual parameter list.

11. A value-returning method returns a value. Therefore, a value-returning method is typically used (called) in either an expression or an output statement, or as a parameter in a method call.

12. The general syntax of a value-returning method is:

```
modifier(s) returnType  methodName(formal parameter list)
{
     statements
}
```

13. The line:

```
modifier(s) returnType methodName(formal parameter list)
```

is called the method heading (or method header). Statements enclosed between braces, { and }, are called the body of the method.

14. The method heading and the body of the method are called the definition of the method.

15. If a method has no parameters, you still need the empty parentheses in both the method heading and the method call.

16. A value-returning method returns its value via the `return` statement.

17. A method can have more than one `return` statement. However, whenever a `return` statement executes in a method, the remaining statements are skipped and the method exits.

18. When a program executes, the execution always begins with the first statement in the method `main`.

19. User-defined methods execute only when they are called.

20. A call to a method transfers control from the caller to the called method.

21. In a method call statement, you specify only the actual parameters, not their data type or the method type.

22. When a method exits, control goes back to the caller.

23. A method that does not have a return data type is called a `void` method.

24. A return statement without any value can be used in a `void` method.

25. If a return statement is used in a `void` method, it is typically used to exit the method early.

26. In Java, `void` is a reserved word.

27. A `void` method may or may not have parameters.

28. To call a `void` method, you use the method name together with the actual parameters in a stand-alone statement.

29. A formal parameter receives a copy of its corresponding actual parameter.

30. If a formal parameter is of the primitive data type, it directly stores the value of the actual parameter.

31. If a formal parameter is a reference variable, it copies the value of its corresponding actual parameter, which is the address of the object where the actual data is stored. Therefore, if a formal parameter is a reference variable, both the formal and actual parameters refer to the same object.

32. The scope of an identifier refers to those parts of the program where it is accessible.

33. Java does not allow the nesting of methods. That is, you cannot include the definition of one method in the body of another method.

34. Within a method or a block, an identifier must be declared before it can be used. Note that a block is a set of statements enclosed within braces. A method's definition can contain several blocks. The body of a loop or an `if` statement also forms a block.

35. Within a class, outside every method definition (and every block), an identifier can be declared anywhere.

36. Within a method, an identifier used to name a variable in the outer block of the method cannot be used to name any other variable in an inner block of the method.

37. The scope rules of an identifier declared within a class and accessed within a method (block) of the class are as follows:

- An identifier **x** declared within a method (block) is accessible:

  - Only within the block from the point at which it is declared until the end of the block.

  - By those blocks that are nested within that block.

- Suppose **x** is an identifier declared within a class and outside every method's definition (block):

  - If **x** is declared without the reserved word `static` (such as a named constant or a method name), then it cannot be accessed within a `static` method.

  - If **x** is declared with the reserved word `static` (such as a named constant or a method name), then it can be accessed within a method (block), provided the method (block) does not have any other identifier named **x**.

38. Two methods are said to have different formal parameter lists if both methods have:

    - A different number of formal parameters, or
    - If the number of formal parameters is the same, then the data type of the formal parameters, in the order you list, must differ in at least one position.

39. The signature of a method consists of the method name and its formal parameter list. Two methods have different signatures if they have either different names or different formal parameter lists.

40. If a method is overloaded, then in a call to that method, the signature, that is, the formal parameter list of the method, determines which method to execute.

EXERCISES

1. Mark the following statements as true or false:

   a. To use a predefined method of a `class` contained in the package `java.lang` in a program, you only need to know what the name of the method is and how to use it.

   b. A value-returning method returns only one value via the return statement.

   c. Parameters allow you to use different values each time the method is called.

d. When a `return` statement executes in a user-defined method, the method immediately exits.

e. A value-returning method returns only integer values.

f. If a Java method does not use parameters, parentheses around the empty parameter list are still needed.

g. In Java, the names of the corresponding formal and actual parameters must be the same.

h. In Java, method definitions can be nested; that is, the definition of one method can be enclosed in the body of another method.

2. Determine the value of each of the following expressions:

a. `Character.toUpperCase('b')`

b. `Character.toUpperCase('7')`

c. `Character.toUpperCase('K')`

d. `Character.toUpperCase('*')`

e. `Character.toLowerCase('D')`

f. `Character.toLowerCase('8')`

g. `Character.toLowerCase('h')`

h. `Character.toLowerCase('$')`

3. Determine the value of each of the following expressions. (Format your answer with two decimal places.)

a. `Math.abs(-4)`

b. `Math.abs(10.8)`

c. `Math.abs(-2.5)`

d. `Math.pow(3.2, 2)`

e. `Math.pow(2.5, 3)`

f. `Math.sqrt(25.0)`

g. `Math.sqrt(6.25)`

h. `Math.pow(3.0, 4.0) / Math.abs(-9)`

i. `Math.floor(28.95)`

j. `Math.ceil(35.2)`

4. Using the methods described in Table 7-1, write each of the following as a Java expression:

a. $2.0^{5.2}$

b. $\sqrt{x + y}$

c. $u^{v - 3}$

d. $\frac{-b+\sqrt{b^2-4ac}}{2a}$

e. $|x + 2.5|$

5. a. What is the return type of the method `main`?

   b. What is the return type of the method `floor` of the `class Math`?

   c. What is the return type of the method `isUpperCase` of the `class Character`?

6. What is the output of the following Java program?

```
import static java.lang.Math.*;

public class Exercise6
{
    public static void main(String[] args)
    {
        for (int counter = 1; counter <= 100; counter++)
            if (pow(floor(sqrt(counter)), 2) == counter)
                System.out.print(counter + " ");

        System.out.println();
    }
}
```

7. Which of the following method headings are valid? If they are invalid, explain why.

```
public static one(int a, int b)
public static int thisone(char x)
public static char another(int a, b)
public static double yetanother
```

8. Consider the following statements:

```
double num1, num2, num3;
int int1, int2, int3;
double value;

num1 = 5.0; num2 = 6.0; num3 = 3.0;
int1 = 4; int2 = 7; int3 = 8;
```

and the method heading:

```
public static double cube(double a, double b, double c)
```

Which of the following statements are valid? If they are invalid, explain why.

   a. `value = cube (num1, 15.0, num3);`

   b. `System.out.println(cube(num1, num3, num2));`

   c. `System.out.println(cube(6.0, 8.0, 10.5));`

   d. `System.out.println(num1 + " " + num3);`

   e. `System.out.println(cube(num1, num3));`

   f. `value = cube(num1, int2, num3);`

   g. `value = cube(7, 8, 9);`

7

9. Identify and correct errors in the following program:

```java
public class Chapter7Ex9
{
    public static void main(String[] args)
    {
        System.out.println(signum(12));
        System.out.println(signum(-11));
        System.out.println(signum(20.5));
        System.out.println(signum(0));
    }

    public static int signum(int x)
    {
        if (x > 0)
            return 1;
        else if (x == 0)
            return 0;
        else
            return -1;
    }
}
```

10. Find and correct error(s) in the following method definition:

```java
public static void doubleNum(int x)
{
    return 2 * x;
}
```

11. Find and correct error(s) in the following method definition:

```java
public static int squareNum(double x)
{
    return x * x;
}
```

12. Consider the following program:

```java
import java.util.*;

public class Chapter7Ex12
{
    static Scanner console = new Scanner(System.in);

    public static void main(String[] args)
    {
        double num1;
        double num2;

        System.out.print("Enter two integers: ");
        num1 = console.nextInt();
        num2 = console.nextInt();
        System.out.println();
```

```
if (num1 != 0 && num2 != 0)
    System.out.printf("%.2f\n",
                Math.sqrt(Math.abs(num1 + num2 + 0.0)));
else if (num1 != 0)
    System.out.printf("%.2f\n", Math.floor(num1 + 0.0));
else if (num2 != 0)
    System.out.printf("%.2f\n",Math.ceil(num2 + 0.0));
else
    System.out.println(0);
}
}
```

a.   What is the output if the input is 12 4?

b.   What is the output if the input is 3 27?

c.   What is the output if the input is 25 0?

d.   What is the output if the input is 0 49?

13.   Consider the following methods:

```
public static int secret(int x)
{
    int i, j;

    i = 2 * x;

    if (i > 10)
        j = x / 2;
    else
        j = x / 3;

    return j - 1;
}

public static int another(int a, int b)
{
    int i, j;

    j = 0;

    for (i = a; i <= b; i++)
        j = j + i;

    return j;
}
```

What is the output of each of the following program segments?

a.   ```
x = 10;
System.out.println(secret(x));
```

b.   ```
x = 5; y = 8;
System.out.println(another(x, y));
```

c.   `x = 10; k = secret(x);`
     `System.out.println(x + " " + k + " "`
                    `+ another(x, k));`

d.   `x = 5; y = 8;`
     `System.out.println(another(y, x));`

14. Consider the following method headings:

```
public static int test(int x, char ch, double d, int y)
public static double two(double d1, double d2)
public static char three(int x, int y, char ch, double d)
```

Answer the following questions:

a. How many parameters does the method `test` have? What is the type of the method `test`?

b. How many parameters does method `two` have? What is the type of the method `two`?

c. How many parameters does method `three` have? What is the type of the method `three`?

d. How many actual parameters are needed to call the method `test`? What is the type of each parameter, and in what order should you use these parameters in a call to the method `test`?

e. Write a Java statement that prints the value returned by the method `test` with the actual parameters 5, 5, 7.3, and `'z'`.

f. Write a Java statement that prints the value returned by method `two` with the actual parameters `17.5` and `18.3`, respectively.

g. Write a Java statement that prints the character that comes after the one returned by the method `three`. (Use your own actual parameters.)

15. Consider the following method:

```
public static int mystery(int x, double y, char ch)
{
    int u;

    if ('A' <= ch && ch <= 'R')
        return (2 * x + (int)(y));
    else
        return ((int)(2 * y) - x);
}
```

What is the output of the following Java statements?

a. `System.out.println(mystery(5, 4.3, 'B'));`

b. `System.out.println(mystery(4, 9.7, 'v'));`

c. `System.out.println(2 * mystery(6, 3.9, 'D'));`

16. Consider the following method:

```
public static int secret(int one)
{
    int i;
    int prod = 1;

    for (i = 1; i <= 3; i++)
        prod = prod * one;

    return prod;
}
```

a. What is the output of the following Java statements?

   i.   `System.out.println(secret(5));`

   ii. `System.out.println(2 * secret(6));`

b. What does the method `secret` do?

17. Can a void method have a return statement? If your answer is yes, in what form?

18. Write appropriate method headings for the following methods:

a. Calculate and return the sum of two decimal numbers.

b. Compute and return the average speed of a car, given the distance traveled (as in `int`) and traveling time (in hours and minutes of type `int`).

c. Given the radius of a circle, output the area of the circle.

d. Given a student's name and three test scores (of type `int`), output the student's name and average test score.

e. Given a number, return `true` if the number is a prime; otherwise, return `false`.

f. Given the cost of an item and the sales tax (as a decimal number), return the total sale price.

g. Given a decimal number, output the square root if the number is nonnegative; otherwise, output an appropriate error message.

19. What is the output of the following program?

```
public class Chapter7Ex19
{
    public static void main(String[] args)
    {
        System.out.println(mystery(7, 8, 3));
        System.out.println(mystery(10, 5, 30));
        System.out.println(mystery(9, 12, 11));
        System.out.println(mystery(5, 5, 8));
        System.out.println(mystery(10, 10, 10));
    }
```

7

```
public static int mystery(int x, int y, int z)
{
    if (x <= y && x <= z)
        return (y + z - x);
    else if (y <= z && y <= x)
        return (z + x - y);
    else
        return (x + y - z);
}
}
```

20. Write the definition of a method that takes as input three numbers and returns the sum of the first two numbers multiplied by the third number. (Assume that the three numbers are of type double.)

21. Show the output of the following program:

```
public class MysteryClass
{
    public static void main(String[] args)
    {
        int n;

        for (n = 1; n <= 5; n++)
            System.out.println(mystery(n));
    }

    public static int mystery(int k)
    {
        int x, y;

        y = k;

        for (x = 1; x <= (k - 1); x++)
            y = y * (k - x);

        return y;
    }
}
```

22. Explain how a reference variable as a formal parameter works.

23. In the following program fragment, identify the following items: method heading, method body, method definition, formal parameters, actual parameters, method call, and local variables.

```
public class Exercise23                          //Line 1
{                                                //Line 2
    public static void main(String[] args)       //Line 3
    {                                            //Line 4
        int x;                                   //Line 5
        double y;                                //Line 6
        char z;                                  //Line 7
        //...                                    //Line 8
        hello(x, y, z);                          //Line 9
```

```
        //...                                    //Line 10
        hello(x + 2, y - 3.5, 'S');              //Line 11
        //...                                    //Line 12
    }                                            //Line 13

    public static void hello(int first, double second,  //Line 14
                             char ch)            //Line 15
    {                                            //Line 16
        int num;                                 //Line 17
        double y;                                //Line 18
        //...                                    //Line 19
    }                                            //Line 20
}                                                //Line 21
```

24. For the program in Exercise 23, fill in the blanks below with variable names to show the matching that occurs between the actual and the formal parameter list in each of the two calls.

First Call to hello			**Second Call to hello**	
Formal	**Actual**		**Formal**	**Actual**
1. _____	_____	1. _____	_____
2. _____	_____	2. _____	_____
3. _____	_____	3. _____	_____

25. What is the output of the following program?

```
public class Exercise25
{
    public static void main(String[] args)
    {
        int num1;
        int num2;

        num1 = 5;
        num2 = 10;
        num2 = test(24, num2);
        num2 = test(num1, num2);
        num2 = test(num1 * num1, num2);
        num2 = test(num1 + num1, num2);
    }

    public static int test(int first, int second)
    {
        int third;

        third = first + second * second + 2;
        first = second - first;
        second = 2 * second;
        System.out.println(first + " " + second + " "
                        + third);
        return second;
    }
}
```

26. In the following program, number the marked statements to show the order in which they will execute (the logical order of execution):

```java
import java.util.*;

public class Exercise26
{
    static Scanner console = new Scanner(System.in);

    public static void main(String[] args)
    {
        int num1;
        int num2;

_____ System.out.println("Please enter two integers "
                            + "on separate lines");

_____ num1 = console.nextInt();

_____ num2 = console.nextInt();

_____ func (num1, num2);

_____ System.out.println("The two integers are " + num1
                            + ", " + num2);
    }

    public static void func (int val1, int val2)
    {
        int val3;
        int val4;

_____ val3 = val1 + val2;

_____ val4 = val1 * val2;

_____ System.out.println("The sum and product are " + val3
                            + " and " + val4);
    }
}
```

27. Consider the following program:

```java
import java.util.*;

public class Chapter7Ex27
{
    static Scanner console = new Scanner(System.in);

    public static void main(String[] args)
    {
        int num;
```

```
                System.out.print("Enter 1 or 2: ");
                num = console.nextInt();
                System.out.println();

                System.out.print("Take ");

                if (num == 1)
                    func1();
                else if (num == 2)
                    func2();
                else
                    System.out.println("Invalid input. "
                                        + "You must enter a 1 or 2");
            }

        public static void func1()
        {
            System.out.println("Programming I.");
        }

        public static void func2()
        {
            System.out.println("Programming II.");
        }
    }
```

a. What is the output if the input is 1?

b. What is the output if the input is 2?

c. What is the output if the input is 3?

d. What is the output if the input is -1?

28. Consider the following program:

```
import java.util.*;

public class Chapter7Ex28
{
    static Scanner console = new Scanner(System.in);

    public static void main(String[] args)
    {
        double one, two;

        System.out.print("Enter two numbers: ");
        one = console.nextDouble();
        two = console.nextDouble();
        System.out.println();

        traceMe(one, two);
        traceMe(two, one);
    }
```

```
public static void traceMe(double x, double y)
{
    double z;

    if (x != 0)
        z = Math.sqrt(y) / x;
    else
    {
        System.out.print("Enter a nonzero number: ");
        x   = console.nextDouble();
        System.out.println();
        z = Math.floor(Math.pow(y, x));
    }

    System.out.printf("%.2f, %.2f, %.2f, %n", x, y, z);
}
```

a. What is the output if the input is 3 625?

b. What is the output if the input is 24 1024?

c. What is the output if the input is 0 196?

29. In Exercise 28, determine the scope of each identifier.

30. Write the definition of a void method that takes as input a decimal number and outputs 3 times the value of the decimal number. Format your output to two decimal places.

31. Write the definition of a void method that takes as input two decimal numbers. If the first number is nonzero, it outputs the second number divided by the first number; otherwise, it outputs a message indicating that the second number cannot be divided by the first number because the first number is 0.

32. Write the definition of a method that takes as input two parameters of type `int`, say `sum` and `testScore`. The method updates the value of `sum` by adding the value of `testScore`, and then returns the updated value of `sum`.

PROGRAMMING EXERCISES

1. Write a value-returning method, `isVowel`, that returns the value `true` if a given character is a vowel, and otherwise returns `false`. Also write a program to test your method.

2. Write a program that prompts the user to input a sequence of characters and outputs the number of vowels. (Use the method `isVowel` written in Programming Exercise 1.)

3. Write a program that uses the method `sqrt` of the `class` `Math` and outputs the square roots of the first 25 positive integers. (Your program must output each number and its square root.)

4. Consider the following program segment:

```java
public class Ch7_PrExercise4
{
    public static void main(String[] args)
    {
        int    num;
        double dec;
        .
        .
        .
    }

    public static int one(int x, int y)
    {
        .
        .
        .
    }

    public static double two(int x, double a)
    {
        int first;
        double z;
        .
        .
        .
    }
}
```

a. Write the definition of method one so that it returns the sum of x and y if x is greater than y; otherwise, it should return x minus 2 times y.

b. Write the definition of method two as follows:

   i. Read a number and store it in z.

   ii. Update the value of z by adding the value of a to its previous value.

   iii. Assign the variable first the value returned by method one with the parameters 6 and 8.

   iv. Update the value of first by adding the value of x to its previous value.

   v. If the value of z is more than twice the value of first, return z; otherwise, return 2 times first minus z.

c. Write a Java program that tests parts a and b. (Declare additional variables in the method main, if necessary.)

5. The following program is designed to find the area of a rectangle, the area of a circle, or the volume of a cylinder. However, (a) the statements are in the

incorrect order; (b) the method calls are incorrect; (c) the logical expression in the `while` loop is incorrect; and (d) method definitions are incorrect. Rewrite the program so that it works correctly. Your program must be properly indented. (Note that the program is menu driven and allows the user to run the program as long as the user wishes.)

```java
import java.util.*;

public class Ch7_PrExercise5
{
    static Scanner console = new Scanner(System.in);

    public static void main(String[] args)
    {
        double radius;
        double height;

        System.out.println("This program can calculate "
                            + "the area of a rectangle, the area "
                            + "of a circle, or volume of a cylinder.");
        System.out.println("To run the program enter: ");
        System.out.println("1: To find the area of rectangle.");
        System.out.println("2: To find the area of a circle.");
        System.out.println("3: To find the volume of a cylinder.");
        System.out.println("-1: To terminate the program.");
        choice = console.nextInt();
        System.out.println();

        int choice;

        while (choice == -1)
        {
        {
            case 1:
                System.out.print("Enter the radius of the base and "
                                + "the height of the cylinder: ");
                radius = console.nextDouble();
                height = console.nextDouble();
                System.out.println();

                System.out.printf("Area = %.2f%n",
                                circle(length, height));
                break;

            case 3:
                double length, width;
                System.out.print("Enter the radius of the circle: ");
                radius = console.nextDouble();
                System.out.println();
```

```
            System.out.printf("Area = %.2f%n", rectangle(radius));
            break;

        case 2:
            System.out.print("Enter the length and the width "
                            + "of the rectangle: ");
            length = console.nextDouble();
            width  = console.nextDouble();
            System.out.println();

            System.out.printf("Volume = %.2f%n",
                            cylinder(radius, height));
            break;
        default:
            System.out.println("Invalid choice!");
        }
        switch (choice)
    }

    System.out.println("To run the program enter: ");
    System.out.println("2: To find the area of a circle.");
    System.out.println("1: To find the area of rectangle.");
    System.out.println("3: To find the volume of a cylinder.");
    System.out.println("-1: To terminate the program.");
    choice = console.nextInt();
    System.out.println();
    }

    public static double rectangle(double l, double w)
    {
        return l * r;
    }

    public static double circle(double r)
    {
        return Math.PI * r * w;
    }

    public static double cylinder(double bR, double h)
    {
        return Math.PI * bR * bR * l;
    }
}
```

6. Write a method, reverseDigit, that takes an integer as a parameter and returns the number with its digits reversed. For example, the value of reverseDigit(12345) is 54321. Also, write a program to test your method.

7. Modify the `RollDice` program, Example 7-3, so that it allows the user to enter the desired sum of the numbers to be rolled. Also allow the user to call the `rollDice` method as many times as the user desires.

8. Write a program to test the method `isPalindrome` discussed in Example 7-4.

9. The following formula gives the distance between two points (x_1, y_1) and (x_2, y_2) in the Cartesian plane:

$$\sqrt{(x_2 - x_1)^2 + (y_2 - y_1)^2}.$$

Given the center and a point on a circle, you can use this formula to find the radius of the circle. Write a program that prompts the user to enter the center and a point on the circle. The program should then output the circle's radius, diameter, circumference, and area. Your program must have at least the following methods:

a. `distance`: This method takes as its parameters four numbers that represent two points in the plane and returns the distance between them.

b. `radius`: This method takes as its parameters four numbers that represent the center and a point on the circle, calls the method `distance` to find the radius of the circle, and returns the circle's radius.

c. `circumference`: This method takes as its parameter a number that represents the radius of the circle and returns the circle's circumference. (If r is the radius, the circumference is $2\pi r$.)

d. `area`: This method takes as its parameter a number that represents the radius of the circle and returns the circle's area. (If r is the radius, the area is πr^2.)

e. Assume that $\pi = 3.1416$.

10. Rewrite the program in Programming Exercise 15 from Chapter 4 (cell phone) so that it uses the following methods to calculate the billing amount. (In this programming exercise, do not output the number of minutes during which the service is used.)

a. `regularBill`: This method calculates and returns the billing amount for regular service.

b. `premiumBill`: This method calculates and returns the billing amount for premium service.

11. A nonnegative integer is called a **palindrome** if it reads forward and backward in the same way. For example, the numbers 5, 121, 3443, and 123454321 are palindromes. Write a method that takes as input a nonnegative integer and returns `true` if the number is a palindrome; otherwise, it returns `false`. (When determining whether the number is a palindrome, do not convert the number into a string.) Also write a program to test your method.

12. Programming Exercise 7 (Chapter 5) asks you to write a program that determines whether a positive integer is a prime number. Redo this programming exercise by writing a method that takes as input a positive integer and returns `true` if the number is a prime number; otherwise, it returns `false`.

13. Write a program that determines whether a positive integer is a prime number. If the number is a prime number, then the program also outputs whether the number is a palindrome. Use the methods developed in Programming Exercises 11 and 12 of this chapter.

14. A prime number whose reversal is also a prime is called *emirp*. For example 11, 13, 79, and 359 are emirps. Write a program that outputs the first 100 emirps. Your program must contain a method that returns `true` if a number is prime; `false` otherwise; and another method that returns the reversal of a positive number. Your program should also prompt the user to enter a positive integer and then should output whether the positive integer is an emirp.

15. Write a program that takes as input five numbers and outputs the mean (average) and standard deviation of the numbers. If the numbers are x_1, x_2, x_3, x_4, and x_5, then the mean is $x = (x_1 + x_2 + x_3 + x_4 + x_5) / 5$ and the standard deviation is:

$$s = \sqrt{\frac{(x_1 - x)^2 + (x_2 - x)^2 + (x_3 - x)^2 + (x_4 - x)^2 + (x_5 - x)^2}{5}}.$$

Your program must contain at least the following method: A method that calculates and returns the mean and a method that calculates the standard deviation.

16. You are given a file consisting of students' names in the following form: `lastName firstName middleName`. (Note that a student may not have a middle name.) Write a program that converts each name to the following form: `firstName middleName lastName`. Your program must read each student's entire name in an object and must consist of a method that takes as input a string, consisting of a student's name, and returns the string consisting of the altered name. Use the string method `index` to find the index of `,`, the method `length` to find the length of the string, and the method `substring` to extract the `firstName`, `middleName`, and `lastName`. (String methods are described in Chapter 3.)

17. When you borrow money to buy a house, a car, or for some other purpose, then you typically repay it by making periodic payments. Suppose that the loan amount is L, r is the interest rate per year, m is the number of payments in a year, and the loan is for t years. Suppose that $i = (r / m)$ and r is in decimal. Then the periodic payment is:

$$R = \frac{L_i}{1 - (1 + i)^{-mt}}.$$

7

You can also calculate the unpaid loan balance after making certain payments. For example, the unpaid balance after making k payments is:

$$L' = R\left[\frac{1-(1+i)^{-(mt-k)}}{i}\right],$$

where R is the periodic payment. (Note that if the payments are monthly, then $m = 12$.)

18. During the tax season, every Friday, J&J accounting firm provides assistance to people who prepare their own tax returns. Their charges are as follows:
    a. If a person has low income ($<= 25,000$) and the consulting time is less than or equal to 30 minutes, there are no charges; otherwise the service charges are 40% of the regular hourly rate for the time over 30 minutes.
    b. For others, if the consulting time is less than or equal to 20 minutes, there are no service charges; otherwise, service charges are 70% of the regular hourly rate for the time over 20 minutes.

    (For example, suppose that a person has low income, spent 1 hour and 15 minutes, and the hourly rate is $70.00. Then the billing amount is 70.00 × 0.40 × (45 / 60) = $21.00.)

    Write a program that prompt the user to enter the hourly rate, the total consulting time, and if the person has low income. The program should output the billing amount. Your program must contain a method that takes as input the hourly rate, the total consulting time, and a value indicating if the person has low income. The method should return the billing amount. Your program may prompt the user to enter the consulting time in minutes.

19. The cost to become a member of a fitness center is as follows: (a) the Senior citizens discount is 30%; (b) if the membership is bought and paid for 12 or more months in advance, the discount is 15%; or (c) if more than 5 personal training sessions are purchased, the discount on each session is 20%.

    Write a menu driven program that determines the cost of a new membership. Your program must contain a method that displays the general information about the fitness center and its charges, a method to get all the necessary information to determine the membership cost, and a method to determine the membership cost. Use appropriate parameters to pass information in and out of a method.

20. Write a program that outputs inflation rates for two successive years and whether the inflation rates are increasing or decreasing. Ask the user to input the current price of an item and its price one year and two years ago. To calculate the inflation rate for a year, subtract the price of the item for that year from the price of the item one year ago and then divide the result by the price a year ago. Your program must contain a method to calculate the results. Use appropriate parameters to pass the information in and out of the method. Do not use any global variables.

21. **(The box problem)** You have been given a flat cardboard of area, say, 70 square inches, to make an open box by cutting a square from each corner and folding the sides (see Figure 7-17). Your objective is to determine the dimension, that is, the length and width, and the side of the square to be cut from the corners so that the resulting box is of maximum volume.

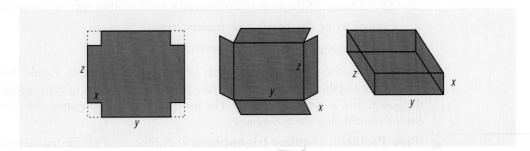

FIGURE 7-17 Cardboard box

Write a program that prompts the user to enter the area of the flat cardboard. The program then outputs the length and width of the cardboard and the length of the side of the square to be cut from the corner so that the resulting box is of maximum volume. Calculate your answer to three decimal places. Your program must contain a method that takes as input the length and width of the cardboard and returns the side of the square that should be cut to maximize the volume. The method also returns the maximum volume.

22. **(The Power Station Problem)** A power station is on one side of a river that is one-half miles wide, and a factory is 8 miles downstream on the other side of the river (see Figure 7-18). It costs $7 per foot to run power lines

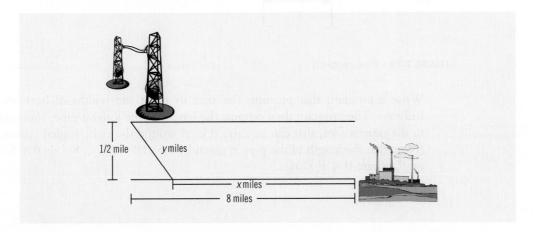

FIGURE 7-18 Power station, river, and factory

7

overland and $9 per foot to run them underwater. Your objective is to determine the most economical path to lay the power line. That is, determine how long the power line should run underwater and how long it should run over land, to achieve the minimum total cost of laying the power line. Write a program that prompts the user to enter the following:

a.   The width of the river.

b.   The distance of the factory downstream on the other side of the river.

c.   Cost of laying the power line underwater.

d.   Cost of laying the power line overland.

The program then outputs the length of the power line that should run underwater and the length that should run over land, so the cost of constructing the power line is at the minimum. The program should also output the total cost of constructing the power line.

23. **(Pipe Problem, requires trigonometry)** A pipe is to be carried around the right-angled corner of two intersecting corridors. Suppose that the widths of the two intersecting corridors are 5 feet and 8 feet (see Figure 7-19). Your objective is to find the length of the longest pipe, rounded to the nearest foot, that can be carried level around the right-angled corner.

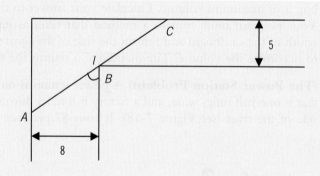

FIGURE 7-19 Pipe problem

Write a program that prompts the user to input the widths of both the hallways. The program then outputs the length of the longest pipe, rounded to the nearest foot, that can be carried level around the right-angled corner. (Note that the length of the pipe is given by $l = AB + BC = 8 / \sin \theta + 5 / \cos \theta$, where $0 < \theta < \pi/2$.)

CHAPTER 8

USER-DEFINED CLASSES AND ADTs

In the preceding chapters, you learned how to use various classes and their methods to manipulate data. Java does not provide all the classes that you will ever need, so it permits you to design and implement your own classes. Therefore, you must learn how to create your own classes. This chapter discusses how to create classes and objects of those classes.

Classes and Objects

Recall, from Chapter 1, that the first step in problem-solving using object-oriented design (OOD) is to identify the components called classes and objects. An *object* of a class has both data and operations that can be performed on that data. The mechanism in Java that allows you to combine data and operations on the data in a single unit is called a *class*. (Combining data and operations on the data is called *encapsulation*—the first principle of OOD.) Now that you know how to store and manipulate data in computer memory and how to construct your own methods, you are ready to learn how classes and objects are constructed.

In Chapter 3, we described the `class` String and illustrated how to use the various String methods. Using the `class` String, you can create various String objects, each storing a different string, and using the methods of the `class` String, each object can manipulate its string. The `class` String allows us to group data, which are strings, and operations on that data in a convenient way. We can use the `class` String in any Java program that requires the manipulation of strings, without re-creating it for a specific program. In fact, the Java programming language provides a wealth of pre-defined classes that can be effectively used in any program. For example, in Chapter 7 we discussed how to use the `class`es Math and Character, and in Chapter 6, we used various classes, such as JFrame, JText, and JLabel, to create GUI programs. However, Java does not provide all the classes that we will ever need as it does not know the specific needs of a programmer. Therefore, we must learn how to create our own classes.

Before discussing how to design your own classes, let's first learn how the `class` String looks. In skeleton form the `class` String has the following form:

```
public final class String
{
    //variables to store a string
    ...

    public int compareTo(String anotherString)
    {
        //code to compare two strings
    }

    public String concat(String str)
    {
        //code to join two strings
    }
```

```
    public String toLowerCase()
    {
        //code to convert all the characters of a string to lowercase
    }

    ...
}
```

As you can see, the `class` `String` has quite a few members. It has methods to implement operations such as compare strings and concatenation operations to join strings. In general, to design a class you must know what data you need to manipulate and what operations you need to manipulate the data. For example, suppose that you want to design the `class` `Circle` that implements the basic properties of a circle. Now every circle has a radius, which can be a floating-point value. Therefore, when you create an object of the `class` `Circle`, then you must store the radius of the circle into that object. Next, the two basic operations that are performed on a circle are to find the area and circumference of the circle. Thus, the `class` `Circle` must provide these two operations. This class needs to provide a few other operations to effectively use this class in a program. In skeleton form, the definition of the `class` `Circle` is as follows:

```
public class Circle
{
    private double radius;

    public double area()
    {
        //code to determine the area of the circle
    }

    public double perimeter()
    {
        //code to determine the perimeter of the circle
    }

    //Additional methods as needed
    ...
}
```

At this point you don't need to be concerned with this definition of the `class` `Circle`. We will create such a class in Example 8-4, of this chapter.

Considering the definition of the `class` `Circle`, it is apparent that to design your own class you need to be familiar with several things. For example, in the definition of the `class` `Circle`, the variable `radius` is declared with the keyword `private` and the methods `area` and `perimeter` are declared with the keyword `public`. Also, notice that the methods `area` and `perimeter` have no parameters. You will learn these and various other characteristics of a class in this chapter.

Next, we give the syntax of a Java class and describe its various parts.

A **class** is a collection of a specific number of components. The components of a `class` are called the **members** of the `class`.

The general syntax for defining a `class` is:

```
modifier(s) class ClassIdentifier modifier(s)
{
    classMembers
}
```

where `modifier(s)` are used to alter the behavior of the class and, usually, `classMembers` consist of named constants, variable declarations, and/or methods, but can even include other classes. That is, usually a member of a `class` can be a variable (to store data) or a method or an inner class. Some of the modifiers that we have encountered are `public`, `private`, and `static`.

- If a member of a class is a named constant, you declare it just like any other named constant.
- If a member of a class is a variable, you declare it just like any other variable.
- If a member of a class is a method, you define it just like any other method.
- If a member of a class is a method, it can (directly) access any member of the class—both data members and methods. Therefore, when you write the definition of a method, you can directly access any data member of the class (without passing it as a parameter).
- Later, we'll describe class members, which themselves are classes, called inner classes.

In Java, `class` is a reserved word. It only defines a data type and it announces the declaration of a class. In Java, the data members of a `class` are also called **fields**.

The members of a `class` are classified into four categories. The three typically used categories are `private`, `public`, and `protected`. (The fourth category is described in the next note.) This chapter discusses the `private` and `public` categories. Chapter 10 discusses `protected` members.

The following are some facts about `private` and `public` members of a class:

- If a member of a class is `private`, you *cannot* access it outside the class.
- If a member of a class is `public`, you *can* access it outside the class.

 NOTE Recall that a package is a collection of related classes. Appendix D describes how to create your own packages. If a class member is declared/defined without any modifiers, then that class member can be accessed from anywhere in the package. (This is the fourth category of class members and is called the *default* visibility of class members. However, this type of visibility should be avoided.)

In Java, `private`, `protected`, and `public` are reserved words.

Suppose that we want to define the `class Clock` to represent the time of day in a program. Further suppose that the time is represented as a set of three integers: one to represent the hours, one to represent the minutes, and one to represent the seconds. We also want to perform the following operations on the time:

1. Set the time.
2. Return the hours.
3. Return the minutes.
4. Return the seconds.
5. Print the time.
6. Increment the time by one hour.
7. Increment the time by one minute.
8. Increment the time by one second.
9. Compare the two times for equality.
10. Copy the time.
11. Return a copy of the time.

To implement these 11 operations, we write algorithms, which we implement as methods—11 methods to implement 11 operations. So far, the `class Clock` has 14 members: 3 data members and 11 methods. Suppose that the 3 data members are `hr`, `min`, and `sec`, each of type `int`.

Some members of the `class Clock` will be `private`, others will be `public`. Deciding which members to make `private` and which to make `public` depends on the nature of each member. The general rule is that any member that needs to be accessed from outside the class is declared `public`; any member that should not be accessed directly by the user should be declared `private`. For example, the user should be able to set the time and print the time. Therefore, the methods that set the time and print the time should be declared `public`.

Similarly, the method to increment the time and compare the times for equality should be declared `public`. On the other hand, users should not control the *direct* manipulation of the data members `hr`, `min`, and `sec`, so we will declare them `private`. Note that if the user has direct access to the data members, methods such as `setTime` are not needed. (However, in general, the user should never be provided with direct access to the variables.)

The data members for the `class Clock` are:

```
private int hr;  //store the hours
private int min; //store the minutes
private int sec; //store the seconds
```

The (non-`static`) data members—variables declared without using the modifier (reserved word) `static`—of a `class` are called **instance variables**. Therefore, the variables `hr`, `min`, and `sec` are the instance variables of the `class Clock`.

Suppose that the 11 methods to implement the 11 operations are as follows (we also specify the headings of the methods):

1. `setTime` sets the time to the time specified by the user. The method heading is:

   `public void setTime(int hours, int minutes, int seconds)`

2. `getHours` returns the hours. The method heading is:

   `public int getHours()`

3. `getMinutes` returns the minutes. The method heading is:

   `public int getMinutes()`

4. `getSeconds` returns the seconds. The method heading is:

   `public int getSeconds()`

5. `printTime` prints the time in the form hh:mm:ss. The method heading is:

   `public void printTime()`

6. `incrementHours` increments the time by one hour. The method heading is:

   `public void incrementHours()`

7. `incrementMinutes` increments the time by one minute. The method heading is:

   `public void incrementMinutes()`

8. `incrementSeconds` increments the time by one second. The method heading is:

   `public void incrementSeconds()`

9. `equals` compares two times to determine whether they are equal. The method heading is:

   `public boolean equals(Clock otherClock)`

10. `makeCopy` copies the time of one `Clock` object into another `Clock` object. The method heading is:

    `public void makeCopy(Clock otherClock)`

11. `getCopy` returns a copy of the time. A copy of the object's time is created and a reference to the copy is returned. The method heading is:

    `public Clock getCopy()`

The objective of the method `setTime` is to set the values of the instance variables. In other words, it changes the values of the instance variables. Such methods are called *mutator* methods. On the other hand, the method `getHours` only accesses the value of an instance variable; that is, it does not change the value of the instance variable. Such methods are called *accessor* methods. These methods are described in detail later in this chapter.

The (non-`static`) methods of a class are called the **instance methods** of the class.

NOTE — In the definition of the `class` Clock, all the data members are `private` and all the method members are `public`. However, a method can also be `private`. For example, if a method is only used to support other methods of the class, and the user of the class does not need to access this method, you make it `private`.

Notice that we have not yet written the definitions of the methods of the `class` Clock. (You will learn how to write them in the section Definitions of the Constructors and Methods of the `class` Clock.) Also notice that the method `equals` has only one parameter, although you need two things to make a comparison. Similarly, the method `makeCopy` has only one parameter. An example later in this chapter will help explain why.

Before giving the definition of the `class` Clock, we first introduce another important concept related to classes—constructors.

Constructors

In addition to the methods necessary to implement operations, every class can have *special* types of methods called constructors. A **constructor** has the same name as the class, and it executes automatically when an object of that class is created. Constructors are used to guarantee that the instance variables of the class are initialized.

There are two types of constructors: those with parameters and those without parameters. The constructor without parameters is called the **default constructor**.

Constructors have the following properties:

- The name of a constructor is the same as the name of the class.
- A constructor, even though it is a method, has no return type. That is, it is neither a value-returning method nor a `void` method.
- A class can have more than one constructor. However, all constructors of a class have the same name. That is, the constructors of a class can be overloaded.
- If a class has more than one constructor, the constructors must have different *signatures*.
- Constructors execute automatically when class objects are instantiated. Because they have no types, they cannot be called like other methods.
- If there are multiple constructors, the constructor that executes depends on the type of values passed to the class object when the class object is instantiated.

For the `class` Clock, we will include two constructors: the default constructor and a constructor with parameters. The default constructor initializes the instance variables used to store the hours, minutes, and seconds, each to 0. Similarly, the constructor with parameters initializes the instance variables to the values specified by the user. We will illustrate shortly how constructors are invoked.

8

The heading of the default constructor is:

```
public Clock()
```

The heading of the constructor with parameters is:

```
public Clock(int hours, int minutes, int seconds)
```

The definition of the **class** Clock has 16 members: 11 methods to implement the 11 operations, 2 constructors, and 3 instance variables to store the hours, minutes, and seconds.

 NOTE If you do not include any constructor in a class, then Java *automatically* provides the default constructor. Therefore, when you create an object, the instance variables are initialized to their default values. For example, **int** variables are initialized to 0. If you provide at least one constructor and do not include the default constructor, then Java *will not automatically* provide the default constructor. Generally, if a class includes constructors, you should also include the default constructor.

Unified Modeling Language Class Diagrams

A class and its members can be described graphically using **Unified Modeling Language (UML)** notation. For example, Figure 8-1 shows the UML diagram of the **class** Clock. Also, what appears in the figure is called the **UML class diagram** of the class.

```
                       Clock
         -hr: int
         -min: int
         -sec: int

         +Clock()
         +Clock(int, int, int)
         +setTime(int, int, int): void
         +getHours(): int
         +getMinutes(): int
         +getSeconds(): int
         +printTime(): void
         +incrementSeconds(): int
         +incrementMinutes(): int
         +incrementHours(): int
         +equals(Clock): boolean
         +makeCopy(Clock): void
         +getCopy(): Clock
```

FIGURE 8-1 UML class diagram of the **class** clock

The top box in the UML diagram contains the name of the class. The middle box contains the data members and their data types. The last box contains the method names, parameter list, and return types. The + (plus) sign in front of a member indicates that it is a `public` member; the − (minus) sign indicates that it is a `private` member. The # symbol before a member name indicates that it is a `protected` member.

Variable Declaration and Object Instantiation

Once a `class` is defined, you can declare reference variables of that `class` type. For example, the following statements declare `myClock` and `yourClock` to be reference variables of type `Clock`:

```
Clock myClock;          //Line 1
Clock yourClock;        //Line 2
```

These statements *do not* allocate memory spaces to store the hours, minutes, and seconds. Next, we explain how to allocate memory space to store the hours, minutes, and seconds, and how to access that memory space using the variables `myClock` and `yourClock`.

The `class` `Clock` has three instance variables. To store the hours, minutes, and seconds, we need to create a `Clock` object, which is accomplished by using the operator `new`.

The general syntax for using the operator `new` is:

```
new className()                                        //Line 3
```

or:

```
new className(argument1, argument2, ..., argumentN)    //Line 4
```

The expression in Line 3 instantiates the object and initializes the instance variables of the object using the default constructor. The expression in Line 4 instantiates the object and initializes the instance variables using a constructor with parameters.

For the expression in Line 4:

- The number of arguments and their type should match the formal parameters (in the order given) of one of the constructors.
- If the type of the arguments does not match the formal parameters of any constructor (in the order given), Java uses type conversion and looks for the best match. For example, an integer value might be converted to a floating-point value with a zero decimal part. Any ambiguity will result in a compile-time error.

Consider the following statements (notice that `myClock` and `yourClock` are as declared in Lines 1 and 2):

```
myClock = new Clock();          //Line 5
yourClock = new Clock(9, 35, 15);   //Line 6
```

The statement in Line 5 allocates memory space for a `Clock` object, initializes each instance variable of the object to 0, and stores the address of the object into `myClock`. The statement in Line 6 allocates memory space for a `Clock` object; initializes the instance variables `hr`, `min`, and `sec` of the object to 9, 35, and 15, respectively; and stores the address of the object into `yourClock` (see Figure 8-2).

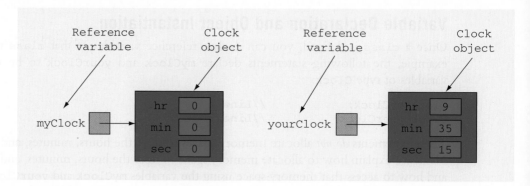

FIGURE 8-2 Variables `myClock` and `yourClock` and associated `Clock` objects

To be specific, we call the object to which `myClock` points the object `myClock` and the object to which `yourClock` points the object `yourClock` (see Figure 8-3).

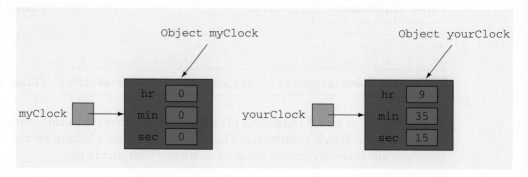

FIGURE 8-3 Objects `myClock` and `yourClock`

Of course, you can combine the statements to declare the variable and instantiate the object into one statement. For example, the statements in Lines 1 and 5 can be combined as:

```
Clock myClock = new Clock();    //declare and instantiate myClock
```

That is, the preceding statement declares `myClock` to be a reference variable of type `Clock` and instantiates the object `myClock` to store the hours, minutes, and seconds. Each instance variable of the object `myClock` is initialized to 0 by the default constructor.

Similarly, the statements in Lines 2 and 6 can be combined as:

```
Clock yourClock = new Clock(9, 35, 15);   //declare and
                                          //instantiate yourClock
```

That is, the preceding statement declares `yourClock` to be a reference variable of type `Clock` and instantiates the object `yourClock` to store the hours, minutes, and seconds. The instance variables `hr`, `min`, and `sec` of the object `yourClock` are initialized to 9, 35, and 15, respectively, by the constructor with parameters.

NOTE   When we use phrases such as "create an object of a `class` type" we mean to: (i) declare a reference variable of the `class` type, (ii) instantiate the `class` object, and (iii) store the address of the object into the reference variable declared. For example, the following statements create the object `tempClock` of the `Clock` type:

```
Clock tempClock = new Clock();
```

The object `tempClock` is accessed via the reference variable `tempClock`.

Recall from Chapter 3 that a `class` object is called an **instance** of that `class`.

Accessing Class Members

Once an object of a class is created, the object can access the members (as explained in the next paragraph, after the syntax) of the `class`. The general syntax for an object to access a data member or a method is:

```
referenceVariableName.memberName
```

The class members that the class object can access depend on where the object is created.

- If the object is created in the definition of a method of the class, then the object can access both the `public` and `private` members. We will elaborate on this when we write the definitions of the methods `equals`, `makeCopy`, and `getCopy` of the `class` `Clock` later in this chapter.

- If the object is created elsewhere (for example, in a user's program), then the object can access *only* the `public` members of the class.

Recall that in Java, the dot `.` (period) is called the **member access operator**.

Example 8-1 illustrates how to access the members of a class.

EXAMPLE 8-1

Suppose that the objects `myClock` and `yourClock` have been created as before. Consider the following statements:

```
myClock.setTime(5, 2, 30);
myClock.printTime();
yourClock.setTime(x, y, z);    //Assume x, y, and z are variables
                               //of type int that have been
                               //initialized.
```

```
if (myClock.equals(yourClock))
    .
    .
    .
```

These statements are legal; that is, they are syntactically correct. Note the following:

- In the first statement, `myClock.setTime(5, 2, 30);`, the method `setTime` is executed. The values 5, 2, and 30 are passed as parameters to the method `setTime`, and the method uses these values to set the values of `hr`, `min`, and `sec` of the object `myClock` to 5, 2, and 30, respectively.

- Similarly, the second statement executes the method `printTime` and outputs the values of `hr`, `min`, and `sec` of the object `myClock`.

- In the third statement, the values of the variables `x`, `y`, and `z` are used to set the values of `hr`, `min`, and `sec` of the object `yourClock`.

- In the fourth statement, the method `equals` executes and compares the instance variables of the object `myClock` with the corresponding instance variables of the object `yourClock`. Because in this statement the method `equals` is invoked by the variable `myClock`, it has direct access to the instance variables of the object `myClock`. So it needs one more object to compare, which, in this case, is the object `yourClock`. This explains why the method `equals` has only one parameter.

The objects `myClock` and `yourClock` can access only `public` members of the class. The following statements are illegal because `hr` and `min` are `private` members of the `class` `Clock` and, therefore, cannot be accessed by `myClock` and `yourClock`:

```
myClock.hr = 10;                    //illegal
myClock.min = yourClock.min;        //illegal
```

Built-in Operations on Classes

Most of Java's built-in operations do not apply to classes. You cannot perform arithmetic operations on class objects. For example, you cannot use the operator + to add the values of two `Clock` objects. Also, you cannot use relational operators to compare two class objects in any meaningful way.

The built-in operation that is valid for classes is the dot operator (`.`). A reference variable uses the dot operator to access `public` members; classes can use the dot operator to access `public static` members.

Assignment Operator and Classes: A Precaution

This section discusses how the assignment operator works with reference variables and objects.

Suppose that the objects `myClock` and `yourClock` are as shown in Figure 8-4.

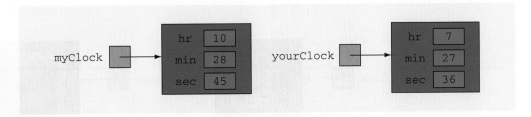

FIGURE 8-4 `myClock` and `yourClock`

The statement:

`myClock = yourClock;`

copies the value of the reference variable `yourClock` into the reference variable `myClock`. After this statement executes, both `yourClock` and `myClock` refer to the same object. Figure 8-5 illustrates this situation.

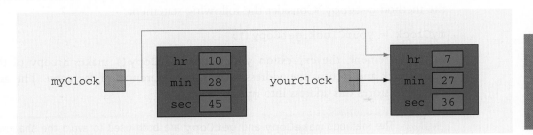

FIGURE 8-5 `myClock` and `yourClock` after the statement `myClock = yourClock;` executes

This is called the shallow copying of data. In **shallow copying**, two or more reference variables of the same type point to the same object; that is, two or more reference variables become aliases. Note that the object originally referred to by `myClock` becomes inaccessible.

To copy the instance variables of the object `yourClock` into the corresponding instance variables of the object `myClock`, you need to use the method `makeCopy`. This is accomplished by the following statement:

`myClock.makeCopy(yourClock);`

After this statement executes:

1. The value of `yourClock.hr` is copied into `myClock.hr`.
2. The value of `yourClock.min` is copied into `myClock.min`.
3. The value of `yourClock.sec` is copied into `myClock.sec`.

In other words, the values of the three instance variables of the object yourClock are copied into the corresponding instance variables of the object myClock, as shown in Figure 8-6.

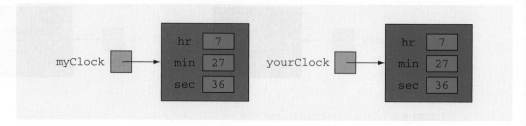

FIGURE 8-6 Objects myClock and yourClock after the statement myClock.makeCopy(yourClock); executes

This is called the deep copying of data. In **deep copying**, each reference variable refers to its *own* object, as in Figure 8-6, *not* the same object, as in Figure 8-5.

Another way to avoid the shallow copying of data is to have the object being copied create a copy of itself, and then return a reference to the copy. This is accomplished by the method getCopy. Consider the following statement:

```
myClock = yourClock.getCopy();
```

In this statement, the expression yourClock.getCopy() makes a copy of the object yourClock and returns the address, that is, the reference, of the copy. The assignment statement stores this address into myClock.

 NOTE The methods makeCopy and getCopy are both used to avoid the shallow copying of data. The main difference between these two methods is: To use the method makeCopy, both objects—the object whose data is being copied and the object that is copying the data—must be instantiated before invoking this method. To use the method getCopy, the object whose data is being copied must be instantiated before invoking this method, while the object of the reference variable receiving a copy of the data need not be instantiated. Note that makeCopy and getCopy are *user-defined* methods.

It is important to understand the difference between the shallow and deep copying of data and when to use which. Shallow copying can produce unintended results, especially by beginning Java programmers.

Class Scope

A reference variable follows the same scope rules as other variables. A member of a class is local to the class. You access a **public class** member outside the **class** through the reference variable name or the **class** name (for **static** members) and the member access operator (.).

Methods and Classes

Reference variables can be passed as parameters to methods and returned as method values. Recall from Chapter 7 that when a reference variable is passed as a parameter to a method, both the formal and actual parameters point to the same object.

Definitions of the Constructors and Methods of the `class Clock`

We now give the definitions of the methods of the `class` Clock, then we will write the complete definition of this class. First, note the following:

1. The `class` Clock has 11 methods: setTime, getHours, getMinutes, getSeconds, printTime, incrementHours, incrementMinutes, incrementSeconds, equals, makeCopy, and getCopy. It has two constructors and three instance variables: hr, min, and sec.

2. The three instance variables—hr, min, and sec—are `private` to the `class` and cannot be accessed directly outside the `class`.

3. The 11 methods—setTime, getHours, getMinutes, getSeconds, printTime, incrementHours, incrementMinutes, incrementSeconds, equals, makeCopy, and getCopy—can directly access the instance variables (hr, min, and sec). In other words, we do not pass instance variables or data members as parameters to these methods. Similarly, constructors directly access the instance variables.

Let's first write the definition of the method setTime. The method setTime has three parameters of type int. This method sets the instance variables to the values specified by the user, which are passed as parameters to this function. The definition of the method setTime follows:

```
public void setTime(int hours, int minutes, int seconds)
{
    if (0 <= hours && hours < 24)
        hr = hours;
    else
        hr = 0;

    if (0 <= minutes && minutes < 60)
        min = minutes;
    else
        min = 0;

    if (0 <= seconds && seconds < 60)
        sec = seconds;
    else
        sec = 0;
}
```

8

Note that the definition of the method setTime checks for the valid values of hours, minutes, and seconds. If any of these values is out of range, the corresponding instance variable is initialized to 0. Now let's look at how the method setTime works.

The method setTime is a **void** method and has three parameters. Therefore:

- A call to this method is a stand-alone statement.
- We must use three parameters in a call to this method.

Furthermore, recall that because setTime is a member of the **class** Clock, it can directly access the instance variables hr, min, and sec, as shown in the definition of setTime.

Suppose that the object myClock is as shown in Figure 8-7.

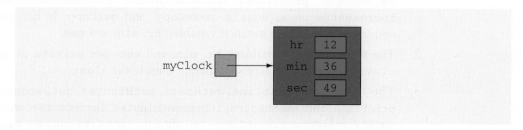

FIGURE 8-7 Object myClock

Consider the following statement:

```
myClock.setTime(3, 48, 52);
```

The variable myClock accesses the member setTime. In the statement myClock.setTime(3, 48, 52);, setTime is accessed by the variable myClock. Therefore, the three variables—hr, min, and sec—referred to in the body of the method setTime are the three instance variables of the object myClock. Thus, the values 3, 48, and 52, which are passed as parameters in the preceding statement, are assigned to the three instance variables of the object myClock by the method setTime (see the body of the method setTime). After the previous statement executes, myClock is as shown in Figure 8-8.

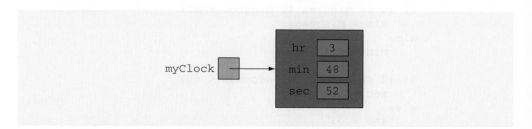

FIGURE 8-8 myClock after statement myClock.setTime(3,48,52); executes

Next, let's give the definitions of the other methods of the `class` Clock. These definitions are simple and easy to follow.

```java
public int getHours()
{
    return hr;          //return the value of hr
}

public int getMinutes()
{
    return min;         //return the value of min
}

public int getSeconds()
{
    return sec;         //return the value of sec
}

public void printTime()
{
    if (hr < 10)
        System.out.print("0");
    System.out.print(hr + ":");

    if (min < 10)
        System.out.print("0");
    System.out.print(min + ":");

    if (sec < 10)
        System.out.print("0");
    System.out.print(sec);
}

public void incrementHours()
{
    hr++;               //increment the value of hr by 1

    if (hr > 23)        //if hr is greater than 23,
        hr = 0;         //set hr to 0
}

public void incrementMinutes()
{
    min++;              //increment the value of min by 1

    if (min > 59)       //if min is greater than 59
    {
        min = 0;        //set min to 0
        incrementHours();  //increment hours
    }
}
```

8

```
public void incrementSeconds()
{
    sec++;                    //increment the value of sec by 1

    if (sec > 59)      //if sec is greater than 59
    {
        sec = 0;                   //set sec to 0
        incrementMinutes();   //increment minutes
    }
}
```

From the definitions of the methods incrementMinutes and incrementSeconds, you can see that a method of a class can call other methods of the class.

The method equals has the following definition:

```
public boolean equals(Clock otherClock)
{
    return (hr == otherClock.hr
            && min == otherClock.min
            && sec == otherClock.sec);
}
```

Let's see how the method equals works.

Suppose that myClock and yourClock are as shown in Figure 8-9.

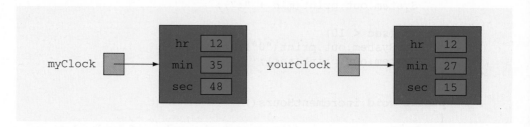

FIGURE 8-9 Objects myClock and yourClock

Consider the following statement:

```
if (myClock.equals(yourClock))
    .
    .
    .
```

In the expression:

```
myClock.equals(yourClock)
```

myClock accesses the method equals. The value of the parameter yourClock is passed to the formal parameter otherClock, as shown in Figure 8-10.

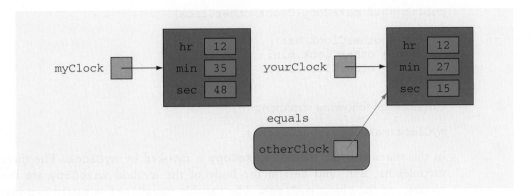

FIGURE 8-10 Object myClock and parameter otherClock

Note that otherClock and yourClock refer to the same object. The instance variables hr, min, and sec of the object otherClock have the values 12, 27, and 15, respectively. In other words, when the body of the method equals executes, the value of otherClock.hr is 12, the value of otherClock.min is 27, and the value of otherClock.sec is 15. The method equals is a member of myClock. When the method equals executes, the variables hr, min, and sec in the body of the method equals are the instance variables of the object myClock. Therefore, the instance variable hr of the object myClock is compared with otherClock.hr, the instance variable min of the object myClock is compared with otherClock.min, and the instance variable sec of the object myClock is compared with otherClock.sec.

Once again, in the expression:

```
myClock.equals(yourClock)
```

the method equals is invoked by myClock and compares the object myClock with the object yourClock. It follows that the method equals needs only one parameter.

Let us again take a look at the definition of the method equals. Notice that within the definition of this method, the object otherClock accesses the data members hr, min, and sec. However, these data members are **private**. So is there any violation? The answer is no. The method equals is a member of the **class** Clock and hr, min, and sec are the data members. Moreover, otherClock is an object of the **class** Clock. Therefore, the object otherClock can access its **private** data members within the definition of the method equals. The same is true for any method of a class.

That is, in general, when you write the definition of a method, say, dummyMethod, of a **class**, say, DummyClass, and the method uses an object, dummyObject of the **class** DummyClass, then within the definition of dummyMethod the object dummyObject can access its **private** data members (in fact, any **private** member of the class).

The method makeCopy copies the instance variables of its parameter, otherClock, into the corresponding instance variables of the object referenced by the variable using this method. Its definition is:

```
public void makeCopy(Clock otherClock)
{
    hr = otherClock.hr;
    min = otherClock.min;
    sec = otherClock.sec;
}
```

Consider the following statement:

```
myClock.makeCopy(yourClock);
```

In this statement, the method `makeCopy` is invoked by `myClock`. The three instance variables `hr`, `min`, and `sec` in the body of the method `makeCopy` are the instance variables of the object `myClock`. The variable `yourClock` is passed as a parameter to `makeCopy`. Therefore, `yourClock` and `otherClock` refer to the same object, which is the object `yourClock`. Thus, after the preceding statement executes, the instance variables of the object `yourClock` are copied into the corresponding instance variables of the object `myClock`. (Note that as in the case of the method `equals`, the parameter `otherClock` can directly access the private data members of the object it points to.)

The method `getCopy` creates a copy of an object's `hr`, `min`, and `sec` and returns the address of the copy of the object. That is, the method `getCopy` creates a new `Clock` object, initializes the instance variables of the object, and returns the address of the object created. The definition of the method `getCopy` is:

```
public Clock getCopy()
{
    Clock temp = new Clock();    //Line 1

    temp.hr = hr;                //Line 2
    temp.min = min;             //Line 3
    temp.sec = sec;             //Line 4

    return temp;                //Line 5
}
```

The following illustrates how the method `getCopy` works. Suppose that `yourClock` is as shown in Figure 8-11.

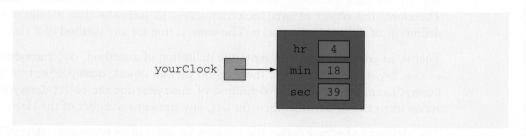

FIGURE 8-11 Object `yourClock`

Consider the following statement:

```
myClock = yourClock.getCopy();          //Line A
```

In this statement, because the method `getCopy` is invoked by `yourClock`, the three variables `hr`, `min`, and `sec` in the body of the method `getCopy` are the instance variables of the object `yourClock`. The body of the method `getCopy` executes as follows. The statement in Line 1 creates the `Clock` object `temp`. The statements in Lines 2 through 4 copy the instance variables of the object `yourClock` into the corresponding instance variables of `temp`. In other words, the object referenced by `temp` is a copy of the object `yourClock` (see Figure 8-12).

FIGURE 8-12   Objects `temp` and `yourClock`

The statement in Line 5 returns the value of `temp`, which is the address of the object holding a copy of the data. The value returned by the method `getCopy` is copied into `myClock`. Therefore, after the statement in Line A executes, `myClock` and `yourClock` are as shown in Figure 8-13.

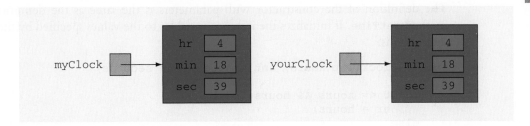

FIGURE 8-13   Objects `myClock` and `yourClock`

Note that as in the case of the methods `equals` and `makeCopy`, the reference variable `temp`—in the definition of the method `getCopy`—can directly access the private data members of the object it points to because `getCopy` is a method of the **class** `Clock`.

NOTE

The definition of the method `getCopy` can also be written as:

```
public Clock getCopy()
{
    Clock temp = new Clock(hr, min, sec);

    return temp;
}
```

This definition of the method `getCopy` uses the constructor with parameters, described below, to initialize the instance variables of the object `temp`.

Next, we give the definitions of the constructors. The default constructor initializes each instance variable to 0. Its definition is:

```
public Clock()
{
    hr = 0;
    min = 0;
    sec = 0;
}
```

You can also write the definition of the default constructor using the method `setTime` as follows:

```
public Clock()
{
    setTime(0, 0, 0);
}
```

The definition of the constructor with parameters is the same as the definition of the method `setTime`. It initializes the instance variables to the values specified by the user. Its definition is:

```
public Clock(int hours, int minutes, int seconds)
{
    if (0 <= hours && hours < 24)
        hr = hours;
    else
        hr = 0;

    if (0 <= minutes && minutes < 60)
        min = minutes;
    else
        min = 0;

    if (0 <= seconds && seconds < 60)
        sec = seconds;
    else
        sec = 0;
}
```

As in the case of the default constructor, you can write the definition of the constructor with parameters using the method `setTime` as follows:

```
public Clock(int hours, int minutes, int seconds)
{
    setTime(hours, minutes, seconds);
}
```

This definition of the constructor with parameters makes debugging easier, because only the code for the method `setTime` needs to be checked.

DEFINITION OF THE Class Clock

Now that we have defined the methods of the **class** `Clock`, we can give the complete definition of the **class** `Clock`. Before the definition of a method, we include comments specifying the preconditions and/or postconditions.

Precondition: A statement specifying the condition(s) that must be true before the function is called.

Postcondition: A statement specifying what is true after the function call is completed.

The definition of the **class** `Clock` is:

```
public class Clock
{
    private int hr;   //store hours
    private int min;  //store minutes
    private int sec;  //store seconds

        //Default constructor
        //Postcondition: hr = 0; min = 0; sec = 0
    public Clock()
    {
        setTime(0, 0, 0);
    }

        //Constructor with parameters, to set the time
        //The time is set according to the parameters.
        //Postcondition: hr = hours; min = minutes;
        //               sec = seconds
    public Clock(int hours, int minutes, int seconds)
    {
        setTime(hours, minutes, seconds);
    }

        //Method to set the time
        //The time is set according to the parameters.
        //Postcondition: hr = hours; min = minutes;
        //               sec = seconds
```

8

```java
public void setTime(int hours, int minutes, int seconds)
{
    if (0 <= hours && hours < 24)
        hr = hours;
    else
        hr = 0;

    if (0 <= minutes && minutes < 60)
        min = minutes;
    else
        min = 0;

    if (0 <= seconds && seconds < 60)
        sec = seconds;
    else
        sec = 0;
}

    //Method to return the hours
    //Postcondition: the value of hr is returned
public int getHours()
{
    return hr;
}

    //Method to return the minutes
    //Postcondition: the value of min is returned
public int getMinutes()
{
    return min;
}

    //Method to return the seconds
    //Postcondition: the value of sec is returned
public int getSeconds()
{
    return sec;
}

    //Method to print the time
    //Postcondition: Time is printed in the form hh:mm:ss
public void printTime()
{
    if (hr < 10)
        System.out.print("0");
    System.out.print(hr + ":");

    if (min < 10)
        System.out.print("0");
    System.out.print(min + ":");
```

```java
    if (sec < 10)
        System.out.print("0");
    System.out.print(sec);
}


    //Method to increment the time by one second
    //Postcondition: The time is incremented by one second
    //If the before-increment time is 23:59:59, the time
    //is reset to 00:00:00
public void incrementSeconds()
{
    sec++;

    if (sec > 59)
    {
        sec = 0;
        incrementMinutes(); //increment minutes
    }
}


    //Method to increment the time by one minute
    //Postcondition: The time is incremented by one minute
    //If the before-increment time is 23:59:53, the time
    //is reset to 00:00:53
public void incrementMinutes()
{
    min++;

    if (min > 59)
    {
        min = 0;
        incrementHours(); //increment hours
    }
}


    //Method to increment the time by one hour
    //Postcondition: The time is incremented by one hour
    //If the before-increment time is 23:45:53, the time
    //is reset to 00:45:53
public void incrementHours()
{
    hr++;

    if (hr > 23)
        hr = 0;
}


    //Method to compare two times
    //Postcondition: Returns true if this time is equal to
    //               otherClock; otherwise returns false
public boolean equals(Clock otherClock)
```

8

```java
    {
        return (hr == otherClock.hr
               && min == otherClock.min
               && sec == otherClock.sec);
    }

    //Method to copy time
    //Postcondition: The instance variables of otherClock
    //               copied into the corresponding data
    //               are members of this time.
    //               hr = otherClock.hr;
    //               min = otherClock.min;
    //               sec = otherClock.sec;
    public void makeCopy(Clock otherClock)
    {
        hr = otherClock.hr;
        min = otherClock.min;
        sec = otherClock.sec;
    }

    //Method to return a copy of time
    //Postcondition: A copy of the object is created and
    //               a reference of the copy is returned
    public Clock getCopy()
    {
        Clock temp = new Clock();

        temp.hr = hr;
        temp.min = min;
        temp.sec = sec;

        return temp;
    }
}
```

NOTE   In a class definition, it is a common practice to list all the instance variables, named constants, other data members, or variable declarations first, then the constructors, and then the methods.

Once a class is properly defined and implemented, it can be used in a program. A program or software that uses and manipulates the objects of a class is called a **client** of that class.

EXAMPLE 8-2

```java
//Program to test various operations of the class Clock

import java.util.*;

public class TestProgClock
```

```
{
    static Scanner console = new Scanner(System.in);

    public static void main(String[] args)
    {
        Clock myClock = new Clock(5, 4, 30);            //Line 1
        Clock yourClock = new Clock();                  //Line 2

        int hours;                                      //Line 3
        int minutes;                                    //Line 4
        int seconds;                                    //Line 5

        System.out.print("Line 6: myClock: ");          //Line 6
        myClock.printTime();                            //Line 7
        System.out.println();                           //Line 8
        System.out.print("Line 9: yourClock: ");        //Line 9
        yourClock.printTime();                          //Line 10
        System.out.println();                           //Line 11

        yourClock.setTime(5, 45, 16);                   //Line 12

        System.out.print("Line 13: After setting "
                       + "the time, yourClock: ");       //Line 13
        yourClock.printTime();                          //Line 14
        System.out.println();                           //Line 15

        if (myClock.equals(yourClock))                  //Line 16
            System.out.println("Line 17: Both the "
                        + "times are equal.");          //Line 17
        else                                            //Line 18
            System.out.println("Line 19: The two "
                        + "times are not "
                        + "equal.");                    //Line 19

        System.out.print("Line 20: Enter hours, "
                       + "minutes, and seconds: ");      //Line 20
        hours = console.nextInt();                      //Line 21
        minutes = console.nextInt();                    //Line 22
        seconds = console.nextInt();                    //Line 23
        System.out.println();                           //Line 24

        myClock.setTime(hours, minutes, seconds);       //Line 25

        System.out.print("Line 26: New time of "
                       + "myClock: ");                   //Line 26
        myClock.printTime();                            //Line 27
        System.out.println();                           //Line 28

        myClock.incrementSeconds();                     //Line 29
```

8

```
        System.out.print("Line 30: After "
                    + "incrementing the time by "
                    + "one second, myClock: ");        //Line 30
        myClock.printTime();                            //Line 31
        System.out.println();                           //Line 32

        yourClock.makeCopy(myClock);                    //Line 33

        System.out.print("Line 34: After copying "
                    + "myClock into yourClock, "
                    + "yourClock: ");                    //Line 34
        yourClock.printTime();                          //Line 35
        System.out.println();                           //Line 36
    }//end main
}
```

Sample Run: (In this sample run, the user input is shaded.)

```
Line 6: myClock: 05:04:30
Line 9: yourClock: 00:00:00
Line 13: After setting the time, yourClock: 05:45:16
Line 19: The two times are not equal.
Line 20: Enter hours, minutes, and seconds: 11 22 59

Line 26: New time of myClock: 11:22:59
Line 30: After incrementing the time by one second, myClock: 11:23:00
Line 34: After copying myClock into yourClock, yourClock: 11:23:00
```

A walk-through of the preceding program is left as an exercise for you.

EXAMPLE 8-3

Consider the following class definition:

```
public class Inventory
{
    private String name;
    private int itemNum;
    private double price;
    private int unitsInStock;

    public Inventory()                                  //Constructor 1
    {
        name = "";
        itemNum = -1;
        price = 0.0;
        unitsInStock = 0;
    }
```

```
    public Inventory(String n)                          //Constructor 2
    {
        name = n;
        itemNum = -1;
        price = 0.0;
        unitsInStock = 0;
    }

    public Inventory(String n, int iNum,
                     double cost)                       //Constructor 3
    {
        name = n;
        itemNum = iNum;
        price = cost;
        unitsInStock = 0;
    }

    public Inventory(String n, int iNum, double cost,
                     int inStock)                       //Constructor 4
    {
        name = n;
        itemNum = iNum;
        price = cost;
        unitsInStock = inStock;
    }

    //Add additional methods
}
```

This class has four constructors and four instance variables.

Consider the following declarations:

```
Inventory item1 = new Inventory();
Inventory item2 = new Inventory("Dryer");
Inventory item3 = new Inventory("Washer", 2345, 278.95);
Inventory item4 = new Inventory("Toaster", 8231, 34.49, 200);
```

For item1, the default constructor in the line labeled //Constructor 1 executes because no value is passed to this variable. For item2, the constructor in the line labeled //Constructor 2 executes because only one parameter, which is of type String, is passed and it matches with that constructor. For item3, the constructor in the line labeled //Constructor 3 executes because three parameters are passed to item3 and they match with that constructor. Similarly, for item4, the constructor in the line labeled //Constructor 4 executes (see Figure 8-14).

item1

name	⟶
itemNum	-1
price	0.0
unitsInStock	0

item2

name	⟶ Dryer
itemNum	-1
price	0.0
unitsInStock	0

item3

name	⟶ Washer
itemNum	2345
price	278.95
unitsInStock	0

item4

name	⟶ Toaster
itemNum	8231
price	34.49
unitsInStock	200

FIGURE 8-14   Effect of constructors on objects

 NOTE   If the values passed to a class object do not match the parameters of any constructor, and if no type conversion is possible, a compile-time error will be generated.

Classes and the Method `toString`

Suppose that **x** is an **int** variable and the value of **x** is 25. The statement:

`System.out.println(x);`

outputs:

25

However, the output of the statement:

`System.out.println(myClock);`

is:

`Clock@11b86e7`

which looks strange. (Note that when you execute a similar statement, you are likely to get a different but similar output.) This is because whenever you create a **class**, the Java system provides the method `toString` to that **class**. The method `toString` is used to convert an object to a **String** object. When an object reference is provided as a parameter to the methods `print`, `println`, and `printf`, the `toString` method is called.

The default definition of the method `toString` creates a string that is the name of the object's `class`, followed by the hash code of the object. For example, in the preceding statement, `Clock` is the name of the object `myClock`'s `class` and the hash code for the object referenced by `myClock` is `@11b86e7`.

The method `toString` is a `public` value-returning method. It does not take any parameters and returns the address of a `String` object. The heading of the method `toString` is:

```
public String toString()
```

You can *override* the default definition of the method `toString` to convert an object to a desired string. Suppose that for the objects of the `class Clock` you want the method `toString` to create the string hh:mm:ss—the string consists of the object's hour, minutes, seconds, and the colons as shown. The string created by the method `toString` is the same as the string output by the method `printTime` of the `class Clock`. This is easily accomplished by providing the following definition of the method `toString`:

```
public String toString()
{
    String str = "";

    if (hr < 10)
        str = "0";
    str = str + hr + ":";

    if (min < 10)
        str = str + "0" ;
    str = str + min + ":";

    if (sec < 10)
        str = str + "0";
    str = str + sec;

    return str;
}
```

In the preceding code, `str` is a `String` variable used to create the required string.

The preceding definition of the method `toString` must be included in the `class Clock`. In fact, after including the method `toString` in the `class Clock`, we can remove the method `printTime`. If the values of the instance variables `hr`, `min`, and `sec` of `myClock` are 8, 25, and 56, respectively, then the output of the statement:

```
System.out.println(myClock)
```

is:

```
08:25:56
```

You can see that the method `toString` is useful for outputting the values of the instance variables. Note that the method `toString` only returns the (formatted) string; the methods `print`, `println`, or `printf` output the string.

EXAMPLE 8-4

In this example, we give the complete definition of the **class** Circle, which was briefly discussed in the beginning of this chapter.

```
public class Circle
{
    private double radius;

    //Default constructor
    //Sets the radius to 0
    Circle()
    {
        radius = 0;
    }

    //Constructor with a parameter
    //Sets the radius to the value specified by the parameter r.
    Circle(double r)
    {
        radius = r;
    }

    //Method to set the radius of the circle.
    //Sets the radius to the value specified by the parameter r.
    public void setRadius(double r)
    {
        radius = r;
    }

    //Method to return the radius of the circle.
    //Returns the radius of the circle.
    public double getRadius()
    {
        return radius;
    }

    //Method to compute and return the area of the circle.
    //Computes and returns the area of the circle.
    public double area()
    {
        return Math.PI * Math.PI * radius;
    }

    //Method to compute and return the perimeter of the circle.
    //Computes and returns the area of the circle.
    public double perimeter()
    {
        return 2 * Math.PI * radius;
    }

    //Method to return the radius, area, perimeter of the circle
    //as a string.
```

```java
public String toString()
{
    return String.format("Radius = %.2f, Perimeter = %.2f"
                + ", Area = %.2f%n", radius, perimeter(),
                area());
}
}
```

We leave the UML class diagram of the `class` Circle as an exercise for you.

The following program shows how to use the `class` Circle in a program.

```java
// Program to test various operations of the class Circle.

import java.util.*;                                       //Line 1

public class TestProgCircle                               //Line 2
{                                                         //Line 3
    static Scanner console = new Scanner(System.in);      //Line 4

    public static void main(String[] args)                //Line 5
    {                                                     //Line 6
        Circle firstCircle = new Circle();                //Line 7
        Circle secondCircle = new Circle(12);             //Line 8

        double radius;                                    //Line 9

        System.out.println("Line 10: firstCircle: "
                    + firstCircle);                       //Line 10

        System.out.println("Line 11: secondCircle: "
                    + secondCircle);                      //Line 11

        System.out.print("Line 12: Enter the radius: ");  //Line 12
        radius = console.nextDouble();                    //Line 13
        System.out.println();                             //Line 14

        firstCircle.setRadius(radius);                    //Line 15

        System.out.println("Line 16: firstCircle: "
                    + firstCircle );                      //Line 16

        if (firstCircle.getRadius()
                > secondCircle.getRadius())               //Line 17
            System.out.println("Line 18: The radius of "
                + "the first circle is greater than "
                + "the radius of the second circle. ");   //Line 18
        else if (firstCircle.getRadius()
                < secondCircle.getRadius())               //Line 19
            System.out.println("Line 20: The radius of "
                + "the first circle is less than the "
                + "radius of the second circle. ");       //Line 20
```

8

```
        else                                          //Line 21
            System.out.println("Line 22: The radius of "
                + "both the circles are the same.");   //Line 22
    }//end main                                        //Line 23
}                                                      //Line 24
```

Sample Run: (In this sample run, the user input is shaded.)

```
Line 10: firstCircle: Radius = 0.00, Perimeter = 0.00, Area = 0.00

Line 11: secondCircle: Radius = 12.00, Perimeter = 75.40, Area = 118.44

Line 12: Enter the radius: 10

Line 16: firstCircle: Radius = 10.00, Perimeter = 62.83, Area = 98.70

Line 20: The radius of the first circle is less than the radius of the
second circle.
```

The preceding program works as follows. The statement in Line 7 creates the object firstCircle and using the default constructor sets the radius to 0. The statement in Line 8 creates the object secondCircle and sets the radius to 12. The statement in Line 9 declares the **double** variable radius. The statement in Line 10 outputs the radius, area, and perimeter of the firstCircle. Similarly, the statement in Line 11 outputs the radius, area, and perimeter of the secondCircle The statement in Line 12 prompts the user to enter the value of radius. The statement in Line 13 stores the value entered by the user in the variable radius. The statement in Line 15 uses the value of radius to set the radius of firstCircle. The statement in Line 16 outputs the radius, area, and perimeter of the firstCircle. The statements in Lines 17 to 23 compare the radius of firstCircle and secondCircle and output the appropriate result.

EXAMPLE 8-5

In Example 7–3, the method rollDice rolls a pair of dice until the sum of the numbers rolled is a given number and returns the number of times the dice are rolled to get the desired sum. In fact, we can design a class that implements the basic properties of a die. Consider the definition of the following **class** RollDie.

```
public class RollDie
{
    private int num;

        //Default constructor
        //Sets the default number rolled by a die to 1
    RollDie()
    {
        num = 1;
    }
```

```
    //Method to roll a die.
    //This method uses a random number generator to randomly
    //generate a number between 1 and 6, and stores the number
    //in the instance variable num and returns the number.
    public int roll()
    {
        num = (int) (Math.random() * 6) + 1;

        return num;
    }

    //Method to return the number on the top face of the die.
    //Returns the value of the instance variable num.
    public int getNum()
    {
        return num;
    }

    //Returns the value of the instance variable num as a string.
    public String toString()
    {
        return "" + num;
    }
}
```

We leave the UML class diagram of the `class` `RollDie` as an exercise for you.

The following program shows how to use the `class` `RollDie` in a program:

```
// Program to test various operations of the class RollDie.

import java.util.*;                                    //Line 1

public class TestProgRollDie                           //Line 2
{                                                      //Line 3
    static Scanner console = new Scanner(System.in);   //Line 4

    public static void main(String[] args)             //Line 5
    {                                                  //Line 6
        RollDie die1 = new RollDie();                  //Line 7
        RollDie die2 = new RollDie();                  //Line 8

        System.out.println("Line 9: die1: " + die1);   //Line 9

        System.out.println("Line 10: die2: " + die2);  //Line 10

        System.out.println("Line 11: After rolling "
                    + "die1: " + die1.roll());          //Line 11

        System.out.println("Line 12: After rolling "
                    + "die2: " + die2.roll());          //Line 12

        System.out.println("Line 13: Sum of the "
                + "numbers rolled by the dice is: "
                + (die1.getNum() + die2.getNum()));     //Line 13
```

8

```
          System.out.println("Line 14: After again rolling "
                    + "the sum of the numbers rolled is: "
                    + (die1.roll() + die2.roll()));         //Line 14
      }//end main                                           //Line 15
}                                                           //Line 16
```

Sample Run:

```
Line 9: die1: 1
Line 10: die2: 1
Line 11: After rolling die1: 5
Line 12: After rolling die2: 3
Line 13: Sum of the numbers rolled by the dice is: 8
Line 14: After again rolling the sum of the numbers rolled is: 4
```

The preceding program works as follows. The statements in Lines 7 and 8 create the objects die1 and die2, and using the default constructor set both the dice to 1. The statements in Lines 9 and 10 output the number of both the dice. The statement in Line 11 rolls die1 and outputs the number rolled. Similarly, the statement in Line 12 rolls die2 and outputs the number rolled. The statement in Line 13 outputs the sum of the numbers rolled by die1 and die2. The statement in Line 14 again rolls both the dice and outputs the sum of the numbers rolled.

Copy Constructor

Suppose that you have the following statement:

```
Clock myClock = new Clock(8, 45, 22);         //Line 1
```

You can use the object myClock to declare and instantiate another Clock object. Consider the following statement:

```
Clock aClock = new Clock(myClock);            //Line 2
```

This statement declares aClock to be a reference variable of type Clock, instantiates the object aClock, and initializes the instance variables of the object aClock using the values of the corresponding instance variables of the object myClock. However, to successfully execute the statement in Line 2, you need to include a special constructor, called a **copy constructor**, in the class Clock. The copy constructor executes when an object is instantiated and initialized using an existing object.

The syntax of the heading of the copy constructor is:

```
public ClassName(ClassName otherObject)
```

For example, the heading of the copy constructor for the class Clock is:

```
public Clock(Clock otherClock)
```

The definition of the copy constructor for the **class** Clock is:

```
public Clock(Clock otherClock)
{
    hr = otherClock.hr;
    min = otherClock.min;
    sec = otherClock.sec;
}
```

If you include this definition of the copy constructor in the **class** Clock, then the statement in Line 2 declares aClock to be a reference variable of type Clock, instantiates the object aClock, and initializes the instance variables of the object aClock using the values of the instance variables of the object myClock.

> **NOTE** The definition of the copy constructor of the **class** Clock can also be written as:
>
> ```
> public Clock(Clock otherClock)
> {
>     setTime(otherClock.hr, otherClock.min, otherClock.sec);
> }
> ```

The copy constructor is useful and will be included in most of the classes.

Static Members of a Class

In Chapter 7, we described the **class**es Math and Character. In Example 7-1 (of Chapter 7), we used several methods of the **class**es Math and Character; however, we did not need to create any objects to use these methods. We simply used the import statement:

```
import static java.lang.Math.*;
```

and then called the method with an appropriate actual parameter list. For example, to use the method pow of the **class** Math, we used expressions such as:

```
pow(5, 3)
```

Recall from Chapter 7 that if you are using versions of Java lower than Java 5.0 or you do not include the preceding **import** statement, then you call the method pow as follows:

```
Math.pow(5, 3)
```

That is, we can simply call the method using the name of the class and the dot operator.

We cannot use the same approach with the **class** Clock. Although the methods of the **class** Math are **public**, they also are defined using the modifier **static**. For example, the heading of the method pow of the **class** Math is:

```
public static double pow(double base, double exponent)
```

The modifier **static** in the heading specifies that the method can be invoked by using the name of the **class**. Similarly, if a data member of a **class** is declared using the modifier **static**, it can be accessed by using the name of the **class**.

The following example clarifies the effect of the modifier `static`.

EXAMPLE 8-6

Consider the following definition of the `class Illustrate`:

```
public class Illustrate
{
    private int x;
    private static int y;
    public static int count;

        //Default constructor
        //Postcondition: x = 0;
    public Illustrate()
    {
        x = 0;
    }

        //Constructor with parameters
        //Postcondition: x = a;
    public Illustrate(int a)
    {
        x = a;
    }

        //Method to set x.
        //Postcondition: x = a;
    void setX(int a)
    {
        x = a;
    }

        //Method to return the values of the instance
        //and static variables as a string
        //The string returned is used by the methods
        //print, println, or printf to print the values
        //of the instance and static variables.
        //Postcondition: The values of x, y, and count
        //are returned as a string.
    public String toString()
    {
        return("x = " + x + ", y = " + y
            + ", count = " + count);
    }

        //Method to increment the value of the private
        //static member y
        //Postcondition: y is incremented by 1.
```

```
    public static void incrementY()
    {
        y++;
    }
}
```

Suppose that you have the following declaration:

```
Illustrate illusObject = new Illustrate();
```

The reference variable `illusObject` can access any `public` member of the `class` `Illustrate`.

The method `incrementY` is `static` and `public`, so the following statement is legal:

```
Illustrate.incrementY();
```

Similarly, because the data member `count` is `static` and `public`, the following statement is legal:

```
Illustrate.count++;
```

In essence, `public static` members of a `class` can be accessed either by an object, that is, by using a reference variable of the `class` type, or using the `class` name and the dot operator.

static **Variables (Data Members) of a Class**

Suppose that you have a `class`, say, `MyClass`, with data members (`static` and non-`static`). When you instantiate the objects of type `MyClass`, only the non-`static` data members of the `class` `MyClass` become the data members of each object. What about the memory for the `static` data members of `MyClass`? For each `static` data member of the `class`, Java allocates memory space only once. All `MyClass` objects refer to the same memory space. In fact, `static` data members of a `class` *exist* even when no object of the `class` type is instantiated. Moreover, `static` variables are initialized to their default values. You can access the `public static` data members outside the `class`, as explained in the previous section.

The following example further clarifies how memory space is allocated for `static` and non-`static` data members of a class.

Suppose that you have the `class` `Illustrate`, as given in Example 8-6. Then, memory space exists for the `static` data members `y` and `count`.

Consider the following statements:

```
Illustrate illusObject1 = new Illustrate(3);    //Line 1
Illustrate illusObject2 = new Illustrate(5);    //Line 2
```

The statements in Lines 1 and 2 declare `illusObject1` and `illusObject2` to be reference variables of type `Illustrate` and instantiate these objects (see Figure 8-15).

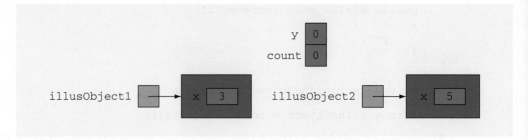

FIGURE 8-15 illusObject1 and illusObject2

Now consider the following statement:

```
Illustrate.incrementY();
Illustrate.count++;
```

After these statements execute, the objects and static members are as shown in Figure 8-16.

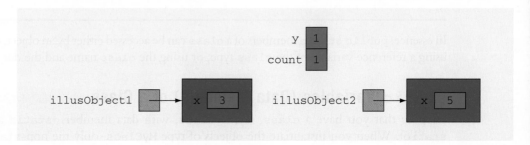

FIGURE 8-16 illusObject1 and illusObject2 after the statements Illustrate.incrementY(); and Illustrate.count++; execute

The output of the statement:

```
System.out.println(illusObject1);
```

is:

```
x = 3, y = 1, count = 1
```

Similarly, the output of the statement:

```
System.out.println(illusObject2);
```

is:

```
x = 5, y = 1, count = 1
```

Now consider the statement:

```
Illustrate.count++;
```

After this statement executes, the objects and static members are as shown in Figure 8-17.

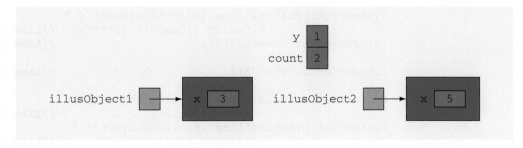

FIGURE 8-17 illusObject1 and illusObject2 after the statement Illustrate.count++; executes

The output of the statements:

```
System.out.println(illusObject1);
System.out.println(illusObject2);
```

is:

```
x = 3, y = 1, count = 2
x = 5, y = 1, count = 2
```

The program in Example 8-7 further illustrates how **static** members of a class work.

EXAMPLE 8-7

```
public class StaticMembers
{
    public static void main(String[] args)
    {
        Illustrate illusObject1 = new Illustrate(3);    //Line 1
        Illustrate illusObject2 = new Illustrate(5);    //Line 2

        Illustrate.incrementY();                        //Line 3
        Illustrate.count++;                             //Line 4

        System.out.println("Line 5: illusObject1: "
                        + illusObject1);                //Line 5
        System.out.println("Line 6: illusObject2: "
                        + illusObject2);                //Line 6

        System.out.println("Line 7: ***Increment y "
                        + "using illusObject1***");     //Line 7
        illusObject1.incrementY();                      //Line 8

        illusObject1.setX(8);                           //Line 9

        System.out.println("Line 10: illusObject1: "
                        + illusObject1);                //Line 10
```

8

```
        System.out.println("Line 11: illusObject2: "
                    + illusObject2);                  //Line 11

        System.out.println("Line 12: ***Increment y "
                    + "using illusObject2***");        //Line 12
        illusObject2.incrementY();                     //Line 13

        illusObject2.setX(23);                         //Line 14

        System.out.println("Line 15: illusObject1: "
                    + illusObject1);                   //Line 15
        System.out.println("Line 16: illusObject2: "
                    + illusObject2);                   //Line 16
    }
}
```

Sample Run:

```
Line 5: illusObject1: x = 3, y = 1, count = 1
Line 6: illusObject2: x = 5, y = 1, count = 1
Line 7: ***Increment y using illusObject1***
Line 10: illusObject1: x = 8, y = 2, count = 1
Line 11: illusObject2: x = 5, y = 2, count = 1
Line 12: ***Increment y using illusObject2***
Line 15: illusObject1: x = 8, y = 3, count = 1
Line 16: illusObject2: x = 23, y = 3, count = 1
```

The preceding program works as follows: The `static` data members `y` and `count` are initialized to 0. The statements in Lines 1 and 2 create the `Illustrate` objects `illusObject1` and `illusObject2`. The instance variable `x` of `illusObject1` is initialized to 3; the instance variable `x` of `illusObject2` is initialized to 5.

The statement in Line 3 uses the name of the `class Illustrate` and the method `incrementY` to increment `y`. Because `count` is a `public static` member of the `class Illustrate`, the statement in Line 4 uses the name of the `class Illustrate` to directly access `count`, and increments it by 1. The statements in Lines 5 and 6 output the data stored in the objects `illusObject1` and `illusObject2`. Note that the value of `y` for both objects is the same. Similarly, the value of `count` for both objects is the same.

The statement in Line 7 is an output statement. The statement in Line 8 uses the object `illusObject1` and the method `incrementY` to increment `y`. The statement in Line 9 sets the value of the instance variable `x` of `illusObject1` to 8. Lines 10 and 11 output the data stored in the objects `illusObject1` and `illusObject2`. Note that the value of `y` for both objects is the same. Similarly, the value of `count` for both objects is the same. Moreover, notice that the statement in Line 9 only changes the value of the instance variable `x` of `illusObject1` because `x` is *not* a `static` member of the `class Illustrate`.

The statement in Line 13 uses the object `illusObject2` and the method `incrementY` to increment `y`. The statement in Line 14 sets the value of the instance variable `x` of `illusObject2` to 23. Lines 15 and 16 output the data stored in the objects `illusObject1` and `illusObject2`. Notice that the value of `y` for both objects is the same. Similarly, the value of count for both objects is the same. Note that the statement in Line 14 only changes the value of the instance variable x of illusObject2 because x is *not* a static member of the class Illustrate.

> **NOTE** Here are some additional comments on static members of a class. As you have seen in this section, a static method of a class does not need any object to be invoked. It can be called using the name of the class and the dot operator. Therefore, a static method cannot use anything that depends on a calling object. In other words, in the definition of a static method, you cannot use a non-static data member or a non-static method, unless there is a locally declared object that accesses the non-static data member or the non-static method.

Finalizers

Like constructors, **finalizers** are also special types of methods. However, a finalizer is a void method. A class can have only one finalizer, and the finalizer cannot have any parameters. The name of the finalizer is finalize. The method finalize automatically executes when the class object goes out of scope. A typical use of a finalizer is to free up the memory allocated by the object of a class.

Accessor and Mutator Methods

Earlier in this chapter, we defined the terms mutator method and accessor method. This section discusses these terms in detail and explains why such methods are needed to construct a class.

Let us look at the methods of the class Clock. The method setTime sets the values of the data members to the values specified by the user. In other words, it alters or modifies the values of the instance variables. Similarly, the methods incrementHours, incrementMinutes, and incrementSeconds also modify the instance variables. However, methods such as getHours, getMinutes, getSeconds, printTime, and equals only access the values of the data members; they *do not* modify the data members. We can, therefore, divide the methods of the class Clock into two categories: methods that modify the data members, and methods that access, but do not modify, the data members.

This is typically true for any class. That is, almost every class has methods that only access and do not modify the data members, called **accessor methods**, and methods that modify the data members, called **mutator methods**.

Accessor Method: A method of a class that only accesses (that is, does not modify) the value(s) of the data member(s).

Mutator Method: A method of a class that modifies the value(s) of one or more data member(s).

8

Typically, the instance variables of a class are declared `private` so that the user of a class does not have direct access to them. In general, every class has a set of accessor methods to work with the instance variables. If the data members need to be modified, then the class also has a set of mutator methods. Conventionally, mutator methods begin with the word `set` and accessor methods begin with the word `get`. You might wonder why we need both mutator and accessor methods when we can simply make the instance variables `public`. However, look closely, for example, at the mutator method `setTime` of the `class` `Clock`. Before setting the time, it validates the time. On the other hand, if the instance variables are all `public`, then the user of the class can put any values in the instance variables. Similarly, the accessor methods only return the value(s) of an instance variable(s); that is, they do not modify the values. A well-designed class uses `private` instance variables, accessor methods, and (if needed) mutator methods to implement the OOD principle of encapsulation.

Example 8-8 further illustrates how classes are designed and implemented. The `class` `Person` that we create in this example is very useful; we will use this `class` in subsequent chapters.

EXAMPLE 8-8

Two common attributes of a person are the person's first name and last name. The typical operations on a person's name are to set the name and print the name. The following statements define a `class` with these properties (see Figure 8-18).

```
public class Person
{
    private String firstName; //store the first name
    private String lastName;  //store the last name

        //Default constructor;
        //Initialize firstName and lastName to empty string.
        //Postcondition: firstName = ""; lastName = "";
    public Person()
    {
        firstName = "";
        lastName = "";
    }

        //Constructor with parameters
        //Set firstName and lastName according to the parameters.
        //Postcondition: firstName = first; lastName = last;
    public Person(String first, String last)
    {
        setName(first, last);
    }
```

```
    //Method to output the first name and last name
    //in the form firstName lastName
public String toString()
{
    return (firstName + " " + lastName);
}

    //Method to set firstName and lastName according to
    //the parameters
    //Postcondition: firstName = first; lastName = last;
public void setName(String first, String last)
{
    firstName = first;
    lastName = last;
}

    //Method to return the firstName
    //Postcondition: the value of firstName is returned
public String getFirstName()
{
    return firstName;
}

    //Method to return the lastName
    //Postcondition: the value of lastName is returned
public String getLastName()
{
    return lastName;
}
}
```

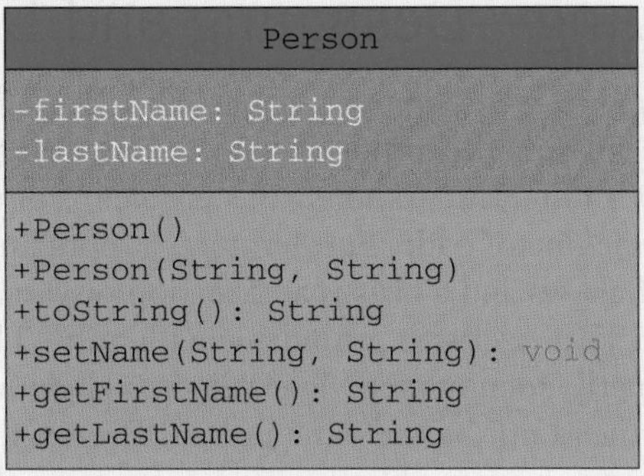

FIGURE 8-18 UML class diagram of the **class** Person

The following program tests the **class** Person:

```java
public class TestProgPerson
{
    public static void main(String[] args)
    {
        Person name = new Person();                    //Line 1

        Person emp = new Person("Donald", "Jackson");  //Line 2

        System.out.println("Line 3: name: " + name);   //Line 3

        name.setName("Ashley", "Blair");               //Line 4
        System.out.println("Line 5: name: " + name);   //Line 5

        System.out.println("Line 6: emp: " + emp);     //Line 6

        emp.setName("Sandy", "Smith");                 //Line 7
        System.out.println("Line 8: emp: " + emp);     //Line 8
    }//end main
}
```

Sample Run:

```
Line 3: name:
Line 5: name: Ashley Blair
Line 6: emp: Donald Jackson
Line 8: emp: Sandy Smith
```

DEBUGGING

Debugging—Designing and Documenting a Class

Before moving to the design phase, a problem must be thoroughly understood so that the focus is on solving the problem. As emphasized in earlier chapters, especially, as a beginner we must learn to solve the problem completely on a piece of paper before writing a single line of code. Furthermore, as noted in earlier chapters, a Java program is a collection of classes and a class is a collection of variables, methods, and sometimes other classes. So in Java, a class is a fundamental entity. Therefore, once a class is designed, it must be properly documented. Typically in a large project, the designer of a class and the programmer need not be the same person. Even if the designer and the programmer are the same person, it is possible that after some time the person currently working on the problem may move to another project or even to a different job. So the person replacing the person leaving must know exactly what the designer intended to do with the class. Therefore, it is very important to document the class so that it can be correctly programmed in Java, and if needed, in the future it can be modified.

This chapter spent a considerable amount of time designing the **class** Clock. In order to design this class, first we identified the operations and determined that each operation must be implemented using a method. We then identified the data members and their types. We also identified which member should be **public** and which should be **private**. Following the syntax of a method heading, we specified the heading of each method and briefly explained what the method should do. Some methods can be implemented using a single line of code, while others may require a complicated algorithm. In either case, an algorithm must be designed and documented to implement a method. Typically, as shown in the programming example in Chapter 7, the algorithm to implement a method can be written as a pseudocode, which is a mixture of English and the Java language. The means of describing the algorithm is not as important as the clarity of the algorithm. The algorithm should be sufficiently clear so that a programmer can code the algorithm in Java without having to make any further decisions about how to solve the problem.

One way to specify the design of the **class** Clock is:

```java
public class Clock
{
        //data members
    private int hr;
    private int min;
    private int sec;

    //methods

    public Clock()
    {
        // default constructor
        // set time to 0,0,0
    }

    public Clock(int hours, int minutes, int seconds)
    {
        // constructor with parameters
        // set time according to the parameters
    }

    public void setTime(int hours, int minutes, int seconds)
    {
        // set time according to the parameters

    }

    public int getHours()
    {
        // return hr
    }
```

8

```
public int getHours()
{
    //return hr
}

// Similarly document other methods.
}
```

You can write the Java code of the **class** Clock using this specification. You can also specify the design of a class as it is shown in the programming example, Candy Machine, later in this chapter. To become an effective and good programmer, you must avoid the temptation to skip the design phase. It is possible that the first few programs that you write can be coded directly. However, in general, this approach only works for very small programs. As a matter of fact, you will spend less time implementing, debugging, and maintaining a code that is properly designed and documented.

Reference `this` (Optional)

In this chapter, we defined the **class** Clock. Suppose that myClock is a reference variable of type Clock. Suppose that the object myClock has been created. Consider the following statements:

```
myClock.setTime(5, 6, 59);          //Line 1
myClock.incrementSeconds();         //Line 2
```

The statement in Line 1 uses the method setTime to set the instance variables hr, min, and sec of the object myClock to 5, 6, and 59, respectively. The statement in Line 2 uses the method incrementSeconds to increment the time of the object myClock by one second. The statement in Line 2 also results in a call to the method incrementMinutes because, after incrementing the value of sec by 1, the value of sec becomes 60, which then is reset to 0, and the method incrementMinutes is invoked.

How do you think Java makes sure that the statement in Line 1 sets the instance variables of the object myClock and not of another Clock object? How does Java make sure that when the method incrementSeconds calls the method incrementMinutes, the method incrementMinutes increments the value of the instance variable min of the object myClock and not of another Clock object?

The answer is that every object has access to a reference of itself. The name of this reference is this. In Java, this is a reserved word.

Java implicitly uses the reference this to refer to both the instance variables and the methods of a class. Recall that the definition of the method setTime is:

```
public void setTime(int hours, int minutes, int seconds)
{
    if (0 <= hours && hours < 24)
        hr = hours;
    else
        hr = 0;

    if (0 <= minutes && minutes < 60)
        min = minutes;
    else
        min = 0;

    if (0 <= seconds && seconds < 60)
        sec = seconds;
    else
        sec = 0;
}
```

In the method `setTime`, the statement:

```
hr = hours;
```

is, in fact, equivalent to the statement:

```
this.hr = hours;
```

In this statement, the reference **this** is used explicitly. You can explicitly use the reference **this** and write the equivalent definition of the method `setTime` as follows:

```
public void setTime(int hr, int min, int sec)
{
    if (0 <= hr && hr < 24)
        this.hr = hr;
    else
        this.hr = 0;

    if (0 <= min && min < 60)
        this.min = min;
    else
        this.min = 0;

    if (0 <= sec && sec < 60)
        this.sec = sec;
    else
        this.sec = 0;
}
```

Notice that in the preceding definition of the method `setTime`, the name of the formal parameters and the name of the instance variables are the same. In this definition of the method `setTime`, the expression `this.hr` means the instance variable `hr`, not the formal parameter `hr`, and so on. Because the code explicitly uses the reference **this**, the compiler can distinguish between the instance variables and the formal parameters. Of

8

course, you could have kept the name of the formal parameters as before and still used the reference `this` as shown in the code.

Similarly, explicitly using the reference `this`, you can write the definition of the method `incrementSeconds` as follows:

```
public void incrementSeconds()
{
    this.sec++;

    if (this.sec > 59)
    {
        this.sec = 0;
        this.incrementMinutes(); //increment minutes
    }
}
```

Cascaded Method Calls (Optional)

In addition to explicitly referring to the instance variables and methods of an object, the reference `this` has another use—to implement cascaded method calls. We explain this with the help of an example.

In Example 8-8, we designed the `class Person` to implement a person's name in a program. Here, we extend the definition of the `class Person` to individually set a person's first name and last name, and then return a reference to the object, using `this`. The following code is the extended definition of the `class Person`. (The methods `setFirstName` and `setLastName` are added to this definition of the `class Person`.)

```
public class Person
{
    private String firstName; //store the first name
    private String lastName;  //store the last name

        //Default constructor;
        //Initialize firstName and lastName to empty string.
        //Postcondition: firstName = ""; lastName = "";
    public Person()
    {
        firstName = "";
        lastName = "";
    }

        //Constructor with parameters
        //Set firstName and lastName according to the parameters.
        //Postcondition: firstName = first; lastName = last;
    public Person(String first, String last)
    {
        setName(first, last);
    }
```

```
    //Method to return the first name and last name
    //in the form firstName lastName
public String toString()
{
    return (firstName + " " + lastName);
}


    //Method to set firstName and lastName according to
    //the parameters
    //Postcondition: firstName = first; lastName = last;
public void setName(String first, String last)
{
    firstName = first;
    lastName = last;
}


    //Method to set the last name
    //Postcondition: lastName = last;
    //        After setting the last name, a reference
    //        of the object is returned.
public Person setLastName(String last)
{
    lastName = last;

    return this;
}

    //Method to set the first name
    //Postcondition: firstName = first;
    //        After setting the first name, a reference
    //        of the object is returned.
public Person setFirstName(String first)
{
    firstName = first;

    return this;
}

    //Method to return the firstName
    //Postcondition: the value of firstName is returned
public String getFirstName()
{
    return firstName;
}

    //Method to return the lastName
    //Postcondition: the value of lastName is returned
public String getLastName()
{
    return lastName;
}
}
```

Consider the following method `main`:

```
public class CascadedMethodCalls
{
    public static void main(String[] args)
    {
        Person student1 =
                new Person("Angela", "Smith");          //Line 1

        Person student2 = new Person();                 //Line 2

        Person student3 = new Person();                 //Line 3
        System.out.println("Line 4 -- Student 1: "
                            + student1);                //Line 4

        student2.setFirstName("Shelly").
                        setLastName("Malik");           //Line 5

        System.out.println("Line 6 -- Student 2: "
                            + student2);                //Line 6

        student3.setFirstName("Chelsea");               //Line 7

        System.out.println("Line 8 -- Student 3: "
                            + student3);                //Line 8

        student3.setLastName("Tomek");                  //Line 9

        System.out.println("Line 10 -- Student 3: "
                            + student3);                //Line 10

    }
}
```

Sample Run:

```
Line 4 -- Student 1: Angela Smith
Line 6 -- Student 2: Shelly Malik
Line 8 -- Student 3: Chelsea
Line 10 -- Student 3: Chelsea Tomek
```

The statements in Lines 1, 2, and 3 declare the variables `student1`, `student2`, and `student3` and also instantiate the objects. The instance variables of the objects `student2` and `student3` are initialized to empty strings. The statement in Line 4 outputs the value of `student1`. The statement in Line 5 works as follows. In the statement:

```
student2.setFirstName("Shelly").setLastName("Malik");
```

first the expression:

```
student2.setFirstName("Shelly")
```

is executed because the associativity of the dot operator is from left to right. This expression sets the first name to `"Shelly"` and returns a reference to the object, which is the object `student2`. Thus, the next expression executed is:

```
student2.setLastName("Malik")
```

which sets the last name of the object `student2` to `"Malik"`. The statement in Line 6 outputs the value of `student2`. The statement in Line 7 sets the first name of `student3` to `"Chelsea"`, and the statement in Line 8 outputs `student3`. Notice the output in Line 8. The output shows only the first name, not the last name, because we have not yet set the last name of the object `student3`. The last name of the object `student3` is still empty, which was set by the statement in Line 3 when `student3` was declared. Next, the statement in Line 9 sets the last name of the object `student3`, and the statement in Line 10 outputs `student3`.

Inner Classes

The classes defined thus far in this chapter are said to have file scope, that is, they are contained within a file, but not within another class. In Chapter 6, while designing the `class RectangleProgram`, we defined the `class CalculateButtonHandler` to handle an action event. The definition of the `class CalculateButtonHandler` is contained within the `class RectangleProgram`. Classes that are defined within other classes are called **inner classes**.

An inner class can be either a complete class definition, such as the `class CalculateButtonHandler`, or an anonymous inner class definition. Anonymous classes are classes with no name.

One of the main uses of inner classes is to handle events—as we did in Chapter 6. A full discussion of inner classes is beyond the scope of this book. In this book, our main use of inner classes is to handle events in a GUI program. For example, see the programming example in Chapter 6 and the GUI part of the programming example in this chapter.

Abstract Data Types

To help you understand an abstract data type (ADT) and how it might be used, we'll provide an analogy. The following items seem unrelated:

- A deck of playing cards
- A set of index cards containing contact information
- Telephone numbers stored in your cellular phone

All three of these items share the following structural properties:

- Each one is a collection of elements.
- There is a first element.

8

- There is a second element, third element, and so on.
- There is a last element.
- Given an element other than the last element, there is a "next" element.
- Given an element other than the first element, there is a "previous" element.
- An element can be removed from the collection.
- An element can be added to the collection.
- A specified element can be located in the collection by systematically going through the collection.

In your programs, you may want to keep a collection of various elements, such as addresses, students, employees, departments, and projects. This structure commonly appears in various applications, and it is worth studying in its own right. We call this organization a *list*, which is an example of an ADT.

There is a data type called `Vector` (discussed in Chapter 9) with basic operations such as:

- Insert an item.
- Delete an item.
- Find an item.

You can use a `Vector` object to create an address book. You would not need to write a program to insert an address, delete an address, or find an item in your address book. Java also allows you to create your own abstract data types through classes.

An ADT is an abstraction of a commonly appearing data structure, along with a set of defined operations on the data structure.

Abstract data type (ADT): A data type that specifies the logical properties without concern for the implementation details.

Historically, the concept of ADT in computer programming developed as a way of abstracting the common data structure and the associated operations. Along the way, ADT provided **information hiding**. That is, ADT *hides* the implementation details of the operations and the data from the users of the ADT. Users can use the operations of an ADT without knowing how the operation is implemented.

PROGRAMMING EXAMPLE: Candy Machine

A new candy machine is bought for the cafeteria and a program is needed to make the machine function properly. The machine sells candies, chips, gum, and cookies. In this programming example, we write a program to create a Java application program for the candy machine so that it can be put into operation.

We implement this program in two ways. First, we show how to design a non-GUI application program. Then, we show how to design an application program that will create a GUI to make the candy machine operational.

The non-GUI application program should do the following:

1. Show the customer the different products sold by the candy machine.
2. Let the customer make the selection.
3. Show the customer the cost of the item selected.
4. Accept the money from the customer.
5. Release the item.

Input: The item selection and the cost of the item

Output: The selected item

In the next section, we design the candy machine's basic components, which are required by either type of application program—GUI or non-GUI. The difference between the two types is evident when we write the main program to put the candy machine into operation.

PROBLEM ANALYSIS AND ALGORITHM DESIGN

A candy machine has three main components: a built-in cash register, several dispensers to hold and release the products, and the candy machine itself. Therefore, we need to define a class to implement the cash register, a class to implement the dispenser, and a class to implement the candy machine. First, we describe the classes to implement the cash register and dispenser, and then we use these classes to describe the candy machine.

Cash Register

Let's first discuss the properties of a cash register. The register has some cash on hand, it accepts the amount from the customer, and if the amount entered is more than the cost of the item, then—if possible—it returns the change. For simplicity, we assume that the user enters the exact amount for the product. The cash register should also be able to show the candy machine's owner the amount of money in the register at any given time. Let's call the class implementing the cash register CashRegister.

The members of the **class** `CashRegister` are listed below and shown in Figure 8-19.

Instance
Variables

```
private int cashOnHand;
```

Constructors
and Methods

```
public CashRegister()
    //Default constructor
    //To set the cash in the register 500 cents
    //Postcondition: cashOnHand = 500;

public CashRegister(int cashIn)
    //Constructor with parameters
    //Postcondition: cashOnHand = cashIn;

public int currentBalance()
    //Method to show the current amount in the cash register
    //Postcondition: The value of the instance variable
    //               cashOnHand is returned

public void acceptAmount(int amountIn)
    //Method to receive the amount deposited by
    //the customer and update the amount in the register
    //Postcondition: cashOnHand = cashOnHand + amountIn
```

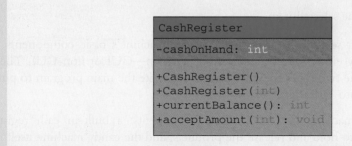

FIGURE 8-19 UML class diagram of the **class** `CashRegister`

Next, we give the definitions of the methods to implement the operations of the **class** `CashRegister`. The definitions of these methods are simple and easy to follow.

The method `currentBalance` shows the current amount in the cash register. The amount stored in the cash register is in cents. Its definition is:

```
public int currentBalance()
{
    return cashOnHand;
}
```

The method `acceptAmount` accepts the amount entered by the customer. It updates the cash in the register by adding the amount entered by the customer to the previous amount in the cash register. The definition of this method is:

```
public void acceptAmount(int amountIn)
{
    cashOnHand = cashOnHand + amountIn;
}
```

The constructor with the parameter sets the value of the instance variable to the value specified by the user. The value is passed as a parameter to the constructor. The definition of the constructor with the parameter is:

```
public CashRegister(int cashIn)
{
    if (cashIn >= 0)
        cashOnHand = cashIn;
    else
        cashOnHand = 500;
}
```

Note that the definition of the constructor checks for valid values of the parameter `cashIn`. If the value of `cashIn` is less than 0, the value assigned to the instance variable `cashOnHand` is 500.

The default constructor sets the value of the instance variable `cashOnHand` to 500 cents. Its definition is:

```
public CashRegister()
{
    cashOnHand = 500;
}
```

Now that we have the definitions of all the methods necessary to implement the operations of the `class` `CashRegister`, we can give the definition of `CashRegister`. Its definition is:

```
//class cashRegister

public class CashRegister
{
    private int cashOnHand;    //variable to store the cash
                               //in the register

        //Default constructor to set the cash
        //in the register to 500 cents
        //Postcondition: cashOnHand = 500
    public CashRegister()
    {
        cashOnHand = 500;
    }
```

8

```
              //Constructor with parameters to set the cash in
              //the register to a specific amount
              //Postcondition: cashOnHand = cashIn
        public CashRegister(int cashIn)
        {
           if (cashIn >= 0)
                cashOnHand = cashIn;
           else
              cashOnHand = 500;
        }

              //Method to show the current amount in the cash register
              //Postcondition: The value of the instance variable
              //               cashOnHand is returned.
        public int currentBalance()
        {
            return cashOnHand;
        }

              //Method to receive the amount deposited by
              //the customer and update the amount in the register
              //Postcondition: cashOnHand = cashOnHand + amountIn
        public void acceptAmount(int amountIn)
        {
            cashOnHand = cashOnHand + amountIn;
        }
    }
```

Dispenser The dispenser releases the selected item if it is not empty. It should show the number of items in the dispenser and the cost of the item. Let's call the class implementing a dispenser `Dispenser`. The members necessary to implement the `class Dispenser` are listed next and shown in Figure 8-20.

Instance Variables

```
private int numberOfItems; //variable to store the number of
                           //items in the dispenser

private int cost;  //variable to store the cost of an item
```

Constructors and Methods

```
public Dispenser()
   //Default constructor to set the cost and number of
   //items to the default values
   //Postcondition: numberOfItems = 50; cost = 50;

public Dispenser(int setNoOfItems, int setCost)
   //Constructor with parameters to set the cost and number
   //of items in the dispenser specified by the user
   //Postcondition: numberOfItems = setNoOfItems;
   //               cost = setCost;
```

```
public int getCount()
   //Method to show the number of items in the dispenser
   //Postcondition: The value of the instance variable
   //               numberOfItems is returned

public int getProductCost()
   //Method to show the cost of the item
   //Postcondition: The value of the instance
   //               variable cost is returned

public void makeSale()
   //Method to reduce the number of items by 1
   //Postcondition: numberOfItems = numberOfItems - 1;
```

```
                    Dispenser

          -numberOfItems: int
          -cost: int

          +Dispenser()
          +Dispenser(int, int)
          +getCount(): int
          +getProductCost(): int
          +makeSale(): void
```

FIGURE 8-20 UML class diagram of the **class** Dispenser

Because the candy machine sells four types of items, we will create four objects of type Dispenser. The statement:

```
Dispenser chips = new Dispenser(100, 65);
```

creates the object chips, sets the number of chip bags in this dispenser to 100, and sets the cost of each chip bag to 65 cents (see Figure 8-21).

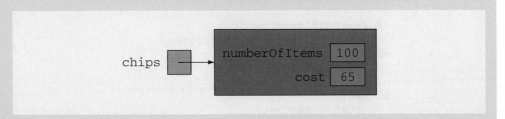

FIGURE 8-21 The object chips

Next, we discuss the definitions of the methods to implement the operations of the class Dispenser.

The method getCount returns the number of items of a particular product. Because the number of items currently in the dispenser is stored in the instance variable numberOfItems, the method getCount returns the value of the instance variable numberOfItems. The definition of this method is:

```
public int getCount()
{
    return numberOfItems;
}
```

The method getProductCost returns the cost of a product. Because the cost of a product is stored in the instance variable cost, it returns the value of the instance variable cost. The definition of this method is:

```
public int getProductCost()
{
    return cost;
}
```

When a product is sold, the number of items in that dispenser is reduced by 1. Therefore, the method makeSale reduces the number of items in the dispenser by 1. That is, it decrements the value of the instance variable numberOfItems by 1. The definition of this method is:

```
public void makeSale()
{
    numberOfItems--;
}
```

The definition of the constructor checks for valid values of the parameters. If these values are less than 0, the default values are assigned to the instance variables. The definition of the constructor is:

```
    //constructor with parameters
public Dispenser(int setNoOfItems, int setCost)
{
    if (setNoOfItems >= 0)
        numberOfItems = setNoOfItems;
    else
        numberOfItems = 50;

    if (setCost >= 0)
        cost = setCost;
    else
        cost = 50;
}
```

The default constructor assigns the default values to the instance variables:

```
public Dispenser()
{
    numberOfItems = 50;
    cost = 50;
}
```

The definition of the class Dispenser is:

```
//class Dispenser

public class Dispenser
{
    private int numberOfItems;   //variable to store the number of
                                 //items in the dispenser
    private int cost;     //variable to store the cost of an item

        //Default constructor to set the cost and number of
        //items to the default values
        //Postcondition: numberOfItems = 50; cost = 50;
    public Dispenser()
    {
        numberOfItems = 50;
        cost = 50;
    }

        //Constructor with parameters to set the cost and number
        //of items in the dispenser specified by the user
        //Postcondition: numberOfItems = setNoOfItems;
        //                cost = setCost;
    public Dispenser(int setNoOfItems, int setCost)
    {
        if (setNoOfItems >= 0)
            numberOfItems = setNoOfItems;
        else
            numberOfItems = 50;

        if (setCost >= 0)
            cost = setCost;
        else
            cost = 50;
    }

        //Method to show the number of items in the dispenser
        //Postcondition: The value of the instance variable
        //                numberOfItems is returned.
    public int getCount()
    {
        return numberOfItems;
    }
```

8

```java
        //Method to show the cost of the item
        //Postcondition: The value of the instance
        //                variable cost is returned.
    public int getProductCost()
    {
        return cost;
    }


        //Method to reduce the number of items by 1
        //Postcondition: numberOfItems = numberOfItems - 1
    public void makeSale()
    {
        numberOfItems--;
    }
}
```

Main Program   When the program executes, it must do the following:

1. Show the different products sold by the candy machine.
2. Show how to select a particular product.
3. Show how to terminate the program.

Furthermore, these instructions must be displayed after processing each selection (except when exiting the program), so that the user need not remember what to do if he or she wants to buy additional items. Once the user makes the appropriate selection, the candy machine must act accordingly. If the user opts to buy an available product, the candy machine should show the cost of the product and ask the user to deposit the money. If the money deposited is at least the cost of the item, the candy machine should sell the item and display an appropriate message.

This discussion translates into the following algorithm:

1. Show the selection to the customer.
2. Get the selection.
3. If the selection is valid and the dispenser corresponding to the selection is not empty, sell the product.

We divide this program into three functions—showSelection, sellProduct, and main.

Method
showSelection   This method displays the necessary information to help the user select and buy a product. Essentially, it contains the following output statements (we assume that the candy machine sells four types of products):

```
*** Welcome to Shelly's Candy Shop ***
To select an item, enter
1 for Candy
2 for Chips
```

```
3 for Gum
4 for Cookies
9 to exit
```

The definition of the function `showSelection` is:

```java
public static void showSelection()
{
    System.out.println("*** Welcome to Shelly's "
                      + "Candy Shop ***");
    System.out.println("To select an item, enter ");
    System.out.println("1 for Candy");
    System.out.println("2 for Chips");
    System.out.println("3 for Gum");
    System.out.println("4 for Cookies");
    System.out.println("9 to exit");
}//end showSelection
```

Next, we describe the method `sellProduct`.

Method sellProduct This method attempts to sell a particular product selected by the customer. The candy machine contains four dispensers, which correspond to the four products. The first thing this method does is check whether the dispenser holding the product is empty. If the dispenser is empty, the method informs the customer that this product is sold out. If the dispenser is not empty, it tells the user to deposit the necessary amount to buy the product. For simplicity, we assume that this program does not return the extra money deposited by the customer. Therefore, the cash register is updated by adding the money entered by the user.

From this discussion, it follows that the method `sellProduct` must have access to the dispenser holding the product (to decrement the number of items in the dispenser by 1 and to show the cost of the item) as well as access to the cash register (to update the cash). Therefore, this method has two parameters: one corresponding to the dispenser and the other corresponding to the cash register.

In pseudocode, the algorithm for this method is:

1. If the dispenser is not empty

   a. Get the product cost.

   b. Set the variable `coinsRequired` to the price of the product.

   c. Set the variable `coinsInserted` to 0.

   d. While `coinsRequired` is greater than 0:

      i. Show and prompt the customer to enter the additional amount.

      ii. Calculate the total amount entered by the customer.

      iii. Determine the amount needed.

e. Update the amount in the cash register.

f. Sell the product—that is, decrement the number of items in the dispenser by 1.

g. Display an appropriate message.

2. If the dispenser is empty, tell the user that this product is sold out.

The definition of the method sellProduct is:

```
public static void sellProduct(Dispenser product,
                               CashRegister cRegister)
{
    int price;          //variable to hold the product price
    int coinsInserted;  //variable to hold the amount entered
    int coinsRequired;  //variable to show the extra amount
                        //needed

    if (product.getCount() > 0)                     //Step 1
    {
        price = product.getProductCost();           //Step 1a
        coinsRequired = price;                       //Step 1b
        coinsInserted = 0;                           //Step 1c

        while (coinsRequired > 0)                    //Step 1d
        {
            System.out.print("Please deposit "
                             + coinsRequired
                             + " cents: ");          //Step 1d.i

            coinsInserted = coinsInserted
                            + console.nextInt();      //Step 1d.ii

            coinsRequired = price
                            - coinsInserted;          //Step 1d.iii
        }

        System.out.println();

        cRegister.acceptAmount(coinsInserted);      //Step 1e
        product.makeSale();                          //Step 1f

        System.out.println("Collect your item "
                           + "at the bottom and "
                           + "enjoy.\n");            //Step 1g
    }
    else
        System.out.println("Sorry this item "
                           + "is sold out.\n");     //Step 2
}//end sellProduct
```

Method
main

The algorithm for the method `main` follows:

1. Create the cash register—that is, create and initialize a `CashRegister` object.

2. Create four dispensers—that is, create and initialize four objects of type `Dispenser`. For example, the statement:

   ```
   Dispenser candy = new Dispenser(100, 50);
   ```

   creates a dispenser object, `candy`, to hold the candies. The number of items in the dispenser is `100`, and the cost of an item is `50` cents.

3. Declare additional variables as necessary.

4. Show the selection; call the method `showSelection`.

5. Get the selection.

6. While not done (a selection of 9 exits the program):

   a. Sell the product; call the method `sellProduct`.

   b. Show the selection; call the method `showSelection`.

   c. Get the selection.

The definition of the method `main` follows:

```
public static void main(String[] args)
{
    CashRegister cashRegister = new CashRegister();    //Step 1
    Dispenser candy = new Dispenser(100, 50);          //Step 2
    Dispenser chips = new Dispenser(100, 65);          //Step 2
    Dispenser gum = new Dispenser(75, 45);             //Step 2
    Dispenser cookies = new Dispenser(100, 85);        //Step 2

    int choice;  //variable to hold the selection      //Step 3

    showSelection();                                   //Step 4
    choice = console.nextInt();                        //Step 5

    while (choice != 9)                                //Step 6
    {
        switch (choice)                                //Step 6a
        {
        case 1:
            sellProduct(candy, cashRegister);
            break;

        case 2:
            sellProduct(chips, cashRegister);
            break;
```

8

```
        case 3:
            sellProduct(gum, cashRegister);
            break;

        case 4:
            sellProduct(cookies, cashRegister);
            break;

        default:
            System.out.println("Invalid Selection");
        }//end switch

        showSelection();                                    //Step 6b
        choice = console.nextInt();                         //Step 6c
    }//end while
}//end main
```

MAIN PROGRAM LISTING

```
//Program: Candy Machine

import java.util.*;

public class CandyMachine
{
    static Scanner console = new Scanner(System.in);

    //Place the definition of the method main as given above here.

    //Place the definition of the method showSelection as
    //given above here.

    //Place the definition of the method sellProduct as
    //given above here.
}
```

Sample Run: (In this sample run, the user input is shaded.)

```
*** Welcome to Shelly's Candy Shop ***
To select an item, enter
1 for Candy
2 for Chips
3 for Gum
4 for Cookies
9 to exit
1
Please deposit 50 cents: 50

Collect your item at the bottom and enjoy.
```

```
*** Welcome to Shelly's Candy Shop ***
To select an item, enter
1 for Candy
2 for Chips
3 for Gum
4 for Cookies
9 to exit
3
Please deposit 45 cents: 45

Collect your item at the bottom and enjoy.

*** Welcome to Shelly's Candy Shop ***
To select an item, enter
1 for Candy
2 for Chips
3 for Gum
4 for Cookies
9 to exit
9
```

CANDY
MACHINE:
CREATING
A GUI

 NOTE If you skipped the GUI part of Chapter 6, you can skip this section.

We will now design an application program that creates the GUI shown in Figure 8-22.

FIGURE 8-22 GUI for the candy machine

The program should do the following:

1. Show the customer the above GUI.

2. Let the customer make the selection.

3. When the user clicks on a product, show the customer its cost, and prompt the customer to enter the money for the product using an input dialog box, as shown in Figure 8-23.

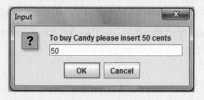

FIGURE 8-23   Input dialog box to enter money for the candy machine

4. Accept the money from the customer.

5. Make the sale and display a dialog box, as shown in Figure 8-24.

FIGURE 8-24   Output dialog box to show the output of the candy machine

In the first part of this programming example, we designed and implemented the classes CashRegister and Dispenser. Our final step is to revise the main program of the first part to create a GUI.

MAIN
PROGRAM

We now describe how to create the candy machine using the classes CashRegister and Dispenser and the GUI components. When the program executes, it must display the GUI shown earlier in Figure 8-22.

The GUI contains a window, two labels, and five buttons. The labels and buttons are placed in the content pane of the window. As you learned in Chapter 6, to create the window, the application program is created by extending the definition of the class JFrame. Thus, we need the following GUI components:

```
private JLabel headingMainL;     //label for the first line

private JLabel selectionL;       //label for the second line

private JButton exitB, candyB, chipsB, gumB, cookiesB;
```

The following statements create and instantiate these labels and button objects:

```
headingMainL = new JLabel("WELCOME TO SHELLY'S CANDY SHOP",
                          SwingConstants.CENTER);

selectionL = new JLabel("To Make a Selection, "
                     + "Click on the Product Button",
                       SwingConstants.CENTER);

candyB = new JButton("Candy");

chipsB = new JButton("Chips");

gumB = new JButton("Gum");

cookiesB = new JButton("Cookies");

exitB = new JButton("Exit");
```

These components are to be placed in the content pane of the window. The seven components—labels and buttons—are arranged in seven rows. Therefore, the content pane layout will be a grid of 7 rows and 1 column. The following statements get the content pane and add these components to the content pane:

```
Container pane = getContentPane();
setSize(300, 300);

pane.setLayout(new GridLayout(7,1));

pane.add(headingMainL);
pane.add(selectionL);
pane.add(candyB);
pane.add(chipsB);
pane.add(gumB);
pane.add(cookiesB);
pane.add(exitB);
```

EVENT HANDLING

When the user clicks on a product button, it generates an action event. There are five buttons, each generating an action event. To handle these action events, we use the same process that we used in Chapter 6. That is:

1. Create a class implementing the `interface` `ActionListener`.
2. Provide the definition of the method `actionPerformed`.
3. Create and instantiate an object, action listener, of the class type created in Step 1.
4. Register the listener of Step 3 to each button.

In Chapter 6, we created a separate class for each of the buttons and then created a separate listener for each button. In this new program, rather than create a separate class for each button, we create only one class. Recall that the heading of the method `actionPerformed` is:

```
public void actionPerformed(ActionEvent e)
```

In Chapter 6, while providing the definition of this method, we ignored the formal parameter e. The formal parameter e is a reference variable of the `ActionEvent` type. The `class` `ActionEvent` contains `getActionCommand` (a method without parameters), which can be used to identify which button generated the event. For example, the expression:

```
e.getActionCommand()
```

returns the string containing the label of the component generating the event. We can now use the appropriate `String` method to determine the button generating the event.

If the user clicks on one of the product buttons, then the candy machine attempts to sell the product. Therefore, the action of clicking on a product button is to sell. For this, we write the method `sellProduct` (discussed later in this programming example). If the user clicks on the `Exit` button, the program should terminate. Let's call the class to handle these events `ButtonHandler`. Its definition is:

```
private class ButtonHandler implements ActionListener
{
    public void actionPerformed (ActionEvent e)
    {
        if (e.getActionCommand().equals("Exit"))
            System.exit(0);
        else if (e.getActionCommand().equals("Candy"))
            sellProduct(candy, "Candy");
        else if (e.getActionCommand().equals("Chips"))
            sellProduct(chips, "Chips");
        else if (e.getActionCommand().equals("Gum"))
            sellProduct(gum, "Gum");
        else if (e.getActionCommand().equals("Cookies"))
            sellProduct(cookies, "Cookies");
    }
}
```

You can now declare, instantiate, and register the listener as follows:

```
private ButtonHandler pbHandler;   //declare the listener

pbHandler = new ButtonHandler();   //instantiate the object

     //register the listener with each button
candyB.addActionListener(pbHandler);
chipsB.addActionListener(pbHandler);
gumB.addActionListener(pbHandler);
cookiesB.addActionListener(pbHandler);
exitB.addActionListener(pbHandler);
```

Next, we describe the method `sellProduct`.

Method
llProduct

The definition of this method is similar to the one we designed for the non-GUI program. (We give the definition here for the sake of completeness.) This method attempts to sell a particular product selected by the customer. The candy machine contains four dispensers, which correspond to the four products. These dispensers will be declared as instance variables. Therefore, the dispenser of the product to be sold and the name of the product are passed as parameters to this method. Because the cash register will be declared as an instance variable, this method can directly access the cash register.

This definition of the method `sellProduct` is:

```
private void sellProduct(Dispenser product, String productName)
{
    int coinsInserted = 0;
    int price;
    int coinsRequired;
    String str;

    if (product.getCount() > 0)
    {
        price = product.getProductCost();
        coinsRequired = price - coinsInserted;

        while (coinsRequired > 0)
        {
            str = JOptionPane.showInputDialog("To buy "
                            + productName
                            + " please insert "
                            + coinsRequired + " cents");
            coinsInserted = coinsInserted
                        + Integer.parseInt(str);
            coinsRequired = price - coinsInserted;
        }
```

8

```
        cashRegister.acceptAmount(coinsInserted);
        product.makeSale();

        JOptionPane.showMessageDialog(null,"Please pick up your "
                              + productName + " and enjoy",
                               "Thank you, Come again!",
                              JOptionPane.PLAIN_MESSAGE);
    }
    else            //dispenser is empty
        JOptionPane.showMessageDialog(null,"Sorry "
                              + productName
                              + " is sold out\n" +
                              "Make another selection",
                              "Thank you, Come again!",
                              JOptionPane.PLAIN_MESSAGE);
}//end sellProduct
```

We have described the method `sellProduct` and the other necessary components, so next we will write the Java application program for the candy machine.

The algorithm is as follows:

1. Create the cash register—that is, declare a reference variable of type `CashRegister` and instantiate the object.

2. Create four dispensers—that is, declare four reference variables of type `Dispenser` and instantiate the appropriate `Dispenser` objects. For example, the statement:

```
Dispenser candy = new Dispenser(100, 50);
```

declares `candy` to be a reference variable of the `Dispenser` type and instantiates the object `candy` to hold the candies. The number of items in the object `candy` is 100, and the cost of a candy is 50 cents.

3. Create the other objects, such as labels and buttons, as previously described.

4. Display the GUI showing the candy machine, as described at the beginning of this programming example.

5. Get and process the selection.

The complete programming listing is available with the Additional Student Files at *www.cengagebrain.com.*

QUICK REVIEW

1. A `class` is a collection of a specific number of components.
2. Components of a `class` are called the members of the class.
3. Members of a `class` are accessed by name.
4. In Java, `class` is a reserved word, and it defines only a data type; no memory is allocated.
5. Members of a class are classified into four categories. The three typically used categories are `private`, `protected`, or `public`.
6. The `private` members of a class are not directly accessible outside the class.
7. The `public` members of a class are accessible outside the class.
8. The `public` members are declared using the modifier `public`.
9. The `private` members are declared using the modifier `private`.
10. A member of a class can be a method, a variable, or an inner class.
11. If any member of a class is a variable, it is declared like any other variable.
12. In Java, a `class` is a definition.
13. Non-`static` variables of a `class` are called instance variables of that `class`.
14. Non-`static` methods of a class are called instance methods.
15. Constructors permit the data members to be initialized when an object is declared.
16. The name of a constructor is the same as the name of the class.
17. A class can have more than one constructor.
18. A constructor without parameters is called the default constructor.
19. Constructors automatically execute when a class object is created.
20. In a UML class diagram, the top box contains the name of the class. The middle box contains the data members and their data types. The bottom box contains the methods' names, parameter list, and return type. A + (plus) sign in front of a member indicates that the member is a `public` member; a − (minus) sign indicates that this is a `private` member. The # symbol before a member name indicates that the member is a `protected` member.
21. In shallow copying, two or more reference variables of the same type refer to the same object.
22. In deep copying, each reference variable refers to its own object.
23. A reference variable follows the same scope rules as other variables.
24. A member of a class is local to the class.
25. You access a `public class` member outside the `class` through the reference variable name or the `class` name (for `static` members) and the member access operator (`.`).

8

26. The copy constructor executes when an object is instantiated and initialized using an existing object.

27. The method `toString` is a `public` value-returning method. It does not take any parameters and returns the address of a `String` object.

28. The methods `print`, `println`, and `printf` output the string created by the method `toString`.

29. The default definition of the method `toString` creates a `String` that is the name of the object's `class` name followed by the object's hash code.

30. The modifier `static` in the heading of the method of a class specifies that the method can be invoked by using the name of the class.

31. If a data member of a class is declared using the modifier `static`, that data member can be invoked by using the name of the class.

32. `static` data members of a `class` *exist* even when no object of the `class` type is instantiated. Moreover, `static` variables are initialized to their default values.

33. Finalizers automatically execute when a class object goes out of scope.

34. A `class` can have only one finalizer, and the finalizer has no parameters.

35. The name of the finalizer is `finalize`.

36. A method of a class that only accesses (that is, does not modify) the value(s) of the data member(s) is called an accessor method.

37. A method of a class that modifies the value(s) of the data member(s) is called a mutator method.

38. Java implicitly uses the reference `this` to refer to both the instance variables and the methods of a class.

39. Classes that are defined within another class are called inner classes.

40. A data type that specifies the logical properties without the implementation details is called an abstract data type (ADT).

EXERCISES

1. Mark the following statements as true or false:

   a. The instance variables of a class must be of the same type.

   b. The methods of a class must be `public`.

   c. A class can have more than one constructor.

   d. A constructor can return a value of the `int` type.

   e. An accessor method of a class accesses and modifies the data members of the class.

2. Figure 8-25 gives the UML class diagram of a class. Answer the following questions.

```
                    State
-name: String
-population: int
-area: double

+State()
+State(String, int, double)
+setName(String): void
+getName(): String
+setPopulation(int): void
+getPopulation(): int
+setArea(double): void
+getArea(): double
+toString(): String
+makeCopy(State): void
+getCopy(): State
```

FIGURE 8-25 UML diagram

a. What is the name of the class?

b. What are the instance variables?

c. What are the methods?

d. What are the private members?

e. What are the public members?

3. Find the syntax errors in the definition of the following class:

```
public class AA
{
    private int x;
    private int y;

    public void print()
    {
        System.out.println(x + " " + y);
    }
    public int sum()
    {
        return x + y;
    }
```

8

```
        public AA()
        {
            x = 0;
            y = 0;
        }

        public int AA(int a, int b)
        {
            x = a;
            y = b;
        }
    }
```

4. Find the syntax errors in the definition of the following class:

```
    public class BB
    {
        private int one;
        private int two;

        public boolean equal()
        {
            return (one == two);
        }

        public print()
        {
            System.out.println(one + " " + two);
        }

        public BB(int a, int b)
        {
            one = a;
            two = b;
        }
    }
```

5. Consider the definition of the following class:

```
    class CC
    {
        private int u;
        private int v;
        private double w;

        public CC()                          //Line 1
        {
        }

        public CC(int a)                     //Line 2
        {
        }
```

```
        public CC(int a, int b)          //Line 3
        {
        }

        public CC(int a, int b, double d)    //Line 4
        {
        }
}
```

a. Give the line number containing the constructor that is executed in each of the following declarations:

   i.   `CC one = new CC();`

   ii.   `CC two = new CC(5, 6);`

   iii.   `CC three = new CC(2, 8, 3.5);`

b. Write the definition of the constructor in Line 1 so that the instance variables are initialized to 0.

c. Write the definition of the constructor in Line 2 so that the instance variable u is initialized according to the value of the parameter, and the instance variables v and w are initialized to 0.

d. Write the definition of the constructor in Line 3 so that the instance variables u and v are initialized according to the values of the parameters a and b, respectively, and the instance variable w is initialized to 0.0.

e. Write the definitions of the constructors in Line 4 so that the instance variables u, v, and w are initialized according to the values of the parameters a, b, and d, respectively.

6. What is a constructor? Why would you include a constructor in a class?

7. Suppose that `Automobile` is the name of a class. What is the name of a constructor of this class?

8. What is the return type of a constructor?

9. How many default constructors can a class have?

10. What are some of the differences between a method and a constructor?

11. Suppose that `c1` and `c2` are reference variables of type `Clock`. What is the effect of each of the following statements?

a. `c1 = new Clock();`

b. `c2 = new Clock(5, 12, 30);`

c. `c1.setTime(3, 24, 36);`

d. `c2.setHours(9);`

12. Consider the UML diagram of the class given in Figure 8-25. Suppose that `myState` is a reference variable of the class type given in this figure. Answer the following questions:

8

a. Write a statement to instantiate the object `myState` with the values `"Alaska"`, `626932`, and `586412.00`, respectively.

b. Write a statement that outputs the value of the instance variable `name` of the object `myState`.

c. Write a statement that changes the value of the instance variable `population` of the object `myState` to `627000`.

13. Explain why we need both `public` and `private` members in a class?

14. Write a Java statement that creates the object `mysteryClock` of the `Clock` type and initializes the instance variables `hr`, `min`, and `sec` of `mysteryClock` to 7, 18, and 39, respectively.

15. Given the statements:

```
Clock firstClock = new Clock(2, 6, 35);
Clock secondClock = new Clock(6, 23, 17);
firstClock = secondClock;
```

what is the output of the following statements?

```
firstClock.print();
System.out.println();
secondClock.print();
System.out.println();
```

16. Consider the following declarations:

```
public class XClass
{
    private int u;
    private double w;

    public XClass()
    {
    }

    public XClass(int a, double b)
    {
    }

    public void func()
    {
    }

    public void print()
    {
    }
}

XClass x = new XClass(10, 20.75);
```

a. How many members does `class XClass` have?

b. How many `private` members does `class XClass` have?

c. How many constructors does class XClass have?

d. Write the definition of the member func so that u is set to 10 and w is set to 15.3.

e. Write the definition of the member print that prints the contents of u and w.

f. Write the definition of the default constructor of the class XClass so that the instance variables are initialized to 0.

g. Write the definition of the constructor with parameters of the class XClass so that the instance variable u is initialized to the value of a and the instance variable w is initialized to the value of b.

h. Write a Java statement that prints the values of the instance variables of x.

i. Write a Java statement that creates the XClass object t and initializes the instance variables of t to 20 and 35.0, respectively.

17. Explain shallow copying.

18. Explain deep copying.

19. Suppose that two reference variables, say aa and bb, of the same type point to two different objects. What happens when you use the assignment operator to copy the value of aa into bb?

20. Assume that the method toString is defined for the class Clock as given in this chapter. What is the output of the following statements?

```
Clock firstClock;
Clock secondClock = new Clock(6, 23, 17);

firstClock = secondClock.getCopy();

System.out.println(firstClock);
```

21. What is the purpose of the copy constructor?

22. How does Java use the reference this?

23. Can you use the relational operator == to determine whether two different objects of the same class type contain the same data?

24. Consider the definition of the following class:

```
class TestClass
{
    private int x;
    private int y;

    //Default constructor to initialize
    //the instance variables to 0
    public TestClass()
    {
    }
```

8

```
    //Constructors with parameters to initialize the
    //instance variables to the values specified by
    //the parameters
    //Postcondition: x = a; y = b;
TestClass(int a, int b)
{
}

    //return the sum of the instance variables
public int sum()
{
}

    //print the values of the instance variables
public void print()
{
}
}
```

a. Write the definitions of the methods as described in the definition of the class TestClass.

b. Write a test program to test various operations of the class TestClass.

25. Write the definition of a class that has the following properties:

a. The name of the class is Stock.

b. The class Stock has four instance variables: name of type String, previousPrice and closingPrice of type double, and numberOfShares of type int.

c. The class Stock has the following methods:

toString—to return the data stored in the data members with the appropriate titles as a string

setName—method to set the name

setPreviousPrice—method to set the previous price of a stock. (This is the closing price of the previous day.)

setClosingPrice—method to set the closing price of a stock

setNumberOfShare—method to set the number of shares owned by the stock

getName—value-returning method to return the name

getPreviousPrice—value-returning method to return the previous price of the stock

getClosingPrice—value-returning method to return the closing price of the stock

getNumberOfShare—value-returning method to return the number of shares owned by the stock percentGain—value-returning method to return the change in the stock value from the previous closing price and today's closing price as a percentage

shareValues—value-returning method to calculate and return the total values of the shares owned

default constructor—the default value of name is the empty string ""; the default values of previousPrice, closingPrice, and numberOfShares are 0.

constructor with parameters—sets the values of the instance variables name, previousPrice, closingPrice, and numberOfShares to the values specified by the user

d. Write the definitions of the methods and constructors of the class Stock as described in part c.

26. Consider the following definition of the class MyClass:

```
class MyClass
{
    private int x;
    private static int count;

        //default constructor
        //Postcondition: x = 0
    public MyClass()
    {
        //write the definition
    }

        //constructor with a parameter
        //Postcondition: x = a
    public MyClass(int a)
    {
        //write the definition
    }

        //Method to set the value of x
        //Postcondition: x = a
    public void setX(int a);
    {
        //write the definition
    }

        //Method to output x.
    public void printX()
    {
        //write the definition
    }
```

8

```
    //Method to output count
    public static void printCount()
    {
        //write the definition
    }

    //Method to increment count
    //Postcondition: count++
    public static int incrementCount()
    {
        //write the definition
    }
}
```

a. Write a Java statement that increments the value of count by 1.

b. Write a Java statement that outputs the value of count.

c. Write the definitions of the methods and the constructors of the class MyClass as described in its definition.

d. Write a Java statement that declares myObject1 to be a MyClass object and initializes its instance variable x to 5.

e. Write a Java statement that declares myObject2 to be a MyClass object and initializes its instance variable x to 7.

f. Which of the following statements are valid? (Assume that myObject1 and myObject2 are as declared in parts d and e.)

```
myObject1.printCount();         //Line 1
myObject1.printX();             //Line 2
MyClass.printCount();           //Line 3
MyClass.printX();               //Line 4
MyClass.count++;                //Line 5
```

g. Assume that myObject1 and myObject2 are as declared in parts d and e. After you have written the definition of the methods of the class MyClass, what is the output of the following Java code?

```
myObject1.printX();
myObject1.incrementCount();
MyClass.incrementCount();
myObject1.printCount();
myObject2.printCount();
myObject2.printX();
myObject1.setX(14);
myObject1.incrementCount();
myObject1.printX();
myObject1.printCount();
myObject2.printCount();
```

PROGRAMMING EXERCISES

1. The class Clock given in the chapter only allows the time to be incremented by one second, one minute, or one hour. Rewrite the definition of the class Clock by including additional members so that time can also be decremented by one second, one minute, or one hour. Also write a program to test your class.

2. Write a program that converts a number entered in Roman numerals to decimal. Your program should consist of a class, say, Roman. An object of type Roman should do the following:

   a. Store the number as a Roman numeral.

   b. Convert and store the number into decimal.

   c. Print the number as a Roman numeral or decimal number as requested by the user.

      The decimal values of the Roman numerals are:

M	1000
D	500
C	100
L	50
X	10
V	5
I	1

   d. Your class must contain the method romanToDecimal to convert a Roman numeral into its equivalent decimal number

   e. Test your program using the following Roman numerals: MCXIV, CCCLIX, and MDCLXVI.

3. Design and implement the class Day that implements the day of the week in a program. The class Day should store the day, such as Sun for Sunday. The program should be able to perform the following operations on an object of type Day:

   a. Set the day.

   b. Print the day.

   c. Return the day.

   d. Return the next day.

   e. Return the previous day.

   f. Calculate and return the day by adding certain days to the current day. For example, if the current day is Monday and we add four days, the day to be returned is Friday. Similarly, if today is Tuesday and we add 13 days, the day to be returned is Monday.

   g. Add the appropriate constructors.

   h. Write the definitions of the methods to implement the operations for the class Day, as defined in a through g.

   i. Write a program to test various operations on the class Day.

4. a. Example 8-8 defined the `class` `Person` to store the name of a person. The methods that we included merely set the name and print the name of a person. Redefine the `class` `Person` so that, in addition to what the existing `class` does, you can:

    i.   Set the last name only.

    ii. Set the first name only.

    iii. Set the middle name.

    iv. Check whether a given last name is the same as the last name of this person.

    v.   Check whether a given first name is the same as the first name of this person.

    vi. Check whether a given middle name is the same as the middle name of this person.

    b. Add the method `equals` that returns true if two objects contain the same first, middle, and last name.

    c. Add the method `makeCopy` that copies the instance variables of a `Person` object into another `Person` object.

    d. Add the method `getCopy` that creates and returns the address of the object, which is a copy of another `Person` object.

    e. Add the copy constructor.

    f. Write the definitions of the methods of the `class` `Person` to implement the operations for this `class`.

    g. Write a program that tests various operations of the `class` `Person`.

5. Redo Example 7-3, Chapter 7, so that it uses the `class` `RollDie` to roll a die.

6. Write the definition of a `class`, `swimmingPool`, to implement the properties of a swimming pool. Your class should have the instance variables to store the length (in feet), width (in feet), depth (in feet), the rate (in gallons per minute) at which the water is filling the pool, and the rate (in gallons per minute) at which the water is draining from the pool. Add appropriate constructors to initialize the instance variables. Also add member functions, to do the following: Determine the amount of water needed to fill an empty or partially filled pool; the time needed to completely or partially fill the pool, or empty the pool; add water or drain for a specific amount of time.

7. The equation of a line in standard form is $ax + by = c$, where a and b both cannot be zero, and a, b, and c are real numbers. If $b \neq 0$, then $-a / b$ is the slope of the line. If $a = 0$, then it is a horizontal line, and if $b = 0$, then it is a vertical line. The slope of a vertical line is undefined. Two lines are parallel if they have the same slope or both are vertical lines. Two lines are perpendicular if one of the lines is horizontal and another is vertical, or if the product of their slopes is -1. Design the `class` `Line` to store a line. To store a line,

you need to store the values of a (coefficient of x), b (coefficient of y), and c. Your class must contain the following operations:

a. If a line is nonvertical, then determine its slope.

b. Determine if two lines are equal. (Two lines $a_1x + b_1y = c_1$ and $a_2x + b_2y = c_2$ are equal if either $a_1 = a_2$, $b_1 = b_2$, and $c_1 = c_2$ or $a_1 = ka_2$, $b_1 = kb_2$, and $c_1 = kc_2$ for some real number k.)

c. Determine if two lines are parallel.

d. Determine if two lines are perpendicular.

e. If two lines are not parallel, then find the point of intersection.

Add appropriate constructors to initialize variables of `Line`. Also write a program to test your class.

8. Rational fractions are of the form $a\,/\,b$, where a and b are integers and $b \neq 0$. In this exercise, by "fractions" we mean rational fractions. Suppose that $a\,/\,b$ and $c\,/\,d$ are fractions. Arithmetic operations on fractions are defined by the following rules:

$$a\,/\,b + c\,/\,d = (ad + bc)\,/\,bd$$
$$a\,/\,b - c\,/\,d = (ad - bc)\,/\,bd$$
$$a\,/\,b \times c\,/\,d = ac\,/\,bd$$
$$(a\,/\,b)\,/\,(c\,/\,d) = ad\,/\,bc, \text{ where } c\,/\,d \neq 0$$

Fractions are compared as follows: $a\,/\,b$ op $c\,/\,d$ if ad op bc, where op is any of the relational operations. For example, $a\,/\,b < c\,/\,d$ if $ad < bc$.

Design the **class** `Fraction` that can be used to manipulate fractions in a program. Among others, the **class** `Fraction` must include methods to add, subtract, multiply, and divide fractions. When you add, subtract, multiply, or divide fractions, your answer need not be in the lowest terms. Also, override the method `toString` so that the fractions can be output using the output statement.

Write a Java program that, using the **class** `Fraction`, performs operations on fractions.

8

CHAPTER

9

ARRAYS

IN THIS CHAPTER, YOU WILL:

- Learn about arrays
- Explore how to declare and manipulate data in arrays
- Learn about the instance variable `length`
- Understand the meaning of "array index out of bounds"
- Become aware of how the assignment and relational operators work with array names
- Discover how to pass an array as a parameter to a method
- Learn how to search an array
- Discover how to manipulate data in a two-dimensional array
- Learn about multidimensional arrays
- Become acquainted with the `class` Vector

In previous chapters, you worked with primitive data types and learned how to construct your own classes. Recall that a variable of a primitive data type can store only one value at a time; on the other hand, a `class` can be defined so that its objects can store more than one value at a time. This chapter introduces a special data structure called an array, which allows the user to group data items of the same type and process them in a convenient way.

Why Do We Need Arrays?

Before we formally define an array, let's consider the following problem. We want to write a Java program that reads five numbers, finds their sum, and prints the numbers in reverse order.

In Chapter 5, you learned how to read numbers, print them, and find their sum. What's different here is that we want to print the numbers in reverse order. We cannot print the first four numbers until we have printed the fifth, and so on. This means that we need to store all the numbers before we can print them in reverse order. From what we have learned so far, the following program accomplishes this task:

```java
//Program to read five numbers, find their sum, and print the
//numbers in the reverse order.

import java.util.*;

public class ReversePrintI
{
    static Scanner console = new Scanner(System.in);

    public static void main(String[] args)
    {
        int item0, item1, item2, item3, item4;
        int sum;

        System.out.println("Enter five integers: ");
        item0 = console.nextInt();
        item1 = console.nextInt();
        item2 = console.nextInt();
        item3 = console.nextInt();
        item4 = console.nextInt();

        sum = item0 + item1 + item2 + item3 + item4;

        System.out.println("The sum of the numbers = " + sum);
        System.out.print("The numbers in reverse order are: ");
        System.out.println(item4 + " " + item3 + " " + item2
                           + " " + item1 + " " + item0);
    }
}
```

This program works fine. However, to read 100 (or more) numbers and print them in reverse order, you would have to declare 100 or more variables and write many input and output statements. Thus, for large amounts of data, this type of program is not desirable.

Note the following in the preceding program:

1. Five variables must be declared because the numbers are to be printed in reverse order.

2. All variables are of type `int`—that is, of the same data type.

3. The way in which these variables are declared indicates that the variables to store these numbers have the same name except for the last character, which is a number.

From 1, it follows that you have to declare five variables. From 3, it follows that it would be convenient if you could somehow put the last character, which is a number, into a counter variable and use one `for` loop to count from 0 to 4 for reading, and use another `for` loop to count from 4 to 0 for printing. Finally, because all the variables are of the same type, you should be able to specify how many variables must be declared—as well as their data type—with a simpler statement than the one used previously.

The data structure that lets you do all of these things in Java is called an array.

Arrays

An **array** is a collection (sequence) of a fixed number of variables called **elements** or **components**, wherein all the elements are of the same data type. A **one-dimensional array** is an array in which the elements are arranged in a list form. The remainder of this section discusses one-dimensional arrays. Arrays of two or more dimensions are discussed later in this chapter.

The general form to declare a one-dimensional array is:

```
dataType[] arrayName;        //Line 1
```

where `dataType` is the element type.

In Java, an array is an object, just like the objects discussed in Chapter 8. Because an array is an object, `arrayName` is a reference variable. Therefore, the preceding statement only declares a reference variable. Before we can store the data, we must instantiate the array object.

The general syntax to instantiate an array object is:

```
arrayName = new dataType[intExp];        //Line 2
```

where `intExp` is any expression that evaluates to a positive integer. Also, the value of `intExp` specifies the number of elements in the array.

You can combine the statements in Lines 1 and 2 into one statement as follows:

```
dataType[] arrayName = new dataType[intExp];    //Line 3
```

We typically use statements similar to the one in Line 3 to create arrays to manipulate data.

NOTE When an array is instantiated, Java automatically initializes its elements to their default values. For example, the elements of numeric arrays are initialized to 0, the elements of `char` arrays are initialized to the null character, which is `'\u0000'`, the elements of `boolean` arrays are initialized to `false`.

EXAMPLE 9-1

The statement:

```
int[] num = new int[5];
```

declares and creates the array `num` consisting of 5 elements. Each element is of type `int`. The elements are accessed as `num[0]`, `num[1]`, `num[2]`, `num[3]`, and `num[4]`. Figure 9-1 illustrates the array `num`.

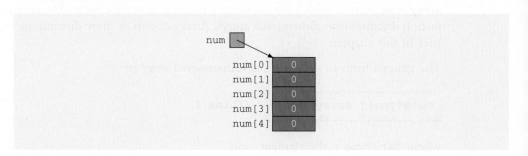

FIGURE 9-1 Array num

> **NOTE** To save space, we also draw an array, as shown in Figures 9-2(a) and 9-2(b).

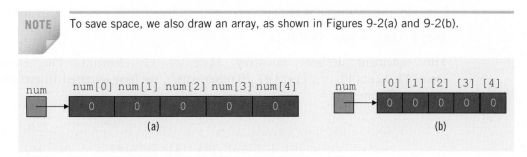

FIGURE 9-2 Array num

Alternate Ways to Declare an Array

Java allows you to declare arrays as follows:

```
int list[];          //Line 1
```

Here, the operator `[]` appears after the identifier `list`, not after the data type `int`.

You should be careful when declaring arrays as in Line 1. Consider the following statements:

```
int alpha[], beta;    //Line 2
int[] gamma, delta;   //Line 3
```

The statement in Line 2 declares the variables `alpha` and `beta`. Similarly, the statement in Line 3 declares the variables `gamma` and `delta`. However, the statement in Line 2 declares only `alpha` to be an array reference variable, while the variable `beta` is an `int` variable. On the other hand, the statement in Line 3 declares both `gamma` and `delta` to be array reference variables.

Traditionally, Java programmers declare arrays as shown in Line 3. We recommend that you do the same.

Accessing Array Elements

The general form (syntax) used to access an array element is:

```
arrayName[indexExp]
```

where `indexExp`, called the **index**, is an expression whose value is a nonnegative integer less than the size of the array. The index value specifies the position of the element in the array. In Java, the array index starts at 0.

In Java, `[]` is an operator called the **array subscripting operator**.

Consider the following statement:

```
int[] list = new int[10];
```

This statement declares an array `list` of 10 elements. The elements are `list[0]`, `list[1]`, ..., `list[9]`. In other words, we have declared 10 variables of type `int` (see Figure 9-3).

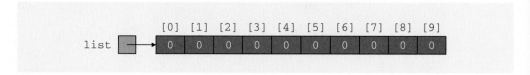

FIGURE 9-3 Array `list`

The assignment statement:

```
list[5] = 34;
```

stores 34 into `list[5]`, which is the sixth element of the array `list` (see Figure 9-4).

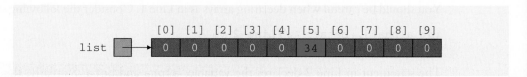

FIGURE 9-4 Array `list` after the execution of the statement `list[5]= 34;`

Suppose `i` is an `int` variable. Then, the assignment statement:

```
list[3] = 63;
```

is equivalent to the assignment statements:

```
i = 3;
list[i] = 63;
```

If `i` is 4, then the assignment statement:

```
list[2 * i - 3] = 58;
```

stores 58 into `list[5]`, because `2 * i - 3` evaluates to 5. The index expression is evaluated first, giving the position of the element in the array.

Next, consider the following statements:

```
list[3] = 10;
list[6] = 35;
list[5] = list[3] + list[6];
```

The first statement stores 10 into `list[3]`, the second statement stores 35 into `list[6]`, and the third statement adds the contents of `list[3]` and `list[6]` and stores the result into `list[5]` (see Figure 9-5).

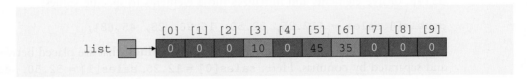

FIGURE 9-5 Array `list` after the execution of the statements `list[3]= 10;`, `list[6]= 35;`, and `list[5] = list[3] + list[6];`

EXAMPLE 9-2

You can also declare arrays as follows:

```
final int ARRAY_SIZE = 10;
int[] list = new int[ARRAY_SIZE];
```

That is, you can first declare a named constant of an integral type, such as `int`, and then use the value of the named constant to specify the size of the array.

Specifying Array Size during Program Execution

When you include a statement in a program to instantiate an array object, it is not necessary to know the size of the array at compile time. During program execution, you can first prompt the user to specify the size of the array and then instantiate the object. The following statements illustrate this concept (suppose that `console` is a `Scanner` object initialized to the standard input device):

```
int arraySize;                                      //Line 1

System.out.print("Enter the size of the array: ");  //Line 2
arraySize = console.nextInt();                      //Line 3
System.out.println();                               //Line 4

int[] list = new int[arraySize];                    //Line 5
```

The statement in Line 2 asks the user to enter the size of the array when the program executes. The statement in Line 3 inputs the size of the array into `arraySize`. During program execution, the system uses the value of the variable `arraySize` to instantiate the object `list`. For example, if the value of `arraySize` is 15, `list` is an array of size 15.

Array Initialization during Declaration

Like any other primitive data type variable, an array can also be initialized with specific values when it is declared. For example, the following Java statement declares an array, `sales`, of five elements and initializes those elements to specific values:

```
double[] sales = {12.25, 32.50, 16.90, 23, 45.68};
```

The **initializer list** contains values, called **initial values**, that are placed between braces and separated by commas. Here, `sales[0] = 12.25`, `sales[1] = 32.50`, `sales[2] = 16.90`, `sales[3] = 23.00`, and `sales[4]= 45.68`.

Note the following about declaring and initializing arrays:

- When declaring and initializing arrays, the size of the array is determined by the number of initial values in the initializer list within the braces.

- If an array is declared and initialized simultaneously, we *do not* use the operator `new` to instantiate the array object.

Arrays and the Instance Variable `length`

Recall that an array is an object; therefore, to store data, the array object must be instantiated. Associated with each array that has been instantiated (that is, for which memory has been allocated to store data), there is a `public` (`final`) instance variable `length`. The variable `length` contains the size of the array. Because `length` is a `public` member, it can be directly accessed in a program using the array name and the dot operator.

Consider the following declaration:

```
int[] list = {10, 20, 30, 40, 50, 60};
```

This statement creates the array `list` of six elements and initializes the elements using the values given. Here, `list.length` is 6.

Consider the following statement:

```
int[] numList = new int[10];
```

This statement creates the array `numList` of 10 elements and initializes each element to 0. Because the number of elements of `numList` is 10, the value of `numList.length` is 10. Now consider the following statements:

```
numList[0] = 5;
numList[1] = 10;
numList[2] = 15;
numList[3] = 20;
```

These statements store 5, 10, 15, and 20, respectively, in the first four elements of `numList`. Even though we put data into only the first four elements, the value of `numList.length` is 10, the total number of array elements.

You can store the number of filled elements (that is, the actual number of elements) in the array in a variable, say `numOfElements`. Programs commonly keep track of the number of filled elements in an array. Also, the filled elements are, typically, in the front of the array, and the empty elements are at the bottom.

NOTE   Once an array is instantiated, its size remains fixed. In other words, if you have instantiated an array of 5 elements, the number of elements of the array remains 5. If you need to increase the size of the array, then you must instantiate another array of the desired size and copy the data stored in the first array into the new array. In the next section, we show how to copy the elements of one array into another array.

Processing One-Dimensional Arrays

Some basic operations performed on a one-dimensional array are initializing the array, reading data into the array, storing output data in the array, and finding the largest and/or smallest element in the array. If the data type of an array element is numeric, some common operations are to find the sum and average of the elements of the array. Each of these operations requires the ability to step through the elements of the array, which is easily accomplished by using a loop. Suppose that we have the following statements:

```
int[] list = new int[100];   //list is an array of size 100
```

The following `for` loop steps through each element of the array `list`, starting at the first element of `list`:

```
for (int i = 0; i < list.length; i++)                //Line 1
    //process list[i], the (i + 1)th element of list //Line 2
```

If processing `list` requires inputting data into `list`, the statement in Line 2 takes the form of an input statement, such as in the following code. The following statements read 100 numbers from the keyboard and store the numbers into `list`:

```
for (int i = 0; i < list.length; i++)    //Line 1
    list[i] = console.nextInt();          //Line 2
```

Similarly, if processing `list` requires outputting data, then the statement in Line 2 takes the form of an output statement. The following `for` loop outputs the elements of `list`:

```
for (int i = 0; i < list.length; i++)    //Line 1
    System.out.print(list[i] + " ");      //Line 2
```

Example 9-3 further illustrates how to process one-dimensional arrays.

EXAMPLE 9-3

This example shows how loops are used to process arrays. The following declaration is used throughout this example:

```
double[] sales = new double[10];
double largestSale, sum, average;
```

The first statement creates the array `sales` of 10 elements, with each element of type `double`. The meaning of the other statements is clear. Also, notice that the value of `sales.length` is 10.

Loops can be used to process arrays in several ways:

1. **Initializing an array to a specific value:** Suppose that you want to initialize every element of the array `sales` to `10.00`. You can use the following loop:

```
for (int index = 0; index < sales.length; index++)
    sales[index] = 10.00;
```

2. **Reading data into an array:** The following loop inputs data into the array `sales`. For simplicity, we assume that the data is entered at the keyboard one number per line.

```
for (int index = 0; index < sales.length; index++)
    sales[index] = console.nextDouble();
```

3. **Printing an array:** The following loop outputs the elements of array `sales`. For simplicity, we assume that the output goes to the screen.

```
for (int index = 0; index < sales.length; index++)
    System.out.print(sales[index] + " ");
```

4. **Finding the sum and average of an array:** Because the array `sales`, as its name implies, represents certain sales data, it may be desirable to find the total sale and average sale amounts. The following Java code finds the sum of the elements of the array `sales` (total sales) and the average sale amount:

```
sum = 0;

for (int index = 0; index < sales.length; index++)
    sum = sum + sales[index];

if (sales.length != 0)
    average = sum / sales.length;
else
    average = 0.0;
```

5. **Determining the largest element in the array:** We now discuss an algorithm to find the largest element in an array—that is, the array element with the largest value. However, the user is typically more interested in determining the location of the largest element in the array. Of course, if you know the location (the index of the largest element in the array), you can easily determine the value of the largest element in the array. Let's describe the algorithm to determine the index of the largest element in an array—in particular, the index of the largest sale amount in the array `sales`.

We assume that `maxIndex` will contain the index of the largest element in the array `sales`. The general algorithm is as follows. Initially, we assume that the first element in the list is the largest element, so `maxIndex` is initialized to 0. We then compare the element to which `maxIndex` points with every element in the list. Whenever we find an element in the array larger than the element to which `maxIndex` points, we update `maxIndex` so that it stores the index of the new larger element. The code to implement this algorithm is as follows:

```
maxIndex = 0;

for (int index = 1; index < sales.length; index++)
    if (sales[maxIndex] < sales[index])
        maxIndex = index;

largestSale = sales[maxIndex];
```

The way this code works can be demonstrated with an example. Suppose the array `sales` is as given in Figure 9-6, and we want to determine the largest element in the array.

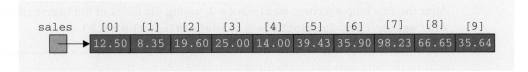

sales [0]   [1]   [2]   [3]   [4]   [5]   [6]   [7]   [8]   [9]

12.50 8.35 19.60 25.00 14.00 39.43 35.90 98.23 66.65 35.64

FIGURE 9-6 Array `sales`

Before the `for` loop begins, `maxIndex` is initialized to 0 and the `for` loop initializes `index` to 1. In Table 9-1, we show the values of `maxIndex`, `index`, and certain array elements during each iteration of the `for` loop:

TABLE 9-1 Values of `sales` Array Elements during `for` Loop Iterations

index	maxIndex	sales [maxIndex]	sales [index]	sales[maxIndex] < sales[index]
1	0	12.50	8.35	12.50 < 8.35 is false
2	0	12.50	19.60	12.50 < 19.60 is true; maxIndex = 2
3	2	19.60	25.00	19.60 < 25.00 is true; maxIndex = 3
4	3	25.00	14.00	25.00 < 14.00 is false
5	3	25.00	39.43	25.00 < 39.43 is true; maxIndex = 5
6	5	39.43	35.90	39.43 < 35.90 is false
7	5	39.43	98.23	39.43 < 98.23 is true; maxIndex = 7
8	7	98.23	66.65	98.23 < 66.65 is false
9	7	98.23	35.64	98.23 < 35.64 is false

After the `for` loop executes, `maxIndex = 7`, giving the index of the largest element in the array `sales`. Thus, `largestSale = sales[maxIndex] = 98.23`.

NOTE In an array, if the largest element occurs more than once, then the previous algorithm will find the index of the first occurrence of the largest element. The algorithm to find the smallest element in an array is similar to the algorithm for finding the largest element in an array. (See Programming Exercise 2 at the end of this chapter.)

Now that we know how to declare and process arrays, let's rewrite the program that we discussed in the beginning of this chapter. Recall that this program reads five numbers, finds the sum, and prints the numbers in reverse order.

EXAMPLE 9-4

```java
//Program to read five numbers, find their sum, and
//print the numbers in the reverse order.

import java.util.*;

public class ReversePrintII
{
    static Scanner console = new Scanner(System.in);

    public static void main(String[] args)
    {
        int[] items = new int[5]; //declare an array item of
                                  //five elements
        int sum;

        System.out.println("Enter five integers:");

        sum = 0;

        for (int counter = 0; counter < items.length;
                                        counter++)
        {
            items[counter] = console.nextInt();
            sum = sum + items[counter];
        }

        System.out.println("The sum of the numbers = "
                        + sum);
        System.out.print("The numbers in the reverse "
                    + "order are: ");

            //print the numbers in the reverse order
        for (int counter = items.length - 1; counter >= 0;
                                        counter--)
            System.out.print(items[counter] + " ");

        System.out.println();

    }
}
```

Sample Run: (In this sample run, the user input is shaded.)

```
Enter five integers:
12 76 34 52 89
The sum of the numbers is: 263
The numbers in the reverse order are: 89 52 34 76 12
```

Array Index Out of Bounds Exception

Consider the following declaration:

```
double[] num = double[10];
int i;
```

The element `num[i]` is valid, that is, `i` is a valid index if `i` = 0, 1, 2, 3, 4, 5, 6, 7, 8, or 9.

The index—say, `index`—of an array is **in bounds** if `index >= 0` and `index <= arraySize - 1`. If either `index < 0` or `index > arraySize - 1`, then we say that the index is **out of bounds**.

In Java, if an array index goes out of bounds during program execution, it throws an `ArrayIndexOutOfBoundsException` exception. If the program does not handle this exception, the program terminates with an appropriate error message.

A loop such as the following can set the index out of bounds:

```
for (i = 0; i <= 10; i++)
    list[i] = 0;
```

Here, we assume that `list` is an array of 10 elements. When `i` becomes 10, the loop test condition `i <= 10` evaluates to `true`, the body of the loop executes, and the program tries to access `list[10]`, which does not exist.

BASE ADDRESS OF AN ARRAY

The **base address** of an array is the address (memory location) of the first array element. For example, if `list` is a one-dimensional array, then the base address of `list` is the address of the element `list[0]`. The value of the variable `list` is the base address of the array—the address of `list[0]`. It follows that when you pass an array as a parameter, the base address of the actual array is passed to the formal parameter.

Declaring Arrays as Formal Parameters to Methods

Just like other data types, you can declare arrays as formal parameters to methods. A general syntax to declare an array as a formal parameter is:

```
dataType[] arrayName
```

For example, consider the following method:

```
public static void arraysAsFormalParameter(int[] listA,
                                           double[] listB,
                                           int num)
{
    //...
}
```

This method has three formal parameters. The formal parameters `listA` and `listB` are arrays, and `num` is of type `int`.

Suppose that you have the following statements:

```
int[] intList = new int[10];

double[] doubleNumList = new double[15];

int number;
```

The following statement calls the method with actual parameters intList, doubleNumList, and number:

```
arraysAsFormalParameter(intList, doubleNumList, number);
```

Assignment Operator, Relational Operators, and Arrays: A Precaution

Consider the following statements:

```
int[] listA = {5, 10, 15, 20, 25, 30, 35};     //Line 1
int[] listB = new int[listA.length];           //Line 2
```

The statement in Line 1 creates the array listA of size 7 and also initializes the array. Note that the value of listA.length is 7. The statement in Line 2 uses the value of listA.length to create the array listB of size 7 (see Figure 9-7).

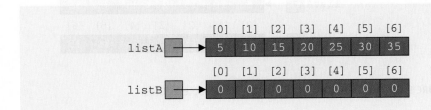

FIGURE 9-7 Arrays listA and listB

You can use the assignment operator to assign listA to listB and the relational operators to compare listA with listB. However, the results obtained might not be what you expect.

For example, consider the following statement:

```
listB = listA;
```

Here, you might expect that the elements of listA are copied into the corresponding elements of listB. However, this is not the case. Because listA is a reference variable, its value is a reference, that is, a memory address. Therefore, the preceding statement copies the value of listA into listB, and so after this statement executes, both listA and listB refer to the same array (see Figure 9-8).

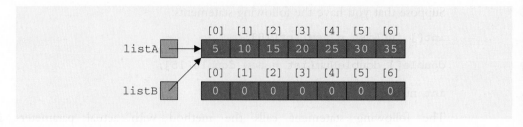

FIGURE 9-8 Arrays after the statement `listB = listA;` executes

Recall that this is called the *shallow copying* of data.

To copy the elements of `listA` into the corresponding elements of `listB`, you need to provide an element-by-element copy, as shown by the following loop:

```
for (int index = 0; index < listA.length; index++)
    listB[index] = listA[index];
```

After this statement executes, `listA` and `listB` each refers to its own array and the elements of `listA` are copied into the corresponding elements of `listB` (see Figure 9-9).

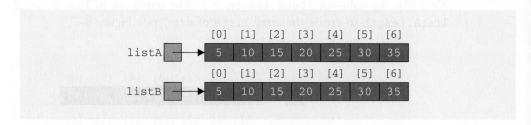

FIGURE 9-9 `listA` and `listB` after the `for` loop executes

Recall that this is called the *deep copying* of data.

In addition to the assignment operator, you can use the relational operators `==` and `!=` to compare arrays. However, you must be aware of what you are comparing. For example, in the statement:

```
if (listA == listB)
...
```

the expression `listA == listB` determines whether the values of `listA` and `listB` are the same, and thus determines whether `listA` and `listB` refer to the same array. That is, this statement does *not* determine whether `listA` and `listB` contain the same elements (when `listA` and `listB` refer to arrays stored at different locations).

To determine whether `listA` and `listB` contain the same elements when they refer to arrays stored at different locations, you need to compare them element by element. You can, in fact, write a method that returns **true** if two **int** arrays contain the same elements. For example, consider the following method:

```
boolean areEqualArrays(int[] firstArray, int[] secondArray)
{
    if (firstArray.length != secondArray.length)
        return false;

    for (int index = 0; index < firstArray.length; index++)
        if (firstArray[index] != secondArray[index]) //the
                                            //corresponding elements
                                            //are different
            return false;

    return true;
}
```

Now consider the following statement:

```
if (areEqualArrays(listA, listB))
...
```

The expression `areEqualArrays(listA, listB)` evaluates to `true` if the arrays `listA` and `listB` contain the same elements; `false` otherwise.

Arrays as Parameters to Methods

Just like other objects, arrays can be passed as parameters to methods. The following method takes as an argument any `int` array and outputs the data stored in each element:

```
public static void printArray(int[] list)
{
    for (int index = 0; index < list.length; index++)
        System.out.print(list[index] + " ");
}
```

Methods such as the preceding one process the data of an entire array. Sometimes the number of elements in the array might be less than the length of the array. For example, the number of elements in an array storing student data might increase or decrease as students drop or add courses. In situations like this, we only want to process the elements of the array that hold actual data. To write methods to process such arrays, in addition to declaring an array as a formal parameter, we declare another formal parameter specifying the number of valid elements in the array, as in the following method:

```
public static void printArray(int[] list, int numOfElements)
{
    for (int index = 0; index < numOfElements; index++)
        System.out.print(list[index] + " ");
}
```

The first parameter of the method `printArray` is an `int` array of any size. When the method `printArray` is called, the number of valid elements in the actual array is passed as the second parameter of the method `printArray`.

9

EXAMPLE 9-5

To access the methods to process a one-dimensional array conveniently, we create the class OneDimArrayMethods and put these methods in this class.

```java
// This class contains methods to manipulate data in a
// one-dimensional array.

import java.util.*;

public class OneDimArrayMethods
{
        //Method to input data and store in an int array.
        //The array to store the data and its size are passed as
        //parameters. The parameter numOfElements specifies the
        //number of elements to be read.
    public static void fillArray(int[] list, int numOfElements)
    {
        Scanner console = new Scanner(System.in);

        for (int index = 0; index < numOfElements; index++)
            list[index] = console.nextInt();
    }

        //Method to print the elements of an int array.
        //The array to be printed and the number of elements are
        //passed as parameters. The parameter numOfElements
        //specifies the number of elements to be printed.
    public static void printArray(int[] list, int numOfElements)
    {
        for (int index = 0; index < numOfElements; index++)
            System.out.print(list[index] + " ");
    }

        //Method to find and return the sum of the elements of an
        //int array. The parameter numOfElements specifies the
        //number of elements to be added.
    public static int sumArray(int[] list, int numOfElements)
    {
        int sum = 0;

        for (int index = 0; index < numOfElements; index++)
            sum = sum + list[index];

        return sum;
    }

        //Method to find and return the index of the first occurrence
        //of the largest element, if it repeats, in an int array.
        //The parameter numOfElements specifies the number of
        //elements in the array.
    public static int indexLargestElement(int[] list,
                                          int numOfElements)
```

```
    {
         int maxIndex = 0;  //Assume first element is the largest

         for (int index = 1; index < numOfElements; index++)
             if (list[maxIndex] < list[index])
                 maxIndex = index;

          return maxIndex;
    }

    //Method to copy some or all the elements of one array
    //into another array. Starting at the position specified
    //by src, the  elements of list1 are copied into list2
    //starting at the position specified by tar. The parameter
    //numOfElements specifies the number of elements of list1 to
    //be copied into list2. Starting at the position specified
    //by tar, list2 must have enough components to copy the
    //elements of list1. The following call copies all the
    //elements of list1 into the corresponding positions in
    //list2:  copyArray(list1, 0, list2, 0, numOfElements);.
    public static void copyArray(int[] list1, int src, int[] list2,
                                 int tar, int numOfElements)
    {
         for (int index = src; index < src + numOfElements; index++)
         {
             list2[index] = list1[tar];
             tar++;
         }
    }
}
```

Because the methods of the **class** `OneDimArrayMethods` are **public** and **static**, they can be called by using the name of the class and the dot operator. For example, if `myList` is an array of 10 elements of type `int`, the following statement outputs the elements of `myList`:

```
OneDimArrayMethods.printArray(myList, myList.length);
```

NOTE   Just as arrays can be passed as parameters to methods, individual elements of the array can also be passed as parameters to methods. For example, suppose that you have the following statement:

```
int[] list = {2, 3, 5};
```

and the method:

```
public static int sumNum(int firstNum, int secondNum)
{
     return firstNum + secondNum;
}
```

The following statement outputs the sum of the first two elements of the array `list`:
```
System.out.println("Sum = " + sumNum(list[0], list[1]));
```

9

The following program illustrates how arrays are passed as actual parameters in a method call.

EXAMPLE 9-6

```java
// This program illustrates how arrays are passed as parameters
// to methods.

import java.util.*;                                      //Line 1

public class ArraysAsParameters                          //Line 2
{                                                        //Line 3
    static final int ARRAY_SIZE = 10;                    //Line 4

    public static void main(String[] args)               //Line 5
    {                                                    //Line 6
        int[] listA = new int[ARRAY_SIZE];               //Line 7
        int[] listB = new int[ARRAY_SIZE];               //Line 8

        System.out.print("Line 9: listA elements: ");    //Line 9

            //output the elements of listA using
            //the method printArray
        OneDimArrayMethods.printArray(listA,
                            listA.length);               //Line 10
        System.out.println();                            //Line 11

        System.out.print("Line 12: Enter " + listA.length
                    + " integers: ");                    //Line 12

            //input data into listA using the method fillArray
        OneDimArrayMethods.fillArray(listA,
                            listA.length);               //Line 13
        System.out.println();                            //Line 14

        System.out.print("Line 15: After filling "
                    + "listA, the elements are:"
                    + "\n          ");                   //Line 15

            //output the elements of listA
        OneDimArrayMethods.printArray(listA,
                            listA.length);               //Line 16
        System.out.println();                            //Line 17

            //find and output the sum of the elements of listA
        System.out.println("Line 18: The sum of the "
                    + "elements of listA is: "
                    + OneDimArrayMethods.sumArray(listA,
                            listA.length));              //Line 18

            //find and output the position of the (first)
            //largest element in listA
```

```
        System.out.println("Line 19: The position of "
                + "the largest element in "
                + "listA is: "
                + OneDimArrayMethods.indexLargestElement
                           (listA, listA.length));      //Line 19

            //find and output the largest element in listA
        System.out.println("Line 20: The largest element "
            + "in listA is: "
            + listA[OneDimArrayMethods.indexLargestElement
                          (listA, listA.length)]);   //Line 20

            //copy the elements of listA into listB
            //using the method copyArray
        OneDimArrayMethods.copyArray(listA, 0, listB, 0,
                               listA.length);      //Line 21
        System.out.print("Line 22: After copying the "
                + "elements of listA into listB\n"
                + "            listB elements are: ");   //Line 22

            //output the elements of listB
        OneDimArrayMethods.printArray(listB,
                               listB.length);      //Line 23
        System.out.println();                       //Line 24
    } //end main                                    //Line 25
}                                                   //Line 26
```

Sample Run: (In this sample run, the user input is shaded.)

```
Line 9: listA elements: 0 0 0 0 0 0 0 0 0 0
Line 12: Enter 10 integers: 33 77 25 63 56 48 98 39 5 12

Line 15: After filling listA, the elements are:
        33 77 25 63 56 48 98 39 5 12
Line 18: The sum of the elements of listA is: 456
Line 19: The position of the largest element in listA is: 6
Line 20: The largest element in listA is: 98
Line 22: After copying the elements of listA into listB
         listB elements are: 33 77 25 63 56 48 98 39 5 12
```

The statement in Line 7 creates the array listA of 10 elements and initializes each element of listA to 0. Similarly, the statement in Line 8 creates the array listB of 10 elements and initializes each element of listB to 0. The statement in Line 10 calls the method printArray and outputs the values stored in listA. The statement in Line 13 calls the method fillArray to input the data into array listA. The statement in Line 18 calls the method sumArray and outputs the sum of all the elements of listA. The statement in Line 19 calls the method indexLargestElement to find the index of (the first occurrence of) the largest element in listA. Similarly, the statement in Line 20 outputs the value of the largest element in listA. The statement in Line 21 calls the method copyArray to copy the elements of listA into listB, and the statement in Line 23 outputs the elements of listB.

Searching an Array for a Specific Item

Searching a list for a given item is one of the most common operations performed on a list. The search algorithm we describe is called the **sequential search** or **linear search**. As the name implies, you search the array sequentially starting from the first array element. You compare searchItem with the elements in the array (the list) and continue the search until either you find the item or no more data is left in the list to compare with searchItem.

Consider the list of seven elements shown in Figure 9-10.

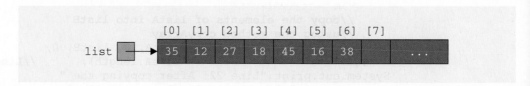

FIGURE 9-10 List of seven elements

Suppose that you want to determine whether 27 is in the list. A sequential search works as follows: First you compare 27 with list[0], that is, compare 27 with 35. Because list[0] ≠ 27, you then compare 27 with list[1] (that is, with 12, the second item in the list). Because list[1] ≠ 27, you compare 27 with the next element in the list, that is, compare 27 with list[2]. Because list[2] = 27, the search stops. This search is successful.

Let's now search for 10. As before, the search starts at the first element in the list, that is, at list[0]. Proceeding as before, we see that this time the search item, which is 10, is compared with every item in the list. Eventually, no more data is left in the list to compare with the search item. This is an unsuccessful search.

It now follows that, as soon as you find an element in the list that is equal to the search item, you must stop the search and report success. (In this case, you usually also report the location in the list where the search item was found.) Otherwise, after the search item is unsuccessfully compared with every element in the list, you must stop the search and report failure.

The following method performs a sequential search on a list. To be specific, and for illustration purposes, we assume that the list elements are of type int.

```
public static int seqSearch(int[] list, int listLength,
                                 int searchItem)
{
    int loc;
    boolean found = false;
    loc = 0;

    while (loc < listLength && !found)
        if (list[loc] == searchItem)
            found = true;
        else
            loc++;
```

```
        if (found)
            return loc;
        else
            return -1;
    }
```

If the method `seqSearch` returns a value greater than or equal to 0, it is a successful search; otherwise, it is an unsuccessful search.

As you can see from this code, you start the search by comparing `searchItem` with the first element in the `list`. If `searchItem` is equal to the first element in the `list`, you exit the loop; otherwise, `loc` is incremented by 1 to point to the next element in the `list`. You then compare `searchItem` with the next element in the `list`, and so on.

You can also include the method `seqSearch` in the **class** `OneDimArrayMethods` just like other methods. Suppose that you have included the method `seqSearch` in this **class**. Example 9-7 shows how to use the method `seqSearch` in a program.

EXAMPLE 9-7

```
// This program illustrates how to use a sequential search in a
// program.

import java.util.*;                                         //Line 1

public class TestSeqSearch                                  //Line 2
{                                                           //Line 3
    static Scanner console = new Scanner(System.in);        //Line 4

    public static void main(String[] args)                  //Line 5
    {                                                       //Line 6
        int[] intList = new int[10];                        //Line 7
        int number;                                         //Line 8
        int index;                                          //Line 9

        System.out.println("Line 10: Enter "
                        + intList.length + " integers.");   //Line 10

        for (index  = 0; index < intList.length; index++)   //Line 11
            intList[index] = console.nextInt();             //Line 12

        System.out.println();                               //Line 13

        System.out.print("Line 14: Enter the number "
                    + "to be searched: ");                  //Line 14
        number  = console.nextInt();                        //Line 15
        System.out.println();                               //Line 16

        index = OneDimArrayMethods.seqSearch(intList,
                            intList.length, number);        //Line 17
```

9

```
        if (index != -1)                                    //Line 18
            System.out.println("Line 19: " + number
                            + " is found at position "
                            + index);                       //Line 19
        else                                                //Line 20
            System.out.println("Line 21: " + number
                            + " is not in the list.");      //Line 21
    }                                                       //Line 22
}                                                           //Line 23
```

Sample Run 1: (In this sample run, the user input is shaded.)

```
Line 10: Enter 10 integers.
2 56 34 25 73 46 89 10 5 16

Line 14: Enter the number to be searched: 25

Line 19: 25 is found at position 3
```

Sample Run 2:

```
Line 10: Enter 10 integers.
2 56 34 25 73 46 89 10 5 16

Line 14: Enter the number to be searched: 38

Line 21: 38 is not in the list.
```

In this program, the statement in Line 7 creates `intList` to be an array of 10 elements. The `for` loop in Lines 11 and 12 inputs the data into `intList`. The statement in Line 14 prompts the user to enter the search item; the statement in Line 15 inputs this search item into `number`. The statement in Line 17 uses the method `seqSearch` to search `intList` for the search item. In Sample Run 1, the search item is 25; in Sample Run 2, it is 38. The statements in Lines 18 through 21 output the appropriate message. Notice that the search in Sample Run 1 is successful, but in Sample Run 2 it is unsuccessful.

Arrays of Objects

In the previous sections, you learned how to use an array to store and manipulate values of the primitive data types, such as `int` and `double`. You can also use arrays to manipulate objects. This section explains how to create and work with arrays of objects.

Arrays of `string` Objects

This section discusses how to create and work with an array of `String` objects. To create an array of strings, you declare an array as follows:

```
String[] nameList = new String[5];    //Line 1
```

This statement declares and instantiates `nameList` to be an array of 5 elements, wherein each element of `nameList` is a reference to a `String` object. (Note that this statement only creates the array `nameList`, which is an array of references. At this point, no `String` object has been created. We will create `String` objects and assign them to array elements next.)

Next, consider the statement:

```
nameList[0] = "Amanda Green";          //Line 2
```

This statement creates a `String` object with the value `"Amanda Green"` and stores the address of the object into `nameList[0]`. Similarly, the following statements assign `String` objects, with the given values, to the other elements of `nameList`:

```
nameList[1] = "Vijay Arora";          //Line 3
nameList[2] = "Sheila Mann";          //Line 4
nameList[3] = "Rohit Sharma";         //Line 5
nameList[4] = "Mandy Johnson";        //Line 6
```

After the statements in Lines 2 through 6 execute, each element of `nameList` is a reference to a `String` object, as shown in Figure 9-11.

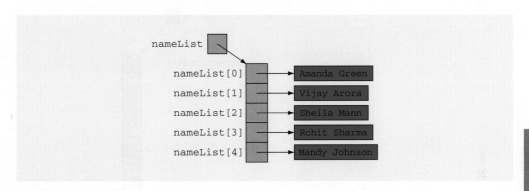

FIGURE 9-11 Array `nameList`

To output the names, you can use a **for** loop as follows:

```
for (int index = 0; index < nameList.length; index++)
    System.out.println(nameList[index]);
```

You can use `String` methods to work with the objects of `nameList`. For example, the expression:

```
nameList[0].equals("Amanda Green")
```

evaluates to **true**, while the expression:

```
nameList[3].equals("Randy Blair")
```

evaluates to **false**.

Similarly, the expression:

```
nameList[4].substring(0, 5)
```

returns a reference to the `String` object with the string `"Mandy"`.

Arrays of Objects of Other Classes

This section discusses, in general, how to create and work with an array of objects.

Suppose that you have 100 employees who are paid on an hourly basis, and you need to keep track of their arrival and departure times. In Chapter 8, we designed and implemented the **class** Clock to implement the time of day in a program. You can declare two arrays—arrivalTimeEmp and departureTimeEmp—of 100 elements each, wherein each element is a reference variable of Clock type. Consider the following statement:

```
Clock[] arrivalTimeEmp = new Clock[100];            //Line 1
```

The statement in Line 1 creates the array shown in Figure 9-12.

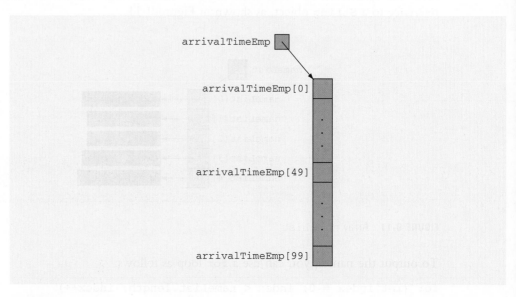

FIGURE 9-12 Array arrivalTimeEmp

The statement in Line 1 creates only the array, not the objects arrivalTimeEmp[0], arrivalTimeEmp[1], ..., arrivalTimeEmp[99]. We still need to instantiate Clock objects for each array element. Consider the following statements:

```
for (int j = 0; j < arrivalTimeEmp.length; j++)   //Line 2
    arrivalTimeEmp[j] = new Clock();               //Line 3
```

The statements in Lines 2 and 3 instantiate the objects arrivalTimeEmp[0], arrivalTimeEmp[1], ..., arrivalTimeEmp[99], as shown in Figure 9-13.

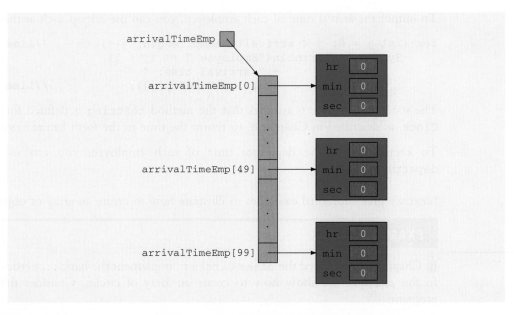

FIGURE 9-13 Array `arrivalTimeEmp` after instantiating objects for each element

You can now use the methods of the **class** `Clock` to manipulate the time for each employee. For example, the following statement sets the arrival time—that is, `hr`, `min`, and `sec`—of employee 49 to 8, 5, and 10, respectively (see Figure 9-14).

```
arrivalTimeEmp[49].setTime(8, 5, 10);                    //Line 4
```

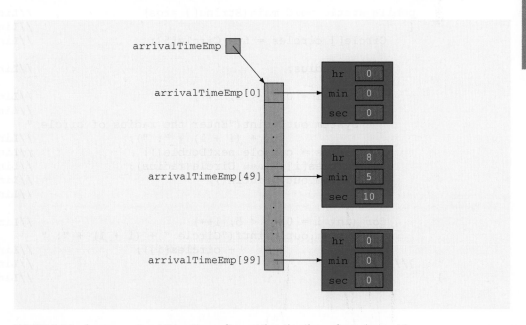

FIGURE 9-14 Array `arrivalTimeEmp` after setting the time of employee 49

To output the arrival time of each employee, you can use a loop such as the following:

```
for (int j = 0; j < arrivalTimeEmp.length; j++)          //Line 5
    System.out.println("Employee " +  (j + 1)
                        + " arrival time: "
                        + arrivalTimeEmp[j]);             //Line 6
```

The statement in Line 6 assumes that the method toString is defined for the class Clock, as described in Chapter 8, to return the time in the form hr:min:sec.

To keep track of the departure time of each employee, you can use the array departureTimeEmp.

Next we give additional examples to illustrate how to create an array of objects.

EXAMPLE 9-8

In Chapter 8, we created the class Circle to implement the basic properties of a circle. In this example, we show how to create an array of circles. Consider the following program:

```
// Program to create an array of circles.

import java.util.*;                                       //Line 1

public class TestProgArrayOfCircles                       //Line 2
{                                                         //Line 3
    static Scanner console = new Scanner(System.in);      //Line 4

    public static void main(String[] args)                //Line 5
    {                                                     //Line 6
        Circle[] circles = new Circle[5];                 //Line 7

        double radius;                                    //Line 8

        for (int i = 0; i < 5; i++)                       //Line 9
        {                                                 //Line 10
            System.out.print("Enter the radius of circle "
                            + (i + 1) + ": ");            //Line 11
            radius = console.nextDouble();                //Line 12
            circles[i] = new Circle(radius);              //Line 13
            System.out.println();                         //Line 14
        }                                                 //Line 15

        for (int i = 0; i < 5; i++)                       //Line 16
            System.out.printf("Circle " + (i + 1) + ": "
                            + circles[i]);                //Line 17
    }//end main                                           //Line 18
}                                                         //Line 19
```

Sample Run: (In this sample run, the user input is shaded.)

```
Enter the radius of circle 1: 7

Enter the radius of circle 2: 4

Enter the radius of circle 3: 8

Enter the radius of circle 4: 9

Enter the radius of circle 5: 6

Circle 1: Radius = 7.00, Perimeter = 43.98, Area = 69.09
Circle 2: Radius = 4.00, Perimeter = 25.13, Area = 39.48
Circle 3: Radius = 8.00, Perimeter = 50.27, Area = 78.96
Circle 4: Radius = 9.00, Perimeter = 56.55, Area = 88.83
Circle 5: Radius = 6.00, Perimeter = 37.70, Area = 59.22
```

The preceding program works as follows. The statement in Line 7 creates the array circles of 5 `Circle` objects. The `for` loop in Line 9 prompts the user to enter the radius of 5 circles (Line 11), inputs the radius of each circle (Line 12), and instantiates and sets the radius of circles (Line 13). The `for` loop in Line 16 outputs the radius, perimeter, and area of each circle. Note that in the `class` `Circle`, the `toString` method returns the radius, perimeter, and area of a circle.

EXAMPLE 9-9

In Chapter 8, we created the `class` `RollDie` to roll a die. The following program uses this class to roll 100 dice and outputs the number of times each number is rolled, the number(s) that are rolled the maximum number of times, and the maximum roll count.

```
// This program rolls 100 dice. It outputs the number of times
// each number is rolled, the number(s) that are rolled the
// maximum number of times, and the maximum roll count.

import java.util.*;                              //Line 1

public class TestProgArrayofDice                 //Line 2
{                                                //Line 3
    static Scanner console = new Scanner(System.in);   //Line 4

    public static void main(String[] args)       //Line 5
    {                                            //Line 6
        RollDie[] dice = new RollDie[100];       //Line 7

        int[] rollCount = new int[6];            //Line 8
        int maxNumRoll = 0;                      //Line 9

        for (int i = 0; i < 100; i++)            //Line 10
```

9

```
    {                                               //Line 11
        dice[i] = new RollDie();                    //Line 12
        dice[i].roll();                             //Line 13
    }                                               //Line 14

    System.out.println("Numbers rolled: ");         //Line 15
    for (int i = 0; i < 100; i++)                   //Line 16
    {                                               //Line 17
        int num = dice[i].getNum();                 //Line 18

        System.out.print(" " + num);                //Line 19
        rollCount[num - 1]++;                       //Line 20
        if ((i + 1) % 34 == 0)                      //Line 21
            System.out.println();                   //Line 22
    }                                               //Line 23

    System.out.println();                           //Line 24
    System.out.println("Num  Roll_Count");          //Line 25

    for (int i = 0; i < 6; i++)                     //Line 26
    {                                               //Line 27
        System.out.println(" " + (i + 1) + "        "
                           + rollCount[i]);         //Line 28
        if (rollCount[i] > rollCount[maxNumRoll])   //Line 29
            maxNumRoll = i;                         //Line 30
    }                                               //Line 31

    System.out.print("The number(s) ");             //Line 32
    for (int i = 0; i < 6; i++)                     //Line 33
        if (rollCount[i] == rollCount[maxNumRoll])  //Line 34
            System.out.print((i + 1) + " ");        //Line 35

    System.out.println("is (are) rolled maximum "
                       + "number of times, which is "
                       + rollCount[maxNumRoll] + "."); //Line 36
    }//end main                                     //Line 37
}                                                   //Line 38
```

Sample Run:

```
Numbers rolled:
 4 6 2 6 5 4 5 2 6 4 2 5 3 1 6 6 1 2 4 5 1 6 6 4 6 3 2 5 3 2 3 5 1 5
 1 6 5 2 1 5 1 6 4 2 4 4 1 1 6 2 4 2 1 3 4 3 5 3 5 1 2 3 5 2 2 2 1 4
 5 1 4 5 6 6 3 6 2 5 5 3 1 4 4 2 3 5 6 4 5 2 3 6 5 3 2 4 2 6 1 3
Num  Roll_Count
 1     15
 2     19
 3     14
 4     16
 5     19
 6     17
The number(s) 2 5 is (are) rolled maximum number of times, which is 19.
```

This program works as follows. The statement in Line 7 creates the array `dice` of 100 elements and each element is a reference to an object of the `class RollDie`. The statement in Line 8 creates the array `rollCount` to store the number of times each number is rolled. The `for` loop in Line 10 instantiates and initializes each element of the array `dice`. The `for` loop in 16 retrieves the number rolled by each die and also counts the number of times each number is rolled. This loop also outputs the numbers rolled with 34 numbers per line. The `for` loop in Line 26 outputs the number of times each number is rolled and also determines the maximum roll count. The `for` loop in Line 33 outputs the numbers that are rolled the maximum number of times.

Arrays and Variable Length Parameter List (Optional)

In Chapter 7, we wrote the method `larger` to determine the larger of two numbers. Similarly, we can write methods to determine the largest of three numbers, four numbers, five numbers, and so on. Moreover, using the mechanism of method overloading, each of these methods can be called `largest`. For example, we can write several such methods with the following headings:

```
public static double largest(double x, double y)
public static double largest(double x, double y, double z)
public static double largest(double x, double y, double z,
                             double u)
public static double largest(double x, double y, double z,
                             double u, double w)
```

9

However, this requires us to write the definitions of each of these methods. Java simplifies this by providing a variable length formal parameter (list). The syntax to declare a variable length formal parameter (list) is:

```
dataType ... identifier
```

where `dataType` is the name of a type, such as the primitive data type or a Java class or a user-defined data type. Note the ellipsis in this syntax; it is part of the syntax. For example, consider the following formal parameter declaration:

```
double ... numList
```

This statement declares `numList` to be a variable length formal parameter. In fact, `numList` is an array wherein each element is of type `double`, and the number of elements in `list` depends on the number of arguments passed to `numList`.

Consider the following method definition:

```
public static double largest(double ... list)
{
    double max;

    if (list.length != 0)
    {
        max = list[0];

        for (int index = 1; index < list.length; index++)
        {
            if (max < list[index])
                max = list[index];
        }

        return max;
    }

    return 0.0;
}
```

The formal parameter `list` of the method `largest` is of variable length. In a call to the method `largest`, you can specify either any number of actual parameters of type `double` or an array of type `double`. If the actual parameters of the method `largest` are of type `double`, then the values of the actual parameters are put in the array `list`. Because the number of actual parameters can be zero, in which case the length of `list` is 0, before determining the largest number in `list` we check whether the length of `list` is 0.

Consider the following statements:

```
double num1 = largest(34, 56);                  //Line 1
double num2 = largest(12.56, 84, 92);           //Line 2
double num3 = largest(98.32, 77, 64.67, 56);    //Line 3
System.out.println(largest(22.50, 67.78,
                        92.58, 45, 34, 56));     //Line 4


double[] numberList = {18.50, 44, 56.23, 17.89,
                        92.34, 112.0, 77, 11, 22,
                        86.62);                   //Line 5
System.out.println(largest(numberList));         //Line 6
```

In Line 1, the method `largest` is called with two parameters; in Line 2 it is called with three parameters; in Line 3 it is called with four parameters; and in Line 4 it is called with six parameters. In Line 6, the actual parameter of the method `largest` is the array `numberList`.

Example 9-10 further illustrates how the method largest can be used in a program.

EXAMPLE 9-10

```java
//Program: Largest of a set of numbers

import java.util.*;

public class LargestNumber
{
    public static void main(String[] args)
    {
        double[] numberList = {23, 45.5, 89, 34, 92.78,
                               36, 90, 120.89, 97, 23,
                               90, 89};                  //Line 1

        System.out.println("Line 2: The larger of 5.6 "
                         + "and 10.8 is "
                         + largest(5.6, 10.8));          //Line 2

        System.out.println("Line 3: The largest of 23, "
                         + "78, and 56 is "
                         + largest(23, 78, 56));         //Line 3

        System.out.println("Line 4: The largest of 93, "
                         + "28, 83, and 66 is "
                         + largest(93, 28, 83, 66));     //Line 4

        System.out.println("Line 5: The largest of 22.5, "
                         + "12.34, 56.34, 78, "
                         + "\n        "
                         + "98.45, 25, 78, 23 and 36 is "
                         + largest(22.5, 12.34, 56.34,
                                   78, 98.45, 25, 78,
                                   23, 36));             //Line 5

        System.out.println("Line 6: The largest "
                         + "number in numList is "
                         + largest(numberList));         //Line 6

        System.out.println("Line 7: A call to the method "
                         + "largest with an empty \n"
                         + "          parameter "
                         + "list returns the value "
                         + largest());                   //Line 7
    }

    public static double largest(double ... numList)
    {
        double max;
```

9

```
        if (numList.length != 0)
        {
            max = numList[0];

            for (int index = 1; index < numList.length; index++)
            {
                if (max < numList [index])
                    max = numList [index];
            }

            return max;
        }

        return 0.0;
    }
}
```

Sample Run:

```
Line 2: The larger of 5.6 and 10.8 is 10.8
Line 3: The largest of 23, 78, and 56 is 78.0
Line 4: The largest of 93, 28, 83, and 66 is 93.0
Line 5: The largest of 22.5, 12.34, 56.34, 78,
        98.45, 25, 78, 23 and 36 is 98.45
Line 6: The largest number in numList is 120.89
Line 7: A call to the method largest with an empty
        parameter list returns the value 0.0
```

In the preceding program, in Line 2, the method `largest` is called with two parameters; in Line 3 it is called with three parameters; in Line 4 it is called with four parameters; and in Line 5 it is called with nine parameters. Note that in Line 6, the method `largest` is called using an array of numbers, but in Line 7 it is called with no parameters.

Just as you can create a method using the primitive data type as a variable length formal parameter, you can also create a method with objects as a variable length formal parameter (list). Examples 9-11 and 9-12 show you how to do this. First, we specify some rules to follow when using a variable length formal parameter list.

1. A method can have both a variable length formal parameter and other formal parameters. For example, consider the following method heading:

```
public static void myMethod(String name, double num,
                            int ... intList)
```

The formal parameter `name` is of type `String`, the formal parameter `num` is of type `double`, and the formal parameter `intList` is of variable length. The actual parameter corresponding to `intList` can be an `int` array or any number of `int` variables and/or `int` values.

2. A method can have, at most, one variable length formal parameter.

3. If a method has both a variable length formal parameter and other types of formal parameters, then the variable length formal parameter must be the last formal parameter of the formal parameter list.

Before giving more examples of methods with a variable length formal parameter list, we note the following.

One way to process the elements of an array one-by-one, starting at the first element, is to use an index variable, initialized to 0, and a loop. For example, to process the elements of an array, `list`, you can use a `for` loop, such as the following:

```
for (int index; index < list.length; index++)
    //process list[index]
```

In fact, this chapter uses these types of loops to process the elements of an array. The most recent version of Java provides a special type of `for` loop to process the elements of an object, such as an array. The syntax to use this `for` loop to process the elements of an array is:

```
for (dataType identifier : arrayName)
    statements
```

where `identifier` is a variable and the data type of `identifier` is the same as the data type of the array elements. This form of the `for` loop is called a **foreach** loop.

For example, suppose `list` is an array and each element is of type `double`, and `sum` is a `double` variable. The following code finds the sum of the elements of `list`:

```
sum = 0;                         //Line 1

for (double num : list)          //Line 2
    sum = sum + num;             //Line 3
```

The `for` statement in Line 2 is read for each num in `list`. The identifier num is initialized to `list[0]`. In the next iteration, the value of num is `list[1]`, and so on.

Using the foreach loop, the `for` loop in the method `largest`, in Example 9-10, can be written as:

```
for (double num : list)
{
    if (max < num)
        max = num;
}
```

(The modified program, named `LargestNumberVersionII.java`, that uses the foreach loop to determine the largest element in `list`, can be found with the Additional Student Files at *www.cengagebrain.com*.)

Example 9-11 shows that the variable length formal parameters (list) of a method can be objects. This example uses the `class` `Clock` designed in Chapter 8.

EXAMPLE 9-11

```java
public class ObjectsAsVariableLengthParameters
{
    public static void main(String[] args)
    {

        Clock myClock = new Clock(12, 5, 10);            //Line 1
        Clock yourClock = new Clock(8, 15, 6);           //Line 2

        Clock[] arrivalTimeEmp = new Clock[10];          //Line 3

        for (int j = 0; j < arrivalTimeEmp.length;
                    j++)                                 //Line 4
            arrivalTimeEmp[j] = new Clock();             //Line 5

        arrivalTimeEmp[5].setTime(8, 5, 10);             //Line 6

        printTimes(myClock, yourClock);                  //Line 7

        System.out.println("\n*****************"
                        + "******* \n");                 //Line 8

        printTimes(arrivalTimeEmp);                      //Line 9
    }

    public static void printTimes(Clock ... clockList)
    {
        for (int i = 0; i < clockList.length; i++)       //Line 10
            System.out.println(clockList[i]);            //Line 11
    }
}
```

Sample Run:

```
12:05:10
08:15:06

***********************

00:00:00
00:00:00
00:00:00
00:00:00
00:00:00
08:05:10
00:00:00
00:00:00
00:00:00
00:00:00
```

In this program, the statements in Lines 1 and 2 create the objects myClock and yourClock. The statement in Line 3 creates the array arrivalTimeEmp of 10 elements, wherein each element is a reference variable of the Clock type. The for loop in the statements in Lines 4 and 5 instantiates the objects of the array arrivalTimeEmp. The statement in Line 6 sets the arrival time of employee 5, which is the sixth element of the array. The statement in Line 7 calls the method printTimes with two actual parameters, and the statement in Line 9 calls this method with arrivalTimeEmp as the actual parameter, an array of 10 elements.

Note that the for loop in Lines 10 and 11 can be replaced with the following foreach loop:

```
for (Clock clockObject : clockList)        //Line 10
    System.out.println(clockObject);    //Line 11
```

Example 9-12 illustrates that a constructor of a class can have a variable length formal parameter list.

EXAMPLE 9-12

Consider the class StudentData:

```
public class StudentData
{
    private String firstName;
    private String lastName;

    private double[] testScores; //array to store
                                 //the test scores
    private char grade;

        //Default constructor
    public StudentData()
    {
        firstName = "";
        lastName = "";
        grade = '*';
        testScores = new double[5];
    }

        //Constructor with parameters
        //The parameter list is of varying length.
        //Postcondition: firstName = fName; lastName = lName;
        //               testScores = list;
        //               Calculate and assign the grade to
        //               grade.
    public StudentData(String fName, String lName,
                       double ... list)
    {
        firstName = fName;
        lastName = lName;
        testScores = list;
```

9

```java
        grade = courseGrade(list); //calculate and store
                                   //the grade in grade
    }

        //Method to calculate the grade
        //Postcondition: The grade is calculated and
        //               returned.
    public char courseGrade(double ... list)
    {
        double sum = 0;
        double average = 0;

        for (double num : list)
            sum = sum + num;     //sum the test scores

        if (list.length != 0)   //find the average
            average = sum / list.length;

        if (average >= 90)      //determine the grade
            return 'A';
        else if (average >= 80)
            return 'B';
        else if (average > 70)
            return 'C';
        else if (average > 60)
            return 'D';
        else
            return 'F';
    }


        //Method to return student's name, test scores,
        //and grades as a string.
        //Postcondition: The string consisting of the first
        //               name, last name, followed by the
        //               test scores, and the course grade is
        //               constructed and returned.
    public String toString()
    {
        String str;

        str = String.format("%-10s %-10s ", firstName,
                            lastName);

        for (double score : testScores)
            str = str + String.format("%7.2f", score);

        str = str + "    " + grade;

        return str;
    }
}
```

Note that the constructor with parameters of the `class` `StudentData` has a variable length formal parameter. The method `courseGrade` also consists of a variable length formal parameter. The following program uses the `class` `Student` to keep track of students' names, test scores, and course grades:

```
public class TestProgStudentData
{
    public static void main(String[] args)
    {
        StudentData student1 =
                new StudentData("John", "Doe",
                        89, 78, 95, 63, 94);

        StudentData student2 =
                new StudentData("Lindsay", "Green",
                        92, 82, 90, 70, 87, 99);

        System.out.println(student1);
        System.out.println(student2);
    }
}
```

Sample Run:

```
John        Doe         89.00  78.00  95.00  63.00  94.00  B
Lindsay     Green       92.00  82.00  90.00  70.00  87.00  99.00  B
```

We leave the details of the preceding output as an exercise.

9

> **NOTE** To learn more about constructors with a variable length formal parameter list, see Exercise 28 at the end of this chapter.

Two-Dimensional Arrays

In the previous section, you learned how to use one-dimensional arrays to manipulate data. If the data is provided in a list form, you can use one-dimensional arrays. However, sometimes data is provided in a table form.

Suppose you want to keep track of how many cars of a particular color a local dealership has in stock. The dealership sells six types of cars in five different colors. Figure 9-15 shows a sample data table.

inStock	[RED]	[BROWN]	[BLACK]	[WHITE]	[GRAY]
[GM]	10	7	12	10	4
[FORD]	18	11	15	17	10
[TOYOTA]	12	10	9	5	12
[BMW]	16	6	13	8	3
[NISSAN]	10	7	12	6	4
[VOLVO]	9	4	7	12	11

FIGURE 9-15 Table `inStock`

You can see that the data is in a table format. The table has 30 entries, and every entry is an integer. Because all the table entries are of the same type, you could declare a one-dimensional array of 30 elements of type `int`. The first five elements of the one-dimensional array could store the data of the first row of the table, the next five elements of the one-dimensional array could store the data of the second row of the table, and so on. In other words, you could simulate the data given in a table format in a one-dimensional array.

If you do so, the algorithms to manipulate the data in the one-dimensional array will be somewhat complicated, because you must carefully note where one row ends and another begins. Also, you would need to correctly compute the index of a particular element from its row and column location. Java simplifies manipulating data in a table format by using **two-dimensional arrays**. This section first discusses how to declare two-dimensional arrays, and then looks at ways to manipulate the data in a two-dimensional array.

Two-dimensional array: A collection of a fixed number of elements arranged in rows and columns (that is, in two dimensions), wherein all the elements are of the same type.

A syntax for declaring a two-dimensional array is:

```
dataType[][] arrayName;
```

where `dataType` is the data type of the array elements.

Because an array is an object, we must instantiate the object to allocate memory space to store the data. The general syntax to instantiate a two-dimensional array object is:

```
arrayName = new dataType[intExp1][intExp2];
```

where `intExp1` and `intExp2` are expressions yielding positive integer values. The two expressions, `intExp1` and `intExp2`, specify the number of rows and the number of columns, respectively, in the array.

The preceding two statements can be combined into one statement, as follows:

```
dataType[][] arrayName = new dataType[intExp1][intExp2];
```

For example, the statement:

```
double[][] sales = new double[10][5];
```

declares a two-dimensional array `sales` of 10 rows and 5 columns, wherein every element is of type `double` initialized to the default value of `0.0`. As in a one-dimensional array, the rows are numbered `0...9` and the columns are numbered `0...4` (see Figure 9-16).

	[0]	[1]	[2]	[3]	[4]
[0]	0.0	0.0	0.0	0.0	0.0
[1]	0.0	0.0	0.0	0.0	0.0
[2]	0.0	0.0	0.0	0.0	0.0
[3]	0.0	0.0	0.0	0.0	0.0
[4]	0.0	0.0	0.0	0.0	0.0
[5]	0.0	0.0	0.0	0.0	0.0
[6]	0.0	0.0	0.0	0.0	0.0
[7]	0.0	0.0	0.0	0.0	0.0
[8]	0.0	0.0	0.0	0.0	0.0
[9]	0.0	0.0	0.0	0.0	0.0

FIGURE 9-16   Two-dimensional array `sales`

9

NOTE From this point forward, whenever we instantiate a two-dimensional array and draw its diagram, all the default values may not be shown as they are in Figure 9-16.

Accessing Array Elements

To access the elements of a two-dimensional array, you need a pair of indices: one for the row position, and one for the column position.

The syntax to access an element of a two-dimensional array is:

```
arrayName[indexExp1][indexExp2]
```

where `indexExp1` and `indexExp2` are expressions yielding nonnegative integer values. `indexExp1` specifies the row position and `indexExp2` specifies the column position. Moreover, the value of `indexExp1` must be nonnegative and less than the number of rows, and the value of `indexExp2` must be nonnegative and less than the number of columns in the array.

The statement:

```
sales[5][3] = 25.75;
```

stores 25.75 into row number 5 and column number 3 (the 6th row and the 4th column) of the array `sales` (see Figure 9-17).

FIGURE 9-17 sales[5][3]

Suppose that:

```
int i = 5;
int j = 3;
```

Then, the previous statement:

```
sales[5][3] = 25.75;
```

is equivalent to:

```
sales[i][j] = 25.75;
```

So the indices can also be variables.

TWO-DIMENSIONAL ARRAYS AND THE INSTANCE VARIABLE `length`

Just as in one-dimensional arrays, you can use the instance variable `length` to determine the number of rows as well as the number of columns (in each row). Consider the following statement:

```
int[][] matrix = new int[20][15];
```

This statement declares and instantiates a two-dimensional array `matrix` of 20 rows and 15 columns. The value of the expression:

```
matrix.length
```

is 20, the number of rows.

Each row of `matrix` is a one-dimensional array; `matrix[0]`, in fact, refers to the first row. Therefore, the value of the expression:

`matrix[0].length`

is 15, the number of columns in the first row. Similarly, `matrix[1].length` gives the number of columns in the second row, which in this case is 15, and so on.

TWO-DIMENSIONAL ARRAYS: SPECIAL CASES

The two-dimensional arrays created in the preceding sections are quite straightforward; each row has the same number of columns. However, Java allows you to specify a different number of columns for each row. In this case, each row must be instantiated separately. Consider the following statement:

`int[][] board;`

Suppose that you want to create the array `board`, as shown in Figure 9-18.

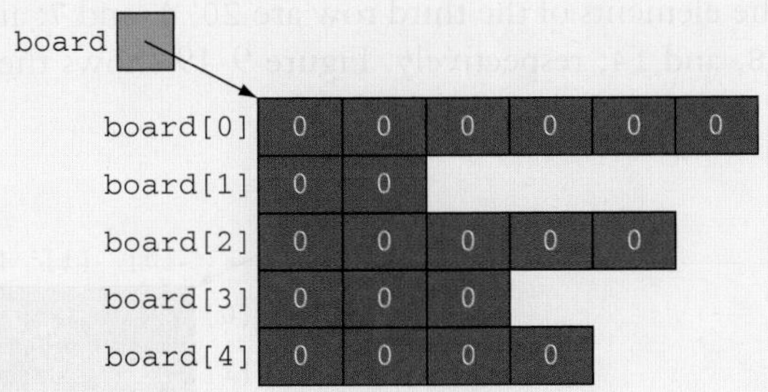

FIGURE 9-18 Array `board`

It follows from Figure 9-18 that the number of rows in `board` is 5, the number of columns in the first row is 6, the number of columns in the second row is 2, the number of columns in the third row is 5, the number of columns in the fourth row is 3, and the number of columns in the fifth row is 4. To create this two-dimensional array, first we create the one-dimensional array `board` of 5 rows. Then, we instantiate each row, specifying the required number of columns, as follows:

```
board = new int[5][];    //Create the number of rows

board[0] = new int[6];   //Create the columns for the first row
board[1] = new int[2];   //Create the columns for the second row
board[2] = new int[5];   //Create the columns for the third row
board[3] = new int[3];   //Create the columns for the fourth row
board[4] = new int[4];   //Create the columns for the fifth row
```

Because the number of columns in each row is not the same, such arrays are called **ragged arrays**. To process these types of two-dimensional arrays, you must know the exact number of columns for each row.

Notice that here `board.length` is 5, the number of rows in the array `board`. Similarly, `board[0].length` is 6, the number of columns in the first row; `board[1].length` is 2, the number of columns in the second row; `board[2].length` is 5, the number of columns in the third row; `board[3].length` is 3, the number of columns in the fourth row; and `board[4].length` is 4, the number of columns in the fifth row.

Two-Dimensional Array Initialization during Declaration

Like one-dimensional arrays, two-dimensional arrays can be initialized when they are declared. The example in the following statement helps illustrate this concept:

```
int[][] board = {{2, 3, 1},
                 {15, 25, 13},
                 {20, 4, 7},
                 {11, 18, 14}};        //Line 1
```

This statement declares `board` to be a two-dimensional array of 4 rows and 3 columns. The elements of the first row are 2, 3, and 1; the elements of the second row are 15, 25, and 13; the elements of the third row are 20, 4, and 7; and the elements of the fourth row are 11, 18, and 14, respectively. Figure 9-19 shows the array `board`.

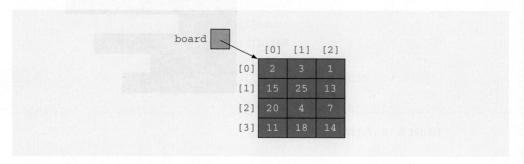

FIGURE 9-19 Two-dimensional array `board`

To initialize a two-dimensional array when it is declared:

- The elements of each row are enclosed within braces and separated by commas.
- All rows are enclosed within braces.

Now consider the following statement:

```
int[][] table = {{2, 1, 3, 5},
                 {15, 25},
                 {4, 23, 45}};
```

Here, you see that the number of values specified for the first row of the array `table` is 4, the number of values specified for the second row is 2, and the number of values specified for the third row is 3. Because the number of values specified for the first row is 4, only four columns are assigned to the first row. Similarly, the number of columns assigned to the second and third rows are 2 and 3, respectively (see Figure 9-20).

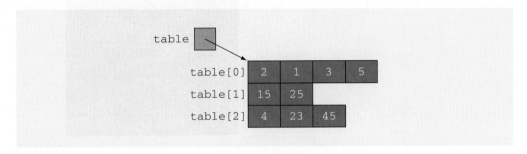

FIGURE 9-20 Array `table`

Processing Two-Dimensional Arrays

In the remainder of this chapter, we assume that the two-dimensional arrays that are being considered are not ragged.

A two-dimensional array can be processed in three common ways:

1. Process the entire array.
2. Process a particular row of the array, called **row processing**.
3. Process a particular column of the array, called **column processing**.

Initializing and printing the array are examples of processing the entire two-dimensional array. Finding the largest element in a row or column, or finding the sum of a row or column, are examples of row (column) processing. We will use the following declarations for our discussion:

```
static final int ROWS = 7;     //this can be set to any number
static final int COLUMNS = 6; //this can be set to any number

int[][] matrix = new int[ROWS][COLUMNS];

int sum;
int largest;
int temp;
```

Figure 9-21 shows the array `matrix`.

9

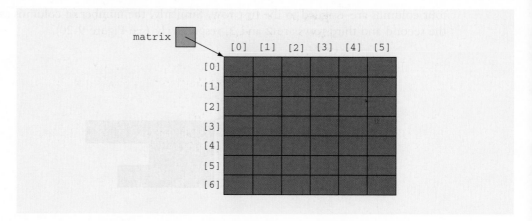

FIGURE 9-21 Two-dimensional array `matrix`

NOTE For the two-dimensional array `matrix`, the value of `matrix.length` is 7, which is the same as the value of the named constant `ROWS`. Also, the values of `matrix[0].length`, `matrix[1].length`, . . ., `matrix[6].length` give the number of columns in row 0, row 1, . . ., row 6, respectively. Notice that the number of columns in each row is 6.

Because all the elements of a two-dimensional array are of the same type, the elements of any row or column are of the same type. This means that in a two-dimensional array, the elements of each row and each column can be processed as a one-dimensional array. Therefore, when processing a particular row or column of a two-dimensional array, we use algorithms similar to those that process one-dimensional arrays. We explain this concept further with the help of the two-dimensional array `matrix`, as declared previously.

Suppose that we want to process row number 5 of `matrix` (the sixth row of `matrix`). The elements of row number 5 of `matrix` are:

`matrix[5][0], matrix[5][1], matrix[5][2], matrix[5][3], matrix[5][4], matrix[5][5]`

In these elements, the first index (the row position) is fixed at 5. The second index (the column position) ranges from 0 to 5. Therefore, we can use the following `for` loop to process row number 5:

```
for (int col = 0; col < matrix[5].length; col++)
    //process matrix[5][col]
```

This `for` loop is equivalent to the following `for` loop:

```
int row = 5;

for (int col = 0; col < matrix[row].length; col++)
    //process matrix[row][col]
```

Similarly, suppose that we want to process column number 2 (the third column) of `matrix`. The elements of this column are:

```
matrix[0][2], matrix[1][2], matrix[2][2], matrix[3][2], matrix[4][2],
matrix[5][2], matrix[6][2]
```

Here, the second index (the column position) is fixed at 2. The first index (the row position) ranges from 0 to 6. In this case, we use the following `for` loop to process column 2 of `matrix`:

```
for (int row = 0; row < matrix.length; row++)
    //process matrix[row][2]
```

This `for` loop is equivalent to the following `for` loop:

```
int col = 2;

for (int row = 0; row < matrix.length; row++)
    //process matrix[row][col]
```

Next, we discuss some specific algorithms for processing two-dimensional arrays.

INITIALIZATION

Suppose that you want to initialize the elements of row number 4 (the fifth row) to 10. As explained earlier, the following `for` loop initializes the elements of row number 4 to 10:

```
int row = 4;
for (int col = 0; col < matrix[row].length; col++)
    matrix[row][col] = 10;
```

If you want to initialize the elements of the entire `matrix` to 10, you can also put the first index (the row position) in a loop. By using the following nested `for` loops, you can initialize each element of `matrix` to 10:

```
for (int row = 0; row < matrix.length; row++)
    for (int col = 0; col < matrix[row].length; col++)
        matrix[row][col] = 10;
```

PRINT

By using a nested `for` loop, you can output the elements of `matrix`. The following nested `for` loops print the elements of `matrix`, one row per line:

```
for (int row = 0; row < matrix.length; row++)
{
    for (int col = 0; col < matrix[row].length; col++)
        System.out.printf("%7d", matrix[row][col]);

    System.out.println();
}
```

INPUT

The following `for` loop inputs data into row number 4 (the fifth row) of `matrix`:

```
int row = 4;

for (int col = 0; col < matrix[row].length; col++)
    matrix[row][col] = console.nextInt();
```

As before, by putting the row number in a loop, you can input data into each element of `matrix`. The following `for` loop inputs data into each element of `matrix`:

```
for (int row = 0; row < matrix.length; row++)
    for (int col = 0; col < matrix[row].length; col++)
        matrix[row][col] = console.nextInt();
```

SUM BY ROW

The following `for` loop finds the sum of the elements of row number 4 of `matrix`; that is, it adds the elements of row number 4:

```
sum = 0;
int row = 4;
for (int col = 0; col < matrix[row].length; col++)
    sum = sum + matrix[row][col];
```

Once again, by putting the row number in a loop, you can find the sum of each row separately. The Java code to find the sum of each individual row follows:

```
    //Sum of each individual row
for (int row = 0; row < matrix.length; row++)
{
    sum = 0;

    for (int col = 0; col < matrix[row].length; col++)
        sum = sum + matrix[row][col];

    System.out.println("The sum of the elements of row "
                     + (row + 1) + " = " + sum);
}
```

SUM BY COLUMN

As in the case of sum by row, the following nested `for` loop finds the sum of the elements of each individual column. (Notice that `matrix[0].length` gives the number of columns in each row.)

```
    //Sum of each individual column
for (int col = 0; col < matrix[0].length; col++)
{
    sum = 0;
    for (int row = 0; row < matrix.length; row++)
        sum = sum + matrix[row][col];
```

```
        System.out.println("The sum of the elements of column "
                            + (col + 1) + " = " + sum);
}
```

(Note that the preceding code to find the sum of the elements of each column assumes that the number of columns in each row is the same. In other words, the two-dimensional array is *not* ragged.)

LARGEST ELEMENT IN EACH ROW AND EACH COLUMN

As stated earlier, another possible operation on a two-dimensional array is finding the largest element in each row and each column. Next, we give the Java code to perform this operation.

The following `for` loop determines the largest element in row number 4:

```
int row = 4;
largest = matrix[row][0]; //assume that the first element of the
                          //row is the largest
for (int col = 1; col < matrix[row].length; col++)
    if (largest < matrix[row][col])
        largest = matrix[row][col];
```

The following Java code determines the largest element in each row and each column:

```
    //The largest element of each row
for (int row = 0; row < matrix.length; row++)
{
    largest = matrix[row][0]; //assume that the first element
                              //of the row is the largest
    for (int col = 1; col < matrix[row].length; col++)
        if (largest < matrix[row][col])
            largest = matrix[row][col];

    System.out.println("The largest element of row "
                        + (row + 1) + " = " + largest);
}


    //The largest element of each column
for (int col = 0; col < matrix[0].length; col++)
{
    largest = matrix[0][col]; //assume that the first element
                              //of the column is the largest
    for (int row = 1; row < matrix.length; row++)
        if (largest < matrix[row][col])
            largest = matrix[row][col];

    System.out.println("The largest element of col "
                        + (col + 1) + " = " + largest);
}
```

Passing Two-Dimensional Arrays as Parameters to Methods

Just like one-dimensional arrays, references to two-dimensional arrays can be passed as parameters to a method.

In the section, Processing Two-Dimensional Arrays, we described various algorithms to process the elements of a two-dimensional array. Using those algorithms, we can write methods that can be used in a variety of applications. In this section, we write some of these methods. For simplicity, we assume that we are processing the entire two-dimensional array.

The following method outputs the elements of a two-dimensional array, one row per line:

```
public static void printMatrix(int[][] matrix)
{
    for (int row = 0; row < matrix.length; row++)
    {
        for (int col = 0; col < matrix[row].length; col++)
            System.out.printf("%7d", matrix[row][col]);

        System.out.println();
    }
}
```

Similarly, the following method outputs the sum of the elements of each row of a two-dimensional array whose elements are of type int:

```
public static void sumRows(int[][] matrix)
{
    int sum;

        //sum of each individual row
    for (int row = 0; row < matrix.length; row++)
    {
        sum = 0;

        for (int col = 0; col < matrix[row].length; col++)
            sum = sum + matrix[row][col];

        System.out.println("The sum of the elements of row "
                        + (row + 1) + " = " + sum);
    }
}
```

The following method determines the largest element in each row:

```
public static void largestInRows(int[][] matrix)
{
    int largest;

        //The largest element in each row
    for (int row = 0; row < matrix.length; row++)
```

```
    {
        largest = matrix[row][0]; //assume that the first
                                  //element of the row is
                                  //the largest
        for (int col = 1; col < matrix[row].length; col++)
            if (largest < matrix[row][col])
                largest = matrix[row][col];

        System.out.println("The largest element of row "
                          + (row + 1) + " = " + largest);
    }
}
```

In a similar fashion, you can write methods to find the sum of the elements of each column, read data into a two-dimensional array, find the largest and/or smallest element in each row or each column, and so on.

As in the case of one-dimensional arrays, to conveniently use the methods to process data in a two-dimensional array, we put the definitions of the methods printArray, sumRows, largestInRows, and other such methods in the **class** TwoDimArraysMethods. The definition of this class is:

```
// This class contains methods to process elements in two-
// dimensional arrays.

public class TwoDimArraysMethods
{
    public static void printMatrix(int[][] matrix)
    {
        for (int row = 0; row < matrix.length; row++)
        {
            for (int col = 0; col < matrix[row].length; col++)
                System.out.printf("%7d", matrix[row][col]);

            System.out.println();
        }
    } //end printMatrix

    public static void sumRows(int[][] matrix)
    {
        int sum;

        //sum of each individual row
        for (int row = 0; row < matrix.length; row++)
        {
            sum = 0;

            for (int col = 0; col < matrix[row].length; col++)
                sum = sum + matrix[row][col];
```

```
        System.out.println("The sum of the elements of row "
                     + (row + 1) + " = " + sum + ".");
    }
} //end sumRows

public static void largestInRows(int[][] matrix)
{
    int largest;

        //Largest element in each row
    for (int row = 0; row < matrix.length; row++)
    {
        largest = matrix[row][0]; //assume that the first
                                  //element of the row is
                                  //largest
        for (int col = 1; col < matrix[row].length; col++)
            if (largest < matrix[row][col])
                largest = matrix[row][col];

        System.out.println("The largest element of row "
                     + (row + 1) + " = " + largest + ".");
    }
} //end largestInRows
}
```

Example 9-13 shows how the preceding methods are used in a program.

EXAMPLE 9-13

The following program illustrates how (references to) two-dimensional arrays are passed as parameters to methods:

```
// This program illustrates how two-dimensional arrays are
// passed as parameters to methods.

public class TwoDimArraysAsParam                         //Line 1
{                                                        //Line 2
    public static void main(String[] args)               //Line 3
    {                                                    //Line 4
        int[][] board ={{23,5,6,15,18},
                        {4,16,24,67,10},
                        {12,54,23,76,11},
                        {1,12,34,22,8},
                        {81,54,32,67,33},
                        {12,34,76,78,9}};                //Line 5

        TwoDimArraysMethods.printMatrix(board);          //Line 6
        System.out.println();                            //Line 7

        TwoDimArraysMethods.sumRows(board);              //Line 8
        System.out.println();                            //Line 9
```

```
        TwoDimArraysMethods.largestInRows(board);        //Line 10
    } //end main                                         //Line 11
}                                                        //Line 12
```

Sample Run:

```
    23      5      6     15     18
     4     16     24     67     10
    12     54     23     76     11
     1     12     34     22      8
    81     54     32     67     33
    12     34     76     78      9
```

```
The sum of the elements of row 1 = 67.
The sum of the elements of row 2 = 121.
The sum of the elements of row 3 = 176.
The sum of the elements of row 4 = 77.
The sum of the elements of row 5 = 267.
The sum of the elements of row 6 = 209.

The largest element of row 1 = 23.
The largest element of row 2 = 67.
The largest element of row 3 = 76.
The largest element of row 4 = 34.
The largest element of row 5 = 81.
The largest element of row 6 = 78.
```

In the preceding program, the statement in Line 5 declares and initializes `board` to be a two-dimensional array of 6 rows and 5 columns. The statement in Line 6 uses the method `printMatrix` to output the elements of `board` (see the first six lines of the Sample Run). The statement in Line 8 uses the method `sumRows` to calculate and print the sum of each row. The statement in Line 10 uses the method `largestInRows` to find and print the largest element in each row.

9

When storing a two-dimensional array in computer memory, Java uses the **row order form**. That is, the first row is stored first, followed by the second row, followed by the third row, and so on.

Multidimensional Arrays

Earlier in this chapter, we defined an array as a collection of a fixed number of variables called elements or components of the same type. A one-dimensional array is an array in which the elements are arranged in a list form; in a two-dimensional array, the elements are arranged in a table form. We can also define three-dimensional or larger arrays. In Java, there is no limit on the dimensions of arrays. The following is the general definition of an array:

n-**dimensional array:** A collection of a fixed number of variables, called elements or components, arranged in n dimensions ($n \geq 1$).

The general syntax for declaring and instantiating an n-dimensional array is:

```
dataType[][]...[] arrayName
                = new dataType[intExp1][intExp2] ... [intExpn];
```

where `intExp1`, `intExp2`, ..., and `intExpn` are constant expressions yielding positive integer values.

The syntax to access an element of an n-dimensional array is:

```
arrayName[indexExp1][indexExp2] ... [indexExpn]
```

where `indexExp1`, `indexExp2`, ..., and `indexExpn` are expressions yielding nonnegative integer values. Moreover, for each `i`, the value of `indexExpi` must be nonnegative and less than the size of the `ith` dimension. `indexExpi` gives the position of the array element in the `ith` dimension.

For example, the statement:

```
double[][][] carDealers = new double[10][5][7];
```

declares `carDealers` to be a three-dimensional array. The size of the first dimension is 10, the size of the second dimension is 5, and the size of the third dimension is 7. The first dimension ranges from 0 to 9, the second dimension ranges from 0 to 4, and the third dimension ranges from 0 to 6. The base address of the array `carDealers` is the address of the first array element—the address of `carDealers[0][0][0]`. The total number of elements in the array `carDealers` is 10 * 5 * 7 = 350.

The statement:

```
carDealers[5][3][2] = 15564.75;
```

sets the value of the element `carDealers[5][3][2]` to `15564.75`.

You can use loops to process multidimensional arrays. For example, the nested `for` loops:

```
for (int i = 0; i < 10; i++)
    for (int j = 0; j < 5; j++)
        for (int k = 0; k < 7; k++)
            carDealers[i][j][k] = 10.00;
```

initialize each element of the array to `10.00`.

During program execution, if an array index goes out of bounds, the program throws an `ArrayIndexOutOfBoundsException`. Exception handling is discussed in detail in Chapter 11.

PROGRAMMING EXAMPLE: Code Detection

When a message is transmitted in secret code over a transmission channel, it is usually transmitted as a sequence of bits, that is, 0s and 1s. Due to noise in the transmission channel, the transmitted message may become corrupted. That is, the message received at the destination is not the same as the message transmitted; some of the bits may have been changed. There are several techniques to check the validity of the transmitted message at the destination. One technique is to transmit the same message twice. At the destination, both copies of the message are compared bit-by-bit. If the corresponding bits are the same, the message is assumed to have been received error-free.

Let's write a program to check whether the message received at the destination is likely error-free. For simplicity, assume that the secret code representing the message is a sequence of digits (0 to 9). Also, the first number in the message is the length of the message. For example, if the secret code is:

7 9 2 7 8 3 5 6

then the actual message is 7 digits long, and it is transmitted twice.

The above message is transmitted as:

7 9 2 7 8 3 5 6 7 9 2 7 8 3 5 6

Input: The secret code and its copy.

Output: The secret code, its copy, and a message—if the received code is error-free—in the following form:

```
Code Digit      Code Digit Copy
    9                  9
    2                  2
    7                  7
    8                  8
    3                  3
    5                  5
    6                  6
Message transmitted OK.
```

The preceding output is to be stored in a file.

PROBLEM ANALYSIS AND ALGORITHM DESIGN

Because we have to compare the corresponding digits of the secret code and its copy, you first read the secret code and store it in an array. Then you read the first digit of the copy and compare it with the first digit of the secret code, and so on. If any corresponding digits are not the same, you indicate this fact by printing a message next to the digits. We use an array to store the secret code. The first number in the secret code, and in the copy of the secret code, indicates the length of the code. This discussion translates into the following algorithm:

1. Prompt and read the length of the secret code.
2. Create an array of appropriate length to store the secret code.
3. Read and store the secret code into an array.
4. Read the length of the copy.
5. If the length of the secret code and its copy are the same, compare the codes. Otherwise, print an error message.

To simplify the definition of the method main, let us write the method, readCode, to read the secret code and another method, compareCode, to compare the codes. Next, we describe these two methods.

readCode The method readCode reads and stores the secret code in an array. This method has one parameter: an array to store the secret code. The definition of the method readCode is as follows:

```
public static void readCode(int[] list)
{
    System.out.print("Enter the secret code: ");

    for (int count = 0; count < list.length; count++)
        list[count] = console.nextInt();

    System.out.println();
}
```

compareCode This method compares the secret code with its copy and prints an appropriate message. Therefore, it must have access to the array containing the secret code. Thus, this method has one parameter: the array containing the secret code. This discussion translates into the following algorithm for the method compareCode:

a. Declare the variables.
b. Set a boolean variable codeOk to true.
c. Read the length of the copy of the secret code.
d. If the length of the secret code and its copy are not the same, output an appropriate error message and terminate the method.
e. Output the heading: Code Digit   Code Digit Copy
f. For each digit in the secret code:
   i. Read the next digit of the copy of the secret code.
   ii. Output the corresponding digits from the secret code and its copy.
   iii. If the corresponding digits are not the same, output an error message and set the boolean variable codeOk to false.

g. if the `boolean` variable `codeOk` is `true`

Output a message indicating that the secret code was transmitted correctly.

else

Output an error message.

Following this algorithm, the definition of the method `compareCode` is

```java
public static void compareCode(int[] list)
{
        //Step a: Declare the variables
    int length2;
    int digit;
    boolean codeOk;

    codeOk = true;                              //Step b

    System.out.println("Enter the length of the copy of "
                    + "the secret code \nand a copy of "
                    + "the secret code: ");

     length2 = console.nextInt();               //Step c

    if (list.length != length2)                 //Step d
    {
        System.out.println("The original code and "
                        + "its copy are not of "
                        + "the same length.");
        return;
    }

    System.out.println("Code Digit    Code Digit "
                    + "Copy");                   //Step e

    for (int count = 0; count < list.length; count++) //Step f
    {
        digit = console.nextInt();              //Step f(i)

        System.out.printf("%5d %15d",
                        list[count], digit);     //Step f(ii)

        if (digit != list[count])               //Step f(iii)
        {
            System.out.println("  corresponding code "
                            + "digits not the same");
            codeOk = false;
        }
```

```
                    else
                        System.out.println();
            }

        if (codeOk)                                      //Step g
            System.out.println("Message transmitted OK.");
        else
            System.out.println("Error in transmission. "
                                + "Retransmit!!");
    }
```

The following is the algorithm for the method `main`.

Main
Algorithm

1. Declare the variable to store the length of the secret code.
2. Prompt the user to enter the length of the secret code.
3. Get the length of the secret code.
4. Create the array to store the secret code.
5. Call the method `readCode` to read the secret code.
6. Call the method `compareCode` to compare the codes.

PROGRAM LISTING

```
//*************************************************************
// Author: D. S. Malik
//
// Program: Code Detection
// This program checks whether the message received at the
// destination is error-free. If there is an error in the
// message, then the program outputs an error message and
// asks for retransmission.
//*************************************************************

import java.util.*;

public class CodeDetection
{
    static Scanner console = new Scanner(System.in);

    public static void main(String[] args)
    {
        int codeLength;                                  //Step 1

        System.out.print("Enter the length "
                        + "of the code: ");       //Step 2
```

```
            codeLength = console.nextInt();        //Step 3
            System.out.println();

            int[] codeArray = new int[codeLength];  //Step 4

            readCode(codeArray);                    //Step 5
            compareCode(codeArray);                 //Step 6
        }

        //Place the definition of the method readCode as
        //described earlier here.
        //Place the definition of the method compareCode as
        //described earlier here.
    }
```

Sample Run: (In this sample run, the user input is shaded.)

```
Enter the length of the code: 7

Enter the secret code: 9 2 7 8 3 5 6

Enter the length of the copy of the secret code
and a copy of the secret code:
7 9 2 7 8 3 5 6

Code Digit    Code Digit Copy
    9               9
    2               2
    7               7
    8               8
    3               3
    5               5
    6               6
Message transmitted OK.
```

9

PROGRAMMING EXAMPLE: Text Processing

Let's now write a program that reads a given text, outputs the text as is, and prints the number of lines and the number of times each letter appears in the text. An uppercase letter and a lowercase letter are treated as being the same; that is, they are tallied together.

Because there are 26 letters, we use an array of 26 elements to perform the letter count. We also need a variable to store the line count.

The text is stored in a file, which we will call `text.txt`. The output will be stored in a file, which we will call `textCh.out`.

Input: A file containing the text to be processed.

Output: A file containing the text, number of lines, and the number of times a letter appears in the text.

PROBLEM
ANALYSIS
AND
ALGORITHM
DESIGN

Based on the desired output, it is clear that we must output the text as is. That is, if the text contains any whitespace characters, they must be output as well.

Let's first describe the variables that are necessary to develop the program. This will simplify the discussion that follows.

Variables

We need to store the letter count and the line count. Therefore, we need a variable to store the line count and 26 variables to store the letter count. We will use an array of 26 elements to perform the letter count. We also need a variable to read and store each character in turn, because the input file will be read character-by-character. Because the data will be read from an input file and the output will be saved in a file, we need an input stream object to open the input file and an output stream object to open the output file. Because the program needs to do a character count, the program should read the input file character-by-character. Moreover, the program should also count the number of lines. Therefore, while reading the data from the input file, the program must capture the newline character. The `Scanner` class does not contain any method that can only read the next character in the input stream, unless the character is delimited by whitespace characters such as blanks. Moreover, using the `Scanner` class, the program should read the entire line or else the newline character will be ignored.

To simplify the character-by-character reading of the input file, we use the Java `class` `FileReader`. (In Chapter 3, we introduced this class to create and initialize a `Scanner` object to the input source.) The `class` `FileReader` contains the method `read` that returns the integer value of the next character. For example, if the next input character is `A`, the method `read` returns 65. We can use the cast operator to change the value 65 to the character `A`. Notice that the method `read` *does not* skip whitespace characters. Also, the method `read` returns −1 when the end of the input file has been reached. We can, therefore, use the value returned by the method `read` to determine whether the end of the input file is reached.

Consider the following statement:

```
FileReader inputStream = new FileReader("text.txt");
```

This statement creates the `FileReader` object `inputStream` and initializes it to the input file `text.txt`. If `nextChar` is a `char` variable, then the following statement reads and stores the next character from the input file into `nextChar`:

```
ch = (char) inputStream.read();
```

It now follows that the method `main` needs (at least) the following variables:

```
int lineCount = 0;      //variable to store the line count

int[] letterCount = new int[26]; //array to store the letter
                                 //count

int next;    //variable to read a character

FileReader inputStream = new FileReader("text.txt");

PrintWriter outfile = new PrintWriter("textCh.out");
```

(Note that the method `read` throws an `IOException` when something goes wrong. At this point, we will ignore this exception by throwing it in the program. Exceptions are covered in detail in Chapter 11.)

In this declaration, `letterCount[0]` stores the A count, `letterCount[1]` stores the B count, and so on. Clearly, the variable `lineCount` and the array `letterCount` must be initialized to `0`.

The algorithm for the program is:

1. Declare and initialize the variables.
2. Create objects to open the input and output files.
3. While there is more data in the input file:
   a. For each character in a line:
      i. Read and write the character.
      ii. Increment the appropriate letter count.
   b. Increment the line count.
4. Output the line count and letter counts.
5. Close the files.

To simplify the method `main`, we divide it into three methods:

1. Method `copyText`
2. Method `chCount`
3. Method `writeTotal`

The following sections describe each method in detail. Then, with the help of these methods, we describe the algorithm for the method `main`.

copyText   This method reads a line and outputs the line. Whenever a nonblank character is found, it calls the method `chCount` to update the letter count. Clearly, this method has four parameters: an input stream object, an output stream object, a variable to read the character, and the array to update the letter count.

Note that the method `copyText` does not perform the letter count, but we still pass the array `letterCount` to it. We do this because this method calls the method `chCount`, which needs the array `letterCount` to update the appropriate letter count. Therefore, we must pass the array `letterCount` to the `copyText` method so that it can pass the array to the method `chCount`.

```
static int copyText(FileReader infile, PrintWriter outfile,
                    int next, int[] letterC) throws IOException
{
    while (next != (int)'\n')
    {
        outfile.print((char)(next));
        chCount((char)(next), letterC);
        next = infile.read();
    }

    outfile.println();

    return next;
}
```

`chCount` This method increments the letter count. To increment the appropriate letter count, the method must know what the letter is. Therefore, the `chCount` method has two parameters: a `char` variable and the array to update the letter count. In pseudocode, this method is:

    a.   Convert the letter to uppercase.

    b.   Find the index of the array corresponding to this letter.

    c.   If the index is valid, increment the appropriate count. At this step, we must ensure that the character is a letter. We are only counting letters, so other characters—such as commas, hyphens, and periods—are ignored.

Following this algorithm, the definition of the method is:

```
static void chCount(char ch, int[] letterC)
{
    int index;

    ch = Character.toUpperCase(ch);    //Step a

    index = (int) ch - 65;             //Step b

    if (index >= 0 && index < 26)      //Step c
        letterC[index]++;
}
```

riteTotal   This method outputs the line count and the letter count. It has three parameters: the output stream object, the line count, and the array to output the letter count. The definition of this method is:

```
static void writeTotal(PrintWriter outfile, int lines,
                       int[] letters)
{

    outfile.println();
    outfile.println("The number of lines = " + lines);

    for (int i = 0; i < 26; i++)
        outfile.println((char)(i + 65) + " count = "
                        + letters[i]);
}
```

We now describe the algorithm for the method main.

MAIN
ALGORITHM

1. Declare and initialize the variables.
2. Open the input and output files.
3. Read the first character.
4. while (not end of the input file):
    a. Process the next line; call the method copyText.
    b. Increment the line count. (Increment the variable lineCount.)
    c. Read the next character.
5. Output the line count and letter count. Call the method writeTotal.
6. Close the files.

9

COMPLETE PROGRAM LISTING

```
//**************************************************************
// Author: D. S. Malik
//
// Program: Line and letter count
// This program reads a given text, outputs the text as
// is, and prints the number of lines and the number of times
// each letter appears in the text. An uppercase letter and a
// lowercase letter are treated as being the same; that is,
// they are tallied together.
//**************************************************************
```

```java
import java.io.*;

public class CharacterCount
{
    public static void main(String[] args)
                    throws FileNotFoundException, IOException
    {
        int lineCount = 0;
        int[] letterCount = new int[26];

        int next;

        FileReader inputStream = new FileReader("text.txt");

        PrintWriter outfile = new PrintWriter("textCh.out");

        next = inputStream.read();

        while (next != -1)
        {
            next = copyText(inputStream, outfile,
                            next, letterCount);
            lineCount++;
            next = inputStream.read();
        }  //end while loop

        writeTotal(outfile, lineCount, letterCount);

        outfile.close();
    }

    //Place the definition of the method copyText, chCount,
    //and writeTotal as described earlier here.
}
```

Sample Run:

Input file (text.txt)

Today we live in an era where information is processed
almost at the speed of light. Through computers, the
technological revolution is drastically changing the way we
live and communicate with one another. Terms such as
"the Internet," which was unfamiliar just a few years ago, are
very common today. With the help of computers you can send
letters to, and receive letters from, loved ones within
seconds. You no longer need to send a resume by mail to apply
for a job; in many cases you can simply submit your job
application via the Internet. You can watch how stocks perform
in real time, and instantly buy and sell them. Students
regularly "surf" the Internet and use computers to design

their classroom projects. They also use powerful word processing software to complete their term papers. Many people maintain and balance their checkbooks on computers.

Output file (textCh.txt)

Today we live in an era where information is processed almost at the speed of light. Through computers, the technological revolution is drastically changing the way we live and communicate with one another. Terms such as "the Internet," which was unfamiliar just a few years ago, are very common today. With the help of computers you can send letters to, and receive letters from, loved ones within seconds. You no longer need to send a resume by mail to apply for a job; in many cases you can simply submit your job application via the Internet. You can watch how stocks perform in real time, and instantly buy and sell them. Students regularly "surf" the Internet and use computers to design their classroom projects. They also use powerful word processing software to complete their term papers. Many people maintain and balance their checkbooks on computers.

```
The number of lines = 15
A count = 53
B count = 7
C count = 30
D count = 19
E count = 83
F count = 11
G count = 10
H count = 29
I count = 41
J count = 4
K count = 3
L count = 31
M count = 26
N count = 50
O count = 59
P count = 21
Q count = 0
R count = 45
S count = 48
T count = 62
U count = 24
V count = 7
W count = 15
X count = 0
Y count = 20
Z count = 0
```

class Vector (Optional)

In addition to arrays, Java provides the **class** Vector to implement a list. Unlike an array, the size of a Vector object can grow and shrink during program execution. Therefore, you need not be concerned about the number of data elements. Before describing how a Vector object is used to manage a list, Table 9-2 describes some of the members of the **class** Vector.

TABLE 9-2 Some Members of the **class** Vector

Instance variables
protected int elementCount;
protected Object[] elementData; //Array of references
Constructors
public **Vector**()   //Creates an empty vector of size 0
public Vector(int size)   //Creates an empty vector of the length specified by size
Methods
public void **addElement**(Object insertObj)   //Add the object insertObj at the end

public void **insertElementAt**(Object insertObj, int index)
  //Inserts the object insertObj at the position specified by index
  //If index is out of range, this method throws
  //ArrayIndexOutOfBoundsException.

public boolean **contains**(Object obj)
  //Returns true if the Vector object contains the element specified
  //by obj; otherwise it returns false

public Object **elementAt**(int index)   //Returns the element of the vector at location specified by index

public int **indexOf**(Object obj)
  //Returns the position of the first occurrence of the element
  //specified by obj in the vector
  //If item is not in the vector, the method returns -1.

```
public int indexOf(Object obj, int index)
   //Starting at index, the method returns the position of the
   //first occurrence of the element specified by obj in the vector.
   //If item is not in the vector, the method returns -1.

public boolean isEmpty()
   //Returns true if the vector is empty; otherwise it returns false

public void removeAllElements()
   //Removes all elements of the vector

public void removeElementAt(int index)
   //If an element at position specified by index exists, it is
   //removed from the vector.
   //If index is out of range, this method throws an
   //ArrayIndexOutOfBoundsException.

public int size()
   //Returns the number of elements in the vector

public String toString()
   //Returns a string representation of this vector
```

From Table 9-2, it follows that every element of a Vector object is a reference variable of type Object. In Java, Object is a predefined class, and a reference variable of the Object type can store the address of any object. Because every element of a Vector object is a reference, to add an element to a Vector object, you must first create the appropriate object and store the data into that object. You can then store the address of the object holding the data into a Vector object element. Because every string in Java is considered a String object, we will illustrate some of the operations on a Vector object using string data.

Consider the following statement:

```
Vector<String> stringList = new Vector<String>();        //Line 1
```

This statement declares stringList to be a reference variable of the Vector type, instantiates an empty Vector object, and stores the address of this object into stringList. The Vector object stringList is used to create a Vector of String objects.

NOTE   In Java 5.0 and higher versions, whenever you declare a Vector object, you should also specify the reference type of the objects that the Vector object will hold. To do this, enclose the reference type of the objects between < and > after the word Vector. For example, in the statement in Line 1, Vector<String> specifies that the Vector object stringList is a Vector of the String object. If you do not specify the reference type after the word Vector, the compiler will generate a warning message indicating an unchecked or unsafe operation.

9

Next, consider the following statements:

```
stringList.addElement("Spring");
stringList.addElement("Summer");
stringList.addElement("Fall");
stringList.addElement("Winter");
```

After these statements execute, `stringList` is as shown in Figure 9-22.

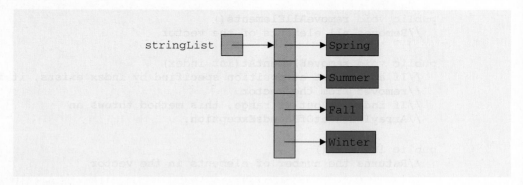

FIGURE 9-22 `stringList` after adding four strings

The statement:

```
System.out.println(stringList);
```

outputs the elements of `stringList` in the following form:

```
[Spring, Summer, Fall, Winter]
```

The **class** `Vector` is contained in the package `java.util`. Therefore, to use the **class** `Vector`, your program must include either the statement:

```
import java.util.*;
```

or the statement:

```
import java.util.Vector;
```

The program in Example 9-14 further illustrates how a `Vector` object works.

EXAMPLE 9-14

```
//StringVectorExample

import java.util.Vector;                              //Line 1

public class StringVectorExample                      //Line 2
{                                                     //Line 3
    public static void main(String[] arg)             //Line 4
```

```
    {                                                     //Line 5
        Vector<String> stringList =
                        new Vector<String>();            //Line 6

        System.out.println("Line 7: Empty stringList?: "
                    + stringList.isEmpty());              //Line 7
        System.out.println("Line 8: Size stringList?: "
                    + stringList.size());                 //Line 8
        System.out.println();                             //Line 9

        stringList.addElement("Spring");                  //Line 10
        stringList.addElement("Summer");                  //Line 11
        stringList.addElement("Fall");                    //Line 12
        stringList.addElement("Winter");                  //Line 13
        stringList.addElement("Sunny");                   //Line 14

        System.out.println("Line 15: **** After adding "
                    + "elements to stringList ****");     //Line 15
        System.out.println("Line 16: Empty stringList?: "
                    + stringList.isEmpty());              //Line 16
        System.out.println("Line 17: Size stringList?: "
                    + stringList.size());                 //Line 17
        System.out.println("Line 18: stringList: "
                    + stringList);                        //Line 18

        System.out.println("Line 19: stringList contains Fall?: "
                    + stringList.contains("Fall"));       //Line 19
        System.out.println();                             //Line 20

        stringList.removeElement("Fall");                 //Line 21
        stringList.removeElementAt(2);                    //Line 22
        System.out.println("Line 23: **** After the remove"
                    + " operations ****");                //Line 23
        System.out.println("Line 24: stringList: "
                    + stringList);                        //Line 24
    }                                                     //Line 25
}                                                         //Line 26
```

Sample Run:

```
Line 7: Empty stringList?: true
Line 8: Size stringList?: 0

Line 15: **** After adding elements to stringList ****
Line 16: Empty stringList?: false
Line 17: Size stringList?: 5
Line 18: stringList: [Spring, Summer, Fall, Winter, Sunny]
Line 19: stringList contains Fall?: true

Line 23: **** After the remove operations ****
Line 24: stringList: [Spring, Summer, Sunny]
```

Primitive Data Types and the `class` `Vector`

As described in the preceding section, every element of a `Vector` object is a reference. Therefore, to create a `Vector` of, say integers, the integers must be wrapped in an object. Recall that Java provides a wrapper class corresponding to each primitive data type. For example, the wrapper class corresponding to type `int` is `Integer`. Therefore, an `int` value can be wrapped in an `Integer` object. As explained in Chapter 6, as of Java 5.0, Java has simplified the wrapping and unwrapping of primitive type values, called the *autoboxing* and *auto-unboxing* of primitive data types. For example, suppose that `x` is an `int` variable and `num` is an `Integer` object.

Consider the statements:

```
num = 25;
num = new Integer(25);
```

After the execution of either of these statements, `num` would point to an `Integer` object with the value 25. Recall that the expression, `num = 25;`, is called the *autoboxing* of the `int` type.

Next, we illustrate how to create a `Vector` of `Integer` objects to store `int` values.

Suppose that you have the declaration:

```
Vector<Integer> list = new Vector<Integer>();
```

The following statements create `Integer` objects with the `int` values 13 and 25 (if there are no other `Integer` objects with these values), and the `Integer` objects are assigned to `list`:

```
list.addElement(13);
list.addElement(25);
```

You can use other `Vector` operations to manipulate the objects of `list`. The program `IntVectorExample.java`, which shows how to create and manipulate a `Vector` of `Integer` objects, can be found with the Additional Student Files at *www.cengagebrain.com*. Also, recall that the wrapper class corresponding to type `char` is `Character`, type `double` is `Double`, type `float` is `Float`, and type `boolean` is `Boolean`.

Vector Objects and the foreach Loop

Recall that a foreach loop can be used to process the elements of a collection object one at a time. Because each `Vector` object is a collection of elements, you can use a foreach loop to process the elements of a `Vector` object. The syntax to use this type of `for` loop to process the elements of a `Vector` object is:

```
for (type identifier : vectorObject)
    statements
```

where `identifier` is a (reference) variable and the data type of (the object that) `identifier` (points to) is the same as the data type of the objects that each `vectorObject` element points to. Also, `type` is either a primitive type or the name of a class.

For example, suppose that you have the following statements:

```
Vector<String> stringList = new Vector<String>();      //Line 1

stringList.addElement("One");                          //Line 2
stringList.addElement("Two");                          //Line 3
stringList.addElement("Three");                        //Line 4

System.out.println("stringList: " + stringList);       //Line 5

for (String str : stringList)                          //Line 6
    System.out.println(str.toUpperCase());             //Line 7
```

The statement in Line 1 creates the `Vector` object `stringList` to create a list of `String` objects. The statements in Lines 2 through 4 add the string objects with the values `"One"`, `"Two"`, and `"Three"`, respectively, to `stringList`. The statement in Line 5 outputs the values of the string objects of `stringList`. Note that the output of the statement in Line 5 is:

```
stringList: [One, Two, Three]
```

The foreach loop in Lines 6 and 7 processes each element of `stringList` one at a time and outputs each string in uppercase letters. More specifically, the output is:

```
ONE
TWO
THREE
```

The program `StringVectorExampleII.java`, which shows how to use a foreach loop to process string `Vector` lists, can be found with the Additional Student Files at *www.cengagebrain.com*. The program `IntVectorExampleII.java` shows how a foreach loop, using the auto-unboxing feature of primitive data types, can be used to process the elements of a `Vector` object of `int` values.

QUICK REVIEW

1. An array is a structured data type with a fixed number of elements. Every element is of the same type, and the elements are accessed using their relative positions in the array.

2. Elements of a one-dimensional array are arranged in the form of a list.

3. An array index can be any expression that evaluates to a nonnegative integer. The value of the index must always be less than the size of the array.

4. In Java, an array index starts with 0.

5. In Java, `[]` is an operator, called the array subscripting operator.

6. When an array object is instantiated, its elements are initialized to their default values.

7. Arrays that are created, that is, instantiated, during program execution are called dynamic arrays.

8. Arrays can be initialized when they are created.

9. A `public` (`final`) instance variable `length` is associated with each array that has been instantiated (that is, for which memory has been allocated to store the data). The variable `length` contains the size of the array.

10. If an array index goes out of bounds, the program throws an `ArrayIndexOutOfBoundsException`.

11. The base address of an array is the address (that is, memory location) of the first array element.

12. Arrays can be passed as parameters to methods.

13. In a method call statement, when passing an array as an actual parameter, you use only its name.

14. Individual array elements can be passed as parameters to methods.

15. The sequential search searches the array sequentially starting from the first array element.

16. You can create an array of objects.

17. The syntax to declare a variable length formal parameter is:

    `dataType ... identifier`

18. A method can have both a variable length formal parameter and other formal parameters.

19. A method can have, at most, one variable length formal parameter.

20. If a method has both a variable length formal parameter and other types of formal parameters, then the variable length formal parameter must be the last formal parameter of the formal parameter list.

21. The most recent version of Java provides a special type of `for` loop, called a foreach loop, to process the elements of an object, such as an array.

22. The syntax to use a foreach loop to process the elements of an array is:

    `for (dataType identifier : arrayName)`

    `    statements`

    where `identifier` is a variable and the data type of `identifier` is the same as the data type of the array elements.

23. A two-dimensional array is an array in which the elements are arranged in a table form.

24. To access an element of a two-dimensional array, you need a pair of indices: one for the row position and one for the column position.

25. In row processing, a two-dimensional array is processed one row at a time.

26. In column processing, a two-dimensional array is processed one column at a time.

27. Java stores two-dimensional arrays in a row order form in computer memory.

28. In addition to arrays, Java provides the `class` Vector to implement a list.

29. Unlike an array, the size of a Vector object can grow and shrink during program execution.

EXERCISES

1. Mark the following statements as true or false.

   a. A `double` type is an example of a primitive data type.

   b. A one-dimensional array is an example of a structured data type.

   c. Arrays can be passed as parameters to a method.

   d. A method can return a value of the type `array`.

   e. The size of an array is determined at compile time.

   f. Given the declaration:

      ```
      int[] list = new int[10];
      ```

      the statement:

      ```
      list[5] = list[3] + list[2];
      ```

      updates the content of the fifth element of the array `list`.

   g. If an array index goes out of bounds, the program terminates in an error.

2. Consider the following declaration:

   ```
   double[] salary = new double[10];
   ```

   In this declaration, identify the following:

   a. The array name.

   b. The array size.

   c. The data type of each array component.

   d. The range of values for the index of the array.

3. Identify error(s), if any, in the following array declarations.

   a. `int[] list = new int[10];`

   b. `final int size = 100;`

      `double[] list = new double[SIZE];`

   c. `int[] numList = new int [0..9];`

   d. `String[] names = new String[20];`

   e. `scores double = new double[50];`

9

4. Determine whether the following array declarations are valid. If a declaration is invalid, give a correct declaration.

    a. `int[75] list;`

    b. `int size;`
        `double[] list = new double[size];`

    c. `int[] test = new int[-10];`

    d. `double[] sales = new double[40.5];`

5. What would be a valid range for the index of an array of size 50?

6. Write Java statements that do the following:

    a. Declare an array `alpha` of 15 elements of type `int`.

    b. Output the value of the tenth element of the array `alpha`.

    c. Set the value of the fifth element of the array `alpha` to 35.

    d. Set the value of the ninth element of the array `alpha` to the sum of the sixth and thirteenth elements of the array `alpha`.

    e. Set the value of the fourth element of the array `alpha` to three times the value of the eighth element, minus 57.

    f. Output `alpha` so that five elements per line are printed.

7. What is the output of the following program segment?

    ```java
    int[] temp = new int[5];

    for (int i = 0; i < 5; i++)
        temp[i] = 2 * i - 3;

    for (int i = 0; i < 5; i++)
        System.out.print(temp[i] + " ");
    System.out.println();

    temp[0] = temp[4];
    temp[4] = temp[1];
    temp[2] = temp[3] + temp[0];

    for (int i = 0; i < 5; i++)
        System.out.print(temp[i] + " ");
    System.out.println();
    ```

8. Suppose `list` is an array of five elements of type `int`. What is stored in `list` after the following Java code executes?

    ```java
    for (i = 0; i < 5; i++)
    {
        list[i] = 2 * i + 5;

        if (i % 2 == 0)
            list[i] = list[i] - 3;
    }
    ```

9. Consider the method headings:

```
void funcOne(int[] alpha, int size)
int funcSum(int x, int y)
void funcTwo(int[] alpha, int[] beta)
```

and the declarations:

```
int[] list = new int[50];
int[] AList = new int[60];
int num;
```

Write Java statements that do the following:

a. Call the method `funcOne` with the actual parameters, `list` and 50, respectively.

b. Print the value returned by the method `funcSum` with the actual parameters, 50 and the fourth element of `list`, respectively.

c. Print the value returned by the method `funcSum` with the actual parameters, the thirtieth and tenth elements of `list`, respectively.

d. Call the method `funcTwo` with the actual parameters, `list` and `AList`, respectively.

10. Correct the following code so that it correctly initializes and outputs the elements of the array `myList`:

```
Scanner console = new Scanner(System.in);

int[] myList = new[10];

for (int i = 1; i <= 10; i++)
    myList = console.nextInt();

for (int i = 1; i <= 10; i++)
    System.out.print(myList[i] + " ");
System.out.println();
```

11. Suppose `list` is an array of six elements of type `int`. What is stored in `list` after the following Java code executes?

```
list[0] = 5;

for (int i = 1; i < 6; i++)
{
    list[i] = i * i + 5;

    if (i > 2)
        list[i] = 2 * list[i] - list[i - 1];
}
```

9

12. What is the output of the following program?

```java
public class Exercise12
{
    public static void main(String[] args)
    {
        int[] alpha = new int[5];

        alpha[0] = 5;
        for (int count = 1; count < 5; count++)
        {
            alpha[count] = 5 * count + 10;
            alpha[count - 1] = alpha[count] - 4;
        }

        System.out.print("List elements: ");

        for (int count = 0; count < 5; count++)
            System.out.print(alpha[count] + " ");
        System.out.println();
    }
}
```

13. What is the output of the following program?

```java
public class Exercise13
{
    public static void main(String[] args)
    {
        int[] one = new int[5];
        int[] two = new int[10];

        for (int j = 0; j < 5; j++)
            one[j] = 5 * j + 3;

        System.out.print("One contains: ");

        for (int j = 0; j < 5; j++)
            System.out.print(one[j] + " ");

        System.out.println();

        for (int j = 0; j < 5; j++)
        {
            two[j] = 2 * one[j] - 1;
            two[j + 5] = one[4 - j] + two[j];
        }

        System.out.print("Two contains: ");

        for (int j = 0; j < 10; j++)
            System.out.print(two[j] + " ");

        System.out.println();
    }
}
```

14. What is an array index out-of-bound? Does Java check for array indices within bound?

15. Suppose that `scores` is an array of 10 components of type `double`, and

    ```
    scores = {2.5, 3.9, 4.8, 6.2, 6.2, 7.4, 7.9, 8.5, 8.5, 9.9}
    ```

    The following is supposed to ensure that the elements of `scores` are in nondecreasing order. However, there are errors in the code. Find and correct the errors.

    ```
    for (int i = 1; i <= 10; i++)
        if (scores[i] >= scores[i + 1])
            System.out.println(i + " and " + (i + 1)
                + " elements of scores are out of order.");
    ```

16. Write Java statements to define and initialize the following arrays.

    a. Array `heights` of 10 components of type `double`. Initialize this array to the following values:

       5.2, 6.3, 5.8, 4.9, 5.2, 5.7, 6.7, 7.1, 5.10, 6.0.

    b. Array `weights` of 7 components of type `int`. Initialize this array to the following values:

       120, 125, 137, 140, 150, 180, 210.

    c. Array `specialSymbols` of type `char`. Initialize this array to the following values:

       '$', '#', '%', '@', '&', '! ', '^'.

    d. Array `seasons` of 4 components of type `String`. Initialize this array to the following values: `"fall"`, `"winter"`, `"spring"`, `"summer"`.

17. Determine whether the following array declarations are valid.

    a. `int[] a = {0, 4, 3, 2, 7};`

    b. `int[10] b = {0, 7, 3, 12};`

    c. `int[] c = {12, 13, , 14, 16, , 8};`

    d. `double[] lengths = {12.7, 13.9, 18.75, 20.78};`

18. Suppose that you have the following declaration:

    ```
    int[] list = {8, 9, 15, 12, 80};
    ```

    What is stored in each components of `list`?

19. What is the output of the following code?

    ```
    int[] list ={6, 8, 2, 14, 13};

    for (int i = 0; i < 4; i++)
        list[i] = list[i] - list[i + 1];

    for (int i = 0; i < 5; i++)
        System.out.println(i + " " + list[i]);
    ```

9

20. Consider the following method heading:

```
public static void tryMe(int[] x, int size);
```

and the declarations:

```
int[] list = new int [100];
int[] score = new int [50];
double[] gpa = new double [50];
```

Which of the following method calls is valid?

a. `tryMe(list, 100);`

b. `tryMe(list, 75);`

c. `tryMe(score, 100);`

d. `tryMe(score, 49);`

e. `tryMe(gpa, 50);`

21. Suppose that you have the following method definition:

```
public static int sum(int x, int y)
{
    return   x + y;
}
```

Consider the following declarations:

```
int[] list1 = new int [10];
int[] list2 = new int [10];
int[] list3 = new int [10];
int a, b, c;
```

Which of the following method calls is valid?

a. `c = sum(a, b);`

b. `a = sum(list1[0], list2[0]);`

c. `c = sum(list1, list2);`

d. `for (int i = 1; i <= 10; i++)`
   `list3[i] = sum(list1[i], list2[i]);`

22. What is the output of the following Java code?

```
double[] salary = {25000, 36500, 85000, 62500, 97000};
double raise = 0.03;

for (int i = 0; i < 5; i++)
    System.out.printf("%d %.2f %.2f %n", (i + 1), salary[i],
                       (salary[i] * raise));
```

23. A car dealership employs 10 salespeople. Each salesperson keeps track of the number of cars sold each month and reports it to the management at the end of the month. The management keeps the data in a file and assigns a number, 1 to 10, to each salesperson. The following statement declares an

array, `cars`, of 10 components of type `int` to store the number of cars sold by each salesperson.

```
int[] cars = new int[10];
```

Write the code so that the number of cars sold by each salesperson is stored in the array `cars`, output the total numbers of cars sold at the end of each month, and output the salesperson number selling the maximum number of cars. (Assume that data is in the file `cars.dat` and that this file has been opened using the `Scanner` object `inFile`.)

24. What is the output of the following program?

```java
import java.util.*;

public class Exercise24
{
    static Scanner console = new Scanner(System.in);

    public static void main(String[] args)
    {
        int count;
        int[] alpha = new int[5];

        alpha[0] = 5;
        for (count = 1; count < 5; count++)
        {
            alpha[count] = 5 * count + 10;
            alpha[count - 1] = alpha[count] - 4;
        }

        System.out.print("List elements: ");
        for (count = 0; count < 5; count++)
            System.out.print(alpha[count] + " ");
        System.out.println();
    }
}
```

25. What is the output of the following program?

```java
public class Exercise25
{
    public static void main(String[] args)
    {
        int[] one = new int[5];
        int[] two = new int[10];

        for (int j = 0; j < 5; j++)
            one[j] = 5 * j + 3;

        System.out.print("One contains: ");
        for (int j = 0; j < 5; j++)
            System.out.print(one[j] + " ");
        System.out.println();
```

9

```
            for (int j = 0; j < 5; j++)
            {
                two[j] = 2 * one[j] - 1;
                two[j + 5] = one[4 - j] + two [j];
            }

            System.out.print("Two contains: ");
            for (int j = 0; j < 10; j++)
                System.out.print(two[j] + " ");
            System.out.println();
        }
    }
```

26. What is the output of the following Java code?

```
final double PI = 3.14159;
double[] cylinderRadii = {3.5, 7.2, 10.5, 9.8, 6.5};
double[] cylinderHeights = {10.7, 6.5, 12.0, 10.5, 8.0};
double[] cylinderVolumes = new double[5];

for (int i = 0; i < 5; i++)
    cylinderVolumes[i] = 2 * PI * cylinderRadii[i]
                            * cylinderHeights[i];

for (int i = 0; i < 5; i++)
    System.out.printf("%d %.2f %.2f %.2f %n",
                (i + 1), cylinderRadii[i], cylinderHeights[i],
                cylinderVolumes[i]);
```

27. When an array is passed as an actual parameter to a method, what is actually being passed?

28. Suppose you have the following class:

```
public class NamesList
{
    private String[] namesList;

        //Constructor with a variable length
        //formal parameter
    public NamesList(String ... names)
    {
        namesList = names;
    }
        //Method to return namesList as a string
    public String toString()
    {
        String str = "";
        for (String name : namesList)
            str = str + name + "\n";

        return str;
    }
}
```

What is the output of the following program?

```java
public class Exercise28
{
    public static void main(String[] args)
    {
        String[] days = {"Sunday", "Monday", "Tuesday",
                         "Wednesday", "Thursday",
                         "Friday", "Saturday"};
        NamesList familyMember =
                    new NamesList("William Johnson",
                              "Linda Johnson",
                              "Susan Johnson",
                              "Alex Johnson");
        NamesList friends =
                    new NamesList("Amy Miller",
                                  "Bobby Gupta",
                                  "Sheila Mann",
                                  "Chris Green",
                                  "Silvia Smith",
                                  "Randy Arora");
        NamesList seasons =
                    new NamesList("Winter", "Spring",
                                  "Summer", "Fall");
        NamesList emptyList = new NamesList();
        NamesList weekDays = new NamesList(days);
        System.out.println("*****  Family Members  "
                + "*****");
        System.out.println(familyMember);
        System.out.println("\n*****  Friends  "
                + "*****");
        System.out.println(friends);
        System.out.println("\n*****  Seasons  "
                + "*****");
        System.out.println(seasons);
        System.out.println("\n*****  Empty Names List  "
                + "*****");
        System.out.println(emptyList);
        System.out.println("\n*****  Week Days  "
                + "*****");
        System.out.println(weekDays);
    }
}
```

29. Consider the following declarations:

```java
static final int CAR_TYPES = 5;
static final int COLOR_TYPES = 6;

double[][] sales = new double[CAR_TYPES][COLOR_TYPES];
```

a. How many elements does the array sales have?

b. What is the number of rows in the array sales?

c. What is the number of columns in the array `sales`?

d. To sum the sales by `CAR_TYPES`, what kind of processing is required?

e. To sum the sales by `COLOR_TYPES`, what kind of processing is required?

30. Write Java statements that do the following:

a. Declare an array `alpha` of 10 rows and 20 columns of type `int`.

b. Initialize each element of the array `alpha` to 5.

c. Store 1 in the first row and 2 in the remaining rows.

d. Store 5 in the first column, and the value in each remaining column is twice the value of the previous column.

e. Print the array `alpha` one row per line.

f. Print the array `alpha` one column per line.

31. Consider the following declaration:

```
int[][] beta = new int[3][3];
```

What is stored in `beta` after each of the following statements executes?

a.
```
for (int i = 0; i < 3; i++)
    for (int j = 0; j < 3; j++)
        beta[i][j] = 0;
```

b.
```
for (int i = 0; i < 3; i++)
    for (int j = 0; j < 3; j++)
        beta[i][j] = i + j;
```

c.
```
for (int i = 0; i < 3; i++)
    for (int j = 0; j < 3; j++)
        beta[i][j] = i * j;
```

d.
```
for (int i = 0; i < 3; i++)
    for (int j = 0; j < 3; j++)
        beta[i][j] = 2 * (i + j) % 4;
```

32. In Java, as an actual parameter, can an array be passed by value?

33. Define a two-dimensional array named `temp` of 3 rows and 4 columns of type `int` such that the first row is initialized to 6, 8, 12, 9; the second row is initialized to 17, 5, 10, 6; and the third row is initialized to 14, 13, 16, 20.

34. Suppose that array `temp` is as defined in Exercise 33. Write Java statements to accomplish the following:

a. Output the contents of the first row and first column element of `temp`.

b. Output the contents of the first row and last column element of `temp`.

c. Output the contents of the last row and first column element of `temp`.

d. Output the contents of the last row and last column element of `temp`.

35. Suppose that you have the following declarations:

```
int[][] times = new int[30][7];
int[][] speed = new int[15][7];
int[][] trees = new int[100][7];
int[][] students = new int[50][7];
```

a. Write the definition of the method print that can be used to output the contents of these arrays.

b. Write the Java statements that call the method print to output the contents of the arrays times, speed, trees, and students.

36. What is the effect of the following statement?

```
Vector<Double> list = new Vector<Double>();
```

37. Suppose that you have the following Vector object list:

```
list = ["One", "Two", "Three", "Four"];
```

What are the elements of list after the following statements execute?

```
list.addElement("Five");
list.insertElementAt("Six", 1);
```

38. Suppose that you have the following Vector object names:

```
names = ["Gwen", "Donald", "Michael", "Peter", "Susan"];
```

What are the elements of names after the following statements execute?

```
names.removeElementAt(1);
names.removeElement("Peter");
```

39. What is the output of the following program?

```
import java.util.Vector;

public class Exercise39
{
    public static void main(String[] arg)
    {
        Vector<String> strList = new Vector<String>();
        Vector<Integer> intList = new Vector<Integer>();

        strList.addElement("Hello");
        intList.addElement(10);
        strList.addElement("Happy");
        intList.addElement(20);
        strList.addElement("Sunny");
        intList.addElement(30);

        System.out.println("strList: " + strList);
        System.out.println("intList: " + intList);

        strList.insertElementAt("Joy", 2);

        intList.removeElement(20);
```

9

```
        System.out.println("strList: " + strList);
        System.out.println("intList: " + intList);
    }
}
```

PROGRAMMING EXERCISES

1. Write a Java program that declares an array `alpha` of 50 elements of type `double`. Initialize the array so that the first 25 elements are equal to the square of the index variable, and the last 25 elements are equal to three times the index variable. Output the array so that 10 elements per line are printed.

2. Write a Java method, `smallestIndex`, that takes as its parameters an `int` array and its size, and returns the index of the (first occurrence of the) smallest element in the array. Also, write a program to test your method.

3. Write a Java method, `lastLargestIndex`, that takes as parameters an `int` array and its size and returns the index of the last occurrence of the largest element in the array. Also, write a program to test your method.

4. Write a program that reads a file consisting of students' test scores in the range 0–200. It should then determine the number of students having scores in each of the following ranges: 0–24, 25–49, 50–74, 75–99, 100–124, 125–149, 150–174, and 175–200. Output the score ranges and the number of students. Run your program with the following input data: 76, 89, 150, 135, 200, 76, 12, 100, 150, 28, 178, 189, 167, 200, 175, 150, 87, 99, 129, 149, 176, 200, 87, 35, 157, 189.

5. Write a program that prompts the user to input a string and then outputs the string in uppercase letters. (Use an array of characters [or `char`] to store the string.)

6. The history teacher at your school needs help grading a True/False test. The students' IDs and test answers are stored in a file. The first entry in the file contains the answers to the test in the following form:

    TFFTFFTTTTFFTFTFTFTT

    Every other entry in the file is the student's ID, followed by a blank, followed by the student's response. For example, the entry:

    ABC54301 TFTFTFTT TFTFTFFTTFT

    indicates that the student's ID is ABC54301 and the answer to question 1 is True, the answer to question 2 is False, and so on. This student did not answer question 9. The exam has 20 questions, and the class has more than 150 students. Each correct answer is awarded two points, each wrong answer gets -1 point, and no answer gets 0 points. Write a program that processes the test data. The output should be the student's ID, followed by the answers, followed by the test score, followed by the test grade. Assume the following grade scale: 90% – 100%, A; 80% – 89.99%, B; 70% – 79.99%, C; 60% – 69.99%, D; and 0% – 59.99%, F.

7. Write a program that allows the user to enter the last names of five candidates in a local election and the votes received by each candidate. The program should then output each candidate's name, the votes received by that candidate, and the percentage of the total votes received by the candidate. Your program should also output the winner of the election. A sample output is:

```
Candidate     Votes Received        % of Total Votes
Johnson            5000                   25.91
Miller             4000                   20.73
Duffy              6000                   31.09
Robinson           2500                   12.95
Ashtony            1800                    9.33
Total             19300
The Winner of the Election is Duffy.
```

8. Write a program that allows the user to enter students' names followed by their test scores and outputs the following information (assume that the maximum number of students in the class is 50):

   a. Class average

   b. Names of all the students whose test scores are below the class average, with an appropriate message

   c. Highest test score and the names of all the students having the highest score

9. Programming Exercise 15, in Chapter 7, asks you to find the mean and standard deviation of five numbers. Extend this programming exercise to find the mean and standard deviation of up to 100 numbers. Suppose that the mean (average) of n numbers $x_1, x_2, \ldots, x_n$ is x. Then the standard deviation of these numbers is:

$$s = \sqrt{\frac{(x_1-x)^2+(x_2-x)^2+\cdots+(x_i-x)^2+\cdots+(x_n-x)^2}{n}}.$$

10. **(Adding Large Integers)** In Java, the largest `int` value is 2147483647. So an integer larger than this cannot be stored and processed as an integer. Similarly, if the sum or product of two positive integers is greater than 2147483647, then the result will be incorrect. One way to store and manipulate large integers is to store each individual digit of the number in an array. Write a program that inputs two positives and outputs the sum of the numbers. Your program must contain a method to find and output the sum of the numbers. (*Hint*: Read numbers as strings and store the digits of the number in the reverse order.)

9

11. Write a program that uses a two-dimensional array to store the highest and lowest temperatures for each month of the year. The program should output the average high, average low, and highest and lowest temperatures of the year. Your program must consist of the following methods:

    a. Method `getData`: This method reads and stores the data in the two-dimensional array.

    b. Method `averageHigh`: This method calculates and returns the average high temperature of the year.

    c. Method `averageLow`: This method calculates and returns the average low temperature of the year.

    d. Method `indexHighTemp`: This method returns the index of the highest temperature in the array.

    e. Method `indexLowTemp`: This method returns the index of the lowest temperature in the array.

    (These methods must all have the appropriate parameters.)

12. Jason, Samantha, Ravi, Sheila, and Ankit are preparing for an upcoming marathon. Each day of the week they run certain miles and write them into a notebook. At the end of the week, they would like to know the number of miles run each day, the total miles for the week, and average miles run each day. Write a program to help them analyze their data. Your program must contain parallel arrays: An array to store the names of the runners and a two-dimensional array of 5 rows and 7 columns to store the number of miles run by each runner each day. Furthermore, your program must contain at least the following methods: a method to read and store the runners name and the number of miles run each day; a method to find the total miles run by each runner and the average number of miles run each day; and a method to output the results. (You may assume that the input data is stored in a file and each line of data is in the following form:

    ```
    runnerName milesDay1 milesDay2 milesDay3 milesDay4 milesDay5
    milesDay6 milesDay7.)
    ```

13. a. Write the definition of the class `Tests` such that an object of this class can store a student's first name, last name, five test scores, average tests score, and grade. (Use an array to store the test scores.) Add constructors and methods to manipulate data stored in an object. Among other things, your class must contain methods to calculate test averages, return test averages, calculate grades, return grades, and modify individual test scores. The method `toString` must return test data (including student's name, five test scores, average, and grade) as a string.

    b. Write a program to calculate students' average test scores and the grade. You may assume the following input data:

```
Jack Johnson 85 83 77 91 76
Lisa Aniston 80 90 95 93 48
Andy Cooper 78 81 11 90 73
Ravi Gupta 92 83 30 69 87
Bonny Blair 23 45 96 38 59
Danny Clark 60 85 45 39 67
Samantha Kennedy 77 31 52 74 83
Robin Bronson 93 94 89 77 97
Sheila Sunny 79 85 28 93 82
Kiran Smith 85 72 49 75 63
```

Use an array of objects of the **class** Tests (designed in part (a)) to store each student's data. The program should output data as close as possible to the following form:

First_Name	Last_Name	Test1	Test2	Test3	Test4	Test5	Average	Grade
Jack	Johnson	85.00	83.00	77.00	91.00	76.00	82.40	B
Lisa	Aniston	80.00	90.00	95.00	93.00	48.00	81.20	B
Andy	Cooper	78.00	81.00	11.00	90.00	73.00	66.60	D
Ravi	Gupta	92.00	83.00	30.00	69.00	87.00	72.20	C
Bonny	Blair	23.00	45.00	96.00	38.00	59.00	52.20	F
Danny	Clark	60.00	85.00	45.00	39.00	67.00	59.20	F
Samantha	Kennedy	77.00	31.00	52.00	74.00	83.00	63.40	D
Robin	Bronson	93.00	94.00	89.00	77.00	97.00	90.00	A
Sheila	Sunny	79.00	85.00	28.00	93.00	82.00	73.40	C
Kiran	Smith	85.00	72.00	49.00	75.00	63.00	68.80	D

```
Class average = 70.94
```

14. Write a program that uses the **class** RollDie to roll a pair of dice 1000 times (or 1000 pairs of dice). The program then outputs the pair of numbers rolled by the dice, the sum of the numbers rolled by each pair of dice, the number of times each sum is rolled, and the sums that are rolled the maximum number of times. (Use a two-dimensional array to create 1000 pairs of dice and to store the pairs of numbers rolled by each pair of dice.)

15. **Airplane Seating Assignment:** Write a program that can be used to assign seats for a commercial airplane. The airplane has 13 rows, with 6 seats in each row. Rows 1 and 2 are first class, rows 3 to 7 are business class, and rows 8 to 13 are economy class. Your program prompts the user to enter the following information:

a. Ticket type (first class, business class, or economy class)

b. Desired seat

Output the seating plan in the following format:

```
      A B C   D E F
Row 1  * * X   * X X
Row 2  * X *   X * X
Row 3  * * X   X * X
Row 4  X * X   * X X
```

9

```
Row 5     * X *   X * *
Row 6     * X *   * * X
Row 7     X * *   * X X
Row 8     * X *   X X *
Row 9     X * X   X * X
Row 10    * X *   X X X
Row 11    * * X   * X *
Row 12    * * X   X * X
Row 13    * * *   * X *
```

Here, * indicates that the seat is available; x indicates that the seat has been assigned. Make this a menu-driven program; show the user's choices and allow the user to make the appropriate choices.

CHAPTER 10

INHERITANCE AND POLYMORPHISM

IN THIS CHAPTER, YOU WILL:

- · Learn about inheritance
- · Learn about subclasses and superclasses
- · Explore how to override the methods of a superclass
- · Examine how constructors of superclasses and subclasses work
- · Learn about polymorphism
- · Examine abstract classes
- · Become familiar with interfaces
- · Learn about composition

Classes were introduced in Chapter 8. Using classes, you can combine data and operations on that data in a single unit, a process called *encapsulation*. Through encapsulation, an object becomes a self-contained entity. Operations can (directly) access the data, but the internal state of an object cannot be manipulated directly.

In addition to implementing encapsulation, classes have other capabilities. For instance, you can create new classes from existing classes. This important feature encourages code reuse and saves programmers an enormous amount of time. In Java, you can relate two or more classes in more than one way. This chapter examines two common ways to relate classes—**inheritance** and **composition (aggregation)**.

Inheritance

Suppose that you want to design a `class`, `PartTimeEmployee`, to implement and process the characteristics of a part-time employee. The main features associated with a part-time employee are the name, pay rate, and number of hours worked. In Example 8-8 (Chapter 8), we designed the `class` `Person` to implement a person's name. Every part-time employee is a person. Therefore, rather than design the `class` `PartTimeEmployee` from scratch, we want to be able to extend the definition of the `class` `Person` from Example 8-8 by adding additional members (data and/or methods).

Of course, we do not want to make the necessary changes directly to the `class` `Person`—that is, edit the `class` `Person` and add and/or delete members. We want to create a new `class` `PartTimeEmployee` without making any physical changes to the `class` `Person`, by adding only the members that are necessary to `class` `PartTimeEmployee`. For example, because the `class` `Person` already has data members to store the first name and last name, we will not include any such members in the `class` `PartTimeEmployee`. In fact, these data members will be *inherited* from the `class` `Person`. (We will design the `class` `PartTimeEmployee` in Example 10-3.)

In Chapter 8, we extensively studied and designed the `class` `Clock` to implement the time of day in a program. The `class` `Clock` has three data members (instance variables) to store the hours, minutes, and seconds. Certain applications might require that we also store the time zone. In this case, we want to *extend* the definition of the `class` `Clock` and create a `class`, `ExtClock`, to accommodate this new information. That is, we want to derive the `class` `ExtClock` by adding a data member—`timeZone`—and the necessary method members to manipulate the time.

In Java, the mechanism that allows us to extend the definition of a class without making any physical changes to the existing class is **inheritance**. Inheritance can be viewed as an "is-a" relationship. For example, every (part-time) employee *is a* person. Similarly, every extended clock, `ExtClock`, *is a* `Clock`.

Inheritance lets you create new classes from existing classes. Any new class that you create from an existing class is called a **subclass** or **derived class**; existing classes are called **superclasses** or **base classes**. The inheritance relationship enables a subclass to inherit features from its superclass. Furthermore, the subclass can add new features of its own. Therefore, rather than create completely new classes from scratch, you can take advantage of inheritance and reduce software complexity.

Inheritance can be viewed as a treelike, or hierarchical, structure wherein a superclass is shown with its subclasses. Consider the diagram in Figure 10-1, which shows the relationship between various shapes.

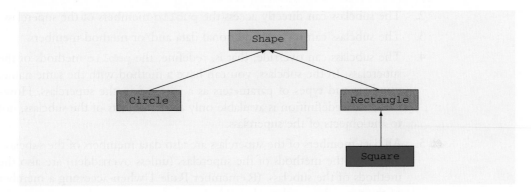

FIGURE 10-1 Inheritance hierarchy

In this diagram, Shape is the superclass. The classes Circle and Rectangle are derived from Shape, and the class Square is derived from Rectangle. Every Circle and every Rectangle is a Shape. Every Square is a Rectangle.

The general syntax to derive a class from an existing class is:

```
modifier(s) class ClassName extends ExistingClassName modifier(s)
{
    memberList
}
```

In Java, **extends** is a reserved word.

EXAMPLE 10-1

Suppose that we have defined a class called Shape. The following statements specify that the class Circle is derived from Shape:

```
public class Circle extends Shape
{
    .
    .
    .
}
```

The following rules about superclasses and subclasses should be kept in mind:

1. The `private` members of the superclass are `private` to the superclass; hence, the members of the subclass(es) cannot access them directly. In other words, when you write the definitions of the methods of the subclass, you cannot access the `private` members of the superclass directly. (The next section explains how to access the `private` members of a superclass in its subclass.)

2. The subclass can directly access the `public` members of the superclass.

3. The subclass can include additional data and/or method members.

4. The subclass can override, that is, redefine, the `public` methods of the superclass. In the subclass, you can have a method with the same name, number, and types of parameters as a method in the superclass. However, this redefinition is available only to the objects of the subclass, not to the objects of the superclass.

5. All data members of the superclass are also data members of the subclass. Similarly, the methods of the superclass (unless overridden) are also the methods of the subclass. (Remember Rule 1 when accessing a member of the superclass in the subclass.)

Each subclass, in turn, may become a superclass for a future subclass. Inheritance can be either single or multiple. In **single inheritance**, the subclass is derived from a single superclass; in **multiple inheritance**, the subclass is derived from more than one superclass. Java *supports only single inheritance*; that is, in Java a class can *extend* the definition of only one class.

The next sections describe two important issues related to inheritance. The first issue is using the methods of a superclass in its subclass. While discussing this issue, we will also address how to access the `private` (data) members of the superclass in the subclass. The second key inheritance issue is related to the constructor. The constructor of a subclass *cannot directly access* the `private` data members of the superclass. Thus, you must ensure that `private` data members that are inherited from the superclass are initialized when a constructor of the subclass executes.

Using Methods of the Superclass in a Subclass

Suppose that a `class` SubClass is derived from a `class` SuperClass. Further assume that both SubClass and SuperClass have some data members. It then follows that the data members of the `class` SubClass are its own data members, together with the data members of SuperClass. Similarly, in addition to its own methods, the subclass also inherits the methods of the superclass. The subclass can give some of its methods the same signature as given by the superclass. For example, suppose that SuperClass contains a method, print, that prints the values of the data members of SuperClass. SubClass contains data members in addition to the data members inherited from SuperClass. Suppose that you want to include a method in SubClass that prints the data members of

SubClass. You can give any name to this method. However, in the `class SubClass`, you can also name this method `print` (the same name used by `SuperClass`). This is called **overriding**, or **redefining**, the method of the superclass.

To override a `public` method of the superclass in the subclass, the corresponding method in the subclass must have the same name, the same type, and the same formal parameter list. That is, to override a method of a superclass, in the subclass the method must be defined using the same signature and the same return type as in its superclass. If the corresponding method in the superclass and the subclass has the same name but different parameter lists, then this is method *overloading* in the subclass, which is also allowed.

Whether you override or overload a method of the superclass in the subclass, you must know how to specify a call to the method of the superclass that has the same name as that used by a method of the subclass. We illustrate these concepts with the help of an example.

Consider the definition of the following class:

```java
public class Rectangle
{
    private double length;
    private double width;

    public Rectangle()
    {
        length = 0;
        width = 0;
    }

    public Rectangle(double l, double w)
    {
        setDimension(l, w);
    }

    public void setDimension(double l, double w)
    {
        if (l >= 0)
            length = l;
        else
            length = 0;

        if (w >= 0)
            width = w;
        else
            width = 0;
    }

    public double getLength()
    {
        return length;
    }
```

```java
    public double getWidth()
    {
        return width;
    }

    public double area()
    {
        return length * width;
    }

    public double perimeter()
    {
        return 2 * (length + width);
    }

    public String toString()
    {
        return ("Length = " + length + "; Width = " + width);
    }
}
```

Figure 10-2 shows the UML class diagram of the **class** Rectangle.

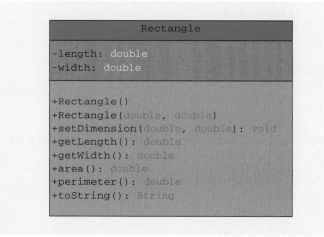

FIGURE 10-2   UML class diagram of the **class** Rectangle

The **class** Rectangle has 10 members.

Now consider the following definition of the **class** Box, derived from the **class** Rectangle:

```
public class Box extends Rectangle
{
    private double height;

    public Box()
    {
        //The definition is as given below
    }

    public Box(double l, double w, double h)
    {
        //The definition is as given below
    }

    public void setDimension(double l, double w, double h)
    {
        //Sets the length, width, and height of the box
        //The definition is as given below
    }

    public double getHeight()
    {
        return height;
    }

    public double area()
    {
        //Returns the surface area
        //The definition is as given below
    }

    public double volume()
    {
        //Returns the volume
        //The definition is as given below
    }

    public String toString()
    {
        //Returns length, width, and height of the box as
        //a string. The definition is as given below.
    }
}
```

Figure 10-3 shows the UML class diagram of the **class** Box and the inheritance hierarchy.

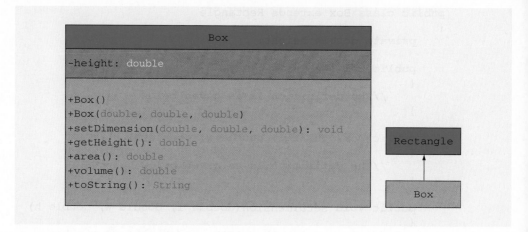

FIGURE 10-3 UML class diagram of the `class` Box and the inheritance hierarchy

From the definition of the **class** Box, it is clear that the **class** Box is derived from the **class** Rectangle. Therefore, all **public** members of Rectangle are **public** members of Box. The **class** Box overrides the methods toString and area, and overloads the method setDimension.

In general, when writing the definitions of the methods of a subclass to specify a call to a **public** method of a superclass, you do the following:

- If the subclass overrides a **public** method of the superclass, then you must specify a call to that **public** method of the superclass by using the reserved word **super**, followed by the dot operator, followed by the method name with an appropriate parameter list. In this case, the general syntax to call a method of the superclass is:

```
super.methodName(parameters);
```

- If the subclass does not override a **public** method of the superclass, you can specify a call to that **public** method by using the name of the method and an appropriate parameter list.

Next, let's write the definition of the method toString of the **class** Box.

The **class** Box has three instance variables: length, width, and height. The method toString of the **class** Box prints the values of these three instance variables. To write the definition of the method toString of the **class** Box, remember the following:

- The instance variables length and width are **private** members of the **class** Rectangle and so cannot be directly accessed in the **class** Box. Therefore, when writing the definition of the method toString of the **class** Box, you cannot directly reference length and width.

- The instance variables `length` and `width` of the `class Rectangle` are accessible in the `class Box` through the `public` methods of the `class Rectangle`. Therefore, when writing the definition of the method `toString` of the `class Box`, you first call the method `toString` of the `class Rectangle` to print the values of `length` and `width`. After printing the values of `length` and `width`, you output the value of `height`.

As stated above, to call the method `toString` of `Rectangle` in the definition of the method `toString` of `Box`, you must use the following statement:

```
super.toString ();
```

This statement ensures that you call the method `toString` of the superclass `Rectangle`, not of the `class Box`.

The definition of the method `toString` of the `class Box` is:

```
public String toString()
{
    return super.toString()      //retrieve length and width
            + "; Height = " + height;
}
```

Let's write the definitions of the remaining methods of the `class Box`:

```
public void setDimension(double l, double w, double h)
{
    super.setDimension(l, w);

    if (h >= 0)
        height = h;
    else
        height = 0;
}
```

 NOTE
The `class Box` overloads the method `setDimension` of the `class Rectangle`. Therefore, in the preceding definition of the method `setDimension` of the `class Box`, you can also specify a call to the method `setDimension` of the `class Rectangle` without the reserved word **super** and the dot operator.

The definition of the method `getHeight` is:

```
public double getHeight()
{
    return height;
}
```

The method `area` of the `class Box` determines the surface area of the box. To do so, we need to access the length and width of the box, which are declared as **private** members of the `class Rectangle`. Therefore, we use the methods `getLength` and `getWidth` of the `class Rectangle` to retrieve the length and width, respectively. Because the `class`

Box does not override the methods `getLength` and `getWidth`, we can call these methods of the `class` Rectangle without using the reserved word `super`.

```
public double area()
{
    return  2 * (getLength() * getWidth()
                + getLength() * height
                + getWidth() * height);
}
```

The method `volume` of the `class` Box determines the volume of the box. To determine the box's volume, you multiply the length, width, and height of the box or multiply the area of the base of the box by its height. Let's write the definition of the method `volume` by using the second alternative. To do so, you can use the method `area` of the `class` Rectangle to determine the area of the base. Because the `class` Box overrides the method `area`, to specify a call to the method `area` of the `class` Rectangle, we use the reserved word `super`, as shown in the following definition:

```
public double volume()
{
    return super.area() * height;
}
```

In the next section, we discuss how to specify a call to the constructor of the superclass when writing the definition of a constructor of the subclass.

NOTE | If a method of a class is declared `final`, it cannot be overridden in any subclass. The following is an example of a `final` method:

```
public final void doAnything()
{
}
```

Constructors of the Superclass and Subclass

A subclass can have its own `private` data members, so a subclass can also have its own constructors. A constructor typically serves to initialize the instance variables. When we instantiate a subclass object, this object inherits the instance variables of the superclass, but the subclass object cannot directly access the `private` instance variables of the superclass. The same is true for the methods of a subclass. That is, the methods of the subclass cannot directly access the `private` members of the superclass.

As a consequence, the constructors of the subclass can and should (directly) initialize only the instance variables of the subclass. Thus, when a subclass object is instantiated, to initialize the (`private` and other) instance variables—both its own and its ancestor class(es)—the subclass object must also automatically execute one of the constructors of the superclass. A call to a constructor of the superclass is specified in the definition of a subclass constructor by using the reserved word `super`. The general syntax to call a constructor of a superclass is:

```
super(parameters);
```

In the preceding section, we defined the class Rectangle and derived the class Box from it. Moreover, we illustrated how to override a method of the class Rectangle. We now discuss how to write the definitions of the constructors of the class Box.

The class Rectangle has two constructors and two instance variables. The class Box has three instance variables: length, width, and height. The instance variables length and width are inherited from the class Rectangle.

To write the definitions of the constructors of the class Box, we first write the definition of the default constructor of the class Box. Recall that if a class contains the default constructor and no values are specified during object instantiation, the default constructor executes and initializes the object. Because the class Rectangle contains the default constructor, when we write the definition of the default constructor of the class Box, to (explicitly) specify a call to the default constructor of the class Rectangle, we use the reserved word super with no parameters, as shown in the following code. Also, a call to the (default) constructor of the superclass *must* be the first statement.

```
public Box()
{
    super();
    height = 0;
}
```

Next, we discuss how to write the definitions of the constructors with parameters. (Note that if you do not include the statement super();, then, by default, the default constructor of the superclass (if any), will be called.)

To specify a call to a constructor with parameters of the superclass, we use the reserved word super with the appropriate parameters. A call to the constructor of the superclass must be the first statement.

Consider the following definition of the constructor with parameters of the class Box:

```
public Box(double l, double w, double h)
{
    super(l, w);
    height = h;
}
```

This definition specifies the constructor of Rectangle with two parameters. When this constructor of Box executes, it triggers the execution of the constructor with two parameters of type double of the class Rectangle.

(Note that invoking a superclass constructor's name in a subclass will result in a syntax error. Also, because a call to a constructor of the superclass must be the first statement, within the definition of a constructor of a subclass only one constructor of the superclass can be invoked.)

As an exercise, try writing the complete definition of the class Box.

Consider the following statements:

```
Rectangle myRectangle = new Rectangle(5, 3);   //Line 1
Box myBox = new Box(6, 5, 4);                  //Line 2
```

The statement in Line 1 creates the `Rectangle` object `myRectangle`. Thus, the object `myRectangle` has two instance variables: `length` and `width`. The statement in Line 2 creates the `Box` object `myBox`. Thus, the object `myBox` has three instance variables: `length`, `width`, and `height` (see Figure 10-4).

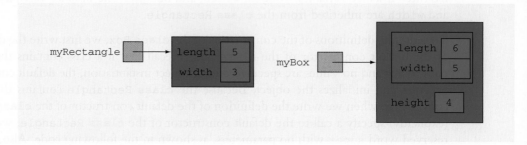

FIGURE 10-4 Objects `myRectangle` and `myBox`

Consider the following statements:

```
System.out.println(myRectangle); //Line 3
System.out.println(myBox);       //Line 4
```

In the statement in Line 3, the method `toString` of the **class** `Rectangle` is executed; in the statement in Line 4, the method `toString` associated with the **class** `Box` is executed. Recall that if a subclass overrides a method of the superclass, the redefinition applies only to the objects of the subclass. Thus, the output of the statement in Line 3 is:

```
Length = 5.0; Width = 3.0
```

The output of the statement in Line 4 is:

```
Length = 6.0; Width = 5.0; Height = 4.0
```

A call to a constructor of a superclass is specified in the definition of a constructor of the subclass. When a subclass constructor executes, first a constructor of the superclass executes to initialize the data members inherited from the superclass and then the constructor of the subclass executes to initialize the data members declared by the subclass. So first the constructor of the **class** `Rectangle` executes to initialize the instance variables `length` and `width` and then the constructor of the **class** `Box` executes to initialize the instance variable `height`.

The program in Example 10-2 shows how the objects of a superclass and a base class work.

EXAMPLE 10-2

Consider the following Java application program:

```
// This program illustrates how the objects of a superclass and a
// base class work.
```

```
public class SubClassSuperClassMethods          //Line 1
{                                                //Line 2
    public static void main(String[] args)       //Line 3
    {                                            //Line 4
        Rectangle myRectangle1 = new Rectangle();      //Line 5
        Rectangle myRectangle2 = new Rectangle(8, 6);  //Line 6

        Box myBox1 = new Box();                  //Line 7
        Box myBox2 = new Box(10, 7, 3);          //Line 8

        System.out.println("Line 9: myRectangle1: "
                            + myRectangle1);     //Line 9

        System.out.println("Line 10: Area of myRectangle1: "
                            + myRectangle1.area());  //Line 10

        System.out.println("Line 11: myRectangle2: "
                            + myRectangle2);     //Line 11
        System.out.println("Line 12: Area of myRectangle2: "
                            + myRectangle2.area());  //Line 12

        System.out.println("Line 13: myBox1: " + myBox1); //Line 13

        System.out.println("Line 14: Surface Area of myBox1: "
                            + myBox1.area());    //Line 14
        System.out.println("Line 15: Volume of myBox1: "
                            + myBox1.volume());  //Line 15

        System.out.println("Line 16: myBox2: " + myBox2); //Line 16

        System.out.println("Line 17: Surface Area of myBox2: "
                            + myBox2.area());    //Line 17
        System.out.println("Line 18: Volume of myBox2: "
                            + myBox2.volume());  //Line 18
    }                                            //Line 19
}                                                //Line 20
```

Sample Run:

```
Line 9: myRectangle1: Length = 0.0; Width = 0.0
Line 10: Area of myRectangle1: 0.0
Line 11: myRectangle2: Length = 8.0; Width = 6.0
Line 12: Area of myRectangle2: 48.0
Line 13: myBox1: Length = 0.0; Width = 0.0; Height = 0.0
Line 14: Surface Area of myBox1: 0.0
Line 15: Volume of myBox1: 0.0
Line 16: myBox2: Length = 10.0; Width = 7.0; Height = 3.0
Line 17: Surface Area of myBox2: 242.0
Line 18: Volume of myBox2: 210.0
```

The preceding program works as follows: The statement in Line 5 creates the Rectangle object myRectangle1 and initializes its instance variables to 0. The statement in Line 6 creates the Rectangle object myRectangle2 and initializes its instance variables length and width to 8.0 and 6.0, respectively.

The statement in Line 7 creates the `Box` object `myBox1` and initializes its instance variables to 0. The statement in Line 8 creates the `Box` object `myBox2` and initializes its instance variables `length`, `width`, and `height` to `10.0`, `7.0`, and `3.0`, respectively.

The statements in Lines 9 and 10 output the length, width, and area of `myRectangle1`. Because the instance variables of `myRectangle1` are initialized to 0 by the default constructor, the area of the rectangle is `0.0` square units, as shown in the output of Line 10.

The statements in Lines 11 and 12 output the length, width, and area of `myRectangle2`. Because the instance variables `length` and `width` of `myRectangle2` are initialized to `8.0` and `6.0`, respectively, by the constructor with parameters, this rectangle's area is `48.0` square units. See the output of Line 12.

The statements in Lines 13, 14, and 15 output the length, width, height, surface area, and volume of `myBox1`. Because the instance variables of `myBox1` are initialized to `0.0` by the default constructor, this box's surface area is `0.0` square units and the volume is `0.0` cubic units. See the output of Lines 14 and 15.

The statements in Lines 16, 17, and 18 output the length, width, height, surface area, and volume of `myBox2`. Because the instance variables `length`, `width`, and `height` of `myBox2` are initialized to `10.0`, `7.0`, and `3.0`, respectively, by the constructor with parameters, this box's surface area is `242.0` square units and the volume is `210.0` cubic units. See the output of Lines 17 and 18.

The output of this program demonstrates that the redefinition of the methods `toString` and `area` in the `class` Box applies only to the objects of type `Box`.

NOTE **(Shadowing Variables)** Suppose that the `class` SubClass is derived from the `class` SuperClass and SuperClass has a variable named `temp`. You can declare a variable named `temp` in the `class` SubClass. In this case, the variable `temp` of SubClass is called a **shadowing variable**. The concept of a shadowing variable is similar to the concept of overriding a method, but it causes confusion. Now the SubClass is derived from SuperClass, so it inherits the variable `temp` of SuperClass. Because a variable named `temp` is already available in SubClass, there is seldom if ever any reason to override it. Furthermore, it is poor programming practice to override a variable in the SubClass. Anyone reading code with a shadowed variable will have two different declarations of a variable seeming to apply to the shadowed variable of the SubClass. This causes confusion and should be avoided. In general, you should avoid shadowing variables.

Next, we give another example illustrating how to create a subclass.

EXAMPLE 10-3

Suppose that you want to define a class to group the attributes of an employee. There are full-time employees and part-time employees. Part-time employees are paid based on the number of hours worked and an hourly rate. Suppose that you want to define a class to keep track of a part-time employee's information, such as the name, pay rate, and hours worked. You can then print the employee's name, together with his or her wages. Recall that Example 8-8 (Chapter 8) defined the `class Person` to store the first name and the last name together with the necessary operations on `name`. Because every employee is a person, we can define a `class PartTimeEmployee` derived from the `class Person`. You can also override the method `toString` of the `class Person` to print the appropriate information.

The members of the `class PartTimeEmployee` are as follows:

Instance Variables:

```
private double payRate;     //store the pay rate

private double hoursWorked; //store the hours worked
```

Instance Methods:

```
public void setNameRateHours(String first, String last,
                             double rate, double hours)
   //Method to set the first name, last name, payRate,
   //and hoursWorked according to the parameters.
   //The parameters first and last are passed to the
   //superclass.
   //Postcondition: firstName = first; lastName = last;
   //               payRate = rate; hoursWorked = hours;

public double getPayRate()
   //Method to return the pay rate
   //Postcondition: The value of payRate is returned

public double getHoursWorked()
   //Method to return the number of hours worked
   //Postcondition: The value of hoursWorked is returned

public double calculatePay()
   //Method to calculate and return the wages

public String toString()
   //Method to return the string consisting of the
   //first name, last name, and the wages in the form:
   //firstName lastName wages are $$$$.$$

public PartTimeEmployee(String first, String last,
                        double rate, double hours)
   //Constructor with parameters
   //Set the first name, last name, payRate, and
   //hoursWorked according to the parameters.
   //Parameters first and last are passed to the
   //superclass.
   //Postcondition: firstName = first; lastName = last;
   //               payRate = rate; hoursWorked = hours;
```

```
public PartTimeEmployee()
    //Default constructor
    //Set the first name, last name, payRate, and
    //hoursWorked to the default values.
    //The first name and last name are initialized to an empty
    //string by the default constructor of the superclass.
    //Postcondition: firstName = ""; lastName = "";
    //                payRate = 0; hoursWorked = 0;
```

Figure 10-5 shows the UML class diagram of the **class** PartTimeEmployee and the inheritance hierarchy.

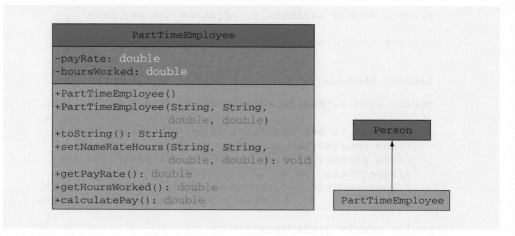

FIGURE 10-5 UML class diagram of the **class** PartTimeEmployee and the inheritance hierarchy

The definitions of the member methods of the **class** PartTimeEmployee are as follows:

```
public String toString()
{
    return (super.toString() + "\'s wages are: $" + calculatePay());
}

public double getPayRate()
{
    return payRate;
}

public double getHoursWorked()
{
    return hoursWorked;
}

public double calculatePay()
{
    return (payRate * hoursWorked);
}
```

```
public void setNameRateHours(String first, String last,
                             double rate, double hours)
{
    setName(first, last);
    payRate = rate;
    hoursWorked = hours;
}
```

The definition of the constructor with parameters is as follows. (Note that the body contains a call to the superclass's constructor with parameters.)

```
public PartTimeEmployee(String first, String last,
                        double rate, double hours)
{
    super(first, last);
    payRate = rate;
    hoursWorked = hours;
}
```

The definition of the default constructor is:

```
public PartTimeEmployee()
{
    super();
    payRate = 0;
    hoursWorked = 0;
}
```

The definition of the class PartTimeEmployee is:

```
public class PartTimeEmployee extends Person
{
   private double payRate;    //store the pay rate
   private double hoursWorked; //store the hours worked

      //Default constructor
      //Set the first name, last name, payRate, and
      //hoursWorked to the default values.
      //The first name and last name are initialized to an empty
      //string by the default constructor of the superclass.
      //Postcondition: firstName = ""; lastName = "";
      //                payRate = 0; hoursWorked = 0;
   public PartTimeEmployee()
   {
      super();
      payRate = 0;
      hoursWorked = 0;
   }

      //Constructor with parameters
      //Set the first name, last name, payRate, and
      //hoursWorked according to the parameters.
      //Parameters first and last are passed to the
      //superclass.
```

```java
    //Postcondition: firstName = first; lastName = last;
    //                payRate = rate; hoursWorked = hours;
public PartTimeEmployee(String first, String last,
                        double rate, double hours)
{
    super(first, last);
    payRate = rate;
    hoursWorked = hours;
}

    //Method to return the string consisting of the
    //first name, last name, and the wages in the form:
    //firstName lastName wages are $$$$.$$
public String toString()

    return (super.toString() + "\'s wages are: $" + calculatePay());
}

    //Method to calculate and return the wages
public double calculatePay()
{
    return (payRate * hoursWorked);
}

    //Method to set the first name, last name, payRate,
    //and hoursWorked according to the parameters.
    //The parameters first and last are passed to the
    //superclass.
    //Postcondition: firstName = first; lastName = last;
    //                payRate = rate; hoursWorked = hours;
public void setNameRateHours(String first, String last,
                             double rate, double hours)

{
    setName(first, last);
    payRate = rate;
    hoursWorked = hours;
}

    //Method to return the pay rate
    //Postcondition: The value of payRate is returned
public double getPayRate()
{
    return payRate;
}

    //Method to return the number of hours worked
    //Postcondition: The value of hoursWorked is returned
public double getHoursWorked()
{
    return hoursWorked;
}
}
```

The definition of the subclass is typically placed in a separate file. Recall that the name of the file must be the same as the name of the class, and the file extension must be `java`.

Protected Members of a Class

The `private` members of a class are `private` to the class and cannot be directly accessed outside the class. Only methods of that class can access the `private` members directly. As discussed previously, the subclass cannot access the `private` members of the superclass directly. However, sometimes it may be necessary for a subclass to access a `private` member of a superclass. If you make a `private` member `public`, then anyone can access that member. Recall that the members of a class are classified into three categories: `public`, `private`, and `protected`. So, if a member of a superclass needs to be (directly) accessed in a subclass and yet still prevent its direct access outside the class, such as in a user program, you must declare that member using the modifier `protected`. Thus, the accessibility of a `protected` member of a class falls between `public` and `private`. A subclass can directly access the `protected` member of a superclass.

To summarize, if a member of a superclass needs to be accessed directly (only) by a subclass, that member is declared using the modifier `protected`.

Example 10-4 illustrates how the methods of a subclass can directly access a `protected` member of the superclass.

EXAMPLE 10-4

Consider the following definitions of the classes `BClass` and `DClass`:

```java
public class BClass
{
    protected char bCh;
    private double bX;

        //Default constructor
    public BClass()
    {
        bCh = '*';
        bX = 0.0;
    }

        //Constructor with parameters
    public BClass(char ch, double u)
    {
        bCh = ch;
        bX = u;
    }
```

10

```java
    public void setData(double u)
    {
        bX = u;
    }

    public void setData(char ch, double u)
    {
        bCh = ch;
        bX = u;
    }

    public String toString()
    {
        return ("Superclass: bCh = " + bCh + ", bX = "
                + bX + '\n');
    }
}
```

The definition of the **class** BClass contains the **protected** instance variable bCh of type **char**, and the **private** instance variable bX of type **double**. It also contains an overloaded method setData; one version of setData is used to set both the instance variables, and the other version is used to set only the **private** instance variable. The **class** BClass also has a constructor with default parameters.

Next, we derive a **class** DClass from the **class** BClass. The **class** DClass contains a **private** instance variable dA of type **int**. It also contains a method setData, with three parameters, and the method toString.

```java
public class DClass extends BClass
{
    private int dA;

    public DClass()
    {
        //The definition is as shown later in this section
    }

    public DClass(char ch, double v, int a)
    {
        //The definition is as shown later in this section
    }

    public void setData(char ch, double v, int a)
    {
        //The definition is as shown later in this section
    }

    public String toString()
    {
        //The definition is as shown later in this section
    }
}
```

Let's now write the definition of the method setData of the class DClass. Because bCh is a **protected** instance variable of the class BClass, it can be directly accessed in the definition of the method setData. However, because bX is a **private** instance variable of the class BClass, the method setData of the class DClass *cannot* directly access bX. Thus, the method setData of the class DClass must set bX by using the method setData of the class BClass. The definition of the method setData of the class DClass can be written as follows:

```
public void setData(char ch, double v, int a)
{
    super.setData(v);

    bCh = ch;    //initialize bCh using the assignment
                 //statement
    dA = a;
}
```

Note that the definition of the method setData contains the statement:

```
super.setData(v);
```

to call the method setData with one parameter (of the superclass), to set the instance variable bX, and then directly set the value of bCh.

Next, let's write the definition of the method toString (of the class DClass):

```
public String toString()
{
    return (super.toString() + "Subclass dA = " + dA + '\n');
}
```

The constructors' definitions are:

```
public DClass()
{
    super();
    dA = 0;
}

public DClass(char ch, double v, int a)
{
    super(ch, v);
    dA = a;
}
```

The following program shows how the objects of BClass and DClass work:

```
public class ProtectedMemberProg
{
    public static void main(String[] args)
    {
        BClass bObject = new BClass();              //Line 1

        DClass dObject = new DClass();              //Line 2
```

```
        System.out.println("Line 3: " + bObject);      //Line 3

        System.out.println("Line 4: ***   "
                      + "Subclass object ***");     //Line 4

        dObject.setData('&', 2.5, 7);                   //Line 5

        System.out.println("Line 6: " + dObject);       //Line 6
    }
}
```

Sample Run:

```
Line 3: Superclass: bCh = *, bX = 0.0

Line 4: ***   Subclass object ***
Line 6: Superclass: bCh = &, bX = 2.5
Subclass dA = 7
```

When you write the definitions of the methods of the class DClass, the protected instance variable bCh can be accessed directly. However, DClass objects *cannot* directly access bCh. That is, the following statement is illegal (it is, in fact, a syntax error):

```
dObject.bCh = '&';  //Illegal
```

 NOTE In an inheritance hierarchy, the public and protected members of a superclass are directly accessible, in a subclass, across any number of generations, that is, at any level. To be explicit, if class Three is derived from class Two and class Two is derived from class One, then the protected and public members of class One are directly accessible in class Two as well as in class Three. Even though the (public and) protected data members of a super class are directly accessible in a subclass, in the inheritance hierarchy, it should be the responsibility of the superclass to properly initialize these data members. (Also note that, in fact, a class member declared with the modifier protected may be accessed by any class in the same package.)

Protected Access vs Package Access

As noted in Chapter 2, a package is a collection of classes. Appendix D explains how to create a package. Typically a member of a class is declared with the modifier public, private, or protected to give appropriate access to that member. For example, if a member of a class is declared private, then it cannot be directly accessed outside of the class, and if a member is declared protected, it can be directly accessed in the class as well as in any subclass. You can also declare a member without any of these modifiers. If a class member is declared without any of the modifiers public, private, or protected, then the Java system gives to that member the default package access. That is, that member can be directly accessed in any class contained in that package. So there is a subtle difference between package access and protected accesses of a member. If a member of a class has a package access, that member can be directly accessed in any class contained in that package, but not in any class that is not contained in that package even if a subclass is derived from the class containing that member and the subclass is not contained in that package. On the other hand if a member of a class is **protected**, that member can be directly accessed in any subclass even if the subclass is contained in a different package.

Consider the following class definition:

```java
public class Rectangle
{
    double length;
    double width;

    public Rectangle()
    {
        length = 0;
        width = 0;
    }

    double area()
    {
        return length * width;
    }
    .
    .
    .
}
```

In this class definition, the data members `length` and `width` and the method `area` have package access.

class Object

In Chapter 8, we defined the **class** Clock and later included the method toString to return the time as a string. When we included the method toString, we noted that every Java class (built-in or user-defined) is automatically provided the method toString. If a user-defined class does not provide its own definition of the method toString, then the default definition of the method toString is invoked. The methods print and println use the method toString to determine what to print. As shown in Chapter 8, the default definition of the method toString returns the class name followed by the hash code of the object. You might ask, where is the method toString defined?

The method toString comes from the Java **class** Object, and it is a **public** member of this class. In Java, if you define a class and do not use the reserved word **extends** to derive it from an existing class, then the class you define is automatically considered to be derived from the **class** Object. Therefore, the **class** Object directly or indirectly becomes the superclass of every class in Java. From this, it follows that the definition of the **class** Clock (previously given in Chapter 8):

```
public class Clock
{
    //Declare instance variables as given in Chapter 8
    //Definition of instance methods as given in Chapter 8
    //...
}
```

is, in fact, equivalent to the following:

```
public class Clock extends Object
{
    //Declare instance variables as given in Chapter 8
    //Definition of instance methods as given in Chapter 8
    //...
}
```

Using the mechanism of inheritance, every `public` member of the `class Object` can be overridden and/or invoked by every object of any class type. Table 10-1 describes some of the constructors and methods of the `class Object`.

TABLE 10-1 Constructors and Methods of the `class Object`

```
public Object()
//Constructor
```

```
public String toString()
//Method to return a string to describe the object
```

```
public boolean equals(Object obj)
//Method to determine if two objects are the same
//Returns true if the object invoking the method and the object
//specified by the parameter obj refer to the same memory space;
//otherwise it returns false.
```

```
protected Object clone()
//Method to return a reference to a copy of the object invoking
//this method
```

```
protected void finalize()
//The body of this method is invoked when the object goes out of scope.
```

Because every Java class is directly or indirectly derived from the `class Object`, it follows from Table 10-1 that the method `toString` becomes a `public` member of every Java class. Therefore, if a class does not override this method, whenever this method is invoked, the method's default definition executes. As indicated previously, the default definition returns the class name followed by the hash code of the object as a string. Usually, every Java class overrides the method `toString`. The `class String` overrides it so that the string stored in the object is returned. The `class Clock` overrides it so that the string containing the time in the form hh:mm:ss is returned. Similarly, the **class** Person also overrides it.

The method equals is also a very useful method of the **class** Object. This method's definition, as given in the **class** Object, determines whether the object invoking this method and the object passed as a parameter refer to the same memory space, that is, whether they point to data in the same memory space. The method equals determines whether the two objects are aliases. As in the case of the method toString, to implement its own needs, every user-defined **class** also usually overrides the method equals. For example, in the **class** Clock, in Chapter 8, the method equals was overridden to determine whether the instance variables (hr, min, and sec) of two Clock objects contained the same value. (You may review the definition of the method equals of the **class** Clock to see how this method may be written for a class.)

As usual, the default constructor is used to initialize an object. The method clone makes a copy of the object and returns a reference to the copy. However, the method clone makes only a memberwise (that is, field-by-field) copy of the object. In other words, the method clone provides a shallow copy of the data.

Java Stream Classes

In Chapter 2, we used the **class** Scanner for inputting data from the standard input device. Chapter 3 described in detail how to perform input/output (I/O) using Java stream classes, such as FileReader and PrintWriter. In Java, stream classes are implemented using the inheritance mechanism, as shown in Figure 10-6.

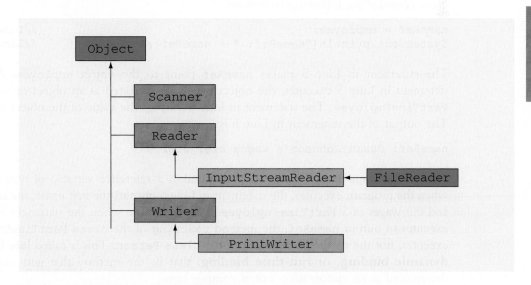

FIGURE 10-6 Java stream classes hierarchy

From Figure 10-6, it follows that the `class`es `Scanner`, `Reader`, and `Writer` are derived from the `class` `Object`. The `class` `InputStreamReader` is derived from the `class` `Reader`, and the `class` `FileReader` is derived from the `class` `InputStreamReader`. Similarly, the `class` `PrintWriter` is derived from the `class` `Writer`.

Polymorphism

Java allows us to treat an object of a subclass as an object of its superclass. In other words, a reference variable of a superclass type can point to an object of its subclass. There are situations when this feature of Java can be used to develop generic code for a variety of applications.

Consider the following statements. (The `class`es `Person` and `PartTimeEmployee` are as previously defined.)

```
Person name, nameRef;                              //Line 1
PartTimeEmployee employee, employeeRef;            //Line 2

name = new Person("John", "Blair");                //Line 3
employee = new PartTimeEmployee("Susan", "Johnson",
                        12.50, 45);                //Line 4
```

The statement in Line 1 declares `name` and `nameRef` to be reference variables of type `Person`. Similarly, the statement in Line 2 declares `employee` and `employeeRef` to be reference variables of type `PartTimeEmployee`. The statement in Line 3 instantiates the object `name` and the statement in Line 4 instantiates the object `employee`.

Now consider the following statements:

```
nameRef = employee;                                //Line 5
System.out.println("nameRef: " + nameRef);         //Line 6
```

The statement in Line 5 makes `nameRef` point to the object `employee`. After the statement in Line 5 executes, the object `nameRef` is treated as an object of the `class` `PartTimeEmployee`. The statement in Line 6 outputs the value of the object `nameRef`. The output of the statement in Line 6 is:

```
nameRef: Susan Johnson's wages are: $562.5
```

Notice that even though `nameRef` is declared as a reference variable of type `Person`, when the program executes, the statement in Line 6 outputs the first name, the last name, and the wages of a `PartTimeEmployee`. This is because when the statement in Line 6 executes to output `nameRef`, the method `toString` of the `class` `PartTimeEmployee` executes, not the method `toString` of the `class` `Person`. This is called **late binding**, **dynamic binding**, or **run-time binding**; that is, the method that gets executed is determined at execution time, not at compile time.

Suppose that `class C` is a subclass of `class B` and that `class B` is a subclass of `class A`. Then, a reference variable of `class A` can point to an object of `class B` as well as to an object of `class C`. Thus, a reference variable of a superclass can point to an object of any of its descendent classes.

In a class hierarchy, several methods may have the same name and the same formal parameter list. Also, a reference variable of a class can refer to either an object of its own class or an object of its subclass. Therefore, a reference variable can invoke, that is, execute, a method of its own class or of its subclass(es). Binding means associating a method definition with its invocation, that is, determining which method definition gets executed. In *early binding*, a method's definition is associated with its invocation when the code is compiled. In *late binding*, a method's definition is associated with the method's invocation at execution time, that is, when the method is executed. Except for a few (special) cases (noted following Example 10-5), Java uses late binding for all methods. Furthermore, the term **polymorphism** means associating multiple (potential) meanings with the same method name. In Java, polymorphism is implemented using late binding.

The reference variable `name` or `nameRef` can point to any object of the `class Person` or the `class PartTimeEmployee`. Loosely speaking, we say that these reference variables have many forms, that is, they are **polymorphic reference** variables. They can refer to objects of their own class or to objects of the subclasses inherited from their class.

The following example further illustrates polymorphism.

EXAMPLE 10-5

```java
public class RectangleFigure
{
    private double length;
    private double width;

    public RectangleFigure()
    {
        length = 0;
        width = 0;
    }

    public RectangleFigure(double l, double w)
    {
        setDimension(l, w);
    }

    public void setDimension(double l, double w)
    {
        if (l >= 0)
            length = l;
```

10

```
        else
            length = 0;

        if (w >= 0)
            width = w;
        else
            width = 0;
    }

    public double getLength()
    {
        return length;
    }

    public double getWidth()
    {
        return width;
    }

    public double area()
    {
        return length * width;
    }

    public double perimeter()
    {
        return 2 * (length + width);
    }

    public String toString()
    {
        return ("Length = "  + length
                + "; Width = " + width + "\n"
                + "Area = " + area());
    }
}
```

Note that the definition of the `class` `RectangleFigure` is similar to the definition of the `class` `Rectangle` given previously. The method `toString` of the `class` `RectangleFigure`, in addition to returning the length and width, also prints the area of the rectangle.

```
public class BoxFigure extends RectangleFigure
{
    private double height;

    public BoxFigure()
    {
        super();
        height = 0;
    }
```

```java
    public BoxFigure(double l, double w, double h)
    {
        super(l, w);
        if (h >= 0)
            height = h;
        else
            height = 0;
    }

    public void setDimension(double l, double w, double h)
    {
        super.setDimension(l, w);

        if (h >= 0)
            height = h;
        else
            height = 0;
    }

    public double getHeight()
    {
        return height;
    }

    public double area()
    {
        return 2 * (getLength() * getWidth()
                    + getLength() * height
                    + getWidth() * height);
    }

    public double volume()
    {
        return super.area() * height;
    }

    public String toString()
    {
        return ("Length = "  + getLength()
            + "; Width = " + getWidth()
            + "; Height = " + height
            + "\n"
            + "Surface Area = " + area()
            + "; Volume = " + volume());
    }
}
```

Note that the **class** BoxFigure is derived from the **class** RectangleFigure. The definition of the **class** BoxFigure is similar to the definition of the **class** Box given previously. The method toString of the **class** BoxFigure, in addition to returning the length, width, and height, also returns the surface area and volume of the box.

Consider the following application program:

```
// This program illustrates how polymorphic reference variables
// work.

public class Polymorphism                              //Line 1
{                                                      //Line 2
    public static void main(String[] args)             //Line 3
    {                                                  //Line 4
        RectangleFigure rectangle, shapeRef;           //Line 5

        BoxFigure box;                                 //Line 6

        rectangle  = new RectangleFigure(8, 5);        //Line 7
        box = new BoxFigure(10, 7, 3);                 //Line 8

        shapeRef = rectangle;                          //Line 9
        System.out.println("Line 10: Rectangle:\n"
                        + shapeRef);                   //Line 10
        System.out.println();                          //Line 11

        shapeRef = box;                                //Line 12
        System.out.println("Line 13: Box:\n"
                        + shapeRef);                   //Line 13
        System.out.println();                          //Line 14
    } //end main                                       //Line 15
}                                                      //Line 16
```

Sample Run:

```
Line 10: Rectangle:
Length = 8.0; Width = 5.0
Area = 40.0

Line 13: Box:
Length = 10.0; Width = 7.0; Height = 3.0
Surface Area = 242.0; Volume = 210.0
```

In the preceding program, shapeRef is a reference variable of the RectangleFigure type. Because the class BoxFigure is derived from the class RectangleFigure, the reference variable shapeRef can point to an object of the class RectangleFigure or to an object of the class BoxFigure.

The statement in Line 7 instantiates a RectangleFigure object and stores the address of this object in the reference variable rectangle. Similarly, the statement in Line 8 instantiates a BoxFigure object and stores the address of this object in the reference variable box.

After the statement in Line 9 executes, shapeRef points to the object rectangle. The statement in Line 10 executes the method toString. Because shapeRef points to an object of the class RectangleFigure, the method toString of the class RectangleFigure executes. When the method toString of the class RectangleFigure executes, it also executes the method area. In this case, the method area of the class RectangleFigure executes.

After the statement in Line 12 executes, `shapeRef` points to the object box. The statement in Line 13 executes the method `toString`. Because `shapeRef` points to an object of the `class BoxFigure`, the method `toString` of the `class BoxFigure` executes. When the method `toString` of the `class BoxFigure` executes, it also executes the method `area`. In this case, the method `area` of the `class BoxFigure` executes, which outputs the surface area of the box.

NOTE

If a method of a `class` is declared final, it cannot be overridden with a new definition in a derived class. You declare a method of a class final by using the keyword `final`. For example, the following method is final:

```
public final void doSomeThing()
{
    //...
}
```

Similarly, you can also declare a `class` final using the keyword `final`. If a class is declared final, then no other `class` can be derived from this `class`; that is, it cannot be the superclass of any other classes.

Java does *not* use late binding for methods that are marked `private`, `final`, or `static`.

As illustrated above, a reference variable of a superclass type can point to an object of its subclass. However, you cannot automatically consider a superclass object to be an object of a subclass. In other words, you *cannot* automatically make a reference variable of a subclass type point to an object of its superclass.

Suppose that `supRef` is a reference variable of a superclass type. Moreover, suppose that `supRef` points to an object of its subclass. You can use an appropriate cast operator on `supRef` and make a reference variable of the subclass point to the object. On the other hand, if `supRef` does not point to a subclass object and you use a cast operator on `supRef` to make a reference variable of the subclass point to the object, then Java will throw a `ClassCastException`—indicating that the `class` cast is not allowed.

Suppose `name`, `nameRef`, `employee`, and `employeeRef` are as declared in the begining of this section, that is:

```
Person name, nameRef;                                //Line 1
PartTimeEmployee employee, employeeRef;              //Line 2

name = new Person("John", "Blair");                  //Line 3
employee = new PartTimeEmployee("Susan", "Johnson",
                          12.50, 45);                //Line 4
nameRef = employee;                                  //Line 5
```

Now consider the following statement:

```
employeeRef = (PartTimeEmployee) name;       //Illegal
```

This statement will throw a `ClassCastException` because `name` points to an object of the `class` `Person`. It does not refer to an object of the `class` `PartTimeEmployee`. However, the following statement is legal:

```
employeeRef = (PartTimeEmployee) nameRef;
```

Because `nameRef` refers to the object `employee` (as set by the statement in Line 5), and `employee` is a reference variable of the `PartTimeEmployee` type, this statement would make `employeeRef` point to the object `employee`. Therefore, the output of the statement:

```
System.out.println(employeeRef);
```

is:

```
Susan Johnson's wages are: $562.50
```

Operator `instanceof`

As previously described, an object of a subclass type can be considered an object of the superclass type. Moreover, by using an appropriate cast operator, you can treat an object of a superclass type as an object of a subclass type. To determine whether a reference variable that points to an object is of a particular class type, Java provides the operator `instanceof`. Consider the following expression (suppose that `p` is an object of a class type):

```
p instanceof BoxShape
```

This expression evaluates to `true` if `p` points to an object of the `class` `BoxShape`; otherwise, it evaluates to `false`. The `class` `BoxShape` is defined in Example 10-6, which further illustrates how the operator `instanceof` works.

EXAMPLE 10-6

Consider the following classes: (The `classes` `RectangleShape` and `BoxShape` are the same as the `classes` `Rectangle` and `Box` given earlier in this chapter. The only difference is that the instance variables of the `classes` `Rectangle` and `Box` are `private`. Because the instance variables of the `class` `RectangleShape` are `protected`, they can be directly accessed in the `class` `BoxShape`. Therefore, the definitions of the methods `area` and `volume` of the `class` `BoxShape` directly access the instance variables `length` and `width` of the `class` `RectangleShape`.)

```java
public class RectangleShape
{
    protected double length;
    protected double width;

    public RectangleShape()
    {
        length = 0;
        width = 0;
    }
}
```

```
    public RectangleShape(double l, double w)
    {
       setDimension(l, w);
    }

    public void setDimension(double l, double w)
    {
        if (l >= 0)
            length = l;
        else
            length = 0;

        if (w >= 0)
            width = w;
        else
            width = 0;
    }

    public double getLength()
    {
        return length;
    }

    public double getWidth()
    {
        return width;
    }

    public double area()
    {
        return length * width;
    }

    public double perimeter()
    {
        return 2 * (length + width);
    }

    public String toString()
    {
        return("Length = "  + length
            + ", Width = " + width
            + ", Perimeter = " + perimeter()
            + ", Area = " + area());
    }
}
```

The **class** BoxShape, given next, is derived from the **class** RectangleShape.

```
public class BoxShape extends RectangleShape
```

```
{
    protected double height;

    public BoxShape()
    {
        super();
        height = 0;
    }

    public BoxShape(double l, double w, double h)
    {
        super(l, w);
        height = h;
    }

    public void setDimension(double l, double w, double h)
    {
        super.setDimension(l, w);

        if (h >= 0)
            height = h;
        else
            height = 0;
    }

    public double getHeight()
    {
        return height;
    }

    public double area()
    {
        return  2 * (length * width + length * height + width * height);
    }

    public double volume()
    {
        return length * width * height;
    }

    public String toString()
    {
        return ("Length = "  + length
                + ", Width = " + width
                + ", Height = " + height
                + ", Surface Area = " + area()
                + ", Volume = " + volume());
    }
}
```

Next, consider the following application program:

```
public class SuperSubClassObjects
{
    public static void main(String[] args)
    {
        RectangleShape  rectangle, rectRef;              //Line 1
        BoxShape box, boxRef;                            //Line 2

        rectangle = new RectangleShape(12, 4);           //Line 3
        System.out.println("Line 4: Rectangle \n"
                        + rectangle+ "\n");              //Line 4
        box = new BoxShape(13, 7, 4);                    //Line 5
        System.out.println("Line 6: Box\n"
                        + box+ "\n");                    //Line 6
        rectRef = box;                                   //Line 7
        System.out.println("Line 8: Box via rectRef\n"
                        + rectRef+ "\n");                //Line 8


        boxRef = (BoxShape) rectRef;                     //Line 9
        System.out.println("Line 10: Box via boxRef\n"
                        + boxRef + "\n");                //Line 10

        if (rectRef instanceof BoxShape)                 //Line 11
            System.out.println("Line 12: rectRef is "
                        + "an instance of BoxShape");    //Line 12
        else                                             //Line 13
            System.out.println("Line 14: rectRef is not "
                        + "an instance of BoxShape");    //Line 14

        if (rectangle instanceof BoxShape)               //Line 15
            System.out.println("Line 16: rectangle is "
                        + "an instance of BoxShape");    //Line 16
        else                                             //Line 17
            System.out.println("Line 18: rectangle is not "
                        + "an instance of BoxShape");    //Line 18
    }
}
```

Sample Run:

```
Line 4: Rectangle
Length = 12.0, Width = 4.0, Perimeter = 32.0, Area = 48.0

Line 6: Box
Length = 13.0, Width = 7.0, Height = 4.0, Surface Area = 342.0, Volume = 364.0

Line 8: Box via rectRef
Length = 13.0, Width = 7.0, Height = 4.0, Surface Area = 342.0, Volume = 364.0
```

```
Line 10: Box via boxRef
Length = 13.0, Width = 7.0, Height = 4.0, Surface Area = 342.0, Volume = 364.0

Line 12: rectRef is an instance of BoxShape
Line 18: rectangle is not an instance of BoxShape
```

The preceding program works as follows: The statement in Line 1 declares `rectangle` and `rectRef` to be reference variables of the `RectangleShape` type. Similarly, the statement in Line 2 declares `box` and `boxRef` to be reference variables of the `BoxShape` type.

The statement in Line 3 instantiates the object `rectangle` and initializes the instance variables `length` and `width` to `12.0` and `4.0`, respectively. The statement in Line 4 outputs the length, width, perimeter, and area of `rectangle`.

The statement in Line 5 instantiates the object `box` and initializes the instance variables `length`, `width`, and `height` to `13.0`, `7.0`, and `4.0`, respectively. The statement in Line 6 outputs the length, width, height, surface area, and volume of `box`.

The statement in Line 7 copies the value of `box` into `rectRef`. After this statement executes, `rectRef` points to the object `box`. Notice that `rectRef` is a reference variable of the `RectangleShape` (the superclass) type and `box` is a reference variable of the `BoxShape` (the subclass of `RectangleShape`) type.

The statement in Line 8 outputs the length, width, height, surface area, and volume of `box` via the reference variable `rectRef`. Notice that `rectRef` is a reference variable of the `RectangleShape` type. However, when the statement in Line 8 executes to output `rectRef`, the method `toString` of the `class` `BoxShape` executes, not the method `toString` of the `class` `RectangleShape`.

Because the reference variable `rectRef` points to an object of `BoxShape`, the statement in Line 9 uses the cast operator and copies the value of `rectRef` into `boxRef`. (If the reference variable `rectRef` did not point to an object of type `BoxShape`, then the statement in Line 9 would result in an error.) The statement in Line 10 outputs the length, width, height, surface area, and volume of the object to which `boxRef` points.

The statements in Lines 11 through 14 determine whether `rectRef` is an instance of `BoxShape`, that is, if `rectRef` points to an object of the `BoxShape` type. Similarly, the statements in Lines 15 through 18 determine whether the reference variable `rectangle` is an instance of `BoxShape`.

Abstract Methods and Classes

An **abstract method** is a method that has only the heading with no body. The heading of an abstract method contains the reserved word **abstract** and ends with a semicolon. The following are examples of abstract methods:

```
public void abstract print();
public abstract object larger(object, object);
void abstract insert(int insertItem);
```

An **abstract class** is a class that is declared with the reserved word **abstract** in its heading. Following are some facts about abstract classes:

- An abstract class can contain instance variables, constructors, the finalizer, and nonabstract methods.

- An abstract class can contain an abstract method(s).

- If a class contains an abstract method, then the class must be declared abstract.

- You cannot instantiate an object of an abstract class. You can only declare a reference variable of an abstract class type.

- You can instantiate an object of a subclass of an abstract class, but only if the subclass gives the definitions of *all* the abstract methods of the superclass.

The following is an example of an abstract class:

```
public abstract class AbstractClassExample
{
    protected int x;

    public abstract void print();

    public void setX(int a)
    {
        x = a;
    }

    public AbstractClassExample()
    {
        x = 0;
    }
}
```

Abstract classes are used as superclasses from which other subclasses within the same context can be derived. They serve as placeholders to store members common to all subclasses. They can be used to force subclasses to provide certain methods, as illustrated in Example 10-7.

EXAMPLE 10-7

Banks offer various types of accounts, such as savings, checking, certificate of deposits, and money market, to attract customers as well as to meet their specific needs. In this example, we illustrate how to use abstract classes and polymorphism for processing different kinds of bank accounts.

Two of the most commonly used accounts are savings and checking. Each of these accounts has various options. For example, you may have a savings account that requires no minimum balance, but has a lower interest rate. Similarly, you may have a checking account that limits the number of checks that you can write each month. Another type of account that is used to save money for the long term is a certificate of deposit (CD). To illustrate how abstract classes are designed and how polymorphism works we assume that the bank offers three types of accounts—savings, checking, and certificate of deposit, as described next.

Savings accounts: Suppose that the bank offers two types of savings accounts: one that has no minimum balance and has a lower interest rate and another that requires a minimum balance and has a higher interest rate.

Checking accounts: Suppose that the bank offers three types of checking accounts: one with a monthly service charge, a limited number of monthly check writing, no minimum balance, and no interest; another with no monthly service charge, requires a minimum balance, allows an unlimited number of monthly check writing, pays lower interest; and a third with no monthly service charge, requires a higher minimum balance, has a higher interest rate, and allows an unlimited number of monthly check writing.

Certificate of deposit (CD): In an account of this type, money is left for some time and these accounts draw higher interest rates than either savings or checking accounts. Suppose that you purchase a CD for six months. Then we say that the CD will mature in six months. Furthermore, the penalty for early withdrawal is stiff.

Figure 10-7 shows the inheritance hierarchy of these bank accounts.

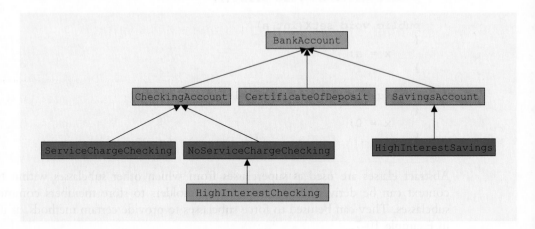

FIGURE 10-7   Inheritance hierarchy of bank accounts

Note that the classes `BankAccount` and `CheckingAccount` are abstract. That is, we cannot instantiate objects of these classes. Typically, common characteristics are placed as high as possible in the inheritance hierarchy and these characteristics are inherited by the subclasses. The other classes in Figure 10-7 are not abstract. Next we describe each of these classes in more detail.

`BankAccount`: Every bank account has an account number, the name of the owner, and a balance. Therefore, instance variables `name`, `accountNumber`, and `balance` are declared in the abstract **class** BankAccount. Some operations common to all types of accounts are to retrieve the account owner's name, the account number, the account balance, make deposits, withdraw money, and create a monthly statement. So we include methods to implement these operations. Furthermore, some of these methods will be abstract. We also include the method toString to return the appropriate information about the class as a string. The UML class diagram of the **class** BankAccount is shown in Figure 10-8.

```
BankAccount (Abstract class)

#accountNumber: int
#name: String
#balance: double

+BankAccount(String, int, double)
+getAccountNumber(): int
+getBalance(): double
+getName(): String
+setName(String): void
+withdraw(double): void
+deposit(double): void
+createMonthlyStatement(): abstract void
+String toString()
```

FIGURE 10-8 UML class diagram of the **class** BankAccount

CheckingAccount: A checking account *is a* bank account. Therefore, it inherits all the properties of a bank account. Because one of the objectives of a checking account is to be able to write checks, we include the abstract method **writeCheck** to write checks. The UML class diagram for **class** CheckingAccount is shown in Figure 10-9.

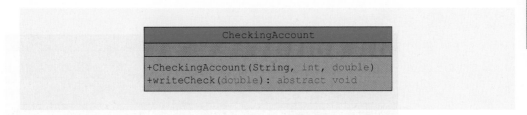

```
CheckingAccount

+CheckingAccount(String, int, double)
+writeCheck(double): abstract void
```

FIGURE 10-9 UML class diagram of the **class** CheckingAccount

ServiceChargeChecking: A service charge checking account *is a* checking account. Therefore, it inherits all the properties of a checking account. For simplicity we assume that this type of account does not pay any interest, allows the account holder to write a limited number of checks each month, and does not require any minimum balance. The named constants, instance variables, and methods of this class are described in Figure 10-10, which also shows the UML class diagram of the **class** ServiceChargeChecking.

```
                    ServiceChargeChecking
-ACCOUNT_SERVICE_CHARGE = 10.00: static final double
-MAXIMUM_NUM_OF_CHECKS = 5: static final int
-SERVICE_CHARGE_EXCESS_NUM_OF_CHECKS = 5: static final double
#serviceChargeAccount: double
#serviceChargeCheck: double
#numberOfChecksWritten: int

+ServiceChargeChecking(String, int, double)
+ServiceChargeChecking(String, int, double, double, double)
+getServiceChargeAccount(): double
+setServiceChargeAccount(double): void
+getServiceChargeChecks(): double
+setServiceChargeChecks(double): void
+getNumberOfChecksWritten(): int
+setNumberOfChecksWritten(int): void
+postServiceCharge(): void
+writeCheck(double): void
+createMonthlyStatement(): void
+toString(): String
```

FIGURE 10-10 UML class diagram of the **class** ServiceChargeChecking

NoServiceChargeChecking: A checking account with no monthly service charge *is a* checking account. Therefore, it inherits all the properties of a checking account. Furthermore, this type of account pays interest, allows the account holder to write checks, and requires a minimum balance. The named constants, instance variables, and methods of this class are described in Figure 10-11, which also shows the UML class diagram of the **class** NoServiceChargeChecking.

```
                   NoServiceChargeChecking
-MIN_BALANCE = 1000.00: static final double
-INTEREST_RATE = 0.02: static final double
#minimumBalance: double
#interestRate: double

+NoServiceChargeChecking(String, int, double)
+NoServiceChargeChecking(String, int, double, double, double)
+getMinimumBalance(): double
+setMinimumBalance(double): void
+verifyMinimumBalance(double): boolean
+writeCheck(double): void
+withdraw(double): void
+createMonthlyStatement(): void
+toString(): String
```

FIGURE 10-11 UML class diagram of the **class** NoServiceChargeChecking

HighInterestChecking: A checking account with high interest *is a* checking account with no monthly service charge. Therefore, it inherits all the properties of a no service charge checking account. Furthermore, this type of account pays higher interest and requires higher minimum balance than the no service charge checking account. The named constants, instance variables, and methods of this class are described in Figure 10-12, which also shows the UML class diagram of the **class HighInterestChecking**.

```
HighInterestChecking

-INTEREST_RATE = 0.05: static final double
-MIN_BALANCE = 5000.00: static final double

+HighInterestChecking(String, int, double)
+HighInterestChecking(String, int, double, double, double)
+getInterestRate(): double
+setInterestRate(double): void
+postInterest(): void
+createMonthlyStatement(): void
+toString(): String
```

FIGURE 10-12 UML class diagram of the **class** HighInterestChecking

SavingsAccount: A savings account *is a* bank account. Therefore, it inherits all the properties of a bank account. Furthermore, a savings account also pays interest. The named constants, instance variables, and methods of this class are described in Figure 10-13, which also shows the UML class diagram of the **class SavingsAccount**.

```
SavingsAccount

-INTEREST_RATE = 0.03: static final double
#interestRate: double

+SavingsAccount(String, int, double)
+SavingsAccount(String, int, double, double)
+getInterestRate(): double
+setInterestRate(double): void
+postInterest(): void
+createMonthlyStatement(): void
+toString(): String
```

FIGURE 10-13 UML class diagram of the **class** SavingsAccount

HighInterestSavings: A high interest savings account *is a* savings account. Therefore, it inherits all the properties of a savings account. It also requires a minimum balance. The named constants, instance variables, and methods of this class are described in Figure 10-14, which also shows the UML class diagram of the **class HighInterestSavings**.

```
                    HighInterestSavings
-MINIMUM_BALANCE = 2500.00: static final double
-INTEREST_RATE = 0.05: static final double
#minimumBalance: double

+HighInterestSavings(String, int, double)
+HighInterestSavings(String, int, double, double, double)
+getMinimumBalance(): double
+verifyMinimumBalance(double): boolean
+withdraw(double): void
+toString(): String
```

FIGURE 10-14 UML class diagram of the **class** HighInterestSavings

CertificateOfDeposit: A certificate of deposit account *is a* bank account. Therefore, it inherits all the properties of a bank account. In addition, it has instance variables to store the number of CD maturity months, the interest rate, and the current CD month. The named constants, instance variables, and methods of this class are listed in Figure 10-15, which also shows the UML class diagram of the **class** CertificateOfDeposit.

```
                   CertificateOfDeposit
-INTEREST_RATE = 0.05: static final double
-NUMBER_OF_MATURITY_MONTHS = 6: static final int
-interestRate: double
-maturityMonths: int
-cdMonth: int

+CertificateOfDeposit(String, int, double)
+CertificateOfDeposit(String, int, double, double, int)
+getInterestRate(): double
+setInterestRate(double): void
+getCurrentCDMonth(): double
+setCurrentCDMonth(int): void
+getMaturityMonths(): double
+setMaturityMonths(int): void
+postInterest():void
+withdraw(double): void
+withdraw(): void
+createMonthlyStatement(): void
+toString(): String
```

FIGURE 10-15 UML class diagram of the **class** CertificateOfDeposit

To create various types of accounts, we can use a **Vector** object. Recall from Chapter 9 that a **Vector** object can increase in size if additional accounts are needed to be created. The elements of the **Vector** are of type **BankAccount**, and six different kinds of bank accounts can be instantiated. The following statement created the `Vector` object `accountsList` and the element type is `BankAccount`:

```
Vector <BankAccount> accountsList = new Vector <BankAccount>();
```

We leave it as an exercise for you to write the definitions of the classes described in this example as well as a program to test these classes. (See Programming Exercise 14 at the end of this chapter.)

Interfaces

In Chapter 6, you learned that the `class ActionListener` is a special type of class called an `interface`. Several other classes in Java are similar to the `interface ActionListener`. For example, window events are handled by the `interface WindowListener`, and mouse events are handled by the `interface MouseListener`. The obvious question is: Why does Java have these interfaces? After all, they are similar to classes. The answer is that Java *does not* support multiple inheritance; a class can extend the definition of only one class. In other words, a class can be derived from *only* one existing class. However, a Java program might contain a variety of GUI components and thus generate a variety of events, such as window events, mouse events, and action events. These events are handled by separate interfaces. Therefore, a program might need to use more than one such interface.

Until now, we have handled events by using the mechanism of the inner class. For example, action events were processed by using inner classes. There are two more ways, discussed in Chapter 11, to process events in a Java program—by using anonymous classes and by making the class containing the application program implement the appropriate interface.

When we created an inner class to process an action event, the inner class was built on top of the `interface ActionListener` by using the mechanism of `implements`. Rather than use the inner class mechanism, the class containing the Java program can itself be created on top of ("by implementing") an interface, just as we created the GUI program by extending the `class JFrame`. For example, for the `RectangleProgram` in Chapter 6, we could have defined the `class RectangleProgram` as follows:

```
public class RectangleProgram extends JFrame implements
                                              ActionListener
{
    //...
}
```

Of course, doing so would also require us to register the listener using the reference `this`, which was explained in Chapter 8.

To be able to handle a variety of events, Java allows a class to implement more than one interface. This is, in fact, how Java implements a *form* of multiple inheritance, *which is not true multiple inheritance*. In the remainder of this section, we provide a few facts about interfaces.

10

You already know that an interface is a special type of class. How does an interface differ from an actual class?

An **interface** is a type of class that contains only abstract methods and/or named constants. Interfaces are defined using the reserved word `interface` in place of the reserved word `class`. For example, the definition of the `interface` `WindowListener` is:

```
public interface WindowListener
{
    public void windowOpened(WindowEvent e);
    public void windowClosing(WindowEvent e);
    public void windowClosed(WindowEvent e);
    public void windowIconified(WindowEvent e);
    public void windowDeiconified(WindowEvent e);
    public void windowActivated(WindowEvent e);
    public void windowDeactivated(WindowEvent e);
}
```

The definition of the `interface` `ActionListener` is:

```
public interface ActionListener
{
    public void actionPerformed(ActionEvent e);
}
```

EXAMPLE 10-8

The following `class` implements the `interfaces` `ActionListener` and `WindowListener`:

```
public class ExampleInterfaceImp implements ActionListener,
                                             WindowListener
{
    //....
}
```

 NOTE Recall that if a `class` contains an `abstract` method, it must be declared `abstract`. Moreover, you cannot instantiate an object of an `abstract class`. Therefore, if a `class` implements an `interface`, it must provide definitions for each of the methods of the `interface`; otherwise, you cannot instantiate an object of that class type.

Polymorphism Via Interfaces

As stated above, one of the main uses of interfaces is to allow GUI programs to handle more than one type of event such as window events, mouse events, and action events. These events are handled by separate interfaces. An interface can also be used in the implementation of abstract data types. Like some other languages, such as C++, you cannot separate the definition of a class from the definitions of its methods. If the user of a class looks at the definition of the class, the user can also look at the definitions of the methods. That is, implementation details of a class cannot be (directly) separated from its specification details. In reality, the user of a class should only be concerned with the specification, not the implementation. One way to accomplish this is to define an interface that contains the methods headings and/or named constants. Then you can define the class that implements the interface. The user can look at the interface and see what operations are implemented by the class.

Just as you can create polymorphic references to classes in an inheritance hierarchy, you can also create polymorphic references using interfaces. You can use an interface name as the type of a reference variable, and the reference variable can point to any object of any class that implements the interface. However, because an interface contains only method headings and/or named constants, *you cannot create an object of an interface*.

Suppose that you have the following interface:

```
public interface Employee
{
    public double wages();
    public String department();
}
```

Now you declare a reference variable using the `interface` `Employee`. For example, the following statement declares `newEmployee` to be a reference variable of type `Employee`:

```
Employee newEmployee;
```

However, the following statement is illegal because you cannot instantiate an object of an `interface`:

```
newEmployee = new Employee();      //illegal
```

Suppose that you have two types of employees—part-time and full-time. You can define the `class` `FullTimeEmployee` that implements the `interface` `Employee`. You can use the reference variable `newEmployee` to create an object of the `class` `FullTimeEmployee`. For example, the following statement creates an object of this class:

```
newEmployee = new FullTimeEmployee();
```

The following statement invokes the methods wages:

```
double salary = newEmployee.wages();
```

In a similar manner, if the `class` `PartTimeEmployee` implements the `interface` `Employee`, the following statement creates an object of this class:

```
newEmployee = new PartTimeEmployee();
```

In addition to implementing methods of the `interface` `Employee`, the `class` `FullTimeEmployee` can contain additional methods. Suppose that the `class` `FullTimeEmployee` contains the method

10

```
public void upDatePayRate(double increment)
{
    //...
}
```

Then the following statement will generate a compiler error:

```
newEmployee.upDatePayRate(25);    //causes compiler error
```

The reason for this error is that, because `newEmployee` is a reference variable of type `Employee`, it can point to an object of the `class FullTimeEmployee` or an object of the `class PartTimeEmployee`, but it can only guarantee that the object it points to can use the methods `wages` and `department`. However, if we know that `newEmployee` points to an object of the `class FullTimeEmployee`, then using an appropriate cast operator, we can call the method `upDatePayRate` as follows:

```
((FullTimeEmployee)newEmployee).upDatePayRate(25);
```

You can expand or extend the hierarchy as needed to accommodate additional kinds of employees. For example, a board member might be another kind of employee, expanding the hierarchy. Or, there might be two kinds of full-time employees: those who receive a fixed salary and those who are paid by the hour. Java provides the flexibility to accommodate the expansion and extension, and to represent these kinds of class relationships.

You can also use an `interface` name to declare a parameter to a method. In this case, any reference variable of any class that implements that interface can be passed as an (actual) parameter to that method.

Composition (Aggregation)

Composition is another way to relate two classes. In **composition (aggregation)**, one or more members of a class are objects of one or more other classes. Composition can be viewed as a "has-a" relation; for example, "every person has a date of birth."

The `class Person`, as defined in Chapter 8, Example 8-8, stores a person's first name and last name. Suppose we want to keep track of additional information, such as a personal ID and date of birth. Because every person has a personal ID and a date of birth, we can define a new `class PersonalInfo`, in which one of the members is an object of type `Person`. We can declare additional members to store the personal ID and date of birth for the `class PersonalInfo`.

First, we define another `class`, `Date`, to store only a person's date of birth, and then construct the `class PersonalInfo` from the `class`es `Person` and `Date`. This way, we can demonstrate how to define a new class using two classes.

To define the `class Date`, we need three instance variables to store the month, day number, and year. Some of the operations that need to be performed on a date are to set the date and to print the date. The following statements define the `class Date`:

```java
public class Date
{
    private int dMonth;      //variable to store the month
    private int dDay;        //variable to store the day
    private int dYear;       //variable to store the year

        //Default constructor
        //The instance variables dMonth, dDay, and dYear are set to
        //the default values.
        //Postcondition: dMonth = 1; dDay = 1; dYear = 1900;
    public Date()
    {
        dMonth = 1;
        dDay = 1;
        dYear = 1900;
    }

        //Constructor to set the date
        //The instance variables dMonth, dDay, and dYear are set
        //according to the parameters.
        //Postcondition: dMonth = month; dDay = day;
        //                     dYear = year;
    public Date(int month, int day, int year)
    {
        dMonth = month;
        dDay = day;
        dYear = year;
    }

        //Method to set the date
        //The instance variables dMonth, dDay, and dYear are set
        //according to the parameters.
        //Postcondition: dMonth = month; dDay = day;
        //                     dYear = year;
    public void setDate(int month, int day, int year)
    {
        dMonth = month;
        dDay = day;
        dYear = year;
    }

        //Method to return the month
        //Postcondition: The value of dMonth is returned.
    public int getMonth()
    {
        return dMonth;
    }

        //Method to return the day
        //Postcondition: The value of dDay is returned.
```

```
public int getDay()
{
    return dDay;
}

    //Method to return the year
    //Postcondition: The value of dYear is returned.
public int getYear()
{
    return dYear;
}

    //Method to return the date in the form mm-dd-yyyy
public String toString()
{
    return (dMonth + "-" + dDay + "-" + dYear);
}
}
```

Figure 10-16 shows the UML diagram of the **class** Date.

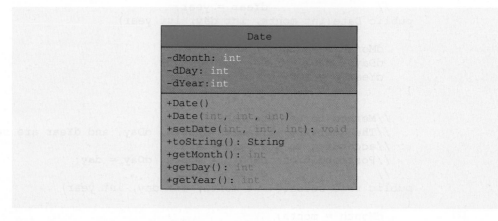

FIGURE 10-16 UML class diagram of the **class** Date

The definition of the method setDate, before storing the date into the data members, does not check to see if the date is valid. That is, it does not confirm that month is between 1 and 12, year is greater than 0, and day is valid (for example, for January, day should be between 1 and 31). In Programming Exercise 2 at the end of this chapter, you are asked to rewrite the definition of the method setDate so that the date is validated before storing it in the data members. Similarly, in Programming Exercise 2, you are asked to rewrite the definition of the constructor with parameters so that it checks for valid values of month, day, and year before storing the date into the data members.

Next, we specify the members of the **class** PersonalInfo.

Instance Variables:

```
private Person name;
private Date bDay;
private int personID;
```

Constructors and Instance Methods:

```
public void setPersonalInfo(String first, String last, int month,
                            int day, int year, int ID)
   //Method to set the personal information
   //Instance variables are set according to the parameters
   //Postcondition: firstName = first; lastName = last;
   //        dMonth = month; dDay = day; dYear = year;
   //        personID = ID;

public String toString()
   //Method to return the string containing personal information

public PersonalInfo(String first, String last, int month,
                    int day, int year, int ID)
   //Constructor with parameters
   //Instance variables are set according to the parameters
   //Postcondition: firstName = first; lastName = last;
   //     dMonth = month; dDay = day; dYear = year;
   //     personID = ID;

public PersonalInfo()
   //Default constructor
   //Instance variables are set to the default values
   //Postcondition: firstName = ""; lastName = "";
   //                dMonth = 1; dDay = 1; dYear = 1900;
   //                personID = 0;
```

Figure 10-17 shows the UML class diagram of the `class` `PersonalInfo`.

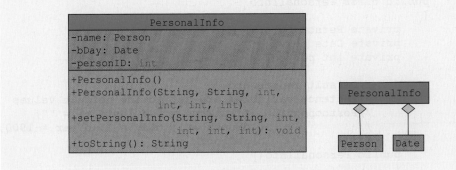

FIGURE 10-17 UML class diagram of the `class` `PersonalInfo`

The definitions of the methods of the `class` `PersonalInfo` follow:

```
public void setPersonalInfo(String first, String last, int month,
                            int day, int year, int ID)
{
    name.setName(first, last);
    bDay.setDate(month, day, year);
    personID = ID;
}

public String toString()
{

    return ("Name: " + name.toString() + "\n"
           + "Date of birth: " + bDay.toString() + "\n"
           + "Personal ID: " + personID);
}

public PersonalInfo(String first, String last, int month,
                    int day, int year, int ID)
{
    name = new Person(first, last);   //instantiate and
                                      //initialize the object name
    bDay = new Date(month, day, year);   //instantiate and
                                         //initialize the object bDay
    personID = ID;
}

public PersonalInfo()
{
    name = new Person();
    bDay = new Date();
    personID = 0;
}
```

Next, we give the definition of the `class` `PersonalInfo`:

```
public class PersonalInfo
{
    private Person name;
    private Date bDay;
    private int personID;

        //Default constructor
        //Instance variables are set to the default values
        //Postcondition: firstName = ""; lastName = "";
        //               dMonth = 1; dDay = 1; dYear = 1900;
        //               personID = 0;
    public PersonalInfo()
    {
        name = new Person();
        bDay = new Date();
        personID = 0;
    }
```

```
    //Constructor with parameters
    //Instance variables are set according to the parameters
    //Postcondition: firstName = first; lastName = last;
    //                dMonth = month; dDay = day; dYear = year;
    //                personID = ID;
public PersonalInfo(String first, String last, int month,
                    int day, int year, int ID)
{
    name = new Person(first, last);  //instantiate and
                                     //initialize the object name
    bDay = new Date(month, day, year);//instantiate and
                                     //initialize the object bDay
    personID = ID;
}

    //Method to set the personal information
    //Instance variables are set according to the parameters
    //Postcondition: firstName = first; lastName = last;
    //                dMonth = month; dDay = day; dYear = year;
    //                personID = ID;
public void setPersonalInfo(String first, String last, int month,
                            int day, int year, int ID)
{
    name.setName(first, last);
    bDay.setDate(month, day, year);
    personID = ID;
}

    //Method to return the string containing personal information
public String toString()
{
    return ("Name: " + name.toString() + "\n"
        + "Date of birth: " + bDay.toString() + "\n"
        + "Personal ID: " + personID);
}
}
```

NOTE The definitions of the classes Person, Date, and PersonalInfo, as well as a program that shows how to use these classes can be found in the Additional Student Files folder at *www.cengagebrain.com*. The folder Composition contains the necessary files.

PROGRAMMING EXAMPLE: Grade Report

This programming example further illustrates the concepts of inheritance and composition.

The midsemester point at your college or university is approaching. The registrar's office wants to prepare the grade reports as soon as the students' grades are recorded. Some of the enrolled students have not yet paid their tuition, however.

If a student has paid the tuition, the student's grades are shown on the grade report with the grade-point average (GPA).

If a student has not paid the tuition, the grades are not printed. For these students, the grade report contains a message indicating that the grades are being held for non-payment of tuition. The grade report also shows the billing amount.

The registrar's office and the business office want you to help write a program that can analyze the students' data and print the appropriate grade reports.

The program is divided into two parts. In the first part, we create the application program that generates the grade report in the window's console environment and stores the output in a file.

In the second part, which is available in the Additional Student Files folder at *www.cengagebrain.com.*, we create a GUI to display the students' grade reports, as shown in the section Student Grade Report: GUI Design.

For this report, the data is stored in a file in the following form:

PART I:
STUDENT
GRADE
REPORT:
CONSOLE
DISPLAY

```
noOfStudents tuitionRate
studentName studentID isTuitionPaid numberOfCourses
courseName courseNumber creditHours grade
courseName courseNumber creditHours grade
.
.
.

studentName studentID isTuitionPaid numberOfCourses
courseName courseNumber creditHours grade
courseName courseNumber creditHours grade
.
.
.
```

The first line indicates the number of students enrolled and the tuition rate per credit hour. The students' data is given thereafter.

A sample input file follows:

```
3 345
Lisa Miller 890238 Y 4
Mathematics MTH345 4 A
Physics PHY357 3 B
ComputerSci CSC478 3 B
History HIS356 3 A
  .
  .
  .
```

The first line indicates that 3 students are enrolled and the tuition rate is $345 per credit hour. Next, the course data for student Lisa Miller is given: Lisa Miller's ID is 890238, she has paid the tuition, and is taking 4 courses. The course number for the mathematics class she is taking is MTH345, the course has 4 credit hours, her mid-semester grade is A, and so on. The output of the program is of the following form:

```
Student Name: Lisa Miller
Student ID: 890238
Number of courses enrolled: 4

Course No   Course Name   Credits Grade
CSC478      ComputerSci      3      B
HIS356      History          3      A
MTH345      Mathematics      4      A
PHY357      Physics          3      B

Total number of credit hours: 13
Midsemester GPA: 3.54
```

It is clear from this output that the courses must be ordered according to the course number. To calculate the GPA, we assume that the grade A is equivalent to 4 points, B is equivalent to 3 points, C is equivalent to 2 points, D is equivalent to 1 point, and F is equivalent to 0 points.

Input: A file containing the data in the form given previously. For easy reference in the rest of the discussion, let's assume that the name of the input file is stData.txt.

Output: A file containing the output of the form given previously.

PROBLEM ANALYSIS AND ALGORITHM DESIGN

We must first identify the main components of the program. The college or university has students, and every student takes courses. Thus, the two main components are the student and the course.

Let's first describe the component Course.

Course

The main characteristics of a course are the course name, course number, and number of credit hours.

Some of the basic operations that need to be performed on an object of the course type are:

1. Set the course information.
2. Print the course information.
3. Show the credit hours.
4. Show the course number.

Next, we define the members of the `class` Course.

Instance Variables:

```
private String courseName;    //object to store the course name
private String courseNo;      //object to store the course number
private int courseCredits;    //variable to store the course
                              //credits
```

Constructors and Instance Methods:

```
public void setCourseInfo(String cName, String cNo,
                          int credits)
   //Method to set the course information
   //The course information is set according to the
   //incoming parameters.
   //Postcondition: courseName = cName; courseNo = cNo;
   //                courseCredits = credits;

public void setCourseName(String cName)
   //Method to set the course Name
   //Postcondition: courseName = cName;

public void setCourseNumber(String cNo)
   //Method to set the course Number
   //Postcondition: courseNo = cNo;

public void setCourseCredits(int credits)
   //Method to set the course credits
   //Postcondition: courseCredits = credits;

public String toString()
  //Method to return the course information as a string
  //Postcondition: The course information is returned
  //               as a string.

public String getCourseName()
   //Method to return the course name
   //Postcondition: The value of courseName is returned.

public String getCourseNumber()
   //Method to return the course number
   //Postcondition: The value of courseNo is returned.
```

```
public int getCredits()
   //Method to return the credit hours
   //Postcondition: The value of courseCredits is returned.

public void copyCourseInfo(Course otherCourse)
   //Method to copy a course's information.
   //otherCourse is copied into this course
   //Postcondition: courseName = otherCourse.courseName;
   //               courseNo = otherCourse.courseNo;
   //               courseCredits = otherCourse.courseCredits;

public Course()
   //Default Constructor
   //The object is initialized to the default values.
   //Postcondition: courseName = ""; courseNo = "";
   //               courseCredits = 0;
public Course(String cName, String cNo, int credits)
   //Constructor
   //The object is initialized according to the parameters.
   //Postcondition: courseName = cName; courseNo = cNo;
   //               courseCredits = credits;
```

Figure 10-18 shows the UML class diagram of the class Course.

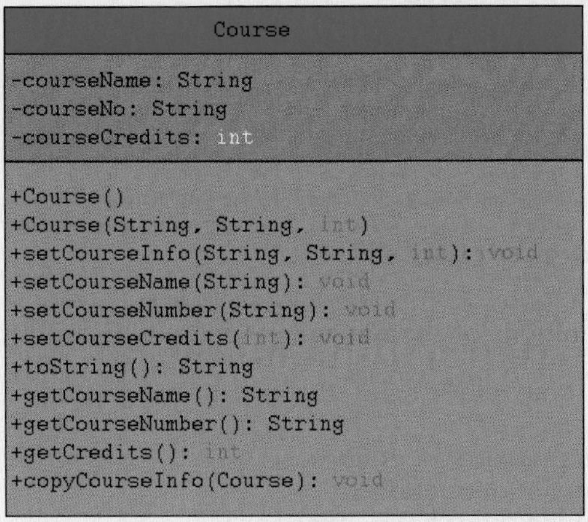

FIGURE 10-18 UML class diagram of the class Course

Next, we discuss the definition of the methods to implement the operations of the class Course.

The method `setCourseInfo` sets the values of the instance variables according to the values of the parameters. Its definition is:

```
public void setCourseInfo(String cName, String cNo,
                          int credits)
{
    courseName = cName;
    courseNo = cNo;
    courseCredits = credits;
}
```

The definitions of the methods `setCourseName`, `setCourseNumber`, and `setCourseCredits` are similar to the method `setCourseInfo`. Their definitions are:

```
public void setCourseName(String cName)
{
    courseName = cName;
}

public void setCourseNumber(String cNo)
{
    courseNo = cNo;
}

public void setCourseCredits(int credits)
{
    courseCredits = credits;
}
```

The method `toString` returns the course information as a string. Its definition is:

```
public String toString()
{
    return String.format("%-12s%-15s%4s", courseNo,
                         courseName, courseCredits);
} //end toString
```

The definitions of the remaining methods and constructors are as follows:

```
public Course(String cName, String cNo, int credits)
{
    courseName = cName;
    courseNo = cNo;
    courseCredits = credits;
}

public Course()
{
    courseName = "";
    courseNo = "";
    courseCredits = 0;
}
```

```java
public String getCourseName()
{
    return courseName;
}

public String getCourseNumber()
{
    return courseNo;
}

public int getCredits()
{
    return courseCredits;
}

public void copyCourseInfo(Course otherCourse)
{
    courseName = otherCourse.courseName;
    courseNo = otherCourse.courseNo;
    courseCredits = otherCourse.courseCredits;
}
```

The definition of the `class` Course looks like the following: (You can complete the definition of this class as an exercise.)

```java
import java.io.*;

public class Course
{
    private String courseName;   //object to store the
                                 //course name
    private String courseNo;     //object to store the
                                 //course number
    private int courseCredits;   //variable to store the
                                 //course credits
    //Place the definitions of the instance methods
    //as discussed here.
}
```

Next, we discuss the component `Student`.

The main characteristics of a student are the student name, student ID, number of courses in which the student is enrolled, courses in which the student is enrolled, and the grade for each course. Because every student must pay tuition, we also include a member to indicate whether the student has paid the tuition.

Every student is a person, and every student takes courses. We have already designed a `class` Person to process a person's first and last name. We have also designed a class to process the course information. Thus, we see that we can derive the `class` Student to keep track of a student's information from the `class` Person, and one member of the `class` Student is of type Course. We can add more members as needed.

The basic operations to be performed on an object of type Student are as follows:

1. Set the student information.
2. Print the student information.
3. Calculate the number of credit hours taken.
4. Calculate the GPA.
5. Calculate the billing amount.
6. Because the grade report will print the courses in ascending order, sort the courses according to the course number.

Next, we define the members of the `class` Student.

Instance Variables:

```
private int sId;                    //variable to store the
                                    //student ID
private int numberOfCourses;        //variable to store the number
                                    //of courses
private boolean isTuitionPaid;      //variable to indicate if
                                    //the tuition is paid

private Course [] coursesEnrolled;  //array to store
                                            //the courses
private char [] courseGrades;       //array to store the
                                    //course grades
```

Constructors and Instance Methods:

```
public void setInfo(String fName, String lName, int ID,
                int nOfCourses, boolean isTPaid,
                Course[] courses, char[] cGrades)
    //Method to set a student's information
    //Postcondition: The instance variables are set according
    //                  to the parameters.

public void setStudentId(int ID)
    //Method to set a student ID
    //Postcondition: sId = ID;

public void setIsTuitionPaid(boolean isTPaid)
    //Method to set whether tuition is paid
    //Postcondition: isTuitionPaid = isTPaid;

public void setNumberOfCourses(int nOfCourses)
    //Method to set number of courses taken
    //Postcondition: numberOfCourses = nOfCourses;
```

```
public void setCoursesEnrolled(Course[] courses,
                               char[] cGrades)
   //Method to set courses enrolled
   //Postcondition: array courses is copied into the array
   //       coursesEnrolled, array cGrades is copied into
   //       the array courseGrades, and these arrays are
   //       sorted.

public String toString()
   //Method to return a student's grade report as a string
   //Postcondition: If the instance variable isTuitionPaid
   //        is true, the grades are returned; otherwise
   //        three stars are returned.

public int getStudentId()
   //Method to get a student ID
   //Postcondition: The value of sId is returned.

public boolean getIsTuitionPaid()
   //Method to return a value specifying if the tuition is paid
   //Postcondition: The value of isTuitionPaid is returned.

public int getNumberOfCourses()
   //Method to get the number of courses taken
   //Postcondition: The value of numberOfCourses is returned.

public char getGrade(int i)
   //Method to return a course grade
   //Postcondition: The value of courseGrades[i] is returned.

public Course getCourse(int i)
   //Method to get a copy of a course taken
   //Postcondition: A copy of coursesEnrolled[i]
   //               is returned.

public int getHoursEnrolled()
   //Method to return the credit hours in which a
   //student is enrolled
   //Postcondition: Total credits are calculated
   //               and returned.

public double getGpa()
   //Method to return the grade point average
   //Postcondition: GPA is calculated and returned.

public double billingAmount(double tuitionRate)
   //Method to return the tuition fees
   //Postcondition: The billing amount is calculated
   //               and returned.
```

10

```
private void sortCourses()
    //Method to sort the courses
    //Postcondition: The array coursesEnrolled is sorted.
    //                The grades for each course, in the
    //                array courseGrades, are also reorganized.

public Student()
    //Default constructor
    //Postcondition: The instance variables are initialized.
```

Figure 10-19 shows the UML class diagram of the class Student.

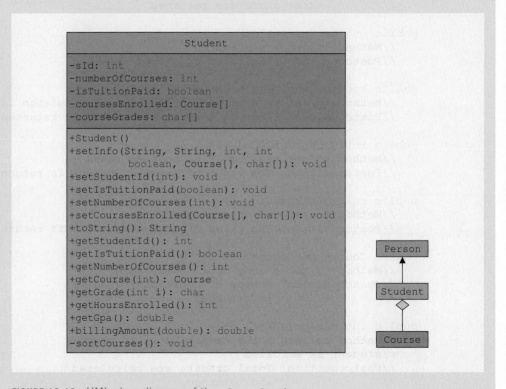

FIGURE 10-19 UML class diagram of the class Student

Note that the method sortCourses to sort the array coursesEnrolled is a private member of the class Student. This is because this method is needed for internal data manipulation, and the user of the class does not need to access this member.

Next, we discuss the definitions of the methods to implement the operations of the class Student.

The method setInfo first initializes the private data members according to the incoming parameters. This method then calls the method sortCourses to sort the array coursesEnrolled by course number. The class Student is derived from the class Person, and the variables to store the first and last name are private members of that class. Therefore, we call the method setName of the class Person, and we pass the appropriate variables to set the first and last names. The definition of the method setInfo is as follows:

```java
public void setInfo(String fName, String lName, int ID,
                    int nOfCourses, boolean isTPaid,
                    Course[] courses, char[] cGrades)
{
    setName(fName, lName);               //set the name

    sId = ID;                            //set the student ID
    isTuitionPaid = isTPaid;             //set isTuitionPaid
    numberOfCourses = nOfCourses ;       //set the number of courses

    for (int i = 0; i < numberOfCourses; i++) //set the array
    {
        coursesEnrolled[i].copyCourseInfo(courses[i]);
        courseGrades[i] = cGrades[i];
    }

    sortCourses();            //sort the array coursesEnrolled
}
```

The definitions of the methods setStudentId, setIsTuitionPaid, setNumberOfCourses, and setCoursesEnrolled are similar to the definition of the method setInfo, and are given next.

```java
public void setStudentId(int ID)
{
    sId = ID;
}

public void setIsTuitionPaid(boolean isTPaid)
{
    isTuitionPaid = isTPaid;
}

public void setNumberOfCourses(int nOfCourses)
{
    numberOfCourses = nOfCourses ;
}

public void setCoursesEnrolled(Course[] courses,
                               char[] cGrades)
```

```
    {
        for (int i = 0; i < numberOfCourses; i++)
        {
            coursesEnrolled[i].copyCourseInfo(courses[i]);
            courseGrades[i] = cGrades[i];
        }

        sortCourses();
    }
```

The default constructor initializes the instance variables to their default values.

```
public Student()
{
    super();
    numberOfCourses = 0;
    sId = 0;
    isTuitionPaid = false;

    coursesEnrolled = new Course[6];

    for (int i = 0; i < 6; i++)
        coursesEnrolled[i] = new Course();

    courseGrades = new char[6];

    for (int i = 0; i < 6; i++)
        courseGrades[i] = '*';
}
```

The method **toString** returns the grade report as a string. If the student has paid his or her tuition, the grades and the GPA are returned. Otherwise, three stars are returned in place of each grade. The definition of this method is:

```
public String toString()
{
    String gReport;

    gReport = "Student Name: "
            + super.toString() + "\r\n"
            + "Student ID: " + sId + "\r\n"
            + "Number of courses enrolled: "
            + numberOfCourses + "\r\n"
            + String.format("%-12s%-15s%-8s%-6s%n",
                        "Course No", "Course Name",
                        "Credits", "Grade");

    for (int i = 0; i < numberOfCourses; i++)
    {
        gReport = gReport + coursesEnrolled[i];

        if (isTuitionPaid)
            gReport = gReport
                    + String.format("%8s%n", courseGrades[i]);
```

```
        else
            gReport = gReport
                    + String.format("%8s%n", "***");
    }

    gReport = gReport
            + "\r\nTotal number of credit hours: "
            + getHoursEnrolled() + "\r\n";

    return gReport;
} //end toString
```

The definitions of the methods getStudentId, getIsTuitionPaid, getNumberOfCourses, getCourse, and getGrade are given next:

```
public int getStudentId()
{
    return sId;
}

public boolean getIsTuitionPaid()
{
    return isTuitionPaid;
}

public int getNumberOfCourses()
{
    return numberOfCourses;
}

public Course getCourse(int i)
{
    Course temp = new Course();

    temp.copyCourseInfo(coursesEnrolled[i]);

    return temp;
}

public char getGrade(int i)
{
    return courseGrades[i];
}
```

The method getHoursEnrolled calculates and returns the total credit hours that a student is taking. These credit hours are needed to calculate both the GPA and the billing amount. The total credit hours are calculated by adding the credit hours of each course in which the student is enrolled. Because the credit hours for a course are in the private data member of an object of type Course, we use the method getCredits of the class Course to retrieve the credit hours. The definition of this method is:

```
public int getHoursEnrolled()
{
    int totalCredits = 0;

    for (int i = 0; i < numberOfCourses; i++)
        totalCredits += coursesEnrolled[i].getCredits();

    return totalCredits;
}
```

If a student has not paid the tuition, the method `billingAmount` calculates and returns the amount due, based on the number of credit hours enrolled. The definition of this method is:

```
public double billingAmount(double tuitionRate)
{
    return tuitionRate * getHoursEnrolled();
}
```

We now discuss the method `getGpa`. This method calculates a student's GPA. To find the GPA, we find the equivalent points for each grade, add the points, and then divide the sum by the total credit hours the student is taking. The definition of this method is:

```
public double getGpa()
{
    double sum = 0.0;

    for (int i = 0; i < numberOfCourses; i++)
    {
        switch (courseGrades[i])
        {
        case 'A':
            sum += coursesEnrolled[i].getCredits() * 4;
            break;

        case 'B':
            sum += coursesEnrolled[i].getCredits() * 3;
            break;

        case 'C':
            sum += coursesEnrolled[i].getCredits() * 2;
            break;

        case 'D':
            sum += coursesEnrolled[i].getCredits() * 1;
            break;

        case 'F':
            break;
```

```
        default:
            System.out.println("Invalid Course Grade");
        }
    }

    return sum / getHoursEnrolled();
}
```

The method `sortCourses` sorts the array `coursesEnrolled` by course number. To sort the array, we use a selection sort algorithm. Because we will compare the course numbers, which are the strings and `private` data members of the `class` Course, we first retrieve and store the course numbers in the local variables. Moreover, this method also rearranges the course grades because the course grades are stored in a separate array. The definition of this method is:

```
private void sortCourses()
{
    int minIndex;
    Course temp = new Course();    //variable to swap data
    String course1;
    String course2;

    char tempGrade;

    for (int i = 0; i < numberOfCourses - 1; i++)
    {
        minIndex = i;

        for (int j = i + 1; j < numberOfCourses; j++)
        {
            //get course numbers
            course1 =
                coursesEnrolled[minIndex].getCourseNumber();
            course2 = coursesEnrolled[j].getCourseNumber();

            if (course1.compareTo(course2) > 0)
                minIndex = j;
        }//end for

        temp.copyCourseInfo(coursesEnrolled[minIndex]);
        coursesEnrolled[minIndex].copyCourseInfo(coursesEnrolled[i]);
        coursesEnrolled[i].copyCourseInfo(temp);

        tempGrade = courseGrades[minIndex];
        courseGrades[minIndex] = courseGrades[i];
        courseGrades[i] = tempGrade;
    }//end for
}//end sortCourses
```

1
0

The definition of the `class` Student has the following form: (You can complete the definition of this class as an exercise.)

```
import java.io.*;

public class Student extends Person
{
        private int sId;                    //variable to store the
                                            //student ID
        private int numberOfCourses;        //variable to store the number
                                            //of courses
        private boolean isTuitionPaid;      //variable to indicate if
                                            //the tuition is paid
        private Course [] coursesEnrolled;  //array to store
                                                   //the courses
        private char [] courseGrades;       //array to store the
                                            //course grades
        //Place the definitions of the instance methods
        //as discussed here.
        //...
}
```

MAIN PROGRAM

Now that we have designed the `class`es Course and Student, we will use these classes to complete the program.

Because the `toString` method of the `class` Student does the necessary computations to print the final grade report, the main program has very little work to do. In fact, all the main program must do is create the objects to hold the students' data, load the data into these objects, and then print the grade reports. Because the input is in a file and the output will be sent to a file, we create appropriate objects to access the input and output files. Essentially, the main algorithm for the program is:

1. Declare the variables.
2. Open the input file.
3. Open the output file.
4. Get the number of students registered and the tuition rate.
5. Load the students' data.
6. Print the grade reports.

Variables

This program first reads the number of students from the input file and then creates the array, `studentList`, to hold the students' data. The size of `studentList` is equal to the number of students.

```
Student[] studentList;

int noOfStudents;
double tuitionRate;
```

```
Scanner inFile = new Scanner(new FileReader("stData.txt"));
PrintWriter outFile = new PrintWriter("sDataOut.out");
```

To simplify the complexity of the method main, we write a method, getStudentData, to load the students' data.

Method getStudent Data

This method has two parameters: one to access the input file and one to access the array studentList. In pseudocode, the definition of this method is as follows:

For each student in the university:

1. Get the first name, last name, student ID, and isPaid.

2. if isPaid is 'Y'
      set isTuitionPaid to true
    else
      set isTuitionPaid to false

3. Get the number of courses the student is taking.

4. For each course:

    a. Get the course name, course number, credit hours, and grade.

    b. Load the course information into a Course object.

5. Load the data into a Student object.

We need to declare several local variables to read and store the data. The definition of the method getStudentData is:

```
public static void getStudentData(Scanner inpFile,
                                  Student[] sList)
{
        //Local variables
    String fName;      //variable to store the first name
    String lName;      //variable to store the last name
    int ID;            //variable to store the student ID
    int noOfCourses;   //variable to store the number of courses
    char isPaid;       //variable to store Y/N; that is,
                       //is the tuition paid?

    boolean isTuitionPaid;    //variable to store true/false

    String cName;    //variable to store the course name
    String cNo;      //variable to store the course number
    int credits;     //variable to store the course credit hours
    char grade;      //variable to store the course grade

    Course[] courses = new Course[6]; //array of objects to
                                      //store the course
                                      //information
```

1
0

```java
        char[] courseGrades = new char[6];

        for (int i = 0; i < 6; i++)
            courses[i] = new Course();

        for (int count = 0; count < sList.length; count++)
        {
                    //Step 1
            fName = inpFile.next();
            lName = inpFile.next();
            ID = inpFile.nextInt();
            isPaid = inpFile.next().charAt(0);

            if (isPaid == 'Y')                              //Step 2
                isTuitionPaid = true;
            else
                isTuitionPaid = false;

            noOfCourses = inpFile.nextInt();                //Step 3

            for (int i = 0; i < noOfCourses; i++)           //Step 4
            {
                cName = inpFile.next();
                cNo = inpFile.next();
                credits = inpFile.nextInt();
                courseGrades[i] = inpFile.next().charAt(0);

                courses[i].setCourseInfo(cName, cNo, credits);
            }

            sList[count].setInfo(fName, lName, ID,
                            noOfCourses, isTuitionPaid,
                            courses, courseGrades);   //Step 5
        }//end for
    } //end getStudentData
```

Method printGrade Reports

This method prints the grade reports. The definition of the method printGradeReports is:

```java
public static void printGradeReports(PrintWriter outpFile,
                            Student[] sList,
                            double tuitionRate)
{
    for (int count = 0; count < sList.length; count++)
    {
        outpFile.print(sList[count]);

        if (sList[count].getIsTuitionPaid())
            outpFile.printf("Midsemester GPA: %.2f%n",
                            sList[count].getGpa());
```

```
        else
        {
            outpFile.println("*** Grades are being held for "
                    + "not paying the tuition. ***");
            outpFile.printf("Amount Due: $%.2f%n",
                    sList[count].billingAmount(tuitionRate));
        }

        outpFile.println("-*-*-*-*-*-*-*-*-*-*-*-*-*-*-"
                + "*-*-*-*-*-*-*-*-*-*-\r\n");
    }
} //end printGradeReports
```

PROGRAM LISTING

```
//***********************************************************
// Author: D.S. Malik
//
// Program: Student Grade Report
// This program reads students' data from a file and outputs
// the grades. If a student has not paid the tuition, the
// grades are not shown, and an appropriate message is output.
// The output is stored in a file.
//***********************************************************

import java.io.*;
import java.util.*;

public class GradeReportProgram
{
    public static void main(String[] args) throws
                                    FileNotFoundException
    {
        int noOfStudents;
        double tuitionRate;

        Scanner inFile =
                new Scanner(new FileReader("stData.txt"));
        PrintWriter outFile =
                new PrintWriter("sDataOut.out");

        noOfStudents = inFile.nextInt();    //get the number
                                            //of students
        tuitionRate = inFile.nextDouble();  //get the tuition
                                            //rate

        Student[] studentList =
                new Student[noOfStudents];

        for (int i = 0; i < studentList.length; i++)
            studentList[i] = new Student();

        getStudentData(inFile, studentList);
        printGradeReports(outFile, studentList, tuitionRate);
```

```
            inFile.close();
            outFile.close();
    }

        //Place the definition of the method getStudentData as
        //described above

        //Place the definition of the method printGradeReports as
        //described above
}
```

Sample Run:

```
Student Name: Lisa Miller
Student ID: 890238
Number of courses enrolled: 4
Course No   Course Name   Credits Grade
CSC478      ComputerSci      3       B
HIS356      History          3       A
MTH345      Mathematics      4       A
PHY357      Physics          3       B

Total number of credit hours: 13
Midsemester GPA: 3.54
_*_*_*_*_*_*_*_*_*_*_*_*_*_*_*_*_*_*_*_*_*_*_*_*_

Student Name: Bill Wilton
Student ID: 798324
Number of courses enrolled: 5
Course No   Course Name   Credits Grade
BIO234      Biology          4      ***
CHM256      Chemistry        4      ***
ENG378      English          3      ***
MTH346      Mathematics      3      ***
PHL534      Philosophy       3      ***

Total number of credit hours: 17
*** Grades are being held for not paying the tuition. ***
Amount Due: 5865.00
_*_*_*_*_*_*_*_*_*_*_*_*_*_*_*_*_*_*_*_*_*_*_*_*_

Student Name: Dandy Goat
Student ID: 746333
Number of courses enrolled: 6
Course No   Course Name   Credits Grade
BUS128      Business         3       C
CHM348      Chemistry        4       B
CSC201      ComputerSci      3       B
ENG328      English          3       B
HIS101      History          3       A
MTH137      Mathematics      3       A

Total number of credit hours: 19
Midsemester GPA: 3.16
_*_*_*_*_*_*_*_*_*_*_*_*_*_*_*_*_*_*_*_*_*_*_*_*_
```

Input File

```
3 345
Lisa Miller 890238 Y 4
Mathematics MTH345 4 A
Physics PHY357 3 B
ComputerSci CSC478 3 B
History HIS356 3 A
Bill Wilton 798324 N 5
English ENG378 3 B
Philosophy PHL534 3 A
Chemistry CHM256 4 C
Biology BIO234 4 A
Mathematics MTH346 3 C

Dandy Goat 746333 Y 6
History HIS101 3 A
English ENG328 3 B
Mathematics MTH137 3 A
Chemistry CHM348 4 B
ComputerSci CSC201 3 B
Business BUS128 3 C
```

 NOTE A GUI version of this program is available with the Additional Student Files at *www.cengagebrain.com*.

QUICK REVIEW

1. Inheritance and composition (aggregation) are meaningful ways to relate two or more classes.

2. Inheritance can be viewed as an "is-a" relationship.

3. In single inheritance, the subclass is derived from only one existing class, called the superclass.

4. In multiple inheritance, a subclass is derived from more than one superclass. Java does not support true multiple inheritance; that is, in Java, a class can only *extend* the definition of one class.

5. The `private` members of a superclass are `private` to the superclass. The subclass cannot directly access them.

6. A subclass can override the methods of a superclass, but this redefinition is available only to the objects of the subclass.

7. In general, while writing the definitions of the methods of a subclass to specify a call to a `public` method of a superclass, we do the following:

   - If the subclass overrides a `public` method of a superclass, then you specify a call to that `public` method of the superclass by using the reserved word `super`, followed by the dot operator, followed by the method name with an appropriate parameter list.

   - If the subclass does not override a `public` method of the superclass, you can specify a call to that `public` method by using the name of the method and an appropriate parameter list.

8. If a method of a class is declared `final`, it cannot be overridden in any subclass.

9. While writing the definition of a constructor of a subclass, a call to a constructor of the superclass is specified using the reserved word `super` with an appropriate parameter list. Moreover, the call to a constructor of the superclass must be the first statement.

10. Typically, when a subclass constructor executes, first a constructor of the superclass executes to initialize the data members inherited from the superclass and then the constructor of the subclass executes to initialize the data members declared by the subclass.

11. For a superclass to give direct access to its member(s), to its subclass(es), and still prevent its direct access outside the class, such as in a user program, you must declare that member using the modifier `protected`. In fact, a class member declared with the modifier `protected` may be accessed by any class in the same package.

12. If a member of a class has a package access, that member can be directly accessed in any class contained in that package, but not in any class that is not contained in that package even if a subclass is derived from the class containing that member and the subclass is not contained in that package.

13. If you define a class and do not use the reserved word `extends` to derive it from an existing class, then the class you define is automatically considered to be derived from the `class Object`.

14. The `class Object` directly or indirectly becomes the superclass of every class in Java.

15. The `classes Scanner`, `Reader`, and `Writer` are derived from the `class Object`. The `class InputStreamReader` is derived from the `class Reader`, and the `class FileReader` is derived from the `class InputStreamReader`. Similarly, the `class PrintWriter` is derived from the `class Writer`.

16. Java allows us to treat an object of a subclass as an object of a superclass; that is, a reference variable of a superclass type can point to an object of a subclass type.

17. In a class hierarchy, several methods can have the same name and the same formal parameter list.

18. A reference variable of a class can refer to either an object of its own class or an object of its subclass.

19. In early binding, a method's definition is associated with its invocation when the code is compiled.

20. In late binding, a method's definition is associated with its invocation at execution time, that is, when the method is executed.

21. Except for a few (special) cases, Java uses late binding for all methods.

22. The term polymorphism means assigning multiple meanings to the same method. In Java, polymorphism is implemented using late binding.

23. You *cannot* automatically consider a superclass object to be an object of a subclass. In other words, you *cannot* automatically make a reference variable of a subclass type point to an object of a superclass type.

24. Suppose that `supRef` is a reference variable of a superclass type. Moreover, suppose that `supRef` points to an object of a subclass. You can use an appropriate cast operator on `supRef` and make a reference variable of the subclass point to the object. On the other hand, if `supRef` does not point to a subclass object, and you use a cast operator on `supRef` to make a reference variable of the subclass point to the object, then Java will throw a `ClassCastException`—indicating that the class cast is not allowed.

25. An abstract method is a method that has only the heading, not the body. Moreover, the heading of an abstract method is terminated with a semicolon.

26. An abstract class is a class that is declared with the reserved word `abstract` in its heading.

27. The following are some of the facts about abstract classes:

    - An abstract class can contain instance variables, constructors, a finalizer, and nonabstract methods.
    - An abstract class can contain an abstract method(s).
    - If a class contains an abstract method, then the class must be declared abstract.
    - You cannot instantiate an object of an abstract class. You can only declare a reference variable of an abstract class type.
    - You can instantiate an object of a subclass of an abstract class, but only if the subclass gives the definitions of *all* the abstract methods of the superclass.

28. An `interface` is a class that contains only abstract methods and/or named constants.

29. Java allows a class to implement more than one interface. This is, in fact, the way to implement a form of multiple inheritance in Java.

30. In composition, one or more members of a class are objects of one or more other classes.

31. Composition (aggregation) can be viewed as a "has-a" relationship.

EXERCISES

1. Mark the following statements as true or false.

   a. The constructor of a subclass specifies a call to the constructor of the superclass in the heading of the constructor's definition.

   b. The constructor of a subclass specifies a call to the constructor of the superclass using the name of the class.

   c. A subclass must define a constructor.

   d. In Java, polymorphism is implemented using late binding.

2. Draw a class hierarchy in which several classes are subclasses of a single superclass.

3. Suppose that a `class` Employee is derived from the `class` Person (see Example 8-8, in Chapter 8). Give examples of data and method members that can be added to the `class` Employee.

4. Identify the superclass and the subclass in each of the following pairs of classes.

   a. `Employee, Person`   d. `BankAccount, SavingsAccount`

   b. `Vehicle, Truck`   e. `GradStudent, Student`

   c. `Circle, Cylinder`   f. `Dog, Animal`

5. Draw the inheritance hierarchy diagram that shows the inheritance relationship between the classes `Person`, `Student`, `Employee`, and `Instructor`.

6. Draw the inheritance hierarchy diagram that shows the inheritance relationship between the classes `Vehicle`, `Car`, `Sedan`, `Truck`, `PickupTruck`, `Object`, and `Animal`.

7. Consider the following statement:

   ```java
   public class Dog extends Animal
   {
       . . .
   }
   ```

   In this declaration, which class is the base class and which class is the derived class.

8. Consider the following class definitions:

   ```java
   class Circle                        public class Cylinder extends Circle
   {                                   {
       private double radius;              private double height;

       public Circle(double)               public Cylinder()
       {                                   {
       }                                   }

       public Circle()                     public Cylinder(double, double)
       {                                   {
       }                                   }
   ```

```
public String toString()              public String toString()
{                                      {
}                                      }

public void setRadius(double)         public void setHeight(double)
{                                      {
}                                      }

public double getRadius()             public double getHeight()
{                                      {
}                                      }

public double area()                  public double volume()
{                                      {
}                                      }
}
                                      public double area()
                                      {
                                      }
                                 }
```

Suppose that you have the declaration:

```
Cylinder newCylinder = new Cylinder();
```

Determine the private members of the object `newCylinder`.

9. Consider the following class definitions:

```
public class AClass
{
    private int u;
    private int v;

    public void print()
    {
    }

    public void set(int x, int y)
    {
    }

    public AClass()
    {
    }

    public AClass(int x, int y)
    {
    }
}
```

What is wrong with the following class definitions?

```
class BClass AClass
{
    private int w;

    public void print()
    {
        System.out.println("u + v + w = " + (u + v + w));
    }

    public BClass()
    {
        super();
        w = 0;
    }

    public BClass(int x, int y, int z)
    {
        super(x, y);
        w = z;
    }
}
```

10. Consider the following statements:

```
public class YClass
{
    private int a;
    private int b;

    public void one()
    {
    }

    public void two(int x, int y)
    {
    }

    public YClass()
    {
    }
}

class XClass extends YClass
{
    private int z;

    public void one()
    {
    }

    public XClass()
    {
    }
}
```

```
YClass yObject;
XClass xObject;
```

a. The **private** members of YClass are **public** members of XClass. True or False?

b. Mark the following statements as valid or invalid. If a statement is invalid, explain why.

    i. The following is a valid definition of the method one of YClass.

```
public void one()
{
    System.out.println(a + b);
}
```

    ii. yObject.a = 15;

    iii. xObject.b = 30;

    iv. The following is a valid definition of the method one of XClass:

```
public void one()
{
    a = 10;
    b = 15;
    z = 30;
    System.out.println(a + b + z);
}
```

    v. System.out.println(yObject.a + " " + yObject.b + " "
             + xObject.z);

11. Assume the declaration of Exercise 10.

a. Write the definition of the default constructor of YClass so that the instance variables of YClass are initialized to 0.

b. Write the definition of the default constructor of XClass so that the instance variables of XClass are initialized to 0.

c. Write the definition of the method two of YClass so that the instance variable a is initialized to the value of the first parameter of two and the instance variable b is initialized to the value of the second parameter of two.

12. Suppose that class Three is derived from class Two and class Two is derived from class One and each class has instance variables. Suppose that an object of class Three enters its scope, so the constructors of these classes will execute. Determine the order in which the constructors of these classes will execute.

13. What is the difference between overloading a method name and overriding a method name?

14. Name two situations in which you would use the reserved word super.

15. Suppose that the class GradStudent is derived from the class Student and the class Student has the following method:

```
public void printGrades()
```

10

Further suppose that the `class` `GradStudent` has the following method:

```
public void printGrades(String status)
```

How many `printGrade` methods will the `class` `GradStudent` have and what are their headings?

16. Suppose that you have the following class:

```
public class classA
{
    private int x;                          //Line 1
    protected void setX(int a)              //Line 2
    {                                       //Line 3
        x = a;                              //Line 4
    }
}
```

What is wrong with the following code?

```
public class Exercise16                          //Line 5
{
    public static void main(String[] args) //Line 6
    {
        classA aObject;                          //Line 7

        aObject.setX(4);                         //Line 8
    }
}
```

17. Suppose that you have the following class definitions:

```
public class One
{
    private int x;
    private int y;

    public void print()
    {
        System.out.println(x + " " + y);
    }
    protected void setData(int u, int v)
    {
        x = u;
        y = v;
    }
}
```

Consider the following class definitions:

```
public class Two extends One
{
    private int z;
```

```
public void setData(int a, int b, int c)
{
    //Postcondition: x = a; y = b; z = c;
}

public void print()
{
    //Output the values of x, y, and z
}
}
```

a. Write the definition of the method `setData` of the `class Two` as described in the class definition.

b. Write the definition of the method `print` of the `class Two` as described in the class definition.

18. Explain the difference between the `private` and `protected` members of a class.

19. Explain the difference between the `public` and `protected` members of a class.

20. Suppose that you have the following class definitions:

```
public class SuperClass
{
    protected int x;

    private String str;

    public void print()
    {
        System.out.println(x + " " + str);
    }

    public SuperClass()
    {
        str = "";
        x = 0;
    }

    public SuperClass(String s, int a)
    {
        str = s;
        x = a;
    }
}

public class SubClass extends SuperClass
{
    private int y;

    public void print()
```

```
    {
        System.out.println("SubClass: " + y);
        super.print();
    }

    public SubClass()
    {
        super();
        y = 0;
    }

    public SubClass(String s, int a, int b)
    {
        super("Hello Super", a + b);
        y = b;
    }
}
```

What is the output of the following Java code?

```
SuperClass superObject = new SuperClass("This is superclass", 2);
SubClass subObject = new SubClass("DDDDDD", 3, 7);

superObject.print();
subObject.print();
```

21. Suppose that class Student is derived from the class Person, and the classes UndergraduateStudent and GradStudent are derived from the class Student. (The class Person is defined in Chapter 8.) Consider the following method heading:

```
public void printName(Student st)
{
    System.out.println(st.getFirstName() + " " + st.getLastName());
}
```

Suppose that student1 is an object of the class UndergraduateStudent and student2 is an object of the class GradStudent. Determine whether the following statements are legal. Justify your answer.

```
printName(student1);
printName(student2);
```

22. What does the operator instanceof do?

23. What is an abstract method?

24. What is the difference between an abstract class and an interface?

25. Why does Java allow a class to implement more than one interface?

PROGRAMMING EXERCISES

1. In Chapter 8, the class Clock was designed to implement the time of day in a program. Certain applications, in addition to hours, minutes, and seconds, might require you to store the time zone. Derive the class ExtClock from the class Clock by adding a data member to store the time zone. Add the necessary methods and constructors to make the class functional. Also, write the definitions of the methods and the constructors. Finally, write a test program to test your class.

2. In this chapter, the class Date was designed to implement the date in a program, but the method setDate and the constructor with parameters do not check whether the date is valid before storing the date in the data members. Rewrite the definitions of the method setDate and the constructor with parameters so that the values of month, day, and year are checked before storing the date into the data members. Add a method isLeapYear to check whether a year is a leap year. Then, write a test program to test your class.

3. A point in the x-y plane is represented by its x-coordinate and y-coordinate. Design the class Point that can store and process a point in the x-y plane. You should then perform operations on a point, such as showing the point, setting the coordinates of the point, printing the coordinates of the point, returning the x-coordinate, and returning the y-coordinate. Also, write a test program to test various operations on a point.

4. Every circle has a center and a radius. Given the radius, we can determine the circle's area and circumference. Given the center, we can determine its position in the x-y plane. The center of a circle is a point in the x-y plane. Design the class Circle that can store the radius and center of the circle. Because the center is a point in the x-y plane and you designed the class to capture the properties of a point in Programming Exercise 3, you must derive the class Circle from the class Point. You should be able to perform the usual operations on a circle, such as setting the radius, printing the radius, calculating and printing the area and circumference, and carrying out the usual operations on the center.

5. Every cylinder has a base and height, where the base is a circle. Design the class Cylinder that can capture the properties of a cylinder and perform the usual operations on a cylinder. Derive this class from the class Circle designed in Programming Exercise 4. Some of the operations that can be performed on a cylinder are as follows: calculate and print the volume, calculate and print the surface area, set the height, set the radius of the base, and set the center of the base.

6. Using classes, design an online address book to keep track of the names, addresses, phone numbers, and birthdays of family members, close friends, and certain business associates. Your program should be able to handle a maximum of 500 entries.

   a. Define the class Address that can store a street address, city, state, and zip code. Use the appropriate methods to print and store the address. Also, use constructors to automatically initialize the data members.

b. Define the `class ExtPerson` using the `class Person` (as defined in Example 8-8, Chapter 8), the `class Date` (as designed in this chapter's Programming Exercise 2), and the `class Address`. Add a data member to this class to classify the person as a family member, friend, or business associate. Also, add a data member to store the phone number. Add (or override) methods to print and store the appropriate information. Use constructors to automatically initialize the data members.

c. Define the `class AddressBook` using previously defined classes. An object of type `AddressBook` should be able to process a maximum of 500 entries.

The program should perform the following operations:

i.   Load the data into the address book from a disk.

ii. Sort the address book by last name.

iii. Search for a person by last name.

iv. Print the address, phone number, and date of birth (if available) of a given person.

v.   Print the names of the people whose birthdays are in a given month or between two given dates.

vi. Print the names of all the people between two last names.

7. In Programming Exercise 2, the `class Date` was designed and implemented to keep track of a date, but it has very limited operations. Redefine the `class Date` so that, in addition to the operations already defined, it can perform the following operations on a date:

a. Set the month.

b. Set the day.

c. Set the year.

d. Return the month.

e. Return the day.

f. Return the year.

g. Test whether the year is a leap year.

h. Return the number of days in the month. For example, if the date is 3-12-2015, the number of days to be returned is 31, because there are 31 days in March.

i. Return the number of days passed in the year. For example, if the date is 3-18-2015, the number of days passed in the year is 77. Note that the number of days returned also includes the current day.

j. Return the number of days remaining in the year. For example, if the date is 3-18-2015, the number of days remaining in the year is 288.

k. Calculate the new date by adding a fixed number of days to the date. For example, if the date is 3-18-2015 and the days to be added are 25, the new date is 4-12-2015.

l. Return a reference to the object containing a copy of the date.

m.   Make a copy of another date. Given a reference to an object containing a date, copy the data members of the object into the corresponding data members of this object.

n.   Write the definitions of the methods to implement the operations defined for the `class Date`.

8.   The `class Date` defined in Programming Exercise 7 prints the date in numerical form. Some applications might require the date to be printed in another form, such as March 24, 2015. Derive the `class ExtDate` so that the date can be printed in either form.

Add a data member to the `class ExtDate` so that the month can also be stored in string form. Add a method to output the month in the string format followed by the year—for example, in the form March 2015.

Write the definitions of the methods to implement the operations for the `class ExtDate`.

9.   Using the `class`es `ExtDate` (Programming Exercise 8) and `Day` (Chapter 8, Programming Exercise 3), design the `class Calendar` so that, given the month and the year, we can print the calendar for that month. To print a monthly calendar, you must know the first day of the month and the number of days in that month. Thus, you must store the first day of the month, which is of the form `Day`, and the month and the year of the calendar. Clearly, the month and the year can be stored in an object of the form `ExtDate` by setting the day component of the date to 1, and the month and year as specified by the user. Thus, the `class Calendar` has two data members: an object of type `Day` and an object of type `ExtDate`.

Design the `class Calendar` so that the program can print a calendar for any month starting January 1, 1500. Note that the day for January 1 of the year 1500 was a Monday. To calculate the first day of a month, you can add the appropriate number of days to Monday, January 1, 1500.

For the `class Calendar`, include the following operations:

a.   Determine the first day of the month for which the calendar will be printed. Call this operation `firstDayOfMonth`.

b.   Set the month.

c.   Set the year.

d.   Return the month.

e.   Return the year.

f.   Print the calendar for the particular month.

g.   Add the appropriate constructors to initialize the data members.

10. a.   Write the definitions of the methods of the `class Calendar` (designed in Programming Exercise 9) to implement the operations of the `class Calendar`.

b.   Write a test program to print the calendar for either a particular month or a particular year. For example, the calendar for September 2014 is:

```
                    September 2014
       Sun    Mon    Tue    Wed    Thu    Fri    Sat
               1      2      3      4      5      6
        7      8      9     10     11     12     13
       14     15     16     17     18     19     20
       21     22     23     24     25     26     27
       28     29     30
```

11. In the Grade Report programming example, the class Student contains two array instance variables, coursesEnrolled and courseGrades, to store the courses a student is taking and the grades in those courses. Redo the Grade Report programming example by defining the class CourseAndGrade that has two instance variables—courseEnrolled of type Course and courseGrade of type char. Add appropriate constructors and methods in this class to manipulate the instance variables. In the class Student, use an array instance variable coursesEnrolled of type CourseAndGrade to store the courses a student is taking and the grade for each course.

12. In the Grade Report programming example, we created the classes Course and Student, and in the main program we created an array to hold student data. Redo this programming example by defining the class StudentList with an instance variable to hold students' data, an instance variable to store the number of students, and an instance variable to store the tuition rate. This class contains methods to load students' data in the array and output grade reports and the appropriate constructors. The method main in a separate class uses the class StudentList to create grade reports. Also, write a program to test your class.

13. In this exercise, you will design various classes and write a program to computerize the billing system of a hospital.

    a. Design the class Doctor, inherited from the class Person, defined in Chapter 8, with an additional data member to store a doctor's specialty. Add appropriate constructors and methods to initialize, access, and manipulate the data members.

    b. Design the class Bill with data members to store a patient's ID and the patient's hospital charges such as pharmacy charges for medicine, the doctor's fee, and the room charges. Add appropriate constructors and methods to initialize, access, and manipulate the data members.

    c. Design the class Patient, inherited from the class Person, defined in Chapter 8, with additional data members to store a patient's ID, age, date of birth, attending physician's name, the date when the patient was admitted in the hospital, and the date when the patient was discharged from the hospital. (Use the class Date to store the date of birth, admit date, discharge date, and the class Doctor to store the attending physician's name.) Add appropriate constructors and methods to initialize, access, and manipulate the data members.

    Write a program to test your classes.

14. Complete Example 10-7 by writing the definitions of the eight classes. Also write a program to test your classes.

HANDLING EXCEPTIONS AND EVENTS

IN THIS CHAPTER, YOU WILL:

- · Learn what an exception is
- · Learn how to use a **try/catch** block to handle exceptions
- · Become acquainted with the hierarchy of exception classes
- · Learn about checked and unchecked exceptions
- · Learn how to handle exceptions within a program
- · Discover how to throw and rethrow an exception
- · Learn how to handle events in a program

The File Input/Output section in Chapter 3 defined an *exception* as an occurrence of an undesirable situation that can be detected during program execution. For example, division by zero and inputting invalid data are exceptions. Similarly, trying to open an input file that does not exist is an exception, as is an array index that is outside the bounds of the array.

Until now, our programs have not included any code to handle exceptions. If exceptions occurred during program execution, the program terminated with an appropriate error message. However, there are situations when an exception occurs and you don't want the program to simply ignore the exception and terminate. For example, a program that monitors stock performance should not automatically sell if the value of the stock exceeds a certain threshold. It should inform the stockholder and request an appropriate action.

This chapter provides more detail about exceptions and describes how they are handled in Java. You will learn about different kinds of exceptions and the options available to programmers for dealing with them. You'll also extend what you learned in Chapters 6 and 10 about event handling.

Handling Exceptions Within a Program

Chapter 2 stated that if you try to input incompatible data into a variable, the program will terminate with an error message indicating that an exception has occurred. For example, inputting a letter or number containing a nondigit character into an `int` variable would cause an exception to occur. Before we discuss how to handle exceptions, let us give some examples that show what can happen if an exception is not handled.

The program in Example 11-1 shows what happens when division by zero is attempted or an invalid input occurs and the problem is not addressed.

EXAMPLE 11-1

```java
import java.util.*;

public class ExceptionExample1
{
    static Scanner console = new Scanner(System.in);

    public static void main(String[] args)
    {
        int dividend, divisor, quotient;          //Line 1

        System.out.print("Line 2: Enter the "
                    + "dividend: ");               //Line 2
        dividend = console.nextInt();             //Line 3
        System.out.println();                     //Line 4
```

```
        System.out.print("Line 5: Enter the "
                    + "divisor: ");              //Line 5
        divisor = console.nextInt();             //Line 6
        System.out.println();                    //Line 7

        quotient = dividend / divisor;           //Line 8

        System.out.println("Line 9: Quotient = "
                    + quotient);                 //Line 9
    }
}
```

Sample Run 1:

Line 2: Enter the dividend: 12

Line 5: Enter the divisor: 5

Line 9: Quotient = 2

Sample Run 2:

Line 2: Enter the dividend: 24

Line 5: Enter the divisor: 0

Exception in thread "main" java.lang.ArithmeticException: / by zero
        at ExceptionExample1.main(ExceptionExample1.java:22)

Sample Run 3:

Line 2: Enter the dividend: 2e
Exception in thread "main" java.util.InputMismatchException
        at java.util.Scanner.throwFor(Unknown Source)
        at java.util.Scanner.next(Unknown Source)
        at java.util.Scanner.nextInt(Unknown Source)
        at java.util.Scanner.nextInt(Unknown Source)
        at ExceptionExample1.main(ExceptionExample1.java:14)

In Sample Run 1, the value of divisor is nonzero, so no exception occurred. The program calculated and printed the quotient and terminated normally.

In Sample Run 2, the value entered for divisor is 0. The statement in Line 8 divides dividend by the divisor. However, the program does not check whether divisor is 0 before attempting to divide dividend by divisor. So the program terminates with the message as shown.

In Sample Run 3, the value entered is 2e. This input cannot be expressed as an int value; therefore, the method nextInt in Line 3 throws an InputMismatchException and the program terminates with the error message as shown.

On some systems, you may get the following output for Sample Run 3:

```
Line 2: Enter the dividend: 2e
Exception in thread "main" java.util.InputMismatchException
        at java.util.Scanner.throwFor(Scanner.java:819)
        at java.util.Scanner.next(Scanner.java:1431)
        at java.util.Scanner.nextInt(Scanner.java:2040)
        at java.util.Scanner.nextInt(Scanner.java:2000)
        at ExceptionExample1.main(ExceptionExample1.java:14)
```

Next, consider Example 11-2. This is the same program as in Example 11-1, except that in Line 8, using an `if` statement, a common programming practice, the program checks whether `divisor` is zero. (Later in this chapter we will explain how to use Java's mechanism to handle an `InputMismatchException`.)

EXAMPLE 11-2

```java
import java.util.*;

public class ExceptionExample2
{
    static Scanner console = new Scanner(System.in);

    public static void main(String[] args)
    {
        int dividend, divisor, quotient;              //Line 1

        System.out.print("Line 2: Enter the "
                        + "dividend: ");              //Line 2
        dividend = console.nextInt();                 //Line 3
        System.out.println();                         //Line 4

        System.out.print("Line 5: Enter the "
                        + "divisor: ");               //Line 5
        divisor = console.nextInt();                  //Line 6
        System.out.println();                         //Line 7

        if (divisor != 0)                             //Line 8
        {
            quotient = dividend / divisor;            //Line 9
            System.out.println("Line 10: "
                              + "Quotient = "
                              + quotient);            //Line 10
        }
        else
            System.out.println("Line 11: Cannot "
                              + "divide by zero.");   //Line 11
    }
}
```

Sample Run 1:

```
Line 2: Enter the dividend: 12

Line 5: Enter the divisor: 5

Line 10: Quotient = 2
```

Sample Run 2:

```
Line 2: Enter the dividend: 24

Line 5: Enter the divisor: 0

Line 11: Cannot divide by zero.
```

In Sample Run 1, the value of `divisor` is nonzero, so no exception occurred. The program calculated and printed the quotient and terminated normally.

In Sample Run 2, the value entered for `divisor` is 0. In Line 8, the program checks whether `divisor` is 0. Because `divisor` is zero, the expression in the `if` statement fails and the `else` part executes, which outputs the third line of the sample run.

Java's Mechanism of Exception Handling

Example 11-1 shows what happens when a division by zero or an input mismatch exception occurs in a program and is not processed. Example 11-2 shows a way to handle a division by zero exception. However, suppose that division by zero occurs in more than one place within the same block. In this case, using `if` statements may not be the most effective way to handle the exception.

Next, we describe how to handle exceptions using Java's exception handling mechanism. However, first let's note the following.

When an exception occurs, an object of a particular exception `class` is created. For example, in Sample Run 2 of Example 11-1, an object of the `class` `ArithmeticException` is created. Java provides several exception classes to effectively handle certain common exceptions, such as division by zero, invalid input, and file not found. For example, division by zero is an arithmetic error and is handled by the `class ArithmeticException`. Therefore, when a division by zero exception occurs, the program creates an object of the `class ArithmeticException`. Similarly, when a `Scanner` object is used to input data into a program, any invalid input errors are handled using the `class InputMismatchException`. Note that the `class Exception` (directly or indirectly) is the superclass of all the exception classes in Java.

NOTE The section titled Java Exception Hierarchy describes the hierarchy of Java's various built-in exception classes. The section titled Java's Exception Classes describes some of the built-in exception classes and their methods. Both sections appear later in this chapter.

try/catch/finally **Block**

Statements that might generate an exception are placed in a `try` block. The `try` block might also contain statements that should not be executed if an exception occurs. The `try` block is followed by zero or more `catch` blocks. A `catch` block specifies the type of exception it can catch and contains an exception handler. The last `catch` block may or may not be followed by a `finally` block. Any code contained in a `finally` block always executes, regardless of whether an exception occurs, except when the program exits early from a `try` block by calling the method `System.exit`. If a `try` block has no `catch` block, then it *must* have the `finally` block.

As noted previously, when an exception occurs, Java creates an object of a specific exception class. For example, if a division by zero exception occurs, then Java creates an object of the `ArithmeticException` **class**.

The general syntax of the `try/catch/finally` block is:

```
try
{
    //statements
}
catch (ExceptionClassName1 objRef1)
{
    //exception handler code
}
catch (ExceptionClassName2 objRef2)
{
    //exception handler code
}
...
catch (ExceptionClassNameN objRefN)
{
    //exception handler code
}
finally
{
    //statements
}
```

(A `try` block contains code for normal circumstances, while a `catch` block contains code to handle an exception(s).)

Note the following about `try/catch/finally` blocks:

- If no exception is thrown in a `try` block, all `catch` blocks associated with the `try` block are ignored and program execution resumes after the last `catch` block.

- If an exception is thrown in a `try` block, the remaining statements in the `try` block are ignored. The program searches the `catch` blocks in the order in which they appear after the `try` block and looks for an appropriate exception handler.

- If the type of the thrown exception matches the parameter type in one of the `catch` blocks, the code of that `catch` block executes and the remaining `catch` blocks after this `catch` block are ignored.

- If there is a `finally` block after the last `catch` block, the `finally` block executes regardless of whether an exception occurs.

As noted, when an exception occurs, an object of a particular exception class type is created. The type of exception handled by a `catch` block is declared in the `catch` block heading, which is the statement between the parentheses after the keyword `catch`.

Consider the following `catch` block:

```
catch (ArithmeticException aeRef)
{
    //exception handler code
}
```

This `catch` block catches an exception of type `ArithmeticException`. The identifier `aeRef` is a reference variable of type `ArithmeticException`. If an exception of type `ArithmeticException` is thrown by the `try` block associated with this `catch` block, and control reaches this `catch` block, then the reference parameter `aeRef` contains the address of the exception object thrown by the `try` block. Because `aeRef` contains the address of the exception object, you can access the exception object through the variable `aeRef`. The object `aeRef` stores a detailed description of the thrown exception. You can use the method `toString` (or the method `getMessage`) to retrieve the message containing the description of the thrown exception. Example 11-3 illustrates how to use the method `toString` to retrieve the description of the thrown exception.

ORDER OF `catch` BLOCKS

A `catch` block can catch either all exceptions of a specific type or all types of exceptions. The heading of a `catch` block specifies the type of exception it handles. As discussed in Chapter 10, a reference variable of a superclass type can point to an object of its subclass. Therefore, if in the heading of a `catch` block you declare an exception using the `class` `Exception`, then that `catch` block can catch all types of exceptions because the `class` `Exception` is the superclass of all exception classes.

Suppose that an exception occurs in a `try` block and that exception is caught by a `catch` block. Then, the remaining `catch` blocks associated with that `try` block are ignored.

Therefore, you should be careful about the order in which you list `catch` blocks following a `try` block (putting more specific exceptions before less specific exceptions). For example, consider the following sequence of `try`/`catch` blocks:

```
try                                          //Line 1
{
    //statements
}
catch (Exception eRef)                       //Line 2
{
    //statements
}
catch (ArithmeticException aeRef)            //Line 3
{
    //statements
}
```

Suppose that an exception is thrown in the `try` block. Because the `catch` block in Line 2 can catch exceptions of all types, the `catch` block in Line 3 cannot be reached. This sequence of `try`/`catch` blocks would, in fact, result in a compile-time error. In general, if a `catch` block of a superclass appears before a `catch` block of a subclass, a compilation error will occur. Therefore, in a sequence of `catch` blocks following a `try` block, a `catch` block declaring an exception of a subclass type should be placed before `catch` blocks declaring exceptions of a superclass type. Often it is useful to make sure that all exceptions that might be thrown by a `try` block are caught. In this case, you should make the `catch` block that declares an exception of the `class Exception` type the last `catch` block.

USING `try/catch` BLOCKS IN A PROGRAM

Next, we give some examples to illustrate how `try/catch` blocks might appear in a program.

As shown in Example 11-1, a common error that might occur while inputting numeric data is typing a nonnumeric character, such as a letter. If the input is invalid, the methods `nextInt` and `nextDouble` throw an `InputMismatchException`. Similarly, another error that might occur when performing numeric calculations is division by zero with integer values. In this case, the program throws an exception of the `class ArithmeticException`. The following program shows how to handle these exceptions.

EXAMPLE 11-3

```java
import java.util.*;

public class ExceptionExample3
{
    static Scanner console = new Scanner(System.in);

    public static void main(String[] args)              //Line 1
    {
        int dividend, divisor, quotient;                //Line 2
```

```
        try                                        //Line 3
        {
            System.out.print("Line 4: Enter the "
                             + "dividend: ");       //Line 4
            dividend = console.nextInt();          //Line 5
            System.out.println();                  //Line 6

            System.out.print("Line 7: Enter the "
                             + "divisor: ");        //Line 7
            divisor = console.nextInt();           //Line 8
            System.out.println();                  //Line 9

            quotient = dividend / divisor;         //Line 10
            System.out.println("Line 11: Quotient = "
                             + quotient);           //Line 11
        }
        catch (ArithmeticException aeRef)          //Line 12
        {
            System.out.println("Line 13: Exception "
                             + aeRef.toString());   //Line 13
        }
        catch (InputMismatchException imeRef)      //Line 14
        {
            System.out.println("Line 15: Exception "
                             + imeRef.toString()); //Line 15
        }
    }
}
```

Sample Run: (In these sample runs, the user input is shaded.)

Sample Run 1:

```
Line 4: Enter the dividend: 45

Line 7: Enter the divisor: 2

Line 11: Quotient = 22
```

Sample Run 2:

```
Line 4: Enter the dividend: 18

Line 7: Enter the divisor: 0

Line 13: Exception java.lang.ArithmeticException: / by zero
```

Sample Run 3:

```
Line 4: Enter the dividend: 2753

Line 7: Enter the divisor: 2f1
Line 15: Exception java.util.InputMismatchException
```

This program works as follows: The method `main` starts at Line 1. The statement in Line 2 declares the `int` variables `dividend`, `divisor`, and `quotient`. The `try` block starts at Line 3. The statement in Line 4 prompts the user to enter the value of the dividend; the statement in Line 5 stores this number in the variable `dividend`. The statement in Line 7 prompts the user to enter the value of `divisor`, and the statement in Line 8 stores this number in the variable `divisor`. The statement in Line 10 divides the value of `dividend` by the value of `divisor` and stores the result in `quotient`. The statement in Line 11 outputs the value of `quotient`.

The first `catch` block, which starts at Line 12, catches an `ArithmeticException`. The next `catch` block, which starts at Line 14, catches an `InputMismatchException`.

In Sample Run 1, the program did not throw any exceptions because the user entered valid data.

In Sample Run 2, the entered value of `divisor` is 0. Therefore, when the `dividend` is divided by the `divisor`, the statement in Line 10 throws an `ArithmeticException`, which is caught by the `catch` block starting at Line 12. The statement in Line 13 outputs the appropriate message.

In Sample Run 3, the value entered in Line 8 for the variable `divisor` contains the letter `f`, a nondigit character. Because this value cannot be converted to an integer, the statement in Line 8 throws an `InputMismatchException`. Notice that the `InputMismatchException` is thrown by the method `nextInt` of the `class` `Scanner`. The `catch` block starting at Line 14 catches this exception, and the statement in Line 15 outputs the appropriate message.

Consider again Sample Run 3. In this sample run, the input for the divisor is `2f1`, which, of course, is invalid. When the expression:

```
console.nextInt()
```

in Line 8 executes, it throws an `InputMismatchException` because the input, `2f1`, cannot be expressed as an integer. Note that because `2f1` cannot be expressed as an integer, it stays as the next input token in the input stream. That is, if the input token is invalid, then the method `nextInt` does not remove that input token from the input stream. To capture this invalid input and print it, you can read it as a string in the `catch` block, in Line 14, and then output the string. To be specific, if you replace the `catch` block starting at Line 14 with the following `catch` block:

```
catch (InputMismatchException imeRef)                //Line 14
{
    String str;                                      //Line 15

    str = console.next();                            //Line 16
    System.out.println("Line 17: Exception "
                + imeRef.toString()
                + " " + str );                       //Line 17
}
```

and rerun the program with the same input as in Sample Run 3, then this sample run is:

Sample Run 3 (with the modified catch block):

```
Line 4: Enter the dividend: 2753

Line 7: Enter the divisor: 2f1
Line 17: Exception java.util.InputMismatchException 2f1
```

The modified program, named `ExceptionExample3A.java`, can be found with the Additional Student Files at *www.cengagebrain.com.*

As noted, when an exception occurs in a program, the program throws an object of a specific exception class. Example 11-3 illustrates how to handle an arithmetic exception and an input mismatch exception. We also noted that the `class Exception` (directly or indirectly) becomes the superclass of the exception classes. Because Java provides many classes for handling exceptions, before giving more examples of exception handling, the next few sections describe the hierarchy of Java's exception classes as well as some of the exception classes in more detail.

Java Exception Hierarchy

In the preceding sections, you learned ways to handle exceptions in a program. Chapter 8 discussed how to create your own classes. Every class you design can potentially cause exceptions. Java provides extensive support for exception handling by providing a number of exception classes. Java also allows users to create and implement their own exception classes to handle exceptions not covered by Java's exception classes. This section discusses the exception classes provided by Java.

The `class Throwable`, which is derived from the `class Object`, is the superclass of the `class Exception`, as shown in Figure 11-1.

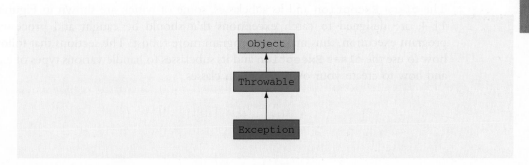

FIGURE 11-1 Java exception hierarchy

The **class** Throwable contains various constructors and methods, some of which are described in Table 11-1.

TABLE 11-1   Constructors and Methods of the **class** Throwable

```
public Throwable()
  //Default constructor
  //Creates an instance of Throwable with an empty message string
```

```
public Throwable(String strMessage)
  //Constructor with parameters
  //Creates an instance of Throwable with message string
  //specified by the parameter strMessage
```

```
public String getMessage()
  //Returns the detailed message stored in the object
```

```
public void printStackTrace()
  //Method to print the stack trace showing the sequence of
  //method calls when an exception occurs
```

```
public void printStackTrace(PrintWriter stream)
  //Method to print the stack trace showing the sequence of
  //method calls when an exception occurs. Output is sent
  //to the stream specified by the parameter stream.
```

```
public String toString()
  //Returns a string representation of the Throwable object
```

The methods getMessage, printStackTrace, and toString are **public** and are inherited by the subclasses of the **class** Throwable.

The **class** Exception and its subclasses, some of which are shown in Figures 11-2 to 11-4, are designed to catch exceptions that should be caught and processed during program execution, thus making a program more robust. The sections that follow discuss how to use the **class** Exception and its subclasses to handle various types of exceptions, and how to create your own exception classes.

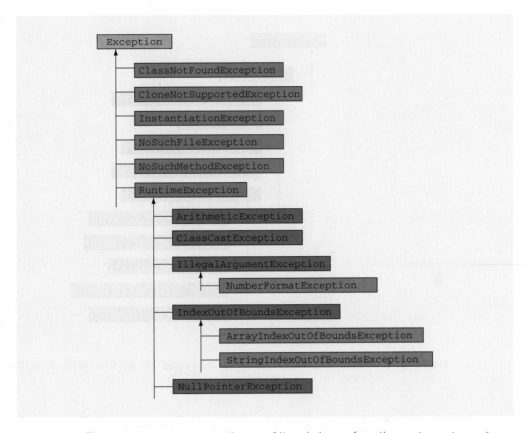

FIGURE 11-2 The **class** Exception and some of its subclasses from the **package** java.lang

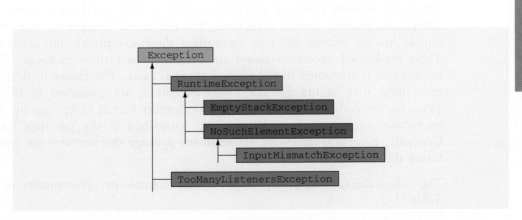

FIGURE 11-3 The **class** Exception and some of its subclasses from the **package** java.util. (Note that the **class** RuntimeException is in the **package** java.lang)

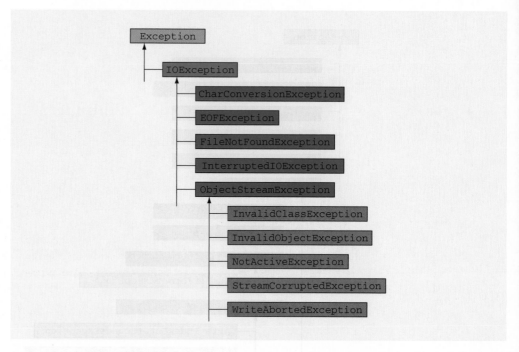

FIGURE 11-4 The **class** IOException and some of its subclasses from the **package** java.io

Java's Exception Classes

The **class** Exception is the superclass of the classes designed to handle exceptions. There are various types of exceptions, such as I/O exceptions, input mismatch exceptions, number format exceptions, file not found exceptions, and array index out of bounds exceptions. Java categorizes these exceptions into separate classes. These predefined exception classes are contained in various packages. The **class** Exception is contained in the **package** java.lang. The classes to deal with I/O exceptions, such as the file not found exception, are contained in the **package** java.io. Similarly, the classes to deal with number format exceptions and arithmetic exceptions, such as division by zero, are contained in the **package** java.lang. Generally, exception classes are placed in the package that contains the methods that throw these exceptions.

The **class** Exception is very simple. It only contains two constructors, as shown in Table 11-2.

TABLE 11-2 `class` Exception and its Constructors

```
public Exception()
 //Default constructor
 //Creates a new instance of the class Exception

public Exception(String str)
 //Constructor with parameters
 //Creates a new instance of the class Exception. The parameter
 //str specifies the message string.
```

Because the `class Exception` is a subclass of the `class Throwable`, the `class Exception` and its subclasses inherit the methods `getMessage`, `printStackTrace`, and `toString`. The method `getMessage` returns the string containing the detailed message stored in the exception object. The method `toString` returns the detailed message stored in the exception object as well as the name of the exception class. The method `printStackTrace` is discussed later in this chapter.

The `class RuntimeException` is the superclass of the classes designed to deal with exceptions, such as division by zero, array index out of bounds, and number format (see Figure 11-2).

Table 11-3 lists some of the exception classes and the type of exceptions they throw.

TABLE 11-3 Some of Java's Exception Classes

Exception Class	Description
ArithmeticException	Arithmetic errors such as division by zero
ArrayIndexOutOfBoundsException	Array index is either less than 0 or greater than or equal to the length of the array.
FileNotFoundException	Reference to a file that cannot be found
IllegalArgumentException	Calling a method with illegal arguments
IndexOutOfBoundsException	An array or a string index is out of bounds.
NullPointerException	Reference to an object that has not been instantiated

1
1

TABLE 11-3 Some of Java's Exception Classes (continued)

Exception Class	Description
NumberFormatException	Use of an illegal number format
StringIndexOutOfBoundsException	A string index is either less than 0 or greater than or equal to the length of the string.
InputMismatchException	Input (token) retrieved does not match the pattern for the expected type, or the token is out of range for the expected type.

The Java application programs in the preceding chapters used the **class** Scanner and its methods nextInt, nextDouble, next, and nextLine to input data into the programs. As shown by Sample Run 3 of Example 11-1, if the user enters an invalid value, the program terminates with an error message indicating an InputMismatchException. This exception is thrown by the method nextInt. In addition to the InputMismatchException, the methods nextInt and nextDouble can throw other exceptions, as shown in Tables 11-4 and 11-5.

TABLE 11-4 Exceptions Thrown by the Method nextInt

Exception Thrown	Description
InputMismatchException	If the next input (token) is not an integer or is out of range
NoSuchElementException	If the input is exhausted
IllegalStateException	If this scanner is closed

TABLE 11-5 Exceptions Thrown by the Method nextDouble

Exception Thrown	Description
InputMismatchException	If the next input (token) is not a floating-point number or is out of range
NoSuchElementException	If the input is exhausted
IllegalStateException	If this scanner is closed

The methods `nextInt` and `nextDouble` both throw an `InputMismatchException` if the input is invalid. The `class InputMismatchException` is a subclass of the `class NoSuchElementException`, which is a subclass of the `class RuntimeException`. The `class InputMismatchException` has only two constructors, as described in Table 11-6.

TABLE 11-6 `class InputMismatchException` and its Constructors

```
public InputMismatchException()
//Default constructor
//Creates a new instance of the class InputMismatchException.
//The error message is null.


public InputMismatchException(String str)
//Constructor with parameters
//Creates a new instance of the class InputMismatchException. The
//parameter str specifies the message string that is to be retrieved
//by the method getMessage.
```

Tables 11-7 and 11-8 show the exceptions thrown by the methods `next` and `nextLine` of the `class` Scanner.

TABLE 11-7 Exceptions Thrown by the Method `next`

Exception Thrown	Description
NoSuchElementException	If there is no more input (tokens)
IllegalStateException	If this scanner is closed

TABLE 11-8 Exceptions Thrown by the Method `nextLine`

Exception Thrown	Description
NoSuchElementException	If the input is exhausted
IllegalStateException	If this scanner is closed

In an end-of-file (EOF)–controlled **while** loop, we use the method `hasNext` of the `class` Scanner to determine whether there is a token in the input stream. Table 11-9 shows the exception thrown by the method `hasNext`.

TABLE 11-9 Exceptions Thrown by the Method `hasNext`

Exception Thrown	Description
IllegalStateException	If this scanner is closed

As we have seen in the previous chapters, as an input to a dialog box or a text field, Java programs accept only strings as input. Numbers, integer or decimal, are entered as strings. We then use the method `parseInt` of the **class** `Integer` to convert an integer string into the equivalent integer. If the string containing the integer contains only digits, the method `parseInt` will return the integer. However, if the string contains a letter or any other nondigit character, the method `parseInt` throws a `NumberFormatException`. Similarly, the method `parseDouble` also throws this exception if the string does not contain a (valid) number. The programs that we've written up to this point ignored these exceptions. Later in this chapter we show how to handle these and other exceptions.

Tables 11-10, 11-11, and 11-12 list some of the exceptions thrown by the methods of the **class**es `Integer`, `Double`, and `String`.

TABLE 11-10 Exceptions Thrown by the Methods of the **class** `Integer`

Method	Exception Thrown	Description
`parseInt(String str)`	`NumberFormatException`	The string `str` does not contain an `int` value.
`valueOf(String str)`	`NumberFormatException`	The string `str` does not contain an `int` value.

TABLE 11-11 Exceptions Thrown by the Methods of the **class** `Double`

Method	Exception Thrown	Description
`parseDouble(String str)`	`NumberFormatException`	The string `str` does not contain a `double` value.
`valueOf(String str)`	`NumberFormatException`	The string `str` does not contain a `double` value.

TABLE 11-12 Exceptions Thrown by the Methods of the **class** String

Method	Exception Thrown	Description
String(String str)	NullPointerException	str is null.
charAt(int a)	StringIndexOutOfBounds Exception	The value of a is not a valid index.
indexOf(String str)	NullPointerException	str is null.
lastIndexOf(String str)	NullPointerException	str is null.
substring(int a)	StringIndexOutOfBounds Exception	The value of a is not a valid index.
substring(int a, int b)	StringIndexOutOfBounds Exception	The value of a and/or b is not a valid index.

Checked and Unchecked Exceptions

In discussing file input/output, Chapter 3 stated that if an input file does not exist when the program executes, the program throws a FileNotFoundException. Similarly, if a program cannot create or access an output file, the program throws a FileNotFoundException. Until now, the program we have used ignored this type of exception by including the **throws** FileNotFoundException clause in the heading of the method. If we did not include this **throws** clause in the heading of the method **main**, the compiler would generate a syntax (compile-time) error.

On the other hand, in programs that used the methods nextInt and nextDouble, we did not include the code to check whether the input was valid or a **throws** clause (there was no need to do so) in the method heading to ignore these exceptions, and the compiler did not generate a syntax error. Also, we were not concerned about situations such as division by zero or array index out of bounds. If these types of errors occurred during program execution, the program terminated with an appropriate error message. For these types of exceptions, we did not need to include a **throws** clause in the heading of any method. So, the obvious question is: What types of exceptions need the **throws** clause in a method heading?

Java's predefined exceptions are divided into two categories: checked exceptions and unchecked exceptions. Any exception that the compiler can recognize is called a **checked exception**. For example, FileNotFoundExceptions are checked exceptions.

1
1

The constructors of the **class**es `FileReader` and `PrintWriter` that we used throw a `FileNotFoundException`. Therefore, these constructors throw a checked exception. When the compiler encounters the statements to open an input or output file, it checks whether the program handles `FileNotFoundExceptions`, or reports them by throwing them. Enabling the compiler to check for these types of exceptions reduces the number of exceptions not properly handled by the program. Because our programs so far were not required to handle `FileNotFoundExceptions` or other types of predefined exceptions, the programs handled the checked exceptions by throwing them. (Another common checked exception that can occur during program execution is known as `IOExceptions`. For example, the method `read` used in the Text Processing programming example, in Chapter 9, may throw an `IOException`.)

When a program is being compiled, the compiler may not be able to determine whether exceptions—such as division by zero, index out of bounds, or the next input is invalid—will occur. Therefore, the compiler does not check these types of exceptions, called **unchecked exceptions**. To significantly improve the correctness of programs, programmers must check for these types of exceptions.

Because the compiler does not check for unchecked exceptions, the program does not need to declare them using a `throws` clause or provide the code within the program to deal with them. The exceptions belonging to a subclass of the **class** `RuntimeException` are *unchecked exceptions*. Because `InputMismatchException` is a subclass of the **class** `RuntimeException`, the exceptions thrown by the methods `nextInt` and `nextDouble` are unchecked. Therefore, in all the programs that used the methods `nextInt` and `nextDouble`, we did not use the `throws` clause to throw these exceptions. If a program does not provide the code to handle an unchecked exception, the exception is handled by Java's default exception handler.

In the method heading, the `throws` clause lists the types of exceptions thrown by the method. The syntax of the `throws` clause is:

```
throws ExceptionType1, ExceptionType2, ...
```

where `ExceptionType1`, `ExceptionType2`, and so on, are the names of the exception classes.

For example, consider the following method:

```
public static void exceptionMethod()
                throws InputMismatchException, FileNotFoundException
{
    //statements
}
```

The method `exceptionMethod` throws exceptions of type `InputMismatchException` and `FileNotFoundException`.

More Examples of Exception Handling

Because Java accepts only strings as input in input dialog boxes and text fields, inputting data into a string variable won't cause any problems. However, when we use the methods parseInt, parseFloat, or parseDouble to convert a numeric string into its respective numeric form, the program may terminate with a number format error. This is because the methods parseInt, parseFloat, and parseDouble each **throw** a number format exception if the numeric string does not contain a number. For example, if the numeric string does not contain an **int** value, then when the method parseInt tries to determine the numeric form of the integer string, it throws a NumberFormatException.

EXAMPLE 11-4

This example shows how to catch and handle number format and division by zero exceptions in programs that use input dialog boxes and/or text fields.

```java
import javax.swing.JOptionPane;

public class ExceptionExample4
{
    public static void main(String[] args)             //Line 1
    {
        int dividend, divisor, quotient;               //Line 2
        String inpStr;                                 //Line 3

        try                                            //Line 4
        {
            inpStr =
                JOptionPane.showInputDialog
                    ("Enter the dividend: ");          //Line 5
            dividend = Integer.parseInt(inpStr);       //Line 6

            inpStr =
                JOptionPane.showInputDialog
                    ("Enter the divisor: ");           //Line 7
            divisor = Integer.parseInt(inpStr);        //Line 8

            quotient = dividend / divisor;             //Line 9

            JOptionPane.showMessageDialog(null,
                    "Line 10:\nDividend = " + dividend
                + "\nDivisor = " + divisor
                + "\nQuotient =" + quotient,
                    "Quotient",
                JOptionPane.INFORMATION_MESSAGE);      //Line 10
        }
```

11

```
        catch (ArithmeticException aeRef)               //Line 11
        {
            JOptionPane.showMessageDialog(null,
                    "Line 12: Exception "
                    + aeRef.toString(),
                    "ArithmeticException",
                    JOptionPane.ERROR_MESSAGE);          //Line 12
        }
        catch (NumberFormatException nfeRef)            //Line 13
        {
            JOptionPane.showMessageDialog(null,
                    "Line 14: Exception "
                    + nfeRef.toString(),
                    "NumberFormatException",
                    JOptionPane.ERROR_MESSAGE);          //Line 14
        }

        System.exit(0);                                 //Line 15
    }
}
```

Sample Runs: Figures 11-5 to 11-7 show various sample runs.

Sample Run 1:

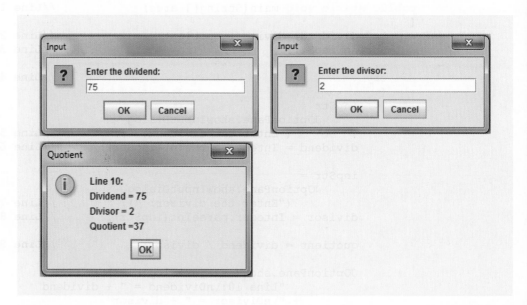

FIGURE 11-5 Sample Run 1 of the program `ExceptionExample4`

Sample Run 2:

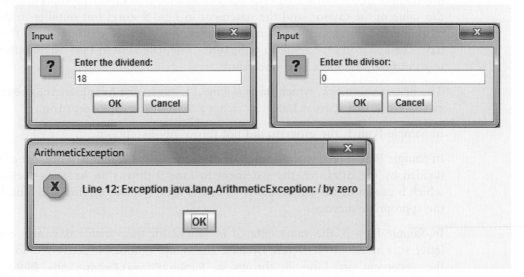

FIGURE 11-6   Sample Run 2 of the program `ExceptionExample4`

Sample Run 3:

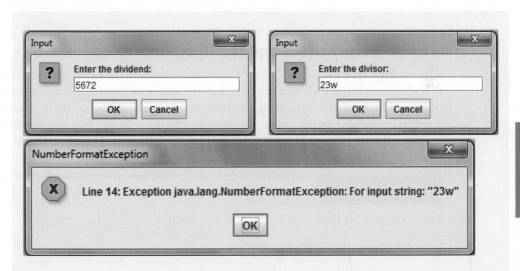

FIGURE 11-7   Sample Run 3 of the program `ExceptionExample4`

This program works as follows: The method `main` starts at Line 1. The statement in Line 2 declares the `int` variables `dividend`, `divisor`, and `quotient`. The statement in Line 3 declares the `String` variable `inpStr`. The `try` block starts at Line 4. The statement in

Line 5 prompts the user to enter the value of the dividend; the statement in Line 6 stores this number in the variable `dividend`. The statement in Line 7 prompts the user to enter the value of the divisor, and the statement in Line 8 stores this number in the variable `divisor`. The statement in Line 9 divides the value of `dividend` by the value of `divisor` and stores the result in `quotient`. The statement in Line 10 outputs the values of `dividend`, `divisor`, and `quotient`.

The first `catch` block, which starts at Line 11, catches an `ArithmeticException`. The `catch` block that starts at Line 13 catches a `NumberFormatException`.

In Sample Run 1, the program did not throw any exceptions.

In Sample Run 2, the entered value of `divisor` is 0. Therefore, when the `dividend` is divided by the `divisor`, the statement in Line 9 throws an `ArithmeticException`, which is caught by the `catch` block starting at Line 11. The statement in Line 12 outputs the appropriate message.

In Sample Run 3, the value entered in Line 7 for the variable `divisor` contains the letter w, a nondigit character. Because this value cannot be converted to an integer, the statement in Line 8 throws a `NumberFormatException`. Note that the `NumberFormatException` is thrown by the method `parseInt` of the `class Integer`. The `catch` block starting at Line 13 catches this exception, and the statement in Line 14 outputs the appropriate message.

class **Exception** and the **Operator** `instanceof`

The program in Example 11-3 uses two `catch` blocks to handle two types of exceptions. Recall from Chapter 10 that a reference variable of a superclass type can point to the objects of its subclasses, and using the operator `instanceof`, you can determine whether a reference variable points to an object of a particular `class`. You can use this facility to combine the two `catch` blocks of the program in Example 11-3 into one `catch` block, as shown by the program in Example 11-5.

EXAMPLE 11-5

```java
import java.util.*;

public class ExceptionExample5
{
    static Scanner console = new Scanner(System.in);

    public static void main(String[] args)          //Line 1
    {
        int dividend, divisor, quotient;            //Line 2

        try                                         //Line 3
```

```
    {
        System.out.print("Line 4: Enter the "
                         + "dividend: ");                    //Line 4
        dividend = console.nextInt();                        //Line 5
        System.out.println();                                //Line 6

        System.out.print("Line 7: Enter the "
                         + "divisor: ");                     //Line 7
        divisor = console.nextInt();                         //Line 8
        System.out.println();                                //Line 9

        quotient = dividend / divisor;                       //Line 10
        System.out.println("Line 11: Quotient = "
                           + quotient);                      //Line 11
    }
    catch (Exception eRef)                                   //Line 12
    {
        if (eRef instanceof ArithmeticException)             //Line 13
            System.out.println("Line 14: Exception "
                               + eRef.toString());           //Line 14
        else if (eRef instanceof InputMismatchException)     //Line 15
            System.out.println("Line 16: Exception "
                               + eRef.toString());           //Line 16
    }
    }
}
```

This program works the same way as the program in Example 11-3. This program, however, has only one `catch` block, which can catch all types of exceptions (see the statement in Line 12). This is because, directly or indirectly, the `class` Exception is the superclass of all the exception classes, and a reference variable of a superclass can point to an object of its subclasses. The parameter `eRef` of the `catch` block in Line 12 is a reference variable of the Exception type. The statement in Line 13 determines whether `eRef` is an instance of the `class` ArithmeticException—that is, if it points to an object of the `class` ArithmeticException. Similarly, the statement in Line 15 determines whether `eRef` is an instance of the `class` InputMismatchException. If `eRef` is an instance of ArithmeticException, then the statement in Line 14 executes, and so on.

EXAMPLE 11-6

The Student Grade programming example in Chapter 3 calculates a student's grade. It reads the data from a file and writes the output to a file. The program given in Chapter 3 throws a `FileNotFoundException` and other exceptions. Now that we know how to handle exceptions in a program, we can rewrite the program to handle the exceptions.

```
//Program: Calculate the average test score
//This program shows how to handle a FileNotFoundException
//or any other exception.
```

```java
import java.io.*;
import java.util.*;

public class StudentGrade
{
    public static void main(String[] args)
    {

        //Declare and initialize the variables    //Step 1
        double test1, test2, test3, test4, test5;
        double average;
        String firstName;
        String lastName;

        try
        {
            Scanner inFile = new Scanner
                (new FileReader("test.txt"));    //Step 2

            PrintWriter outFile =
                new PrintWriter("testavg.out");    //Step 3

            firstName = inFile.next();                //Step 4
            lastName = inFile.next();                 //Step 4

            outFile.println("Student Name: "
                        + firstName + " "
                        + lastName);                  //Step 5

                //Step 6 - retrieve the five test scores
            test1 = inFile.nextDouble();
            test2 = inFile.nextDouble();
            test3 = inFile.nextDouble();
            test4 = inFile.nextDouble();
            test5 = inFile.nextDouble();

            outFile.printf("Test scores: %5.2f %5.2f %5.2f "
                    + "%5.2f %5.2f %n", test1,
                        test2, test3, test4,
                        test5);                       //Step 7

            average = (test1 + test2 + test3 + test4
                    + test5) / 5.0;                   //Step 8

            outFile.printf("Average test score: %5.2f %n",
                        average);                     //Step 9

            outFile.close();                          //Step 10

        }
        catch (FileNotFoundException fnfeRef)
        {
            System.out.println(fnfeRef.toString());
        }
```

```
    catch (Exception eRef)
    {
        System.out.println(eRef.toString());
    }
  }
}
```

Sample Run: If the input file does not exist, the following message is printed:

```
java.io.FileNotFoundException: test.txt (The system cannot find the
file specified)
```

The `try` block contains statements that open both the input and output files. It also contains input and output statements. The first `catch` block catches a `FileNotFoundException`, the second `catch` block catches all types of exceptions. As shown in the sample run, if the input file does not exist, the statement in Step 2 in the `try` block throws a `FileNotFoundException`, which is caught and handled by the first `catch` block.

Rethrowing and Throwing an Exception

When an exception occurs in a `try` block, control immediately passes to the first matching `catch` block. Typically, a `catch` block does one of the following:

- Completely handles the exception.
- Partially processes the exception. In this case, the `catch` block either rethrows the same exception or throws another exception for the calling environment to handle the exception.
- Rethrows the same exception for the calling environment to handle the exception.

The `catch` blocks in Examples 11-3 to 11-6 handled the exception. The mechanism of rethrowing or throwing an exception is quite useful in cases when a `catch` block catches the exception, but the `catch` block is unable to handle the exception, or if the `catch` block decides that the exception should be handled by the calling environment. This allows the programmer to provide the exception handling code in one place.

Rethrowing an exception or throwing an exception is accomplished by the `throw` statement. A `throw` statement can throw either a checked or an unchecked exception.

Exceptions are objects of a specific `class` type. Therefore, if you have a reference to an exception object, you can use the reference to throw the exception. In this case, the general syntax to rethrow an exception caught by a `catch` block is:

```
throw exceptionReference;
```

11

Example 11-7 shows how to rethrow an exception caught by a `catch` block.

EXAMPLE 11-7

Consider the following Java code:

```java
//RethrowExceptionExmp1

import java.util.*;

public class RethrowExceptionExmp1
{
    static Scanner console = new Scanner(System.in);

    public static void main(String[] args)          //Line 1
    {
        int number;                                  //Line 2

        try                                          //Line 3
        {
            number = getNumber();                    //Line 4
            System.out.println("Line 5: number = "
                                + number);           //Line 5
        }
        catch (InputMismatchException imeRef)        //Line 6
        {
            System.out.println("Line 7: Exception "
                            + imeRef.toString());    //Line 7
        }
    }

    public static int getNumber()
                    throws InputMismatchException    //Line 8
    {
        int num;                                     //Line 9

        try                                          //Line 10
        {
            System.out.print("Line 11: Enter an "
                            + "integer: ");          //Line 11
            num = console.nextInt();                 //Line 12
            System.out.println();                    //Line 13

            return num;                              //Line 14
        }
        catch (InputMismatchException imeRef)        //Line 15
        {
            throw imeRef;                            //Line 16
        }
    }
}
```

Sample Runs:

Sample Run 1: (In this sample run, the user input is shaded.)

```
Line 11: Enter an integer: 56
Line 5: number = 56
```

Sample Run 2: (In this sample run, the user input is shaded.)

```
Line 11: Enter an integer: 56t7
Line 7: Exception java.util.InputMismatchException
```

The preceding program contains the method getNumber, which reads an integer and returns it to the method main. If the number entered by the user contains a nondigit character, the method getNumber throws an InputMismatchException. The catch block in Line 15 catches this exception. Rather than handle this exception, the method getNumber rethrows this exception (see the statement in Line 16).

The catch block in Line 6 of the method main also catches the InputMismatchException.

In Sample Run 1, the method getNumber successfully reads the number and returns it to the method main. In Sample Run 2, the user enters an invalid number. The statement in Line 12 throws an InputMismatchException, which is caught and rethrown by the catch block starting at Line 15. After the statement in Line 16 executes, control goes back to the method main (Line 4), which throws an InputMismatchException thrown by the method getNumber. The catch block in Line 6 catches this exception, and the statement in Line 7 outputs the appropriate message.

Example 11-7 illustrates how to rethrow the same exception caught by a catch block. When an exception occurs, the system creates an object of a specific exception class. In fact, you can also create your own exception objects and throw them using the throw statement. In this case, the general syntax used for the throw statement is:

```
throw new ExceptionClassName(messageString);
```

Of course, you could have first created the object and then used the reference to the object in the throw statement.

Example 11-8 illustrates how to create and throw an exception object.

EXAMPLE 11-8

```
//RethrowExceptionExmp2

import java.util.*;

public class RethrowExceptionExmp2
{
    static Scanner console = new Scanner(System.in);
```

```
public static void main(String[] args)          //Line 1
{
    int number;                                 //Line 2

    try                                         //Line 3
    {
        number = getNumber();                   //Line 4
        System.out.println("Line 5: number = "
                        + number);              //Line 5
    }
    catch (InputMismatchException imeRef)       //Line 6
    {
        System.out.println("Line 7: Exception "
                        + imeRef.toString());   //Line 7
    }
}

public static int getNumber()
            throws InputMismatchException       //Line 8
{
    int num;                                    //Line 9

    try                                         //Line 10
    {
        System.out.print("Line 11: Enter an "
                        + "integer: ");         //Line 11
        num = console.nextInt();                //Line 12
        System.out.println();                   //Line 13

        return num;                             //Line 14
    }
    catch (InputMismatchException imeRef)       //Line 15
    {
        System.out.println("Line 16: Exception "
                        + imeRef.toString());   //Line 16
        throw new InputMismatchException
                        ("getNumber");          //Line 17
    }
}
}
```

Sample Run: (In this sample run, the user input is shaded.)

```
Line 11: Enter an integer: 563r9
Line 16: Exception java.util.InputMismatchException
Line 7: Exception java.util.InputMismatchException: getNumber
```

The preceding program works similarly to the program in Example 11-7. The difference is in the `catch` block starting at Line 15, in the method `getNumber`. The `catch` block in Line 15 catches an `InputMismatchException`, outputs an appropriate message in Line 16, and then in Line 17 creates an `InputMismatchException` object with the message string `"getNumber"` and throws the object. The `catch` block starting at Line 6 in the method `main` catches the thrown object. The statement in Line 7 outputs the appropriate message. Notice that the output of the statement in Line 16 (the second line of the sample run) does not output the string `getNumber`, whereas the statement in Line 7 (the third line of the sample run) does output the string `getNumber`. This is because the statement in Line 17 creates and throws an object that is different from the `InputMismatchException` object thrown by the statement in Line 12. The message string of the object thrown by the statement in Line 12 is null; the object thrown by the statement in Line 17 contains the message string `"getNumber"`.

The programs in Examples 11-7 and 11-8 illustrate how a method can rethrow the same exception object, or create an exception object and throw it for the calling method to handle. This mechanism is quite useful; it allows a program to handle all the exceptions in one location rather than spreading exception-handling code throughout the program.

Method `printStackTrace`

Suppose that method `A` calls method `B`, method `B` calls method `C`, and an exception occurs in method `C`. Java keeps track of this sequence of method calls. Recall that the `class Exception` is a subclass of the `class Throwable`. As shown in Table 11-1, the `class Throwable` contains the `public` method `printStackTrace`. Because the method `printStackTrace` is `public`, every subclass of the `class Throwable` inherits this method. When an exception occurs in a method, you can use the method `printStackTrace` to determine the order in which the methods were called and where the exception was handled.

EXAMPLE 11-9

This example shows the use of the method `printStackTrace` to show the order in which methods are called and exceptions handled.

```java
import java.io.*;

public class PrintStackTraceExample1
{
    public static void main(String[] args)
    {
        try
        {
            methodA();
        }
        catch (Exception e)
        {
            System.out.println(e.toString() + " caught in main");
            e.printStackTrace();
        }
    }
```

```
public static void methodA() throws Exception
{
    methodB();
}

public static void methodB() throws Exception
{
    methodC();
}

public static void methodC() throws Exception
{
    throw new Exception("Exception generated in method C");
}
}
```

Sample Run:

```
java.lang.Exception: Exception generated in method C caught in main
java.lang.Exception: Exception generated in method C
        at PrintStackTraceExample1.methodC(PrintStackTraceExample1.java:30)
        at PrintStackTraceExample1.methodB(PrintStackTraceExample1.java:25)
        at PrintStackTraceExample1.methodA(PrintStackTraceExample1.java:20)
        at PrintStackTraceExample1.main(PrintStackTraceExample1.java:9)
```

The preceding program contains the methods methodA, methodB, methodC, and main. The method methodC creates and throws an object of the **class** Exception. The method methodB calls methodC, methodA calls methodB, and the method main calls methodA. Because the methods methodA and methodB do not handle the exception thrown by methodC, they contain the **throws** Exception clause in their heading. The method main handles the exception thrown by methodC, which was propagated first by methodB and then by methodA. The **catch** block in the method main first outputs the message contained in the exception object and the string " caught in main", then it calls the method printStackTrace to trace the method calls (see the last four lines of the output).

The program in Example 11-10 is similar to the program in Example 11-9. The main difference is that the exception thrown by methodC is caught and handled in methodA. Note that the heading of methodA does not contain any **throws** clause.

EXAMPLE 11-10

```
import java.io.*;

public class PrintStackTraceExample2
{
    public static void main(String[] args)
    {
        methodA();
    }
```

```
public static void methodA()
{
    try
    {
        methodB();
    }
    catch (Exception e)
    {
        System.out.println(e.toString() + " caught in methodA");
        e.printStackTrace();
    }
}

public static void methodB() throws Exception
{
    methodC();
}

public static void methodC() throws Exception
{
    throw new Exception("Exception generated in method C");
}
}
```

Sample Run:

```
java.lang.Exception: Exception generated in method C caught in methodA
java.lang.Exception: Exception generated in method C
        at PrintStackTraceExample2.methodC(PrintStackTraceExample2.java:30)
        at PrintStackTraceExample2.methodB(PrintStackTraceExample2.java:25)
        at PrintStackTraceExample2.methodA(PrintStackTraceExample2.java:14)
        at PrintStackTraceExample2.main(PrintStackTraceExample2.java:7)
```

Exception-Handling Techniques

When an exception occurs in a program, usually the programmer has three choices—terminate the program, fix the error and continue, or log the error and continue. The following sections discuss each situation.

Terminate the Program

In some cases, it is best to let the program terminate when an exception occurs. Suppose you have written a program that inputs data from a file. If the input file does not exist when the program executes, then there is no point in continuing with the program. In this case, the program can output an appropriate error message and terminate.

Fix the Error and Continue

In other cases, you will want to handle the exception and let the program continue. Suppose you have a program that takes as input an integer. If a user inputs a character in place of a digit, the program will throw an `InputMismatchException`. This is a situation where you can include the necessary code to keep prompting the user to input a number until the entry is valid. Example 11-11 illustrates this concept.

EXAMPLE 11-11

The following program continues to prompt the user until the user enters a valid integer.

```java
import java.util.*;

public class FixErrorAndContinue
{
    static Scanner console = new Scanner(System.in);

    public static void main(String[] args)
    {
        int number;                                     //Line 1
        boolean done;                                   //Line 2
        String str;                                     //Line 3

        done = false;                                   //Line 4

        do                                              //Line 5
        {
            try                                         //Line 6
            {
                System.out.print("Line 7: Enter an "
                                 + "integer: ");        //Line 7
                number = console.nextInt();             //Line 8
                System.out.println();                   //Line 9
                done = true;                            //Line 10

                System.out.println("Line 11: number = "
                                   + number);           //Line 11
            }
            catch (InputMismatchException imeRef)       //Line 12
            {
                str = console.next();                   //Line 13

                System.out.println("Line 14: Exception "
                                   + imeRef.toString()
                                   + " " + str);         //Line 14
            }
        }
        while (!done);                                  //Line 15
    }
}
```

Sample Run: (In this sample run, the user input is shaded.)

```
Line 7: Enter an integer: 34t5
Line 14: Exception java.util.InputMismatchException 34t5
Line 7: Enter an integer: 398se2
Line 14: Exception java.util.InputMismatchException 398se2
Line 7: Enter an integer: r45
Line 14: Exception java.util.InputMismatchException r45
Line 7: Enter an integer: 56

Line 11: number = 56
```

In the preceding program, the statement in Line 7 prompts the user to enter an integer. The statement in Line 8 inputs the integer entered by the user into the variable `number`. If the user enters a valid integer, then that integer is stored in `number`. Then, the statement in Line 10 sets the `boolean` variable `done` to `true`. After the statement in Line 11 executes, the next statement executed is the expression `!done` in Line 15. If `done` is `true`, then `!done` is `false`, so the `while` loop terminates.

Suppose that the user does not enter a valid integer. Because the next input (token) cannot be expressed as an integer, the statement in Line 8 throws an `InputMismatchException` and control is transferred to the `catch` block starting at Line 12. Notice that the invalid number entered by the user is still the next input (token) in the input stream. Therefore, the statement in Line 13 reads that invalid number and assigns that input (token) to `str`. The statement in Line 14 outputs the exception as well as the invalid input. Notice that we can output the invalid input because the program captured the invalid input at Line 13. The `do...while` loop continues to prompt the user until the user inputs a valid integer.

Notice that in the sample run, the first, second, and third inputs are `34t5`, `398se2`, and `r45`, which contain nondigit characters. The fourth input, which is `56`, is a valid integer.

Log the Error and Continue

A program that terminates when an exception occurs usually assumes that the termination is reasonably safe. On the other hand, if your program is designed to run a nuclear reactor or continuously monitor a satellite, it cannot be terminated if an exception occurs. These programs should report the exception, but the program must continue to run.

For example, consider a program that analyzes airline-ticketing transactions. Because a large number of ticketing transactions take place each day, a program is run daily to validate that day's transactions. This type of program would take an enormous amount of time to process the transactions. Therefore, when an exception occurs, the program should write the exception into a file and continue to analyze the transactions.

Creating Your Own Exception Classes

When you create your own classes or write programs, exceptions are likely to occur. As you have seen, Java provides a substantial number of exception classes to deal with these situations. However, it does not provide all the exception classes you will ever need. Therefore, Java enables programmers to create exception classes to handle the exceptions not covered by Java's exception classes or to handle their own exceptions. This section describes how to create your own exception classes.

Java's mechanism to process the exceptions you define is the same as that for built-in exceptions. However, you must throw your own exceptions using the `throw` statement.

The exception class that you define extends either the `class Exception` or one of its subclasses. Also, a subclass of the `class Exception` is either a predefined class or a user-defined class. In other words, if you have created an exception class, you can define other exception classes by extending the definition of the exception class you created.

Typically, constructors are the only methods that you include when you define your own exception class. Because the exception class you define is a subclass of an existing exception class, either built-in or user-defined, the exception class that you define inherits the members of the superclass. Therefore, objects of the exception classes can use the `public` members of the superclasses.

Because the `class Exception` is derived from the `class Throwable`, it inherits the methods `getMessage` and `toString` of the `class Throwable`. These methods are `public`, so they are also inherited by the subclasses of the `class Exception`.

EXAMPLE 11-12

This example shows how to create your own division by the zero exception class.

```java
public class MyDivisionByZeroException extends Exception
{
    public MyDivisionByZeroException()
    {
        super("Cannot divide by zero");
    }

    public MyDivisionByZeroException(String strMessage)
    {
        super(strMessage);
    }
}
```

The program in Example 11-13 uses the class MyDivisionByZeroException designed in Example 11-12.

EXAMPLE 11-13

```java
import java.util.*;

public class MyDivisionByZeroExceptionTestProg
{
    static Scanner console = new Scanner(System.in);

    public static void main(String[] args)
    {
        double numerator;                               //Line 1
        double denominator;                             //Line 2

        try                                             //Line 3
        {
            System.out.print("Line 4: Enter the "
                        + "numerator: ");               //Line 4
            numerator = console.nextDouble();           //Line 5
            System.out.println();                       //Line 6

            System.out.print("Line 7: Enter the "
                        + "denominator: ");             //Line 7
            denominator = console.nextDouble();         //Line 8
            System.out.println();                       //Line 9

            if (denominator == 0.0)                     //Line 10
                throw new MyDivisionByZeroException();  //Line 11

            System.out.println("Line 12: Quotient = "
                        + (numerator / denominator));   //Line 12
        }
        catch (MyDivisionByZeroException mdbze)          //Line 13
        {
            System.out.println("Line 14: "
                        + mdbze.toString());            //Line 14
        }
        catch (Exception e)                             //Line 15
        {
            System.out.println("Line 16: "
                        + e.toString());                //Line 16
        }
    }
}
```

Sample Runs:

Sample Run 1: (In this sample run, the user input is shaded.)

Line 4: Enter the numerator: 25

Line 7: Enter the denominator: 4

Line 12: Quotient = 6.25

Sample Run 2: (In this sample run, the user input is shaded.)

Line 4: Enter the numerator: 20

Line 7: Enter the denominator: 0

Line 14: MyDivisionByZeroException: Cannot divide by zero

NOTE If the exception class you create is a direct subclass of the `class` Exception—or a direct subclass of an exception class whose exceptions are checked exceptions—then the exceptions of the class you created are checked exceptions.

Event Handling

The previous sections discussed in detail Java's mechanism of exception handling. You learned that Java offers extensive support for handling exceptions by providing a number of exception classes. In previous chapters, you learned that Java also provides powerful yet easy-to-use GUI components to create programs that can visually interact with the user. A major item that is required in creating a GUI is the handling of events. In Chapter 6, you learned that when you click a button or press the Enter key in a text field, it generates an action event. In fact, when you press a mouse button to click a button, in addition to generating an action event, a mouse event is generated. Similarly, when you press the Enter key in a text field, in addition to the action event, it generates a key event. Therefore, a GUI program can simultaneously generate more than one event. In the remainder of this section, you will learn how to handle other action events, such as windows and mouse events.

As described in Chapter 6, Java provides various `interfaces` to handle different events. For example, to handle action events, you use the `interface` ActionListener and to handle mouse events, you use the `interface` MouseListener. Key events are handled by the `interface` KeyListener; and window events are handled by the `interface` WindowListener. These and other interfaces contain methods that are executed when a particular event occurs. For example, when an action event occurs, the method actionPerformed of the `interface` ActionListener is executed.

To handle an event, we create an appropriate object and register it with the GUI component. Recall that the methods of an interface are `abstract`. That is, they contain only the headings of the methods. Therefore, you cannot instantiate an object of an interface. To create an object to handle an event, first you create a class that implements an appropriate interface.

Chapter 6 discussed in detail how to handle action events. Recall that to handle an action event, we do the following:

1. Create a class that implements the **interface** ActionListener. For example, in Chapter 6, for the JButton calculateB, we created the **class** CalculateButtonHandler.

2. Provide the definition of the method actionPerformed within the class that you created in Step 1. The method actionPerformed contains the code that the program executes when the specific event is generated. For example, in Chapter 6, when you click the JButton calculateB, the program should calculate and display the area and perimeter of the rectangle.

3. Create and instantiate an object of the class created in Step 1. For example, in Chapter 6, for the JButton calculateB, we created the object cbHandler.

4. Register the event handler created in Step 3 with the object that generates an action event using the method addActionListener. For example, in Chapter 6, for the JButton calculateB, the following statement registers the object cbHandler to listen for and register the action event:

```
calculateB.addActionListener(cbHandler);
```

Just as you create objects of the class that extends the **interface** ActionListener to handle action events, to handle window events you first create a class that implements the **interface** WindowListener and then create and register objects of that class. You take similar steps to handle mouse events.

In Chapter 6, to terminate the program when the close window button is clicked, we used the method setDefaultCloseOperation with the predefined named constant EXIT_ON_CLOSE. If you want to provide your own code to terminate the program when the window is closed, or if you want the program to take a different action when the window closes, then you use the **interface** WindowListener. That is, first you create a class that implements the **interface** WindowListener, provide the appropriate definition of the method windowClosed, create an appropriate object of that class, and then register the object created with the program.

Let's look at the definition of the **interface** WindowListener:

```
public interface WindowListener
{
    void windowActivated(WindowEvent e);
      //This method executes when a window is activated.
    void windowClosed(WindowEvent e);
      //This method executes when a window is closed.
    void windowClosing(WindowEvent e);
      //This method executes when a window is closing,
      //just before a window is closed.
    void windowDeactivated(WindowEvent e);
      //This method executes when a window is deactivated.
```

11

```
void windowIconified(WindowEvent e);
   //This method executes when a window is iconified.
void windowOpened(WindowEvent e);
   //This method executes when a window is opened.
}
```

As you can see, the `interface` `WindowListener` contains several `abstract` methods. Therefore, to instantiate an object of the class that implements the `interface` `WindowListener`, that class must provide the definition of each method of the `interface` `WindowListener`, even if a method is not used. Of course, if a method is not used, you could provide an empty body for that method. Recall that if a class contains an `abstract` method, you cannot instantiate an object of that class.

In Chapter 6, we used the mechanism of the inner class to handle events. That is, the class that implemented the interface was defined within the class containing the application program. Chapter 10 noted that rather than create an inner class to implement the interface, the class containing the application program can itself implement the interface. Now a program can generate various types of events, such as action events and window events. Java allows a class to implement more than one interface. However, Java does not allow a class to extend the definition of more than one class; that is, Java does not support multiple inheritance.

For interfaces such as `WindowListener` that contain more than one method, Java provides the `class` `WindowAdapter`. The `class` `WindowAdapter` implements the `interface` `WindowListener` by providing an empty body for each method of the `interface` `WindowListener`. The definition of the `class` `WindowAdapter` is:

```
public class WindowAdapter implements WindowListener
{
    void windowActivated(WindowEvent e)
    {
    }

    void windowClosed(WindowEvent e)
    {
    }
    void windowClosing(WindowEvent e)
    {
    }

    void windowDeactivated(WindowEvent e)
    {
    }

    void windowIconified(WindowEvent e)
    {
    }

    void windowOpened(WindowEvent e)
    {
    }
}
```

If you use the inner class mechanism to handle a window event, you can create the class by extending the definition of the class `WindowAdapter` and provide the definition of only the methods that the program needs. Similarly, to handle window events, if the class containing the application program does not extend the definition of another class, you can make that class extend the definition of the class `WindowAdapter`.

Chapter 6 discussed in detail how to use the inner class mechanism. The GUI part of the programming example in Chapter 10, which can be found in the Additional Student Files folder at *www.cengagebrain.com,* explained how to make the class containing the application program implement more than one interface. As stated in Chapter 10, there is one more way to handle events in a program—using the mechanism of anonymous classes. This mechanism is quite useful to handle events such as window and mouse events because the corresponding interfaces contain more than one method, and the program might want to use only one method.

Recall from Chapter 6 that to register an action listener object to a GUI component, you use the method `addActionListener`. To register a `WindowListener` object to a GUI component, you use the method `addWindowListener`. The `WindowListener` object being registered is passed as a parameter to the method `addWindowListener`.

Consider the following code:

```
this.addWindowListener(new WindowAdapter()
        {
            public void windowClosing(WindowEvent e)
            {
                System.exit(0);
            }
        }
);
```

The preceding statements create an object of the anonymous class, which extends the class `WindowAdapter` and overrides the method `windowClosing`. The object created is passed as an argument to the method `addWindowListener`. The method `addWindowListener` is invoked by explicitly using the reference `this`.

Similarly, you can handle mouse events by using the interface `MouseListener`. The definition of the interface `MouseListener` and the class `MouseAdapter` is:

```
public interface MouseListener
{
    void mouseClicked(MouseEvent e);
      //This method executes when a mouse button is clicked
      //on a component.
    void mouseEntered(MouseEvent e);
      //This method executes when the mouse enters a component.
    void mouseExited(MouseEvent e);
      //This method executes when the mouse exits a component.
    void mousePressed(MouseEvent e);
      //This method executes when a mouse button is
      //is pressed on a component.
```

```
    void mouseReleased(MouseEvent e);
        //This method executes when a mouse button is released
        //on a component.
}

public class MouseAdapter implements MouseListener
{
    void mouseClicked(MouseEvent e)
    {
    }

    void mouseEntered(MouseEvent e)
    {
    }

    void mouseExited(MouseEvent e)
    {
    }

    void mousePressed(MouseEvent e)
    {
    }

    void mouseReleased(MouseEvent e)
    {
    }
}
```

To register a `MouseListener` object to a GUI component, you use the method `addMouseListener`. The `MouseListener` object being registered is passed as a parameter to the method `addMouseListener`.

In addition to the GUI components with which you have worked, Chapter 12 introduces other GUI components such as check boxes, option buttons, menu items, and lists. These GUI components also generate events. Table 11-13 summarizes the various events generated by GUI components. It also shows the GUI component, the listener interface, and the name of the method of the interface to handle the event.

TABLE 11-13 Events Generated by a GUI Component, the Listener Interface, and the Name of the Method of the Interface to Handle the Event

GUI Component	Event Generated	Listener Interface	Listener Method
JButtton	ActionEvent	ActionListener	actionPerformed
JCheckBox	ItemEvent	ItemListener	itemStateChanged
JCheckboxMenuItem	ItemEvent	ItemListener	itemStateChanged
JChoice	ItemEvent	ItemListener	itemStateChanged
JComponent	ComponentEvent	ComponentListener	componentHidden
JComponent	ComponentEvent	ComponentListener	componentMoved

TABLE 11-13 Events Generated by a GUI Component, the Listener Interface, and the Name of the Method of the Interface to Handle the Event (continued)

GUI Component	Event Generated	Listener Interface	Listener Method
JComponent	ComponentEvent	ComponentListener	componentResized
JComponent	ComponentEvent	ComponentListener	componentShown
JComponent	FocusEvent	FocusListener	focusGained
JComponent	FocusEvent	FocusListener	focusLost
Container	ContainerEvent	ContainerListener	componentAdded
Container	ContainerEvent	ContainerListener	componentRemoved
JList	ActionEvent	ActionListener	actionPerformed
JList	ItemEvent	ItemListener	itemStateChanged
JMenuItem	ActionEvent	ActionListener	actionPerformed
JScrollbar	AdjustmentEvent	AdjustmentListener	adjustmentValueChanged
JTextComponent	TextEvent	TextListener	textValueChanged
JTextField	ActionEvent	ActionListener	actionPerformed
Window	WindowEvent	WindowListener	windowActivated
Window	WindowEvent	WindowListener	windowClosed
Window	WindowEvent	WindowListener	windowClosing
Window	WindowEvent	WindowListener	windowDeactivated
Window	WindowEvent	WindowListener	windowDeiconified
Window	WindowEvent	WindowListener	windowIconified
Window	WindowEvent	WindowListener	windowOpened

Even though key and mouse are not GUI components, they do generate events. Table 11-14 summarizes the events generated by the key and mouse components.

TABLE 11-14 Events Generated by key and mouse Components

	Event Generated	Listener Interface	Listener Method
key	KeyEvent	KeyListener	keyPressed
key	KeyEvent	KeyListener	keyReleased
key	KeyEvent	KeyListener	keyTyped
mouse	MouseEvent	MouseListener	mouseClicked

11

TABLE 11-14 Events Generated by `key` and `mouse` Components (continued)

	Event Generated	Listener Interface	Listener Method
mouse	MouseEvent	MouseListener	mouseEntered
mouse	MouseEvent	MouseListener	mouseExited
mouse	MouseEvent	MouseListener	mousePressed
mouse	MouseEvent	MouseListener	mouseReleased
mouse	MouseEvent	MouseMotionListener	mouseDragged
mouse	MouseEvent	MouseMotionListener	mouseMoved

NOTE The section Key and Mouse Events in Chapter 12 gives examples of how to handle key and mouse events.

PROGRAMMING EXAMPLE: Calculator

In this programming example, we design a program that simulates a calculator. The program will provide the basic integer arithmetic operations +, −, *, and /. When the program executes, it displays the GUI shown in Figure 11-8.

FIGURE 11-8 Calculator program GUI

Input: Integers via pressing various digit buttons, arithmetic operations via pressing operation buttons, the equal sign via pressing the button containing the symbol = on the calculator panel, and clearing inputs by pressing the C button.

Output: The result of the operation or an appropriate error message if something goes wrong.

As shown in Figure 11-8, the GUI contains 16 buttons, a text field, and a window. The buttons and the text field are placed in the content pane of the window. The user enters the input using the various buttons, and the program displays the result in the text field. To create the 16 buttons, you use 16 reference variables of type `JButton`, and to create the text field, you use a reference variable of type `JTextField`. You also need a reference variable to access the content pane of the window. As we did in previous GUI programs (in Chapters 6, 8, and 10), we create the class containing the application program by extending the definition of the `class JFrame`, which also allows you to create the necessary window to create the GUI. Thus, we use the following variables to create the GUI components and to access the content pane of the window:

```
private JTextField displayText = new JTextField(30);
private JButton[] button = new JButton[16];

Container pane = getContentPane(); //to access the content pane
```

As you can see from Figure 11-8, the GUI components are nicely organized. To place the GUI components as shown in the figure, we first set the layout of the content pane to `null` and then use the methods `setSize` and `setLocation` to place the GUI components at various locations in the content pane. The following statement instantiates the `JTextField` object `displayText` and places it in the content pane:

```
displayText.setSize(200, 30);
displayText.setLocation(10, 10);
pane.add(displayText);
```

The size of `displayText` is set to 200 pixels wide and 30 pixels high and it is placed at position `(10, 10)` in the content pane.

To assign labels to the buttons, rather than write 16 statements, we use an array of strings and a loop. Consider the following statement:

```
private String[] keys = {"7", "8", "9", "/",
                         "4", "5", "6", "*",
                         "1", "2", "3", "-",
                         "0", "C", "=", "+"};
```

Because the size of the `displayText` is 200 pixels wide and each row has four `JButton`s, we set the width of each `JButton` to 50 pixels wide. To keep the height of each `JButton` the same as the height of `displayText`, we set the height of each `JButton` to 30 pixels.

The user enters input via the buttons. Therefore, each button can generate an action event. To respond to the events generated by a button, we will create and register an appropriate object. In Chapters 6, 8, and 10, we used the mechanism of the inner class to create and register a listener object. In this program, we make the class containing the application program implement the `interface ActionListener`. Therefore, we only need to provide the definition of the method `actionPerformed`, which will be described later in this section. Because the class containing the application program implements the `interface` `ActionListener`, we do not need to explicitly instantiate a listener object. We can simply use the reference `this` as an argument to the method `addActionListener` to register the listener.

The following statements instantiate the 16 `JButtons`, place them in the content pane at the proper locations, and register the listener object:

```
int x, y;

x = 10;
y = 40;

for (int ind = 0; ind < 16; ind++)
{
    button[ind] = new JButton(keys[ind]); //instantiate the
                                          //JButton and assign
                                          //it a label
    button[ind].addActionListener(this);  //register the
                                          //listener object
    button[ind].setSize(50,30);           //set the size
    button[ind].setLocation(x, y);        //set the location
    pane.add(button[ind]);                //place the button
                                          //in the content pane

        //determine the coordinates of the next JButton
    x = x + 50;

    if ((ind + 1) % 4 == 0)
    {
        x = 10;
        y = y + 30;
    }
}
```

The inputs to the program are integers, various operations, and the equal symbol. The numbers are entered via the buttons whose labels are digits, and the operations are specified via the buttons whose labels are operations. When the user presses the button with the label =, the program displays the results. The user can also press the button with the label C to clear the numbers.

Because Java accepts only strings as inputs in a GUI component, we need two `String` variables to store the number strings. Before performing the operation, the strings will be converted to their numeric form.

To input numbers, the user presses various digit buttons, one at a time. For example, to specify that a number is 235, the user presses the buttons labeled 2, 3, and 5 in sequence. After pressing each button, the number is displayed in the text field. Each number is entered as a string and therefore concatenated with the previous string. When the user presses an operation button, it indicates that the user is about to enter the second number. Therefore, we use a `boolean` variable, which is set to `false` after the first number is input. We will need the following variables:

```
private String numStr1 = "";
private String numStr2 = "";

private char op;
private boolean firstInput = true;
```

When an event is generated by a button, the method `actionPerformed` is executed. So when the user clicks the = button, the program must display the result. Similarly, when the user clicks an operation button, the program should prepare to receive the second number, and so on. We, therefore, see that the instructions to receive the inputs and operations and display the results will be placed in the method `actionPerformed`. Next, we describe this method.

Method action Performed

As described above, the method `actionPerformed` is executed when the user presses any button. Several things can go wrong while using the calculator. For example, the user might press an operation button without specifying the first number, or the user might press the equal button either without specifying a number or after inputting the first number. Of course, we must also address division by zero. Therefore, the method `actionPerformed` must appropriately respond to the errors.

Suppose that the user wants to add three numbers. After adding the first two numbers, the third number can be added to the sum of the first two numbers. In this case, when the third number is added, the first number is the sum of the first two numbers and the second number becomes the third number. Therefore, after each operation, we will set the first number as the result of the operation. The user can click the C button to start a different calculation. This discussion translates into the following algorithm:

1. Declare the appropriate variables.

2. Use the method `getActionCommand` to identify the button clicked. Retrieve the label of the button, which is a string.

3. Retrieve the character specifying the button label and store it in the variable `ch`.

4. a. If `ch` is a digit and `firstInput` is `true`, append the character at the end of the first number string; otherwise, append the character at the end of the second number string.

   b. If `ch` is an operation, set `firstInput` to `false` and set the variable `op` to `ch`.

   c. If `ch` is = and there is no error, perform the operation, display the result, and set the first number as the result of the operation. If an error occurred, display an appropriate message.

   d. If `ch` is C, set both number strings to blank and clear the `displayText`.

To perform the operation, we write the method `evaluate`, which is described in the next section.

The definition of the method `actionPerformed` is:

```java
public void actionPerformed(ActionEvent e)
{
    String resultStr;                               //Step 1

    String str
        = String.valueOf(e.getActionCommand());     //Steps 1 and 2

    char ch = str.charAt(0);                         //Steps 1 and 3

    switch (ch)                                      //Step 4
    {
    case '0':                                        //Step 4a
    case '1':
    case '2':
    case '3':
    case '4':
    case '5':
    case '6':
    case '7':
    case '8':
    case '9':
        if (firstInput)
        {
            numStr1 = numStr1 + ch;
            displayText.setText(numStr1);
        }
        else
        {
            numStr2 = numStr2 + ch;
            displayText.setText(numStr2);
        }
        break;

    case '+':                                        //Step 4b
    case '-':
    case '*':
    case '/':
        op = ch;
        firstInput = false;
        break;
    case '=':                                        //Step 4c
        resultStr = evaluate();
        displayText.setText(resultStr);
        numStr1 = resultStr;
        numStr2 = "";
        firstInput = false;
        break;
```

```
            case 'C':
                displayText.setText("");              //Step 4d
                numStr1 = "";
                numStr2 = "";
                firstInput = true;
        }
    }
```

Method
evaluate
The method `evaluate` performs an operation and returns the result of the operation as a string. This method also handles various exceptions, such as division by zero and number format error (which occurs if one of the number strings is empty). The definition of this method is:

```
private String evaluate()
{
    final char beep = '\u0007';

    try
    {
        int num1 = Integer.parseInt(numStr1);
        int num2 = Integer.parseInt(numStr2);
        int result = 0;

        switch (op)
        {
        case '+':
            result = num1 + num2;
            break;

        case '-':
            result = num1 - num2;
            break;

        case '*':
            result = num1 * num2;
            break;

        case '/':
            result = num1 / num2;
        }

        return String.valueOf(result);
    }
    catch (ArithmeticException e)
    {
        System.out.print(beep);
        return "E R R O R: " + e.getMessage();
    }
    catch (NumberFormatException e)
    {
        System.out.print(beep);
```

```
                if (numStr1.equals(""))
                    return "E R R O R: Invalid First Number" ;
                else
                    return "E R R O R: Invalid Second Number" ;
        }
        catch (Exception e)
        {
            System.out.print(beep);
            return "E R R O R";
        }
}
```

Before writing the complete program, we must do one more thing. When the user clicks the window closing button, the program must terminate. Clicking the window closing button generates a window event. Therefore, we must create a WindowListener object and register the object of the class containing the application program because this class extends the definition of the class JFrame. The window events are handled by the interface WindowListener. To terminate the program when the user clicks the window closing button, we must provide the definition of the method windowClosing of the interface WindowListener. Because the interface WindowListener contains more than one method and we only want to use the method windowClosing, we use the mechanism of the anonymous class to create and register the window event object. To do so, we make the class containing the application program use the class WindowAdapter to create and register the window event object. Creating and registering the window event object is accomplished by the following statements:

```
this.addWindowListener(new WindowAdapter()
        {
            public void windowClosing(WindowEvent e)
            {
                System.exit(0);
            }
        }
);
```

We can now outline the program listing.

PROGRAM LISTING

```
//***********************************************************
// Author: D.S. Malik
//
// GUI Calculator Program
// This program implements the arithmetic operations.
//***********************************************************
```

```java
import javax.swing.*;
import java.awt.*;
import java.awt.event.*;
import java.io.*;

public class Calculator extends JFrame implements
                                        ActionListener
{
    private JTextField displayText = new JTextField(30);
    private JButton[] button = new JButton[16];

    private String[] keys = {"7", "8", "9", "/",
                             "4", "5", "6", "*",
                             "1", "2", "3", "-",
                             "0", "C", "=", "+"};

    private String numStr1 = "";
    private String numStr2 = "";

    private char op;
    private boolean firstInput = true;

    public Calculator()
    {
        setTitle("My Calculator");
        setSize(230, 200);
        Container pane = getContentPane();

        pane.setLayout(null);

        displayText.setSize(200,30);
        displayText.setLocation(10,10);
        pane.add(displayText);

        int x, y;

        x = 10;
        y = 40;

        for (int ind = 0; ind < 16; ind++)
        {
            button[ind] = new JButton(keys[ind]);
            button[ind].addActionListener(this);
            button[ind].setSize(50,30);
            button[ind].setLocation(x, y);
            pane.add(button[ind]);
            x = x + 50;

            if ((ind + 1) % 4 == 0)
            {
                x = 10;
                y = y + 30;
            }
        }
```

```
        this.addWindowListener(new WindowAdapter()
            {
                public void windowClosing(WindowEvent e)
                {
                    System.exit(0);
                }
            }
        );

        setVisible(true);
    }

    //Place the definition of the method actionPerformed
    //as described here

    //Place the definition of the method evaluate
    //as described here

    public static void main(String[] args)
    {
        Calculator C = new Calculator();
    }
}
```

Sample Run 1: In this sample run (see Figure 11-9), the user entered the numbers 34 and 25, the operation +, and =. The result is shown in the bottom screen.

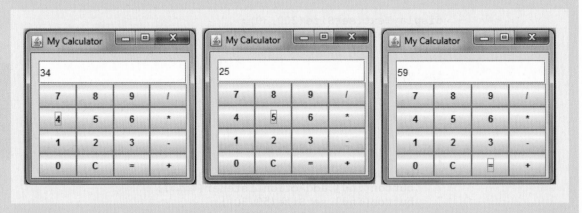

FIGURE 11-9 Adding numbers 34 and 25

Sample Run 2: In this sample run (see Figure 11-10), the user attempted to divide by 0, resulting in an error message.

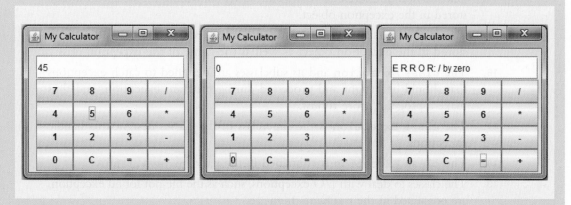

FIGURE 11-10 An attempt to divide by 0

QUICK REVIEW

1. An exception is an object of a specific exception class. Java provides extensive support for exception handling by providing several exception classes. Java also allows users to create and implement their own exception classes.

2. The `try/catch/finally` block is used to handle exceptions within a program.

3. Statements that may generate an exception are placed in a `try` block. The `try` block also contains statements that should not be executed if an exception occurs.

4. A `try` block is followed by zero or more `catch` blocks.

5. A `catch` block specifies the type of exception it can catch and contains an exception handler.

6. The last `catch` block may or may not be followed by a `finally` block.

7. The code contained in the `finally` block always executes, regardless of whether an exception occurs, except when the program exits early from a `try` block by calling the method `System.exit`.

8. If a `try` block is not followed by a `catch` block, then it must have the `finally` block.

9. When an exception occurs, an object of a specific exception class is created.

10. A `catch` block can catch either all exceptions of a specific type or all types of exceptions.

11. The heading of a `catch` block specifies the type of exception it handles.

12. The class `Throwable`, which is derived from the class `Object`, is the superclass of the class `Exception`.

13. The methods `getMessage`, `printStackTrace`, and `toString` of the class `Throwable` are `public` and so are inherited by the subclasses of the class `Throwable`.

14. The method `getMessage` returns the string containing the detailed message stored in the exception object.

15. The method `toString` (in `class Exception`) returns the detailed message stored in the exception object as well as the name of the exception class.

16. The `class Exception` and its subclasses are designed to catch exceptions that should be caught and processed during program execution, and thus make a program more robust.

17. The `class Exception` is the superclass of the classes designed to handle exceptions.

18. The `class Exception` is contained in the package `java.lang`.

19. The classes to deal with I/O exceptions, such as the file not found exception, are contained in the `package java.io`.

20. The `class InputMismatchException` is contained in the package `java.util`.

21. The classes to deal with number format exceptions and arithmetic exceptions, such as division by zero, are contained in the `package java.lang`.

22. Generally, exception classes are placed in the package that contains the methods that throw these exceptions.

23. Java's predefined exceptions are divided into two categories—checked exceptions and unchecked exceptions.

24. Any exception that can be recognized by the compiler is called a checked exception.

25. Unchecked exceptions are exceptions that are not recognized by the compiler.

26. Typically, a `catch` block does one of the following:
    - Completely handles the exception.
    - Partially processes the exception. In this case, the `catch` block either rethrows the same exception or throws another exception for the calling environment to handle the exception.
    - Rethrows the same exception for the calling environment to handle the exception.

27. The general syntax to rethrow an exception caught by a `catch` block is:
    `throw exceptionReference;`

28. The general syntax to throw your own exception object is:
    `throw new ExceptionClassName(messageString);`

29. The method `printStackTrace` is used to determine the order in which the methods were called and where the exception was handled.

30. The exception class that you define extends the `class Exception` or one of its subclasses.

31. Action events are handled by appropriately implementing the `interface ActionListener`.

32. Window events are handled by appropriately implementing the `interface` `WindowListener`.

33. The `class WindowAdapter` implements the `interface WindowListener` by providing empty bodies to the methods.

34. To register a window listener object to a GUI component, you use the method `addWindowListener`. The window listener object being registered is passed as a parameter to the method `addWindowListener`.

35. Mouse events are handled by appropriately implementing the `interface` `MouseListener`.

36. The `class MouseAdapter` implements the `interface MouseListener` by providing empty bodies to the methods.

37. To register a mouse listener object to a GUI component, you use the method `addMouseListener`. The mouse listener object being registered is passed as a parameter to the method `addMouseListener`.

38. Key events are handled by appropriately implementing the `interface` `KeyListener`.

EXERCISES

1. Mark the following statements as true or false.

   a. The block `finally` is always executed.

   b. Division by zero is a checked exception.

   c. File not found is an unchecked exception.

   d. Exceptions are thrown either in a `try` block in a method or from a method called directly or indirectly from a `try` block.

   e. The order in which `catch` blocks are listed is not important.

   f. An exception can be caught either in the method where it occurred or in any one of the methods that led to the invocation of this method.

   g. One way to handle an exception is to print an error message and exit the program.

   h. All exceptions must be reported to avoid compilation errors.

   i. An event handler is a method.

   j. A GUI component can generate only one type of event.

2. What is the difference between a `try` block and a `catch` block?

3. What will happen if an exception is thrown but not caught?

4. What happens if no exception is thrown in a `try` block?

5. What happens if an exception is thrown in a `try` block?

6. Suppose that `console` is a `Scanner` object initialized to the standard input device. Consider the following Java code:

```
double balance;

try
{
    System.out.print("Enter balance: ");
    balance = console.nextDouble();
    System.out.println();

    if (balance < 1000.00)
        throw new Exception("Balance must be greater than 1000.00");

    System.out.println("Leaving try block.");
}
catch (Exception obj)
{
    System.out.println("Balance must be greater than 1000.00");
}
```

a. In this code, identify the `try` block.

b. In this code, identify the `catch` block.

c. In this code, identify the `catch` block parameter and its type.

d. In this code, identify the `throw` statement.

7. Assume the code given in Exercise 6.

a. What is the output if the input is 1200?

b. What is the output if the input is 975?

c. What is the output if the input is -2000?

8. Consider the following Java code:

```
int lowerLimit;
...
try
{
    System.out.println("Entering the try block.");

    if (lowerLimit < 100)
        throw new Exception("Lower limit violation.");

    System.out.println("Exiting the try block.");
}
catch (Exception e)
{
    System.out.println("Exception: " + e.getMessage());
}

System.out.println("After the catch block");
```

What is the output if:

a. The value of `lowerLimit` is 50?

b. The value of `lowerLimit` is 150?

9. Consider the following Java code:

```java
int lowerLimit;
int divisor;
int result;

try
{
    System.out.println("Entering the try block.");

    result = lowerLimit / divisor;

    if (lowerLimit < 100)
        throw new Exception("Lower limit violation.");

    System.out.println("Exiting the try block.");
}
catch (ArithmeticException e)
{
    System.out.println("Exception: " + e.getMessage());

    result = 110;
}
catch (Exception e)
{
    System.out.println("Exception: " + e.getMessage());
}

System.out.println("After the catch block");
```

What is the output if:

a. The value of `lowerLimit` is 50 and the value of `divisor` is 10?

b. The value of `lowerLimit` is 50 and the value of `divisor` is 0?

c. The value of `lowerLimit` is 150 and the value of `divisor` is 10?

d. The value of `lowerLimit` is 150 and the value of `divisor` is 0?

10. Rewrite the Java code given in Exercise 9 so that the new equivalent code has exactly one `catch` block.

11. If you define your own exception class, what is typically included in that class?

12. What type of statement is used to rethrow an exception?

13. Correct any compile-time errors in the following code:

```java
import java.io.*;
import java.util.*;

public class SAverage
{
    public static void main(String[] args)
    {
        double test1, test2, test3, test4;
        double average;

        try
```

1
1

```
        {
            Scanner inFile = new
                Scaner(new FileReader("test.txt"));

            PrintWriter outFile =
                        new PrintWriter("testavg.out");

            test1 = inFile.nextDouble();
            test2 = inFile.nextDouble();
            test3 = inFile.nextDouble();
            test4 = inFile.nextDouble();

            outFile.printf("Test scores: %.2f %.2f %.2f %.2f %n",
                        test1, test2, test3, test4);

            average = (test1 + test2 + test3 + test4) / 4.0;
            outFile.println("Average test score: %.2f",
                        average);

            outFile.close();

        }
        catch (Exception e)
        {
            System.out.println(e.toString());
        }
        catch (FileNotFoundException e)
        {
            System.out.println(e.toString());
        }
    }
}
```

14. Define the exception **class** TornadoException. The class should have two constructors, including one default constructor. If the exception is thrown with the default constructor, the method getMessage should return:

    "Tornado! Take cover immediately!"

    The other constructor has a single parameter, say, m, of type **int**. If the exception is thrown with this constructor, the method getMessage should return:

    "Tornado m miles away and approaching!"

15. Write a Java program to test the **class** TornadoException specified in Exercise 14.

16. Suppose the exception **class** MyException is defined as follows:

```
public class MyException extends Exception
{
    public MyException()
    {
        super("MyException thrown!");

        System.out.println("Immediate attention required!");
    }
```

```
public MyException(String msg)
{
    super(msg);

    System.out.println("Attention required!");
}
}
```

What output will be produced if the exception is thrown with the default constructor? What output will be produced if the exception is thrown by the constructor with parameter with the actual parameter "May Day, May Day"?

17. If a method throws an exception, how does it specify that exception?

18. Name three exception handling techniques.

19. What are the three different ways you can implement an interface?

PROGRAMMING EXERCISES

1. Write a program that prompts the user to enter the length in feet and inches and outputs the equivalent length in inches and in centimeters. If the user enters a negative number or a nondigit number, throw and handle an appropriate exception and prompt the user to enter another set of numbers.

2. Redo the Text Processing programming example in Chapter 9 so that if the array index goes out of bounds when the program accesses the array `letterCount`, it throws and handles the `ArrayIndexOutOfBoundsException`.

3. Write a program that prompts the user to enter time in 12-hour notation. The program then outputs the time in 24-hour notation. Your program must contain three exception `class`es: `InvalidHrExcep`, `InvalidMinExcep`, and `InvalidSecExcep`. If the user enters an invalid value for hours, then the program should throw and catch an `InvalidHr` object. Similar conventions for the values of minutes and seconds.

4. Write a program that prompts the user to enter a person's date of birth in numeric form such as 8-27-1980. The program then outputs the date of birth in the form: August 27, 1980. Your program must contain at least two exception `class`es: `InvalidDayExcep` and `InvalidMonthExcep`. If the user enters an invalid value for day, then the program should throw and catch an `InvaliDayExcep` object. Similar conventions for the values of month and year. (Note that your program must handle a leap year.)

5. Redo Programming Exercise 7 of Chapter 8 so that your program handles exceptions such as division by zero.

6. Extend the Calculator programming example of this chapter by adding three buttons with the labels M, R, and E as follows: If the user clicks the button M, the number currently in the `displayText` field is stored in the variable, say, `memory`; if the user clicks the button R, the number stored in memory is displayed and also becomes the first number (so that another number can be

added, subtracted, multiplied, or divided); and if the user clicks the button E, the program terminates.

7. The Calculator programming example of this chapter is designed to perform operations on integers. Write a similar program that can be used to perform operations on decimal numbers. (*Note*: If division by zero occurs with values of the `int` data type, the program throws a division by zero exception. However, if you divide a decimal number by zero, Java does not throw the division by zero exception; it returns the answer as `infinity`. However, if division by zero occurs, your calculator program must output the message `ERROR: / by zero`.)

8. In Programming Exercise 2 in Chapter 8, we defined a `class Roman` to implement Roman numerals in a program. In that exercise, we also implemented the method `romanToDecimal` to convert a Roman numeral into its equivalent decimal number.

   a. Modify the definition of the `class Roman` so that the data members are declared as `protected`. Also include the method `decimalToRoman`, which converts the decimal number (the decimal number must be a positive integer) to an equivalent Roman numeral format. Write the definition of the method `decimalToRoman`. Your definition of the `class Roman` must contain the method `toString`, which returns the string containing the number in Roman format. For simplicity, we assume that only the letter `I` can appear in front of another letter and that it appears only in front of the letters `V` and `X`. For example, 4 is represented as `IV`, 9 is represented as `IX`, 39 is represented as `XXXIX`, and 49 is represented as `XXXXIX`. Also, 40 is represented as `XXXX`, 190 is represented as `CLXXXX`, and so on.

   b. Derive the `class ExtendedRoman` from the `class Roman` to do the following. In the `class ExtendedRoman`, include the methods `add`, `subtract`, `multiply`, and `divide` so that arithmetic operations can be performed on Roman numerals.

   To add (subtract, multiply, or divide) Roman numerals, add (subtract, multiply, or divide, respectively) their decimal representations and then convert the result to the Roman numeral format. For subtraction, if the first number is smaller than the second number, throw the exception, "`Because the first number is smaller than the second, the numbers cannot be subtracted`". Similarly, for division, the numerator must be larger than the denominator.

   c. Write the definitions of the methods `add`, `subtract`, `multiply`, and `divide` as described in Part b. Also, your definition of the `class ExtendedRoman` must contain the method `toString` that returns the string containing the number in Roman format.

   d. Write a program to test various operations on your `class ExtendedRoman`.

ADVANCED GUIS AND GRAPHICS

IN THIS CHAPTER, YOU WILL:

- Learn about applets
- Explore the **class** Graphics
- Learn about the **class** Font
- Explore the **class** Color
- Learn how to use additional Layout managers
- Become familiar with more GUI components
- Learn how to create menu-based programs
- Learn how to handle key and mouse events

There are two types of Java programs—applications and applets. Up to this point, we have created only application programs. Even the programs we've created that use GUI components are application programs. Java **applets** are small applications that can be embedded in an HTML page. In this chapter, you will learn how to create an applet. You will also learn how to convert a GUI application to a Java applet. This chapter also shows you how to use fonts, colors, and geometric shapes to enhance the output of your programs.

In Chapter 6, you learned how to use GUI components, such as `JFrame`, `JLabel`, `JTextField`, and `JButton`, to make your programs attractive and user-friendly. In this chapter, you will learn about other commonly used GUI components. The `class` `JComponent` is the superclass of the classes used to create various GUI components. Figure 12-1 shows the inheritance hierarchy of the GUI classes that you have used in previous chapters, plus the ones you will encounter in this chapter. The package containing the definition of a particular class is also shown.

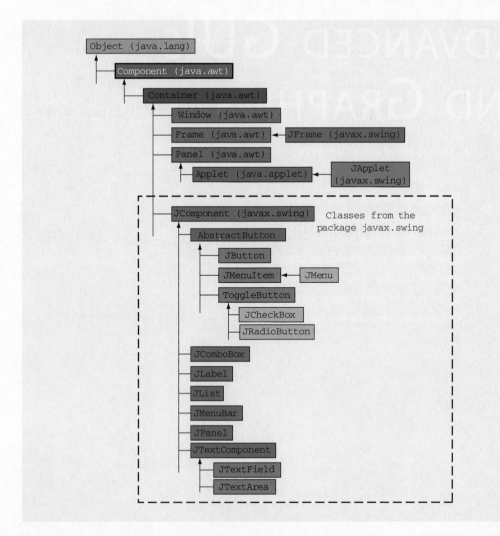

FIGURE 12-1 Inheritance hierarchy of GUI classes (classes shown in the dotted rectangle are from the `package` `javax.swing`)

As shown in Figure 12-1, the `class` `Container`, which is a subclass of the `class` `Component`, is the superclass of all the classes designed to provide GUIs—and, therefore, all `public` members of these classes are inherited by their subclasses. Moreover, both the `Container` and `Component` classes are `abstract`.

The `class` `Component` contains many methods that are inherited by its subclasses. You have used methods such as `setSize` and `setLocation` in various GUI programs. Table 12-1 describes some of the constructors and methods of the `class` `Component`.

TABLE 12-1 Constructors and Methods of the `class` `Component`

```
protected Component()
   //Constructor
   //Creates a new instance of a component.
```

```
public void addComponentListener(ComponentListener lis)
   //Adds the component listener specified by lis.
```

```
public void addFocusListener(FocusListener lis)
   //Adds the focus listener specified by lis.
```

```
public void addKeyListener(KeyListener lis)
   //Adds the key listener specified by lis.
```

```
public void addMouseListener(MouseListener lis)
   //Adds the mouse listener specified by lis.
```

```
public void addMouseMotionListener(MouseMotionListener lis)
   //Adds the mouse motion listener specified by lis.
```

```
public void removeComponentListener(ComponentListener lis)
   //Removes the component listener specified by lis.
```

```
public void removeKeyListener(KeyListener lis)
   //Removes the key listener specified by lis.
```

```
public void removeMouseListener(MouseListener lis)
   //Removes the mouse listener specified by lis.
```

```
public void removeMouseMotionListener(MouseMotionListener lis)
   //Removes the mouse motion listener specified by lis.
```

```
public Color getBackground()
   //Returns the background color of this component.
```

```
public Color getForeground()
   //Returns the foreground color of this component.
```

```
public void setBackground(Color c)
   //Sets the background color of this component to color c.
```

1
2

TABLE 12-1 Constructors and Methods of the **class** Component (continued)

```
public void setForeground(Color c)
  //Sets the foreground color of this component to color c.
```

```
public Font getFont()
  //Returns the font of this component.
```

```
public void setFont(Font ft)
  //Sets the font of this component to ft.
```

```
public void setSize(int w, int h)
  //Sets the size of this component to width w and height h
```

```
public boolean isVisible()
  //Returns true if the component is visible; false otherwise.
```

```
public void setVisible(boolean tog)
  //If tog is true, sets the component to visible;
  //if tog is false, the component is not shown.
```

```
public void paint(Graphics g)
  //Paints the component with the graphic component specified by g.
```

```
public void repaint()
  //Repaints the component.
```

```
public void repaint(int x, int y, int wid, int ht)
  //Repaints the rectangular portion of the component from (x, y)
  //to (x + wid, y + ht)
```

```
public void setLocation(int x, int y)
  //Sets the component at the location (x, y).
```

```
public String toString()
  //Returns a string representation of this component.
```

```
public void update(Graphics g)
  //Invokes the paint method.
```

```
public void validate()
  //Validates this container and all of its subcomponents; the
  //method validate is used to cause a container to lay out its
  //subcomponents once more. Typically called after the components
  //it contains have been added to or modified.
```

The **class** Container inherits all the methods of the **class** Component. In addition to the methods listed in Table 12-1, Table 12-2 shows some commonly used methods of the **class** Container.

TABLE 12-2 Methods of the **class** Container

```
public Component add(Component comp)
   //Appends the specified component to the end of this container.
```

```
public Component add(Component comp, int index)
   //Adds the specified component to this container at the
   //position specified by index.
```

```
public void paint(Graphics g)
   //Paints the container with the graphics component specified by g.
```

```
public void update(Graphics g)
   //Invokes the paint method.
```

```
public void validate()
   //Validates this container and all of its subcomponents. The
   //method validate is used to cause a container to lay out its
   //subcomponents once more. Typically called after the components
   //it contains have been added to or modified.
```

In the remainder of this chapter, whenever we list the methods of a class, we will not show the methods that are inherited from the **class**es Component and Container.

Next, we discuss how to create a Java applet. For the most part, the programs in this chapter are Java applets.

Applets

The term *applet* refers to a little application. In Java, an **applet** is a Java program that is embedded within an HTML document and executed by a Web browser. You create an applet by extending the **class** JApplet, which is contained in the **package** javax.swing.

Table 12-3 describes some commonly used methods of the **class** JApplet.

TABLE 12-3 Some Members of the **class** JApplet (**package** javax.swing)

```
public void init()
   //Called by the browser or applet viewer to inform this applet
   //that it has been loaded into the system.
```

```
public void start()
   //Called by the browser or applet viewer to inform this applet
   //that it should start its execution. It is called after the init
   //method and each time the applet is revisited in a Web page.
```

```
public void stop()
   //Called by the browser or applet viewer to inform this applet
   //that it should stop its execution. It is called before the
   //method destroy.
```

1
2

TABLE 12-3 Some Members of the **class** JApplet (**package** javax.swing) (continued)

```
public void destroy()
   //Called by the browser or applet viewer. Informs this applet that
   //it is being reclaimed and that it should destroy any resources
   //that it has allocated. The method stop is called before destroy.
```

```
public void showStatus(String msg)
   //Displays the string msg in the status bar.
```

```
public Container getContentPane()
   //Returns the ContentPane object for this applet.
```

```
public JMenuBar getJMenuBar()
   //Returns the JMenuBar object for this applet.
```

```
public URL getDocumentBase()
   //Returns the URL of the document that contains this applet.
```

```
public URL getCodeBase()
   //Returns the URL of this applet.
```

```
public void update(Graphics g)
   //Calls the paint() method.
```

```
protected String paramString()
   //Returns a string representation of this JApplet; mainly used
   //for debugging.
```

Unlike Java application programs, Java applets do not have the method main. Instead, when a browser runs an applet, the methods init, start, and paint are guaranteed to be invoked in sequence. Therefore, as a programmer, to develop an applet, all you have to do is override one or all of the methods init, start, and paint. Of these three methods, the paint method has one argument, which is a Graphics object. This allows you to use the **class** Graphics without actually creating a Graphics object. Later in this chapter, when the **class** Graphics is presented in detail, you will notice that it is an **abstract** class; therefore, you cannot create an instance of this class. For now, all you need to do is import the **package** java.awt so that you can use various methods of the **class** Graphics in the paint method. To do so, you need the following two import statements:

```
import java.awt.Graphics;
import javax.swing.JApplet;
```

Because you create an applet by extending the **class** JApplet, a Java applet in skeleton form looks something like this:

```
import java.awt.Graphics;
import javax.swing.JApplet;

public class WelcomeApplet extends JApplet
{

}
```

As a general rule, you keep all statements to be executed only once in the `init` method. The `paint` method is used to draw various items, including strings, in the content pane of the applet. Thus, in the applets presented in this chapter, we use `init` to:

- Initialize variables
- Get data from the user
- Place various GUI components

The `paint` method is used to create the output. The `init` and `paint` methods need to share common data items, so these items are the data members of the applet.

Let's now create an applet that will display a welcome message. Because no initialization is required, all you need to do is override the method `paint` so that it draws the welcome message. Sometimes when you override a method, it is a good idea to invoke the corresponding method of the parent `class`. Whenever you override the `paint` method, the first Java statement is:

```
super.paint(g);
```

where g is a `Graphics` object. Recall that `super` is a reserved word in Java and refers to the instance of the parent class.

To display the string containing the welcome message, we use the method `drawString` of the `class` `Graphics`. The method `drawString` is an overloaded method. One of the headings of the method `drawString` is:

```
public abstract void drawString(String str, int x, int y)
```

The method `drawString` displays the string specified by `str` at the horizontal position x pixels away from the upper-left corner of the applet, and the vertical position y pixels away from the upper-left corner of the applet. In other words, the applet has an x-y coordinate system, with x = 0, y = 0 at the upper-left corner; the x value increases from left to right and the y value increases from top to bottom. Thus, the method `drawString`, as given previously, draws the string `str` starting at the position (x, y).

The following Java applet displays a welcome message:

```
//Welcome Applet

import java.awt.Graphics;
import javax.swing.JApplet;

public class WelcomeApplet extends JApplet
{
    public void paint(Graphics g)
    {
        super.paint(g);                                    //Line 1

        g.drawString("Welcome to Java Programming",
                30, 30);                                   //Line 2
    }
}
```

In the preceding applet, the statement in Line 1 invokes the `paint` method of the **class** `JApplet`. Notice that the method `paint` uses a `Graphics` object `g` as the argument. Recall that the **class** `Graphics` is an **abstract** class, and for this reason, you cannot create an instance of the **class** `Graphics`. The system will create a `Graphics` object for you; you need not be concerned about it. The statement in Line 2 draws the string `"Welcome to Java Programming"` at the coordinate position (30, 30).

Until now, when we created a GUI application program, we used methods such as `setTitle` and `setSize`. As you can see in the preceding applet, such methods are not used in an applet. Note the following about applets:

- The method `setTitle` is not used in applets because applets do not have titles. An applet is embedded in an HTML document, and the applet itself does not have a title. The HTML document may have a title, which is set by the document.

- The method `setSize` is not used in applets because the applet's size is determined in the HTML document, not by the applet. You do not need to set the size of the applet.

- You do not need to invoke the method `setVisible`.

- You do not need to close the applet. When the HTML document containing the applet is closed, the applet is destroyed.

- There is no method `main`.

As with an application, you compile an applet and produce a `.class` file. Once the `.class` file is created, you need to place it in a Web page to run the applet. For example, you can create a file with the `.html` extension, say, `WelcomeApplet.html`, with the following lines in the same folder where the `WelcomeApplet.class` file resides:

```
<HTML>
  <HEAD>
    <TITLE>WELCOME APPLET</TITLE>
  </HEAD>
  <BODY>
    <OBJECT code = "WelcomeApplet.class" width = "250"
                                         height = "60">
    </OBJECT>
  </BODY>
</HTML>
```

Once the HTML file is created, you can run your applet either by opening `WelcomeApplet.html` with a Web browser, or you can enter:

```
appletviewer WelcomeApplet.html
```

at a command-line prompt, if you are using the JDK (Java Development Kit).

Sample Run: Figure 12-2 shows the output of the `WelcomeApplet` produced by the Applet Viewer in Windows 7 Professional.

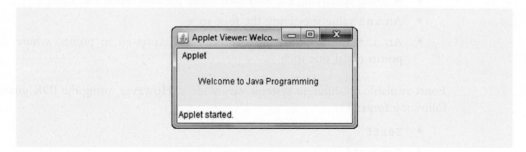

FIGURE 12-2 Output of the `WelcomeApplet`

You terminate the applet by clicking the close button in the upper-right corner of the Applet Viewer, or by closing the HTML document in which the applet is embedded.

Two ways to make your applets more attractive are to vary the type font and color. Next, we introduce the `class`es `Font` and `Color`, contained in the `package java.awt`.

class Font

The GUI programs we have created so far have used only the default font. To show text in different fonts when the program executes, Java provides the `class Font`. The `class Font` is contained in the `package java.awt`, so you need to use the following `import` statement in your program:

```
import java.awt.*;
```

The `class Font` contains various constructors, methods, and constants, some of which are described in Table 12-4.

TABLE 12-4 Some Constructors and Methods of the `class Font`

```
public Font(String name, int style, int size)
  //Constructor
  //Creates a new Font from the specified name, style, and point
  //size.

public String getFamily()
  //Returns the family name of this Font.

public String getFontName()
  //Returns the font face name of this Font.
```

1
2

Typically, you use only the constructor of the **class** Font. As shown in Table 12-4, the constructor of the **class** Font takes the following three arguments:

- A string specifying the font face name (or font name for short)
- An **int** value specifying the font style
- An **int** value specifying the font size expressed in points, where 72 points equal one inch

Fonts available on different systems vary widely. However, using the JDK guarantees the following fonts:

- Serif
- SanSerif
- Monospaced
- Dialog
- DialogInput

If you want to know which fonts are available on your system, you can run the program given next. (This program uses a graphics environment, which is covered later in this chapter.)

```java
import java.awt.*;

public class FontNames
{
    public static void main(String[] args)
    {
        String[] listOfFontNames =
            GraphicsEnvironment.getLocalGraphicsEnvironment()
                    .getAvailableFontFamilyNames();

        for (int i = 0; i < listOfFontNames.length; i++)
            System.out.println(listOfFontNames[i]);
    }
}
```

The **class** Font contains the constants Font.PLAIN, Font.ITALIC, and Font.BOLD, which you can apply to change the style of a font. For example, the Java statement:

new Font("Serif", Font.ITALIC, 12)

creates a 12-point Serif italic font. Likewise, the statement:

new Font("Dialog", Font.ITALIC + Font.BOLD, 36)

creates a 36-point Dialog italic and bold font.

The applet given in Example 12-1 illustrates how to change fonts in text.

EXAMPLE 12-1

```
//FontsDisplayed Applet

import java.awt.*;
import javax.swing.JApplet;

public class FontsDisplayed extends JApplet
{
    public void paint(Graphics g)
    {
        super.paint(g);

        g.setFont(new Font("Courier", Font.BOLD, 24));
        g.drawString("Courier bold 24pt font", 30, 36);

        g.setFont(new Font("Arial", Font.PLAIN, 30));
        g.drawString("Arial plain 30pt font", 30, 70);

        g.setFont(new Font("Dialog", Font.BOLD + Font.ITALIC,
                           36));
        g.drawString("Dialog italic bold 36pt font", 30, 110);

        g.setFont(new Font("Serif", Font.ITALIC, 30));
        g.drawString("Serif italic 42pt font", 30, 156);
    }
}
```

The HTML file that invokes this applet contains the following code:

```
<HTML>
  <HEAD>
    <TITLE>Four Fonts</TITLE>
  </HEAD>
  <BODY>
    <OBJECT code = "FontsDisplayed.class" width = "500"
                                          height = "190">
    </OBJECT>
  </BODY>
</HTML>
```

Sample Run: Figure 12-3 shows the output of the FontsDisplayed applet in Applet Viewer.

FIGURE 12-3 Output of the `FontsDisplayed` applet

class Color

So far, we have used only the default colors in our GUI programs. For example, the text always appeared as black. You may want to show the text in different colors or change the background color of a component. Java provides the **class** Color to accomplish this. The **class** Color is contained in the **package** java.awt, so you need to use the **import** statement:

```
import java.awt.*;
```

Table 12-5 shows various constructors and methods of the **class** Color.

TABLE 12-5 Some Constructors and Methods of the **class** Color

```
Color(int r, int g, int b)
   //Constructor
   //Creates a Color object with the red value r, green value g,
   //and blue value b. In this case, r, g, and b can be
   //between 0 and 255.
   //Example: new  Color(0, 255, 0)
   //        creates a color with no red or blue component.
```

```
Color(int rgb)
   //Constructor
   //Creates a Color object with the red value r, green value g,
   //and blue value b; RGB value consisting of the red component
   //in bits 16-23, the green component in bits 8-15, and the
   //blue component in bits 0-7.
   //Example: new  Color(255)
   //        creates a color with no red or green component.
```

TABLE 12-5 Some Constructors and Methods of the **class** Color (continued)

```
Color(float r, float g, float b)
  //Constructor
  //Creates a Color object with the red value r, green value g,
  //and blue value b. In this case, r, g, and b can be between 0
  //and 1.0.
  //Example: new  Color(1.0, 0, 0)
  //         creates a color with no green or blue component.
```

```
public Color brighter()
  //Returns a Color that is brighter.
```

```
public Color darker()
  //Returns a Color that is darker.
```

```
public boolean equals(Object o)
  //Returns true if the color of this object is the same as the
  //color of the object o; false otherwise.
```

```
public int getBlue()
  //Returns the value of the blue component.
```

```
public int getGreen()
  //Returns the value of the green component.
```

```
public int getRed()
  //Returns the value of the red component.
```

```
public int getRGB()
  //Returns the RGB value.
```

```
public String toString()
  //Returns a string with the information about the color.
```

You can use the methods `setBackground` and `setForeground`, described in Table 12-1, to set the background and foreground color of a component.

Java uses the color scheme known as RGB, where R stands for red, G for green, and B for blue, respectively. You create instances of `Color` by mixing red, green, and blue hues in various proportions. The **class** `Color` contains three constructors, as shown in Table 12-5. In the first constructor, an RGB value is represented as three `int` values. The second constructor specifies an RGB value as a single integer. In either form, the closer an r, g, or b value is to 255, the more hue is mixed into the color. For example, if you use the first constructor, pure red is produced by mixing red 255, green 0, and blue 0 parts each. To produce the color red, you use the first constructor as follows:

```
Color redColor = new Color(255, 0, 0);
```

Various tones of black, white, and gray can be created by mixing all three colors in the same proportion. For example, the color white has the RGB values 255, 255, 255, and black has the RGB values 0, 0, 0. An RGB value of 100, 100, 100 creates a gray color darker than one with an RGB value of 200, 200, 200.

In addition to the methods shown in Table 12-5, the **class** Color defines a number of standard colors as constants. Table 12-6 shows the color name in bold and its values for easy reference.

TABLE 12-6 Constants Defined in the **class** Color

Color.**black**: (0, 0, 0)	Color.**magenta**: (255, 0, 255)
Color.**blue**: (0, 0, 255)	Color.**orange**: (255, 200, 0)
Color.**cyan**: (0, 255, 255)	Color.**pink**: (255, 175, 175)
Color.**darkGray**: (64, 64, 64)	Color.**red**: (255, 0, 0)
Color.**gray**: (128, 128, 128)	Color.**white**: (255, 255, 255)
Color.**green**: (0, 255, 0)	Color.**yellow**: (255, 255, 0)
Color.**lightGray**: (192, 192, 192)	

A simple applet to illustrate the use of the **class** Color is given in Example 12-2. In this example, we use the **class** GridLayout, described in Chapter 6, to place the GUI components. Recall that GridLayout divides the container into a grid of rows and columns, allowing you to place the components in rows and columns. Every component placed in a GridLayout will have the same width and height. The components are placed from left to right in the first row, followed by left to right in the second row, and so on.

The **class** GridLayout is contained in the **package** java.awt. Most often, we use the following constructor of the **class** GridLayout:

GridLayout(**int** row, **int** col)

where row specifies the number of rows and col specifies the number of columns in the grid, respectively. For example, to create a grid with 10 rows and 5 columns, and set it as the layout of the container c, you use the following Java statement:

c.setLayout(**new** GridLayout(10, 5));

In our next applet, we use a grid with 2 rows and 2 columns. Therefore, we use the statement:

c.setLayout(**new** GridLayout(2, 2));

Example 12-2 uses the method random of the **class** Math that returns a random value between 0 and 1. For example, the statement:

Math.random();

returns a random `double` value between 0 and 1. Note that the third constructor of the Color class (see Table 12-5) takes three `float` values, each between 0 and 1, as parameters. Therefore, we use the explicit cast operator `(float)` to convert the `double` value returned by the `random` method. Thus, we use the following statements to randomly generate a value for the colors red, green, and blue:

```
red = (float) Math.random();
green = (float) Math.random();
blue = (float) Math.random();
```

These statements assign random `float` values between 0 and 1 to the `float` variables red, green, and blue. Suppose that `bottomrightJL` is a `JLabel`. The statement:

```
bottomrightJL.setForeground(new Color(red, green, blue));
```

creates a color and assigns it as the foreground color of the label `bottomrightJL`.

EXAMPLE 12-2

This example gives the complete program listing and a sample run that shows how to set the colors of a text and GUI components.

```
//ColorsDisplayed Applet

import java.awt.*;
import javax.swing.*;

public class ColorsDisplayed extends JApplet
{
    JLabel topleftJL, toprightJL, bottomleftJL, bottomrightJL;

    int i;
    float red, green, blue;

    public void init()
    {
        Container c = getContentPane();

        c.setLayout(new GridLayout(2, 2));
        c.setBackground(Color.white);

        topleftJL = new JLabel("Red", SwingConstants.CENTER);
        toprightJL = new JLabel("Green", SwingConstants.CENTER);
        bottomleftJL = new JLabel("Blue",
                                SwingConstants.CENTER);
        bottomrightJL = new JLabel("Random",
                                SwingConstants.CENTER);

        topleftJL.setForeground(Color.red);
        toprightJL.setForeground(Color.green);
        bottomleftJL.setForeground(Color.blue);
```

1
2

```
    red = (float) Math.random();
    green = (float) Math.random();
    blue = (float) Math.random();
    bottomrightJL.setForeground(new Color(red, green, blue));

    c.add(topleftJL);
    c.add(toprightJL);
    c.add(bottomleftJL);
    c.add(bottomrightJL);
  }
}
```

The HTML file that invokes this applet contains the following code:

```
<HTML>
  <HEAD>
    <TITLE>Four Colors</TITLE>
  </HEAD>
  <BODY>
    <OBJECT code = "ColorsDisplayed.class" width = "400"
                                           height = "200">

    </OBJECT>
  </BODY>
</HTML>
```

Sample Run: Figure 12-4 shows the output of the `ColorsDisplayed` applet.

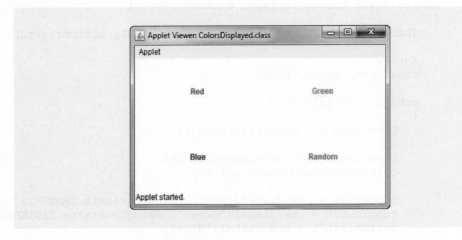

FIGURE 12-4 Output of the `ColorsDisplayed` applet

You can use both the **class** Font and the **class** Color to enhance your presentation of an applet. For example, consider the `GrandWelcome` applet given in Example 12-3, which shows the complete program listing followed by a sample run.

EXAMPLE 12-3

```java
//GrandWelcome Applet

import java.awt.*;
import javax.swing.JApplet;

public class GrandWelcome extends JApplet
{
    public void paint(Graphics g)
    {
        super.paint(g);

        g.setColor(Color.red);
        g.setFont(new Font("Courier", Font.BOLD, 24));
        g.drawString("Welcome to Java Programming", 30, 30);
    }
}
```

The HTML file for this program contains the following code:

```html
<HTML>
  <HEAD>
    <TITLE>WELCOME</TITLE>
  </HEAD>
  <BODY>
    <OBJECT code = "GrandWelcome.class" width = "440"
                                        height = "50">
    </OBJECT>
  </BODY>
</HTML>
```

Sample Run: Figure 12-5 shows the output of the GrandWelcome applet.

FIGURE 12-5 Output of the GrandWelcome applet

class Graphics

This section presents a glimpse of the **class** Graphics, which is contained in the **package** java.awt. The **class** Graphics provides methods for drawing items such as lines, ovals, and rectangles on the screen. Some methods of the **class** Graphics draw shapes; others draw bitmap images. This class also contains methods to set the properties of graphic elements including fonts and colors. Table 12-7 shows some of the constructors and methods of the **class** Graphics.

TABLE 12-7   Some Constructors and Methods of the **class** Graphics

```
protected Graphics()
  //Constructs a Graphics object that defines a context in which the
  //user can draw. This constructor cannot be called directly.
```

```
public void draw3DRect(int x, int y, int w, int h, boolean t)
  //Draws a 3D rectangle at (x, y) of the width w and height h. If t is
  //true, the rectangle will appear raised.
```

```
public abstract void drawArc(int x, int y, int w, int h,
                             int sangle, int aangle)
  //Draws an arc in the rectangle at the position (x, y) of width w
  //and height h. The arc starts at the angle sangle with an arc angle
  //aangle. Both angles are measured in degrees.
```

```
public abstract boolean drawImage(Image img, int xs1, int ys1,
                  int xs2, int ys2, int xd1, int yd1,
                  int xd2, int yd2, Color c, ImageObserver ob)
  //Draws the image specified by img from the area defined by the
  //bounding rectangle, (xs1, ys1) to (xs2, ys2), in the area defined
  //by the rectangle (xd1, yd1) to (xd2, yd2). Any transparent color
  //pixels are drawn in the color c. The ob monitors the progress of
  //the image.
```

```
public abstract void drawLine(int xs, int ys, int xd, int yd)
  //Draws a line from (xs, ys) to (xd, yd).
```

```
public abstract void drawOval(int x, int y, int w, int h)
  //Draws an oval at the position (x, y) of width w and height h.
```

```
public abstract void drawPolygon(int[] x, int[] y, int num)
  //Draws a polygon with the points (x[0], y[0]), ...,
  //(x[num - 1], y[num - 1]). Here num is the number of points in
  //the polygon.
```

```
public abstract void drawPolygon(Polygon poly)
  //Draws a polygon as defined by the object poly.
```

```
public abstract void drawRect(int x, int y, int w, int h)
  //Draws a rectangle at the position (x, y) of width w and
  //height h.
```

TABLE 12-7 Some Constructors and Methods of the **class** Graphics (continued)

public abstract void **drawRoundRect**(int x, int y, int w, int h,
                                    int arcw, int arch)
  //Draws a round-cornered rectangle at the position (x, y) having a
  //width w and height h. The shape of the rounded corners is
  //determined by the arc with the width arcw and the height arch.

public abstract void **drawString**(String s, int x, int y)
  //Draws the string s at (x, y).

public void **fill3DRect**(int x, int y, int w, int h, boolean t)
  //Draws a 3D filled rectangle at (x, y) of width w height h.
  //If t is true, the rectangle will appear raised. The rectangle is
  //filled with the current color.

public abstract void **fillArc**(int x, int y, int w, int h,
                               int sangle, int aangle)
  //Draws a filled arc in the rectangle at the position (x, y) of
  //width w and height h starting at angle sangle with the arc
  //angle aangle. Both angles are measured in degrees. The arc is
  //filled with the current color.

public abstract void **fillOval**(int x, int y, int w, int h)
  //Draws a filled oval at the position (x, y) having a width w and
  //height h. The oval is filled with the current color.

public abstract void **fillPolygon**(int[] x, int[] y, int num)
  //Draws a filled polygon with the points (x[0], y[0]), ...,
  //(x[num - 1], y[num - 1]). Here num is the number of points in
  //the polygon. The polygon is filled with the current color.

public abstract void **fillPolygon**(Polygon poly)
  //Draws a filled polygon as defined by the object poly. The polygon
  //is filled with the current color.

public abstract void **fillRect**(int x, int y, int w, int h)
  //Draws a filled rectangle at the position (x, y) of width w
  //and height h. The rectangle is filled with the current color.

public abstract void **fillRoundRect**(int x, int y, int w, int h,
                                     int arcw, int arch)
  //Draws a filled, round-cornered rectangle at the position (x, y)
  //of width w and height h. The shape of the rounded corners
  //is determined by the arc with the width arcw and the height arch.
  //The rectangle is filled with the current color.

public abstract Color **getColor**()
  //Returns the current color for this graphics context.

public abstract void **setColor**(Color c)
  //Sets the current color for this graphics context to c.

1
2

TABLE 12-7 Some Constructors and Methods of the **class** Graphics (continued)

public abstract Font **getFont**() //Returns the current font for this graphics context.
public abstract void **setFont**(Font f) //Sets the current font for this graphics context to f.
public void String **toString**() //Returns a string representation of this graphics context.

Before drawing in Java, let us first explain Java's coordinate system, which is used to identify every point on the screen. The coordinates of the upper-left corner of a GUI component, such as the content pane, are (0, 0); this point is called the **origin**. Every coordinate pair has an x-coordinate and a y-coordinate. The x-coordinate specifies the horizontal position, moving from left to right relative to the origin; the y-coordinate specifies the vertical position, moving from top to bottom relative to the origin. The x-axis specifies every x-coordinate and the y-axis specifies every y-coordinate. Figure 12-6 illustrates Java's coordinate system.

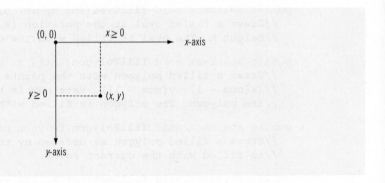

FIGURE 12-6 Java's coordinate system

You have already used the drawString method to output a string. Other draw methods are used in a similar manner. For example, to draw a line from (10, 10) to (10, 40), you use the method drawLine as follows:

```
g.drawLine(10, 10, 10, 40);     //left line
```

where g is a Graphics object.

Let us draw three more lines, so that our welcome message is inside a box.

```
g.drawLine(10, 40, 430, 40);    //bottom line
g.drawLine(430, 40, 430, 10);   //right line
g.drawLine(430, 10, 10, 10);    //top line
```

Placing these lines in our GrandWelcome applet of Example 12-3 gives us the program shown in Example 12-4.

EXAMPLE 12-4

```
//GrandWelcomeLine Applet

import java.awt.*;
import javax.swing.JApplet;

public class GrandWelcomeLine extends JApplet
{
    public void paint( Graphics g)
    {
        super.paint(g);

        g.setColor(Color.red);

        g.setFont(new Font("Courier", Font.BOLD, 24));
        g.drawString("Welcome to Java Programming", 30, 30);

        g.drawLine(10, 10, 10, 40);      //left line
        g.drawLine(10, 40, 430, 40);     //bottom line
        g.drawLine(430, 40, 430, 10);    //right line
        g.drawLine(430, 10, 10, 10);     //top line
    }
}
```

The HTML file for this program contains the following code:

```
<HTML>
  <HEAD>
    <TITLE>WELCOME</TITLE>
  </HEAD>
  <BODY>
    <OBJECT code = "GrandWelcomeLine.class" width = "440"
                                            height = "50">
    </OBJECT>
  </BODY>
</HTML>
```

Sample Run: Figure 12-7 shows the output of the GrandWelcomeLine applet.

FIGURE 12-7 Output of the GrandWelcomeLine applet

In the applet of Example 12-4, you could have used the method `drawRect` to draw a rectangle rather than four lines. In that case, you could use the following statement:

```
g.drawRect(10, 10, 430, 40);    //draw rectangle
```

The program in Example 12-5 further illustrates how to use various methods of the `Graphics class`. In this example, we create a random collection of geometric shapes. The program uses the method `random` of the `class` `Math` to randomly determine the number of figures. We want to have at least 5 and at most 14 figures. Therefore, we declare an `int` variable and initialize it as follows:

```
int numOfFigures;

numOfFigures = 5 + (int)(Math.random() * 10); //determine the
                                              //number of figures
```

For each figure, we want a random color, random anchor point, random width, and random height. Further, we want a random shape from a set of possible options. This applies to all figures. Therefore, we need to have a loop similar to the following:

```
for (i = 0; i < numOfFigures; i++)
{
    //...
}
```

Inside the preceding loop, we determine a random color. We can use the method `random` of the `class` `Math` to get red, green, and blue values between 0 and 255 and use them to create a random color. Therefore, we need the following statements (assume that g is a reference variable of the `Graphics` type):

```
int red;
int green;
int blue;

red = (int)(Math.random() * 256);    //red component
green = (int)(Math.random() * 256);  //green component
blue = (int)(Math.random() * 256);   //blue component

g.setColor(new Color(red, green, blue));  //color for
                                          //this figure
```

We also need to compute four more values for `x`, `y`, and the width and height between, say, 0 and 200. Furthermore, to make the program easier to modify, we use the named constant `SIZE`, initialized to 200. Thus, we need the following Java statements:

```
private final int SIZE = 200;
int x;
int y;
int width;
int height;
int red;
```

```
x = (int)(Math.random() * SIZE);        //x value
y = (int)(Math.random() * SIZE);        //y value
width = (int)(Math.random() * SIZE);    //width
height = (int)(Math.random() * SIZE);   //height
```

Now all that is left is to randomly select a shape among, say, rectangle, filled rectangle, oval, and filled oval. So let's assign the values:

- 0 for rectangle
- 1 for filled rectangle
- 2 for oval
- 3 for filled oval

A `switch` statement can be used to invoke the appropriate method, as shown in the following:

```
shape = (int)(Math.random() * 4);

switch (shape)
{
case 0 :
    g.drawRect(x, y, width, height);
    break;

case 1 :
    g.fillRect(x, y, width, height);
    break;

case 2 :
    g.drawOval(x, y, width, height);
    break;

case 3 :
    g.fillOval(x, y, width, height);
    break;
}
```

Putting it all together, we have the Java applet shown in Example 12-5.

EXAMPLE 12-5

```
//Java applet to draw ovals and rectangles

import java.awt.*;
import javax.swing.*;

public class OvalRectApplet extends JApplet
{
    private final int SIZE = 200;
```

```java
public void paint(Graphics g)
{
    int shape;
    int numOfFigures;
    int x;
    int y;
    int width;
    int height;
    int red;
    int green;
    int blue;

    int i;

            //determine the number of figures
    numOfFigures = 5 + (int)(Math.random() * 10);

    for (i = 0; i < numOfFigures; i++)
    {
        red = (int)(Math.random() * 256);   //red component
        green = (int)(Math.random() * 256);//green component
        blue = (int)(Math.random() * 256); //blue component

        g.setColor(new Color(red, green, blue)); //color for
                                                 //this figure

        x = (int)(Math.random() * SIZE);      //x value
        y = (int)(Math.random() * SIZE);      //y value
        width = (int)(Math.random() * SIZE);  //width
        height = (int)(Math.random() * SIZE); //height

        shape = (int)(Math.random() * 4);

        /**
         *    0 : Rectangle
         *    1 : Filled Rectangle
         *    2 : Oval
         *    3 : Filled Oval
         *
         **/

        switch (shape)
        {
        case 0:
            g.drawRect(x, y, width, height);
            break;

        case 1:
            g.fillRect(x, y, width, height);
            break;
```

```
            case 2:
                g.drawOval(x, y, width, height);
                break;

            case 3:
                g.fillOval(x, y, width, height);
        }//end switch
    }//end for
    }
}
```

The HTML file for this program contains the following code:

```
<HTML>
  <HEAD>
    <TITLE>WELCOME APPLET</TITLE>
  </HEAD>
  <BODY>
    <OBJECT code = "OvalRectApplet.class" width = "400"
                                          height = "300">
    </OBJECT>
  </BODY>
</HTML>
```

Sample Run: Figure 12-8 shows a sample run of `OvalRectApplet`.

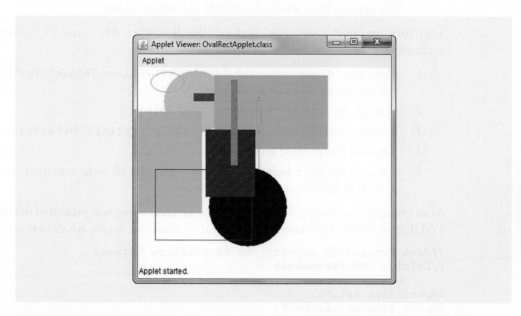

FIGURE 12-8   Sample Run of `OvalRectApplet`

Note that in this sample run, a figure drawn later has visual priority over a figure drawn earlier.

Converting an Application Program to an Applet

At this point, you might wonder whether there is a simple scheme to convert GUI applications to applets. An applet class shares many features of a GUI application. The main differences are:

- An applet class is derived from the **class** JApplet, whereas a GUI application class is created by extending the **class** JFrame.

- Applets do not have the method main. Instead, an applet invokes the init, start, paint, stop, and destroy methods in sequence. Quite often, you place the initialization code in init and the output is produced by the method paint.

- Applets do not use constructors. Instead, they use the method init to initialize various GUI components and data members.

- Applets do not require methods such as setVisible. Applets are embedded in HTML documents, and it is the HTML document that displays the applet.

- Applets do not use the method setTitle; the HTML document sets the title.

- Applets do not use the method setSize; the HTML document specifies the size of the applet.

- Applets do not have to be closed. In particular, there is no Exit button. The applet closes when the HTML document closes.

Therefore, in most cases, you perform the following five steps to convert a GUI application to an applet:

1. Make your **class** extend the definition of the **class** JApplet. In other words, change JFrame to JApplet.

2. Change the constructor to the method init.

3. Remove method calls such as setVisible, setTitle, and setSize.

4. Remove the method main.

5. Remove the Exit button, if you have one, and all code associated with it, such as the action listener, and so on.

As an example, we modify the temperature conversion program presented in Chapter 6 as a GUI application. The statements changed to create an applet are shown as comments.

```
//Java program to convert the temperature between
//Celsius and Fahrenheit.

import java.awt.*;
import java.awt.event.*;
import javax.swing.*;
```

```
      //public class TempConversion extends JFrame
      //
      //Replace JFrame with JApplet
      //
  public class TempConvertApplet extends JApplet
  {
      private JLabel celsiusLabel;
      private JLabel fahrenheitLabel;
      private JTextField celsiusTF;
      private JTextField fahrenheitTF;
      private CelsHandler celsiusHandler;
      private FahrHandler fahrenheitHandler;

      private static final int WIDTH = 500;
      private static final int HEIGHT = 50;
      private static final double FTOC = 5.0 / 9.0;
      private static final double CTOF = 1.8;    // 9 / 5
      private static final int OFFSET = 32;

        //public TempConversion()
        //
        //Replace this constructor with the init method
        //
      public void init()
      {
            //setTitle("Temperature Conversion");
            //
            //Delete setTitle
            //

          Container c = getContentPane();
          c.setLayout(new GridLayout(1, 4));

          celsiusLabel = new JLabel("Enter Celsius",
                              SwingConstants.RIGHT);
          fahrenheitLabel = new JLabel("Enter Fahrenheit ",
                              SwingConstants.RIGHT);

          celsiusTF = new JTextField(7);
          fahrenheitTF = new JTextField(7);

          c.add(celsiusLabel);
          c.add(celsiusTF);
          c.add(fahrenheitLabel);
          c.add(fahrenheitTF);

          celsiusHandler = new CelsHandler();
          fahrenheitHandler = new FahrHandler();
          celsiusTF.addActionListener(celsiusHandler);
          fahrenheitTF.addActionListener(fahrenheitHandler);
```

```
        //setSize(WIDTH, HEIGHT);
        //Delete: setSize(WIDTH, HEIGHT);

        //setDefaultCloseOperation(EXIT_ON_CLOSE);
        //Delete: setDefaultCloseOperation(EXIT_ON_CLOSE);

        //setVisible(true);
        //Delete: setVisible(true);
    }

    private class CelsHandler implements ActionListener
    {
        public void actionPerformed(ActionEvent e)
        {
            double celsius, fahrenheit;

            celsius =
                    Double.parseDouble(celsiusTF.getText());
            fahrenheit = celsius * CTOF + OFFSET;
            fahrenheitTF.setText(""+
                        String.format("%.2f", fahrenheit));
        }
    }

    private class FahrHandler implements ActionListener
    {
        public void actionPerformed(ActionEvent e)
        {
            double celsius, fahrenheit;

            fahrenheit =
                Double.parseDouble(fahrenheitTF.getText());

            celsius = (fahrenheit - OFFSET) * FTOC;
            celsiusTF.setText(""+
                        String.format("%.2f", celsius));
        }
    }

    //public static void main(String[] args)
    //{
    //     TempConversion tempConv = new TempConversion();
    //}
    //
    //Delete the method main
    //
}//end TempConvertApplet
```

The HTML file for this program contains the following code:

```
<HTML>
  <HEAD>
    <TITLE>TEMPCONVERT APPLET</TITLE>
  </HEAD>
  <BODY>
    <OBJECT code = "TempConvertApplet.class" width = "500"
                                             height = "50">
    </OBJECT>
  </BODY>
</HTML>
```

Additional GUI Components

The remainder of this chapter introduces GUI components in addition to those introduced in Chapter 6. For the most part, these additional GUI components are used in the same way as the ones introduced earlier. For example, you create an instance (or object) using the operator `new`. If the program needs to respond to an event occurring in a GUI component, such as `JTextField` or `JButton`, you must add an event listener and provide the associated method that needs to be invoked, commonly called the event handler. We will also illustrate the use of various methods of the `class Graphics`.

JTextArea

The GUI programs in previous chapters extensively used the `class JTextField` to display a line of text. However, there are situations when the program must display multiple lines of text. For example, an employee's address is shown in three or more lines. Because an object of the `class JTextField` can display only one line of text, you cannot use an object of this class to display multiple lines of text. Java provides the `class JTextArea` to either collect multiple lines of input from the user or to display multiple lines of output. Using an object of this class, the user can type multiple lines of text, which are separated by pressing the Enter key. In Java, each line ends with the newline character '\n'.

The GUI part of the Student Grade Report programming example in Chapter 10, (available with the Additional Student Files at *www.cengagebrain.com*) uses a `JTextArea` to display multiple lines of text to show the various courses taken by a student and the student's grade for each course. This section discusses the capabilities of the `class JTextArea` in some detail.

Both `JTextField` and `JTextArea` are derived from the `class JTextComponent` and, as such, share many common methods. However, you cannot create an instance of the `class JTextComponent` because it is an `abstract` class. Table 12-8 lists some of the constructors and methods of the `class JTextArea`.

TABLE 12-8 Commonly Used Constructors and Methods of the **class** JTextArea

```
public JTextArea(int r, int c)
  //Constructor
  //Creates a new JTextArea with r number of rows and
  //c number of columns.
```

```
public JTextArea(String t, int r, int c)
  //Constructor
  //Creates a new JTextArea with r number of rows, c number
  //of columns, and the initial text t.
```

```
public void setColumns(int c)
  //Sets the number of columns to c.
```

```
public void setRows(int r)
  //Sets the number of rows to r.
```

```
public void append(String t)
  //Concatenates the text already in the JTextArea with t.
```

```
public void setLineWrap(boolean b)
  //If b is true, the lines are wrapped.
```

```
public void setTabSize(int c)
  //Sets tab stops every c columns.
```

```
public void setWrapStyleWord(boolean b)
  //If b is true, the lines are wrapped at the word boundaries.
  //If b is false, the word boundaries are not considered.
```

Table 12-9 shows the methods, which you have used with a JTextField object, that are inherited by the **class** JTextArea from the parent **class** JTextComponent.

TABLE 12-9 Methods Inherited by the **class** JTextArea from the Parent **class** JTextComponent

```
public void setText(String t)
  //Changes the text of the text area to t.
```

```
public String getText()
  //Returns the text contained in the text area.
```

```
public void setEditable(boolean b)
  //If b is false, the user cannot type in the text area. In this case,
  //the text area is used as a tool to display the result.
```

EXAMPLE 12-6

The program in this example illustrates the use of `JTextArea`. It creates the GUI shown in Figure 12-9.

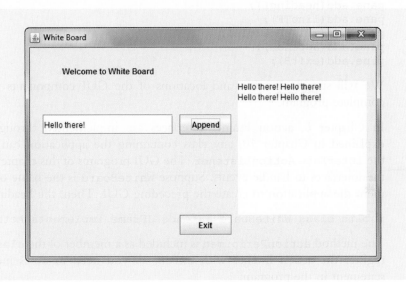

FIGURE 12-9 White Board GUI

As shown in Figure 12-9, the GUI contains a `JLabel`, two `JButtons`, a text field, and a text area. The user can type a line of text in the text field. Similarly, if the user clicks the `Append` button, the text in the text field is appended to the text in the text area. When the user clicks the `Exit` button, the program terminates.

In this example, we write the program as a GUI application. A corresponding applet is left as an exercise for you; see Programming Exercise 8 at the end of this chapter.

As in the previous GUI application program, we create the necessary labels, text fields, and text areas, and place them in the content pane. We also create and place two buttons, `exitB` and `appendB`, in the content pane. The following statements access the content pane, create the GUI components, and place the GUI components in the content pane:

```
private JLabel headingL;
headingL = new JLabel("Welcome to White Board");

private JTextField lineTF;
lineTF = new JTextField(20);

private JTextArea whiteBoardTA;
whiteBoardTA = new JTextArea(10, 20);
```

```
private JButton exitB, appendB;
exitB = new JButton("Exit");
appendB = new JButton("Append");

Container pane = getContentPane();

pane.add(headingL);
pane.add(lineTF);
pane.add(whiteBoardTA);
pane.add(appendB);
pane.add(exitB);
```

We will specify the sizes and locations of the GUI components when we write the complete program.

In Chapter 6, action listener interfaces are implemented through inner classes. As explained in Chapter 10, any class containing the application can directly implement the `interface` ActionListener. The GUI programs of this chapter directly implement the interfaces to handle events. Suppose WhiteBoard is the name of the class to implement the application to create the preceding GUI. Then, the heading of this class is:

```
public class WhiteBoard extends JFrame implements ActionListener
```

The method `actionPerformed` is included as a member of the `class` WhiteBoard. To register the action listener with `exitB`, all you need to do is include the following statement in the program:

```
exitB.addActionListener(this);
```

Of course, the necessary code is placed in the method `actionPerformed`.

Because action events are generated by the two buttons, the method `actionPerformed` uses the methods `getActionCommand` and `equals` to identify the source of the event. The definition of this method is:

```
public void actionPerformed(ActionEvent e)
{
    if (e.getActionCommand().equals("Append"))       //Line 1
        whiteBoardTA.append(lineTF.getText());       //Line 2
    else if (e.getActionCommand().equals("Exit"))    //Line 3
        System.exit(0);                              //Line 4
}
```

If the user clicks the Append button, the `if` statement in Line 1 evaluates to `true`. In this case, the statement in Line 2 retrieves the line of text from the text field object `lineTF` and appends it to the text in the text area object `whiteBoardTA`. When the user clicks the Exit button, the `if` statement in Line 3 evaluates to `true` and the statement in Line 4 terminates the program.

The complete program listing follows:

```
import javax.swing.*;
import java.awt.*;
import java.awt.event.*;
```

```
public class WhiteBoard extends JFrame
                        implements ActionListener
{
    private static int WIDTH = 550;
    private static int HEIGHT = 350;

    private int row = 10;
    private int col = 20;

        //GUI components
    private JLabel headingL;
    private JTextField lineTF;
    private JTextArea whiteBoardTA;
    private JButton exitB, appendB;

    public WhiteBoard()
    {
        setTitle("White Board");
        Container pane  = getContentPane();
        setSize(WIDTH,HEIGHT);

        headingL = new JLabel("Welcome to White Board");
        lineTF = new JTextField(20);

        whiteBoardTA = new JTextArea(row, col);
        exitB = new JButton("Exit");
        exitB.addActionListener(this);

        appendB = new JButton("Append");
        appendB.addActionListener(this);

        pane.setLayout(null);

        headingL.setLocation(50, 20);
        lineTF.setLocation(20, 100);
        whiteBoardTA.setLocation(320, 50);
        appendB.setLocation(230, 100);
        exitB.setLocation(230, 250);

        headingL.setSize(200, 30);
        lineTF.setSize(200, 30);
        whiteBoardTA.setSize(200, 200);
        appendB.setSize(80, 30);
        exitB.setSize(80, 30);

        pane.add(headingL);
        pane.add(lineTF);
        pane.add(whiteBoardTA);
        pane.add(appendB);
        pane.add(exitB);
```

1
2

```
        setVisible(true);
        setDefaultCloseOperation(EXIT_ON_CLOSE);
    } //end of the constructor

  public static void main(String[] args)
  {
        WhiteBoard board = new WhiteBoard();
  }

   public void actionPerformed(ActionEvent e)
   {
        if (e.getActionCommand().equals("Append"))
            whiteBoardTA.append(lineTF.getText());
        else if (e.getActionCommand().equals("Exit"))
            System.exit(0);
   }
}
```

Sample Run: Figure 12-10 shows a sample run of this program. (To get the new line in the text area, click the mouse to position the insertion point in the text area, then press the Enter key. The next append should now be in the next line.)

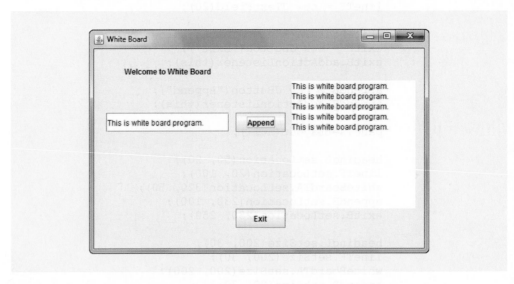

FIGURE 12-10 Sample run of the White Board program

JCheckBox

In the previous section, you learned how to use text fields and text areas to collect input from the user. When you use a text field or a text area to input data, users can type anything they want. However, sometimes you want the user to select from a set of predefined values. For example, to specify gender, the user would select either male or female; similarly, a student would select either undergraduate or graduate. In addition to freeing the user from typing in such values, to get precise input, you want the user to select a value from a given set.

The JCheckBox and JRadioButton classes allow a user to select a value from a set of given values. These classes are both subclasses of the abstract class ToggleButton. The class JCheckBox is described in this section; the class JRadioButton is discussed in the next section.

Table 12-10 shows some of the constructors and methods of the class JCheckBox.

TABLE 12-10 Some Constructors and Methods of the class JCheckBox

```
public JCheckBox()
  //Creates an initially unselected check box button
  //with no label and no icon.
  //Example: JCheckBox myJCheckBox = new JCheckBox()
  //         myJCheckBox points to the check box with no label
  //         and no icon.

public JCheckBox(Icon icon)
  //Creates an initially unselected check box button with
  //the specified icon and no label.
  //Example: JCheckBox myJCheckBox = new JCheckBox(anIcon);
  //         myJCheckBox points to the check box with the
  //         icon "anIcon".

public JCheckBox(Icon icon, boolean selected)
  //Creates a check box with the specified
  //image and selection state, but with no label.
  //Example: JCheckBox myJCheckBox =
  //                     new JCheckBox(anIcon, true);
  //         myJCheckBox points to the selected check box with
  //         anIcon as the icon.

public JCheckBox(String text)
  //Creates an unselected check box with
  //the specified label.
  //Example: JCheckBox myJCheckBox = new JCheckBox("Box");
  //         myJCheckBox points to the unselected check box with
  //         the label "Box".

public JCheckBox(String text, boolean selected)
  //Creates a check box with the specified
  //label and selection state.
  //Example: JCheckBox myJCheckBox =
  //                     new JCheckBox("Box", false);
  //         myJCheckBox points to the unselected check box with
  //         the label "Box".
```

1
2

TABLE 12-10 Some Constructors and Methods of the **class** JCheckBox (continued)

```
public JCheckBox(String text, Icon icon)
   //Creates a check box with the specified image
   //and specified label.
   //Example: JCheckBox myJCheckBox =
   //                  new JCheckBox("Box", anIcon);
   //     myJCheckBox points to the unselected check box with
   //     the label "Box" and anIcon as the icon.

public JCheckBox(String text, Icon icon, boolean selected)
   //Creates a check box with the specified image
   //and selection state, and with the specified text.
   //Example: JCheckBox myJCheckBox =
   //                  new JCheckBox("Box", anIcon, true);
   //     myJCheckBox points to the selected check box with
   //     the label "Box" and anIcon as the icon.

public boolean isSelected()
   //This method is inherited from the AbstractButton class
   //and is used to retrieve the state of a button.
   //Example: if(myJCheckBox.isSelected() == true)
   //     The "if" block will be executed, provided that myJCheckBox
   //     is checked.

public boolean setSelected(boolean b)
   //This method is inherited from the AbstractButton class
   //and is used to set the state of a button.
   //Example: myJCheckBox.setSelected(true);
   //     myJCheckBox gets checked.
```

Similar to buttons, check boxes also come with their own identifying labels. Consider the following statements:

```
JCheckBox italicCB;                     //Line 1
italicCB = new JCheckBox("Italic");   //Line 2
```

The statement in Line 1 declares italicCB to be a reference variable of JCheckBox type. The statement in Line 2 creates the object italicCB and assigns it the label Italic. After the statement in Line 2 executes, the check box shown in Figure 12-11 results.

FIGURE 12-11 Check box with label

In Figure 12-11, the box to the left of the label `Italic` is a check box. The user clicks it to select or deselect it. For example, clicking the check box in Figure 12-11 produces the result shown in Figure 12-12.

☑ Italic

FIGURE 12-12 Result of clicking the check box

If you click the check box shown in Figure 12-12, the checkmark disappears. A check box is an example of a toggle button. If it is not selected and you click it, then the box is selected and a checkmark appears. If it is selected and you click it, the checkmark disappears.

When you click a `JCheckBox`, it generates an **item event**. Item events are handled by the `interface ItemListener`. The `interface ItemListener` contains only the `abstract` method `itemStateChanged`. The heading of the method is:

```
public void itemStateChanged(ItemEvent e)
```

To make the program respond to the event generated by clicking a check box, you write the code that needs to be executed in the body of the method `itemStateChanged` and register an item listener object to the check box.

Next, we write an applet that has two check boxes and also displays a line of text. The first check box is used to indicate the selection of bold style and the second to indicate the selection of italic style. The user can click the check boxes to change the font and style of the text. We create two check boxes with the labels `"Bold"` and `"Italic"` and place them in the content pane of the applet. The method `init` contains the statements needed for these initializations. Therefore, the `init` method can be written as follows:

```
public void init()
{
    Container c = getContentPane();   //get the container
    c.setLayout(null);                //set the layout to null
       //create the check boxes with the appropriate labels
    boldCB = new JCheckBox("Bold");
    italicCB = new JCheckBox("Italic");

       //set the sizes of the check boxes
    boldCB.setSize(100, 30);
    italicCB.setSize(100, 30);

       //set the location of the check boxes
    boldCB.setLocation(100, 100);
    italicCB.setLocation(300, 100);
```

1
2

```
    //register the item listener to the check boxes
    boldCB.addItemListener(this);
    italicCB.addItemListener(this);

    //add the check boxes to the pane
    c.add(boldCB);
    c.add(italicCB);
}
```

To specify the font and style of the text, we use two `int` variables: `intBold` and `intItalic`. These variables are set to `Font.PLAIN` when the check boxes are not checked. They are set to `Font.BOLD` and `Font.ITALIC`, respectively, if the corresponding check boxes are checked. To create bold and italic fonts, you simply add the values of the variables `bold` and `italic`. In other words, you can create desired fonts by just using `intBold + intItalic` as the style value. Note that because `Font.PLAIN` has a value of zero, `Font.PLAIN + Font.PLAIN` remains `Font.PLAIN`. The `paint` method can be used to set the color and font, and to display the welcome message. The definition of the method `paint` can be written as follows:

```
public void paint(Graphics g)
{
    super.paint(g);
    g.setColor(Color.red);
    g.setFont(new Font("Courier", intBold + intItalic, 24));
    g.drawString("Welcome to Java Programming", 30, 30);
}
```

To make the program respond to the events generated by the check boxes, next we write the definition of the method `itemStateChanged`. As shown earlier, the method `itemStateChanged` has one parameter, `e`, of the type `ItemEvent`. Because there are two check boxes, we use the method `getSource` to identify the box generating the event.

The expression:

```
e.getSource() == boldCB
```

is `true` if the check box associated with `boldCB` generated the event. Similarly, the expression:

```
e.getSource() == italicCB
```

is `true` if the check box associated with `italicCB` generated the event.

After identifying the check box that generated the event, we determine whether the user selected or deselected the check box. For this, we use the method `getStateChange` of the `class` `ItemEvent` that returns either the constant `ItemEvent.SELECTED` or the constant `ItemEvent.DESELECTED`, which are defined in the `class` `ItemEvent`. For example, the expression:

```
e.getStateChange() == ItemEvent.SELECTED
```

is `true` if the event `e` corresponds to selecting the check box.

Finally, every time an event happens, you want to change the font accordingly. This can be achieved by invoking the `paint` method. To call the `paint` method, you need a `Graphics` object. So, you invoke the `repaint` method, which in turn invokes the `paint` method. Therefore, you need to call the `repaint` method before leaving the event handler method.

The definition of the method `itemStateChanged` is:

```java
public void itemStateChanged(ItemEvent e)
{
    if (e.getSource() == boldCB)
    {
        if (e.getStateChange() == ItemEvent.SELECTED)
            intBold = Font.BOLD;
        if (e.getStateChange() == ItemEvent.DESELECTED)
            intBold = Font.PLAIN;
    }

    if (e.getSource() == italicCB)
    {
        if (e.getStateChange() == ItemEvent.SELECTED)
            intItalic = Font.ITALIC;
        if (e.getStateChange() == ItemEvent.DESELECTED)
            intItalic = Font.PLAIN;
    }

    repaint();
}
```

Now that the necessary components are written, we can write the complete program.

```java
//Welcome Applet with check boxes

import java.awt.*;
import java.awt.event.*;
import javax.swing.*;

public class GrandWelcomeCheckBox extends JApplet implements
                                                    ItemListener
{
    private int intBold = Font.PLAIN;
    private int intItalic = Font.PLAIN;
    private JCheckBox boldCB, italicCB;

    public void init()
    {
        Container c = getContentPane();
        c.setLayout(null);
        boldCB = new JCheckBox("Bold");
        italicCB = new JCheckBox("Italic");
```

1
2

```
        boldCB.setSize(100, 30);
        italicCB.setSize(100,30);

        boldCB.setLocation(100, 100);
        italicCB.setLocation(300, 100);

        boldCB.addItemListener(this);
        italicCB.addItemListener(this);

        c.add(boldCB);
        c.add(italicCB);
    }

    public void paint( Graphics g)
    {
        super.paint(g);
        g.setColor(Color.red);
        g.setFont(new Font("Courier", intBold + intItalic, 24));
        g.drawString("Welcome to Java Programming", 30, 30);
    }

    public void itemStateChanged(ItemEvent e)
    {
        if (e.getSource() == boldCB)
        {
            if (e.getStateChange() == ItemEvent.SELECTED)
                intBold = Font.BOLD;
            if (e.getStateChange() == ItemEvent.DESELECTED)
                intBold = Font.PLAIN;
        }

        if (e.getSource() == italicCB)
        {
            if (e.getStateChange() == ItemEvent.SELECTED)
                intItalic = Font.ITALIC;
            if (e.getStateChange() == ItemEvent.DESELECTED)
                intItalic = Font.PLAIN;
        }

        repaint();
    }
}
```

The HTML file for this program contains the following code:

```
<HTML>
  <HEAD>
    <TITLE>WELCOME</TITLE>
  </HEAD>
  <BODY>
    <OBJECT code = "GrandWelcomeCheckBox.class" width = "440"
                                                height = "200">
    </OBJECT>
  </BODY>
</HTML>
```

Sample Run: Figure 12-13 shows a sample run of the applet with check boxes.

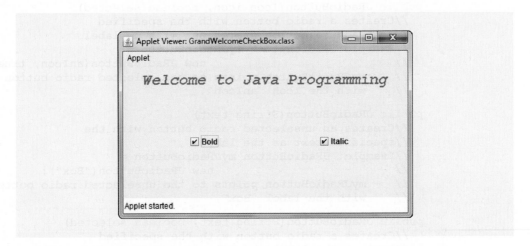

FIGURE 12-13 Welcome applet with check boxes

JRadioButton

Check boxes allow the user to select values from a given set of values. The program in the previous section used two check boxes. The user could select or deselect one or both check boxes. However, there are situations in which you want the user to make only one selection from a set of values. For example, if the user needs to select the gender of a person, the user selects either female or male, but not both. If you want the user to select only one of the options presented, you use radio buttons. To make such selections possible, Java provides the `class` JRadioButton.

Table 12-11 shows some of the constructors and methods of the `class` JRadioButton.

TABLE 12-11 Some Constructors and Methods of the `class` JRadioButton

```
public JRadioButton()
  //Creates an initially unselected radio button
  //with no label and no icon.
  //Example: JRadioButton myJRadioButton = new JRadioButton();
  //    myJRadioButton points to the radio button with no label
  //    and no icon.

public JRadioButton(Icon icon)
  //Creates an initially unselected radio button
  //with the specified icon and no label.
  //Example: JRadioButton myJRadioButton =
  //            new JRadioButton(anIcon);
  //    myJRadioButton points to the radio button with the
  //    icon "anIcon".
```

1
2

TABLE 12-11 Some Constructors and Methods of the **class** JRadioButton (continued)

```
public JRadioButton(Icon icon, boolean selected)
  //Creates a radio button with the specified
  //icon and selection state, but with no label.
  //Example:JRadioButton myJRadioButton =
  //                    new JRadioButton(anIcon, true);
  //    myJRadioButton points to the selected radio button
  //    with the icon "anIcon".
```

```
public JRadioButton(String text)
  //Creates an unselected radio button with the
  //specified text as the label.
  //Example: JRadioButton myJRadioButton =
  //                    new JRadioButton("Box");
  //    myJRadioButton points to the unselected radio button
  //    with the label "Box".
```

```
public JRadioButton(String text, boolean selected)
  //Creates a radio button with the specified
  //text as the label and selection state.
  //Example: JRadioButton myJRadioButton =
  //              new JRadioButton("Box", false);
  //        myJRadioButton points to the unselected radio
  //        button with the label "Box".
```

```
public JRadioButton(String text, Icon icon)
  //Creates a radio button with the specified
  //icon and the specified text as the label.
  //Example: RadioButton myJRadioButton =
  //                    new JRadioButton("Box", anIcon);
  //    myJRadioButton points to the unselected radio button
  //    with the label "Box" and the icon "anIcon".
```

```
public JRadioButton(String text, Icon icon, boolean selected)
  //Creates a radio button with the specified icon and
  //selection state, and with the specified text as the label
  //Example: JRadioButton myJRadioButton =
  //                    new JRadioButton("Box", anIcon, true);
  //        myJRadioButton points to the selected radio button
  //        with the label "Box" and the icon "anIcon".
```

```
public boolean isSelected()
  //This method is inherited from the AbstractButton class
  //and is used to retrieve the state of a button.
  //Example: if (myJRadioButton.isSelected() == true)
  //        The "if" block will be executed provided
  //        myJRadioButton is checked.
```

```
public boolean setSelected(boolean b)
  //This method is inherited from the AbstractButton class
  //and is used to set the state of a button.
  //Example: myJRadioButton.setSelected(true);
  //        myJRadioButton gets checked.
```

Radio buttons are created the same way check boxes are created. Consider the following statements:

```
private JRadioButton redRB, greenRB, blueRB;        //Line 1
redRB = new JRadioButton("Red");                    //Line 2
greenRB = new JRadioButton("Green");                //Line 3
blueRB = new JRadioButton("Blue");                  //Line 4
```

The statement in Line 1 declares `redRB`, `greenRB`, and `blueRB` to be reference variables of the `JRadioButton` type. The statement in Line 2 instantiates the object `redRB` and assigns it the label `"Red"`. Similarly, the statements in Lines 3 and 4 instantiate the objects `greenRB` and `blueRB` and with the labels `"Green"` and `"Blue"`, respectively.

As with check boxes, we create and place radio buttons in the content pane of the applet. However, in this case, to force the user to select only one radio button at a time, we create a button group and group the radio buttons. Consider the following statements:

```
private ButtonGroup ColorSelectBGroup;              //Line 5

ColorSelectBGroup = new ButtonGroup();              //Line 6
ColorSelectBGroup.add(redRB);                       //Line 7
ColorSelectBGroup.add(greenRB);                     //Line 8
ColorSelectBGroup.add(blueRB);                      //Line 9
```

The statements in Lines 5 and 6 create the object `ColorSelectBGroup`, and the statements in Lines 7, 8, and 9 add the radio buttons `redRB`, `greenRB`, and `blueRB` to this object. The statements in Lines 1 through 9 create and group the radio buttons, as shown in Figure 12-14.

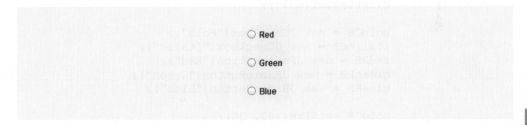

FIGURE 12-14 Radio buttons

Because the radio buttons `redRB`, `greenRB`, and `blueRB` are grouped, the user can select only one of these buttons. Similarly to JCheckBox, JRadioButton also generates an `ItemEvent`. So we use the **interface** `ItemListener` and its method `itemStateChanged` to handle the events.

In the following example, we start with the applet we created in the section JCheckBox and add three radio buttons so that the text color can be selected from the list: red, green, or blue.

Grouping buttons enforces the constraint that only one radio button can be selected at any time. This also affects how you write the event handler. Because only one button can be selected, once you know the source of the event, you can conclude that the associated radio button is selected. Thus, the relevant code for handling the events generated by these radio buttons can be written as follows:

```
if (e.getSource() == redRB)
    currentColor = Color.red;
else if (e.getSource() == greenRB)
    currentColor = Color.green;
else if (e.getSource() == blueRB)
    currentColor = Color.blue;
```

The complete program, along with the sample run, follows:

```java
import java.awt.*;
import java.awt.event.*;
import javax.swing.*;

public class GrandWelcomeRButton extends JApplet implements
                                        ItemListener
{
    private int intBold = Font.PLAIN;
    private int intItalic = Font.PLAIN;
    private Color currentColor = Color.black;
    private JCheckBox boldCB, italicCB;
    private JRadioButton redRB, greenRB, blueRB;
    private ButtonGroup ColorSelectBGroup;

    public void init()
    {
        Container c = getContentPane();
        c.setLayout(null);

        boldCB = new JCheckBox("Bold");
        italicCB = new JCheckBox("Italic");
        redRB = new JRadioButton("Red");
        greenRB = new JRadioButton("Green");
        blueRB = new JRadioButton("Blue");

        boldCB.setSize(100, 30);
        italicCB.setSize(100, 30);
        redRB.setSize(100, 30);
        greenRB.setSize(100, 30);
        blueRB.setSize(100, 30);

        boldCB.setLocation(100, 70);
        italicCB.setLocation(100, 150);
        redRB.setLocation(300, 70);
        greenRB.setLocation(300, 110);
        blueRB.setLocation(300, 150);

        boldCB.addItemListener(this);
        italicCB.addItemListener(this);
        redRB.addItemListener(this);
```

```java
        greenRB.addItemListener(this);
        blueRB.addItemListener(this);

        c.add(boldCB);
        c.add(italicCB);
        c.add(redRB);
        c.add(greenRB);
        c.add(blueRB);

        ColorSelectBGroup = new ButtonGroup();
        ColorSelectBGroup.add(redRB);
        ColorSelectBGroup.add(greenRB);
        ColorSelectBGroup.add(blueRB);
    }

    public void paint(Graphics g)
    {
        super.paint(g);
        g.setColor(Color.orange);
        g.drawRoundRect(75, 50, 125, 140, 10, 10);
        g.drawRoundRect(275, 50, 125, 140, 10, 10);
        g.setColor(currentColor);
        g.setFont(new Font("Courier", intBold + intItalic, 24));
        g.drawString("Welcome to Java Programming", 30, 30);
    }

    public void itemStateChanged(ItemEvent e)
    {
        if (e.getSource() == boldCB)
        {
            if (e.getStateChange() == ItemEvent.SELECTED)
                intBold = Font.BOLD;
            if (e.getStateChange() == ItemEvent.DESELECTED)
                intBold = Font.PLAIN;
        }

        if (e.getSource() == italicCB)
        {
            if (e.getStateChange() == ItemEvent.SELECTED)
                intItalic = Font.ITALIC;
            if (e.getStateChange() == ItemEvent.DESELECTED)
                intItalic = Font.PLAIN;
        }

        if (e.getSource() == redRB)
            currentColor = Color.red;
        else if (e.getSource() == greenRB)
            currentColor = Color.green;
        else if (e.getSource() == blueRB)
            currentColor = Color.blue;

        repaint();
    }
}
```

The HTML file for this program contains the following code:

```
<HTML>
  <HEAD>
    <TITLE>WELCOME</TITLE>
  </HEAD>
  <BODY>
    <OBJECT code = "GrandWelcomeRButton.class" width = "440"
                                              height = "200">
    </OBJECT>
  </BODY>
</HTML>
```

Sample Run: Figure 12-15 is a sample run showing check boxes and radio buttons.

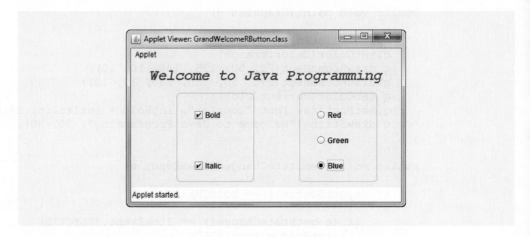

FIGURE 12-15   Sample run showing check boxes and radio buttons

JComboBox

A **combo box**, also known as a drop-down list, is used to select an item from a list of possibilities. A JComboBox generates an ItemEvent monitored by an ItemListener, which invokes the method itemStateChanged exactly as in JCheckBox or JRadioButton.

Table 12-12 lists some constructors of the class JComboBox.

TABLE 12-12 Some Constructors of the `class` JComboBox

```
public JComboBox()
  //Creates a JComboBox with no items to select.
  //Example: JComboBox selectionList = new JComboBox();
  //          selectionList is created but has no selectable items.
```

```
public JComboBox(Vector<?> v)
  //Creates a JComboBox to display the elements
  //in the vector provided as an input parameter.
  //Example: JComboBox selectionList = new JComboBox(v);
  //          selectionList points to the combo box that lists the
  //          elements contained in Vector v.
```

```
public JComboBox(Object[] o)
  //Constructor:  Creates a JComboBox that displays the
  //elements in the object array provided as an input parameter.
  //Example: JComboBox selectionList = new JComboBox(o);
  //      selectionList points to the combo box that lists the
  //      elements contained in the array o.
```

In the previous two sections, we created an applet that uses check boxes and radio buttons to change the font and style of the text. In this section, we add a JComboBox to the program so that the user can select a font from a list of font names, and apply that font to the text.

To create a combo box, we first declare a reference variable as follows:

```
private JComboBox fontFaceDD;                              //Line 1
```

Next, we create an array of strings and initialize it with the list of font names. The corresponding Java statement is:

```
private String fontNames[] = {"Dialog", "Century Gothic",
                              "Courier", "Serif"};        //Line 2
```

Next, we use the variable fontFaceDD, declared in Line 1, and the array of strings fontNames, created in Line 2, to create a combo box. Consider the following statement:

```
fontFaceDD = new JComboBox(fontNames);                    //Line 3
```

This statement creates the object fontFaceDD and initializes this object using the strings in the array fontNames.

The object fontFaceDD has four items. When you click the combo box, it shows you the four choices. You can control the number of choices shown by using the method setMaximumRowCount. For example, the statement:

```
fontFaceDD.setMaximumRowCount(3);
```

sets the number of choices to be shown to 3. Because there are four choices in the combo box `fontFaceDD` and only three choices are shown, a vertical scroll bar appears to the right of the box. You can scroll this bar to see and select the other choices.

When you click an item in the combo box, it generates an item event. To process item events, we use the `interface ItemListener`. As described in the previous section, the item event handler code is placed in the body of the method `itemStateChanged`.

When the user selects an item from a combo box, the index of the selected item can be obtained by using the method `getSelectedIndex()`. For example, the statement:

```
currentFontName = fontNames[fontFaceDD.getSelectedIndex()];
```

assigns the current font name to the string variable `currentFontName`.

Example 12-7 gives the complete program listing for this `JComboBox` example.

EXAMPLE 12-7

```java
//Welcome program with check boxes, radio buttons, and combo box

import java.awt.*;
import java.awt.event.*;
import javax.swing.*;

public class GrandWelcomeFinal extends JApplet implements
                                                    ItemListener
{
    private int intBold = Font.PLAIN;
    private int intItalic = Font.PLAIN;

    private Color currentColor = Color.black;
    private String currentFontName ="Courier";
    private JCheckBox boldCB, italicCB;
    private JRadioButton redRB, greenRB, blueRB;
    private ButtonGroup ColorSelectBGroup;
    private JComboBox fontFaceDD;

    private String[] fontNames
                = {"Dialog", "Century Gothic",
                    "Courier", "Serif"};

    public void init()
    {
        Container c = getContentPane();
        c.setLayout(null);
```

```java
    boldCB = new JCheckBox("Bold");
    italicCB = new JCheckBox("Italic");
    redRB = new JRadioButton("Red");
    greenRB = new JRadioButton("Green");
    blueRB = new JRadioButton("Blue");
    fontFaceDD = new JComboBox(fontNames);
    fontFaceDD.setMaximumRowCount(3);

    boldCB.setSize(80, 30);
    italicCB.setSize(80, 30);
    redRB.setSize(80, 30);
    greenRB.setSize(80, 30);
    blueRB.setSize(80, 30);
    fontFaceDD.setSize(80, 30);

    boldCB.setLocation(100, 70);
    italicCB.setLocation(100, 150);
    redRB.setLocation(300, 70);
    greenRB.setLocation(300, 110);
    blueRB.setLocation(300, 150);
    fontFaceDD.setLocation(200, 70);

    boldCB.addItemListener(this);
    italicCB.addItemListener(this);
    redRB.addItemListener(this);
    greenRB.addItemListener(this);
    blueRB.addItemListener(this);
    fontFaceDD.addItemListener(this);

    c.add(boldCB);
    c.add(italicCB);
    c.add(redRB);
    c.add(greenRB);
    c.add(blueRB);

    c.add(fontFaceDD);
    ColorSelectBGroup = new ButtonGroup();
    ColorSelectBGroup.add(redRB);
    ColorSelectBGroup.add(greenRB);
    ColorSelectBGroup.add(blueRB);
}

public void paint(Graphics g)
{
    super.paint(g);

    g.setColor(Color.orange);
    g.drawRoundRect(75, 50, 324, 140, 10, 10);
    g.drawLine(183, 50, 183, 190);
    g.drawLine(291, 50, 291, 190);
```

```
            g.setColor(currentColor);
            g.setFont(new Font(currentFontName,
                               intBold + intItalic, 24));
            g.drawString("Welcome to Java Programming", 30, 30);
        }

    public void itemStateChanged(ItemEvent e)
    {
        if (e.getSource() == boldCB)
        {
            if (e.getStateChange() == ItemEvent.SELECTED)
                intBold = Font.BOLD;
            if (e.getStateChange() == ItemEvent.DESELECTED)
                intBold = Font.PLAIN;
        }

        if (e.getSource() == italicCB)
        {
            if (e.getStateChange() == ItemEvent.SELECTED)
                intItalic = Font.ITALIC;
            if (e.getStateChange() == ItemEvent.DESELECTED)
                intItalic = Font.PLAIN;
        }

        if (e.getSource() == redRB)
            currentColor = Color.red;
        else if (e.getSource() == greenRB)
            currentColor = Color.green;
        else if (e.getSource() == blueRB)
            currentColor = Color.blue;

        if (e.getSource() == fontFaceDD)
            currentFontName =
                        fontNames[fontFaceDD.getSelectedIndex()];

        repaint();
    }
}
```

The HTML file for this program contains the following code:

```
<HTML>
  <HEAD>
    <TITLE>WELCOME</TITLE>
  </HEAD>
  <BODY>
    <OBJECT code = "GrandWelcomeFinal.class" width = "440"
                                             height = "200">
    </OBJECT>
  </BODY>
</HTML>
```

Sample Run: Figure 12-16 shows a sample run of the Welcome applet with check boxes, a combo box, and radio buttons.

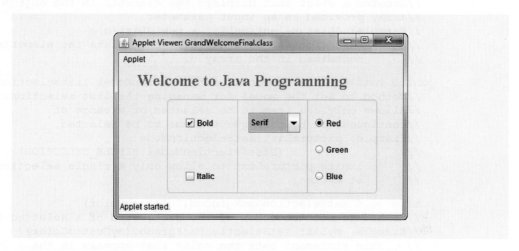

FIGURE 12-16 Welcome applet with check boxes, combo box, and radio buttons

JList

A **list** displays a number of items from which the user can select one or more items. This section illustrates the use of a single selection list. The programming example at the end of this chapter uses a multiple selection list. Table 12-13 shows some constructors and methods of the `class` JList.

TABLE 12-13 Some Constructors and Methods of the `class` JList

```
public JList()
  //Creates a JList with no items to select.
  //Example: JList selectionList = new JList();
  //         selectionList is created but has no selectable items.

public JList(Vector<? extends E> v)
  //Creates a JList to display the elements in the
  //vector provided as an input parameter.
  //Example: JList selectionList = new JList(v);
  //         selectionList is a new list that lists the elements
  //         contained in Vector v.
```

1
2

TABLE 12-13 Some Constructors and Methods of the `class` JList (continued)

```
public JList(Object[] o)
  //Creates a JList that displays the elements in the object
  //array provided as an input parameter.
  //Example: JList selectionList = new JList(o);
  //       selectionList is a new list that lists the elements
  //       contained in the array o.
```

```
public void setSelectionMode(ListSelectionModel listselectionmodel)
  //Method to set the model for managing the list selections.
  //Allows only one item to be selected or a range of
  //contiguous or noncontiguous items to be selected.
  //Example: pictureList.setSelectionMode
  //                 (ListSelectionModel.SINGLE_SELECTION);
  //       limits pictureList to allow only a single selection
  //       at a time.
```

```
public void setSelectionBackground(Color sbColor)
  //Method to set the color of the background of a selected item
  //Example: myList.setSelectionBackground(myCustomColor);
  //    This statement sets the color that appears in the
  //    background of a selected item in myList to the color
  //    represented by the Color object myCustomColor.
```

```
public void addListSelectionListener(ListSelectionListener lsl)
  //Method to add a listener class to take action when an item
  //in the list is selected.
  //Example: pictureList.addListSelectionListener(handler);
  //    This statement adds a new ListSelectionListener object,
  //    named handler, to pictureList to process the events
  //    related to the selection of a list item.
```

```
public int getSelectedIndex()
  //When an item in the list is selected, this method returns
  //the index of that item (0 to the number of items - 1);
  //returns -1 if nothing is selected
  //Example: myLabel.setIcon
  //             (pictures[ pictureList.getSelectedIndex() ]);
  //    This statement sets an icon for a label to the item in
  //    an array of image icons specified by the index of the
  //    selected item in the list.
```

Let's write a program that uses a JList and JLabels to create the GUI as shown in Figure 12-17.

The GUI in Figure 12-17 contains four GUI components: a JList and three JLabels. The JList object contains the list of items, such as Pie Diagram, Line Graph, and Bar Graph. The first JLabel contains the string "Select an Image". Below this label is the JList object, and below the JList object is a JLabel that displays an image. For example, if the user selects Normal Curve, this JLabel object shows the image of a normal curve. Below the label showing an image is a `JLabel` that displays the name of the image. For example, in Figure 12-17, this label displays the text `Normal Curve`.

The top and the bottom labels display a line of text, so they are manipulated using strings as labels. The label showing an image is manipulated using images. For this program, we include five JPEG images. The following statement creates the `JLabel` object `promptJL` with `Select an Image` as its label and sets the justification of the label to center:

```
private JLabel promptJL = new JLabel("Select an Image",
                                     SwingConstants.CENTER);
```

The following statements declare `displayPicJL` and `infoJL` to be reference variables of the `JLabel` type:

```
private JLabel displayPicJL;
private JLabel infoJL;
```

We use `displayPicJL` to display the image and `infoJL` to display the name of the image, as shown in Figure 12-17. The following paragraphs explain how to change the text and image of these labels during program execution.

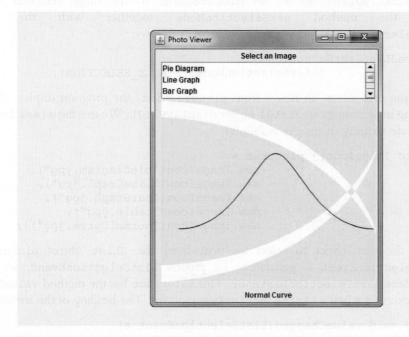

FIGURE 12-17 GUI using `JList` and `JLabel`

We now discuss how to create the `JList` with five items. For the most part, creating a `JList` is similar to creating a `JComboBox`. To create a `JList`, we first declare a reference variable as follows:

```
private JList pictureJList;
```

Next, we create an array of strings consisting of the names of the images. The following statement creates the array `pictureNames` of five components:

```
private String[] pictureNames = {"Pie Diagram",
                                 "Line Graph",
                                 "Bar Graph",
                                 "Table",
                                 "Normal Curve"};
```

Next, we use the array `pictureNames` to create the `JList` object `pictureJList` as follows:

```
pictureJList = new JList(pictureNames);
```

As in the case of combo boxes, you can use the method `setVisibleRowCount` to set the number of visible rows of a `JList`. For example, the following statement sets the number of visible rows of `pictureJList` to 3:

```
pictureJList.setVisibleRowCount(3);
```

In the program we are writing, we want the user to select only one item at a time from `pictureJList`, so we set `pictureJList` to the single selection mode by using the method `setSelectionMode` together with the constant `ListSelectionModel.SINGLE_SELECTION` as follows:

```
pictureJList.setSelectionMode
            (ListSelectionModel.SINGLE_SELECTION);
```

When the user selects an image from `pictureJList`, the program displays the corresponding image using the `JLabel` object `displayPicJL`. We use the **class** `ImageIcon` and create an array of images as follows:

```
private ImageIcon[] pictures =
                    {new ImageIcon("pieDiagram.jpg"),
                     new ImageIcon("lineGraph.jpg"),
                     new ImageIcon("barGraph.jpg"),
                     new ImageIcon("table.jpg"),
                     new ImageIcon("normalCurve.jpg")};
```

When the user clicks to select an item from the `JList` object `pictureJList`, `ListSelectionEvent` is generated. To process `ListSelectionEvent`, we use the **interface** `ListSelectionListener`. This **interface** has the method `valueChanged`, which executes when a `ListSelectionEvent` occurs. The heading of this method is:

```
public void valueChanged(ListSelectionEvent e)
```

We can put the code to display the required image and its name in this method. When the user clicks an item in the `JList`, we can determine the index of the selected item by using the method `getSelectedIndex`. We then use this index to select the corresponding image from the array `pictures` and the name of the image from the array `pictureNames`. We can now use the method `repaint` to repaint the pane. The definition of the method `valueChanged` is:

```
public void valueChanged(ListSelectionEvent e)
{
    displayPicJL.setIcon(
            pictures[pictureJList.getSelectedIndex()]);
    infoJL.setText(
            pictureNames[pictureJList.getSelectedIndex()]);
    repaint();
}
```

Of course, we must register the list selection listener to the `JList`. The following statement accomplishes this:

```
pictureJList.addListSelectionListener(this);
```

There are five items in `pictureJList`. When the program executes, it displays only three of these items in the list at a time. Therefore, we want to attach a vertical scroll bar to `pictureJList`, so that the user can scroll to select an item not currently shown in the list. To do so, we use the **class** `JScrollPane` as follows. First, we create the `JScrollPane` object `selectionJS` and initialize this object using the object `pictureJList`. We then add the object to the pane `selectionJS`. The following statements illustrate this concept:

```
selectionJS = new JScrollPane(pictureJList);
pane.add(selectionJS);
```

We will set the pane layout to **null** and specify the size and location of the GUI components. The complete program listing contains the following statements:

```
//Program to demonstrate JLIST

import java.awt.*;
import javax.swing.*;
import javax.swing.event.*;

public class JListPictureViewer extends JFrame implements
                                    ListSelectionListener
{
    private String[] pictureNames = {"Pie Diagram",
                                     "Line Graph",
                                     "Bar Graph",
                                     "Table",
                                     "Normal Curve"};

    private ImageIcon[] pictures =
                    {new ImageIcon("pieDiagram.jpg"),
                     new ImageIcon("lineGraph.jpg"),
                     new ImageIcon("barGraph.jpg"),
                     new ImageIcon("table.jpg"),
                     new ImageIcon("normalCurve.jpg")};
```

```
      private JList pictureJList;
      private JScrollPane selectionJS;
      private JLabel promptJL;
      private JLabel displayPicJL;
      private JLabel infoJL;

      public JListPictureViewer()
      {
         super("Photo Viewer");

         Container pane = getContentPane();
         pane.setLayout(null);

         promptJL = new JLabel("Select an Image",
                              SwingConstants.CENTER);
         promptJL.setSize(350, 20);
         promptJL.setLocation(10, 0);
         pane.add(promptJL);

         pictureJList = new JList(pictureNames);
         pictureJList.setVisibleRowCount(3);
         pictureJList.setSelectionMode
                    (ListSelectionModel.SINGLE_SELECTION);
         pictureJList.addListSelectionListener(this);

         selectionJS = new JScrollPane(pictureJList);
         selectionJS.setSize(350, 60);
         selectionJS.setLocation(10, 20);
         pane.add(selectionJS);

         displayPicJL = new JLabel(pictures[4]);
         displayPicJL.setSize(350, 350);
         displayPicJL.setLocation(10, 50);

         pane.add(displayPicJL);

         infoJL = new JLabel(pictureNames[4],
                            SwingConstants.CENTER);
         infoJL.setSize(350, 20);
         infoJL.setLocation(10, 380);
         pane.add(infoJL);

         setSize (380, 440);
         setVisible(true);
         setDefaultCloseOperation(EXIT_ON_CLOSE);
      }

      public static void main(String args[])
      {
         JListPictureViewer picViewer = new JListPictureViewer();
      }
```

```
    public void valueChanged(ListSelectionEvent e)
    {
        displayPicJL.setIcon(
            pictures[pictureJList.getSelectedIndex()]);
        infoJL.setText(
            pictureNames[pictureJList.getSelectedIndex()]);
        repaint();
    }
}
```

Sample Run: Figure 12-18 shows a sample run of the `JListPictureViewer` program.

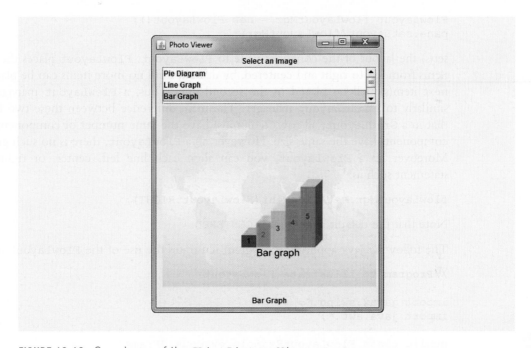

FIGURE 12-18 Sample run of the `JListPictureViewer` program

Layout Managers

In earlier chapters, you saw two layout managers: `GridLayout` and `null`. For `GridLayout`, you specify the number of rows and columns you want, and you can place your components from left to right, row-by-row, or from top to bottom. If you choose the `null` layout, you have to specify the size and location of each component. Java provides many layout managers; this section briefly introduces two more.

FlowLayout

FlowLayout is the default layout manager for a Java application. Creating a FlowLayout manager is similar to creating a GridLayout manager. For example, suppose that you have the following declaration:

```
Container pane = getContentPane();
```

The statement(s):

```
pane.setLayout(new FlowLayout());
```

or:

```
FlowLayout flowLayoutMgr = new FlowLayout();
pane.setLayout(flowLayoutMgr);
```

set(s) the layout of the container pane to FlowLayout. FlowLayout places the components from left to right and centered, by default, until no more items can be placed. The next item(s) will be placed in the second line. Thus, a FlowLayout manager works similarly to a GridLayout manager. The main difference between these two layouts is that in a GridLayout, all rows (columns) have the same number of components and all components have the same size. However, in a FlowLayout, there is no such guarantee. Moreover, in a FlowLayout, you can align each line left, center, or right using a statement such as:

```
flowLayoutMgr.setAlignment(FlowLayout.RIGHT);
```

Note that the default alignment is CENTERED.

The following Java application program illustrates the use of the FlowLayout manager:

```
//Program to illustrate FlowLayout

import javax.swing.*;
import java.awt.*;

public class FlowLayoutExample extends JFrame
{
    private static int WIDTH = 350;
    private static int HEIGHT = 350;

        //Variables to create GUI components
    private JLabel labelJL;
    private JTextField textFieldTF;
    private JButton buttonJB;
    private JCheckBox checkboxCB;
    private JRadioButton radioButtonRB;
    private JTextArea textAreaTA;
```

```
    private FlowLayout flowLayoutMgr;

    public FlowLayoutExample()
    {
        setTitle("FlowLayout Manager");            //Line 1
        Container pane = getContentPane();         //Line 2
        setSize(WIDTH,HEIGHT);                      //Line 3

        flowLayoutMgr = new FlowLayout();          //Line 4
        pane.setLayout(flowLayoutMgr);             //Line 5

        labelJL = new JLabel("First Component");   //Line 6
        textFieldTF = new JTextField(15);          //Line 7
        textFieldTF.setText("Second Component");   //Line 8
        buttonJB = new JButton("Third Component"); //Line 9

        checkboxCB = new JCheckBox("Fourth Component"); //Line 10

        radioButtonRB =
                new JRadioButton("Fifth Component");    //Line 11

        textAreaTA = new JTextArea(10, 20);        //Line 12

        textAreaTA.setText("Sixth Component.\n");  //Line 13

        textAreaTA.append(
            "Use the mouse to resize the window.");    //Line 14

            //place the GUI components into the pane
        pane.add(labelJL);                         //Line 15
        pane.add(textFieldTF);                     //Line 16
        pane.add(buttonJB);                        //Line 17
        pane.add(checkboxCB);                      //Line 18
        pane.add(radioButtonRB);                   //Line 19
        pane.add(textAreaTA);                      //Line 20

        setVisible(true);                          //Line 21
        setDefaultCloseOperation(EXIT_ON_CLOSE);   //Line 22
    }

    public static void main(String[] args)         //Line 23
    {
        FlowLayoutExample flow =
                new FlowLayoutExample();           //Line 24
    }
}
```

Sample Run: Figure 12-19 shows a sample run of the `FlowLayoutExample` program.

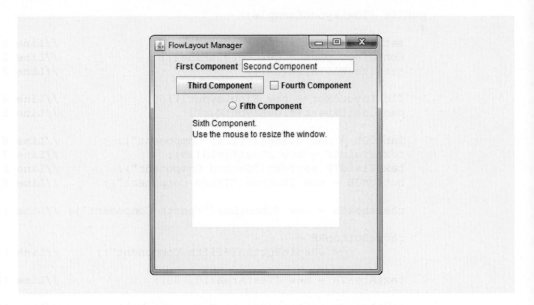

FIGURE 12-19 Sample run of the `FlowLayoutExample` program

The preceding program works as follows: The statement in Line 1 sets the title of the window. The statement in Line 2 accesses the content pane. The statement in Line 3 sets the size of the window. The statement in Line 4 creates the `FlowLayout` object `flowLayoutMgr`; the statement in Line 5 uses this object to set the layout of the pane to `FlowLayout`. (Because we did not specify the layout, the default layout, `CENTERED`, is assumed.) The statement in Line 6 instantiates the `JLabel` object `labelJL`. The statement in Line 7 instantiates the `JTextField` object `textFieldTF`, and the statement in Line 8 sets the text of the object `textFieldTF`. The statement in Line 9 instantiates the `JButton` object `buttonJB`. The statement in Line 10 instantiates the `JCheckBox` object `checkboxCB`. The statement in Line 11 instantiates the `JRadioButton` object `radioButtonRB`. The statement in Line 12 instantiates the `JTextArea` object `textAreaTA` with 10 rows and 20 columns. The statement in Line 13 places the text `Sixth Component` into the text area. The statement in Line 14 appends the text:

`Use the mouse to resize the window.`

The statements in Lines 15 through 20 place the GUI components in the pane. The statement in Line 21 sets the visibility of the window to `true`, and the statement in Line 22 sets the window closing option to close when the program terminates. When the program executes, the statement in Line 24 creates the window with the GUI components shown in the sample run.

BorderLayout

The BorderLayout manager allows you to place items in specific regions. This layout manager divides the container into five regions: NORTH, SOUTH, EAST, WEST, and CENTER. Components placed in the NORTH and SOUTH regions extend horizontally, completely spanning one edge to the other. EAST and WEST components extend vertically between the components in the NORTH and SOUTH regions. The component placed at the CENTER expands to occupy any unused regions.

In the following example, we create five components and place them in the content pane using the BorderLayout manager:

```
//Program to illustrate BorderLayout

import javax.swing.*;
import java.awt.*;

public class BorderLayoutExample extends JFrame
{
    private static int WIDTH = 350;
    private static int HEIGHT = 300;

        //GUI components
    private JLabel labelJL;
    private JTextField textFieldTF;
    private JButton buttonJB;
    private JCheckBox checkboxCB;
    private JRadioButton radioButtonRB;
    private JTextArea textAreaTA;

    private BorderLayout borderLayoutMgr;

    public BorderLayoutExample()
    {
        setTitle("BorderLayout Manager");
        Container pane  = getContentPane();
        setSize(WIDTH, HEIGHT);

        borderLayoutMgr = new BorderLayout(10, 10);
        pane.setLayout(borderLayoutMgr);

        labelJL = new JLabel("North Component");
        textAreaTA = new JTextArea(10, 20);
        textAreaTA.setText("South Component.\n");
        textAreaTA.append(
            "Use the mouse to change the size of the window.");
        buttonJB = new JButton("West Component");
        checkboxCB = new JCheckBox("East Component");
        radioButtonRB = new JRadioButton("Center Component");
```

1
2

```
        pane.add(labelJL, BorderLayout.NORTH);
        pane.add(textAreaTA, BorderLayout.SOUTH);
        pane.add(buttonJB, BorderLayout.EAST);
        pane.add(checkboxCB, BorderLayout.WEST);
        pane.add(radioButtonRB, BorderLayout.CENTER);

        setVisible(true);
        setDefaultCloseOperation(EXIT_ON_CLOSE);
    }

    public static void main(String[] args)
    {
        BorderLayoutExample flow = new BorderLayoutExample();
    }
}
```

Sample Run: A sample run of the `BorderLayoutExample` program is shown in Figure 12-20.

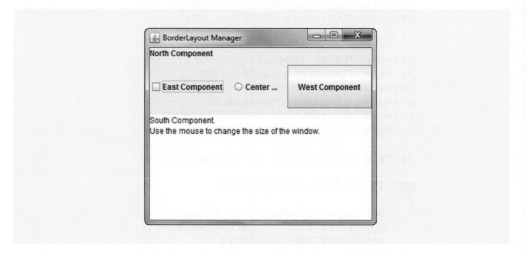

FIGURE 12-20 Sample run of the `BorderLayoutExample` program

Menus

Menus allow you to provide various functions without cluttering the GUI with too many components. Menus can be attached to objects, such as `JFrame` and `JApplet`.

The `classes` `JFrame` and `JApplet` both have the method `setJMenuBar` that allows you to set a menu bar. To set a menu bar, say, `menuMB`, you need statements such as the following:

```
private JMenuBar menuMB = new JMenuBar();  //creates a menu bar

setJMenuBar(menuMB);                              //sets the menu bar
```

Once you have created a menu bar, you can add menus, and in each menu you can add menu items. For instance, to create an `Edit` menu and add it to the menu bar created above, you need the following two statements:

```
JMenu editM = new JMenu("Edit");   //creates a menu "Edit"
menuMB.add(editM);                 //adds the menu to menu bar
                                   //menuMB created above
```

Likewise, if you need to create a `File` menu, you may do so by adding the following lines of code:

```
JMenu fileM = new JMenu("File");

menuMB.add(fileM);
```

Notice that the order in which you add menus to the menu bar determines the order in which they appear. For example, if you want the `File` menu to appear first, you must add it first.

The following program illustrates the use of menus:

```
import java.awt.*;
import java.awt.event.*;
import javax.swing.*;

public class TextEditor extends JFrame implements
                                            ActionListener
{
    private JMenuBar menuMB =
                    new JMenuBar(); //create the menu bar
    private JMenu fileM, editM, optionM;
    private JMenuItem exitI;
    private JMenuItem cutI, copyI, pasteI, selectI;
    private JTextArea pageTA = new JTextArea();
    private String scratchpad = "";

    public TextEditor()
    {
        setTitle("Simple Text Editor");

        Container pane = getContentPane();

        pane.setLayout(new BorderLayout());
        pane.add(pageTA, BorderLayout.CENTER);
        pane.add(new JScrollPane(pageTA));
        pageTA.setLineWrap(true);
```

```
        setJMenuBar(menuMB);
        setFileMenu();
        setEditMenu();
        setSize(300, 200);

        setVisible(true);
        setDefaultCloseOperation(EXIT_ON_CLOSE);
    }

    private void setFileMenu()
    {
        fileM = new JMenu("File");
        menuMB.add(fileM);
        exitI = new JMenuItem("Exit");
        fileM.add(exitI);
        exitI.addActionListener(this);
    }

    private void setEditMenu()
    {
        editM = new JMenu("Edit");
        menuMB.add(editM);
        cutI = new JMenuItem("Cut");
        editM.add(cutI);
        cutI.addActionListener(this);
        copyI = new JMenuItem("Copy");
        editM.add(copyI);
        copyI.addActionListener(this);
        pasteI = new JMenuItem("Paste");
        editM.add(pasteI);
        pasteI.addActionListener(this);
        selectI = new JMenuItem("Select All");
        editM.add(selectI);
        selectI.addActionListener(this);
    }

    public void actionPerformed(ActionEvent e)
    {
        JMenuItem mItem = (JMenuItem) e.getSource();

        if (mItem == exitI)
        {
            System.exit(0);
        }
        else if (mItem == cutI)
        {
            scratchpad = pageTA.getSelectedText();
            pageTA.replaceRange("",
                        pageTA.getSelectionStart(),
                        pageTA.getSelectionEnd());
        }
```

```
        else if (mItem == copyI)
            scratchpad = pageTA.getSelectedText();
        else if (mItem == pasteI)
            pageTA.insert(scratchpad, pageTA.getCaretPosition());
        else if (mItem == selectI)
            pageTA.selectAll();
    }

    public static void main(String args[])
    {
        TextEditor texted = new TextEditor();
    }
}
```

Sample Run: A sample run of the program with menus is shown in Figure 12-21.

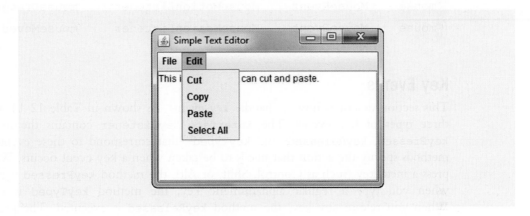

FIGURE 12-21 Sample run of the `TextEditor` program

Key and Mouse Events

In this chapter and in the preceding chapters, you learned how to handle action events when the user clicks a button. Moreover, Chapter 11 noted that when the Enter key is pressed in a text field, an action event is generated. Also, recall that when a mouse button is pressed to click a button, in addition to generating an action event, a mouse event is generated. Likewise, when the Enter key is pressed in a text field, in addition to the action event, a key event is generated. Therefore, a GUI program can simultaneously generate more than one event. This section includes various programs to show how to handle key and mouse events.

Recall from Chapter 11 that key events are handled by the **interface KeyListener**, and mouse events are handled by the **interfaces MouseListener** and **MouseMotionListener**. The key and mouse events and the corresponding event handlers were shown in Table 11-14 and are reproduced in Table 12-14.

1
2

TABLE 12-14 Events Generated by the Keyboard and Mouse

	Event Generated	Listener Interface	Listener Method
key	KeyEvent	KeyListener	keyPressed
key	KeyEvent	KeyListener	keyReleased
key	KeyEvent	KeyListener	keyTyped
mouse	MouseEvent	MouseListener	mouseClicked
mouse	MouseEvent	MouseListener	mouseEntered
mouse	MouseEvent	MouseListener	mouseExited
mouse	MouseEvent	MouseListener	mousePressed
mouse	MouseEvent	MouseListener	mouseReleased
mouse	MouseEvent	MouseMotionListener	mouseDragged
mouse	MouseEvent	MouseMotionListener	mouseMoved

Key Events

This section describes how to handle key events. As shown in Table 12-14, there are three types of key events. The `interface KeyListener` contains the methods—`keyPressed`, `keyReleased`, and `keyTyped`—that correspond to these events. These methods specify the action that needs to be taken when a key event occurs. When you press a meta key (such as Control, Shift, or Alt), the method `keyPressed` is executed; when you type a regular alphanumeric key, the method `keyTyped` is executed. When you release any key, the method `keyReleased` is executed. The program in Example 12-8 shows how to handle key events.

EXAMPLE 12-8

This program displays the character that corresponds to the key typed by the user. For example, if the user presses the key A, the program displays A. We use a `JTextField` object to display the character.

When you type an alphanumeric key, a key event is generated. The key event is handled by the method `keyTyped`. The necessary code to display the key is placed in the body of the method `keyTyped`. Before displaying the key typed by the user, the previous character is removed from the `JTextField` object. In other words, the program displays only one character at a time, corresponding to the key typed. In this program, the font of the character is set to `Courier` and the color of the character is randomly selected.

Because the interface `keyListener` contains three methods and we want to implement only one of these methods, we use the anonymous class mechanism to register a listener object. The complete program listing follows. (Notice that the program uses a message dialog box to inform the user what to do.)

```java
//Key Event

import java.awt.*;
import java.awt.event.*;
import javax.swing.*;

public class OneChar extends JApplet
{
    JTextField oneLetter = new JTextField(1);

    public void init()
    {
        Container c = getContentPane();

          //register the listener object
        oneLetter.addKeyListener(new KeyAdapter()
        {
            public void keyTyped(KeyEvent e)
            {
                float red, green, blue;

                Color fg, bg;

                oneLetter.setText(" ");

                red = (float) Math.random();
                green = (float) Math.random();
                blue = (float) Math.random();

                fg = new Color(red, green, blue);
                bg = Color.white;

                oneLetter.setForeground(fg);
                oneLetter.setBackground(bg);
                oneLetter.setCaretColor(bg);
                oneLetter.setFont(new Font("Courier",
                                        Font.BOLD, 200));
            }
        });

        c.setLayout(new GridLayout(1, 1));
        c.setBackground(Color.white);
        c.add(oneLetter);

        JOptionPane.showMessageDialog
            (null, "Click on the applet, then type a key ",
            "Information", JOptionPane.PLAIN_MESSAGE );
    }
}
```

1
2

The HTML file for this program contains the following code:

```
<HTML>
  <HEAD>
    <TITLE>ONECHAR APPLET</TITLE>
  </HEAD>
  <BODY>
    <OBJECT code = "OneChar.class" width = "350" height = "300">
    </OBJECT>
  </BODY>
</HTML>
```

Sample Run: Figure 12-22 shows a sample run of the `OneChar` applet. (Notice that Figure 12-22 does not show the message dialog box. However, when you execute this program, it first shows the message dialog box.)

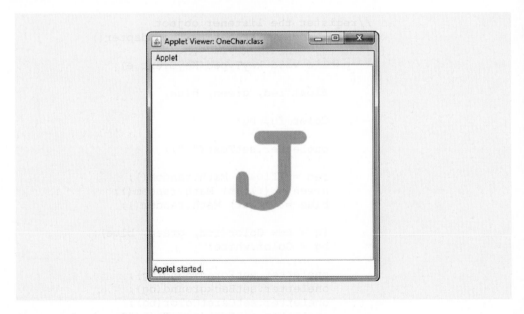

FIGURE 12-22   Sample run of the `OneChar` applet

Mouse Events

This section describes how to handle mouse events. A mouse can generate seven different types of events, as shown previously in Table 12-14. Some mouse events are handled by the **interface** `MouseListener` and others are handled by the **interface** `MouseMotionListener`. Table 12-14 also shows which listener method is executed when a particular mouse event occurs. Example 12-9 illustrates how to handle mouse events.

EXAMPLE 12-9

This example shows how to handle the following mouse events: mouse clicked, mouse entered, mouse exited, mouse pressed, and mouse released. To handle these events, we use the methods of the **interface** MouseListener. The MouseExample program contains six labels corresponding to the five mouse events and one label to display the mouse location. When you run this program and use the mouse, the foreground color of the label corresponding to the generated mouse event changes, and the mouse location where the event occurred is displayed.

```
//Program to illustrate mouse events

import javax.swing.*;
import java.awt.*;
import java.awt.event.*;

public class MouseExample extends JFrame
                          implements MouseListener
{
    private static int WIDTH = 350;
    private static int HEIGHT = 250;

        //GUI components
    private JLabel[] labelJL;

    public MouseExample()
    {
        setTitle("Mouse Events");
        Container pane  = getContentPane();
        setSize(WIDTH,HEIGHT);

        GridLayout gridMgr = new GridLayout(6, 1, 10, 10);
        pane.setLayout(gridMgr);

        labelJL = new JLabel[6];

        labelJL[0] = new JLabel("Mouse Clicked",
                        SwingConstants.CENTER);
        labelJL[1] = new JLabel("Mouse Entered",
                        SwingConstants.CENTER);
        labelJL[2] = new JLabel("Mouse Exited",
                        SwingConstants.CENTER);
        labelJL[3] = new JLabel("Mouse Pressed",
                        SwingConstants.CENTER);
        labelJL[4] = new JLabel("Mouse Released",
                        SwingConstants.CENTER);
        labelJL[5] = new JLabel("",SwingConstants.CENTER);
```

1
2

```java
    for (int i = 0; i < labelJL.length; i++)
    {
        labelJL[i].setForeground(Color.gray);
        pane.add(labelJL[i]);
    }

    pane.addMouseListener(this);

    setVisible(true);
    setDefaultCloseOperation(EXIT_ON_CLOSE);
}

public void mouseClicked(MouseEvent event)
{
    for (int i = 0; i < labelJL.length; i++)
    {
        if (i == 0)
            labelJL[i].setForeground(Color.yellow);
        else
            labelJL[i].setForeground(Color.gray);
    }

    labelJL[5].setText("["+ event.getX() + ","
                        + event.getY()+"]");

}

public void mouseEntered(MouseEvent event)
{
    for (int i = 0; i < labelJL.length; i++)
    {
        if (i == 1)
            labelJL[i].setForeground(Color.green);
        else
            labelJL[i].setForeground(Color.gray);
    }

    labelJL[5].setText("["+ event.getX() + ","
                        + event.getY()+"]");
}

public void mouseExited(MouseEvent event)
{
    for (int i = 0; i < labelJL.length; i++)
    {
        if (i == 2)
            labelJL[i].setForeground(Color.red);
        else
            labelJL[i].setForeground(Color.gray);
    }

    labelJL[5].setText("["+ event.getX() + ","
                        + event.getY()+"]");
}
```

```
    public void mousePressed(MouseEvent event)
    {
        for (int i = 0; i < labelJL.length; i++)
        {
            if (i == 3)
                labelJL[i].setForeground(Color.blue);
            else
                labelJL[i].setForeground(Color.gray);
        }

        labelJL[5].setText("["+ event.getX() + ","
                            + event.getY()+"]");
    }

    public void mouseReleased(MouseEvent event)
    {
        for (int i = 0; i < labelJL.length; i++)
        {
            if (i == 4)
                labelJL[i].setForeground(Color.pink);
            else
                labelJL[i].setForeground(Color.gray);
        }

        labelJL[5].setText("["+ event.getX() + ","
                            + event.getY()+"]");
    }

    public static void main(String[] args)
    {
        MouseExample flow = new MouseExample();
    }
}
```

Sample Run: Figure 12-23 shows a sample run of the `MouseExample` program.

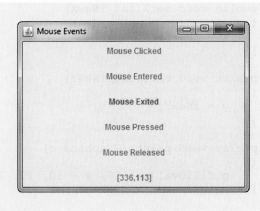

FIGURE 12-23 Sample run of the `MouseExample` program

EXAMPLE 12-10

The program in this example shows how to handle the mouse-dragged event. You can handle the mouse moved event similarly. These events are handled by the interface `MouseMotionListener`, which contains the methods `mouseDragged` and `mouseMoved`, which, in turn, are used to handle the mouse-dragged and mouse-moved events, respectively.

The program starts with some colored dots. If you drag a dot using the mouse, the dot turns into a line. This way, you can "freehand draw" different pictures. What is really happening is that we created small circle objects. The program contains the method `selected` to check whether or not the mouse is on a circle. If you drag a circle, the method `mouseDragged` is invoked and it paints a new circle. The sequence of circles gives the impression of drawing a line. The complete program listing follows:

```java
import javax.swing.*;
import java.awt.event.*;
import java.applet.*;
import java.awt.*;

public class FreeDrawApplet extends JApplet
                            implements MouseMotionListener
{
       //instance variables
    ColorCircle[] myGraph;

    final int NUM_CIRCLES = 7;
    final int WIDTH = 400;
    final int HEIGHT = 400;

    public class ColorCircle
    {
        private int x;
        private int y;

        public void setX(int iNewX)
        {
            x = iNewX;
        }

        public void setY(int iNewY)
        {
            y = iNewY;
        }

        public void paint (Graphics g)
        {
            g.fillOval(x - 10, y - 10, 20, 20);
        }
```

```java
        public boolean selected(int iXcoord, int iYcoord)
        {
            if ((iXcoord >= x - 10) && (iXcoord <= x + 10)
                && (iYcoord >= y - 10) && (iYcoord <= y + 10))
                return true;
            else
                return false;
        }
    }

    public void init ()
    {
        addMouseMotionListener(this);
        myGraph = new ColorCircle[NUM_CIRCLES];

        for (int i = 0; i < NUM_CIRCLES; i++)
        {
            ColorCircle myVertex = new ColorCircle();

            myVertex.setX((int)(Math.random() * (WIDTH-50)));

            myVertex.setY((int)(Math.random() * (HEIGHT - 100)));

            myGraph[i] = myVertex;
        }

        JOptionPane.showMessageDialog(null,
                "Try to drag any one of the colored circles ",
                "Information", JOptionPane.PLAIN_MESSAGE );

    }

    public void paint(Graphics g)
    {
        Color[] myColor = {Color.black, Color.red, Color.blue,
                            Color.green, Color.cyan,
                            Color.orange, Color.yellow};

        if (NUM_CIRCLES > 0)
            for (int i = 0; i < NUM_CIRCLES; i++)
            {
                g.setColor(myColor[i]);
                myGraph[i].paint(g);
            }
    }

    public void mouseDragged(MouseEvent event)
    {
        int iX = event.getX();
        int iY = event.getY();

        for (int i = 0; i < NUM_CIRCLES; i++)
            if (myGraph[i].selected(iX, iY))
```

```
                    {
                        myGraph[i].setX(iX);
                        myGraph[i].setY(iY);
                        break;
                    }

            repaint();

        }

        public void mouseMoved(MouseEvent p1)
        {
        }
    }
```

The HTML file for this program contains the following code:

```html
<HTML>
  <HEAD>
    <TITLE>Drawing Board</TITLE>
  </HEAD>
  <BODY>
    <OBJECT code = "FreeDrawApplet.class" width = "400"
                                          height = "400">
    </OBJECT>
  </BODY>
</HTML>
```

Sample Run: Figure 12-24 shows a sample run of the `FreeDrawApplet`.

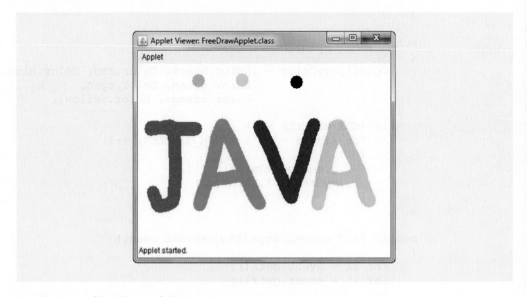

FIGURE 12-24   Sample run of the `FreeDrawApplet`

The program FreeDrawApplet uses small circles to draw lines. Because there is no GUI component we can use, we created the class ColorCircle. This class has two private members x and y of the type int. The point (x, y) specifies the center of the circle, and the radius of the circle is fixed at 10 pixels. In addition to the methods to set the values of x and y, the class ColorCircle has only two other methods: paint and isSelected. The paint method draws a filled circle of radius 10 at the point (x, y). The method isSelected returns true if and only if (iXcoord, iYcoord) lies inside a 20-by-20 square with the point (x, y) as the center. We use this method to check whether the mouse is at, say, (iXcoord, iYcoord) on the circle with the center (x, y). Note that because ColorCircle is not a GUI component, it can generate any event. Therefore, any time a mouseDragged event is generated, we must check whether the mouse is on any of the circles. We do so using the following for loop:

```
for (int i = 0; i < NUM_CIRCLES; i++)
    if (myGraph[i].selected(iX, iY))
    {
        myGraph[i].setX(iX);
        myGraph[i].setY(iY);
        break;
    }
```

Note that if a mouseDragged event occurs on a ColorCircle object, the preceding for loop sets the current mouse position as the new center of the ColorCircle object. This, in effect, moves the ColorCircle object. By continually moving a ColorCircle object, we create a line.

PROGRAMMING EXAMPLE: Java Kiosk

In this programming example, we design a program that simulates a fast food kiosk. The program displays a menu similar to one you might find in a fast food restaurant. The user makes a selection and then presses a JButton to mark the end of the selection process. The program then calculates and displays the bill. A sample output is shown in Figure 12-25.

1
2

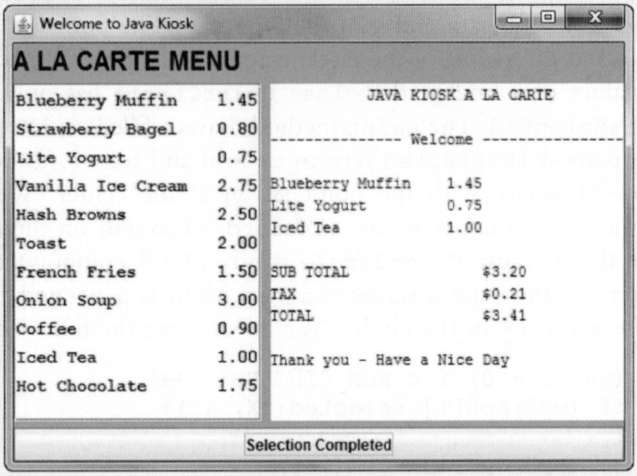

FIGURE 12-25 Sample output of the Java Kiosk program

Input: A list of selected items from the menu shown on the left in Figure 12-25.

Output: A bill shown on the right in Figure 12-25.

PROBLEM
ANALYSIS
AND GUI AND
ALGORITHM
DESIGN

As shown in Figure 12-25, there are five GUI components: a frame, a label, a list, a text area, and a button. All components other than the frame are placed into the content pane of the window. The user selects various list items and then presses the `Selection Completed` button. Recall that when you click a button, it generates an action event, which is processed by using the `interface` ActionListener. Therefore, we will create and register an action listener object with the button.

When the event is generated, the event handler computes the subtotal, tax, and total. The program then displays the result in the text area. To create the label, list, text area, and button, we use reference variables of the types JLabel, JList, JTextArea, and JButton, respectively. We also need a reference variable to access the content pane of the window. As in the GUI programs in previous chapters, we create the class containing the application program by extending the definition of the `class` JFrame; this also allows us to create the necessary window to create the GUI. Thus, we use the following reference variables to create the GUI components and to access the content pane of the window:

```
private JList yourChoices;
private JTextArea bill;
```

```
private Container pane;
JLabel yourChoicesJLabel;
JButton button;
```

The next step is to instantiate four GUI components and initialize the pane using the method `getContentPane`. Recall that, to create a list, we first create an array of strings and then use the array as the argument in the constructor of the `JList`. We can instantiate other GUI components the same way we have done previously. This program uses the `BorderLayout` to neatly place all four GUI components. We place the label in the NORTH region, the list in the WEST region, the text area in the EAST region, and the button in the SOUTH region.

The following statement creates the array of strings to create the menu:

```
static String[] yourChoicesItems =
                      {"Blueberry Muffin     1.45",
                       "Strawberry Bagel     0.80",
                       "Lite Yogurt          0.75",
                       "Vanilla Ice Cream    2.75",
                       "Hash Browns          2.50",
                       "Toast                2.00",
                       "French Fries         1.50",
                       "Onion Soup           3.00",
                       "Coffee               0.90",
                       "Iced Tea             1.00",
                       "Hot Chocolate        1.75"};
```

The following statements create the necessary GUI components and place them in the container:

```
private JList yourChoices;
private JTextArea bill;

private Container pane;

pane = getContentPane();
pane.setBackground(new Color(0, 200, 200));
pane.setLayout(new BorderLayout(5, 5));

        //Create a label and place it in the NORTH region
        //and set the font of this label.
JLabel yourChoicesJLabel = new JLabel("A LA CARTE MENU");
pane.add(yourChoicesJLabel, BorderLayout.NORTH);
yourChoicesJLabel.setFont(new Font("Dialog", Font.BOLD, 20));

        //Create a list and place it in the WEST region
        //and set the font of this list.
yourChoices = new JList(yourChoicesItems);
pane.add(new JScrollPane (yourChoices), BorderLayout.WEST);
yourChoices.setFont(new Font("Courier", Font.BOLD, 14));
```

1
2

```
        //Create a text area and place it in the EAST region
        //and set the font of this text area.
bill = new JTextArea();
pane.add(bill, BorderLayout.EAST);
bill.setFont(new Font("Courier", Font.PLAIN, 12));

        //Create a button and place it in the SOUTH region and
        //add an action listener.
JButton button = new JButton("Selection Completed");
pane.add(button, BorderLayout.SOUTH);
button.addActionListener(this);
```

We need another array to keep track of the prices of the various items.

```
static double[] yourChoicesPrices = {1.45, 0.80, 0.75, 2.75,
                                     2.50, 2.00, 1.50, 3.00,
                                     0.90, 1.00, 1.75};
```

The following statements set the size of the window and set its visibility to true:

```
setSize(500, 360);
setVisible(true);
```

Recall that when an action event is generated by a button, the method actionPerformed is invoked. When the user clicks the button, the program must compute the subtotal, tax, and total, and display the result in the text area. The instructions to perform these tasks are placed in the method actionPerformed, which is described next.

Method actionPerformed

As noted previously, the method actionPerformed is executed when the user clicks the button. The method actionPerformed calculates and displays the bill. We write the method displayBill that computes the bill and displays it using the text area. The method actionPerformed invokes the method displayBill to display the bill. The definition of the method actionPerformed is:

```
public void actionPerformed(ActionEvent event)
{
    if (event.getActionCommand().equals("Selection Completed"))
        displayBill();
}
```

Method displayBill

The method displayBill first needs to identify the items selected by the user. The method getSelectedIndices of the JList will return an array of indices. Because we need an integer array to hold these indices, we might need the following Java statements:

```
int[] listArray = yourChoices.getSelectedIndices();
double localTax = 0.065;
double tax;
double subtotal = 0;
double total;
```

Note that `listArray[0]`, `listArray[1]`, ..., `listArray[listArray.length - 1]` contains the indices of the items selected from the menu list. Therefore, the following `for` loop computes the total cost of the items selected from the menu:

```
for (int index = 0; index < listArray.length; index++)
    subTotal = subTotal + yourChoicesPrices[listArray[index]];
```

Next, we compute the tax and add it to `subTotal` to get the billing amount:

```
tax = localTax * subTotal;
total = subTotal + tax;
```

To display the bill, we append the necessary statements to the `JTextArea` and invoke the `repaint` method to redraw the GUI components. To place another order, we unselect the selected items. The definition of the method `displayBill` is:

```
    // method to display the order and total cost
private void displayBill()
{
    int[] listArray = yourChoices.getSelectedIndices();
    double localTax = 0.065;
    double tax;
    double subtotal = 0;
    double total;

        //Set the text area to nonedit mode
        //and start with an empty string.
    bill.setEditable(false);
    bill.setText("");

        //Calculate the cost of the items ordered.
    for (int index = 0; index < listArray.length; index++)
        subTotal = subTotal + yourChoicesPrices[listArray[index]];

    tax = localTax * subTotal;
    total = subTotal + tax;

        //Display costs.
    bill.append("            JAVA KIOSK A LA CARTE\n\n");
    bill.append("-------------- Welcome ---------------\n\n");

    for (int index = 0; index < listArray.length; index++)
    {
        bill.append(yourChoicesItems[listArray[index]] + "\n");
    }
```

```
        bill.append("\n");
        bill.append("SUB TOTAL\t\t$"
                    + String.format("%.2f", subTotal) + "\n");
        bill.append("TAX        \t\t$"
                    + String.format("%.2f", tax) + "\n");
        bill.append("TOTAL      \t\t$"
                    + String.format("%.2f", total) + "\n\n");
        bill.append("Thank you - Have a Nice Day\n\n");

        //reset the list array
        yourChoices.clearSelection();

        repaint();
}
```

The program listing is as follows:

```
//A la Carte

import java.awt.*;
import java.awt.event.*;
import javax.swing.*;
import javax.swing.event.*;

public class AlaCarte extends JFrame implements ActionListener
{
    static String[] yourChoicesItems =
                            {"Blueberry Muffin     1.45",
                             "Strawberry Bagel     0.80",
                             "Lite Yogurt          0.75",
                             "Vanilla Ice Cream    2.75",
                             "Hash Browns          2.50",
                             "Toast                2.00",
                             "French Fries         1.50",
                             "Onion Soup           3.00",
                             "Coffee               0.90",
                             "Iced Tea             1.00",
                             "Hot Chocolate        1.75"};

    static double[] yourChoicesPrices = {1.45, 0.80, 0.75, 2.75,
                                         2.50, 2.00, 1.50, 3.00,
                                         0.90, 1.00, 1.75};
    private JList yourChoices;
    private JTextArea  bill;

    private Container pane;
```

```java
public AlaCarte()
{
    super("Welcome to Java Kiosk");

        //Get the content pane and set its background color
        //and layout manager.
    pane = getContentPane();
    pane.setBackground(new Color(0, 200, 200));
    pane.setLayout(new BorderLayout(5, 5));

        //Create a label and place it at NORTH. Also
        //set the font of this label.
    JLabel yourChoicesJLabel = new JLabel("A LA CARTE MENU");
    pane.add(yourChoicesJLabel,BorderLayout.NORTH);
    yourChoicesJLabel.setFont(new Font("Dialog",Font.BOLD,20));

        //Create a list and place it at WEST. Also
        //set the font of this list.
    yourChoices = new JList(yourChoicesItems);
    pane.add(new JScrollPane (yourChoices),BorderLayout.WEST);
    yourChoices.setFont(new Font("Courier",Font.BOLD,14));

        //Create a text area and place it at EAST. Also
        //set the font of this text area.
    bill = new JTextArea();
    pane.add(bill,BorderLayout.EAST);
    bill.setFont(new Font("Courier",Font.PLAIN,12));

        //Create a button and place it in the SOUTH region
        //and add an action listener.
    JButton button = new JButton("Selection Completed");
    pane.add(button,BorderLayout.SOUTH);
    button.addActionListener(this);

    setSize(500, 360);
    setVisible(true);
    setDefaultCloseOperation(EXIT_ON_CLOSE);
}

    //method to display the order and the total cost
private void displayBill()
{
    int[] listArray = yourChoices.getSelectedIndices();
    double localTax = 0.065;
    double tax;
    double subTotal = 0;
    double total;

        //Set the text area to nonedit mode and start
        //with an empty string.
    bill.setEditable(false);
    bill.setText("");
```

```
                //Calculate the cost of the items ordered.
        for (int index = 0; index < listArray.length; index++)
            subTotal = subTotal
                        + yourChoicesPrices[listArray[index]];

        tax = localTax * subTotal;
        total = subTotal + tax;

            //Display the costs.
        bill.append("             JAVA KIOSK A LA CARTE\n\n");
        bill.append("--------------- Welcome ----------------\n\n");

        for (int index = 0; index < listArray.length; index++)
        {
            bill.append(yourChoicesItems[listArray[index]] + "\n");
        }

        bill.append("\n");
        bill.append("SUB TOTAL\t\t$"
                    + String.format("%.2f", subTotal) + "\n");
        bill.append("TAX        \t\t$"
                    + String.format("%.2f", tax) + "\n");
        bill.append("TOTAL      \t\t$"
                    + String.format("%.2f", total) + "\n\n");
        bill.append("Thank you - Have a Nice Day\n\n");

            //Reset list array.
        yourChoices.clearSelection();

        repaint();
    }

    public void actionPerformed(ActionEvent event)
    {
        if (event.getActionCommand().equals("Selection Completed"))
            displayBill();
    }

    public static void main(String[] args)
    {
        AlaCarte alc = new AlaCarte();
    }
}
```

Sample Run: Figure 12-26 shows a sample run of the program. (To make more than one selection, click the first selection, hold the Ctrl key, then click the left mouse button on the other selections. To make contiguous selections, click the first item, hold the Shift key, then click the last item you want to select.)

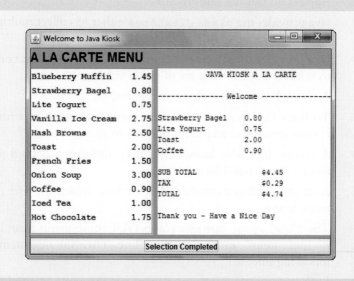

FIGURE 12-26 Sample run of the Java Kiosk program

QUICK REVIEW

1. The term applet means a little application.

2. An applet is a Java program that is embedded within a Web page and executed by a Web browser.

3. You create an applet by extending the `class` JApplet, which is contained in the `package` javax.swing.

4. Unlike a Java application program, a Java applet does not have the `main` method.

5. When a browser runs an applet, the methods `init`, `start`, and `paint` are guaranteed to be invoked in sequence.

6. All statements to be executed only once are kept in the `init` method of an applet.

7. An applet does not have a title.

8. The `class`es Font and Color are contained in the `package` java.awt.

9. Java uses the color scheme known as RGB, where R stands for red, G for green, and B for blue.

10. You create instances of the `class` Color by mixing red, green, and blue hues in various proportions.

11. An applet class is derived from the `class` JApplet, whereas a GUI application class is created by extending the `class` JFrame.

12. Applets do not use constructors.

13. Java provides the `class` JTextArea either to collect multiple lines of input from the user or to display multiple lines of output.

14. Java provides the `classes` JCheckBox and JRadioButton to allow a user to select a value from a set of given values.

15. A check box is also called a toggle button.

16. To force the user to select only one radio button at a time, you create a button group and add radio buttons to the group.

17. A combo box, also known as a drop-down list, is used to select an item from a list of possibilities.

18. A JList displays a number of items from which the user can select one or more items.

19. The FlowLayout manager places GUI components from left to right until no more items can be placed in a line. Then the next item is placed in the following line.

20. In the case of BorderLayout manager, the component placed at the center expands to occupy any unused regions.

21. Menus allow you to provide various functions without cluttering the GUI with components.

22. Menus can be attached to objects such as JFrame and JApplet.

23. Key events are handled by the `interface` KeyListener; mouse events are handled by the `interfaces` MouseListener and MouseMotionListener.

EXERCISES

1. Mark the following statements as true or false.

a. An applet's width and height are specified in the HTML file.

b. In Java, JApplet is a class.

c. To display an applet, you do not need to invoke a method, such as setVisible().

d. You must include an exit button in all Java applets.

e. When an applet is loaded, the method start is invoked before the method init.

f. Check boxes are used to display the output of a program.

g. A radio button always has a label.

h. You use JList to create a combo box.

i. JTextField can be used to output multiple lines of text.

2. Name four GUI components that can be used for input only.

3. Name two GUI components that can be used for both input and output.

4. Name a GUI component that can be used for output only.

5. Why do you need check boxes in a GUI program?

6. Fill in the blanks in each of the following:

   a. The _____ method of the `class Graphics` draws a rectangle.

   b. RGB is short for ____, ____, and _____.

   c. The method _____ is invoked when an item is selected from a combo box and a(n) _____ is registered to handle an event.

   d. The _____ method of the `class Graphics` can be used to draw a circle.

   e. Font sizes are specified in units called _____.

   f. Both `JTextField` and `JTextArea` inherit directly from the `class` _____.

   g. The method `Random` returns a value between _____ and _____.

   h. The method _____ gets the string in the `JTextArea`, and the method _____ changes the string displayed in a `JTextArea`.

   i. The `BorderLayout` manager divides the container into five regions: _____, _____, _____, _____, and _____.

   j. The _____ class is used to create a slider for _____.

   k. You cannot use `System.out.println` inside a(n) _____ method.

7. Write the necessary statements to create the following:

   a. A `JList` with the list items `orange`, `apple`, `banana`, `grape`, and `pineapple`

   b. A check box with the label `draft`

   c. A group of three radio buttons with the labels `home`, `visitor`, and `neutral`

   d. A menu bar

   e. A Courier bold 32-point font

   f. A new color that is not already defined in the `class Color`

8. Correct any syntax errors in the following program:

```
//Grand Welcome Problem Applet

import java.awt.*;
import javax.swing.JApplet;

public class GrandWelcomeProblem extends JApplet
{
    public int()
```

1
2

```
    {
        JLabel myLabel = new JLabel("");
    }

    public void paint( Graphics g)
    {
        super.paint(g);
        Container pane = g.getContentPane();
        pane.setLayout(BORDER_LAYOUT);
        pane.add(BORDER_LAYOUT.CENTER);

        myLabel.setText("A Grand Welcome to "
                        + "Java Programming! ");
    }
}
```

PROGRAMMING EXERCISES

1. Create an applet to draw a digit using the method `fillRect` of the **class**
    `Graphics`. For instance, if the input is 4, the applet will display the digit 4, as
    shown in Figure 12-27.

FIGURE 12-27 Figure for Programming Exercise 1

2. Modify the applet created in Programming Exercise 1 by adding eight radio
    buttons so the user can change the color of the digit drawn.

3. Modify the applet created in Programming Exercise 1 by adding a color menu to change the color of the digit drawn.

4. Modify the applet created in Programming Exercise 1 by adding a `JList` of eight items so the user can change the background color of the applet.

5. Create an applet that will draw a set of ovals similar to that shown in Figure 12-28. The user can specify the number of ovals.

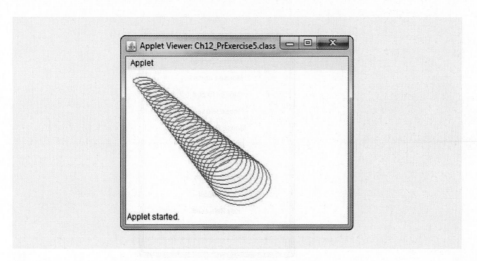

FIGURE 12-28 Figure for Programming Exercise 5

6. Modify the applet in Programming Exercise 5 by adding three different types of GUI components so the user can select from the following:

   a. Number of figures: 1, 2, 4, 8, 16, or various combinations of these numbers

   b. Type of figures: circle, oval, rectangle, or square

   c. Color: red, blue, green, yellow, pink, black, cyan, or magenta

7. Modify the applet in Programming Exercise 5 by adding the necessary menus so the user can select from the following:

   a. Number of figures: 1, 10, 20, 30, or 40

   b. Type of figures: circle, oval, rectangle, or square

   c. Color: red, blue, green, yellow, pink, black, cyan, or magenta

8. Convert the `WhiteBoard` program (presented earlier in this chapter) from an application to an applet.

9. Redo `JListPictureViewer` (presented earlier in this chapter) using one of the layout managers. For this exercise, use a `JList` and one `JLabel` to display the image.

10. Create an applet to draw lines. The user can choose the start and end points of the line to be drawn by clicking the mouse.

11. Create an application to illustrate mouse events, mouse motion events, and keyboard events. Figure 12-29 shows the user interface. The key code corresponding to a key event or the position of the mouse is displayed just above the text field.

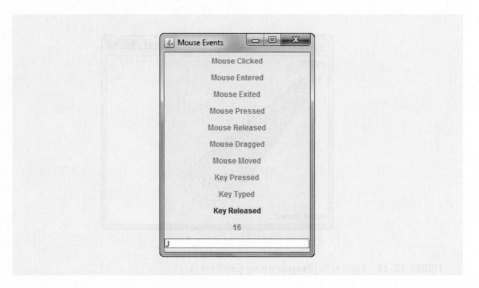

FIGURE 12-29 Figure for Programming Exercise 11

12. Create an applet to draw lines, rectangles, squares, circles, and ovals. The user can select any one of these through a menu. The user can also choose the start and end points of the line to be drawn by clicking the mouse. For other geometric figures, the user chooses the upper-left and lower-right corners by clicking the mouse.

13. Convert the Java Kiosk programming example from an application to an applet.

14. Create an applet that starts with displaying several colored circles that can be moved to different places in the applet by dragging the mouse.

15. Convert the GrandWelcomeFinal program (presented earlier in this chapter) from an applet to an application.

16. Convert the OneChar program (presented earlier in this chapter) from an applet to an application.

17. Write a GUI program that produces the figure shown in Figure 12-30.

FIGURE 12-30 Target practice

18. Write a GUI program that produces the house shown in Figure 12-31.

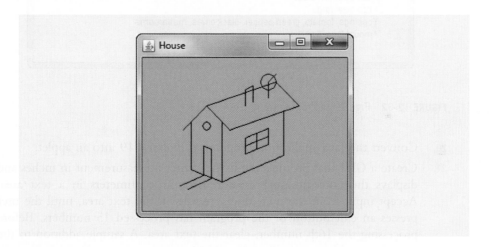

FIGURE 12-31 House

19. Write a GUI application program, to create a menu for a pizza shop. Use check boxes, radio buttons, and a JButton to allow a customer to make selections and process their order. Use a text area to display the customer's order and the amount due. A sample menu and a customer's order is shown in Figure 12-32.

FIGURE 12-32 Figure for Programming Exercise 19

20. Convert the Java application program of Exercise 19 into an applet.

21. Create a GUI that prompts the user to enter a measurement in inches and displays the corresponding measurement in centimeters in a text area. Accept input from the user, display results in the text area, until the user presses an exit button or the program has processed 15 numbers. Before processing the 16th number, clear the text area. A sample addition to the text area might be 2.00 inches = 5.08 centimeters.

22. Enhance the GUI of Programming Exercise 21 by omitting duplicate entries. Also add a scroll bar to the text area so that more than 15 lines can be viewed.

23. Enhance the GUI of Programming Exercises 22 by adding two buttons: one with the label Inches to Centimeters and the other with the label Centimeters to Inches. When the user enters a value and presses one of the two buttons, the appropriate calculation is performed and the results are appended to the text area.

CHAPTER 13

RECURSION

IN THIS CHAPTER, YOU WILL:

- Learn about recursive definitions
- Determine the base case and general case of a recursive definition
- Learn about recursive algorithms
- Learn about recursive methods
- Become familiar with direct and indirect recursion
- Learn how to use recursive methods to implement recursive algorithms

In previous chapters, we used the common technique called iteration to devise problem solutions. For certain problems, however, using the iterative technique to obtain the solution is quite complicated. This chapter introduces another problem-solving technique called recursion and provides several examples demonstrating how recursion works.

Recursive Definitions

The process of solving a problem by reducing it to successively smaller versions of itself is called **recursion**. Recursion is a powerful way to solve certain problems for which the solution can otherwise be very complicated. Let's consider a familiar problem.

In mathematics, the factorial of a nonnegative integer is defined as follows:

$$0! = 1 \qquad\qquad\qquad\qquad (13\text{-}1)$$

$$n! = n \times (n - 1)! \text{ if } n > 0 \qquad\qquad (13\text{-}2)$$

In this definition, $0!$ is defined to be 1, and if n is an integer greater than 0, first we find $(n - 1)!$ and then multiply it by n. To find $(n - 1)!$, we apply the definition again. If $(n - 1) > 0$, we use Equation 13-2; otherwise, we use Equation 13-1. Thus, for an integer n greater than 0, $n!$ is obtained by first finding $(n - 1)!$ (that is, $n!$ is determined in part by a smaller, but similar problem) and then multiplying $(n - 1)!$ by n.

Let's apply this definition to find $3!$. Here, $n = 3$. Because $n > 0$, we use Equation 13-2 to obtain:

$$3! = 3 \times 2!$$

Next we find $2!$. Here, $n = 2$. Because $n > 0$, we use Equation 13-2 to obtain:

$$2! = 2 \times 1!$$

Now, to find $1!$, we again use Equation 13-2 because $n = 1 > 0$. Thus:

$$1! = 1 \times 0!$$

Finally, we use Equation 13-1 to find $0!$, which is 1. Substituting $0!$ into $1!$ gives $1! = 1$. This gives $2! = 2 \times 1! = 2 \times 1 = 2$, which in turn gives $3! = 3 \times 2! = 3 \times 2 = 6$.

Note that the solution in Equation 13-1 is direct—that is, the right side of the equation contains no factorial notation. The solution in Equation 13-2 is given in terms of a smaller version of itself. The definition of the factorial as given in Equations 13-1 and 13-2 is called a **recursive definition**. Equation 13-1 is called the **base case**, the case for which the solution is obtained directly; Equation 13-2 is called the **general case** or **recursive case**.

Recursive definition: A definition in which something is defined in terms of a smaller version of itself.

From the previous example, it is clear that:

1. Every recursive definition must have one (or more) base case(s).
2. The general case must eventually be reduced to a base case.
3. The base case stops the recursion.

The concept of recursion in computer science works similarly. Here, we talk about recursive algorithms and recursive methods. An algorithm that finds the solution to a given problem by reducing the problem to smaller versions of itself is called a **recursive algorithm**. The recursive algorithm must have one or more base cases, and the general solution must eventually be reduced to a base case.

A method that calls itself is called a **recursive method**. That is, the body of the recursive method contains a statement that causes the same method to execute before completing the current call. Recursive algorithms are implemented using recursive methods.

Next, let's write the recursive method that implements the factorial definition:

```java
public static int fact(int num)
{
    if (num == 0)
        return 1;
    else
        return num * fact(num - 1);
}
```

Figure 13-1 traces the execution of the following statement:

```java
System.out.println(fact(4));
```

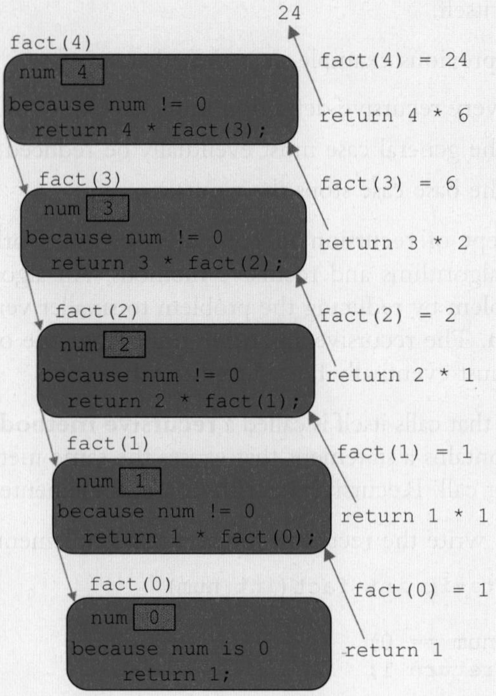

FIGURE 13-1 Execution of `fact(4)`

The output of the previous statement is 24.

In Figure 13-1, the downward arrows represent the successive calls to the method `fact`, and the upward arrows represent the values returned to the caller, that is, the calling method.

While tracing the execution of the recursive method `fact`, note the following:

- Logically, you can think of a recursive method as having unlimited copies of itself.

- Every call to a recursive method—that is, every recursive call—has its own code and its own set of parameters and local variables.

- After completing a particular recursive call, control goes back to the calling environment, which is the previous call. The current (recursive) call must execute completely before control goes back to the previous call. The execution in the previous call begins from the point immediately following the recursive call.

Direct and Indirect Recursion

A method is called **directly recursive** if it calls itself. A method that calls another method and eventually results in the original method call is called **indirectly recursive**. For example, if method A calls method B and method B calls method A, then method A is indirectly recursive. Indirect recursion could be several layers deep. For example, if method A calls method B, method B calls method C, method C calls method D, and method D calls method A, then method A is indirectly recursive.

Indirect recursion requires the same careful analysis as direct recursion. The base cases must be identified and nonrecursive solutions to them must be provided. However, tracing through indirect recursion can be a tedious process. Therefore, extra care must be exercised when designing indirect recursive methods. For simplicity, this book considers only problems that involve direct recursion.

A recursive method in which the last statement executed is the recursive call is called a **tail recursive method**. The method `fact` is an example of a tail recursive method.

Infinite Recursion

Figure 13-1 shows that the sequence of recursive calls reached a call that made no further recursive calls. That is, the sequence of recursive calls eventually reached a base case. However, if every recursive call results in another recursive call, then the recursive method (algorithm) is said to have infinite recursion. In theory, infinite recursion executes forever. However, every call to a recursive method requires the system to allocate memory for the local variables and formal parameters. In addition, the system also saves the information so that after completing a call, control can be transferred back to the caller. Therefore, because computer memory is finite, if you execute an infinite recursive method on a computer, the method will execute until the system runs out of memory, which results in an abnormal termination of the program.

Designing Recursive Methods

Recursive methods (algorithms) must be designed and analyzed carefully. You must make sure that every recursive call eventually reduces to a base case. The following sections give various examples illustrating how to design and implement recursive algorithms.

To design a recursive method, you must:

1. Understand the problem requirements.
2. Determine the limiting conditions. For example, for a list, the limiting condition is determined by the number of elements in the list.
3. Identify the base cases and provide a direct (nonrecursive) solution to each base case.
4. Identify the general cases and provide a solution to each general case in terms of a smaller version of itself.

Typically, all recursive methods have the following characteristics: (a) they use an `if...else` or a `switch` statement that leads to different cases, (b) one or more base cases are used to stop recursion, and (c) each recursive call reduces the problem to a smaller version of itself.

Problem Solving Using Recursion

Examples 13-1 through 13-3 illustrate how recursive algorithms are developed and implemented in Java using recursive methods.

EXAMPLE 13-1 LARGEST ELEMENT IN THE ARRAY

In Chapter 9, we used a loop to find the largest element in an array. This example uses a recursive algorithm to find the largest element in an array. Consider the list given in Figure 13-2.

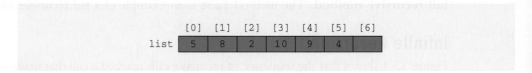

FIGURE 13-2 List with six elements

The largest element in the list given in Figure 13-2 is 10.

Suppose `list` is the name of the array containing the list elements. Also suppose that `list[a]...list[b]` stands for the array elements `list[a]`, `list[a + 1]`, ..., `list[b]`. For example, `list[0]...list[5]` represents the array elements `list[0]`, `list[1]`, `list[2]`, `list[3]`, `list[4]`, and `list[5]`. Similarly, `list[1]...list[5]` represents the array elements `list[1]`, `list[2]`, `list[3]`, `list[4]`, and `list[5]`. To write an algorithm to find the largest element in `list`, let's think recursively.

If `list` is of length 1, then `list` has only one element, which is the largest element. Suppose the length of `list` is greater than 1. To find the largest element in `list[a]...list[b]`, we first find the largest element in `list[a + 1]...list[b]` and then compare this largest element with `list[a]`. That is, the largest element in `list[a]...list[b]` is given by:

`maximum(list[a], largest(list[a + 1]...list[b]))`

Let's apply this formula to find the largest element in the list shown in Figure 13-2. This list has six elements, given by `list[0]...list[5]`. Now the largest element in `list` is:

`maximum(list[0], largest(list[1]...list[5]))`

That is, the largest element in `list` is the maximum of `list[0]` and the largest element in `list[1]...list[5]`. To find the largest element in `list[1]...list[5]`, we use the same formula again because the length of this list is greater than 1. The largest element in `list[1]...list[5]` is then:

`maximum(list[1], largest(list[2]...list[5]))`

and so on. Note that every time we use the preceding formula to find the largest element in a sublist, the length of the sublist in the next call is reduced by one. Eventually, the sublist is of length 1, in which case the sublist contains only one element, which, in turn, is the largest element in the sublist. From this point onward, we backtrack through the recursive calls. This discussion translates into the following recursive algorithm, which is presented in pseudocode:

```
if the size of the list is 1
    the largest element in the list is the only element in the list
else
    to find the largest element in list[a]...list[b]
        a. find the largest element in list[a + 1]...list[b] and call
           it max
        b. compare list[a] and max
            if (list[a] >= max)
                the largest element in list[a]...list[b] is list[a]
            else
                the largest element in list[a]...list[b] is max
```

This algorithm translates into the following Java method to find the largest element in an array:

```java
public static int largest(int[] list,
                          int lowerIndex, int upperIndex)
{
    int max;

    if (lowerIndex == upperIndex)   //size of the sublist is 1
        return list[lowerIndex];
    else
    {
        max = largest(list, lowerIndex + 1, upperIndex);

        if (list[lowerIndex] >= max)
            return list[lowerIndex];
        else
            return max;
    }
}
```

Consider the list given in Figure 13-3.

FIGURE 13-3 List with four elements

Let's trace the execution of the following statement:

```
System.out.println(largest(list, 0, 3));
```

Here, upperIndex = 3 and the list has four elements. Figure 13-4 traces the execution of largest(list, 0, 3).

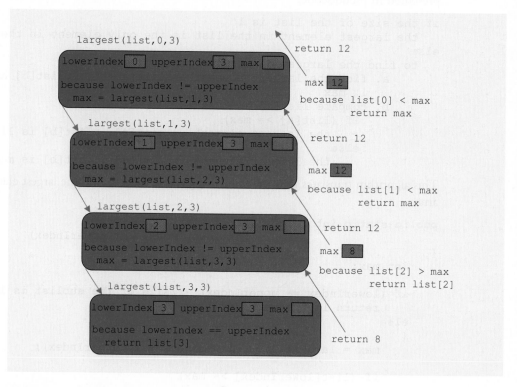

FIGURE 13-4 Execution of largest(list, 0, 3)

The value returned by the expression largest(list, 0, 3) is 12, which is the largest element in list.

The following Java program uses the method largest to determine the largest element in the list:

```java
//Recursion: Largest Element in an Array

import java.io.*;

public class  LargestElementInAnArray
{
    public static void main(String[] args)
    {
        int[]  intArray = {23, 43, 35, 38, 67, 12, 76,
                           10, 34, 8};
```

```
        System.out.println("The largest element in intArray: "
                 + largest(intArray, 0, intArray.length - 1));
    }

    public static int largest(int[] list,
                              int lowerIndex, int upperIndex)
    {
        int max;

        if (lowerIndex == upperIndex)
            return list[lowerIndex];
        else
        {
            max = largest(list, lowerIndex + 1, upperIndex);

            if (list[lowerIndex] >= max)
                return list[lowerIndex];
            else
                return max;
        }
    }
}
```

Sample Run:

```
The largest element in intArray: 76
```

EXAMPLE 13-2 FIBONACCI NUMBER

In Chapter 5, we designed a program to determine the desired Fibonacci number. In this example, we write a recursive method, rFibNum, to determine the desired Fibonacci number. The method rFibNum takes as parameters three numbers representing the first two numbers of the Fibonacci sequence and a number n, the desired nth Fibonacci number. The method rFibNum returns the nth Fibonacci number in the sequence.

Recall that the third Fibonacci number is the sum of the first two Fibonacci numbers. The fourth Fibonacci number in a sequence is the sum of the second and third Fibonacci numbers. Therefore, to calculate the fourth Fibonacci number, we add the second Fibonacci number and the third Fibonacci number (which itself is the sum of the first two Fibonacci numbers). The following recursive algorithm calculates the nth Fibonacci number, where a denotes the first Fibonacci number, b the second Fibonacci number, and n the nth Fibonacci number:

$$rFibNum(a, b, n) = \begin{cases} a & \text{if } n = 1 \\ b & \text{if } n = 2 \\ rFibNum(a, b, n-1) + rFibNum(a, b, n-2) & \text{if } n > 2. \end{cases} \quad (13\text{-}3)$$

Suppose that we want to determine the following:

1. `rFibNum(2, 5, 4)`

    Here, a = 2, b = 5, and n = 4. That is, we want to determine the fourth Fibonacci number of the sequence whose first number is 2 and whose second number is 5. Because n is 4 > 2:

    `rFibNum(2, 5, 4) = rFibNum(2, 5, 3) + rFibNum(2, 5, 2)`

    Next, we determine `rFibNum(2, 5, 3)` and `rFibNum(2, 5, 2)`. Let's first determine `rFibNum(2, 5, 3)`. Here, a = 2, b = 5, and n is 3. Because n is 3:

    1.a. `rFibNum(2, 5, 3) = rFibNum(2, 5, 2) + rFibNum(2, 5, 1)`

    This statement requires that we determine `rFibNum(2, 5, 2)` and `rFibNum(2, 5, 1)`. In `rFibNum(2, 5, 2)`, a = 2, b = 5, and n = 2. Therefore, from the definition given in Equation 13-3, it follows that:

    1.a.1. `rFibNum(2, 5, 2) = 5`

    To find `rFibNum(2, 5, 1)`, note that a = 2, b = 5, and n = 1. Therefore, by the definition given in Equation 13-3:

    1.a.2. `rFibNum(2, 5, 1) = 2`

    We substitute the values of `rFibNum(2, 5, 2)` and `rFibNum(2, 5, 1)` into (1.a) to get:

    `rFibNum(2, 5, 3) = 5 + 2 = 7`

    Next, we determine `rFibNum(2, 5, 2)`. As in (1.a.1), `rFibNum(2, 5, 2) = 5`. We can substitute the values of `rFibNum(2, 5, 3)` and `rFibNum(2, 5, 2)` into (1) to get:

    `rFibNum(2, 5, 4) = 7 + 5 = 12`

The following recursive method implements this algorithm:

```
public static int rFibNum(int a, int b, int n)
{
    if (n == 1)
        return a;
    else if (n == 2)
        return b;
    else
        return rFibNum(a, b, n - 1) + rFibNum(a, b, n - 2);
}
```

Let's trace the execution of the following statement:

```
System.out.println(rFibNum(2, 3, 5));
```

In this statement, the first number is 2, the second number is 3, and we want to determine the 5th Fibonacci number of the sequence. Figure 13-5 traces the execution of the expression `rFibNum(2, 3, 5)`. The value returned is 13, which is the 5th Fibonacci number of the sequence whose first number is 2 and whose second number is 3.

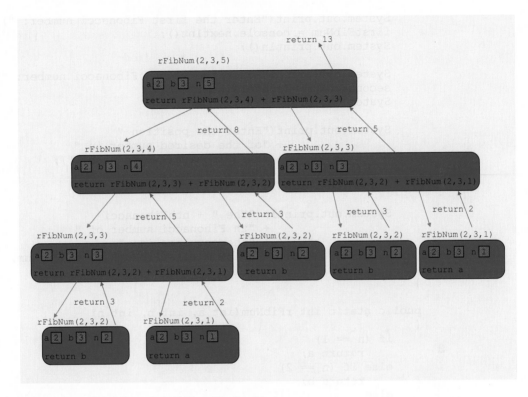

FIGURE 13-5 Execution of rFibNum(2, 3, 5)

From Figure 13-5, we can conclude that the recursive version of the program to calculate a Fibonacci number is not as efficient as the nonrecursive version. In the recursive version, some values are calculated more than once. For example, to calculate `rFibNum(2, 3, 5)`, the value `rFibNum(2, 3, 2)` is calculated three times. So a recursive method may be easier to write, but may not be very efficient. The section Recursion or Iteration?, presented later in this chapter, discusses the differences between these two alternatives.

The following Java program uses the method `rFibNum`:

```
//Recursion: Fibonacci Number

import java.util.*;

public class FibonacciNumber
{
    static Scanner console = new Scanner(System.in);
```

```java
public static void main(String[] args)
{
    int firstFibNum;
    int secondFibNum;
    int nthFibonacci;

    System.out.print("Enter the first Fibonacci number: ");
    firstFibNum = console.nextInt();
    System.out.println();

    System.out.print("Enter the second Fibonacci number: ");
    secondFibNum = console.nextInt();
    System.out.println();

    System.out.print("Enter the position "
                    + "of the desired number in "
                    + "the Fibonacci \nsequence: ");
    nthFibonacci = console.nextInt();
    System.out.println();

    System.out.println("The " + nthFibonacci
                    + "th Fibonacci number of "
                    + "the sequence is: "
                    + rFibNum(firstFibNum, secondFibNum,
                            nthFibonacci));
}

public static int rFibNum(int a, int b, int n)
{
    if (n == 1)
        return a;
    else if (n == 2)
        return b;
    else
        return rFibNum(a, b, n - 1) + rFibNum(a, b, n - 2);
}
}
```

Sample Run: (In this sample run, the user input is shaded.)

```
Enter the first Fibonacci number: 3

Enter the second Fibonacci number: 4

Enter the position of the desired number in the Fibonacci
sequence: 6

The 6th Fibonacci number of the sequence is: 29
```

EXAMPLE 13-3 TOWER OF HANOI

In the nineteenth century, a game called the Tower of Hanoi was popular in Europe. This game is based on a legend regarding the construction of the temple of Brahma. According to this legend, at the creation of the universe, priests in the temple of Brahma were given three diamond needles, with one needle containing 64 golden disks. Each golden disk is slightly smaller than the disk below it. The priests' task was to move all 64 disks from the first needle to the third needle. The rules for moving the disks are as follows:

1. Only one disk can be moved at a time.

2. The removed disk must be placed on one of the needles.

3. A larger disk cannot be placed on top of a smaller disk.

The priests were told that once they had moved all the disks from the first needle to the third needle, the universe would come to an end.

Our objective is to write a program that prints the sequence of moves needed to transfer the disks from the first needle to the third needle. Figure 13-6 shows the Tower of Hanoi problem with three disks.

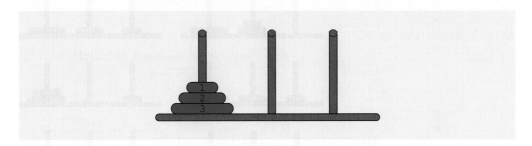

FIGURE 13-6 Tower of Hanoi problem with three disks

As before, we think in terms of recursion. Let's consider the case where the first needle contains only one disk. In this case, the disk can be moved directly from needle 1 to needle 3. Now let's consider the case when the first needle contains only two disks. In this case, we move the first disk from needle 1 to needle 2, and then we move the second disk from needle 1 to needle 3. Finally, we move the first disk from needle 2 to needle 3. Next, we consider the case where the first needle contains three disks, and then generalize this to the case of 64 disks (in fact, to an arbitrary number of disks).

Suppose that needle 1 contains three disks. To move disk number 3 to needle 3, the top two disks must first be moved to needle 2. Disk number 3 can then be moved from needle 1 to needle 3. To move the top two disks from needle 2 to needle 3, we use the same strategy as before. This time, we use needle 1 as the intermediate needle. Figure 13-7 shows a solution to the Tower of Hanoi problem with three disks.

1
3

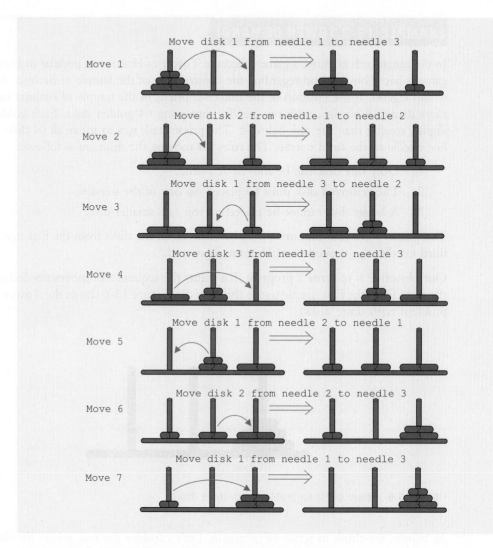

FIGURE 13-7 Solution to Tower of Hanoi problem with three disks

Let's now generalize this problem to the case of 64 disks. To begin, the first needle contains all 64 disks. Disk number 64 cannot be moved from needle 1 to needle 3 unless the top 63 disks are on the second needle. So first we move the top 63 disks from needle 1 to needle 2, and then we move disk number 64 from needle 1 to needle 3. Now the top 63 disks are all on needle 2. To move disk number 63 from needle 2 to needle 3, we first move the top 62 disks from needle 2 to needle 1, and then we move disk number 63 from needle 2 to needle 3. To move the remaining 62 disks, we use a similar procedure. This discussion translates into the following recursive algorithm, given in pseudocode. Suppose that needle 1 contains n disks, where $n \geq 1$.

1. Move the top $n - 1$ disks from needle 1 to needle 2, using needle 3 as the intermediate needle.

2. Move disk number n from needle 1 to needle 3.

3. Move the top $n - 1$ disks from needle 2 to needle 3, using needle 1 as the intermediate needle.

This recursive algorithm translates into the following Java method:

```java
public static void moveDisks(int count, int needle1,
                             int needle3, int needle2)
{
    if (count > 0)
    {
        moveDisks(count-1, needle1, needle2, needle3);
        System.out.println("Move disk " + count
                           + " from needle "
                           + needle1
                           + " to needle " + needle3 + ".");
        moveDisks(count-1, needle2, needle3, needle1);
    }
}
```

Tower of Hanoi: Analysis

Let us determine how long it would take to move all 64 disks from needle 1 to needle 3. If needle 1 contains 3 disks, then the number of moves required to move all 3 disks from needle 1 to needle 3 is $2^3 - 1 = 7$. Similarly, if needle 1 contains 64 disks, then the number of moves required to move all 64 disks from needle 1 to needle 3 is $2^{64} - 1$. Because $2^{10} = 1024 \approx 1000 = 10^3$, we have

$$2^{64} = 2^4 \times 2^{60} \approx 2^4 \times 10^{18} = 1.6 \times 10^{19}$$

The number of seconds in one year is approximately 3.2×10^7. Suppose the priests move one disk per second and they do not rest. Now:

$$1.6 \times 10^{19} = 5 \times 3.2 \times 10^{18} = 5 \times (3.2 \times 10^7) \times 10^{11} = (3.2 \times 10^7) \times (5 \times 10^{11})$$

The time required to move all 64 disks from needle 1 to needle 3 is roughly 5×10^{11} years. It is estimated that our universe is about 15 billion years old (1.5×10^{10}). Also, $5 \times 10^{11} = 50 \times 10^{10} \approx 33 \times (1.5 \times 10^{10})$. This calculation shows that our universe would last about 33 times as long as it already has.

Assume that a computer can generate 1 billion (10^9) moves per second. Then, the number of moves that the computer can generate in one year is:

$$(3.2 \times 10^7) \times 10^9 = 3.2 \times 10^{16}$$

So, the computer time required to generate 2^{64} moves is:

$$2^{64} \approx 1.6 \times 10^{19} = 1.6 \times 10^{16} \times 10^3 = (3.2 \times 10^{16}) \times 500$$

Thus, it would take about 500 years for the computer to generate 2^{64} moves at the rate of 1 billion moves per second.

Recursion or Iteration?

In Chapter 5, we designed a program to determine a desired Fibonacci number. That program used a loop to perform the calculation. In other words, the programs in Chapter 5 used an iterative control structure to repeat a set of statements. More formally, **iterative control structures** use a looping structure, such as `while`, `for`, or `do...while`, to repeat a set of statements. In Example 13-2, we designed a recursive method to calculate a Fibonacci number. From the examples in this chapter, it follows that in recursion, a set of statements is repeated by having the method call itself. Moreover, a selection control structure is used to control the repeated calls in recursion.

Similarly, in Chapter 9, we used an iterative control structure (a `for` loop) to determine the largest element in a list. In this chapter, we used recursion to determine the largest element in a list. In addition, this chapter began by designing a recursive method to find the factorial of a nonnegative integer. Using an iterative control structure, we can also write an algorithm to find the factorial of a nonnegative integer. The only reason we gave a recursive solution to a factorial problem is to illustrate how recursion works.

Often there are two ways to solve a particular problem—recursion or iteration. The obvious question is, Which method is better? There is no simple answer. In addition to the nature of the problem, the other key factor in determining the best solution method is efficiency.

When we traced the execution of the program in Example 7-11 (Chapter 7), we saw that whenever a method is called, memory space for its formal parameters and (automatic) local variables is allocated. When the method terminates, that memory space is then deallocated.

In this chapter, while tracing the execution of recursive methods, we saw that every (recursive) call also had its own set of parameters and local variables. That is, every (recursive) call required that the system allocate memory space for its formal parameters and local variables, and then deallocate the memory space when the method exited. Thus, overhead is associated with executing a (recursive) method, both in terms of memory space and computer time. Therefore, a recursive method executes more slowly than its iterative counterpart. On slower computers, especially those with limited memory space, the (slow) execution of a recursive method would be noticeable.

Today's computers, however, are fast and have ample memory. Therefore, the execution of a recursive method is not so noticeable. Keeping in mind the power of today's computers, the choice between iteration or recursion depends on the nature of the problem. Of course, for problems such as mission control systems, efficiency is absolutely critical and, therefore, the efficiency factor dictates the solution method.

As a general rule, if you think an iterative solution is more obvious and easier to understand than a recursive solution, use the iterative solution, which is more efficient. On the other hand, problems exist for which the recursive solution is more obvious or easier to construct, such as the Tower of Hanoi problem. (In fact, it is difficult to construct an iterative solution for the Tower of Hanoi problem.) Keeping in mind the power of recursion, if the definition of a problem is inherently recursive, then you should consider a recursive solution.

PROGRAMMING EXAMPLE: Decimal to Binary Conversion

This programming example discusses and designs a program that uses recursion to convert a nonnegative integer in decimal format—that is, base 10—into the equivalent binary number—that is, base 2. First, we define some terms.

Let x be a nonnegative integer. We call the remainder of x after division by 2 the **rightmost bit** of x.

Thus, the rightmost bit of 33 is 1 because 33 % 2 is 1, and the rightmost bit of 28 is 0 because 28 % 2 is 0.

We first use an example to illustrate the algorithm to convert an integer in base 10 to the equivalent number in binary format.

Suppose we want to find the binary representation of 35. First, we divide 35 by 2. The quotient is 17 and the remainder—that is, the rightmost bit of 35—is 1. Next, we divide 17 by 2. The quotient is 8 and the remainder—that is, the rightmost bit of 17—is 1. Next, we divide 8 by 2. The quotient is 4 and the remainder—that is, the rightmost bit of 8—is 0. We continue this process until the quotient becomes 0.

The rightmost bit of 35 cannot be printed until we have printed the rightmost bit of 17. The rightmost bit of 17 cannot be printed until we have printed the rightmost bit of 8, and so on. Thus, the binary representation of 35 is the binary representation of 17 (that is, the quotient of 35 after division by 2), followed by the rightmost bit of 35.

Thus, to convert a nonnegative integer num in base 10 into the equivalent binary number, we first convert the quotient num / 2 into an equivalent binary number, and then append the rightmost bit of num to the binary representation of num / 2.

This discussion translates into the following recursive algorithm, where binary(num) denotes the binary representation of num:

1. binary(num) = num if num = 0.
2. binary(num) = binary(num / 2), followed by num % 2 if num > 0.

1
3

The following recursive method implements this algorithm:

```java
public static void decToBin(int num, int base)
{
    if (num == 0)
        System.out.print(0);
    else if (num > 0)
    {
        decToBin(num / base, base);
        System.out.print(num % base);
    }
}
```

Figure 13-8 traces the execution of the following statement:

```java
decToBin(13, 2);
```

where num is 13 and base is 2.

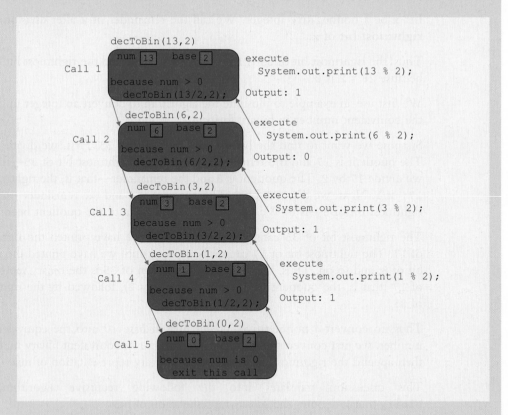

FIGURE 13-8 Execution of decToBin(13, 2)

Because the if statement in Call 5 succeeds, this call prints 0. The second output is produced by Call 4, which prints 1; the third output is produced by Call 3, which prints 1; the fourth output is produced by Call 2, which prints 0; and the fifth output is produced by Call 1, which prints 1. Thus, the output of the statement:

```
decToBin(13, 2);
```

is:

01101

The following Java program tests the method `decToBin`:

```java
//**********************************************************
// Author: D.S. Malik
//
// Recursion: Program - Decimal to Binary
// This program uses recursion to find the binary
// representation of a nonnegative integer.
//**********************************************************

import java.util.*;

public class DecimalToBinary
{
    static Scanner console = new Scanner(System.in);

    public static void main(String[] args)
    {
        int decimalNum;
        int base;

        base = 2;

        System.out.print("Enter a nonnegative integer in "
                        + "decimal: ");
        decimalNum = console.nextInt();
        System.out.println();

        System.out.print("Decimal " + decimalNum + " = ");
        decToBin(decimalNum, base);
        System.out.println(" binary");
    }

    public static void decToBin(int num, int base)
    {
        if (num == 0)
            System.out.print(0);
        else if (num > 0)
        {
            decToBin(num / base, base);
            System.out.print(num % base);
        }
    }
}
```

1
3

Sample Run: (In this sample run, the user input is shaded.)

```
Enter a nonnegative integer in decimal: 57

Decimal 57 = 0111001 binary
```

PROGRAMMING EXAMPLE: Sierpinski Gasket

To draw the shapes of natural scenes, such as mountains, trees, and clouds, graphic programmers typically use special mathematical tools, called **fractals**, related to fractal geometry. Fractal geometry is a major area of research in mathematics in its own right. The term fractal was introduced by the mathematician Benoit Mandelbrot in the mid-1970s. Mandelbrot is credited with the development of systematic fractal geometry, which provides a description of many seemingly complex forms found in nature. One kind of fractal, called a self-similar fractal, is a geometric shape in which certain patterns repeat, sometimes at different scales and with different orientations. Mandelbrot is recognized as the first person to demonstrate that fractals occur in various places in mathematics and nature.

Because certain patterns occur at various places in a fractal, a convenient and effective way to write programs to draw fractals is to use recursion. This section describes a special type of fractal called a **Sierpinski gasket**.

Suppose that you have the triangle *ABC* as given in Figure 13-9(a). Now determine the midpoints *P*, *Q*, and *R* of the sides *AB*, *AC*, and *BC*, respectively. Next, draw the lines *PQ*, *QR*, and *PR*. This creates three triangles, *APQ*, *BPR*, and *CRQ*, as shown in Figure 13-9(b), which have similar shapes as in the triangle *ABC*. The process of finding the midpoints of the sides and then drawing lines through those midpoints is now repeated on each of the triangles *APQ*, *BPR*, and *CRQ*, as shown in Figure 13-9(c). Figure 13-9(a) is called a Sierpinski gasket of order (or level) 0, Figure 13-9(b) is called a Sierpinski gasket of order (or level) 1, Figure 13-9(c) is called a Sierpinski gasket of order (or level) 2, and Figure13-9(d) shows a Sierpinski gasket of order (or level) 3.

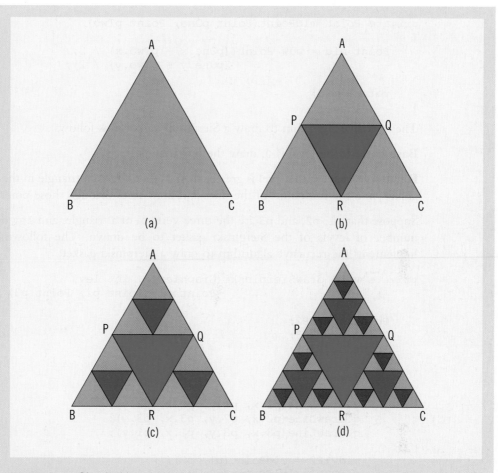

FIGURE 13-9 Sierpinski gaskets of various orders (levels)

Input: A nonnegative integer indicating the level of the Sierpinski gasket.

Output: A triangle shape displaying a Sierpinski gasket of the given order.

PROBLEM
ANALYSIS
AND
ALGORITHM
DESIGN

The problem is as described previously. Initially, we specify the coordinates of the first triangle and then draw the triangle. We use the **class** Point to store the *x-y* coordinates of a point. (The **class** point is a predefined Java class and is contained in the **package** java.awt.) We also use the method drawLine, as described in Chapter 12, to draw a line between two points.

For each triangle, we need three objects of the **class** Point to store the vertices of the triangle, and three more objects to store the midpoints of each side. Because we frequently need to find the midpoints of a line, we write the method midPoint, which returns the coordinates of the midpoint of a line. Its definition is:

```
private Point midPoint(Point pOne, Point pTwo)
{
    Point mid = new Point((pOne.x + pTwo.x) / 2,
                          (pOne.y + pTwo.y) / 2);

    return mid;
}
```

The recursive algorithm to draw a Sierpinski gasket is as follows:

Base case: If the level is 0, draw the first triangle.

Recursive case: If the level is greater than 0, then for each triangle in the Sierpinski gasket, find the midpoints of the sides and draw lines through those points.

Suppose that p1, p2, and p3 are the three vertices of a triangle, and `lev` denotes the number of levels of the Sierpinski gasket to be drawn. The following method implements the recursive algorithm to draw a Sierpinski gasket:

```
private void drawSierpinski(Graphics g, int lev,
                            Point p1, Point p2, Point p3)
{
    Point midP1P2;
    Point midP2P3;
    Point midP3P1;

    if (lev > 0)
    {
        g.drawLine(p1.x, p1.y, p2.x, p2.y);
        g.drawLine(p2.x, p2.y, p3.x, p3.y);
        g.drawLine(p3.x, p3.y, p1.x, p1.y);

        midP1P2 = midPoint(p1, p2);
        midP2P3 = midPoint(p2, p3);
        midP3P1 = midPoint(p3, p1);

        drawSierpinski(g, lev - 1, p1, midP1P2, midP3P1);
        drawSierpinski(g, lev - 1, p2, midP2P3, midP1P2);
        drawSierpinski(g, lev - 1, p3, midP3P1, midP2P3);
    }
}
```

The following program listing provides the complete algorithm to draw a Sierpinski gasket of a given order. Notice that the program uses an input dialog box to get the user's input.

COMPLETE PROGRAM LISTING

```java
//*********************************************************
// Author: D.S. Malik
//
// Program: Drawing a Sierpinski Gasket
// Given the order of a Sierpinski Gasket, this program
// draws a Sierpinski Gasket of that order.
//*********************************************************

import java.awt.*;
import javax.swing.*;

public class SierpinskiGasket extends JApplet
{
    int level = 0;

    public void init()
    {
        String levelStr = JOptionPane.showInputDialog
                        ("Enter the recursion depth: ");

        level = Integer.parseInt(levelStr);
    }

    public void paint(Graphics g)
    {
        Point pointOne = new Point(60, 160);
        Point pointTwo = new Point(220, 160);
        Point pointThree = new Point(140, 20);

        drawSierpinski(g, level, pointOne, pointTwo,
                    pointThree);
    }

    private void drawSierpinski(Graphics g, int lev,
                            Point p1, Point p2, Point p3)
    {
        Point midP1P2;
        Point midP2P3;
        Point midP3P1;

        if (lev > 0)
        {
            g.drawLine(p1.x, p1.y, p2.x, p2.y);
            g.drawLine(p2.x, p2.y, p3.x, p3.y);
            g.drawLine(p3.x, p3.y, p1.x, p1.y);

            midP1P2 = midPoint(p1, p2);
            midP2P3 = midPoint(p2, p3);
            midP3P1 = midPoint(p3, p1);
```

1
3

```
                    drawSierpinski(g, lev - 1, p1, midP1P2, midP3P1);
                    drawSierpinski(g, lev - 1, p2, midP2P3, midP1P2);
                    drawSierpinski(g, lev - 1, p3, midP3P1, midP2P3);
            }
    }

    private Point midPoint(Point pOne, Point pTwo)
    {
        Point mid = new Point((pOne.x + pTwo.x) / 2,
                              (pOne.y + pTwo.y) / 2);

        return mid;
    }
}
```

Sample Run: Figure 13-10 shows a sample run. In this sample run, the user input is entered in the input dialog box.

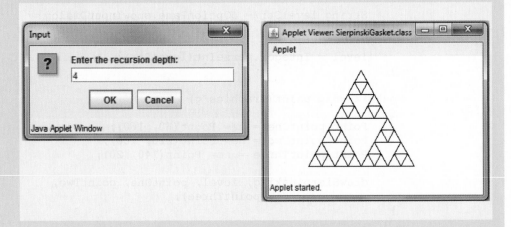

FIGURE 13-10   Recursion depth of 4 produces a Sierpinski gasket of order 3

QUICK REVIEW

1. The process of solving a problem by reducing it to smaller versions of itself is called recursion.

2. A recursive definition defines the problem in terms of smaller versions of itself.

3. Every recursive definition has one or more base cases.

4. A recursive algorithm solves a problem by reducing it to smaller versions of itself.

5. Every recursive algorithm has one or more base cases.

6. The solution to a problem in a base case is obtained directly.

7. A method is recursive if it calls itself.

8. Recursive algorithms are implemented using recursive methods.

9. Every recursive method must have one or more base cases.

10. The general solution breaks a problem into smaller versions of itself.

11. The general case must eventually be reduced to a base case.

12. The base case stops the recursion.

13. While tracing a recursive method:

    a. Logically, you can think of a recursive method as having unlimited copies of itself.

    b. Every call to a recursive method—that is, every recursive call—has its own code and its own set of parameters and local variables.

    c. After completing a particular recursive call, control goes back to the calling environment, which is the previous call. The current (recursive) call must execute completely before control goes back to the previous call. The execution in the previous call continues from the point immediately following the recursive call.

14. A method is directly recursive if it calls itself.

15. A method that calls another method and eventually results in the original method call is indirectly recursive.

16. A recursive method in which the last statement executed is the recursive call is called a tail recursive method.

17. To design a recursive method, you must do the following:

    a. Understand the problem requirements.

    b. Determine the limiting conditions.

    c. Identify the base cases and provide a direct solution to each base case.

    d. Identify the general case(s) and provide a solution to each general case in terms of a smaller version of itself.

EXERCISES

1. Mark the following statements as true or false.

    a. Every recursive definition must have one or more base cases.

    b. Every recursive method must have one or more base cases.

    c. The general case stops the recursion.

d. In the general case, the solution to the problem is obtained directly.

e. A recursive method always returns a value.

2. What is a base case?

3. What is a recursive case?

4. What is direct recursion?

5. What is indirect recursion?

6. What is tail recursion?

7. Consider the following recursive method:

```
public static int mystery(int number)          //Line 1
{
    if (number == 0)                            //Line 2
        return number;                          //Line 3
    else                                        //Line 4
        return(number + mystery(number - 1));   //Line 5
}
```

a. Identify the base case.

b. Identify the general case.

c. What valid values can be passed as parameters to the method mystery?

d. If mystery(0) is a valid call, what is its value? If it is not a valid call, explain why.

e. If mystery(5) is a valid call, what is its value? If not, explain why.

f. If mystery(-3) is a valid call, what is its value? If not, explain why.

8. Consider the following recursive method:

```
public static void funcRec(int u, char v)       //Line 1
{
    if (u == 0)                                 //Line 2
        System.out.print(v);                    //Line 3
    else if(u == 1)                             //Line 4
        System.out.print((char)((int)(v) + 1);  //Line 5
    else                                        //Line 6
        funcRec(u - 1, v);                      //Line 7
}
```

a. Identify the base case.

b. Identify the general case.

c. What is the output of the following statement?

```
funcRec(5,'A');
```

9. Consider the following recursive method:

```
public static void exercise(int x)
{
    if (x > 0 && x < 10)
```

```
    {
        System.out.print(x + " ");
        exercise(x + 1);
    }
}
```

What is the output of the following statements?

a. `exercise(0);`   c. `exercise(10);`

b. `exercise(5);`   d. `exercise(-5);`

10. Consider the following recursive function:

```
public static void recFun(int x)
{
    if (x > 10)
    {
        recFun(x / 10);
        System.out.println(x % 10);
    }
    else
        System.out.println(x);
}
```

What is the output of the following statements?

a. `recFun(258);`   c. `recFun(36);`

b. `recFun(7);`   d. `recFun(-85);`

11. Consider the following recursive function:

```
public static void recFun(int u)
{
    if (u == 1)

        System.out.print("Stop! ");
    else
    {
        System.out.print("Go ");
        recFun(u - 1);;
    }
}
```

What is the output, if any, of the following statements?

a. `recFun(7);` b. `recFun(3);` c. `recFun(-6);`

1
3

12. Consider the following method:

```
public static int test(int x, int y)
{
    if (x == y)
        return x;
    else if (x > y)
        return (x + y);
    else
        return test(x + 1, y - 1);
}
```

What is the output of the following statements?

a. `System.out.println(test(5, 10));`

b. `System.out.println(test(3, 9));`

13. Consider the following method:

```
public static int func(int x)
{
    if (x == 0)
        return 2;
    else if (x == 1)
        return 3;
    else
        return (func(x - 1) + func(x - 2));
}
```

What is the output of the following statements?

a. `System.out.println(func(0));`

b. `System.out.println(func(1));`

c. `System.out.println(func(2));`

d. `System.out.println(func(5));`

14. Suppose that `intArray` is an array of integers and `length` specifies the number of elements in `intArray`. Also, suppose that `low` and `high` are two integers such that 0 <= low < length, 0 <= high < length, and low <= high. That is, `low` and `high` are two indices in `intArray`. Write a recursive definition that reverses the elements in `intArray` between `low` and `high`.

15. Write a recursive definition to multiply two positive integers m and n using repeated addition.

16. Consider the following problem: How many ways can a committee of four people be selected from a group of 10 people? There are many other similar problems, where you are asked to find the number of ways to select a set of items from a given set of items. The general problem can be stated as follows: Find the number of ways r different things can be chosen from a set of n items, where r and n are nonnegative integers and $r \le n$. Suppose

$C(n, r)$ denotes the number of ways r different things can be chosen from a set of n items. Then $C(n, r)$ is given by the following formula:

$$C(n, r) = \frac{n!}{r!(n - r)!}$$

where the exclamation point denotes the factorial function. Moreover, $C(n, 0) = C(n, n) = 1$. It is also known that $C(n, r) = C(n - 1, r - 1) + C(n - 1, r)$.

a. Write a recursive algorithm to determine $C(n, r)$. Identify the base case(s) and the general case(s).

b. Using your recursive algorithm, determine $C(5, 3)$ and $C(9, 4)$.

PROGRAMMING EXERCISES

1. Write a recursive method that takes as a parameter a nonnegative integer and generates the following pattern of stars. If the nonnegative integer is 4, then the pattern generated is:

```
****
***
**
*
*
**
***
****
```

Also, write a program that prompts the user to enter the number of lines in the pattern and uses the recursive method to generate the pattern. For example, specifying the number of lines to be 4 generates the preceding pattern.

2. Write a recursive method to generate the following pattern of stars:

```
    *
   * *
  * * *
 * * * *
  * * *
   * *
    *
```

Also, write a program that prompts the user to enter the number of lines in the pattern and uses the recursive method to generate the pattern. For example, specifying the number of lines to be 4 generates the preceding pattern.

3. Write a recursive method, vowels, that returns the number of vowels in a string. Also, write a program to test your method.

4. Write a recursive function named sumSquares that returns the sum of the squares of the numbers from 0 to num, where num is a nonnegative int variable. Do not use global variables, use appropriate parameters. Also write a program to test your function.

5. Write a recursive method that finds and returns the sum of the elements of an int array. Also, write a program to test your method.

6. A palindrome is a string that reads the same both forward and backward. For example, the string "madam" is a palindrome. Write a program that uses a recursive method to check whether a string is a palindrome. Your program must contain a value-returning recursive method that returns true if the string is a palindrome and false otherwise. Use appropriate parameters in your method.

7. Write a program that uses a recursive method to print a string backward. Your program must contain a recursive method that prints the string backward. Use appropriate parameters in your method.

8. Write a recursive method, reverseDigits, that takes an integer as a parameter and returns the number with the digits reversed. Also, write a program to test your method.

9. Write a recursive method, power, that takes as parameters two integers x and y such that x is nonzero and returns x^y. You can use the following recursive definition to calculate x^y. If $y \geq 0$:

$$power(x, y) = \begin{cases} 1 & \text{if } y = 0 \\ x & \text{if } y = 1 \\ x * power(x, y - 1) & \text{if } y > 1 \end{cases}$$

If $y < 0$:

$$power(x, y) = \frac{1}{power(x, -y)}$$

Also, write a program to test your method.

10. **Greatest Common Divisor.** Given two integers x and y, the following recursive definition determines the greatest common divisor of x and y, written $gcd(x,y)$:

$$gcd(x, y) = \begin{cases} x & \text{if } y = 0 \\ gcd(y, x \% y) & \text{if } y \neq 0 \end{cases}$$

(*Note*: In this definition, % is the mod operator.)
(This algorithm to determine the gcd of two integers is called the **Euclidean algorithm**.) Write a recursive method, gcd, that takes as parameters two integers and returns the greatest common divisor of the numbers. Also, write a program to test your method.

11. **(Ackermann's Function)** Ackermann's function is defined as follows:

$$A(m, n) = \begin{cases} n+1, & \text{if } m = 0 \\ A(m-1, 1), & \text{if } n = 0 \\ A(m-1, A(m, n-1)), & \text{otherwise,} \end{cases}$$

where m and n are nonnegative integers. Write a recursive function to implement Ackermann's function. Also write a program to test your function. What happens when you call the function with $m = 4$ and $n = 3$?

12. Write a recursive method to implement the recursive definition of Exercise 14 (reversing the elements of an array between two indices). Also, write a program to test your method.

13. Write a recursive method to implement the recursive definition of Exercise 15 (multiply two positive integers using repeated addition). Also, write a program to test your method.

14. In the Decimal to Binary Conversion programming example presented in this chapter, you learned how to convert a decimal number into its equivalent binary number. Two more number systems, octal (base 8) and hexadecimal (base 16), are of interest to computer scientists.

The digits in the octal number system are 0, 1, 2, 3, 4, 5, 6, and 7. The digits in the hexadecimal number system are 0, 1, 2, 3, 4, 5, 6, 7, 8, 9, A, B, C, D, E, and F. So, A in hexadecimal is 10 in decimal, B in hexadecimal is 11 in decimal, and so on.

The algorithm to convert a positive decimal number into an equivalent number in octal (or hexadecimal) is the same as that discussed for binary numbers. Here, we divide the decimal number by 8 (for octal) and by 16 (for hexadecimal). Suppose that a_b represents the number a to the base b. For example, 75_{10} means 75 to the base 10 (that is, decimal), and 83_{16} means 83 to the base 16 (that is, hexadecimal). Then:

$753_{10} = 1361_8$

$753_{10} = 2F1_{16}$

The method of converting a decimal number to base 2, or 8, or 16 can be extended to any arbitrary base. Suppose you want to convert a decimal number n into an equivalent number in base b, where b is between 2 and 36. You then divide the decimal number n by b, as in the algorithm for converting decimal to binary.

Note that the digits in, say, base 20, are 0, 1, 2, 3, 4, 5, 6, 7, 8, 9, A, B, C, D, E, F, G, H, I, and J.

Write a program that uses a recursive method to convert a number in decimal to a given base b, where b is between 2 and 36. Your program should prompt the user to enter the number in decimal and in the desired base.

Test your program on the following data:

9098 and base 20

692 and base 2

753 and base 16

15. **Binary to Decimal Conversion.** The language of a computer, called machine language, is a sequence of 0s and 1s. When you press the A key on the keyboard, 01000001 is stored in the computer. Note that the collating sequence of A in the Unicode character set is 65. In fact, the binary representation of A is 01000001 and the decimal representation of A is 65.

The numbering system we use is called the decimal system, or base 10 system. The numbering system that the computer uses is called the binary system, or base 2 system. This chapter described how to convert a decimal number into an equivalent binary number. The purpose of this exercise is to write a program to convert a number from base 2 to base 10.

To convert a number from base 2 to base 10, we first find the weight of each bit in the binary number. The weight of each bit in the binary number is assigned from right to left. The weight of the rightmost bit is 0. The weight of the bit immediately to the left of the rightmost bit is 1, the weight of the bit immediately to the left of it is 2, and so on. Consider the binary number 1001101. The weight of each bit is as follows:

```
weight   6 5 4 3 2 1 0
         1 0 0 1 1 0 1
```

We use the weight of each bit to find the equivalent decimal number. For each bit, we multiply the bit by 2 to the power of its weight and then add all of the numbers. For the above binary number, the equivalent decimal number is:

$$1 \times 2^6 + 0 \times 2^5 + 0 \times 2^4 + 1 \times 2^3 + 1 \times 2^2 + 0 \times 2^1 + 1 \times 2^0$$

$$= 64 + 0 + 0 + 8 + 4 + 0 + 1$$

$$= 77$$

To write a program that converts a binary number into the equivalent decimal number, we note two things: (1) the weight of each bit in the binary number must be known; and (2) the weight is assigned from right to left. Because we do not know in advance how many bits are in the binary number, we must process the bits from right to left. After processing a bit, we can add 1 to its weight, giving the weight of the bit immediately to its left. Also, each bit must be extracted from the binary number and multiplied by 2 to the power of its weight. To extract a bit, you can use the mod operator. Write a method that converts a binary number into an equivalent decimal number. Moreover, write a program and test your method for the following values: 11000101, 10101010, 11111111, 10000000, and 1111100000.

16. Write a program that uses recursion to draw a Koch snowflake fractal of any given order. A Koch snowflake of order 0 is an equilateral triangle. To create the next-higher-order fractal, each line segment in the shape is modified by replacing its middle third with a sharp protrusion made of two line segments, each having the same length as the replaced one, as shown in Figure 13-11.

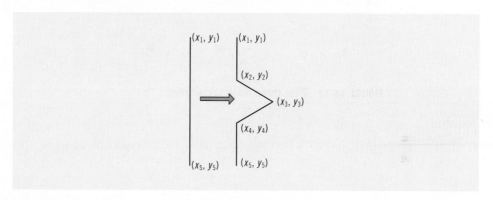

FIGURE 13-11 Line segments for Koch snowflakes

The following is the necessary information to compute the three new points (x_2, y_2), (x_3, y_3), and (x_4, y_4) in terms of (x_1, y_1) and (x_5, y_5).

Let:

$deltaX = x_5 - x_1$

$deltaY = y_5 - y_1$

Then:

$x_2 = x_1 + deltaX/3,$

$y_2 = y_1 + deltaY/3,$

$x_3 = 0.5(x_1 + x_5) + \sqrt{3}(y_1 - y_5)/6,$

$y_3 = 0.5(y_1 + y_5) + \sqrt{3}(x_5 - x_1)/6,$

$x_4 = x_1 + 2 \times deltaX/3,$

$y_4 = y_1 + 2 \times deltaY/3$

1
3

The first three Koch snowflakes produced by the program might look like
Figure 13-12.

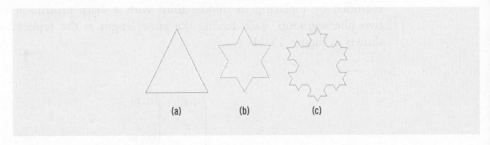

(a)   (b)   (c)

FIGURE 13-12 First three Koch snowflakes

SEARCHING AND SORTING

IN THIS CHAPTER, YOU WILL:

· Explore how to sort an array using the selection sort algorithm

· Explore how to sort an array using the insertion sort algorithm

· Learn how to implement the binary search algorithm

Chapter 9 introduced arrays, a structured data type. Arrays are a convenient way to store and process data values of the same type. You learned how to use loops effectively with arrays for input/output, initialization, and other operations. You also learned how to pass an entire set of values as a single parameter. This chapter continues the discussion of arrays and shows you how to use them effectively for processing lists.

List Processing

A **list** is a set of values of the same type. Because all values are of the same type, it is convenient to store a list in an array, specifically a one-dimensional array. The size of a list is the number of elements in the list. Because a list's size can increase and decrease, the array you use to store the list should be declared to be the maximum size of the list.

Some basic operations performed on a list are:

- Search the list for a given item.
- Sort the list.
- Insert an item in the list.
- Delete an item from the list.

The following sections discuss algorithms to perform some of these operations.

Searching

Chapter 9 described a sequential search algorithm and also illustrated how to use it. Recall that the sequential search searches the array sequentially starting from the first array element.

Suppose that you have a list with 1000 elements, as shown in Figure 14-1.

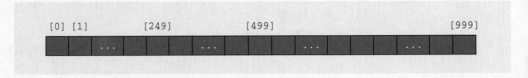

FIGURE 14-1 List of 1000 elements

If the search item is the second item in the list, the sequential search makes two **key comparisons** (also called **item comparisons**) to determine whether the search item is in the list. Similarly, if the search item is the 900th item in the list, the sequential search makes 900 key comparisons to determine whether the search item is in the list. If the search item is not in the list, the sequential search makes 1000 key comparisons.

If searchItem is always at the end of the list, it will take many comparisons to find searchItem. Also, if searchItem is not in the list, then we will compare searchItem with every element in the `list`. A sequential search is therefore not efficient for large lists. In fact, it can be proved that, on average, the number of comparisons (that is, key comparisons) made by a sequential search is equal to half the size of the list. So, for a list of size 1000, on average, the sequential search makes about 500 comparisons. Similarly, for a list of size 1,000,000, on average, the sequential search makes about 500,000 comparisons. (Imagine how much time it will take if you search a telephone book for "Smith" sequentially starting at A's and go through all the records until you find Smith.)

This search algorithm does not assume that the `list` is sorted. If the `list` is sorted, then you can improve the search algorithm. Next, we discuss how to sort a `list`.

Selection Sort

Many sorting algorithms are available in the literature. This section describes the sorting algorithm called the **selection sort**, to sort a list.

In a selection sort, a list is sorted by selecting elements in the list, one at a time, and moving them to their proper positions. This algorithm finds the location of the smallest element in the unsorted portion of the list and moves it to the top of the unsorted portion (i.e., the whole list) of the list. The first time we locate the smallest item in the entire list; the second time we locate the smallest item in the list starting from the second element in the list; and so on. For example, suppose you have the list shown in Figure 14-2.

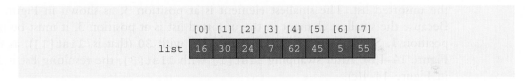

FIGURE 14-2 List of 8 elements

Figure 14-3 shows the elements of `list` in the first iteration.

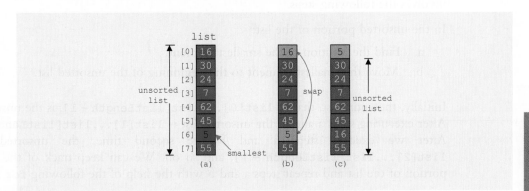

FIGURE 14-3 Elements of `list` during the first iteration

Initially, the entire list is unsorted. So we find the smallest item in the list. The smallest item is at position 6, as shown in Figure 14-3(a). Because this is the smallest item, it must be moved to position 0. So we swap 16 (that is, list[0]) with 5 (that is, list[6]), as shown in Figure 14-3(b). After swapping these elements, the resulting list is as shown in Figure 14-3(c).

Figure 14-4 shows the elements of list in the second iteration.

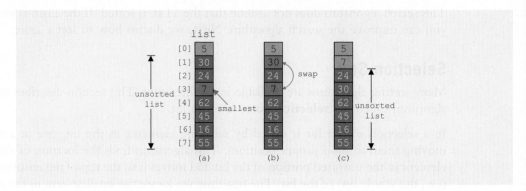

FIGURE 14-4   Elements of list during the second iteration

Now the unsorted list is list[1]...list[7]. So we find the smallest element in the unsorted list. The smallest element is at position 3, as shown in Figure 14-4(a). Because the smallest element in the unsorted list is at position 3, it must be moved to position 1. So we swap 7 (that is, list[3]) with 30 (that is, list[1]), as shown in Figure 14-4(b). After swapping list[1] with list[3], the resulting list is as shown in Figure 14-4(c).

Now the unsorted list is list[2]...list[7]. So we repeat the preceding process of finding the (position of the) smallest element in the unsorted portion of the list and moving it to the beginning of the unsorted portion of the list. The selection sort thus involves the following steps.

In the unsorted portion of the list:

    a.   Find the location of the smallest element.

    b.   Move the smallest element to the beginning of the unsorted list.

Initially, the entire list, that is, list[0]...list[listLength – 1], is the unsorted list. After executing steps a and b, the unsorted list is list[1]...list[listLength – 1]. After we execute steps a and b the second time, the unsorted list is list[2]...list[listLength – 1], and so on. We can keep track of the unsorted portion of the list and repeat steps a and b with the help of the following **for** loop:

```
for (index = 0; index < listLength - 1; index++)
{
    a. find the location, smallestIndex, of the smallest element in
       list[index]...list[listLength].
    b. Swap the smallest element with list[index]. That is, swap
       list[smallestIndex] with list[index].
}
```

The first time through the loop, we locate the smallest element in
`list[0]...list[listLength - 1]` and swap this smallest element with `list[0]`. The
second time through the loop, we locate the smallest element in
`list[1]...list[listLength - 1]` and swap this smallest element with `list[1]`, and so on.

Step a is similar to the algorithm of finding the index of the largest item in the list,
as discussed in Chapter 9. Here, we find the index of the smallest item in the list.
(See Programming Exercise 2 in Chapter 9.) The general form of step a is:

```
smallestIndex = index; //assume that the first element
                       //is the smallest

for (minIndex = index + 1; minIndex < listLength; minIndex++)
    if (list[minIndex] < list[smallestIndex])
        smallestIndex = minIndex; //current element in the list
                                  //is smaller than the smallest so
                                  //far, so update smallestIndex
```

Step b swaps the contents of `list[smallestIndex]` with `list[index]`. The following
statements accomplish this task:

```
temp = list[smallestIndex];
list[smallestIndex] = list[index];
list[index] = temp;
```

It follows that to swap these values, three item assignments are needed. The following
method, `selectionSort`, implements the selection sort algorithm:

```
public static void selectionSort(int[] list, int listLength)
{
    int index;
    int smallestIndex;
    int minIndex;
    int temp;

    for (index = 0; index < listLength - 1; index++)
    {
            //Step a
        smallestIndex = index;

        for (minIndex = index + 1; minIndex < listLength;
                            minIndex++)
            if (list[minIndex] < list[smallestIndex])
                smallestIndex = minIndex;
```

1
4

```
                             //Step b
          temp = list[smallestIndex];
          list[smallestIndex] = list[index];
          list[index] = temp;
     }
}
```

Note that if the list contains duplicates, then while searching for the smallest element, the method `selectionSort` finds the position of the first occurrence of the smallest element, and in the successive iterations finds the positions of other occurrences of this smallest element. Example 14-1 shows how to use the selection sort algorithm in a program.

EXAMPLE 14-1 (SELECTION SORT)

```
// This program illustrates how to use a selection sort algorithm
// in a program.

public class TestSelectionSort                         //Line 1
{                                                      //Line 2
    public static void main(String[] args)            //Line 3
    {
        int list[] = {2, 56, 34, 25, 73, 46, 89,
                      10, 5, 16};                       //Line 4

        selectionSort(list, list.length);              //Line 5

        System.out.println("After sorting, the "
                          + "list elements are:");      //Line 6

        for (int i = 0; i < list.length; i++)          //Line 7
            System.out.print(list[i] + " ");           //Line 8

        System.out.println();                          //Line 9
    }                                                  //Line 10

    //Place the definition of the selection sort algorithm
    //given previously here.
}
```

Sample Run:

```
After sorting, the list elements are:
2 5 10 16 25 34 46 56 73 89
```

The statement in Line 4 creates and initializes `list` to be an array of 10 elements of type `int`. The statement in Line 5 uses the method `selectionSort` to sort `list`. Notice that both `list` and its length are passed as parameters to the method `selectionSort`. The `for` loop in Lines 7 and 8 outputs the elements of `list`.

In this program, to illustrate the selection sort algorithm, we declared and initialized the array `list`. However, you can also prompt the user to input the data during program execution.

For a list of length n, selection sort makes exactly $\frac{n(n-1)}{2}$ key comparisons and $3(n-1)$ item assignments. Therefore, if $n = 1000$, then to sort the list, selection sort makes about 500,000 key comparisons and about 3000 item assignments. The next section presents the insertion sort algorithm that reduces the number of comparisons.

Insertion Sort

As noted in the previous section, for a list of length 1000, selection sort makes 500,000 key comparisons, which is quite high. This section describes the sorting algorithm called the insertion sort, which attempts to reduce the number of key comparisons.

The insertion sort algorithm sorts a list by repeatedly inserting an element in its proper place into a sorted sublist until the whole list is sorted. Consider the list shown in Figure 14-5.

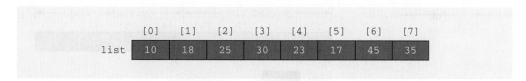

FIGURE 14-5 List

The length of the list is 8. In this list, the elements `list[0]`, `list[1]`, `list[2]`, and `list[3]` are in order. That is, `list[0]...list[3]` is sorted (see Figure 14-6).

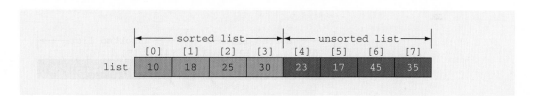

FIGURE 14-6 Sorted and unsorted portion of `list`

Next, we consider the element `list[4]`, the first element of the unsorted list. Because `list[4] < list[3]`, we need to insert the element `list[4]` in its proper location. From this list, it follows that element `list[4]` should be moved to `list[2]` (see Figure 14-7).

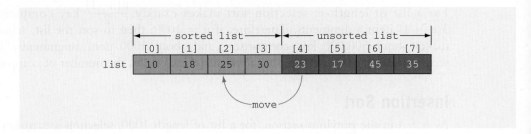

FIGURE 14-7 Move `list[4]` into `list[2]`

To move `list[4]` into `list[2]`, first we copy `list[4]` into `temp`, a temporary memory space (see Figure 14-8).

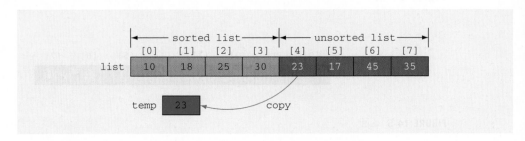

FIGURE 14-8 Copy `list[4]` into `temp`

Next, we copy `list[3]` into `list[4]`, and then `list[2]` into `list[3]` (see Figure 14-9).

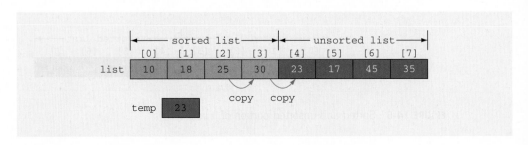

FIGURE 14-9 List before copying `list[3]` into `list[4]`, and then `list[2]` into `list[3]`

After copying `list[3]` into `list[4]` and `list[2]` into `list[3]`, the list is as shown in Figure 14-10.

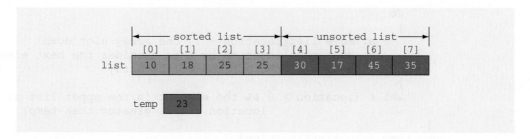

FIGURE 14-10 List after copying `list[3]` into `list[4]`, and then `list[2]` into `list[3]`

We now copy `temp` into `list[2]`. Figure 14-11 shows the resulting list.

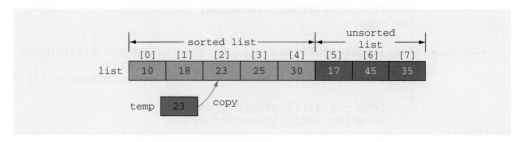

FIGURE 14-11 List after copying `temp` into `list[2]`

Now `list[0]...list[4]` is sorted and `list[5]...list[7]` is unsorted. We repeat this process on the resulting list by moving the first element of the unsorted list into the sorted list in the proper place.

From this discussion, it is clear that during the sorting phase the array containing the list is divided into two sublists: sorted and unsorted. Elements in the sorted sublist are sorted; elements in the unsorted sublist are to be moved to the sorted sublist in their proper places one at a time. We use an index—say, `firstOutOfOrder`—to point to the first element in the unsorted sublist. Initially, `firstOutOfOrder` is initialized to 1.

This discussion translates into the following pseudoalgorithm:

```
for (firstOutOfOrder = 1; firstOutOfOrder < listLength;
                    firstOutOfOrder++)
  if (list[firstOutOfOrder] is less than list[firstOutOfOrder - 1])
  {
      copy list[firstOutOfOrder] into temp

      initialize location to firstOutOfOrder
```

1
4

```
        do
        {
            a. move list[location - 1] one array slot down
            b. decrement location by 1 to consider the next element
               sorted of the portion of the array
        }
        while (location > 0 && the element in the upper list at
                              location - 1 is greater than temp)
    }
copy temp into list[location]
```

The following Java method implements the previous algorithm:

```
public static void insertionSort(int[] list, int listLength)
{
    int firstOutOfOrder, location;
    int temp;

    for (firstOutOfOrder = 1; firstOutOfOrder < listLength;
                              firstOutOfOrder++)
    if (list[firstOutOfOrder] < list[firstOutOfOrder - 1])
    {
        temp = list[firstOutOfOrder];
        location = firstOutOfOrder;

        do
        {
            list[location] = list[location - 1];
            location--;
        }
        while (location > 0 && list[location - 1] > temp);

        list[location] = temp;
    }
} //end insertionSort
```

We leave it as an exercise for you to write a program to test the insertion sort algorithm.

It is known that for a list of length n, on average, an insertion sort makes about $\frac{n^2 + 3n - 4}{4}$ key comparisons and about $\frac{n(n-1)}{4}$ item assignments. Therefore, if $n = 1000$, to sort the list, insertion sort makes about 250,000 key comparisons and about 250,000 item assignments.

This chapter has presented two sorting algorithms, but there are many others. (For example, the Additional Student Files folder at *www.cengagebrain.com* contains a bubble sort and a quick sort algorithm.) Why are there so many different sorting algorithms? The answer is that the performance of each sorting algorithm is different. Some algorithms make more comparisons, some make fewer item assignments, and some algorithms make fewer comparisons as well as fewer item assignments. The preceding sections gave the average number of comparisons and item assignments for this chapter's three sorting algorithms. By analyzing the number of key comparisons and item assignments, the user can decide which algorithm to use in a particular situation.

Binary Search

A sequential search is not efficient for large lists. It typically still searches about half the list. However, if the list is sorted, you can use another search algorithm, called a **binary search**. A binary search is much faster than a sequential search, but a binary search can be performed only on a sorted list. A binary search uses the *divide and conquer* technique to search the list. First, the search item is compared with the middle element of the list. If the search item is not equal to the middle element, and is less than the middle element of the list, the search is restricted to the first half of the list; otherwise, the second half of the list is searched.

Consider the following sorted list of length 12, shown in Figure 14-12.

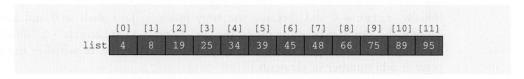

FIGURE 14-12 List of length 12

Suppose that we want to determine whether 75 is in the list. Initially, the entire list is the search list (see Figure 14-13).

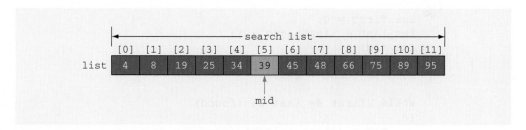

FIGURE 14-13 Search list, `list[0]...list[11]`

First, we compare 75 with the middle element, `list[5]` (which is 39), in the list. Because 75 ≠ `list[5]` and 75 > `list[5]`, next we restrict our search to the list `list[6]...list[11]`, as shown in Figure 14-14.

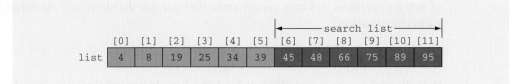

FIGURE 14-14 Search list, `list[6]...list[11]`

The above process is now repeated on the list `list[6]...list[11]`, which is a list of length 6.

Because we frequently need to determine the middle element of the list, the binary search algorithm is usually implemented for array-based lists. To determine the middle element of the list, we add the starting index, `first`, and the ending index, `last`, of the search list and divide by 2 to calculate its index. That is, $mid = \dfrac{first + last}{2}$.

Initially, `first = 0` and (because the array index in Java starts at 0 and `listLength` denotes the number of elements in the list) `last = listLength - 1`. (Note that the formula for calculating the middle element works regardless of whether the list has an even or odd number of elements.)

The following Java method implements the binary search algorithm. If the search item is found in the list, its location is returned. If the search item is not in the list, `-1` is returned.

```java
public static int binarySearch(int[] list, int listLength,
                               int searchItem)
{
    int first = 0;
    int last = listLength - 1;
    int mid;

    boolean found = false;

    while (first <= last && !found)
    {
        mid = (first + last) / 2;

        if (list[mid] == searchItem)
            found = true;
        else if (list[mid] > searchItem)
            last = mid - 1;
        else
            first = mid + 1;
    }
```

```
    if (found)
        return mid;
    else
        return -1;
}//end binarySearch
```

Note that in the binary search algorithm, two key (item) comparisons are made each time through the loop, except in the successful case the last time through the loop, when only one key comparison is made.

Next, we do a walk-through of the binary search algorithm on the list shown in Figure 14-15.

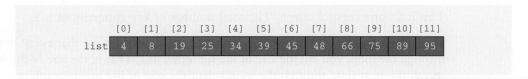

FIGURE 14-15 Sorted list for binary search

The size of the list in Figure 14-15 is 12, that is, listLength = 12. Suppose that the item for which we are searching is 89, that is, searchItem = 89. Before the while loop executes, first = 0, last = 11, and found = false. In the following, we trace the execution of the while loop, showing the values of first, last, and mid, and the number of key comparisons during each iteration:

Iteration	first	last	mid	list[mid]	Number of key comparisons
1	0	11	5	39	2
2	6	11	8	66	2
3	9	11	10	89	1 (found is true)

The item is found at location 10 and the total number of key comparisons is 5.

Next, let's search the list for 34, that is, searchItem = 34. Before the while loop executes, first = 0, last = 11, and found = false. In the following, as before, we trace the execution of the while loop, showing the values of first, last, and mid, and the number of key comparisons during each iteration:

Iteration	first	last	mid	list[mid]	Number of key comparisons
1	0	11	5	39	2
2	0	4	2	19	2
3	3	4	3	25	2
4	4	4	4	34	1 (found is true)

The item is found at location 4 and the total number of key comparisons is 7.

Let's now search for 22, that is, `searchItem = 22`. Before the `while` loop executes, `first = 0`, `last = 11`, and `found = false`. In the following, as before, we trace the execution of the `while` loop, showing the values of `first`, `last`, and `mid`, and the number of key comparisons during each iteration:

Iteration	first	last	mid	list[mid]	Number of key comparisons
1	0	11	5	39	2
2	0	4	2	19	2
3	3	4	3	25	2
4	3	2		the loop stops (because `first > last`) unsuccessful search	

This is an unsuccessful search. The total number of key comparisons is 6.

From these tracings of the binary search algorithm, you can see that every time you go through the loop, you cut the size of the sublist by half. That is, the size of the sublist you search the next time through the loop is half the size of the previous sublist.

PERFORMANCE OF THE BINARY SEARCH

Suppose that L is a sorted list of size 1024 and we want to determine if an item x is in L. From the binary search algorithm, it follows that every iteration of the `while` loop cuts the size of the search list by half. (For example, see Figures 14-13 and 14-14.) Because $1024 = 2^{10}$, the `while` loop will have, at most, 11 iterations to determine whether x is in L. (Note that the symbol $\approx$ means approximately equal to.) Because every iteration of the `while` loop makes two item (key) comparisons, that is, x is compared twice with the elements of L, the binary search will make, at most, 22 comparisons to determine whether x is in L. On the other hand, recall that a sequential search on average will make 512 comparisons to determine whether x is in L.

To better understand how fast binary search is compared to sequential search, suppose that L is of size 1048576. Because $1048576 = 2^{20}$, it follows that the `while` loop in binary search will have at most 21 iterations to determine whether an element is in L. Every iteration of the `while` loop makes two key (that is, item) comparisons. Therefore, to determine whether an element is in L, binary search makes at most 42 item comparisons. On the other hand, on average, a sequential search will make 524,288 key (item) comparisons to determine whether an element is in L. (Because a telephone book is in alphabetical order, it can be searched using a binary search. For example, to search for "Smith," you open the telephone book in the middle to start the search.)

In general, if L is a sorted list of size n, to determine whether an element is in L, the binary search makes at most $2\log_2 n + 2$ key (item) comparisons.

PROGRAMMING EXAMPLE: Election Results

The election for president of the student council of your local university is about to be held. To ensure confidentiality, the election committee chair wants to computerize the voting. The chair is looking for someone to write a program to process the data and report the winner. Let's write a program to help the chair of the election committee.

The university has four major colleges, and each college has several departments. For election purposes, the four colleges are labeled Region 1, Region 2, Region 3, and Region 4. Each department in each college holds its own voting and directly reports the votes received by each candidate to the election committee. The voting is reported in the form:

```
candidate_name region# number_of_votes_for_this_candidate
```

The election committee wants the output in the following tabular form:

```
--------------Election Results--------------

Candidate                    Votes
Name       Region1 Region2 Region3 Region4  Total
----       ------- ------- ------- -------  -----
Ashley          23      89       0     160    272
Danny           25      71      89      97    282
Donald         110     158       0       0    268
 .
 .
 .


Winner: ???,  Votes Received: ???
Total votes polled: ???
```

The names of the candidates in the output must be in alphabetical order.

For this program, we assume that six candidates are running for student council president. This program can be enhanced to any number of candidates. Also, we assume that no two candidates receive the same number of votes, that is, there is no tie. We will leave it as an exercise for you to modify the program so that if more than one candidate receives the maximum number of votes, then the program outputs the names of all such candidates.

The data is provided in two files. One file, candData.txt, consists of the names of the candidates. The names of the candidates in the file are in no particular order. In the second file, voteData.txt, each line consists of the voting results in the following form:

```
candidateName regionNumber numberOfVotesForTheCandidate
```

1
4

That is, each line in the file `voteData.txt` consists of the candidate's name, region number, and the votes received by the candidate in this region. There is one entry per line. For example, the input file containing the voting data looks like:

```
Mia 2 34
Mickey 1 56
Donald 2 56
Mia 1 78
Danny 4 29
Ashley 4 78
.
.
.
```

The first line indicates that `Mia` received 34 votes from region 2.

Input: Two files, one containing the candidates' names and the other containing the voting data, as described previously.

Output: The election results in a tabular form, as described previously, and the winner.

PROBLEM
ANALYSIS AND
ALGORITHM
DESIGN

Looking at the output, it is clear that the program must organize the voting data by regions. The program must also calculate the total votes received by each candidate and the total votes polled for the election. Furthermore, the names of the candidates must appear in alphabetical order.

Because the data type of a candidate's name (which is a string) and the data type of the number of votes (which is an integer) are different, we need separate arrays—one to hold the candidates' names and the other to hold the voting data. The array to hold the names of the candidates is a one-dimensional array, and each element of this array is a string. Instead of using one two-dimensional array to hold the voting data, we will use a two-dimensional array to hold the next four columns of the output, that is, the regional voting data, and we will use a one-dimensional array to hold the total votes received by each candidate. These three arrays are parallel arrays (see Figure 14-16).

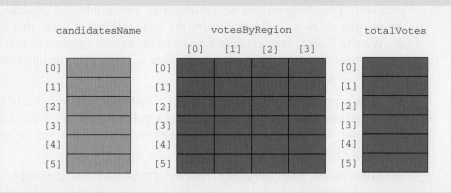

FIGURE 14-16 Parallel arrays `candidatesName`, `votesByRegion`, and `totalVotes`

The data in the first row of these three arrays correspond to the candidate whose name is stored in the first row of the array `candidatesName`, and so on. In the voting-by-region array, column 1 corresponds to Region 1, column 2 corresponds to Region 2, and so on. Recall that, in Java, an array index starts at 0. Therefore, if the name of this array in the program is, say, `votesByRegion`, `votesByRegion[][0]` refers to the first column and thus Region 1, and so on.

For easy reference, for the remainder of this discussion, assume that in the program we are writing, the name of the candidates' name array is `candidatesName`, the name of the voting-by-region array is `votesByRegion`, and the name of the array containing the total votes is `totalVotes`.

The first thing we must do in this program is read the candidates' names from the input file `candData.txt` into the array `candidatesName`. Once the candidates' names are stored in the array `candidatesName`, we must sort this array.

Next, we process the voting data. Every entry in the file `voteData.txt` contains `candidatesName`, `regionNumber`, and `numberOfVotesForTheCandidate`. To process this entry, we find the appropriate entry in the array `votesByRegion` and update this entry by adding `numberOfVotesForTheCandidate` to this entry. Therefore, it follows that the array `votesByRegion` must be initialized to zero. Processing the voting data is described in detail later in this section.

After processing the voting data, the next step is to calculate the total votes received by each candidate. This is accomplished by adding the votes received in each region. Therefore, we must initialize the array `totalVotes` to zero. Finally, we output the results as shown earlier.

This discussion translates into the following algorithm:

1. Read the candidates' names into the array `candidatesName`.
2. Sort the array `candidatesName`.
3. Process the voting data.
4. Calculate the total votes received by each candidate.
5. Output the results as shown earlier.

Note that the arrays `votesByRegion` and `totalVotes` are automatically initialized when they are created. Because the input data is provided in two separate files, in this program, we must open two input files. We open both input files in the method `main`.

To implement the preceding five steps, the program consists of several methods, which are described next.

Method
Candidates
Name

This method reads the data from the input file `candData.txt` and fills the array `candidatesName`. The input file is opened in the method `main`. Note that this method has two parameters: a parameter corresponding to the input file and

1
4

a parameter corresponding to the array `candidatesName`. Essentially, this method is:

```
public static void getCandidatesName(Scanner inp,
                                     String[] cNames)
{
    int i;

    for (i = 0; i < cNames.length; i++)
        cNames[i] = inp.next();
}
```

After a call to this method, the arrays to hold the data are as shown in Figure 14-17.

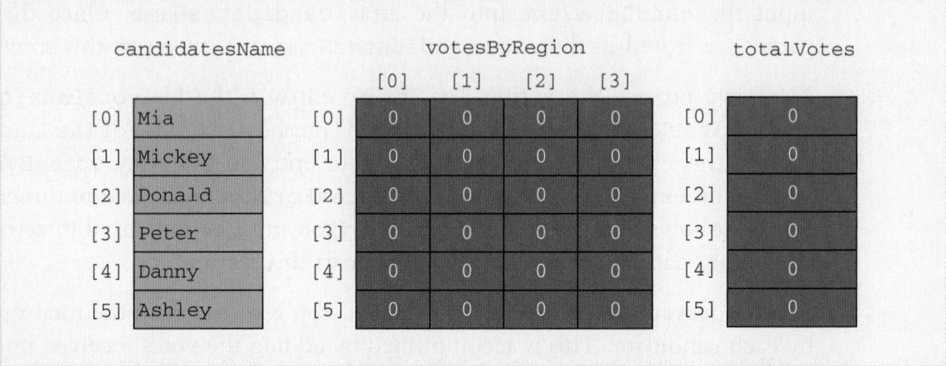

FIGURE 14-17   Arrays `candidatesName`, `votesByRegion`, and `totalVotes` after reading candidates' names

Method sortCandidatesName

This method uses a selection sort algorithm to sort the array `candidatesName`. This method has only one parameter: the parameter corresponding to the array `candidatesName`. Essentially, this method is:

```
public static void sortCandidatesName(String[] cNames)
{
    int i, j;
    int min;
    String temp;

        //selection sort
    for (i = 0; i < cNames.length - 1; i++)
    {
        min = i;

        for (j = i + 1; j < cNames.length; j++)
            if (cNames[j].compareTo(cNames[min]) <  0)
                min = j;
```

```
        temp = cNames[i];
        cNames[i] = cNames[min];
        cNames[min] = temp;
    }
}
```

After a call to this method, the arrays are as shown in Figure 14-18.

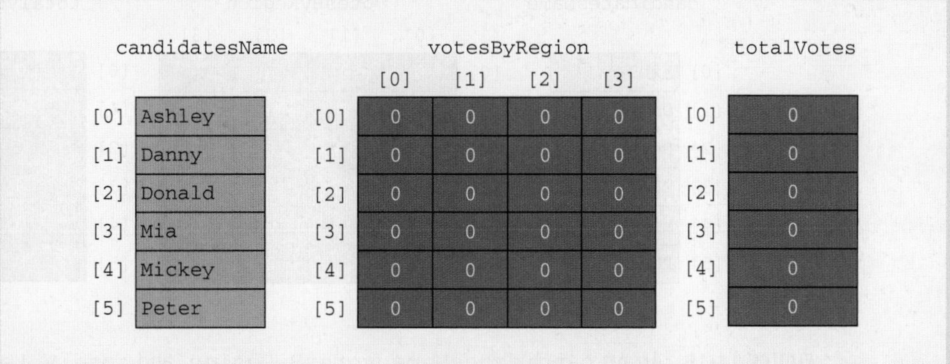

FIGURE 14-18 Arrays candidatesName, votesByRegion, and totalVotes after sorting names

Process Voting Data

Processing the voting data is quite straightforward. Each entry in the file voteData.txt is in the following form:

candidatesName regionNumber numberOfVotesForTheCandidate

The general algorithm to process the voting data follows.

For each entry in the file voteData.txt:

1. Get the candidatesName, regionNumber, and numberOfVotesForTheCandidate.

2. Find the row number in the array candidatesName corresponding to this candidate. This will give the corresponding row number in the array votesByRegion for this candidate.

3. Find the column number in the array votesByRegion corresponding to this regionNumber.

4. Update the appropriate entry in the array votesByRegion by adding numberOfVotesForTheCandidate.

Step 2 requires us to search the array candidatesName to find the location, that is, row number, of a particular candidate. Because the array candidatesName is sorted, we can use the binary search algorithm to find the row number corresponding to a particular candidate. Therefore, the program also includes the method binSearch to implement the binary search algorithm on the array `candidatesName`. We will write the definition of the method `binSearch` shortly. First we discuss how to update the array `votesByRegion`.

Suppose that the three arrays are as shown in Figure 14-19.

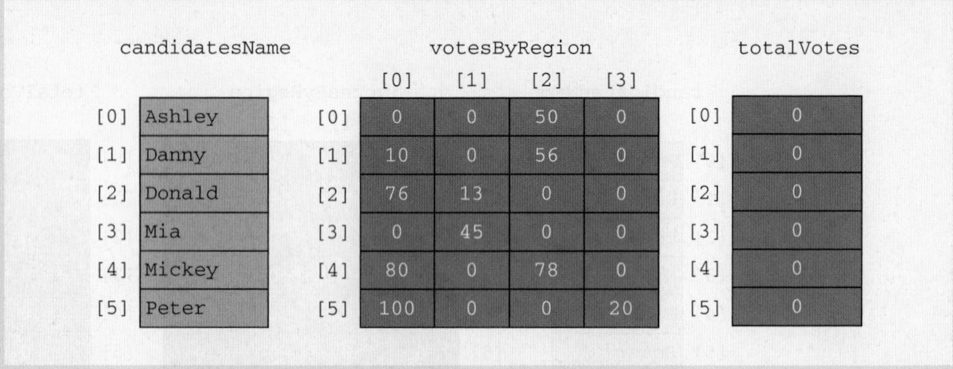

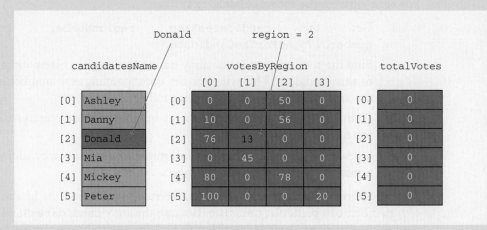

FIGURE 14-19 Arrays `candidatesName`, `votesByRegion`, and `totalVotes`

Further suppose that the next entry read from the input file is:

```
Donald 2 35
```

Next, we locate the row in the preceding grid that corresponds to this candidate. To find the row, we search the array `candidatesName` to find the row that corresponds to this name. Now `Donald` corresponds to row number 2 in the array `candidatesName`, as shown in Figure 14-20.

FIGURE 14-20 Position of `Donald` and region = 2

To process this entry, we access row number 2 of the array `votesByRegion`. Because Donald received 35 votes from Region 2, we access row number 2 and column number 1, that is, `votesByRegion[2][1]`, and update this entry by adding 35 to its previous value. The following statement accomplishes this:

`votesByRegion[2][1] = votesByRegion[2][1] + 35;`

After processing this entry, the three arrays are as shown in Figure 14-21.

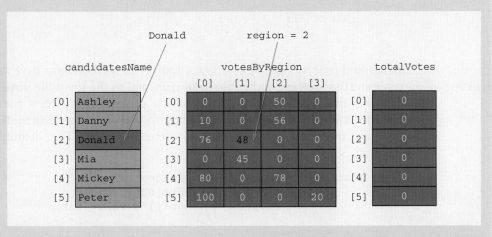

FIGURE 14-21 Arrays `candidatesName`, `votesByRegion`, and `totalVotes` after processing the entry `Donald 2 35`

We now describe the method `binSearch` and the method `processVotes` to process the voting data.

Method **binSearch**

This method implements the binary search algorithm on the array `candidatesName`. It is similar to the method `binarySearch`. Its definition is:

```java
public static int binSearch(String[] cNames, String name)
{
    int first, last;
    int mid = 0;

    boolean found;

    first = 0;
    last = cNames.length - 1;
    found = false;

    while (first <= last && !found)
    {
        mid = (first + last) / 2;
```

1
4

```
        if (cNames[mid].equals(name))
            found = true;
        else if (cNames[mid].compareTo(name) > 0)
            last = mid - 1;
        else
            first = mid + 1;
    }

    if (found)
        return mid;
    else
        return -1;
}
```

Method processVotes

This method processes the voting data. Clearly, this method must have access to the arrays `candidatesName` and `votesByRegion`, and to the input file `voteData.txt`. Thus, this method has three parameters: a parameter to access the input file `voteData.txt`, a parameter corresponding to the array `candidatesName`, and a parameter corresponding to the array `votesByRegion`. The definition of this method is:

```
public static void processVotes(Scanner inp,
                                String[] cNames,
                                int[][] vbRegion)
{
    String candName;
    int region;
    int noOfVotes;
    int loc;

    while (inp.hasNext())
    {
        candName = inp.next();
        region = inp.nextInt();
        noOfVotes = inp.nextInt();

        loc =  binSearch(cNames, candName);

        if (loc != -1)
            vbRegion[loc][region - 1] =
                vbRegion[loc][region - 1] + noOfVotes;
    }
}
```

Calculate Total Votes (Method addRegionsVote)

After processing the voting data, the next step is to calculate the total votes for each candidate. Suppose that after processing the voting data, the arrays are as shown in Figure 14-22.

	candidatesName		votesByRegion [0]	[1]	[2]	[3]		totalVotes
[0]	Ashley	[0]	23	89	0	160	[0]	0
[1]	Danny	[1]	25	71	89	97	[1]	0
[2]	Donald	[2]	110	158	0	0	[2]	0
[3]	Mia	[3]	134	112	156	0	[3]	0
[4]	Mickey	[4]	56	63	67	89	[4]	0
[5]	Peter	[5]	207	56	0	46	[5]	0

FIGURE 14-22 Arrays `candidatesName`, `votesByRegion`, and `totalVotes` after processing the voting data

After calculating the total votes received by each candidate, the three arrays are as shown in Figure 14-23.

	candidatesName		votesByRegion [0]	[1]	[2]	[3]		totalVotes
[0]	Ashley	[0]	23	89	0	160	[0]	272
[1]	Danny	[1]	25	71	89	97	[1]	282
[2]	Donald	[2]	110	158	0	0	[2]	268
[3]	Mia	[3]	134	112	156	0	[3]	402
[4]	Mickey	[4]	56	63	67	89	[4]	275
[5]	Peter	[5]	207	56	0	46	[5]	309

FIGURE 14-23 Arrays `candidatesName`, `votesByRegion`, and `totalVotes` after calculating the total votes received by each candidate

To calculate the total votes received by each candidate, we add the contents of each row in the `votesByRegion` array and store the sum in the corresponding row in the `totalVotes` array. This is accomplished by the method `addRegionsVote`, which is described next.

The method `addRegionsVote` calculates the total votes received by each candidate. This method must access the arrays `votesByRegion` and `totalVotes`. This method has two parameters: a parameter corresponding to the array `votesByRegion` and a parameter corresponding to the array `totalVotes`. The definition of this method is:

```
public static void addRegionsVote(int[][] vbRegion, int[] tVotes)
{

    for (int i = 0; i < tVotes.length; i++)
        for (int j = 0; j < vbRegion[0].length; j++)
            tVotes[i] = tVotes[i] + vbRegion[i][j];
}
```

The remaining methods to get the desired output are described next.

Method printHeading

The method `printHeading` outputs the first four lines of the output, so it contains certain output statements. The definition of this method is:

```
public static void printHeading()
{
    System.out.println("   ---------------Election Results"
                   + "--------------\n");
    System.out.println("Candidate            "
                   + "        Votes");
    System.out.println("Name          Region1 Region2 "
                   + "Region3 Region4   Total");
    System.out.println("----          ------- ------- "
                   + "------- -------   -----");
}
```

Method printResults

The method `printResults` outputs the remaining lines of the output. Clearly, this method must have access to each of the three arrays. (Note that each array has the same number of rows.) Thus, this method has three parameters. Suppose that the parameter cNames corresponds to `candidatesName`, the parameter vbRegion corresponds to `votesByRegion`, and the parameter tVotes corresponds to `totalVotes`.

Further suppose that the variable sumVotes holds the total votes polled for the election, the variable largestVotes holds the largest number of votes received by a candidate, and the variable winLoc holds the index of the winning candidate in the array candidatesName. The algorithm for this method is:

1. Initialize sumVotes, largestVotes, and winLoc to 0.
2. For each row in each array:

   a. `if(largestVotes < tVotes[i])`
      ```
      {
          largestVotes = tVotes[i];
          winLoc = i;
      }
      ```
   b. `sumVotes = sumVotes + tVotes[i];`
   c. Output the data from the corresponding rows of each array.
3. Output the final lines of the output.

The definition of this method is:

```java
public static void printResults(String[] cNames,
                                int[][] vbRegion, int[] tVotes)
{
    int largestVotes = 0;
    int winLoc = 0;
    int sumVotes = 0;

    for (int i = 0; i < tVotes.length; i++)
    {
        if (largestVotes < tVotes[i])
        {
            largestVotes = tVotes[i];
            winLoc = i;
        }

        sumVotes = sumVotes + tVotes[i];

        System.out.printf("%-11s ", cNames[i]);

        for (int j = 0; j < vbRegion[0].length; j++)
            System.out.printf("%6d  ", vbRegion[i][j]);

        System.out.printf("%5d%n", tVotes[i]);
    }

    System.out.println("\n\nWinner: " + cNames[winLoc]
                    + ",   Votes Received: "
                    + tVotes[winLoc]);
    System.out.println("Total votes polled: " + sumVotes);
}
```

Main Algorithm: method main

Suppose that the variables in the method `main` are:

```java
String[] candidatesName = new String[NO_OF_CANDIDATES]; //array
                                    //to store candidates' names

int[][] votesByRegion =
            new int[NO_OF_CANDIDATES][NO_OF_REGIONS]; //array
                            //to hold voting data by region

int[] totalVotes = new int[NO_OF_CANDIDATES]; //array to hold
                                //total votes received by
                                //each candidate

Scanner inFile; //input file variable
```

Further suppose that the candidates' names are in the file `candData.txt`, and the voting data is in the file `voteData.txt`.

The algorithm for the method `main` is:

1. Declare and initialize the variables and the objects.
2. Open the input file `candData.txt`.
3. Read the data from the file `candData.txt` into the array `candidatesName`.
4. Sort the array `candidatesName`.
5. Open the input file `voteData.txt`.
6. Process the voting data and store the results in the array `votesByRegion`.
7. Calculate the total votes received by each candidate and store the results in the array `totalVotes`.
8. Print the heading.
9. Print the results.

PROGRAM LISTING

```
//**************************************************************
// Author: D.S. Malik
//
// Program: Election Results
// Given candidates' voting data, this program determines the
// winner of the election. The program outputs the votes
// received by each candidate and the winner.
//**************************************************************

import java.io.*;
import java.util.*;

public class ElectionResults
{
    final static int NO_OF_CANDIDATES = 6;
    final static int NO_OF_REGIONS = 4;

    public static void main (String[] args) throws
                                    FileNotFoundException
    {
            //Step 1
        String[] candidatesName = new String[NO_OF_CANDIDATES];

        int[][] votesByRegion =
            new int[NO_OF_CANDIDATES][NO_OF_REGIONS];

        int[] totalVotes = new int[NO_OF_CANDIDATES];

        Scanner inFile = new Scanner(new
            FileReader("candData.txt"));        //Step 2
```

```
            getCandidatesName(inFile, candidatesName);      //Step 3
            sortCandidatesName(candidatesName);             //Step 4

            inFile = null;
            inFile = new Scanner(new
                    FileReader("voteData.txt"));            //Step 5

            processVotes(inFile, candidatesName,
                    votesByRegion);                         //Step 6
            addRegionsVote(votesByRegion, totalVotes);      //Step 7

            printHeading();                                 //Step 8
            printResults(candidatesName, votesByRegion,
                    totalVotes);                            //Step 9
    }

    //Place the definitions of the methods getCandidatesName,
    //sortCandidatesName, binSearch, processVotes,
    //addRegionsVote, printHeading, and printResults,
    //as described in this section, here.
}
```

Sample Run: (After placing the definitions of all the methods as described and then executing the program, the output is as follows.)

```
    ---------------Election Results---------------

Candidate                   Votes
Name        Region1 Region2 Region3 Region4  Total
----        ------- ------- ------- -------  -----
Ashley           23      89       0     160    272
Danny            25      71      89      97    282
Donald          110     158       0       0    268
Mia             134     112     156       0    402
Mickey           56      63      67      89    275
Peter           207      56       0      46    309

Winner: Mia,  Votes Received: 402
Total votes polled: 1808
```

Input Files: The files candData.txt and voteData.txt are provided with the Additional Student Files at *www.cengagebrain.com*. The complete program listing of this program can also be found in this folder.

1
4

NOTE The OOD version of this program can be found with the Additional Student Files at *www.cengagebrain.com*. The name of the file containing the Programming Example is Chapter 14_ElectionResults_ OOD_Version.pdf.

QUICK REVIEW

1. A list is a set of elements of the same type.

2. The length of a list is the number of elements in the list.

3. A one-dimensional array is a convenient data structure for storing and processing lists.

4. A sequential search algorithm searches the list for a given item, starting with the first element in the list. It continues comparing this item with the elements in the list until either the item is found, or the list has no more elements left to compare with the search item.

5. On average, a sequential search searches half the list.

6. In a selection sort, a list is sorted by selecting elements in the list, one at a time, and moving them to their proper positions. This algorithm finds the location of the smallest element in the unsorted portion of the list and moves it to the top of the unsorted portion (i.e., the whole list) of the list.

7. For a list of length n, selection sort makes exactly $\dfrac{n(n-1)}{2}$ key comparisons and $3(n-1)$ item assignments.

8. Insertion sort algorithm sorts the list by inserting each element in its proper place.

9. For a list of length n, on average, an insertion sort makes $\dfrac{n^2 + 3n - 4}{4}$ key comparisons and about $\dfrac{n(n-1)}{4}$ item assignments.

10. In general, binary search is much faster than a sequential search.

11. Binary search requires that the list elements are in order, that is, sorted.

EXERCISES

1. Mark the following statements as true or false.

   a. A sequential search of a list assumes that the list is in ascending order.

   b. A binary search of a list assumes that the list is in sorted order.

   c. A binary search is faster on ordered lists and slower on unordered lists.

2. Consider the following list: 63 45 32 98 46 57 28 100

   Using the sequential search (given in Chapter 9), how many comparisons are required to determine whether the following items are in the list? (Recall that comparisons mean item comparisons, not index comparisons.)

   a. 90   b. 57   c. 63   d. 120

3. a. Write a version of the sequential search algorithm that can be used to search a sorted list.

   b. Consider the following list:

   5 12 17 35 46 65 78 85 93 110 115

   Using the sequential search on ordered lists that you designed in (a), how many comparisons are required to determine whether the following items are in the list or not? (Recall that comparisons mean item comparisons, not index comparisons.)

   i. 35   ii. 60   iii. 78   iv. 120

4. Consider the following list:

   2 10 17 45 49 55 68 85 92 98 110

   Using the binary search (given in this chapter), how many comparisons are required to determine whether the following items are in the list? Show the values of `first`, `last`, and `middle`, and the number of comparisons after each iteration of the loop.

   a. 15   b. 49   c. 98   d. 99

5. Sort the following list using the selection sort algorithm as discussed in this chapter. Show the list after each iteration of the outer `for` loop.

   26, 45, 17, 65, 33, 55, 12, 18

6. Sort the following list using the selection sort algorithm as discussed in this chapter. Show the list after each iteration of the outer `for` loop.

   36, 55, 17, 35, 63, 85, 12, 48, 3, 66

7. Assume the following list: 5, 18, 21, 10, 55, 20

   The first three keys are in order. To move 10 to its proper position, using the insertion sort as described in this chapter, exactly how many key comparisons are executed?

8. Assume the following list: 7, 28, 31, 40, 5, 20

   The first four keys are in order. To move 5 to its proper position, using the insertion sort as described in this chapter, exactly how many key comparisons are executed?

9. Assume the following list:

   28, 18, 21, 10, 25, 30, 12, 71, 32, 58, 15

   This list is to be sorted using the insertion sort algorithm as described in this chapter. Show the resulting list after six passes of the sorting phase—that is, after six iterations of the `for` loop.

10. Recall the insertion sort algorithm as discussed in this chapter. Assume the following list of keys:

    18, 8, 11, 9, 15, 20, 32, 61, 22, 48, 75, 83, 35, 3

    Exactly how many key comparisons are executed to sort this list using the insertion sort?

14

11. Suppose that `L` is a list of 10,000 elements. Find the average number of comparisons made by selection sort and insertion sort to sort `L`.

12. Suppose that `L` is a sorted list of 4096 elements. What is the maximum number of comparisons made by a binary search to determine if an item is in `L`?

13. Suppose that the elements of a list are in descending order and they need to be put in ascending order. Write a Java method that takes as input an array of items in descending order and the number of elements in the array. The method rearranges the element of the array in ascending order. Your method must not incorporate any sorting algorithms, that is, no item comparisons should occur.

PROGRAMMING EXERCISES

1. Write a program to test the method `binarySearch`. Use either the method `insertionSort` or `selectionSort` to sort the list before the search.

2. Write a method, `remove`, that takes three parameters: an array of integers, the length of the array, and an integer, say, `removeItem`. The method should find and delete the first occurrence of `removeItem` in the array. If the value does not exist or the array is empty, output an appropriate message. (Note that after deleting the element, the array size is reduced by 1.) You may assume that the array is unsorted.

3. Write a method, `removeAt`, that takes three parameters: an array of integers, the length of the array, and an integer, say, `index`. The method deletes the array element indicated by `index`. If `index` is out of range or the array is empty, output an appropriate message. (Note that after deleting the element, the array size is reduced by 1.) You may assume that the array is unsorted.

4. Write a method, `removeAll`, that takes three parameters: an array of integers, the length of the array, and an integer, say, `removeItem`. The method should find and delete all occurrences of `removeItem` from the array. If the value does not exist or the array is empty, output an appropriate message. (Note that after deleting the element, the array size will be reduced.) You may assume that the array is unsorted.

5. Redo Programming Exercises 2, 3, and 4 for a sorted array.

6. Write a method, `insertAt`, that takes four parameters: an array of integers; the length of the array; an integer, say, `insertItem`; and an integer, say, `index`. The method inserts `insertItem` in the array at the position specified by `index`. If `index` is out of range, output an appropriate message. (Note that `index` must be between 0 and `arraySize`, that is, $0 \leq index < arraySize$.) You may assume that the array is unsorted.

7. Write a version of a sequential search that can be used to search a string `Vector` object. Also, write a program to test your algorithm.

8. Write a version of a selection sort that can be used to sort a string `Vector` object. Also, write a program to test your algorithm.

9. Write a program to test the insertion sort algorithm as given in this chapter.

10. Write a version of the insertion sort algorithm that can be used to sort a string Vector object. Also, write a program to test your algorithm.

11. Write a version of a binary search that can be used to search a string Vector object. Also, write a program to test your algorithm. (Use the selection sort algorithm you developed in Programming Exercise 8 to sort the Vector.)

12. Redo the Programming Example Election Results so that the names of the candidates and the total votes are stored in Vector objects.

13. Write a program to keep track of a hardware store's inventory. The store sells various items. For each item in the store, the following information is kept: item ID, item name, number of pieces ordered, number of pieces currently in the store, number of pieces sold, manufacturer's price of the item, and the store's selling price. At the end of each week, the store manager would like to see a report in the following form:

```
                Friendly Hardware Store

itemID itemName      pOrdered  pInStore pSold manufPrice sellingPrice
4444   Circular Saw      150       150    40      45.00       125.00
3333   Cooking Range      50        50    20     450.00       850.00
  .
  .
  .


Total Inventory: $#########.##
Total number of items in the store: _____
```

The total inventory is the total selling value of all the items currently in the store. The total number of items is the sum of the number of pieces of all the items in the store.

Your program must be menu driven, giving the user various choices, such as: check whether an item is in the store, sell an item, and print the report. After inputting the data, sort it according to the items' names. Also, after an item is sold, update the appropriate counts.

Initially, the number of pieces (of an item) in the store is the same as the number of pieces ordered, and the number of pieces of an item sold is zero. Input to the program is a file consisting of data in the following form:

```
itemID
itemName
pOrdered manufPrice sellingPrice
```

Use seven parallel vectors to store the information. The program must contain at least the following methods—a method to input the data into the vectors, a method to display the menu, a method to sell an item, and a method to print the report for the manager. After inputting the data, sort it according to the items' names.

1
4

JAVA RESERVED WORDS

The following table lists Java reserved words in alphabetical order.

abstract	else	interface	switch
assert	enum	long	synchronized
boolean	extends	native	this
break	false	new	throw
byte	final	null	throws
case	finally	package	transient
catch	float	private	true
char	for	protected	try
class	goto	public	void
const	if	return	volatile
continue	implements	short	while
default	import	static	
do	instanceof	strictfp	
double	int	super	

The reserved words const and goto are *not* currently in use.

OPERATOR
PRECEDENCE

The following table shows the precedence of operators in Java from highest to lowest, and their associativity.

Operator	Description	Precedence Level	Associativity
.	Object member access	1	Left to right
[ ]	Array subscripting	1	Left to right
(parameters)	Method call	1	Left to right
++	Postincrement	1	Left to right
--	Postdecrement	1	Left to right
++	Preincrement	2	Right to left
--	Predecrement	2	Right to left
+	Unary plus	2	Right to left
-	Unary minus	2	Right to left
!	Logical not	2	Right to left
~	Bitwise not	2	Right to left
new	Object instantiation	3	Right to left
(type)	Type conversion	3	Right to left
*	Multiplication	4	Left to right
/	Division	4	Left to right
%	Remainder (modulus)	4	Left to right

Operator	Description	Precedence Level	Associativity
+	Addition	5	Left to right
–	Subtraction	5	Left to right
+	String concatenation	5	Left to right
<<	Left shift	6	Left to right
>>	Right shift with sign extension	6	Left to right
>>>	Right shift with zero extension	6	Left to right
<	Less than	7	Left to right
<=	Less than or equal to	7	Left to right
>	Greater than	7	Left to right
>=	Greater than or equal to	7	Left to right
instanceof	Type comparison	7	Left to right
==	Equal to	8	Left to right
!=	Not equal to	8	Left to right
&	Bitwise AND	9	Left to right
&	Logical AND	9	Left to right
^	Bitwise XOR	10	Left to right
^	Logical XOR	10	Left to right
|	Bitwise OR	11	Left to right
|	Logical OR	11	Left to right
&&	Logical AND	12	Left to right

Operator	Description	Precedence Level	Associativity
||	Logical OR	13	Left to right
? :	Conditional operator	14	Right to left
=	Assignment	15	Right to left
Compound Operators			
+=	Addition, then assignment	15	Right to left
+=	String concatenation, then assignment	15	Right to left
-=	Subtraction, then assignment	15	Right to left
*=	Multiplication, then assignment	15	Right to left
/=	Division, then assignment	15	Right to left
%=	Remainder, then assignment	15	Right to left
<<=	Bitwise left shift, then assignment	15	Right to left
>>=	Bitwise right shift, then assignment	15	Right to left
>>>=	Bitwise unsigned-right shift, then assignment	15	Right to left
&=	Bitwise AND, then assignment	15	Right to left
&=	Logical AND, then assignment	15	Right to left
|=	Bitwise OR, then assignment	15	Right to left
|=	Logical OR, then assignment	15	Right to left
^=	Bitwise XOR, then assignment	15	Right to left
^=	Logical XOR, then assignment	15	Right to left

CHARACTER SETS

This appendix lists and describes the character sets for ASCII (American Standard Code for Information Interchange), which also comprises the first 128 characters of the Unicode character set, and EBCDIC (Extended Binary Coded Decimal Interchange Code).

ASCII (American Standard Code for Information Interchange), the First 128 Characters of the Unicode Character Set

The following table shows the first 128 characters of the Unicode (ASCII) character set.

ASCII										
	0	1	2	3	4	5	6	7	8	9
0	nul	soh	stx	etx	eot	enq	ack	bel	bs	ht
1	lf	vt	ff	cr	so	si	dle	dc1	dc2	dc3
2	dc4	nak	syn	etb	can	em	sub	esc	fs	gs
3	rs	us	b	!	"	#	$	%	&	'
4	(	)	*	+	,	-	.	/	0	1
5	2	3	4	5	6	7	8	9	:	;
6	<	=	>	?	@	A	B	C	D	E
7	F	G	H	I	J	K	L	M	N	O
8	P	Q	R	S	T	U	V	W	X	Y
9	Z	[	\	]	^	_	`	a	b	c
10	d	e	f	g	h	i	j	k	l	m
11	n	o	p	q	r	s	t	u	v	w
12	x	y	z	{	|	}	~	del		

> **NOTE** For more information on the Unicode/ASCII character set, visit the Web site at *http://www.unicode.org*.

Note that the character <u>b</u> at position 32 represents the space character. The first 32 characters, that is, the characters at positions 00–31 and at position 127 are nonprintable characters. The following table shows the abbreviations and meanings of these characters.

nul	null character	ff	form feed	can	cancel
soh	start of header	cr	carriage return	em	end of medium
stx	start of text	so	shift out	sub	substitute
etx	end of text	si	shift in	esc	escape
eot	end of transmission	dle	data link escape	fs	file separator
enq	enquiry	dc1	device control 1	gs	group separator
ack	acknowledge	dc2	device control 2	rs	record separator
bel	bell	dc3	device control 3	us	unit separator
bs	backspace	dc4	device control 4	<u>b</u>	space
ht	horizontal tab	nak	negative acknowledge	del	delete
lf	line feed	syn	synchronous idle		
vt	vertical tab	etb	end of transmitted block		

EBCDIC (Extended Binary Coded Decimal Interchange Code)

The following table shows some of the characters in the EBCDIC character set.

EBCDIC										
	0	1	2	3	4	5	6	7	8	9
6					<u>b</u>					
7						.	<	(	+	|
8	&									
9	!	$	*	)	;	¬	-	/		
10								'	%	_

EBCDIC	0	1	2	3	4	5	6	7	8	9
11	>	?								
12		`	:	#	@	'	=	"		a
13	b	c	d	e	f	g	h	i		
14						j	k	l	m	n
15	o	p	q	r						
16		~	s	t	u	v	w	x	y	z
17										
18	[	]								
19			A	B	C	D	E	F	G	
20	H	I								J
21	K	L	M	N	O	P	Q	R		
22							S	T	U	V
23	W	X	Y	Z						
24	0	1	2	3	4	5	6	7	8	9

The numbers 6–24 in the first column specify the left digit(s) and the numbers 0–9 in the second row specify the right digits of the characters in the EBCDIC data set. For example, the character in the row marked 19 (the number in the first column) and the column marked 3 (the number in the second row) is A. Therefore, the character at position 193 (which is the 194th character) is A. Moreover, the character b̲ at position 64 represents the space character. This table does not show all the characters in the EBCDIC character set. In fact, the characters at positions 00–63 and 250–255 are nonprintable control characters.

The numbers 0–23 in the first column specify the left digits, and the numbers 0–9 in the second row specify the right digits of the characters in the EBCDIC data set. For example, the character in the row marked 19 (the number in the first column) and the column marked 7 (the number in the second row) is A; therefore, the character at position 193 (which is the 194th character) is A. Moreover, the character at position 64 represents the space character. This table does not show all the characters in the EBCDIC character set. In fact, the characters at positions 00–63 and 250–255 are nonprintable control characters.

APPENDIX D
ADDITIONAL
JAVA TOPICS

Binary (Base 2) Representation of a Nonnegative Integer

Converting a Base 10 Number to a Binary Number (Base 2)

Chapter 1 noted that A is the 66th character in the ASCII character set, but its position is 65 because the position of the first character is 0. Furthermore, the binary number 1000001 is the binary representation of 65. The number system that we use daily is called the **decimal number system** or **base 10 system**. The number system that the computer uses is called the **binary number system** or **base 2 system**. In this section, we describe how to find the binary representation of a nonnegative integer and vice versa.

Consider 65. Note that:

$$65 = 1 \times 2^6 + 0 \times 2^5 + 0 \times 2^4 + 0 \times 2^3 + 0 \times 2^2 + 0 \times 2^1 + 1 \times 2^0.$$

Similarly:

$$711 = 1 \times 2^9 + 0 \times 2^8 + 1 \times 2^7 + 1 \times 2^6 + 0 \times 2^5 + 0 \times 2^4 + 0 \times 2^3$$
$$+ 1 \times 2^2 + 1 \times 2^1 + 1 \times 2^0.$$

In general, if m is a nonnegative integer, then m can be written as:

$$m = a_k \times 2^k + a_{k-1} \times 2^{k-1} + a_{k-2} \times 2^{k-2} + \cdots + a_1 \times 2^1 + a_0 \times 2^0,$$

for some nonnegative integer k, and where $a_i = 0$ or 1, for each $i = 0, 1, 2, \ldots, k$. The binary number $a_k a_{k-1} a_{k-2} \ldots a_1 a_0$ is called the **binary** or **base 2 representation** of m. In this case, we usually write:

$$m_{10} = (a_k a_{k-1} a_{k-2} \cdots a_1 a_0)_2$$

and say that m to the base 10 is $a_k a_{k-1} a_{k-2} \ldots a_1 a_0$ to the base 2.

For example, for the integer 65, $k = 6$, $a_6 = 1$, $a_5 = 0$, $a_4 = 0$, $a_3 = 0$, $a_2 = 0$, $a_1 = 0$, and $a_0 = 1$. Thus, $a_6a_5a_4a_3a_2a_1a_0 = 1000001$, so the binary representation of 65 is 1000001, that is:

$$65_{10} = (1000001)_2.$$

If no confusion arises, then we write $(1000001)_2$ as 1000001_2.

Similarly, for the number 711, $k = 9$, $a_9 = 1$, $a_8 = 0$, $a_7 = 1$, $a_6 = 1$, $a_5 = 0$, $a_4 = 0$, $a_3 = 0$, $a_2 = 1$, $a_1 = 1$, and $a_0 = 1$. Thus:

$$711_{10} = 1011000111_2.$$

It follows that to find the binary representation of a nonnegative integer, we need to find the coefficients, which are 0 or 1, of various powers of 2. However, there is an easy algorithm, described next, that can be used to find the binary representation of a nonnegative integer. First, note that:

$$0_{10} = 0_2, \ 1_{10} = 1_2, \ 2_{10} = 10_2, \ 3_{10} = 11_2, \ 4_{10} = 100_2, \ 5_{10} = 101_2, \ 6_{10} = 110_2, \text{ and } 7_{10} = 111_2.$$

Let us consider the integer 65. Note that $65 \ / \ 2 = 32$ and $65 \ \% \ 2 = 1$, where % is the mod operator. Next, $32 \ / \ 2 = 16$, and $32 \ \% \ 2 = 0$, and so on. It can be shown that $a_0 = 65 \ \% \ 2 = 1$, $a_1 = 32 \ \% \ 2 = 0$, and so on. We can show this continuous division and obtain the remainder with the help of Figure D-1.

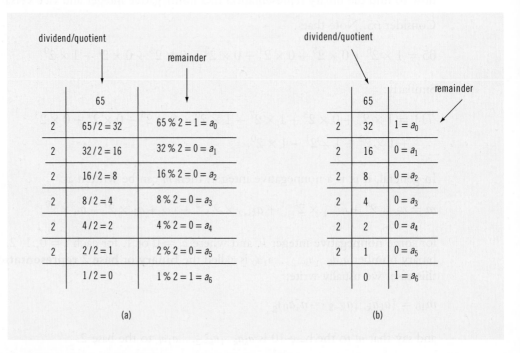

FIGURE D-1 Determining the binary representation of 65

Notice that in Figure D-1(a), starting at the second row, the second column contains the quotient when the number in the previous row is divided by 2, and the third column contains the remainder of that division. For example, in the second row, 65 / 2 = 32, and 65 % 2 = 1. In the third row, 32 / 2 = 16 and 32 % 2 = 0, and so on. For each row, the number in the second column is divided by 2, the quotient is written in the row below the current row, and the remainder appears in the third column. When using a figure such as D-1 to find the binary representation of a nonnegative integer, we typically show only the quotients and remainders, as shown in Figure D-1(b). You can write the binary representation of the number, starting with the last remainder in the third column, followed by the second to the last remainder, and so on. Thus:

$65_{10} = 1000001_2$.

Next, consider the number 711. Figure D-2 shows the quotients and the remainders.

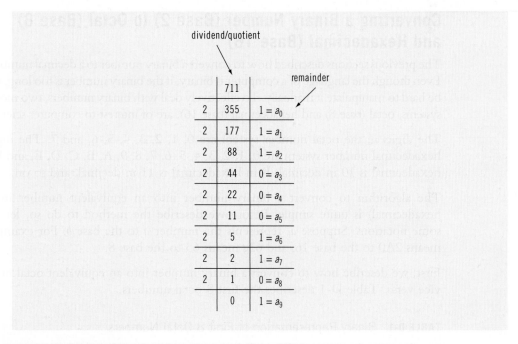

FIGURE D-2   Determining the binary representation of 711

From Figure D-2, it follows that:

$711_{10} = 1011000111_2$.

Converting a Binary Number (Base 2) to Base 10

To convert a number from base 2 to base 10, we first find the weight of each bit in the binary number, which is assigned from right to left. The weight of the rightmost bit is 0.

The weight of the bit immediately to the left of the rightmost bit is 1, the weight of the bit immediately to the left of it is 2, and so on. Consider the binary number 1001101. The weight of each bit is as follows:

Weight	6	5	4	3	2	1	0
	1	0	0	1	1	0	1

We use the weight of each bit to find the equivalent decimal number. For each bit, we multiply the bit by 2 to the power of its weight and then we add all of the numbers. For the above binary number, the equivalent decimal number is:

$$1 \times 2^6 + 0 \times 2^5 + 0 \times 2^4 + 1 \times 2^3 + 1 \times 2^2 + 0 \times 2^1 + 1 \times 2^0$$

$$= 64 + 0 + 0 + 8 + 4 + 0 + 1$$

$$= 77.$$

Converting a Binary Number (Base 2) to Octal (Base 8) and Hexadecimal (Base 16)

The previous sections described how to convert a binary number to a decimal number (base 2). Even though the language of a computer is binary, if the binary number is too long, then it will be hard to manipulate it manually. To effectively deal with binary numbers, two more number systems, octal (base 8) and hexadecimal (base 16), are of interest to computer scientists.

The digits in the octal number system are 0, 1, 2, 3, 4, 5, 6, and 7. The digits in the hexadecimal number system are 0, 1, 2, 3, 4, 5, 6, 7, 8, 9, A, B, C, D, E, and F. So A in hexadecimal is 10 in decimal, B in hexadecimal is 11 in decimal, and so on.

The algorithm to convert a binary number into an equivalent number in octal (or hexadecimal) is quite simple. Before we describe the method to do so, let us review some notations. Suppose a_b represents the number a to the base b. For example, $2A0_{16}$ means 2A0 to the base 16, and 63_8 means 63 to the base 8.

First, we describe how to convert a binary number into an equivalent octal number and vice versa. Table D-1 describes the first 8 octal numbers.

TABLE D-1 Binary Representation of First 8 Octal Numbers

Binary	Octal		Binary	Octal
000	0		100	4
001	1		101	5
010	2		110	6
011	3		111	7

Consider the binary number 1101100010101. To find the equivalent octal number, starting from right to left, we consider three digits at a time and write their octal representation. Note that the binary number 1101100010101 has only 13 digits. So when we consider three digits at a time, at the end, we will be left with only one digit. In this case, we just add two 0s to the left of the binary number; the equivalent binary number is 001101100010101. Thus:

$$1101100010101_2 \ = \ 001101100010101_2$$

$$= \ 001\ 101\ 100\ 010\ 101$$

$$= \ 15425_8 \text{ because } 001_2 = 1_8,\ 101_2 = 5_8,\ 100_2 = 4_8,\ 010_2 = 2_8, \text{ and } 101_2 = 5_8.$$

Thus, $1101100010101_2 = 15425_8$.

To convert an octal number into an equivalent binary number, using Table D-1, write the binary representation of each octal digit in the number. For example:

$$3761_8 \ = \ 011\ 111\ 110\ 001_2$$

$$= \ 0.11111110001_2$$

$$= \ 11111110001_2.$$

Thus, $3761_8 = 11111110001_2$.

Next, we discuss how to convert a binary number into an equivalent hexadecimal number and vice versa. The method to do so is similar to converting a number from binary to octal and vice versa, except that here we work with four binary digits. Table D-2 gives the binary representation of the first 16 hexadecimal numbers.

TABLE D-2 Binary Representation of First 16 Hexadecimal Numbers

Binary	Hexadecimal		Binary	Hexadecimal
0000	0		1000	8
0001	1		1001	9
0010	2		1010	A
0011	3		1011	B
0100	4		1100	C
0101	5		1101	D
0110	6		1110	E
0111	7		1111	F

Consider the binary number 1111101010001010101_2. Now:

$$1111101010001010101_2 = 111\ 1101\ 0100\ 0101\ 0101_2$$

$$= 0111\ 1101\ 0100\ 0101\ 0101_2,\ \text{add one zero to the left}$$

$$= 7D455_{16}.$$

Hence, $1111101010001010101_2 = 7D455_{16}$.

Next, to convert a hexadecimal number into an equivalent binary number, write the four-digit binary representation of each hexadecimal digit into that number. For example:

$$A7F32_{16} = 1010\ 0111\ 1111\ 0011\ 0010_2$$

$$= 10100111111100110010_2.$$

Thus, $A7F32_{16} = 10100111111100110010_2$.

Executing Java Programs Using the Command-Line Statements

When you install JDK 7.0 in the Windows 7.0 environment, the system creates two main subdirectories: `Java\jdk1.7.0` and `Java\jre1.7.0`. These two subdirectories are, typically, created within the directory `c:\Program Files\Java`. However, these subdirectories might also be created in the directory `c:` as `c:\jdk1.7.0` and `c:\jre1.7.0`. (Check your systems documentation.) The files necessary to compile and execute Java programs are placed within these subdirectories, along with other files. For example, the file `javac.exe` to compile a Java program and the file `java.exe` to execute a Java application program are placed within the subdirectory `jdk1.7.0\bin` or `jdk1.7.0\fastdebug\bin`. You can set (or alter) the Windows system environment variable `Path` to add the path where the files `javac.exe` and `java.exe` are located. This will allow you to conveniently compile a Java program from within any subdirectory. In the Windows 7.0 Professional environment, you can also set the environment variable `CLASSPATH` so that when you execute a Java program, the system can find the compiled code of the program. Next, we describe how to set up the `Path`.

Setting the Path in Windows 7.0 (Professional)

To set the `Path` so that you can compile a Java program from within any subdirectory, perform the following steps.

1. Click the `Start` button (lower-left corner of the window.)
2. Select `Control Panel`. A window similar to the window shown in Figure D-3 appears.

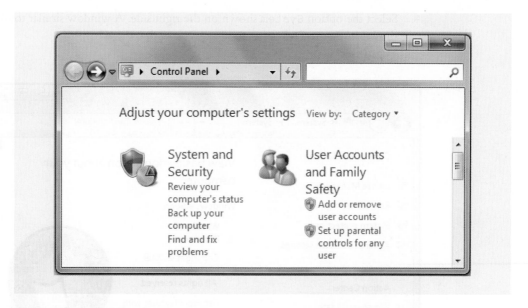

FIGURE D-3 Control Panel

3. Select the `System and Security` option. A window similar to the window shown in Figure D-4 appears.

FIGURE D-4 System and Security window

4. Select the option **System** shown on the right side. A window similar to the window shown in Figure D-5 appears.

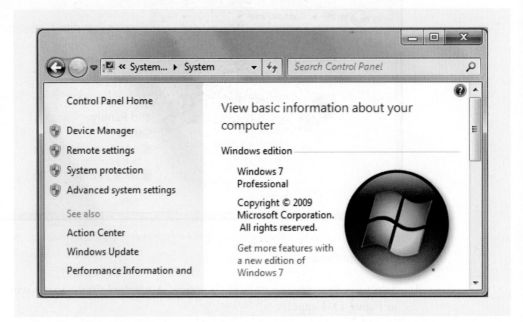

FIGURE D-5 System window

5. Select the option **Advanced system settings** shown on the left side. A window similar to the window shown in Figure D-6 appears.

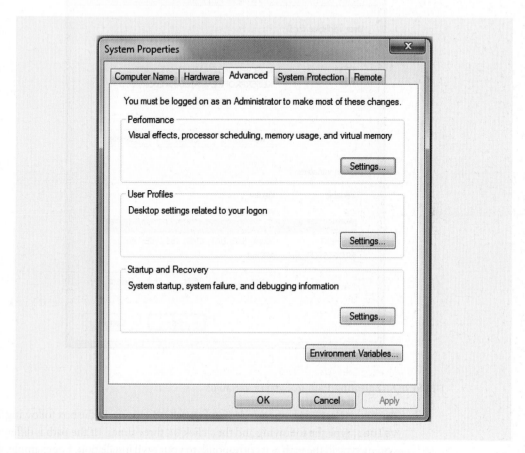

FIGURE D-6 Selecting the Advanced tab

6. In the window in Figure D-6, click **Environment Variables**. A window similar to the one shown in Figure D-7 appears. In this window, in the **System variables** section, scroll down, select **Path**, and then click **Edit**.

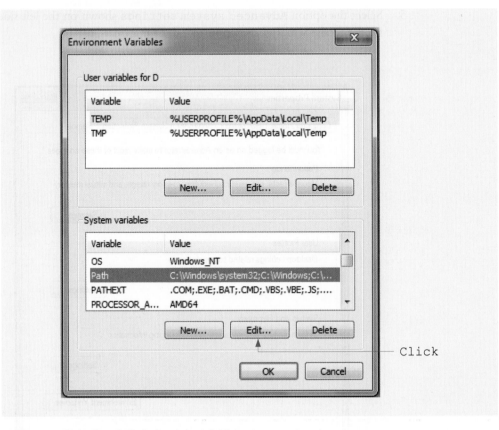

FIGURE D-7   Selecting Path in System variables

7. After you select **Edit**, the window in Figure D-8 appears. In the box following **Variable value:**, type the following and then click **OK** three times. (If the path is different on your system, type in the path as it corresponds to your own installation. For example, the path on your system might be **C:\ Program Files\ Java\ jdk1.7.0\ bin**)

   `;C:\ jdk1.7.0\ fastdebug\ bin`

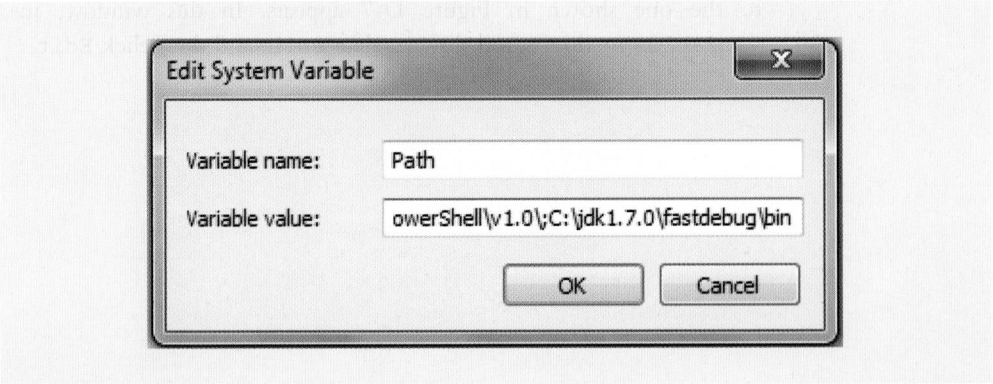

FIGURE D-8   Editing Path

The preceding steps should set the `Path`. To be absolutely certain about the `Path` and also to set the `CLASSPATH`, check your operating system's documentation.

Executing Java Programs

The following discussion assumes that you have set the `Path` so that the files `javac.exe` and `java.exe` can be executed from within any subdirectory.

You can use an editor such as Notepad to create Java programs. The name of the class containing the Java program and the name of the file containing the program must be the same. Moreover, the file containing the Java program must have the extension `.java`.

Suppose that the file `Welcome.java` is in the subdirectory `c:\jpfpatpd` and contains the following Java application program:

```java
public class Welcome
{
    public static void main(String[] args)
    {
        System.out.println("Welcome to Java Programming.");
    }
}
```

We assume that you have switched to the subdirectory `c:\jpfpatpd` (see Figure D-9).

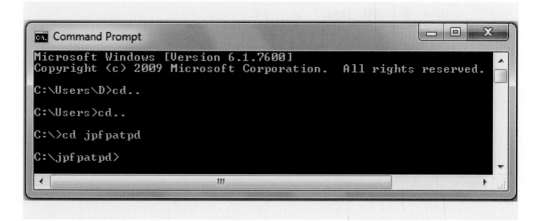

FIGURE D-9 Windows console environment

Figure D-10 shows the files in the subdirectory `c:\jpfpatpd`.

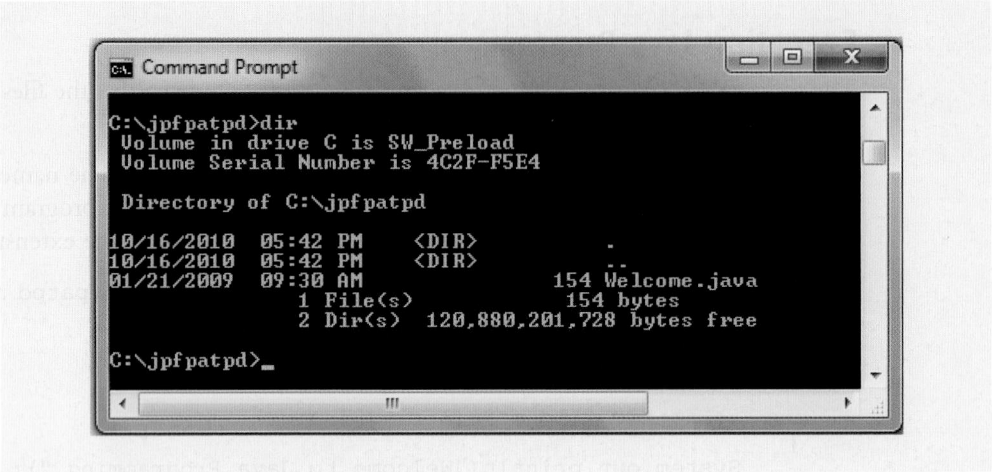

FIGURE D-10   Files in the subdirectory `c:\jpfpatpd`

To place the compiled code of the program `Welcome.java` in the subdirectory `c:\jpfpatpd`, you can execute the following command, as shown in Figure D-11:

`javac Welcome.java`

FIGURE D-11   Compile `Welcome.java` program

The preceding command creates the file `Welcome.class`, which contains the compiled code of the program `Welcome.java` and places it in the subdirectory `c:\jpfpatpd` (see Figure D-12).

FIGURE D-12 The file `Welcome.class` program

You can now issue the following command to execute the **Welcome** program (see Figure D-13):

```
java Welcome
```

FIGURE D-13 Executing `Welcome` program

After this statement executes, the following line appears on the screen, as shown in Figure D-14:

```
Welcome to Java Programming.
```

FIGURE D-14 Execution of the `Welcome` program

The preceding command, after compiling the program, places the compiled code in the same subdirectory as the program. However, when you compile a Java program using the command-line compiler, you can instruct the system to store the program's compiled code in any subdirectory you want. To place the compiled code in a specific directory, you include the option −d and the name of the subdirectory where you want the command code placed when you compile the program. For example, the command:

```
javac -d c:\jdk1.7.0\fastdebug\bin\classes Welcome.java
```

places the compiled code of the program Welcome.java in the subdirectory:

```
c:\jdk1.7.0\fastdebug\bin\classes
```

Note that the subdirectory `c:\jdk1.7.0\fastdebug\bin\classes` must exist before you execute the command to compile the program.

Similarly, the following command places the compiled code of the program `Welcome.java` in the subdirectory `c:\jpfpatpd`:

```
javac -d c:\jpfpatpd Welcome.java
```

To be absolutely certain that the directory path is correct, check your system's documentation.

Suppose that you have placed the file `Welcome.class` within the subdirectory `c:\jdk1.7.0\fastdebug\bin\classes`. In addition, suppose that you have not set the `CLASSPATH` to allow the system to look for the compiled code on specific locations on your computer. In this case, you can use the option −classpath and the name of the subdirectory that contains the compiled code to execute the program. For example, the following command looks for the compiled code of the `Welcome` program in the subdirectory `c:\jdk1.7.0\fastdebug\bin\classes`:

```
java -classpath c:\jdk1.7.0\fastdebug\bin\classes Welcome
```

NOTE If the compiled code of the classes is in the subdirectory, say `c:\jpfpatpd`, you can set the system variable `CLASSPATH` to `c:\jpfpatpd`. If the system variable `CLASSPATH` already exists, you can add the path `c:\jpfpatpd` to it. To be absolutely certain how to set `CLASSPATH` in the Windows environment, check your operating system's documentation. Moreover, if you are using other operating systems, such as `UNIX`, check the documentation to set the variables so that you can conveniently compile and execute a Java program.

The subdirectory `c:\jpfpatpd` also contains the file `ASimpleJavaProgram.java`. Figure D-15 shows the compile command, execute command, and the output of the program.

FIGURE D-15 Compiling and executing the program `ASimpleJavaProgram.java`

Note that the program `ASimpleJavaProgram` is the same as that discussed in Chapter 2.

The subdirectory `c:\jpfpatpd` also contains the file `FirstJavaProgram.java`. Figure D-16 shows the compile command, execute command, and program output.

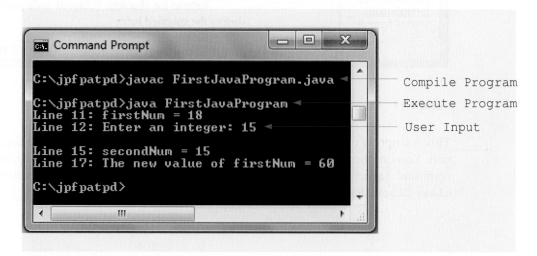

FIGURE D-16 Compiling and executing the program `FirstJavaProgram.java`

Note that the program `FirstJavaProgram` is the same as that discussed in Example 2-26 in Chapter 2.

Java Style Documentation

In this book, whenever we designed a class, among others, we provided an explanation of the methods. We also noted that Java provides a wealth of predefined classes. For example, if you visit the Web site *http://java.sun.com/javase/6/docs/api* or *http://java.sun.com/javase/7/docs/api* you can find a description of the **class** `String` as shown in Figure D-17. (Note that the URL locations of these api documentations may change without any notice.)

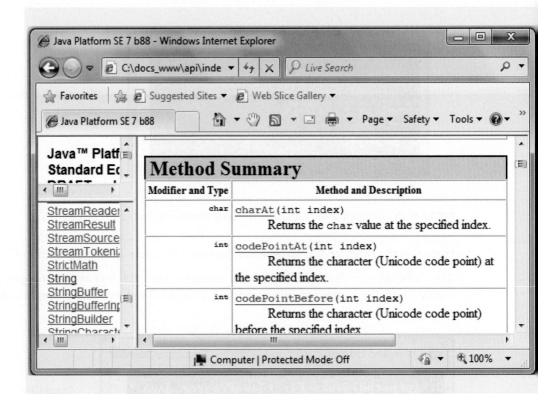

FIGURE D-17 The `class` String

This description of the **class** `String` as shown in Figure D-17 is Java style documentation. You can also produce this type of documentation for the classes you design using the command `javadoc`. We illustrate how to produce the Java style documentation of the **class** `Clock`, designed in Chapter 8.

Suppose that the definition of the `class` `Clock` is in the subdirectory `c:\jpfpatpd`. Next execute the command: `javadoc Clock.java`, see Figure D-18.

FIGURE D-18 Execute the command `javadoc Clock.java`

The preceding command creates a number of files as shown in Figure D-19.

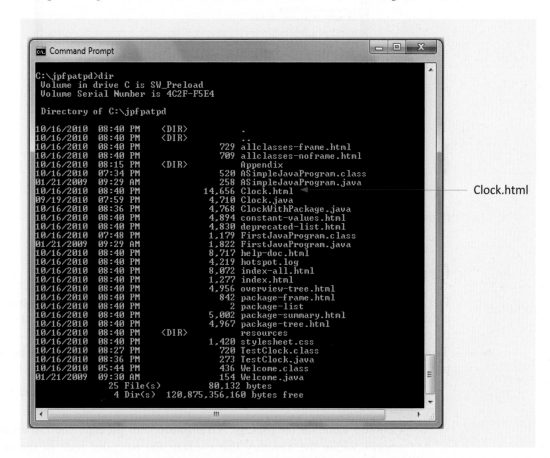

FIGURE D-19 The files produced by the command `javadoc Clock.java`

Next, if you switch to the Windows environment and double click on the file Clock.html, it shows you the Java style documentation of the **class** Clock shown in Figure D-20.

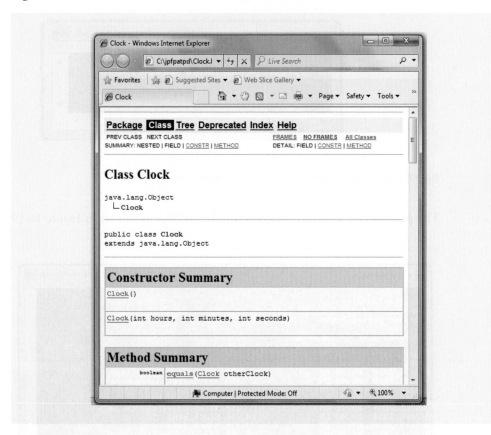

FIGURE D-20   Java style documentation of the **class** Clock

Creating Your Own Packages

Recall that a package is a collection of related classes. As you develop classes, you can create packages and categorize your classes. You can import your classes in the same way that you import classes from the packages provided by Java.

To create a package and add a class to the package so that the class can be used in a program, you do the following:

1. Define the class to be **public**. If the class is not **public**, it can be used only within the package.

2. Choose a name for the package. To organize your package, you can create subdirectories within the directory that contains the compiled code of the classes. For

example, you could create a directory for the classes you create in this book. Because the title of this book is *Java Programming: From Problem Analysis to Program Design*, you could create a directory named `jpfpatpd`. You could then make subdirectories for the classes used in each chapter, such as the subdirectory `Appendix` within the directory `jpfpatpd`.

Suppose that you want to create a `package` to group the classes related to time. You could call this `package` `clockPackage`. To add the `class` `Clock` to this package and to place the package `clockPackage` within the subdirectory `Appendix` of the directory `jpfpatpd`, you include the following package statement with the file containing the `class` `Clock` (Note that the `class` `Clock` is the same as discussed in Chapter 8):

```
package jpfpatpd.Appendix.clockPackage;
```

We put this statement before the definition of the `class`, like this:

```
package jpfpatpd.Appendix.clockPackage;

public class Clock
{
    //put instance variables and methods here
}
```

The next step is to compile the file `Clock.java` using the compile command in the IDE (integrated development environment) you are using.

The following discussion assumes that you have set the `Path` so that the files `javac.exe` and `java.exe` can be executed from within any subdirectory. Suppose that the file `Clock.java` is in the subdirectory `c:\jpfpatpd`. We assume that you have switched to the subdirectory `c:\jpfpatpd`.

If you are using Java 7.0, which contains a command-line compiler, you include the option `-d` to place the compiled code of the program `Clock.java` in a specific directory. For example, the command:

```
javac -d c:\jre1.7.0\lib\classes Clock.java
```

places the compiled code of the program `Clock.java` in the subdirectory:

```
c:\jre1.7.0\lib\classes\jpfpatpd\Appendix\clockPackage
```

Similarly, the following command places the compiled code of the program `Clock.java` in the subdirectory `c:\jpfpatpd\Appendix\clockPackage`:

```
javac -d c:\ Clock.java
```

If the directories `jpfpatpd`, `Appendix`, and `clockPackage` do not exist, then the compiler automatically creates these directories. Note that for the earlier command to execute successfully, the subdirectory `c:\jre1.7.0\lib\classes` must exist. If this subdirectory does not exist, you must first create it. Also, to be absolutely sure about the correct directory path, check your system's documentation. Moreover, if you do not use the `-d` option with the path of the subdirectory to specify the subdirectory in which to store the compiled code, then the compiled code is, typically, stored in the current subdirectory.

Once the `package` is created, you can use the appropriate `import` command in your program to make use of the `class`. For example, to use the `class` `Clock`, as created in the preceding code, you use the following `import` statement in your program:

```
import jpfpatpd.Appendix.clockPackage.Clock;
```

In Java, `package` is a reserved word.

Example D-1 further explains how to use a package in a program. We assume that the `class` `Clock` has been compiled and placed in the subdirectory `c:\jpfpatpd\Appendix\clockPackage`.

EXAMPLE D-1

The following program uses the `class` `Clock`.

```java
import jpfpatpd.Appendix.clockPackage.Clock;

public class TestClock
{
    public static void main(String[] args)
    {
        Clock myClock = new Clock(12,30,45);

        System.out.println("myClock: " + myClock);
    }
}
```

Because this program uses the `class` `Clock`, when you compile the program using the compiler command, you use the option `-classpath` to specify where to find the compiled code of the `class` `Clock`. Suppose that the file `TestClock.java` is in the subdirectory `c:\jpfpatpd`. Consider the following command:

```
javac -classpath c:\ TestClock.java
```

This command finds `Clock.class` in the subdirectory `c:\jpfpatpd\Appendix\clockPackage`. The compiled code `TestClock.class` of the program `TestClock.java` is placed in the current subdirectory. On the other hand, the following command places the compiled code, `TestClock.class`, in the subdirectory `c:\jpfpatpd`:

```
javac -d c:\jpfpatpd -classpath c:\ TestClock.java
```

Suppose the file `TestClock.class` is in the subdirectory `c:\jpfpatpd`. The following command executes the program `TestClock.class`:

```
java -classpath .;c:\ TestClock
```

If you are using an IDE to create Java programs, you need to be familiar with the commands to compile and execute them. Typically, an IDE automatically stores the compiled code of the classes in an appropriate subdirectory.

Multiple-File Programs

In the preceding section, you learned how to create a `package`. Creating a `package` to group related `class`(es) is very useful if the classes are to be used again and again. On the other hand, if a `class` is to be used in only one program, or if you have divided your program so that it uses more than one `class`, rather than create a `package`, you can directly add the file(s) containing the `class`(es) to the program.

The Java IDEs—J++ Builder and JGrasp—put the editor, compiler, and loader all into one program. With one command, a program is compiled. These IDEs also manage multiple-file programs in the form of a project. A **project** consists of several files, called the project files. These IDEs include a command that allows you to add several files to a project. Also, these IDEs usually have commands such as **build**, **rebuild**, or **make** (check your software's documentation) to automatically compile all the files required. When one or more files in the project change, you can use these commands to recompile the files.

Formatting the Output of Decimal Numbers Using the **class DecimalFormat**

Chapter 3 explained how to format the output of floating-point numbers, using the method format of the **class** `String`, to a specific number of decimal places. Chapter 3 also noted that another way to format the output of floating-point numbers is to use the **class** `DecimalFormat`.

Recall that the default output of decimal numbers of the type `float` is up to six decimal places. Similarly, the default output of decimal numbers of the type `double` is up to 15 decimal places. For example, consider the statements in Table D-3; the output is shown to the right.

TABLE D-3 Default Output of Floating-Point Numbers

Statement	Output
`System.out.println(22.0 / 7.0);`	3.142857142857143
`System.out.println(75.0 / 7.0);`	10.714285714285714
`System.out.println((float)(33.0 / 16.0));`	2.0625
`System.out.println((float)(22.0 / 7.0));`	3.142857

As discussed in Chapter 3, sometimes floating-point numbers must be output in a specific way. For example, a paycheck must be printed to two decimal places, whereas the results of a scientific experiment might require the output of floating-point numbers to six, seven, or perhaps even 10 decimal places.

You can use the Java `class` `DecimalFormat` to format decimal numbers in a specific manner. The method `format` of the `class` `DecimalFormat` is applied to the decimal value being formatted. The following steps explain how to use these features to format decimal numbers:

1. Create a `DecimalFormat` object and initialize it to the specific format. Consider the following statement:

   ```
   DecimalFormat twoDecimal = new DecimalFormat("0.00");
   ```

   This statement creates the `DecimalFormat` object `twoDecimal` and initializes it to the string `"0.00"`. Each 0 in the string is a **format flag**. The string `"0.00"` specifies the formatting of the decimal number. This string indicates that the decimal number being formatted with the object `twoDecimal` will have at least one digit to the left of the decimal point and exactly two digits to the right of the decimal point. If the number being formatted does not meet the formatting requirement, that is, it does not have digits at the specified places, those places are automatically filled with 0. Moreover, suppose that you have the following statement:

   ```
   DecimalFormat twoDigits = new DecimalFormat("0.##");
   ```

   The object `twoDigits` can be used to format the number with two decimal places, but the `##` symbols indicate that trailing zeros will appear as spaces.

2. Next, use the method `format` of the `class` `DecimalFormat`. (Assume the first declaration of Step 1.) For example, the statement:

   ```
   twoDecimal.format(56.379);
   ```

   formats the decimal number `56.379` as `56.38` (the decimal number is rounded). The method format returns the string containing the digits of the formatted number.

3. The `class` `DecimalFormat` is included in the `package` `java.text`. You must import this `class` into your program.

Example D-2 illustrates how to format the output of decimal numbers.

EXAMPLE D-2

```
//Program: Formatting output of decimal numbers using
//the class DecimalFormat

import java.text.DecimalFormat;

public class FormattingDecimalNum
{
    public static void main(String[] args)
    {
        double x = 15.674;                          //Line 1
        double y = 235.73;                          //Line 2
        double z = 9525.9864;                       //Line 3
```

```
            DecimalFormat twoDecimal =
                        new DecimalFormat("0.00");      //Line 4
            DecimalFormat threeDecimal =
                        new DecimalFormat("0.000");   //Line 5

            System.out.println("Line 6: Outputting the "
                        + "values of x, y, and z \n"
                        + "          with two decimal "
                        + "places.");                  //Line 6
            System.out.println("Line 7: x = "
                        + twoDecimal.format(x));        //Line 7
            System.out.println("Line 8: y = "
                        + twoDecimal.format(y));        //Line 8
            System.out.println("Line 9: z = "
                        + twoDecimal.format(z));        //Line 9

            System.out.println("Line 10: Outputting the "
                        + "values of x, y, and z \n"
                        + "             with three "
                        + "decimal places.");           //Line 10
            System.out.println("Line 11: x = "
                        + threeDecimal.format(x));      //Line 11
            System.out.println("Line 12: y = "
                        + threeDecimal.format(y));      //Line 12
            System.out.println("Line 13: z = "
                        + threeDecimal.format(z));      //Line 13
        }
}
```

Sample Run:

```
Line 6: Outputting the values of x, y, and z
        with two decimal places.
Line 7: x = 15.67
Line 8: y = 235.73
Line 9: z = 9525.99
Line 10: Outputting the values of x, y, and z
        with three decimal places.
Line 11: x = 15.674
Line 12: y = 235.730
Line 13: z = 9525.986
```

The statements in Lines 1, 2, and 3 declare and initialize x, y, and z to 15.674, 235.73, and 9525.9864, respectively. The statement in Line 4 creates and initializes the DecimalFormat object twoDecimal to output decimal numbers to two decimal places. Similarly, the statement in Line 5 creates and initializes the DecimalFormat object threeDecimal to output decimal numbers with three decimal places.

The statements in Lines 7, 8, and 9 output the values of x, y, and z to two decimal places, respectively. Note that the printed values of x in Line 7 and z in Line 9 are rounded.

The statements in Lines 11, 12, and 13 output the values of x, y, and z, respectively, to three decimal places. Note that the value of y in Line 12 is output to three decimal places. Because the number stored in y has only two decimal places, a 0 is printed as the third decimal place.

Packages and User-Defined Classes

Chapter 7 discusses user-defined methods, in particular methods with parameters. As explained in Chapter 3, there are two types of variables in Java—primitive and reference. The program in Example 7-8 illustrates that if a formal parameter is of the primitive type and the corresponding actual parameter is a variable, then the formal parameter cannot change the value of the actual parameter. Changing the value of a formal parameter of a primitive data type has no effect on the actual parameter. However, if a formal parameter is a reference variable, then both the actual and the formal parameter refer to the same object. That is, only formal parameters that are reference variables are capable of passing values outside the function.

Java provides classes corresponding to each primitive data type, so that values of primitive data types can be considered objects. For example, you can use the class Integer to treat int values as objects, class Double to treat double values as objects, and so on. These classes, called wrapper classes, were described in Chapter 6.

As noted in Chapter 7, Java does not provide any class that wraps primitive type values in objects and, when passed as parameters, change their values. If a method returns only one value of a primitive type, then you can write a value-returning method. However, if you encounter a situation that requires you to write a method that needs to pass more than one value of a primitive type, then you should design your own classes. In the next section, we introduce various classes to accomplish this. For example, we design the class IntClass so that values of the int type can be wrapped in an object. The class IntClass also provides methods to change the value of an IntClass object. We use reference variables of the IntClass type to pass int values outside a method.

Primitive Type Classes

This section presents the definitions of the classes IntClass, LongClass, CharClass, FloatClass, DoubleClass, and BooleanClass.

Class: IntClass

```
public class IntClass
{
    private int x;     //variable to store the number

        //default constructor
        //Postcondition: x = 0
    public IntClass()
    {
        x = 0;
    }
```

```java
    //constructor with parameter
    //Postcondition: x = num
public IntClass(int num)
{
    x = num;
}

    //Method to set the data member x
    //Postcondition: x = num
public void setNum(int num)
{
    x = num;
}

    //Method to return the value of x
    //Postcondition: The value of x is returned
public int getNum()
{
    return x;
}

    //Method to update the value of x by adding
    //the value of num
    //Postcondition: x = x + num;
public void addToNum(int num)
{
    x = x + num;
}
    //Method to update the value of x by multiplying
    //the value of x by num
    //Postcondition: x = x * num;
public void multiplyToNum(int num)
{
    x = x * num;
}

    //Method to compare the value of x with the value of num
    //Postcondition: Returns a value < 0 if x < num
    //               Returns 0 if x == num
    //               Returns a value > 0 if x > num
public int compareTo(int num)
{
    return (x - num);
}

    //Method to compare x with num for equality
    //Postcondition: Returns true if x == num;
    //               otherwise it returns false
public boolean equals(int num)
{
    if (x == num)
        return true;
    else
        return false;
}
```

```
        //Method to return the value of x as a string
    public String toString()
    {
        return (String.valueOf(x));
    }
}
```

Consider the following statements:

```
IntClass firstNum = new IntClass();        //Line 1
IntClass secondNum = new IntClass(5);      //Line 2
int num;                                    //Line 3
```

The statement in Line 1 creates the object `firstNum` and initializes it to 0. The statement in Line 2 creates the object `secondNum` and initializes it to 5. The statement in Line 3 declares num to be an `int` variable. Now consider the following statements:

```
firstNum.setNum(24);                        //Line 4
secondNum.addToNum(6);                      //Line 5
num = firstNum.getNum();                    //Line 6
```

The statement in Line 4 sets the value of `firstNum` (in fact, the value of the data member `x` of `firstNum`) to 24. The statement in Line 5 updates the value of `secondNum` to 11 (the previous value 5 is updated by adding 6 to it.) The statement in Line 6 retrieves the value of the object `firstNum` (the value of the data member `x`) and assigns it to num. After this statement executes, the value of num is 24.

The following statements output the values of `firstNum` and `secondNum` (in fact, the values of their data members):

```
System.out.println("firstNum = " + firstNum);
System.out.println("secondNum = " + secondNum);
```

Table D-4 shows how variables of `int` type and the corresponding reference variables of `IntClass` type work.

TABLE D-4 Variables of `int` Type and the Corresponding Reference Variables of `IntClass`

	int	IntClass

Declaration without or with initialization	int x, y = 5;	IntClass x, y;
		x = new IntClass();
		y = new IntClass(5);

Assignment	x = 24;	x.setNum(24);
	y = x;	y.setNum(x.getNum());
Addition	x = x + 10;	x.addToNum(10);
	x = x + y;	x.addToNum(y.getNum());

TABLE D-4 Variables of `int` Type and the Corresponding Reference Variables of `IntClass` (continued)

	int	IntClass
Multiplication	`x = x * 10;`	`x.multiplyToNum(10);`
	`x = x * y;`	`x.multiplyToNum(y.getNum());`
Comparison	`if (x < 10)`	`if (x.compareTo(10) < 0)`
	`if (x < y)`	`if (x.compareTo(y.getNum()) < 0)`
	`if (x <= 10)`	`if (x.compareTo(10) <= 0)`
	`if (x <= y)`	`if (x.compareTo(y.getNum()) <= 0)`

	`if (x == 10)`	`if (x.compareTo(10) == 0)`
		or
		`if (x.equals(10))`

	`if (x == y)`	`if (x.compareTo(y.getNum()) == 0)`
		or
		`if (x.equals(y.getNum()))`

	`if (x > 10)`	`if (x.compareTo(10) > 0)`
	`if (x > y)`	`if (x.compareTo(y.getNum()) > 0)`
	`if (x >= 10)`	`if (x.compareTo(10) >= 0)`
	`if (x >= y)`	`if (x.compareTo(y.getNum()) >= 0)`

	`if (x != 10)`	`if (x.compareTo(10) != 0)`
		or
		`if (!x.equals(10))`

	`if (x != y)`	`if (x.compareTo(y.getNum()) != 0)`
		or
		`if (!x.equals(y.getNum()))`

Output		`System.out.println(x);`
		`System.out.println(x);`

Class: `LongClass`

```java
public class LongClass
{
    private long x;

    public LongClass()
    {
        x = 0;
    }

    public LongClass(long num)
    {
        x = num;
    }

    public void setNum(long num)
    {
        x = num;
    }

    public long getNum()
    {
        return x;
    }

    public void addToNum(long num)
    {
        x = x + num;
    }

    public void multiplyToNum(long num)
    {
        x = x * num;
    }

    public long compareTo(long num)
    {
        return (x - num);
    }

    public boolean equals(long num)
    {
        if (x == num)
            return true;
        else
            return false;
    }

    public String toString()
    {
        return (String.valueOf(x));
    }
}
```

Class: CharClass

```
public class CharClass
{
    private char ch;

    public CharClass()
    {
        ch = ' ';
    }

    public CharClass(char c)
    {
        ch = c;
    }

    public void setChar(char c)
    {
        ch = c;
    }

    public int getChar()
    {
        return ch;
    }

    public char nextChar()
    {
        return (char)((int)ch + 1);
    }

    public char prevChar()
    {
        return (char)((int)ch - 1);
    }

    public String toString()
    {
        return (String.valueOf(ch));
    }
}
```

Class: FloatClass

```
public class FloatClass
{
    private float x;

    public FloatClass()
    {
        x = 0;
    }

    public FloatClass(float num)
    {
        x = num;
    }
```

```java
    public void setNum(float num)
    {
        x = num;
    }

    public float getNum()
    {
        return x;
    }

    public void addToNum(float num)
    {
        x = x + num;
    }

    public void multiplyToNum(float num)
    {
        x = x * num;
    }

    public float compareTo(float num)
    {
        return (x - num);
    }

    public boolean equals(float num)
    {
        if (x == num)
            return true;
        else
            return false;
    }

    public String toString()
    {
        return (String.valueOf(x));
    }
}
```

Class: DoubleClass

```java
public class DoubleClass
{
    private double x;

    public DoubleClass()
    {
        x = 0;
    }

    public DoubleClass(double num)
    {
        x = num;
    }
```

```java
    public void setNum(double num)
    {
        x = num;
    }

    public double getNum()
    {
        return x;
    }

    public void addToNum(double num)
    {
        x = x + num;
    }

    public void multiplyToNum(double num)
    {
        x = x * num;
    }

    public double compareTo(double num)
    {
        return (x - num);
    }

    public boolean equals(double num)
    {
        if (x == num)
            return true;
        else
            return false;
    }

    public String toString()
    {
        return (String.valueOf(x));
    }
}
```

Class: BooleanClass

```java
public class BooleanClass
{
    private boolean flag;

    public BooleanClass()
    {
        flag = false;
    }

    public BooleanClass(boolean f)
    {
        flag = f;
    }
```

```java
    public boolean get()
    {
        return flag;
    }

    public void set(boolean f)
    {
        flag = f;
    }

    public String toString()
    {
        return (String.valueOf(flag));
    }

}
```

Using Primitive Type Classes in a Program

This section describes how to use the classes introduced in the previous section.

The class IntClass can be used in two ways. One way is to keep the file IntClass.java and the program in the same directory. First, compile the file IntClass.java, then compile the program.

The second way is to first create a package, and then put this class in that package. For example, you can create the package:

jpfpatpd.ch07.primitiveTypeClasses

and put the class in this package.

In this case, you place the statement:

package jpfpatpd.ch07.primitiveTypeClasses;

before the definition of the class IntClass.

The class IntClass definition is in the file IntClass.java. We need to compile this file and place the compiled code in the directory: jpfpatpd.ch07. primitiveTypeClasses. To do so, we execute the following command at the command line:

javac -d c:\jre1.7.0\lib\classes IntClass.java

The file IntClass.class is now placed in the subdirectory jpfpatpd\ch07 \primitiveTypeClasses of the directory c:\jre1.7.0\lib\classes.

On the other hand, the command:

javac IntClass.java

places the file IntClass.class in the subdirectory jpfpatpd\ch07\primitive TypeClasses of the same directory. Note that the system automatically creates the subdirectory jpfpatpd\ch07\primitiveTypeClasses if it does not exist.

You can now import this class in a program using the import statement. For example, you can use either of the following statements to use the **class** IntClass in your program:

`import jpfpatpd.ch07.primitiveTypeClasses.*;`

or

`import jpfpatpd.ch07.primitiveTypeClasses.IntClass;`

USING A SOFTWARE DEVELOPMENT KIT (SDK)

If you are using an SDK, such as CodeWarrior or J++ Builder, you can place the file containing the definition of the class in the same directory that contains your program. You do not need to create a package. However, you can also create a package using the SDK. In this case, place the appropriate **package** statement before the definition of the class, and use the compile command provided by the SDK. (In most cases, you do not need to specify a subdirectory.) The compiled file will be placed in the appropriate directory. You can now import the class without adding it to the project.

 NOTE If you have created a package for your classes, to avoid compilation errors, do not add the file containing the definition of the class to the project.

Enumeration Types

Chapter 2 defined a data type as a set of values, combined with a set of operations on those values. It then introduced the primitive data types: **int**, **char**, **double**, and **float**. Using primitive data types, Chapter 8 discussed how to design classes to create your own data types. In other words, primitive data types are the building blocks of classes.

The values belonging to primitive data types are predefined. Java allows programmers to create their own data types by specifying the values of that data type. These are called **enumeration** or **enum** types and are defined using the keyword **enum**. *The values that you specify for the data types are identifiers.* For example, consider the following statement:

`enum Grades {A, B, C, D, F};`

This statement defines Grades to be an **enum** type; the values belonging to this type are A, B, C, D, and F. The values of an **enum** type are called **enumeration** or **enum** constants. Note that the values are enclosed in braces and separated by commas. Also, the **enum** constants within an **enum** type must be unique.

Similarly, the statement:

```
enum Sports {BASEBALL, BASKETBALL, FOOTBALL, GOLF,
             HOCKEY, SOCCER, TENNIS};
```

defines Sports to be an **enum** type and the values belonging to this type, that is, the **enum** constants, are BASEBALL, BASKETBALL, FOOTBALL, GOLF, HOCKEY, SOCCER, and TENNIS.

Each enum type is a *special type of class*, and the values belonging to the enum type are (special types of) objects of that class. For example, Grades is, in fact, a class and A, B, C, D, and F are public static reference variables to objects of the type Grades.

After an enum type is defined, you can declare reference variables of that type. For example, the following statement declares myGrade to be a reference variable of the Grades type:

```
Grades myGrade;
```

Because each of the variables A, B, C, D, and F is public and static, they can be accessed using the name of the class and the dot operator. Therefore, the following statement assigns the object B to myGrade:

```
myGrade = Grades.B;
```

The output of the statement:

```
System.out.println("myGrade: " + myGrade);
```

is:

```
myGrade: B
```

Similarly, the output of the statement:

```
System.out.println("Grades.B: " + Grades.B);
```

is:

```
Grades.B: B
```

Each enum constant in an enum type has a specific value, called the **ordinal value**. The ordinal value of the first enum constant is 0, the ordinal value of the second enum constant is 1, and so on. Therefore, in the enum type Grades, the ordinal value of A is 0 and the ordinal value of C is 2.

Associated with enum type is a set of methods that can be used to work with enum types. Table D-5 describes some of those methods.

TABLE D-5 Methods Associated with enum Types

Method	Description
ordinal()	Returns the ordinal value of an enum constant
name()	Returns the name of the enum value
values()	Returns the values of an enum type as a list

Example D-3 illustrates how these methods work.

EXAMPLE D-3

```java
public class EnumExample1
{
    enum Grades {A, B, C, D, F};                     //Line 1

    enum Sports {BASEBALL, BASKETBALL, FOOTBALL,
                 GOLF, HOCKEY, SOCCER, TENNIS};       //Line 2

    public static void main(String[] args)           //Line 3
    {
        Grades myGrade;                              //Line 4
        Sports mySport;                              //Line 5

        myGrade = Grades.A;                          //Line 6

        mySport = Sports.BASKETBALL;                 //Line 7

        System.out.println("Line 8: My grade: "
                        + myGrade);                  //Line 8
        System.out.println("Line 9: The ordinal "
                        + "value of myGrade is "
                        + myGrade.ordinal());        //Line 9
        System.out.println("Line 10: myGrade name: "
                        + myGrade.name());           //Line 10

        System.out.println("Line 11: My sport: "
                        + mySport);                  //Line 11
        System.out.println("Line 12: The ordinal "
                        + "value of mySport is "
                        + mySport.ordinal());        //Line 12
        System.out.println("Line 13: mySport name: "
                        + mySport.name());           //Line 13

        System.out.println("Line 14: Sports: ");     //Line 14

        for (Sports sp : Sports.values())            //Line 15
            System.out.println(sp + "'s ordinal "
                        + "value is "
                        + sp.ordinal());             //Line 16

        System.out.println();                        //Line 17
    }
}
```

Sample Run:

```
Line 8: My grade: A
Line 9: The ordinal value of myGrade is 0
Line 10: myGrade name: A
Line 11: My sport: BASKETBALL
Line 12: The ordinal value of mySport is 1
Line 13: mySport name: BASKETBALL
Line 14: Sports:
BASEBALL's ordinal value is 0
BASKETBALL's ordinal value is 1
FOOTBALL's ordinal value is 2
GOLF's ordinal value is 3
HOCKEY's ordinal value is 4
SOCCER's ordinal value is 5
TENNIS's ordinal value is 6
```

The preceding program works as follows. The statements in Lines 1 and 2 define the `enum` type `Grades` and `Sports`, respectively. The statement in Line 4 declares `myGrade` to be a reference variable of the type `Grades`, and the statement in Line 5 declares `mySport` to be a reference variable of the type `Sports`. The statement in Line 6 assigns the object `A` to `myGrade`, and the statement in Line 7 assigns the object `BASKETBALL` to `mySport`.

The statement in Line 8 outputs `myGrade`, the statement in Line 9 uses the method `ordinal` to output the ordinal value of `myGrade`, and the statement in Line 10 uses the method `name` to output the name of `myGrade`.

The statement in Line 11 outputs `mySport`, the statement in Line 12 uses the method `ordinal` to output the ordinal value of `mySport`, and the statement in Line 13 uses the method `name` to output the name of `mySport`.

The foreach loop in Line 15 outputs the value of `Sports` and their ordinal values. Note that the method `values`, in the expression `Sports.values()`, returns the value of the `enum` type `Sport` as a list. The loop control variable `sp` ranges over those values one-by-one, starting at the first value.

The beginning of this section noted that an `enum` type is a special type of class, and the `enum` constants are reference variables to the objects of that `enum` type. Because each `enum` type is a class, in addition to the `enum` constants, it can also contain constructors, (`private`) data members, and methods. Before describing enumeration type or `enum` in more detail, let us note the following:

1. Enumeration types are defined using the keyword `enum` rather than `class`.
2. `enum` types are implicitly `final` because `enum` constants should not be modified.
3. `enum` constants are implicitly `static`.

4. Once an **enum** type is created, you can declare reference variables of that type, but you cannot instantiate objects using the operator **new**. In fact, an attempt to instantiate an object using the operator **new** will result in a compilation error.

(Because **enum** objects cannot be instantiated using the operator **new**, the constructor, if any, of an enumeration *cannot* be **public**. In fact, the constructors of an **enum** type are implicitly **private**.)

The **enum** type **Grades** was defined earlier in this section. Let us redefine this **enum** type by adding constructors, data members, and methods. Consider the following definition:

```
public enum Grades
{
    A ("Range 90% to 100%"),
    B ("Range 80% to 89.99%"),
    C ("Range 70% to 79.99%"),
    D ("Range 60% to 69.99%"),
    F ("Range 0% to 59.99%");

    private final String range;

    private Grades()
    {
        range = "";
    }

    private Grades(String str)
    {
        range = str;
    }

    public String getRange()
    {
        return range;
    }
}
```

This **enum** type **Grades** contains the **enum** constants **A, B, C, D,** and **F**. It has a **private** named constant **range** of the type **String**, two constructors, and the method **getRange**. Note that each **Grades** object has the data member **range**. Let us consider the statement:

```
A ("Range 90% to 100%")
```

This statement creates the **Grades** object, using the constructor with parameters, with the string **"Range 90% to 100%"**, and assigns that object to the reference variable **A**. The method **getRange** is used to return the string contained in the object.

It is not necessary to specify the modifier **private** in the heading of the constructor. Each constructor is implicitly **private**. Therefore, the two constructors of the **enum** type **Grades** can be written as:

```
Grades()
{
    range = "";
}

Grades(String str)
{
    range = str;
}
```

Example D-4 illustrates how the enum type Grades works.

EXAMPLE D-4

```
public class EnumExample2
{
    public static void main(String[] args)
    {
        System.out.println("Grade Ranges");        //Line 1

        for (Grades gr : Grades.values())          //Line 2
            System.out.println(gr + " "
                                + gr.getRange());  //Line 3

        System.out.println();                      //Line 4
    }
}
```

Sample Run:

```
Grade Ranges
A Range 90% to 100%
B Range 80% to 89.99%
C Range 70% to 79.99%
D Range 60% to 69.99%
F Range 0% to 59.99%
```

The foreach loop in Line 2 uses the method values to retrieve the enum constants as a list. The method getRange in Line 3 is used to retrieve the string contained in the Grades object.

The following programming example uses an enum type to create a program to play the game of rock, paper, and scissors.

PROGRAMMING EXAMPLE: The Rock, Paper, and Scissors Game

Everyone is familiar with the rock, paper, and scissors game. The game has two players, each of whom chooses one of the three objects: rock, paper, or scissors. If player 1 chooses rock and player 2 chooses paper, player 2 wins the game because paper covers the rock. The game is played according to the following rules:

- If both players choose the same object, this play is a tie.
- If one player chooses rock and the other chooses scissors, the player choosing the rock wins this play because the rock crushes the scissors.
- If one player chooses rock and the other chooses paper, the player choosing the paper wins this play because the paper covers the rock.
- If one player chooses scissors and the other chooses paper, the player choosing the scissors wins this play because the scissors cut the paper.

We write an interactive program that allows two players to play this game.

Input: This program has two types of input:

- The players' responses to play the game
- The players' choices

Output: The players' choices and the winner of each play. After the game is over, the total number of plays and the number of times that each player won should be output as well.

PROBLEM
ANALYSIS
AND
ALGORITHM
DESIGN

Two players play this game. Players enter their choices via the keyboard. Each player enters R or r for Rock, P or p for Paper, or S or s for Scissors. While the first player enters a choice, the second player looks away. Once both entries are in, if the entries are valid, the program outputs the players' choices and declares the winner of the play. The game continues until one of the players decides to quit. After the game ends, the program outputs the total number of plays and the number of times that each player won. This discussion translates into the following algorithm:

1. Provide a brief explanation of the game and how it is played.
2. Ask the users if they want to play the game.
3. Get plays for both players.
4. If the plays are valid, output the plays and the winner.
5. Update the total game count and winner count.
6. Repeat Steps 2–5 while the users continue to play the game.
7. Output the number of plays and times that each player won.

To describe the objects ROCK, PAPER, and SCISSORS, we define the following enum type:

```java
public enum RockPaperScissors
{
    ROCK ("Rock crushes scissors."),
    PAPER ("Paper covers rock."),
    SCISSORS ("Scissors cuts paper.");

    private String mgs;

    private RockPaperScissors()
    {
        mgs = "";
    }

    private RockPaperScissors(String str)
    {
        mgs = str;
    }

    public String getMessage()
    {
        return mgs;
    }
}
```

Variables (Method main) It is clear that you need the following variables in the method main:

```java
int gameCount;        //to count the number of
                      //games played
int winCount1;        //to count the number of
                      //games won by player 1
int winCount2;        //to count the number of
                      //games won by player 2
int gameWinner;
char response;        //to get the user's response
                      //to play the game
char selection1;
char selection2;

RockPaperScissors play1;  //player1's selection
RockPaperScissors play2;  //player2's selection
```

This program is divided into six methods, which the following sections describe in detail.

- **displayRules**: This method displays some brief information about the game and its rules.
- **validSelection**: This method checks whether a player's selection is valid. The only valid selections are R, r, P, p, S, and s.
- **retrievePlay**: This method uses the entered choice (R, r, P, p, S, or s) and returns the appropriate object.
- **gameResult**: This method outputs the players' choices and the winner of the game.
- **winningObject**: This method determines and returns the winning object.
- **displayResults**: After the game is over, this method displays the final results.

Method display Rules

This method has no parameters. It consists only of output statements to explain the game and rules of play. Essentially, this method's definition is:

```
public static void displayRules()
{
    System.out.println("Welcome to the game of Rock, "
                     + "Paper, and Scissors.");
    System.out.println("This is a game for two players. "
                     + "For each game, each player \n"
                     + "selects one of the "
                     + "objects: Rock, Paper or "
                     + "Scissors.");
    System.out.println("The rules for winning the "
                     + "game are: ");
    System.out.println("1. If both players select the "
                     + "same object, it is a tie.");
    System.out.println("2. Rock crushes Scissors: The "
                     + "player who selects Rock wins.");
    System.out.println("3. Paper covers Rock: The "
                     + "player who selects Paper wins.");
    System.out.println("4. Scissors cuts Paper: The "
                     + "player who selects Scissors "
                     + "wins.");
    System.out.println("Enter R or r to select Rock, "
                     + "P or p to select Paper, \n"
                     + "and S or s to select Scissors.");
}
```

Method valid Selection

This method checks whether a player's selection is valid. Let's use a `switch` statement to check for the valid selection. The definition of this method is:

```java
public static boolean validSelection(char selection)
{
    switch (selection)
    {
    case 'R':
    case 'r':
    case 'P':
    case 'p':
    case 'S':
    case 's':
        return true;

    default:
        return false;
    }
}
```

Method retrievePlay This method uses the entered choice (R, r, P, p, S, or s) and returns the appropriate object. The method has one parameter of the type `char`. It is a value-returning method and returns a reference to a `RockPaperScissors` object.

The definition of the method `retrievePlay` is:

```java
public static RockPaperScissors retrievePlay
                                (char selection)
{
    RockPaperScissors obj = RockPaperScissors.ROCK;

    switch (selection)
    {
    case 'R':
    case 'r':
        obj = RockPaperScissors.ROCK;
        break;

    case 'P':
    case 'p':
        obj = RockPaperScissors.PAPER;
        break;

    case 'S':
    case 's':
        obj = RockPaperScissors.SCISSORS;
    }

    return obj;
}
```

Method game Result

This method decides whether a game is a tie or which player is the winner. It outputs the players' selections and the winner of the game. This method has two parameters: player 1's choice and player 2's choice. It returns the number (1 or 2) of the winning player.

The definition of this method is:

```java
public static int gameResult(RockPaperScissors play1,
                             RockPaperScissors play2)
{
    int winner = 0;

    RockPaperScissors winnerObject;

    if (play1 == play2)
    {
        winner = 0;
        System.out.println("Both players selected "
                           + play1
                           + ". This game is a tie.");
    }
    else
    {
        winnerObject = winningObject(play1, play2);

            //Output each player's choice
        System.out.println("Player 1 selected " + play1
                           + " and player 2 selected "
                           + play2 + ".");

            //Decide the winner
        if (play1 == winnerObject)
            winner = 1;
        else if (play2 == winnerObject)
            winner = 2;

            //Output winning object's message
        System.out.println(winnerObject.getMessage());

            //Output the winner
        System.out.println("Player " + winner
                           + " wins this play.");
    }

    return winner;
}
```

Method winning Object

To decide the winner of the game, you look at the players' selections and then at the rules of the game. For example, if one player chooses ROCK and another chooses PAPER, the player who chose PAPER wins. In other words, the winning object is PAPER. The method winningObject, given two objects, decides and returns the winning object. Clearly, this method has two parameters of the type RockPaperScissors, and the value returned by this method is also of the type RockPaperScissors. The definition of this method is:

```java
public static RockPaperScissors winningObject
                        (RockPaperScissors play1,
                         RockPaperScissors play2)
{
    if ((play1 == RockPaperScissors.ROCK &&
        play2 == RockPaperScissors.SCISSORS)
       || (play2 == RockPaperScissors.ROCK &&
          play1 == RockPaperScissors.SCISSORS))
        return RockPaperScissors.ROCK;
    else if ((play1 == RockPaperScissors.ROCK &&
             play2 == RockPaperScissors.PAPER)
            || (play2 == RockPaperScissors.ROCK &&
               play1 == RockPaperScissors.PAPER))
        return RockPaperScissors.PAPER;
    else
        return RockPaperScissors.SCISSORS;
}
```

Method display Results

After the game is over, this method outputs the final results—that is, the total number of plays and the number of plays won by each player. The total number of plays is stored in the variable gameCount, the number of plays by player 1 is stored in the variable winCount1, and the number of plays won by player 2 is stored in the variable winCount2. This method has three parameters corresponding to these three variables. Essentially, the definition of this method is as follows:

```java
public static void displayResults(int gCount, int wCount1,
                                  int wCount2)
{
    System.out.println("The total number of plays: "
                       + gCount);
    System.out.println("The number of plays won by "
                       + "player 1: " + wCount1);
    System.out.println("The number of plays won by "
                       + "player 2: " + wCount2);
}
```

We are now ready to write the algorithm for the method main.

Main Algorithm	1.	Declare the variables.

Main Algorithm

1. Declare the variables.
2. Initialize the variables.
3. Display the rules.
4. Prompt the users to play the game.
5. Get the users' responses to play the game.
6. `while` (response is yes)

    {

    a. Prompt player 1 to make a selection.
    b. Get the play for player 1.
    c. Prompt player 2 to make a selection.
    d. Get the play for player 2.
    e. If both the plays are legal

        {

        i. Retrieve both plays.
        ii. Increment the total game count.
        iii. Declare the winner of the game.
        iv. Increment the winner's game win count by 1.

        }

    f. Prompt the users to determine whether they want to play again.
    g. Get the players' responses.

    }

7. Output the game results.

PROGRAM LISTING

```java
import java.util.*;

public class GameRockPaperScissors
{
    static Scanner console = new Scanner(System.in);

    public static void main(String[] args)
    {
            //Step 1
        int gameCount;  //to count the number of
                        //games played
        int winCount1;  //to count the number of
                        //games won by player 1
        int winCount2;  //to count the number of
                        //games won by player 2
```

```java
        int gameWinner;
        char response;   //to get the user's response
                         //to play the game
        char selection1;
        char selection2;

        RockPaperScissors play1;   //player1's selection
        RockPaperScissors play2;   //player2's selection

            //Initialize the variables; Step 2
        gameCount = 0;
        winCount1 = 0;
        winCount2 = 0;

        displayRules();                                     //Step 3

        System.out.print("Enter Y/y to play "
                    + "the game: ");                        //Step 4
        response = console.nextLine().charAt(0);            //Step 5
        System.out.println();

        while (response == 'Y' || response == 'y')          //Step 6
        {
            System.out.print("Player 1 enter "
                        + "your choice: ");                 //Step 6a
            selection1 =
                console.nextLine().charAt(0);               //Step 6b
            System.out.println();

            System.out.print("Player 2 enter "
                        + "your choice: ");                 //Step 6c
            selection2 =
                console.nextLine().charAt(0);               //Step 6d
            System.out.println();

                //Step 6e
            if (validSelection(selection1) &&
                validSelection(selection2))
            {
                play1 = retrievePlay(selection1);
                play2 = retrievePlay(selection2);
                gameCount++;
                gameWinner = gameResult(play1, play2);

                if (gameWinner == 1)
                    winCount1++;
                else if (gameWinner == 2)
                    winCount2++;
            }//end if
```

```
                System.out.print("Enter Y/y to play "
                            + "the game: ");              //Step 6f
                response = console.nextLine().charAt(0); //Step 6g
                System.out.println();
            }//end while

            displayResults(gameCount, winCount1,
                        winCount2);                       //Step 7

        }//end main

        //Place the definitions of the methods displayRules,
        //validSelection, retrievePlay, winningObject,
        //gameResult, and displayResults here.
    }
```

Sample Run: (In this sample run, the user input is shaded.)

```
Welcome to the game of Rock, Paper, and Scissors.
This is a game for two players. For each game, each player
selects one of the objects: Rock, Paper or Scissors.
The rules for winning the game are:
1. If both players select the same object, it is a tie.
2. Rock crushes Scissors: The player who selects Rock wins.
3. Paper covers Rock: The player who selects Paper wins.
4. Scissors cuts Paper: The player who selects Scissors wins.
Enter R or r to select Rock, P or p to select Paper,
and S or s to select Scissors.
Enter Y/y to play the game: y

Player 1 enter your choice: R

Player 2 enter your choice: S
Player 1 selected ROCK and player 2 selected SCISSORS.
Rock crushes scissors.
Player 1 wins this play.
Enter Y/y to play the game: Y

Player 1 enter your choice: S

Player 2 enter your choice: P
Player 1 selected SCISSORS and player 2 selected PAPER.
Scissors cuts paper.
Player 1 wins this play.
Enter Y/y to play the game: Y

Player 1 enter your choice: R
```

```
Player 2 enter your choice: P
Player 1 selected ROCK and player 2 selected PAPER.
Paper covers rock.
Player 2 wins this play.
Enter Y/y to play the game: n
The total number of plays: 3
The number of plays won by player 1: 2
The number of plays won by player 2: 1
```

ANSWERS TO ODD-NUMBERED EXERCISES

Chapter 1

1. a. False; b. False; c. True; d. False; e. False; f. True; g. True; h. False; i. False; j. True; k. False; l. True

3. Monitor and printer.

5. An operating system monitors the overall activity of the computer and provides services. Some of these services include memory management, input/output activities, and storage management.

7. In machine language the programs are written using the binary codes while in high-level language the programs are closer to the natural language. For execution, a high-level language program is translated into the machine language while a machine language need not be translated into any other language.

9. Syntax errors.

11. Instructions in a high-level language are closer to the natural language, such as English, and therefore, are easier to understand and learn than the machine language.

13. To find the weighted average of four test scores, first you need to know each test score and its weight. Next, you multiply each test score by its weight and then add these numbers to get the average. Therefore:
    1. Get testScore1, weightTestScore1
    2. Get testScore2, weightTestScore2
    3. Get testScore3, weightTestScore3
    4. Get testScore4, weightTestScore4
    5. sum = testScore1 * weightTestScore1 +
            testScore2 * weightTestScore2 +
            testScore3 * weightTestScore3 +
            testScore4 * weightTestScore4;

15. To calculate the selling price of an item, we need to know the original price (the price the store pays to buy it) of the item. We can then the use the following formula to find the selling price:

```
sellingPrice = (originalPrice + originalPrice × 0.80) × 0.90
```

The algorithm is as follows:

a. Get `originalPrice`

b. Calculate the `sellingPrice` using the formula:

```
sellingPrice = (originalPrice + originalPrice × 0.80) × 0.90
```

The information needed to calculate the selling price is the original price and the marked-up percentage.

17. Suppose that `numOfPages` denotes the number of pages to be faxed and `billingAmount` denotes the total charges for the pages faxed. To calculate the total charges, you need to know the number of pages faxed.

    If `numOfPages` is less than or equal to 10, the billing amount is service charges plus (`numOfPages` × 0.20); otherwise, billing amount is service charges plus 10 × 0.20 plus (`numOfPages` − 10) × 0.10.

    You can now write the algorithm as follows:

    a. Get `numOfPages`.

    b. Calculate billing amount using the formula:

```
if (numOfPages is less than or equal to 10)
    billingAmount = 3.00 + (numOfPages × 0.20);
otherwise
    billingAmount = 3.00 + 10 × 0.20 + (numOfPages - 10) × 0.10;
```

Chapter 2

1. a. False; b. False; c. False; d. False; e. True; f. True; g. True; h. False; i. True; j. False

3. a

5. The identifiers `firstName` and `FirstName` are not the same. Java is case sensitive. The first character of `firstName` is lowercase `f` while the first character of `FirstName` is uppercase `F`. So these identifiers are different.

7. a. 3; b. 0.5; c. 4.5; d. 38.5; e. 1; f. 2; g. 2; h. 420.0

9. 7

11. a and c are valid

13. a. `32 * a + b`

    b. `'8'`

    c. `"Julie Nelson"`

    d. `(b * b - 4 * a * c) / (2 * a)`

    e. `(a + b) / c * (e * f) - g * h`

    f. `(-b + (b * b - 4 * a * c)) / (2 * a)`

15. x = 20
    y = 15
    z = 6
    w = 11.5
    t = 4.5

17. a. x = 2, y = 5, z = 6
    b. x + y = 7
    c. Sum of 2 and 6 is 8
    d. z / x = 3
    e. 2 times 2 = 4

19. a. `System.out.println();` or `System.out.print("\n");` or `System.out.print('\n');`
    b. `System.out.println("\t");`
    c. `System.out.println("\"");`

21. a. firstName
    b. discountedPrice
    c. numOfJuiceBottles
    d. milesTravelled
    e. highestTestScore

23. A correct answer is:

```
public class Exercise23
{
    static final int    SECRET_NUM = 11213;
    static final double PAY_RATE = 18.35;

    public static void main(String[] arg)
    {
        int one, two, three;
        double first, second;

        double paycheck, hoursWorked;

        one = 18;
        two = 11;
        three = 3;

        first = 25;
        second = first * three;

        second = 2 * SECRET_NUM;
```

```
            System.out.println(first + " " + second + " " + SECRET_NUM);

            hoursWorked = 35;

            paycheck = hoursWorked * PAY_RATE;

            System.out.println("Wages = " +  paycheck);
        }
    }
```

25. A correct answer is:

```
public class Exercise25
{
    static final char STAR = '*';
    static final int  PRIME = 71;

    public static void main(String[] arg)
    {
        int count = 1;
        int sum = count + PRIME;

        double x = 25.67;
        int newNum = count * PRIME + 2;

        sum = sum + count;
        x = x + sum * count;
        System.out.println(" count = " + count + ", sum = "
                            + sum + ", PRIME = " + PRIME);
    }
}
```

27. The **class** String is contained in the package java.lang. You do not need to import classes from the package java.lang. The system automatically does it for you.

29. a. x = x + 5 - z;

    b. y = y * (2 * x + 5 - z);

    c. w = w + 2 * z + 4;

    d. x = x - (z + y - t);

    e. sum = sum + num;

    f. x = x / (y - 2);

31.

	a	b	c	sum
sum = a + b + (int)c;	3	5	14.1	22
c /= a;	3	5	4.7	22
b += (int)c - a;	3	6	4.7	22
a *= 2 * b + (int)c;	48	6	4.7	22

33. (NOTE: The user input is shaded.)

```
Enter last name: Miller

Enter a two digit number: 34

Enter a positive integer less than 1000: 340

Name: Miller
Id: 3417
Mystery number: 3689
```

35. The program require three inputs. One possible form of input is:
```
number
string
number
```

Another possible form of input is:
```
number string
number
```

Chapter 3

1. a. False; b. True; c. True; d. True

3. An object is an instance of a specific class.

5. `str = new String("Java Programming");`

7. The **class** String is contained in the package java.lang. If a program uses a class contained in this package, the Java system automatically imports that class. Therefore, because **class** String is contained in the package java.lang, it is not necessary to explicitly import this class using the import statement.

9. a. `Going`
   b. `amusement`
   c. `GOING TO THE AMUSEMENT PARK`
   d. `going to the amusement park`
   e. `Going *o *he amusemen* park`

11. a. false
    b. true

13. `name = console.nextLine();`

15. This statement causes the following input dialog box to appear allowing the user to enter the score.

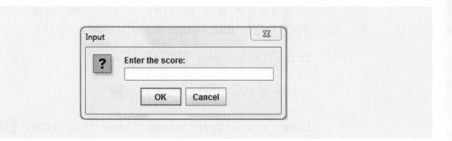

FIGURE E-1 Chapter 3 Exercise 15

17. ```
JOptionPane.showMessageDialog(null,
                    "Current Temperature: 70 degrees",
                    "Temperature",
                    JOptionPane.QUESTION_MESSAGE);
```

19. ```
x = console.nextInt();
ch = console.next().charAt(0);
y = console.nextInt();
```

21. `java.io`

23. ```
acctNumber = infile.nextInt();
accountType = infile.next();
balance = infile.nextDouble();
```

25. a. Same as before.

   b. The file contains the output produced by the program.

   c. The file contains the output produced by the program. Old contents are erased.

   d. The program would prepare the file and store the output in the file.

# Chapter 4

1. a. True; b. False; c. False; d. False; e. False; f. False; g. False; h. False; i. True

3. a. true; b. false; c. true; d. true; e. true

5. `100 200 0`

7. Omit the semicolon after `else`:

```
if (score >= 60)
    System.out.println("You pass.");
else
    System.out.println("You fail.");
```
```

9.   3 1

11.   1 3

13.
```
if (0 < overSpeed && overSpeed <= 5)
        fine = 20.00;
    else if (5 < overSpeed && overSpeed <= 10)
        fine = 75.00;
    else if (10 < overSpeed && overSpeed <= 15)
        fine = 150.00;
    else if (overSpeed > 15)
        fine = 150.00 + 20.00 * (overSpeed - 15);
```

15. a. i.   The output is: Grade is C. The value of score after the if statement executes is 70.

     ii. The expression score = 70 in statement ii will result in a syntax error.

     b. i.   No output. The value of score after the if statement executes is 80.

     ii. The expression score = 70 in statement ii will result in a syntax error.

17. a.
```
if (x < 5)
        y = 10;
    else
        y = 20;
```

     b.
```
if (fuel >= 10)
        drive = 150;
    else
        drive = 30;
```

     c.
```
if (booksBought >= 3)
        discount = 0.15;
    else
        discount = 0.0;
```

19. a is invalid: The expression n <= 2 evaluates to a boolean value, which is not an integral type. The expression in the switch expression must evaluate to an integral value. b is invalid: A case value cannot appear more than once. c and d are valid.

21. 7

23. There is more than one answer. One possible answer is:

```
import java.util.*;

public class Errors
{
    static Scanner console = new Scanner(System.in);

    public static void main(String[] args)
    {
        int a, b;
```

```
        int c;
        boolean found;

        System.out.print("Enter the first integer: ");
        a = console.nextInt();
        System.out.println();

        System.out.print("Enter the second integer: ");
        b = console.nextInt();

        if (a > a * b && 10 < b)
            found = 2 * a > b;
        else
        {
            found = 2 * a < b;
            if (found)
                a = 3;
            c = 15;
            if (b > 0)
            {
                b = 0;
                a = 1;
            }
        }
    }
}
```

25. a. true; b. true; c. false; d. true

Chapter 5

1. a. False; b. True; c. False; d. True; e. True; f. True; g. True; h. False

3. 5

5. When ch > 'Z'

7. Sum = 158

9. Sum = 158

11. 11 18 25

13. Replace the while loop statement with the following:

```
while (response == 'Y' || response == 'y')
```

Replace the output statement:

```
System.out.printf("%.2f + %.2f  = %.2f %n",
                  num1, num2, (num1 - num2));
```

with the following:

```
System.out.printf("%.2f + %.2f  = %.2f %n",
                  num1, num2, (num1 + num2));
```

15. 4 3 2 1

17. 0 3 8 15 24

19. Loop control variable: j
The initialization statement: j = 1;
Loop condition: j <= 10;
Update statement: j++
The statement that updates the value of s: s = s + j * (j - 1);

21. 2 7 17 37 77 157

23. a. *

    b. infinite loop

    c. infinite loop

    d. ****

    e. ******

    f. ***

25. The relationship between x and y is: $3^y = x$.
    Output: x = 19683, y = 10

27. 0 - 24
    25 - 49
    50 - 74
    75 - 99
    100 - 124
    125 - 149
    150 - 174
    175 - 200

29. a. Both; b. do...while; c. while; d. while

31. In a pretest loop, the loop condition is evaluated before executing the body of the loop. In a posttest loop, the loop condition is evaluated after executing the body of the loop. A posttest loop executes at least once, while a pretest loop may not execute at all.

33. (Assume that console is a Scanner object initialized to the standard input device.)

```
int num;
do
{
    System.out.println("Enter a number less than 20 "
                   + "or greater than 75: ");
    num = console.nextInt();
}
while (20 <= num && num <= 75);
```

35.
```
int i = 0, value = 0;
do
{
    if (i % 2 == 0 && i <= 10)
        value = value + i * i;
    else if (i % 2 == 0 && i > 10)
        value = value + i;
    else
        value = value - i;
    i = i + 1;
}
while (i <= 20);

System.out.println("value = " + value);
```

The output is: value = 200

37.
```
number = console.nextInt();

while (number != -1)
{
    total =  total + number;
    number = console.nextInt();
}
```

39. a.
```
number = 1;
while (number <= 10)
{
    System.out.print(number + " ");
    number++;
}

System.out.println();
```
b.
```
number = 1;
do
{
    System.out.print(number + " ");
    number++;
}
while (number <= 10);

System.out.println();
```

41. 11 18 25
43. -1 0 3 8 15 24
45. 12 11 9 7 6 4 2 1

Chapter 6

1. a. True; b. True; c. True; d. True; e. False; f. False; g. True; h. True; i. True; j. False; k. False; l. False

3. `JTextField`

5. To identify other GUI components such as a `JTextField`.

7. Through the process outlined, you have a methodology that will allow you to critically think and plan your problem-solving approach. You may be able to identify the flaws involved in your thinking before you implement it. A well-analyzed problem leads to a well-designed algorithm. Also, a program that is well-analyzed is easier to modify and spot and fix errors. No one would build a house without a blueprint.

9. The answer to this question is available with the Additional Student Files at *www.cengagebrain.com*.

11. a. `JLabel numOfCourses;`
       `numOfCourses = new JLabel("Enter the number of courses");`
    b. `JButton run;`
       `run = new JButton("Run");`
    c. `JTextField oneTextField ;`
       `oneTextField = new JTextField(15);`
    d. `setTitle("Welcome Home!");`
    e. `setSize(200, 400);`
    f. `JTextField oneTextField;`
       `oneTextField = new JTextField(15);`
       `oneTextField.setText("Apple tree");`

13. The answer to this question is available with the Additional Student Files at *www.cengagebrain.com*.

15. `displayWelcome`, `getAcctNo`, `getPin`, `verifyAcct`, `deposit`, `withdraw`, `transfer`, `tenderCash`, `checkAcct`, and so on.

17. Customer: data members include `firstName`, `lastName`, `phone`, `email`, `address`; methods include `set` and `get` methods for data members.
    Account: `accountNumber`, `type`, `currentRate`; methods include `set` and `get` methods for data members.
    Loan: `loanNumber`, `type`, `currentRate`; methods include `set` and `get` methods for data member.
    Manager: data members include `firstName`, `lastName`, `phone`, `email`, `address`; methods include `set` and `get` methods for data members, `createAccount`, `approveLoan`, and so on.

Teller: data members include `firstName`, `lastName`, `phone`, `email`, `address`; methods include `set` and `get` methods for data members, `processCheck`, `tenderCash`, `transferAmt`, and so on.

19. Company: data members include `accountNumber`, `name`, `phone`, `email`, `address`, `status`, `numOpenings`; methods include `set` and `get` methods for data members, `listOpenings`, `requestCandidate`, `cancelPosition`, and so on.

Candidate: data members include `candidateID`, `firstName`, `lastName`, `phone`, `email`, `address`, `wage`; methods include `set` and `get` methods for data members, `listQualifications`, `calculateSalary`, `withholdIncomeTax`, and so on.

Placement: data members include `candidateID`, `companyID`, `openingID`, `startDate`, `endDate`; methods include `set` and `get` methods for data members, `listQualifications`, `calculateSalary`, `informCompany`, `informCandidate`, and so on.

Opening: data members include `openingID`, `companyID`, `startDate`, `endDate`, `qualificationID`, `salary`; methods include `set` and `get` methods for data members.

Qualification: data members include `qualificationID`, `meanSalary`, `maximumSalary`, `minimumSalary`, `category`; methods include `set` and `get` methods for data members.

Chapter 7

1. a. True; b. True; c. True; d. True; e. False; f. True; g. False; h. False

3. a. `4`   b. `10.80`   c. `2.50`   d. `10.24`   e. `15.63`
   f. `5.00`   g. `2.50`   h. `9.00`   i. `28.00`   j. `36.00`

5. a. The method `main` has no return type. It is a **void** method.
   b. `double`
   c. `boolean`

7. a. Invalid; Method type is missing.
   b. Valid
   c. Invalid; Data type for the parameter `b` is missing.
   d. Invalid; Missing parentheses after the method name.

9. The formal parameter `x` of the method `signum` is an integer. In the method call statement `signum(20.5)`, a decimal value is used that is not an integer. So we could replace the expression `signum(20.5)` with the expression `signum(20)`.

11. The method `squareNum` returns an **int** value while the expression `x * x`, in the return statement is a **double** value. One possible solution is to replace the expression `x * x` with the expression `(int) x * x`. Another solution is: In the method heading, change the method type from **int** to **double**.

13.   a. 4; b. 26; c. 10 4 0; d. 0

15.   a. 14; b. 15; c. 30

17.   A **void** method can have a **return** statement. If a **void** method has a **return** statement, then it must be of the form **return;**, it should not return any value.

19.   12
      35
      14
      8
      10

21.   1
      2
      6
      24
      120

23.   Method headings:

```
public static void main(String[] args)
public static void hello(int first, double second,
                         char ch)
```

Method bodies:
      main: starts at Line 4 ends at Line 13
      hello: starts at Line 16 ends at Line 20

Method definitions:
      main: starts at Line 3 ends at Line 13
      hello: starts at Line 14 ends at Line 20

Formal parameters:
      main: args
      hello: first, second, ch

Actual parameters:
      x, y, z
      x + 2, y - 3.5, 'S'

Method calls: Statements in Lines 9 and 11
```
hello(x, y, z);              //Line 9
hello(x + 2, y - 3.5, 'S');  //Line 11
```

Local variables:
      main: x, y, z
      hello: num, y

25. -14 20 126
    15 40 407
    15 80 1627
    70 160 6412

27. a. Take Programming I.
    b. Take Programming II.
    c. Take Invalid input. You must enter a 1 or 2
    d. Take Invalid input. You must enter a 1 or 2

29.

Identifier	Visibility in traceMe	Visibility in main
main	Y	Y
local variables of main	N	Y
traceMe (function name)	Y	Y
x (traceMe's formal parameter)	Y	N
y (traceMe's formal parameter)	Y	N
z (traceMe's local variable)	Y	N

31.
```java
public static void func(double x, double y)
{
    if (x != 0)
        System.out.println(y / x);
    else
        System.out.println("Because the first number is 0, "
                        + "we cannot divide the second "
                        + "number by the first number.");
}
```

Chapter 8

1. a. False; b. False; c. True; d. False; e. False

3. Constructors have no type. Therefore the definition of the constructor with parameters should be:

```java
public AA(int a, int b)
{
    x = a;
    y = b;
}
```

5. a. i. Constructor at Line 1.

    ii. Constructor at Line 3.

    iii. Constructor at Line 4.

    b. ```
    public CC()
    {
        u = 0;
        v = 0;
        w = 0.0;
    }
    ```

    c.  ```
    public CC(int a)
    {
        u = a;
        v = 0;
        w = 0.0;
    }
    ```

    d. ```
    public CC(int a, int b)
    {
        u = a;
        v = b;
        w = 0.0;
    }
    ```

    e.  ```
    public CC(int a, int b, double d)
    {
        u = a;
        v = b;
        w = d;
    }
    ```

7. Automobile

9. One.

11. a. It creates the object c1, and the instance variables hr, min, and sec are initialized to 0.

    b. It creates the object c2. The instance variable hr is initialized to 5, the instance variable min is initialized to 12, and the instance variable sec is initialized to 30.

    c. The values of the instance variables hr, min, and sec of the object c1 are set to 3, 24, and 36, respectively.

    d. The value of the instance variables hr of the object c2 is set to 9.

13. In Java, a class combines data and operations on data in a single unit. Typically, we do not want the user to directly manipulate the data, so data members are declared as private. To allow the users to manipulate the private members of a class, the user is provided with public members. Therefore, we need both public and private members in a class.

15. 06:23:17
    06:23:17

17. In shallow copying, two or more reference variables of the same type point to the same object.

19. Both aa and bb point to the object bb.

21. The purpose of the copy constructor is to initialize an object, when the object is instantiated, using an existing object of the same type.

23. No.

25.
```java
public class Stock
{
    private String name;
    private double previousPrice;
    private double closingPrice;
    private int numberOfShares;

    Stock()
    {
        name = "";
        previousPrice = 0.0;
        closingPrice = 0.0;
        numberOfShares = 0;
    }

    Stock(String n, int prePr, int clPr, double shares)
    {
        name = n;
        previousPrice = prePr;
        closingPrice = clPr;
        numberOfShares = shares;
    }

    public void setName(String n)
    {
        name = n;
    }

    public void setPreviousPrice(double p)
    {
        previousPrice = p;
    }
```

```java
        public void setClosingPrice(double c)
        {
           closingPrice = c;
        }

        public void setNumberOfShare(int ns)
        {
           numberOfShares = ns;
        }


        public String getName()
        {
           return name;
        }

        public int getPreviousPrice()
        {
           return previousPrice;
        }


        public double getClosingPrice()
        {
           return closingPrice;
        }

        public int getNumberOfShare()
        {
           return numberOfShares;
        }

        public double shareValues()
        {
           return numberOfShares * closingPrice;
        }

        public double percentGain()
        {
           return (previousPrice - closingPrice) / previousPrice *   100;
        }
```

```
public String toString()
{
    return ("Stock Name: " + name
        + "\r\n Previous Price: " + previousPrice
        + "\r\n Closing Price: " + closingPrice
        + "\r\n Number Of Shares: " + numberOfShares);
}
}
```

Chapter 9

1. a. True; b. True; c. True; d. True; e. False; f. False; g. True
3. a. This declaration is correct.
   b. The final declaration should be: `final int SIZE = 100;`
   c. This declaration should be: `int[] numList = new int[10]`
   d. This declaration is correct.
   e. This declaration should be: `double[] scores = new double[50];`
5. 0 to 49
7. `-3 -1 1 3 5`
   `5 -1 8 3 -1`
9. a. `funcOne(list, 50);`
   b. `System.out.print(funcSum(50, list[3]));`
   c. `System.out.print(funcSum(list[29], list[9]));`
   d. `funcTwo(list, Alist);`
11. The elements of `list` are: 5, 6, 9, 19, 23, 37
13. `One contains: 3 8 13 18 23`
    `Two contains: 5 15 25 35 45 28 33 38 43 48`
15. ```
    for (int i = 1; i < 9; i++)
        if (scores[i] > scores[i + 1])
            System.out.println(i + " and " + (i + 1)
                + " elements of scores are out of order.");
    ```
17. a. Valid   b. Invalid   c. Invalid   d. Valid
19. `0 -2`
    `1 6`
    `2 -12`
    `3 1`
    `4 13`
21. a. Valid   b. Valid   c. Invalid   d. Valid
    ```

23.
```
int sum = 0;

int maxIndex;
int max;

for (int j = 0; j < 10; j++)
    cars[j] = inFile.nextInt();

for (int j = 0; j < 10; j++)
    sum = sum + cars[j];

System.out.println("The total number of cars sold = " + sum);

max = cars[0];

for (int j = 1; j < 10; j++)
    if (max < cars[j])
        max = cars[j];

System.out.println("The salesperson(s) selling the maximum "
                  + "number of cars: ");

for (int j = 0; j < 10; j++)
    if (max == cars[j])
        System.out.print(j + ", ");
System.out.println();
```

25. One contains: 3 8 13 18 23
Two contains: 5 15 25 35 45 28 33 38 43 48

27. The base address of the array.

29. a. 30
b. 5
c. 6
d. row
e. column

31. a. `beta` is initialized to zero.
b. First row of beta: 0 1 2
Second row of beta: 1 2 3
Third row of beta: 2 3 4
c. First row of beta: 0 0 0
Second row of beta: 0 1 2
Third row of beta: 0 2 4
d. First row of beta: 0 2 0
Second row of beta: 2 0 2
Third row of beta: 0 2 0

33.
```
int[][] temp = {{6, 8, 12, 9},
                {17, 5, 10, 6},
                {14, 13, 16, 20}};
```

35. a.

```
public static void print(int[][] x, int rowSize, int columnSize)
{
    for (int i = 0; i < rowSize; i++)
    {
        for (int j = 0; i < columnSize; j++)
            System.out.print(x[i][j] + " ");

        System.out.println();
    }
}
```

b.
```
print(times, 30, 7);
print(speed, 15, 7);
print(trees, 100, 7);
print(students, 50, 7);
```

37. `list = ["One", "Six", "Two", "Three", "Four", "Five"];`

39.
```
strList: [Hello, Happy, Sunny]
intList: [10, 20, 30]
strList: [Hello, Happy, Joy, Sunny]
intList: [10, 30]
```

Chapter 10

1. a. False; b. False; c. False; d. True

3. Some of the data members that can be added to the **class** Employee are: department, salary, employeeCategory (such as supervisor and president), and employeeID. Some of the methods are: setInfo, getSalary, getEmployeeCategory, and setSalary.

5.

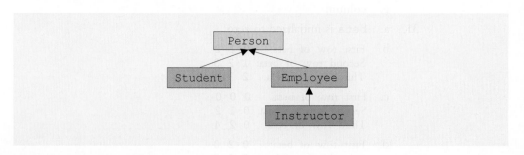

FIGURE E-2 Chapter 10 Exercise 5

7. The **class** Animal is the base class and the **class** Dog is the derived class.

9. a. The statement:

```
class BClass AClass
```

should be:

```
class BClass extends AClass
```

b. Variables u and v are private in **class** AClass and cannot be accessed directly in **class** BClass.

11. a.
```
public YClass()
{
    a = 0;
    b = 0;
}
```

b.
```
public XClass()
{
    super(0, 0);
    z = 0;
}
```

c.
```
public void two(int x, int y)
{
    a = x;
    b = y;
}
```

13. In overloading, two or more methods have the same name but have different formal parameter lists. In overriding, you are redefining a method of a superclass in a subclass. The two methods (the method in the superclass and its redefinition in the subclass) have the same name and formal parameter list.

15. The **class** GradStudent has two printGrades methods and their headings are: **public void** printGrades() and **public void** printGrades(String status)

17. a.
```
public void setData(int a, int b, int c)
{
    super.setData(a, b);
    z = c;
}
```

b.
```
public void print()
{
    super.print();
    System.out.println(z);
}
```

19. The **public** members of a class can be accessed anywhere the class is used. The **protected** members of the base class can be directly accessed only by the methods of the derived class.

21. These statements are legal because a reference variable of a superclass type can point to an object of a subclass. Therefore, the formal parameter st can point to the objects student1 and student2.

23. An abstract method is a method that only has the heading with no body. Moreover, the heading of an abstract method contains the reserved word **abstract** and ends with a semicolon.

25. Java does not support multiple inheritance. That is, a class can only extend the definition of one class. In other words, a class can be derived from only one existing class. However, a Java program might contain a variety of GUI components and thus generate a variety of events such as window events, mouse events, as well as action events. These events are handled by separate interfaces. Therefore, a program might need to use more than one interface.

Chapter 11

1. a. True; b. False; c. False; d. True; e. False; f. True; g. True; h. False; i. True; j. False

3. The program will terminate with an error message.

5. If an exception is thrown in a **try** block, the remaining statements in that **try** block are ignored. The program searches the **catch** blocks in the order they appear after the **try** block, and looks for an appropriate exception handler. If the type of thrown exception matches the parameter type in one of the **catch** blocks, the code of that **catch** block executes and the remaining **catch** blocks after this **catch** block are ignored. If there is a **finally** block after the last **catch** block, the **finally** block executes regardless of whether an exception occurs.

7. a.   Leaving try block.

   b.   Balance must be greater than 1000.00.

   c.   Balance must be greater than 1000.00.

9. a.   Entering the try block.
       Exception: Lower limit violation.
       After the catch block

   b.   Entering the try block.
       Exception: / by zero
       After the catch block

   c.   Entering the try block.
       Exiting the try block.
       After the catch block

   d.   Entering the try block.
       Exception: / by zero
       After the catch block

11. Typically constructors are the only methods that you include when you define your own exception class.

13. The answer to this exercise is available with the Additional Student Files at *www.cengagebrain.com*.

15.
```java
public class Test
{
    public static void main(String[] args)
    {
        int i = 8;

        try
        {
            if (i < 5)
                throw new TornadoException();
            else
                throw new TornadoException(i);
        }
        catch (TornadoException e)
        {
            System.out.println(e.getMessage());
        }
    }
}
```

17. A method specifies the exceptions it throws in its heading using the `throws` clause.

19. Any class can implement an interface. The three different options are to use an inner class, an anonymous inner class, or the application (the applet) program class itself to implement an interface.

Chapter 12

1. a. True; b. True; c. True; d. False; e. False; f. False; g. True; h. False; i. False

3. `JTextField` and `JTextArea`

5. Sometimes you want the user to select from a set of predefined values. In addition to freeing the user from typing in such values, to get a precise input, you want the user to select a value from a set of given values.

7. The answer to this exercise is available with the Additional Student Files at *www.cengagebrain.com*.

Chapter 13

1. a. True; b. True; c. False; d. False; e. False

3. The case in which the solution is defined in terms of smaller versions of itself.

5. A method that calls another method and eventually results in the original method call is said to be indirectly recursive.

7. a. The statements in Lines 2 and 3.

    b. The statements in Lines 4 and 5.

    c. Any nonnegative integer.

    d. It is a valid call. The value of `mystery(0)` is 0.

    e. It is a valid call. The value of `mystery(5)` is 15.

    f. It is an invalid call. It will result in the infinite recursion.

9. a. It does not produce any output.

    b. `5 6 7 8 9`

    c. It does not produce any output.

    d. It does not produce any output.

11. a. `Go Go Go Go Go Go Stop!` b. `Go Go Stop!`
    c. Infinite loop, continuously printing `Go`.

13. a. 2

    b. 3

    c. 5

    d. 21

15. $multiply(m, n) = \begin{cases} 0 & if\ n = 0 \\ m & if\ n = 1 \\ m + multiply(m, n-1) & otherwise \end{cases}$

Chapter 14

1. a. False; b. True; c. False;

3. a.

```
public static int seqOrderedSearch(int[] list, int listLength,
                                   int searchItem)
{
    int loc;
    bool found = false;

    for (loc = 0; loc < listLength; loc++)
```

```
        if (list[loc] >= searchItem)
        {
            found = true;
            break;
        }

    if (found)
        if (list[loc] == searchItem)
            return loc;
        else
            return -1;
    else
        return -1;
}
```

b. i. 5 ii. 7 iii. 8 iv.11

5. List before the first iteration: 26, 45, 17, 65, 33, 55, 12, 18
   List after the first iteration: 12, 45, 17, 65, 33, 55, 26, 18
   List after the second iteration: 12, 17, 45, 65, 33, 55, 26, 18
   List after the third iteration: 12, 17, 18, 65, 33, 55, 26, 45
   List after the fourth iteration: 12, 17, 18, 26, 33, 55, 65, 45
   List after the fifth iteration: 12, 17, 18, 26, 33, 55, 65, 45
   List after the sixth iteration: 12, 17, 18, 26, 33, 45, 65, 55
   List after the seventh iteration: 12, 17, 18, 26, 33, 45, 55, 65

7. 3

9. 10, 12, 18, 21, 25, 28, 30, 71, 32, 58, 15

11. Selection sort: 49,995,000 comparisons; insertion sort: 25,007,499 comparisons

13.

```
public static void descendingToAscending(int[] list, int
length)
{
    int temp;
    int index;
    int last = length - 1;

    for (index = 0; index <= (length - 1) / 2; index++)
    {
        temp = list[index];
        list[index] = list[last];
        list[last] = temp;
        last--;
    }
}
```

INDEX

Note: Page numbers in **boldface type** indicate pages where key terms are defined.